D0891933

Principles
of
Social
Psychology

Third Edition

Principles

—— of ——

SOCIAL PSYCHOLOGY

Third Edition

KELLY G. SHAVER

The College of William and Mary

LEA LAWRENCE ERLBAUM ASSOCIATES, PUBLISHERS
1987 Hillsdale, New Jersey   London

Lawrence Erlbaum Associates, Inc., Publishers
365 Broadway
Hillsdale, New Jersey 07642

Library of Congress Cataloging-in-Publication Data

Shaver, Kelly G., 1941–
   Principles of social psychology.

   Bibliography: p.
   Includes index.
   1. Social psychology.   I. Title.
HM251.S465   1987   302   86-24179
ISBN 0-89859-592-4

Printed in the United States of America
10 9 8 7 6 5 4 3 2 1

To all my former students—
from whom I have learned so much

CONTENTS

CHAPTER THREE   70

ELEMENTS OF SOCIAL PERCEPTION

CHAPTER FOUR   108

SOCIAL COGNITION: CONSTRUCTION OF SOCIAL REALITY

CHAPTER FIVE   150

ATTITUDE ORGANIZATION AND COGNITIVE CONSISTENCY

CHAPTER TEN

COMPETITION AND AGGRESSION

CHAPTER ELEVEN

SOCIAL INFLUENCE

CHAPTER TWELVE

THE INDIVIDUAL AND THE GROUP

CHAPTER THIRTEEN

THE ENVIRONMENT AND SOCIAL BEHAVIOR

PREFACE

The field of social psychology encompasses established theory, recent research, and practical application, and an introductory textbook must choose which of these to emphasize. Like its predecessors, this third edition of *Principles of Social Psychology* concentrates on the ideas that have provided continuity to the discipline through the years. Although this edition has been updated to take account of recent research, that work is selectively described only where it is helpful in making a conceptual point. No attempt has been made to catalogue all research conducted in the last few years. Numerous examples show the relevance of the principles to everyday social behavior, but the book's strong emphasis on theory reflects my belief that concepts need to be taught, whereas practical applications will suggest themselves to people who know the concepts.

The book's approach to social psychology is decidedly cognitive, on the presumption that the way in which an individual views and organizes the world will influence his or her social behavior. Continuing a chapter structure originated in the first edition, this book begins with the internal processes of social perception, social cognition, and attitude organization and change. Next it describes the self and social motivation, then turning to interpersonal phenomena of attraction, competition, aggression, social influence, and group processes. Finally, the book concludes with discussion of two aspects of the larger social context—the physical environment and the criminal justice system—that constrain individual action. The latter chapter is new to this edition, reflecting increased participation by social psychologists in the study of victimization, trial practice and testimony, incarceration and parole.

In addition to the inclusion of a new chapter, there are other changes from the second edition. To streamline the discussion of research techniques without decreasing the book's thorough treatment of method, the two research chapters have been consolidated. Principles of research are now presented in a single chapter, and specific techniques have been included in a Methodological Appendix that also contains a statistical primer and procedures for measurement of implicit personality theory and attitudes. A unique feature of the Methodological Appendix is a comprehensive description of a student-initiated class project on the effects of the matching principle on dating preferences. This example traces the details of conducting research that are usually omitted from studies reported in professional journals, giving students insight into how social psychologists actually practice their craft. The attitude change chapter has been reorganized, with a discussion of prejudice and racism replacing the attitude measurement material moved to the appendix. The social cognition and attitude organization chapters have been expanded to incorporate new material on the purely cognitive processes involved in these areas. Because social psychology is a popular elective choice for students interested in business, business-related examples have been included throughout the text.

Like the previous editions, this book attempts to *teach* the concepts of social psychology and toward that end includes specific tools for learning. Each chapter begins with a chapter outline and a preview of the material to be discussed. Chapters conclude with narrative summaries and suggested additional readings. Key terms are highlighted in boldface in the text and are defined in a Glossary that appears at the end of the book. Both the Glossary and the chapter summary show the page number on which a term was first introduced, so students can quickly locate the conceptual context for the terms. Concepts and theories are thoroughly discussed on their first introduction, but there are over 100 cross-references to places where a point has already been made, or will be expanded. These cross-references help communicate that social psychology is cumulative and interrelated, regardless of whether instructors follow the chapter order presented or choose an alternative order of presentation. Even with these substantial reinforcements to learning, the study of social psychology remains conceptually challenging, and this book reflects that challenge.

Although I bear the responsibility for whatever weaknesses remain in the book, a number of people deserve credit for their assistance in its completion. My thanks first to Jack Burton of Lawrence Erlbaum Associates for his support and encouragement throughout preparation of this edition, and to Lori Baronian for her assistance in its production. Portions of the manuscript were reviewed by Dan Wegner, and the entire book was read by Gene Burnstein, Saul Kassin, and Milt Rosenbaum. I am grateful to all of these people for the improvements suggested by their constructive criticism. Finally, I would like to thank my past undergraduate students at William and Mary, to whom this book is dedicated, for their excellent questions, their novel ideas for class projects, and their enthusiastic interest in social psychology.

CHAPTER ONE

SOCIAL PSYCHOLOGY: ACCOUNTING FOR SOCIAL BEHAVIOR

CONTENTS

PREVIEW

A relatively recent addition to the scientific study of human behavior, social psychology was established as an independent discipline only in the late 1930s. Defined as the "scientific study of the personal and situational factors that affect individual social behavior," social psychology considers the cognitive and motivational processes that affect interpersonal behavior in a larger social context. Social psychologists observe human behavior, construct theories to explain those human actions, and test the validity of their theories in research. Although observations of social activities can be a rich source of hypotheses for study, personal experience alone cannot substitute for the understanding that can be achieved through scientific methods.

"Opposites attract."

This "explanation" for romantic attachment is one of the staples of our popular wisdom about social behavior. Romantic attraction is so fundamental a human phenomenon that few people will be likely to claim they have never been "in love," at least once. From a teenager's temporary infatuation to an elderly couple's celebration of 50 years of marriage, romantic involvements provide us with many of our warmest memories. Unfortunately, attraction can also lead to tragedy: half of the couples who marry in America today will eventually be divorced; some 30% of American couples will report an episode of physical violence occurring at least once in their marriage (Straus, Gelles, & Steinmetz, 1980); estranged lovers or spouses are involved in a large fraction of the murders committed in a year. If a principle as concise as "opposites attract" could explain not only the successes, but also the failures, in romantic relationships, it would truly be the powerful explanatory tool suggested by its longevity in everyday accounts of interaction.

WHAT KIND OF EXPLANATION?

Criteria for Scientific Explanation

Persistent or extensive popular use of a concept does not, however, mean that the concept will necessarily be useful to the discipline of social psychology in its formal study of human interaction. To be scientifically acceptable, an explanatory principle needs (a) to be defined unambiguously, (b) to identify the causal relation between two or more phenomena, and (c) to specify **limiting conditions:** factors in the environment that make it no longer possible for the causal relation to hold. On two of these counts the notion that "opposites attract" falls short.

Clear Definition.   First, consider how the terms might be defined. What, exactly, is the dimension on which the individuals are to be opposite in order to be attracted to one another? Some of the possibilities that immediately suggest themselves are socioeconomic status, religious background, attitudes, personality characteristics, temperament, interests, or physical attractiveness. Some personality attributes – dominance-submissiveness, for example – fit the notion quite well, but "opposite-ness" on many of the other dimensions – attitudes, socioeconomic status, interests – would seem a hindrance to the development of a strong interpersonal bond.

What about the definition of *attract?* Here there are at least two different aspects of the term that need to be distinguished. To begin with the kind of attraction, romantic attraction is different from same-gender friendship, and neither of these is the same as respect for a parent or adulation of a political leader. Friends might find it stimulating to share quite divergent interests, but it is unlikely that people will canonize a political leader whose views on fundamental issues are opposite their own. Turning to the degree of attraction, does the presumed positive effect of different perspectives occur only before there is much mutual commitment to the interaction (novelty is intriguing), only in an intense relationship with a great deal of mutual commitment (novelty adds the "spice" to keep the interaction fresh), or in both instances?

By now it should be clear that what appeared to be elegant simplicity of an explanatory principle was really a failure to include a thorough definition of the terms. Even for a frequent and familiar social behavior like the development of interpersonal attraction, terms that are acceptable in everyday language may be inadequate for scientific purposes. To eliminate the ambiguity, social psychologists employ **operational definitions:** definitions of conceptual variables that are stated in terms of the operations used to measure concepts. In this case "hours per week spent in the company of the other person" would be an operational definition of attraction, and "an average difference of greater than 60 percentage points on each of 12 subscales of a standard personality test" would be an operational definition of oppositeness. No doubt you can think of other operations that could be used to measure oppositeness, or attraction, and social psychologists typically use varying operations in different research studies. But in each instance the definition must be a precise statement of what the investigator did, so that others who wanted to could repeat the operations exactly.

Causal Statements.   The second characteristic of a scientifically acceptable explanation of social behavior is its ability to identify the causal relationship between two or more phenomena. Philosophers of science have debated the notion of causality literally for centuries, but most social psychologists subscribe to a view that involves three separate elements. First, a presumed cause must be contiguous with the presumed effect, in space, in time, or in both. The cause and effect must appear together regularly, and although the effect might sometimes occur without the particular cause (there could have been others), presence of the cause should more reliably produce the effect (in rare cases insurmountable obstacles might prevent the effect). Second, the cause should precede the effect in time. Our very understanding of the words "cause" and "effect" implies temporal precedence of the cause. And third, it is necessary to rule out other factors that might have produced both the effect and what would otherwise appear to be its cause. As we see in later chapters, this elimination of plausible alternatives is one of the critical tasks facing scientific social psychology. For now suffice it to say that the principle "opposites attract" does make a kind of causal claim: the oppositeness comes first, the attraction comes second as a consequence of that oppositeness.

Limiting Conditions. The third aspect of a scientifically acceptable account of social behavior is its specification of the limiting conditions. These limiting conditions can be of two different sorts. First, it is important to be able to tell when the posited causal relationship might not hold. Some of these are inherent in the different definitions noted earlier. For example, the relationship might be limited to friendship, or to oppositeness of temperament. Other limiting conditions are not inherent in the definition selected: with oppositeness defined in terms of personality characteristics, and attraction limited to romantic attachment, it still might be true that the principle would hold for a long-term relationship, but might actually discourage an initial approach. The second sort of limiting condition suggests cases in which the presumed effect (attraction) might be produced by some cause other than the specified oppositeness. For example, one can imagine initial romantic attraction being tied to physical attractiveness, even before anything is known about similarities or differences in other factors.

Implicit Theories of Social Psychology

A Need to Learn the Language. The principle that "opposites attract" does state a causal relationship between two social phenomena, but as previously demonstrated, it does not do so as precisely as is necessary for scientific explanations of social behavior. Similar differences in precision can be shown by comparing ordinary spoken language to the language of any science or technical field: "cook until done in a moderate oven" is fine for a recipe, but inadequate as an instruction for producing a chemical reaction initiated by temperature; "the Stock Market did better today" may be as much description as many people want, but any business economist will need to know about the performance of particular technical market indicators; "my car runs unevenly" is reasonable as a complaint to an understanding friend, but it won't get you a new carburetor needle valve from the auto parts store. What makes social psychology different from other scientific and technical disciplines is not its need for precision, but your recognition of that need.

Usually when you begin to study an unfamiliar academic discipline, you quickly become aware of how little you know. Neither your past experience nor your everyday language can be brought to bear on what you must try to learn. When the physics professor speaks of wave propagation, cascading, and hyperons; when the biology professor describes hydrophytes, indolebutyric acid, or compound racemose inflorescence; or even when the clinical psychologist discusses tardive dyskinesia, lithium therapy, or schizo-affective disorder, you try to take very careful notes so that you won't miss anything. You feel sufficiently uncertain of your background in the area that you find it difficult to formulate intelligent questions, and you wouldn't dream of actually contradicting the professor on the basis of your personal experience. You recognize your limitations, and you realize that you must learn a new language—the technical jargon of the discipline.

The Role of Personal Experience.   What happens when you study social psychology? To begin with, all of your past social experience seems to be relevant. You have engaged in social perception, you have formed friendships, you have dealt with people who have power over you, and you have exercised influence over others. You have changed attitudes, developed a self-concept, and joined groups. Moreover, you have a fairly good idea of the functional relationships between elements of your social world. You know what circumstances, and what individual characteristics, are most likely to lead to one sort of behavior instead of another. You know that your actions around your parents differ from those around your friends (that the situation and your role influence your behavior). You know that there are some people whose attitudes can be changed simply by providing them with information that contradicts their beliefs, but that there are others who will not change unless you appeal to their baser instincts (that some people respond to logical persuasive messages, whereas others only respond to emotional appeals). You know that in any group some people always seem to become leaders whereas others remain followers (that personal characteristics influence emergent leadership). In the course of accumulating all this interpersonal experience, you have developed what can best be described as an *implicit theory of social psychology:*

a haphazard collection of ideas about what situations and personal characteristics are associated with the occurrence of particular kinds of social behavior.

The Trivial and the Counterintuitive.   Your implicit theory of social psychology is derived from your own experience. Because of the subjective validity of that experience for you, you are likely to believe it to be "correct" in some more objective sense. You have observed regularities in the social behavior of people around you, and you may even have verified your experiences by comparing them with those of your friends or acquaintances. There are few things subjectively more real than your own experience, so it is difficult for you to understand that other people might view the same situation in entirely different ways. You may assume that what is real for you must surely generalize to the experience of others as well, and thereby underestimate the extent to which your implicit theory of social psychology represents only your unique viewpoint.

As a result, you compare new information (say, from your social psychology professor) to your implicit theory. When the new information agrees with your theory, you might be tempted to accuse social psychologists of "studying the obvious," wasting a lot of valuable research time to generate findings that are apparent to anyone who has the requisite common sense. In short, you might consider the research results trivial and not worth bothering with. On the other hand, should the new information contradict your implicit theory of social psychology, you might dismiss it as an anomaly. You would regard such a counterintuitive (for you) finding with a good deal of suspicion, again because of the overwhelming reality of your own experience. In either case you would be making a mistake.

The first kind of error has already been illustrated in the discussion of the notion that "opposites attract." There is, indeed, social psychological research that shows people who have complementary personal needs to be attracted to each other (e.g., Kerckhoff & Davis, 1962; Levinger, 1964; Winch, 1958). On the other hand, there are other studies that indicate interpersonal attraction to be a positive function of attitude similarity (e.g., Byrne, 1971; Newcomb, 1961). This latter work would appear to be consistent with the adage that "birds of a feather flock together."

Identification of Limiting Conditions.   If it is so obvious that "opposites attract," how is it possible to explain that "birds of a feather flock together?" Which account is "trivial," and which is "counterintuitive?" At the level of the two everyday proverbs, it is impossible to tell. At the level of research and formal theory, however, the greater precision in definition and the identification of limiting conditions permit a more detailed answer that better reflects the true complexity of social interaction. Specifically, it turns out that the rule is probably a positive relationship between similarity and attraction (greater similarity leads to greater attraction), and "opposites attract" is the exception, limited primarily to personality differences among certain engaged or married couples (Berscheid & Walster, 1969; Kerckhoff & Davis, 1962). Your implicit theory of social psychology can only interpret functional relationships that are obtained, but cannot distinguish between conflicting explanations. In contrast, the formal theory and research of scientific social psychology can be used to identify the limiting conditions that explain apparently contradictory findings. The question "Which relationship is correct?" becomes "What are the circumstances under which one functional relationship changes to the other?"

Counterintuitive Findings: A Study of Obedience

If reliance on an implicit theory of social psychology is a forgiveable mistake when the problem appears trivial, it can be a serious blunder when actual results of research would not agree with expectations. As an example, consider the research by Milgram (1963) dealing with destructive obedience. Milgram tried to study, in the experimental laboratory, some of the factors that might be involved in "following orders" to the extent of causing serious harm to other persons. He argued that the systematic murder practiced by the Nazis during World War II, although perhaps conceived by a single person, "could only be carried out on a massive scale if a very large number of persons had obeyed orders" (p. 371).

The first question, of course, deals with the likelihood that people will actually engage in destructive obedience. Was the Nazi experience based on a combination of the times and some unique flaw in the German national character (your implicit theory of social psychology might well suggest that it was), or could a laboratory analogue be constructed? Could anyone (including your own presumably moral fellow Americans) be induced to follow the orders of a researcher, even though doing so might endanger the health (or perhaps life) of an innocent person?

The Laboratory Setting. To investigate these questions Milgram devised a study in which naive subjects (adult males recruited through advertisements) were asked to administer electric shocks of increasing intensity to another middle-aged male as part of a purported study of the effects of punishment for errors in paired-associate learning. The subject was given the task of teaching a list of word pairs, such as blue-girl, nice-day, and fatneck, to another subject (who was, in fact, a confederate of the experimenter). Every time the learner made an error, he was to receive an electric shock of increasing intensity. These shocks were to be delivered by the teacher (the naive subject), who was to use an authentic-looking shock generator that contained a single row of 30 toggle switches, each one representing a 15-volt increment over the one immediately to its left. The shock scale thus ran from a low of 15 volts to a high of 450, and each toggle switch was marked by the appropriate number of volts. In addition to these numerical designations, groups of four switches were also labeled (from left to right) as follows: Slight Shock, Moderate Shock, Strong Shock, Very Strong Shock, Intense Shock, Extreme Intensity Shock, and Danger: Severe Shock. The last two switches were simply marked XXX. Whenever the teacher depressed a switch, a pilot light went on, an electric buzzing was heard, a blue light labeled "voltage energizer" flashed on, and a needle on a large voltmeter spiked to the right. Just to ensure credibility, each subject was given a sample shock of 45 volts, using the third switch from the left (which was actually wired to a 45-volt battery housed inside the shock generator).

As part of the initial instructions, both the naive subject and the experimental confederate drew slips from a bowl to determine which one of them would be the teacher and which would be the learner. Both slips had the word "teacher" printed on them, and the confederate simply announced that his slip said "learner." After a description of the learning task, the researcher took the learner (the confederate) into an adjoining experimental room, asking the subject to accompany them so that he could see the remainder of the setup. Once in the adjoining room, the learner was seated in a chair and asked to take off his coat and roll up his sleeve. Electrode paste was then applied to his wrist "to avoid blisters and burns," and his arm was strapped to the chair in such a way that his wrist was firmly placed on an electrode plate ostensibly connected to the shock generator. At this point the learner reported that he had recently been diagnosed as having a mild heart condition. He stated that it was nothing to worry about, but wondered how serious the shocks might be. The researcher assured him that although the shocks would be quite painful, there should be no lasting physiological damage. Finally, the researcher took the subject back into the first room, seated him in front of the shock generator, and had him begin teaching the lists of word pairs.

The Distressing Results. In any research, the measured response of conceptual interest is the **dependent variable**, and in this study that dependent variable was the point at which the subject adamantly refused to continue. This could have happened before the first shock had been administered, at any point during the sequence, or not at all. Any subject who continued until the highest voltage level was reached was to be asked to administer that level for several successive errors before the researcher terminated the procedure.

What sort of results would your implicit theory of social psychology predict? Would anyone continue to the end? If not, when would the majority of people refuse to go on? Let me be even more specific, and ask you the kind of question that Milgram asked some senior psychology majors and a number of his professional colleagues: Of 100 American males of diverse occupations, ranging in age from 20 to 50, what percentage would continue until the highest shock level had been reached? None of the estimates was higher than 3%, with the most pessimistic student predicting that 3 out of 100 subjects would continue to increase the shocks until the highest level was reached. These estimates probably correspond fairly well to the estimate that you might have made. To return to the language we have used previously, it is at least counterintuitive, even frightening, to believe that large numbers of subjects would continue to administer ever more severe shocks to a middle-aged man with a possible heart condition long after he has screamed in protest, pounded on the wall, and then fallen silent, refusing to respond to any stimulus word.

Indeed, if we were to rely upon our implicit theories of social psychology, we might never have performed this study in the first place. We might look at the setup and procedures and conclude that so few people would ever begin the series of shocks, much less persist in administering them, that it would be very difficult to obtain useful data. After all, it would be impossible to discover any situational factors, or personality characteristics, that might contribute to compliance with the researcher's demands if no subjects actually followed his orders. Our implicit theories of social psychology would suggest that destructive obedience should occur only under the most extreme circumstances. People whose own lives are threatened might willingly inflict pain on others; the compelling horror of war might lead to infrequent atrocities; occasional psychopaths might find satisfaction in others' discomfort. But we would fervently hope that no laboratory analogue of these situations could be constructed.

Sadly, we would be mistaken. A total of 40 subjects took part in the study just described, and 26 of the participants (65%) obeyed the researcher right up to the bitter end. Only 14 subjects ever refused to continue, and no one did so until after the learner fell silent at the 300-volt level.

How Could it Happen? This study raises several important issues. First, we must wonder why so many subjects disregarded their better judgment and followed the researcher's orders. He had no real power over them, and when they balked at continuing, he only claimed vaguely that "the experiment requires that you continue." Subjects had been paid at the beginning of the session, and were told that they could keep the payment regardless of what happened in the course of the study. It was obvious from the subjects' behavior that many of them were in serious conflict over whether to go along, so why did so many continue?

Perhaps they had faith in the researcher, and in the university (Yale) where the study was conducted, believing that neither would permit serious harm to come to any participants. Perhaps they believed that what they were doing was for the "good of science," a long-term goal that might have justified some temporary suffering. Or perhaps they simply acted without reflecting on the possible consequences of their behavior. It is important to note that none of these possibilities diminishes the force of the conclusion. In real life situations requiring the obedient execution of orders, the source of those orders is most often a legitimate authority, making its demands on the basis of a larger "principle," often without allowing adequate time for reflection and discussion of the potential consequences.

A Question of Ethics. A second set of issues raised by the Milgram study deals not so much with the results themselves as with the methods used to obtain those results. The experiment combined two of the most ethically questionable elements of some research in social psychology: a powerful deception of the subjects, and a procedure that virtually guaranteed that those subjects would learn something negative about themselves as a consequence of taking part in the study. Among other things, the subjects were misled into believing that (a) the learner was simply another subject, (b) there was a real possibility of harm to him, and (c) they had actually caused such harm by shocking him for his incorrect answers. It is clear from the reports of observers of the procedure that administering the shocks was a traumatic experience for subjects. In the words of one observer, "I watched a mature and initially poised businessman enter the laboratory smiling and confident. Within 20 minutes he was reduced to a twitching, stuttering wreck, who was rapidly approaching a point of nervous collapse . . ." (Milgram, 1963, p. 376).

One must wonder whether the debriefing given each subject (including an explanation of the study and a friendly reconciliation with the learner) was sufficient to counteract both the stress of the moment and the impact of the realization that "I am the kind of guy who will obediently follow orders, even though it might cause serious harm to another person." To determine whether there were lingering effects, Milgram (1964) conducted followup surveys among the participants in his research. Not only did he discover no lingering harmful effects, the vast majority of the subjects said that they would be willing to take part in similar studies in the future. But we should not let answers like these make us complacent. People who have engaged in activity that contradicts their existing attitudes or moral codes often need to justify their actions, in some instances by altering their perceptions of how painful the experience really was at the time. For this and other reasons, social psychologists must remain vigilant about the ethical implications of their research, and we shall return to further consideration of these issues in chapter 2.

Implicit Theories are not Enough. The final lesson to be learned from the Milgram study is the discovery that our implicit theories of social psychology will be inadequate predictors of what people will actually *do*. Certainly it is true that our implicit theories contain provisions for people's well-documented inhumanity to one another (and, as the My Lai massacre during the Vietnam war illustrated, Americans take part in atrocities just as do other national groups). But because these provisions suggest the necessity for extreme conditions, they do not prepare us for the revelation that people from all walks of life who are simply participating in an experiment will, with relatively little external justification or pressure, obediently follow orders that conflict with their moral and ethical values.

What Milgram's research teaches us as human beings is that we should be conscious of the relationship between our ethical principles and our behavior, not only in extreme circumstances, but always. What it teaches us as students of social psychology is that we must not rely solely upon our implicit theories: if we seek thorough understanding and accurate prediction of social behavior, we must perform the necessary research. Experience is an excellent source of suggestions and hypotheses, but scientific theory must be grounded on data. The challenge for social psychology is to turn everyday observations into testable theoretical statements.

OBSERVATION AND THEORY

People have been observing human social behavior, and trying to understand it, since before our distant ancestors left the caves, and the philosophical underpinnings of much of social psychology as a discipline can be traced as far back as Plato and Aristotle. The first textbooks on social psychology were published in 1908, one by a psychologist named William McDougall and one by a sociologist named Edward Ross. Each of these books is more important for its historical value than for its lasting theoretical contribution, because most social psychologists regard Kurt Lewin, whose work was first published in the late 1930s and early 1940s, as the intellectual father of the discipline.

Hypothetical Constructs

There is a story, confirmed by at least one observer (Marrow, 1969), that illustrates Lewin's astute observations of human behavior. Lewin and his students at the Psychological Institute of the University of Berlin frequently gathered at the Schwedische Café near the Institute, and the several participants in these informal gatherings typically ordered a variety of foods and drinks. A certain waiter was always able to remember each person's order without the benefit of written notes. When someone asked for the check, the waiter would simply recall exactly what each person had ordered. On one of these occasions, several minutes after the bill had been paid, Lewin asked the waiter to provide another accounting of the orders. The waiter declared indignantly that he could not remember, and that the matter had been settled.

How could something so faithfully remembered then so quickly be forgotten? For Lewin, the question suggested the presence of a psychological tension created with the taking of the order and discharged with the payment of the bill. As long as the tension was present, the waiter would have no difficulty remembering the orders, but as soon as the tension had been discharged, the orders would be forgotten. This internal tension, like many of the explanatory principles in social psychology, cannot be observed directly. Rather, it is a **hypothetical construct**: a conceptual principle that serves as the explanation for an aspect of observable behavior. To test the idea of psychological tension, one of Lewin's students, Bluma Zeigarnik, conducted a series of experiments on recall of completed and uncompleted tasks. The results are the well-known *Zeigarnik effect:* people will recall interrupted tasks much better than finished tasks (from which result we infer that in the case of incompleted tasks some tension still remains).

Although the study of memory is presently regarded as falling in the purview of cognitive psychology, not social psychology, the hypothetical construct of tension assumed a fundamental role in Lewin's *field* theory of social behavior (to be discussed in chapter 12). For now, however, it is sufficient to notice that the sensitive observation of a simple social behavior contributed to the development of a complex psychological theory. Experience cannot be a substitute for systematic methods, but it can be a rich source of hypotheses to be put to the test experimentally.

Study of Ongoing Social Processes

At about the same time that Lewin was outlining the beginnings of his field theory, another pioneer in the field was conducting research that helped to establish experimental social psychology as a separate enterprise. This occurred in 1936, when Muzafer Sherif reported a series of experiments that demonstrated that an ongoing social process—the formation of social norms—could be subjected to the same kind of scrutiny previously directed only toward the outcome of a process (such as the immediate forgetting of material no longer supported by psychological tension). Sherif was intrigued by the emergence of social **norms:** sets of expectations for social behavior in a particular setting, expectations that are applied to any participant in the activity, regardless of that person's individual characteristics. Specifically, Sherif wondered how an individual's judgment might be affected by the opinions of others.

In order to simplify the development of social norms, Sherif employed an experimental task known as the *autokinetic effect.* If you are asked to sit in a darkened room and to look continuously at a pinpoint of light, pretty soon you will think the light is moving. It isn't, of course; the source of the perceived movement is generally agreed to be your eye movements. For Sherif's purposes, however, what was important was that (a) perceived movement does occur; (b) over a long series of trials, subjects will report a relatively stable amount of movement; (c) there are substantial individual differences in these personal distributions of movement; and (d) there is no objective or absolute frame of reference that can be used to establish a "correct" amount of movement. In other words, almost all of the conditions were conducive to social influence over individual judgments of movement. Once again, the researcher began with an observation of a social behavior and translated the essential ingredients of that behavior into procedures that could test a theoretical idea.

Sherif's question was this: How will a person's judgments of the movement when he or she is viewing the light alone compare with judgments made in the presence of others? Will the individual judgments of group members remain disparate, or will they converge into a *common norm* for the group? And how will the person's subsequent judgments made alone be affected by a previously established group norm? To answer these questions, Sherif asked participants to make three separate sets of 100 judgments each set. The first set was made when each participant was alone in the experimental room, and these judgments showed wide variations in the degree to which the autokinetic effect was reported. During the second phase of the research, several participants at a time reported their perceptions out loud, with the result that the individual judgments converged about a common norm for the group. In the third stage of the research, subjects were again tested individually. Interestingly enough, reports from this third set of judgments showed almost no individual differences—the participants had come to agree on a common norm for movement, and they carried this norm with them as a frame of reference for the third stage of the study. This research served not only to establish the efficacy of the experimental method in social psychology, but also to provide the theoretical foundation for later research in social comparison theory (chapter 7) and social influence processes (chapter 12).

The Social Psychology of Research

The goal of social psychology is a more complete understanding of human social behavior, and so far we have seen two early and one more recent example of attempts to address that goal. Building on their intuitions and observations, social psychologists identify principles thought to account for aspects of behavior, and then conduct research designed to test the predictive power of these hypothetical constructs. One reason that research in social psychology is especially challenging is that the very act of conducting research is affected by many of the same interpersonal processes that have been the subject of study in their own right. This fact has come to be represented in a number of different concepts (to be discussed more fully in chapter 2 and the Methodological Appendix), such as evaluation apprehension (Rosenberg, 1965), experimenter expectancy (Rosenthal, 1966), and demand characteristics (Orne, 1962), but the first indication of its influence was in an extensive set of field experiments reported by Roethlisberger and Dickson (1939).

These experiments had been designed to assess the effects of various working conditions on the output of workers who were assembling electrical components at the Hawthorne works of the Western Electric Company. Roethlisberger, a professor at the Harvard Graduate School of Business, and Dickson, a member of Western Electric's research department, and their colleagues began by studying the effects of differences in illumination of the work area. Following proper experimental procedure, they separated the workers into two groups: an experimental group that received varying intensities of illumination and a control group that received a constant intensity of illumination. To the investigators' surprise, there was an increase in output in both groups. Then the researchers tried other variations in illumination, even including telling the experimental group that there would be a change and not actually changing the intensity. Still the output increased. The only decline was observed when the level of illumination was lowered to an amount equivalent to moonlight!

The studies continued for a period of 5 years, changing numerous conditions other than illumination, and using different sets of workers in the plant, with remarkably consistent results. Almost no matter what experimental conditions were imposed, increases in output occurred, and workers typically maintained these increases after all experimental conditions had been removed. The investigators had obviously influenced the subjects' behavior merely by studying it, and this phenomenon has become known as the *Hawthorne effect*. Although reservations have recently been expressed about details of Roethlisberger and Dickson's (1939) procedures, there is no doubt that knowing you are a subject in social psychological research alters your natural pattern of behavior. This "social psychology of the psychological experiment" must be taken into account in all contemporary research, and is one of the major reasons why methodological sophistication is so important to the discipline.

Theory and Application

For our purposes Roethlisberger and Dickson's (1939) work is noteworthy primarily because of the Hawthorne effect, but their research also helped to establish the idea that the methods of social psychology could be brought to bear on important problems in the "real world" outside the laboratory. The relationship between theory and application, like the relationship between observation and theory, is best represented historically in the work of Lewin. Not only was Lewin an astute observer of social behavior, but he also used the theories developed from those observations to solve applied problems, firmly believing that "there is nothing so practical as a good theory" (1951, p. 169).

Nowhere is this relationship between theory and practical application better illustrated than in Lewin's studies of the effects of group discussion and consensus on attitude and behavior change. Lewin's extensive field theory of human behavior led him to conclude that even well-established social attitudes are not permanently fixed. On the contrary, they are dynamic entities, maintained in part by the social support they receive from other people. Consequently, variations in the social climate can produce lasting attitude change, first by **unfreezing** the existing attitude, then by **moving** it, and finally by **refreezing** the attitude at its new position.

Group Discussion and Eating Habits. During World War II Lewin had the opportunity to apply these theoretical notions when he and his associates became involved in a project to change the eating habits of families in order to conserve meats needed for the troops. The subjects were Red Cross volunteers, in groups of 13 to 17, and the purpose of the program was to increase the home use of beef hearts, sweetbreads, and kidneys. There were two experimental conditions—lecture and group decision—and half of the subjects were assigned to each condition. In the Lecture condition the groups heard an interesting lecture linking nutrition problems to the necessity of conserving meat for the war effort, emphasizing the nutritional content of the three meats, and presenting sample recipes along with detailed instructions on preparation of the meats (suggesting ways of minimizing their unattractive characteristics). The lecturer recounted her success in preparing these "delicious dishes" for her own family.

In the Group Decision condition the leader made a few introductory remarks about the nutritional value of the meats and about the war effort, and then started a discussion to involve subjects in the process of deciding whether to serve the dishes. These group discussions concentrated on the obstacles against using beef hearts, sweetbreads, and kidneys (such as the smell during cooking and objections from the family members), and the same remedies and recipes were distributed as in the Lecture condition. At the end of the meeting subjects in the Group Decision condition were asked to indicate by a show of hands how many people intended to try one of the meats during the following week.

A Methodological Contribution. A later interview with all of the groups showed that in the Lecture condition only 3% of the subjects actually served one of the recommended meats, but in the Group Decision condition 32% of the individuals did so. There are, of course, several possible explanations. Perhaps the group decision produces greater involvement; perhaps the public commitment of agreeing to try a previously unattractive food creates an obligation to do so; perhaps the thought of having to return to a group where some consensus has already been established creates social pressure to join in that consensus. Subsequent research with different subjects and different foodstuffs served to rule out some of these alternatives and to narrow the possible explanations to group decision and public commitment, but a later study by Bennett (1955) suggested that these might not be as important as the process of discussion and the degree of perceived consensus.

Despite the qualifications that now appear to be necessary, Lewin's methodological contributions can be seen in contemporary studies of group problem solving (Kelley & Thibaut, 1969) and choice shifts in group discussion (Cartwright, 1971; Kogan & Wallach, 1965). More importantly, Lewin's recognition that cognition and motivation both play a role in interpersonal behavior, and his emphasis on the practical applications for social psychological theory, placed a strong imprint on the later development of the field.

CONSTRUCTING A DEFINITION OF SOCIAL PSYCHOLOGY

Just what is the field of social psychology? At first, it involves interest in social behavior. We want to know why two eyewitnesses to an accident can give completely different accounts of the reasons for its occurrence. We want to learn why people come to hold certain attitudes, and to discover how those attitudes might be changed. We want to determine when a person's needs and motives will affect his or her behavior toward others. Why do people help each other, and what are the social roots of human aggression? Why do our friends like us, and why do some people remain unfriendly? How do people influence each other, and what effects does group membership have on a person's actions?

To one degree or another, we are all interested in social behavior, but interest alone is not enough. As we have seen, the conclusions reached through the systematic methods of social psychology often differ markedly from the predictions that interested individuals would make on the basis of their implicit theories of social behavior. These differences arise because social psychology applies standards for the definition of concepts, the identification of causal connections, and the specification of limiting conditions that are more stringent than the standards typically used by interested individuals. The accumulation of scientific data differs from the satisfaction of individual curiosity primarily in the methods employed.

Level of Analysis

But how can social psychology be distinguished from other disciplines —such as general experimental psychology and sociology—that also employ scientific methods in the study of human behavior? The answer to this question lies in the level of analysis of the field. Social psychology chooses to focus on the meaningful social behaviors of an individual person. Both a person's social milieu (physical and social surroundings) and unique personal characteristics are thought to influence the person's behavior, and this behavior is described in socially meaningful terms that most closely correspond to those of everyday language. In contrast to this emphasis on the socially meaningful actions of an individual person, general experimental psychology is concerned with portions of the individual's behavior (physiological processes, learning, sensation, and perception), whereas sociology is concerned with the structural elements (social roles, formal organizations, social institutions) that are thought to remain essentially unchanged no matter who the particular individuals are.

Consider, for example, the ways in which each discipline might describe a family dinner. Depending on his or her specialty within the discipline, a general experimental psychologist might study the eye-hand coordination necessary to bring the food from the plate to the mouth, the subjective experiences corresponding to the taste and smell of the meal, or perhaps the learning processes involved in getting the children to eat their spinach. For the sociologist, again depending on his or her specialty within the discipline, the most interesting data might be the degree to which the role of "pleasant and conversant spouse" conflicts with the role of "supervising parent," the importance of an evening meal in the daily contact between members of a nuclear family, or the larger social function of the meal for the particular social class or ethnic group of the people involved. The social psychologist, by contrast, might wonder whether the family would conduct itself the same way with invited guests present as it does when eating alone, whether suggestions to the children have more impact when delivered with good food than when delivered at other times, or how a parent's unpleasant interchange with his or her boss during the afternoon might affect enjoyment of the meal and communication with other members of the group.

A Formal Definition

Notice that the experimental psychologist concentrates on the sensory, perceptual, and learning processes of individuals, allowing for some differences between people but virtually ignoring the social nature of the setting in which these processes are observed. The sociologist concentrates on the social significance of the gathering—role strain, maintenance of a social institution (the family), and demographic or cultural variations— virtually ignoring the personal characteristics of the particular individuals involved. For the social psychologist, however, it is the interaction between individual characteristics and social situation that is of paramount importance.

Tasting food ought to be relatively constant across people, but "having dinner" involves both the situation and the person.

Through the years there have been numerous definitions of the field of social psychology, and one of the most widely quoted is that of Allport (1968): "an attempt to understand and explain how the thought, feeling, and behavior of individuals are influenced by the actual, imagined, or implied presence of others" (p. 3). There are, however, two difficulties with this definition. First, it does not suggest how the formal discipline of social psychology differs from the attempts at understanding and explanation that constitute our implicit theories of social behavior. The distinction is, as we have seen, in the methods employed in the two endeavors, and this distinction must be incorporated in the definition of the field. Second, in two important senses Allport's definition is overly restrictive. It suggests that only thoughts, feelings, and interpersonal behavior are of interest to social psychologists, but many social psychologists believe that independently measureable physiological processes, and even physical health, are also affected by social variables. Indeed, this is the rationale for study of behavioral medicine and for research in what is known as social psychophysiology (Cacioppo & Petty, 1983). Allport's definition also suggests that the thoughts, feelings, and behavior will typically be what is measured. In fact, both the historical examples we have already discussed and numerous examples described in later chapters presume that the individual's thoughts, feelings, and other personal characteristics will also produce differences in social behavior. To distinguish social psychology from everyday attempts at understanding, while including a wider array of possible influences on human behavior, I define social psychology as **the scientific study of the personal and situational factors that affect individual social behavior.**

PLAN OF THE BOOK

Fifty Years of Experimental Social Psychology

By a variety of intellectual landmarks, modern experimental social psychology is some 50 years old. The first *Handbook of Social Psychology,* edited by Murchison, was published in 1935, and according to a perceptive history of the field by Jones (1985) the Murchison volume "marked the end of the pre-experimental era in social psychology" (p. 63). A second edition of the *Handbook,* edited by Lindzey, was published in 1954, a third, edited by Lindzey and Aronson, appeared in 1968-69, and a fourth, again edited by Lindzey and Aronson, was released in 1985. Methods still in use for the measurement of social attitudes were first presented by Thurstone and

Chave (1929) and by Likert (1932). Many of Lewin's contributions appeared in the 1930s (e.g. Lewin, Lippitt, & White, 1939), and Sherif's experimental study of norm formation was published in 1936.

Scientific disciplines are rarely isolated from the social events of the time, and social psychology is no exception to this rule. Whole subfields such as social perception, attitude change, and the influence of personality on social behavior, received dramatic impetus as a consequence of World War II. Although the discipline is predominantly an American phenomenon, many of its early founders—including Lewin—were European refugees. Together these developments led one historian of the field (Cartwright, 1979) to name Adolph Hitler as the one person with the greatest influence on the direction of the discipline. In his discussion of the influence of external events, Jones (1985) argues convincingly that other political or social events have also helped to shape modern social psychology—the interest in bargaining and negotiation prompted by concern about nuclear war, and the initiation of research on helping behavior in response to a brutal public murder are just two of the many examples.

Cognition and Motivation

During the last 50 years, and particularly the last 20, the field moved away from the initial questions about motivation and interpersonal behavior with which Lewin and Sherif began. It concentrated instead on the cognitive categorization processes inherent in understanding others, the knowledge structures involved in attitude organization and change, and the cognitive representations of the self and of the social world. There might be numerous explanations for the shift, but one of substantial import is that the discipline assumes that before the individual can engage in social behavior he or she must know about the social world and his or her place in it. For this reason, much of the research and theory to be described in the book deals with cognitive processes that are believed to take place within an individual. In recent years, however, the field has come full circle, with investigators returning to problems of affect, emotion, and interpersonal behavior, but returning with the more powerful conceptual tools that have been developed in the interim. This renewed attention to some of the recurrent problems that have defined the field of social psychology is also discussed in the pages to come.

Overview

In an attempt to show how social psychology addresses the fundamental questions about the causes of social behavior, the book begins with processes and products that are internal to the individual and ends with the effects of the physical environment and of a social system – the law – that plays an ever-increasing role in our daily life. After considering general issues of theory and method (Chapter 2), we start with the essential processes of social perception (Chapter 3) and social cognition (Chapter 4). Next we turn to attitude organization and change (Chapters 5 and 6). Because the social self consists of perceptions, cognitions, and attitudes, but initiates interpersonal actions, Chapter 7 provides a bridge to aspects of interpersonal behavior that begin with theories of social exchange (Chapter 8), and include discussions of interpersonal attraction and helping behavior (Chapter 9), and competition and aggression (Chapter 10). The external influences on social behavior begin with a discussion of power and influence (Chapter 11), and then describe social behavior in the context of other people (Chapter 12), the physical environment (Chapter 13), and the law (Chapter 14). The book concludes with a Methodological Appendix that contains material on experimentation, attitude measurement, and analysis of interpersonal behavior. Thus the book moves from *intra*personal processes to *inter*personal ones, from smaller units of behavior to larger ones. Although many instructors will find such an organization helpful, others may choose to consider the material in a quite different order. Consequently, the level of analysis remains the same throughout: the "midrange" theories of social psychology are applied both to social perception and to environment and law. I have not used "psychological" theories on the one hand and "sociological" theories on the other.

Methodology

Because scientific theories of social psychology differ from implicit theories primarily in their emphasis on careful definition and limiting conditions, a thorough introduction to research and theory is a valuable prelude to the remainder of the book. Chapter 2 begins with the assumptions that underlie social psychological theory; describes procedures for definition and replication; and concludes with a discussion of the ethical and validity ramifications of archival, observational, and experimental methods.

Specific research techniques described throughout the text in previous editions have been collected into a Methodological Appendix in this revision. This Appendix expands on the treatment of experimental design and analysis and contains techniques for the measurement of cognitive structures such as implicit personality theory and attitudes. To illustrate that experimental techniques can also be applied to the study of interpersonal behavior, the chapter concludes with a thorough description of a student-initiated study of romantic attraction.

Section 1: Intrapersonal Processes

Social Perception and Cognition. Much of our knowledge about the world is obtained through social perception and organized according to processes of social cognition. Chapter 3 begins with a discussion of accuracy in social perception, and considers the organizational processes involved in the construction of impressions. The discussion includes the factors involved in the encoding and decoding of facial expressions and nonverbal behavior, and describes the behavioral consequences of social perception.

Chapter 4 considers social cognition in a broader perspective, concentrating on the inferences perceivers make from the information they obtain. Processes of attribution are considered in detail, and the effects of cognitive heuristics and schemata are described. The chapter draws parallels among implicit personality theory and other cognitive structures such as prototypes of particular kinds of persons.

Attitudes and the Self. Remaining on the level of internal phenomena, Chapter 5 describes the affective, cognitive, and behavioral components of social attitudes and presents various models of attitude organization. The dynamic relationships among attitudes are often thought to be governed by a principle of cognitive consistency, which holds that inconsistency is a motivation for change. Two theories of cognitive consistency—dissonance theory and balance theory—are presented in detail.

Chapter 6 begins with a discussion of the attitude of racism, as an example of a social attitude that is resistant to change. The chapter then describes the process of persuasion and other general issues in attitude change. Sources of resistance to influence attempts and sources of facilitation are then considered, including the characteristics of persuasive communication, the relationship of the communication to the individual's existing attitude, and the effects of the target's participation in the process of attitude change.

The emphasis on primarily internal processes concludes, and the study of interpersonal processes begins, in Chapter 7, with discussion of the social self. An individual's self-concept is influenced to a significant degree by comparison with other people, and the results of such comparisons have implications for emotion and intrinsic motivation. Aspects of self-concept influence the person's estimates of the prevalence of his or her own views, the nature of self-presentation, and responses under normal and stressful circumstances. But the self is more than a collection of components. It is also an agent capable of voluntary actions toward other people, and many of these actions are considered in later chapters.

Section 2: Individual Needs
and Social Exchange

Theories of Social Exchange. Even with the shift to interpersonal behavior, the major concerns remain the personal and situational factors that affect social action. Chapter 8 is an overview of several conceptions of action – social learning theory, exchange theory, and equity theory – based generally on the principle of reinforcement. People usually try to maximize their rewards in social interaction, and the continuation of interaction may depend on the individual's belief that his or her outcomes are fair under the circumstances.

Positive Social Behavior. Chapter 9 describes the formation of friendships, the development of romantic attraction, and helping behavior among strangers. Intimacy in any ongoing relationship requires a degree of self-disclosure and a commitment to maintaining the relationship. Close relationships provide not only great personal satisfaction, but also the potential for damaging confrontation. The fact that helping behavior can be characterized in a variety of ways – by reference to the actor's intention, the benefits received by the recipient, or the demands of the situation – illustrates the difficulties encountered in the attempt to build sound research and theory. The costs and rewards involved in all of these positive forms of social behavior are considered.

Competition and Aggression. A different side of human interaction is dealt with in Chapter 10. In the case of both competition and aggression the description of the action in positive or negative terms may depend as much on the viewpoint of the observer as on the nature of the action itself. Competition may be affected by the characteristics of the situation or by internal factors such as the achievement motivation of the participants. The existence of aggression has been attributed to instinctive drives and to frustration, but much of the research evidence suggests that social learning plays an important role in the instigation to, and expression of, aggressive behavior.

Section 3:
Elements of the Social Context

The Social Environment. Chapter 11 begins consideration of the larger context for social behavior, first distinguishing between power and influence, then discussing sources of social power, the potential for resistance, and the difference between compliance and acceptance. The influence of one individual over another is illustrated by studies of Machiavellianism, and the influence of a group over an individual is shown by research on conformity. Even in a relationship between a powerful majority and a less powerful minority, some mutual contingency of action occurs, and this may contribute to social change.

Chapter 12 describes the process of communication within a group, and within a formal organization. Formal structure is distinguished from informal structure, processes of group leadership are described, and the mutual influence that occurs during group problem solving is discussed. Although groups often enable their individual members to achieve goals that would not be possible otherwise, the unquestioning pursuit of a goal can lead the group to lose touch with reality, producing one bad decision after another.

The Physical Environment and the Social System.   Chapter 13 takes into account the fact that all social behavior occurs in the context of a physical environment. Human beings, like other animals, have needs for personal space, territory, and privacy. These needs are strongly affected by cognitive processes, but the importance of both the natural environment and the built environment is demonstrated in a variety of ways.

Chapter 14 concludes the book with a discussion of the ways in which the larger social system, represented in this case by the law, involves individual social behavior. This chapter begins by describing similarities in the conception of human behavior held by social psychology and criminal justice. Then it suggests how agents of the legal system, acting at their discretion, are really behaving not as legal professionals, but as people governed by the principles of social psychology. These principles can be seen in such diverse areas as procedural justice and eyewitness testimony. Theories of attribution and social exchange are especially helpful tools with which to examine the processes involved in the criminal justice system.

SUGGESTED ADDITIONAL READINGS

JONES, E. E. (1985). Major developments in social psychology since 1930. In G. Lindzey & E. Aronson (Eds.), Handbook of social psychology (3rd ed., Vol. 1, pp. 47–108). This chapter on the recent history of social psychology shows how the field of experimental social psychology, which began in America in a few urban settings, has been shaped by its early contributors and by forces in the larger social and political environments.

CHAPTER TWO

THEORY
AND
METHOD

CONTENTS

Systematic Data Collection and Public Conclusions

ASSUMPTIONS OF SOCIAL PSYCHOLOGY

The Psychological Context
The Causes of Social Behavior
The Influence of Internal Processes
Elements of the Structure

DEFINITIONS, OPERATIONS, AND REPLICATION

Defining the Terms
Empirical Replication
Conceptual Replication

VALIDITY OF THE RESEARCH METHOD

Internal Validity: Meaningful Differences
External Validity: Results that Generalize

REACTIVITY IN SOCIAL PSYCHOLOGICAL RESEARCH

The Awareness of Being Tested
Response Biases in Experimenter and Subject

ARCHIVAL METHODS: HISTORY AS SOCIAL PSYCHOLOGY

An Illustration: Identifying Problems
The Importance of Interpretation

OBSERVATIONAL METHODS: BEHAVIOR IN PUBLIC PLACES

Four Observational Techniques
Concealed Participant Observation: The Doomsday Believers
Natural Experiments
Field Experiments

PREVIEW

Like other social and behavioral sciences, social psychology rests on several basic assumptions about the nature of causality and the character of human activity. These assumptions guide the specific theories of social behavior that are tested in archival, observational, and experimental research. Confidence in a particular finding increases when the same operations produce similar results in different settings (empirical replication) and when different operations yield similar conceptual conclusions (conceptual replication). Regardless of the research method chosen, the investigator must try to ensure that the findings obtained have both internal validity (freedom from artifacts) and external validity (generalizability beyond the context in which the research was performed). Archival and observational methods minimize the respondent's awareness that he or she is participating in research, whereas experimental methods provide the control needed for precise tests of theory. In both observational and experimental research, social psychologists must balance the potential benefits of their work against the potential risks to participants in the study. Through the refinement of theory, using methods that are ethically acceptable and methodologically sound, social psychology contributes to our understanding of human behavior.

Explaining social behavior is both a major interest of individuals and the principal task of scientific social psychology, but the different methods used by the two often lead to quite different conclusions. In the course of their experience, people develop implicit theories of social psychology: They observe and categorize social behavior, noting what they believe to be recurrent relationships between behavior and various situations and personal characteristics. These observations, however, are necessarily limited by the individual's own experience and viewpoint. The relevant data are haphazardly gathered, selectively remembered, and privately interpreted in light of preexisting ideas. Evidence that is expected or desired may be observed when it does not really exist, and disconfirming evidence may be overlooked.

Systematic Data Collection and Public Conclusions

In contrast, social psychologists develop formal theories of social behavior based on data gathered systematically. Research procedures are standardized and reported, so that they may be repeated by other investigators. Attempts are made to minimize or eliminate bias in the research process, and conclusions are drawn publicly so that they may be verified (or rejected) by later research. As the results of Milgram's (1963) obedience study so dramatically demonstrated in chapter 1, the conclusions drawn from the informal question "What do I think people will do?" can differ substantially from those based on the research question "What will people actually do?"

The purpose of this chapter is to show how social psychologists employ theories, and conduct research, to answer this latter question. We begin with a description of the assumptions underlying the scientific study of social behavior, then discuss the need for careful definition and replication, and conclude with a comparison of the major research methods in social psychology. A much more detailed description of the conduct of an experiment is given in the Methodological Appendix.

ASSUMPTIONS OF SOCIAL PSYCHOLOGY

The Psychological Context

One of the most important implications of recent work in the history of science (e.g., Holton, 1973; Kuhn, 1962) is that scientific disciplines – like individual people – have particular viewpoints that will affect the problems chosen for study, the methods employed in research, and the conclusions drawn from completed work. To borrow a familiar example from physical science, the very nature of observation and theory in astronomy was fundamentally (and irrevocably) altered when practicing astronomers rejected the belief that the Earth was the center of the planetary system. Note that what changed after acceptance of Copernicus's heliocentric theory of the solar system was not the fundamental structure of the universe. The physical relationships among stars, the sun, and the planets were exactly the same after the heliocentric theory was accepted as they had been before its introduction. What had changed was the belief structure of the people who were trying to give meaning to those physical relationships. Thus, it was the *psychological context* (Shaver, 1985) for the study of astronomy that underwent revolutionary change.

No explanation for social relationships receives the unanimous acceptance within social psychology that the heliocentric account of the solar system enjoys within astronomy. There are, however, a number of fundamental assumptions about social behavior that form the psychological context for current research and theory in social psychology. Almost without exception, social psychologists share common views on two related issues – the nature of causality and the importance of internal processes. Because these assumptions define the problems of interest, set limits for theory, and suggest what data collection methods are appropriate, they need to be specified in greater detail.

The Causes of Social Behavior

Underlying Regularities. In reading chapter 1, you will have noticed that although the formal definition of the discipline of social psychology refers to the behavior of an individual person, all of the research described as representative of the field involved multiple such individuals. This is because the behavior of one research subject is no better as an indication of what individual people in general will do than is your own personal experience. Social psychological studies are designed measure the underlying regularities in behavior that occur across subjects despite the unique personal history that each subject brings to the research.

As obvious as this assertion sounds, it embodies a particular position on a long-standing controversy in the analysis of human behavior – the classical argument between determinism and free will. Are human beings capable of making free choices among possible courses of action, or are what appear to be choices merely illusions, responses determined by prior events? Versions of this question have been debated in philosophy for centuries, and have plagued psychological science since its inception. The argument continues today, and may never be resolved to everyone's satisfaction. But a delicate balance between free will and determinism is part of the psychological context for current theory and research in social psychology.

The Principle of Determinism.   The principle of **determinism** consists of two related elements. First, it asserts that every event has a cause. A firm belief in this part of the principle is a virtual requirement for conducting scientific inquiry of any sort. Why? Consider the other alternatives: "no events have causes," or "some events do not have causes." If the first of these alternatives were true, there would be no underlying regularities to be discovered, either by scientists or by ordinary people trying to "understand" behavior. There would only be the explanation that "all events are random." If the second alternative were true, then there would be some events for which explanations could never be offered. Few scientists, and few nonscientists, would be comfortable admitting that there were phenomena that could, in principle, never be understood. Note that in this context, a view of the world based on religious faith is not in conflict with the scientific view: The only disagreement would be over *which* cause (divine intervention or a physical phenomenon) produced the event. Indeed, a "miracle" is an event for which a supernatural cause is invoked because the ordinary laws of physical causality do not seem to apply. The idea that every event has a cause is clearly not the point of controversy between determinism and free will.

The second assertion contained in the principle of determinism is that complete specification of the causal structure of the universe at one moment in time will permit infallible prediction of all future states of the universe. If there are no uncaused events, and if all of the cause-effect connections can be specified with precision, then by appropriate extrapolation, all future events can be predicted. As a simple example of this principle, imagine that you have designed a computerized robot about to begin to play a game of "rack pool" with an unsuspecting human opponent. The set of 15 billiard balls is arranged in a triangular "rack" on the surface of a rectangular pool table that has a pocket at each of the four corners, a pocket in the center of each of the two long sides, and "cushions" along all four sides.

The object of this game is to "sink" (put into the pockets) as many balls as you can, specifying in advance which ball will go into which pocket. The other player gets a turn only when the first player (your robot) misses a shot or mistakenly sinks the cue ball. When 14 of the 15 balls have been sunk those 14 are again "racked up" in the triangular pattern, and the shot that sinks the 15th ball must also "break" the rack. If your robot had been programmed with the exact resilience of each of the four cushions, the coefficient of drag of the felt surface of the table, the precise position of the triangular rack of balls, and the initial location of the cue ball, then it would be able to break the first rack in precisely the right way to sink a specified ball on the break shot. It would also be able to predict exactly where each of the remaining balls would come to rest after the first shot. Then the robot would take its second shot, making the very same precise predictions once again. This system is entirely deterministic. With its perfect knowledge of all of the conditions and causes, the robot would be able to predict successfully all future states of the balls on the table, and would, much to the dismay of its opponent, be able to continue playing literally forever.

Complexity and Statistical Prediction. The principle of determinism was originally formulated to describe the operation of physical systems, and in a concrete example like that of our mechanical pool hustler, the principle obviously works quite well. What happens when the predictions cannot be as precise, as in the case of a more complex physical system?

As an example of the latter, consider the nightly weather forecast. Enjoy the fancy computer graphics, the color weather radar, and the moving satellite photographs of the cloud cover. Then come sharply back to reality. Listen very carefully to the "predictions" for the next day, and you will hear high temperature ranges announced, not a temperature reading; wind velocity ranges, not a wind speed; and a probability value that there will be showers. After tomorrow is over, however, there will have been a maximum wind velocity, a single maximum and minimum temperature, and it either will or will not have rained.

Think of the sheer amount of television time taken up in describing, on hundreds of local stations, the "weather across the nation," the local temperature, humidity, sunrise, sunset, high and low tides, barometric pressure, sky conditions, and wind velocity and direction. Now think of the vast network of meteorologists making observations, and the banks of sophisticated computers that integrate all of this information. With such an investment of talent and technology, you'd think that you could at least avoid hearing "the weather service forecast calls for partly cloudy skies and a high of 80 this afternoon" as you sit shivering in your car, having just been drenched by a steady downpour that shows no signs of letting up. Can the principle of determinism apply to a phenomenon as unpredictable as the weather?

The answer to this question is, of course, affirmative. The problem is not that weather conditions have no causes, but rather that they have too many causes for accurate prediction to be possible at the current state of the art. Indeed, meteorological models often are used to test the capabilities of new computer systems, because those models are so complex that they can strain the limits of hardware and software alike, while still not including all of the mutually interacting variables known to influence the weather. Consequently, weather predictions must, at present, be statistical predictions, not precise predictions of single occurrences. When the forecaster claims a "20% chance of rain today" that claim cannot be taken literally. Either it will rain (100%) or it will not rain (0%) during the day in question. Rather it means that there has been rain on 20% of past days on which the current conditions have prevailed. Determinism still applies, even though the prediction is a statistical one, because in principle if there were complete information a precise (100% or 0%) prediction could be made.

Statistical Prediction and Multiple Observations. Human social behavior is at least as complex and variable as the weather, and it often is described by the same sort of statistical predictions. Some forecasts of human actions are exceedingly accurate (e.g., the television networks' "exit polls" that are used to predict vote totals in national elections), whereas other forecasts are completely off the mark (e.g., the predictions by several now-failed computer manufacturers that "the home computer will be as common as the telephone"). Moreover, predictions of social behavior made on the basis of research or theory have the same probabilistic form as predictions about the weather. We would, for example, predict on the basis of Milgram's (1963) research that roughly 60% of the subjects in a similar study would administer shocks as they were directed to by the experimenter. Any individual subject either would conform (100%) or not (0%), but given the conditions overall the average would be about 60%. Thus social psychology's search for the underlying regularities in social behavior must of necessity involve observation of more than one individual person. As you see later in the chapter, the concepts of statistical prediction and multiple observations are essential features of all research methods in social psychology.

The Influence of Internal Processes

The second fundamental component of the psychological context for research and theory in social psychology is the assumption that human behavior is governed by internal structures and processes that cannot be observed directly. This assertion would seem to be even more intuitively apparent than the idea that it is possible to discover underlying regularities in social behavior. Advertisers spend millions of dollars every year to change people's opinions about products of all sorts. Many businesses pay their employees on a commission basis, or invite salaried employees to participate in profit-sharing plans, on the assumption that these incentives will increase motivation. Whole systems of legal sanctions are designed to regulate interpersonal conduct by imposing penalties for infractions, in the belief that knowledge of these penalties will act to reduce antisocial activities. How could a discipline that presumes to study much of the same social behavior not concern itself with internal processes?

The answer is, of course, that social psychology does place a high value on the study of internal processes. But in so doing it takes a particular position on an issue that has been controversial in both philosophy and psychology, namely, that unobservable internal states can directly influence overt behavior. In the terms introduced in chapter 1, "opinions," "motivation," and "knowledge" are all *hypothetical constructs*, explanatory concepts that are not themselves directly observable. Some psychologists, notably those who subscribe to Skinner's (1953) version of behaviorism, would argue that the postulation of such internal states merely distracts us from the "true" causes of behavior – all of which are external to the person. For their part, philosophers who subscribe to the *materialist identity* position, which asserts that there is nothing to the mind but the electrochemical activity of the brain, would also object to our including constructs such as opinions, motivation, and knowledge among the possible causes of action.

On the other hand, many of our informal social rules, and much of the formal legal system, are based on the assumption that people make rational choices among possible courses of action. Not all of social behavior is this reflective, and even when choices are being considered factors in the external situation will influence the one actually made. But as Heider (1958) has noted, a person's intentions – internal and not directly observable – are what distinguishes true *personal* causality from the impersonal causality that characterizes a physical system. It is precisely because they can be reflected in intentional actions that social psychology attends to factors like "opinions," "motivation," and "knowledge."

Elements of the Structure

Just as a belief in the possibility of intentional action is part of the psychological context of social psychology, so too is there tacit agreement on three elements of the internal structure that would be needed to carry out such intentional actions: representation, organization, and motivation. Each of us has, at one time or another, done something morally questionable, for which action we have later felt guilt or remorse. Think very carefully about such an instance in your own life, particularly the various pressures on you to do the right thing. Society attempts to reinforce moral action, our parents admonish us to be honest and forthright, and nearly all of us think of ourselves as "good" people. So virtually all of the external pressures would lead us to behave in a morally acceptable manner. Yet occasionally we do not. Using that choice as the object of explanation, let us consider each of the three elements in more detail.

Representation. The first essential structural feature is an internal representation of the external social world, the moral precepts directing you toward one course of action, the temptation directing you toward a different behavior, and the presumed consequences that would follow each choice. Not only moral choices, but virtually all of your other social behavior as well will be based on your **phenomenological experience** of the world around you. By the term *phenomenological experience* social psychologists refer to the internal representations of people, objects, and situations you have constructed from data obtained through your senses (either perceived in the present, or remembered from the past). What governs your actions is not the external world as it is, but that world *as it appears to you.*

Your phenomenological experience may or may not agree with the "objective" world, and the potential for disagreement is one of the factors that limits the predictive usefulness of the personal experience of any individual person. Think about the moral dilemma you faced. Was it one for which there would be almost universal agreement on the "correct" alternative (no differences in phenomenological experience)? Or was part of the problem the very fact that some people you respect thought one choice to be morally correct, whereas other people you respect considered the other choice correct (disagreement among phenomenological experience)? In the first instance accurate predictions might be made for almost anyone's behavior simply from knowing what was involved in the choice. In the second instance, however, accurate predictions of behavior would have to take into account some of the factors—education, religious training, self-concept—that might have led to the differing perceptions of the choices to be made.

Some of the representations that will be important in later chapters are the social perceptions you have of other people and the causes of their actions, the beliefs that you possess about various attitude objects, and the errors can arise when the immediate social world is defined by a tightly knit group of people who have a crucial decision to make.

Organization. Just having representations of the external world is not enough to permit choices among response alternatives. Perceptions and beliefs must be evaluated, categorized, and ce. distinguished from one another. Was the choice you needed to make between two incompatible, but morally laudable aims (for example, do you reveal something told you in confidence by one friend in order to keep another friend from inadvertently saying something that would have hurt the first person)? Or was the choice between a morally approved action and one generally disapproved? Just asking these questions gives some idea of the *organization* that is necessary: there must be a cognitive category for "friends," there must be an internalized set of moral principles against which any of the actions can be compared, there must be a conception of "the future," and the ability to see a relationship between your own actions and the the actions of others.

The behavioral choices you make are seldom between one course of action that is utterly without redeeming moral value and another course of action that is, for every conceivable reason, morally correct. Rather, most of your social actions are the consequence of a choice made between roughly comparable, but imperfect, alternatives. The possibilities must be examined, compared, placed in the larger context provided by your past actions and future plans, and only then can the choice be made. In your dealings with the world you develop both the cognitive structures necessary for these comparisons, and the cognitive processes by which the comparisons can be made. The ideas of structure and process form the foundation for much of what is to come, including the study of social cognition, attitude organization, and the determination of fairness in a social interaction.

Motivation. The final internal element necessary for making choices among alternative courses of action is the concept of motivation. You have an internal representation of the morally approved action and its consequences, and a comparable representation of the morally disapproved action. You have compared the two sets of consequences, and now you choose to take one path instead of the other. Your action implies a preference between the two, which preference could be based entirely on the specifics of the two actions, on more enduring aspects of your goals or self-concept, on your judgment of the meaning that each action would have for other people, or on some combination of all of these factors. It is important to note that whatever its source, the preference is the expression of a motive. Representations of the world and beliefs about the ways in which actions compare are not sufficient in and of themselves for the production of action. These beliefs must be combined with motives for intentional actions to be taken. The idea that social behavior reflects underlying motivation will recur throughout the chapters to come, especially in the areas of attitude change and the social exchange that constitutes interpersonal behavior.

In many disciplines one can find rather sharp divisions based either on theoretical content or on the methodology involved in research. Theoretical physics is different from experimental physics, physical anthropology is different from cultural anthropology, and pitched battles are waged between biologists who accept sociobiology and those who do not. Even personality psychology and clinical psychology are dominated by a few well known theoretical approaches that dictate which problems are considered important and which solutions are most likely to be productive.

Within social psychology, however, the disagreements tend to be drawn more narrowly, often in terms of the value of a particular theory or the efficacy of a specific research technique. Virtually whatever their theoretical or methodological commitments might be, social psychologists will share a psychological context that assumes human behavior to be influenced by structures and processes within the person. The objective of the discipline as a whole is to increase our understanding of these structures and processes, using variations on archival, observational, or experimental methods. Throughout the discussion of methods, we will use selected examples from the research literature to illustrate important concepts. In addition, to provide greater continuity across the various procedures, we take a specific example of a social behavior – cheating in college – and show how each method might be used to study that behavior.

DEFINITIONS, OPERATIONS, AND REPLICATION

Suppose that you are a social psychologist. You are teaching at a college or university, the time for final examinations is fast approaching, and you happen to be discussing with some of your colleagues the need for imposing tight security on the departmental office during preparation of the examinations. You all agree that it is a sad commentary on the state of academic affairs, and one of your colleagues says "All right, you are the social psychologist, why don't you tell us why students cheat?" You might be tempted to give a quick answer such as "To get better grades," or "Because there is such a small chance of getting caught," or (if you have become very cynical) "Why not? Doesn't everyone?" These answers suggest quite different possible explanations and help to illustrate that the example generalizes quite well to other situations – preparation of fraudulent income tax returns, unethical business or political practices, and white collar crime.

In conceptual terms the first rationale is an instrumental one. Dishonesty is seen as the means toward a desired end. The second answer assumes that people's natural evil tendencies can be prevented from affecting their behavior only if the punishment for transgression is swift and sure. That sort of viewpoint should have a familiar ring to anyone who has listened to the justifications for most of our criminal laws. The third answer suggests that morality ought to be defined not in terms of universal principles, but only in relative terms, and further, that to be moral is to put yourself at a competitive disadvantage. That these three rationales for behavior occur frequently suggests that although the example of college cheating is limited in scope, its assumptions about human nature will be relevant for a wide variety of other situations.

Defining the Terms

Restrictions on Meaning. Now, what else can be said about the answers to the question? Although any one of your responses might have been correct, it is important to notice that you have not responded *as a social psychologist*. You have answered with guesses based on your own implicit theory of social psychology. What you should have done, instead, was ask a few questions of your own. What does your colleague mean by the word "cheat"? Does this category of "cheating behavior" include the actions of a student who looks at another's paper during the examination as well as the actions of a student who steals the examination in advance? What about a student who has someone else take the exam in his or her place? Does cheating also include purchasing a term paper? Using the spelling checker that is part of your wordprocessing system? Bringing an electronic calculator to a mathematics exam? Getting special tutoring from the laboratory assistant? Asking questions in class about issues that are almost certain to be on the test? But wait a minute. At least this last possibility sounds like "being a good student," not like "cheating." As a matter of fact, obtaining extra tutoring also sounds more like responsible behavior than like cheating. And using electronic aids available to you may be unfair to the students who cannot afford them, but is it really "cheating?"

The crucial point is that although there might be rather widespread agreement that some of these practices are "cheating," and some are not, certainty can be achieved only with a proper definition. To circumvent the problems created by individualized views of cheating (which individualized views depend to a great degree on different phenomenological experience) the abstract concept of cheating must be reduced to an agreed-upon set of observable behaviors. Let us say that you and I had planned to compare the level of cheating at our two institutions. Suppose that I included using a spelling checker among the prohibited activities and you did not. We would probably find more cheating at my institution than at yours, but that difference would have been spuriously inflated by the differences in definition. Because social psychology relies on statistical prediction, researchers must strive for results that will be *replicable,* or repeatable, in other settings. This goal is difficult enough to reach under the best of circumstances. Without very careful definition of the conceptual propositions under study, the goal is unattainable.

Operational Definition. We have already seen the necessity for constructing a behavioral definition of the concept, so that different researchers will be studying the same set of actions. But is that enough? Suppose that you and I have agreed to exclude from the category of "cheating behavior" everything but "looking at another student's paper during the examination." Now if I take all of my measurements during midterm exams in small classes where the professor remains in the room, and you make all of your observations from the projection booth of a large lecture hall during a final examination conducted without proctors, the amounts of cheating that we observe will almost certainly be different. But is the difference a function of the character of the two schools and their students, or is it attributable to the differences in time and method of measurement? It is clear that for the data from the two settings to be strictly comparable, we must modify our behavioral definition of the concept so that it becomes an **operational definition**: a definition stated in terms of the operations performed to measure the behavior of interest.

Empirical Replication

Strict comparability between two or more settings is especially important when the object of the research is the documentation of the existence or prevalence of a phenomenon. If we seek to test the proposition that "30% of all university students cheat," then we had better make certain that the behaviors included in the definition, and the operations employed to measure cheating, are as similar as we can possibly make them across our sample of universities. If we conduct such a comparison, we will have performed an **empirical replication**: a second (or subsequent) study in which the operations used are as nearly identical as possible to those of the first study. There will, of course, have been differences in place, time, participants, and perhaps researchers, but the procedures will have been the same.

Empirical replications are most useful in permitting us to generalize findings across several populations, but even here we must not forget the social psychology of research. Suppose, for example, that our empirical replication finds similar levels of cheating at two different universities, but that (unbeknownst to us) there has recently been a cheating scandal at one of these institutions. Does the similar level of cheating obtain because students at both institutions are equivalent in personal morality, or because those at the place where the scandal took place are just being more careful than they would otherwise have been? We have failed to take into account that the subjects bring with them into the research setting not only their own internal individual differences, but also their own recent experience. The fact that our procedures have been identical does not in and of itself guarantee that similar behaviors reflect similar personal predilections.

Conceptual Replication

Using the same operations at two different universities we may have obtained reliable evidence about the prevalence of cheating. But remember that the task of social psychology is to discover the personal and situational factors involved in the production of social behavior, not merely to document the existence of various activities. To achieve this more important objective the strict comparability inherent in the empirical replication may not be necessary, or even desirable. In many cases the generality of research findings can be increased by using different procedures in varying settings.

Different Operational Definitions. Suppose that we wanted to determine whether there was more cheating on final examinations than on midterm examinations (presumably because of the greater pressure created by the final exam). You would measure the incidence of cheating at both examination times at your university, and I would observe the incidence of cheating at both times at my university. Each one of us would, of course, have to have the same operational definition of cheating on the final that we had used on the midterm, but we might increase the generality of our results by using different operational definitions in the two universities. If you observed the large lecture class from the projection booth (where you would not be seen) and I observed several small classes from the rear of the room, we would, as indicated earlier, probably discover a larger amount of cheating at your university.

But now the absolute prevalence of cheating is not our primary concern; instead we are interested in the change in cheating from the midterm to the final. The level of cheating observed at midterm would be the base rate for each set of research circumstances (university, class size, presence or absence of observer), and the level of cheating at the final examination would be expressed as a change from this base rate. What we have conducted is an elementary **conceptual replication**: we have both tested the same concept—change in cheating behavior—but have used quite different operations to do so.

Now let us assume that although the midterm base rates differ across the two universities, there is about twice as much cheating on the final examination in each institution as there had been on the midterm. We do not even attempt to interpret the overall differences in levels, because we know that they might have been produced as much by the different measurement techniques as by any intrinsic characteristics of the students. We do compare the two *rates* of increase, find them to be the same, and conclude that final examinations will produce about twice as much cheating as will midterms. Only the timing (midterm-final) variable was constant across the two settings, and so we achieve a higher degree of confidence than we would have, had everything else also been the same.

Problems with Conceptual Replications. Conceptual replications are not, however, free from risks. We stand to gain more precise information if the conceptual replication is successful, but will have a more difficult time interpreting any differences in conclusions. Consider only one of the possible failures to replicate: compared to its midterm level, cheating doubles at the final at your university, but remains at the same low level at mine. Perhaps this is because the presence of an observer is sufficiently threatening that only the most desperate will risk being caught either at midterm or at the final, or perhaps the group solidarity engendered by small classes establishes implicit norms against cheating (again, violated only by the most desperate). Or perhaps the students at my school have more rigid superegos, while the students at your school believe in a situationally based set of ethical principles that permits cheating if the stakes are high enough. The problem with unsuccessful conceptual replication is that we cannot tell from any of the data available which of these possibilities – or others that we have not mentioned – actually produced the difference in results.

Multiple Operationism. What is the solution? The best research strategy should combine elements of both empirical and conceptual replication. As Campbell and Fiske (1959) have argued, the concepts of social psychology are sufficiently complex so that no single operation can serve as a complete definition. As a consequence, sound research procedure would require what Campbell and Fiske have called **multiple operationism**: the use of different operations to define any particular concept. Assuming that we could agree that cheating involved stealing examinations, using crib notes, having others take the tests, copying from another's paper, and a limited number of other specific actions, then our research should incorporate as many of these different operational definitions as possible. In addition to incorporating multiple definitions of the concept under investigation, an ideal study should use multiple measures of the various dependent variables. In the cheating example, reports to the campus honor council, perceptions of the class members about the amount of cheating going on, and anonymous self-reported cheating might be added to the observations that you and I make in the actual classrooms. Because of the uncertainty inherent in the statistical predictions that must be made by social psychology, it is exceedingly important to rule out as much of the methodological uncertainty as possible.

It should be noted, however, that a healthy combination of conceptual and empirical replication, with all the proper controls and with enough auxiliary data to rule out potential alternative explanations of the results, can seldom occur in actual practice. Time, money, subjects, and research assistants are limited; in most cases they are aptly described as meager. As a result, researchers must find ways to compromise on the joint goals of conceptual and empirical replication. They must depend, instead, on lengthy programs of research studies, rather than on single large studies that might answer more of the questions at one time.

VALIDITY
OF THE RESEARCH METHOD

As noted before, the task of scientific social psychology (as compared to the naive social psychology of the individual) is to discover how people actually behave in social situations and to specify the limiting conditions for the principles discovered. This task imposes two requirements on the research conducted: measurement errors must be minimized or eliminated, and the findings need to generalize beyond the specific context of the study. We shall consider each of these requirements in turn.

Internal Validity:
Meaningful Differences

First, the researcher must be certain that the findings obtained are real differences of psychological importance, rather than mere **artifacts**: results produced by errors in procedure. Suppose that you were comparing the level of cheating on a final examination in large classes with the level of cheating on a final in small classes. The variable of conceptual interest might be the students' feelings of anonymity, with less personal identification presumably leading to lowered restraints against a socially undesirable behavior. Let us further suppose that you discovered greater cheating in the large classes. You might be tempted to conclude that anonymity was the "cause" of the difference, until you noticed – much to your dismay – that the final examinations in all of the large classes involved multiple-choice questions, whereas all of the final examinations in the small classes were short answer and essay questions. It could be that the results you obtained had nothing at all to do with anonymity (the variable of psychological interest), but rather with the form of the examination (a measurement artifact).

The more a researcher can be confident that the findings represent differences based on the psychological variable under study, rather than measurement artifacts, the greater the **internal validity** of the research will be. Internal validity thus reflects the degree of control inherent in the research. The better the controls against artifacts, and the more alternative explanations that are ruled out, the more likely it is that the differences obtained in the results reflect the variable actually operationalized.

External Validity:
Results that Generalize

Knowledge that the psychological variable of interest produced the results obtained is exceedingly important, but research will assume practical utility only if the results generalize beyond the observational or laboratory setting in which they were obtained. The extent to which a finding will generalize to other subject samples, times, or settings is the **external validity** of the finding. If this comparison across subjects, times, and settings sounds familiar, it is because the process of conceptual replication is one of the principal means of establishing the external validity of a particular set of results. The more different ways we test a theoretical proposition, provided the results remain the same, the more confident we become of the external validity of the original test of the idea.

Representativeness of Subjects and Experience.   In addition to conceptual replication, there are other ways in which the researcher can enhance the external validity of the findings. The first of these is to ensure that the subjects used in the research are representative of the population to which the findings are to be generalized. This question of **representativeness** is more complex than it would first appear, because some of the phenomena of interest to social psychology generalize more readily than others. For example, if we wish to compare how various descriptive adjectives are combined into a complete impression of a stimulus person (this work is discussed in detail in chapter 4), then the fact that the subjects are college sophomores is only a minor threat to the external validity of the results. There is no a priori reason to believe that these basic processes of impression formation will be substantially different in other people within the same linguistic community as the subjects.

By contrast, if we are attempting to study the factors that lead to jury convictions and acquittals through simulation with college sophomores, the need to ensure external validity is a constant challenge. The class of potential real jurors typically includes all registered voters, and although many college students are voters, many other voters have never been to college. Some of this built-in bias can be taken into account by careful subject selection and use of stimulus materials known to be clear to those without a college education. But not even the most conscientious researcher can guarantee representativeness of experience: experimental juries will always be just that. No matter how "real" we make the simulation of the jury process, it will still be true that no actual defendant's fate or freedom rests on the decision to be made. This crucial difference in experience will limit the external validity of the verdicts rendered by simulated juries. The obtained findings are no less psychologically real (in the internal validity sense), and simulated juries may tell us a great deal about group decision processes. Those findings, however, can only be taken as a rough estimate of what actual juries might do with the same case.

REACTIVITY IN SOCIAL PSYCHOLOGICAL RESEARCH

In most instances, the people who are participating in social psychological research are aware that they are not merely behaving, they are creating data. Because the discipline is interested in the (often intentional) behavior of the individual person, and because that person is presumed to be capable of choice (such as the choice of whether or not to cooperate with the researcher), social psychology is more likely than are other behavioral sciences to have its data affected by the subject's knowledge that he or she is under scrutiny. The extent to which data may be distorted by the unique features of participating in research is referred to as the **reactivity** of the measurement technique. Several sources of reactivity have been identified (Webb, Campbell, Schwartz, & Sechrest, 1966), and for our purposes these may be grouped into two general categories: problems arising from the awareness of being tested, and problems arising from individual response biases.

The Awareness of Being Tested

Although you may be a willing, cooperative, and well-intentioned participant in my research, you are still "behaving like a subject" rather than "behaving naturally." This problem arises whether the research is conducted in an experimental laboratory or in the subject's normal surroundings, and it can take on quite substantial proportions. Webb and his colleagues (1966) cite an incident in which a number of graduate students were sent to a South Side Chicago street that intersected an informal racial boundary. The students were to observe the numbers of blacks and whites in stores, bars, restaurants, and theaters to determine how these proportions might change as one moved from the predominantly white end of the street to the predominantly black end. The observers were simply to make counts, not to question any people on the street. As research goes, this should have been relatively innocuous, yet two merchants were sufficiently upset to place repeated calls to the university to determine whether the observers were performing an official function, or casing their places of business in preparation for a later robbery. The problem is that if the researchers had this much effect on the merchants, their presence must also have affected the actions of the passersby who were being counted.

Demand Characteristics. If behaving like a subject is a problem in field observation, it is even more troublesome in the experimental laboratory. In what was to be a test of the power of hypnosis, Orne (1962) reported a series of pilot studies that had been intended to create a task that nonhypnotized individuals would quickly refuse to continue. (Once such a task had been discovered, Orne would have asked hypnotized subjects to perform it, predicting that these people would continue for a much longer time.) In one of these pilot experiments subjects were asked to sum pairs of adjacent numbers on sheets filled with rows of random digits. To finish even a single sheet would require 224 additions, and each participant was presented with a pile of nearly 2,000 such sheets. After the initial instructions, the experimenter removed the subject's watch and told the person to begin working, claiming that he would "return eventually." After as much as 5 ½ hours the experimenter gave up and returned to stop the subject.

Thinking that subjects might have invented some rationale for this absurd task, Orne then tried to make its meaninglessness even clearer for a second group of pilot subjects. These people were given the same addition task, but now upon completing each page of additions, the subjects were to receive further instructions by turning over the top card in a large stack of index cards. Every card in this stack directed the subject to tear the just-completed sheet of additions into not less than 32 pieces. Surprisingly, subjects persisted in this task for as much as several hours without objection!

As Orne points out, "Just about any request which could conceivably be asked of the subject by a reputable investigator is legitimized by the quasi-magical phrase, 'This is part of an experiment,' and the shared assumption that a legitimate purpose will be served by the subject's behavior" (1962, p. 777). Participation in research can be seen as problem-solving behavior. In order to be helpful (to conform to the experimenter's hypothesis) the subject must first discover what that hypothesis is. To make this decision, the subject presumably relies on what Orne (1959) called the **demand characteristics** of the experimental situation: the sum total of all the cues that convey an experimental hypothesis to the subject.

Note that this need not be the experimenter's true hypothesis, but only one that the subject considers plausible in the circumstances. Indeed, it is just this difference that provides one of the rationales for the use of deception in experimental research. If a good "cover story" suggests a plausible alternative hypothesis, the subject's behavior relative to that hypothesis will be biased, but actions relevant for the true hypothesis will be uncontaminated by demand characteristics. If I could convince you that I was conducting research on people's ability to cope with life stress, you might be more likely to behave "naturally" (that is, to cheat on the final examination, if that was your predilection) than if you thought I was investigating the influence of perceived examination unfairness on people's willingness to cheat.

Evaluation Apprehension. Whether a volunteer or a nonvolunteer, the experimental subject probably approaches the task with mixed feelings. He or she may be taking part to earn money, to help advance psychological science, to obtain course credit, or just to kill some time between classes. In addition to these various motives for participation, the subject may feel some reluctance. The psychologist's business is to learn about people, and the subject may wonder what personal secrets will be revealed by his or her actions in the experiment. Subjects have what Rosenberg (1965) called **evaluation apprehension**: concern about obtaining a positive evaluation from the experimenter. If any cues to the behavior of the "typical" subject are available in the setting, the actual participant will try to respond in the way that "everyone else" is thought to respond. This concern will be heightened in any research involving behavior with moral or value overtones, and would be a particular problem in an experimental study of cheating behavior.

Response Biases
in Experimenter and Subject

Experimenter Expectancy. If demand characteristics and evaluation apprehension are products of the subject's interest in the research, then the set of potential biases known as *experimenter effects* (Rosenthal, 1966) reflects the fact that the researcher also has a stake in the outcome. The most obvious experimenter effects are the infrequent intentional distortions of data that, when brought to light, destroy the career of the researcher, arouse suspicion toward the discipline involved, and provide evidence that dishonesty can be found in any profession. More subtle are *interpreter effects* that take place in the coding of observational data or in the drawing of conclusions. These arise from overreliance on a tenuous theory (the scientific version of "My mind is made up, don't confuse me with the facts"), and are likely to be corrected when less committed investigators (or investigators committed to the opposing theoretical view) attempt to replicate the findings. Somewhat less easily corrected are the *biosocial effects* based on the race, sex, and appearance of the experimenter (e.g., the problem of using white experimenters to test the intelligence of children in an inner-city black neighborhood). The last potential source of experimenter bias–**experimenter expectancy**–is the least available for public scrutiny, and has received the most attention.

An experimenter's values will influence his or her choice of problems for study (for example, will they be prosocial ones or antisocial ones, problems of one segment of society or of another?), choice of methodology (observation or experimentation, deception or some alternative, college or noncollege subjects), and to some extent the particular hypotheses proposed. Research in social psychology, like that in other areas, is seldom conducted as a "fishing expedition" by people who have no interest in the outcome. Rather, it is conducted on limited problems by interested experimenters who have theoretical or practical goals toward which the research is directed. Thus it is not surprising, or even undesirable, that experimenters have definite ideas about what their research might show. Expectancy effects only become troublesome when the experimenter inadvertently communicates those ideas to the subject. In this case, the experimenter's expectation becomes a *self-fulfilling prophecy* (Merton,1957); it is communicated to the subject who, possibly because of a desire to be helpful or a fear of being evaluated, behaves according to the expectancy, even though he or she might not otherwise have done so. Thus the problem for the researcher is not to deny having any notion of how the research might turn out, but rather to make certain that this expectancy is not communicated to the subjects.

Keeping the Experimenter Blind to the Conditions. Contamination of research data by expectancy effects could best be avoided by trying to keep the experimenters as "blind" as possible to the experimental hypotheses and conditions. At first this sounds like an impossible task. But it can be done more easily than it would first seem. If the subjects have been grouped by their scores on some premeasure, the grouping can be accomplished by someone other than the person who will actually deliver the experimental instructions. If those instructions begin with the same general opening statement, and only later diverge for the different experimental conditions, the experimenter can determine which particular treatment is to be administered by turning over the top card of a stack of index cards after the general instructions have been delivered. If the manipulations are contained on videotape, the same card-turning procedure can be used to determine which segment of the tape to play, again, after all of the introductory instructions have been administered. Finally, if the manipulations are to be contained in written materials, the experimenter can randomly intermix those materials, and run sessions in which all of the conditions appear at the same time.

Response Biases in the Subjects. Unfortunately for the social psychologist, the problems created by awareness (demand characteristics and evaluation apprehension) and by experimenter expectancy are not the only reactive effects present in research. The last major problem is the **response set**: a general tendency to respond in a specified way, regardless of the particular circumstances or information content. For example, when people are asked interview questions, they will more frequently agree with a statement than disagree with the statement's opposite (Sletto, 1937). This tendency is referred to as the **acquiescence** response set. Although there is some evidence (Rorer, 1965) that it may not apply to virtually any content, acquiescence does affect measures of importance to social psychologists (Campbell, Siegman, & Rees, 1967). Both for this reason, and because the correction is so simple—word half of the items in a positive direction, half in a negative direction—acquiescence is usually reduced to negligible proportions.

Other response sets such as **social desirability** (Crowne & Marlowe, 1964; Edwards, 1957) are more difficult to deal with. People hold private beliefs that do not always agree with those widely approved in society, and investigators often find most interesting the basically "undesirable" behaviors—cheating, aggression, the raw exercise of even legitimate power. For either or both of these reasons, the researcher runs the risk of obtaining from the subject not true feelings or behavior, but an opinion or behavior the subject believes will meet with the approval of the experimenter.

To complicate the issue still further, social desirability may well be defined by the subjects in terms of the presumed subculture or actual biosocial attributes of the experimenter, rather than in terms of society as a whole. For example, if in my study of academic cheating I employ interviewers who boast of their own exploits (such as "boosting" cars, or "ripping off" large department stores) before asking questions of the respondents, I am likely to get an overestimate of the cheating that actually occurs. In response to the social desirability demands of the interview situation, the subjects have had to prove that they, too, are in a position to take risks.

Threats to internal validity from the social desirability response bias can be minimized, if not eliminated, by reducing the desirability demands inherent in the procedures, by masking the value loadings of questions asked of subjects, and by using standard measures of the response bias (e.g., Crowne & Marlowe, 1964; Edwards, 1957) to remove by statistical methods that portion of the subject's responses that might have been contributed by social desirability. As is the case with all of the other potential threats to internal and external validity, there is no substitute for careful advance planning of the research, regardless of the particular method to be employed.

ARCHIVAL METHODS: HISTORY AS SOCIAL PSYCHOLOGY

We have noted earlier that social psychology involves the search for underlying regularities in social behavior. At the societal level, much of this behavior has been documented, so some historical records can be of use to social psychologists. The ongoing, continuing records of a society are its archives, and although they are usually maintained for some other purpose, such records can help us understand aspects of social behavior.

An Illustration: Identifying Problems

Suppose that you were challenged to show that social psychological research and theory have something to say about important domestic problems in the United States. The first task you would have is to identify those "important domestic problems." With a large research budget you could conduct a national survey, such as those frequently performed by newspapers or television networks. This would involve the construction of standard questions to be asked of some 1,500-2,000 individuals across the country, with later computerized analysis of the responses. At the other extreme, you could consult no one, and rely entirely on your own personal opinion of what the critical problems are. Neither of these methods will really suit your purposes: the first is too expensive for your personal budget, and the second is suspect because it is restricted to your (possibly idiosyncratic) view of the world. Is there a convenient, but inexpensive alternative?

Alternative Operationalizations of the Concept. There is, and it is as close as your university library. Keep in mind that "important domestic problems" is a concept, and a national survey would only be one possible operationalization of that concept. There are others, including, for example, the problems identified by national news magazines. A weekly publication such as *Newsweek* has a "cover story" each week, which story is deemed by the editors to address the most newsworthy event of the week. This editorial judgment of "importance" is obviously affected by the need to sell magazines, a need that has both negative and positive consequences. On the negative side, assuming the truth of the adage that "bad news is news," then the number of problems identified in cover stories is likely to be somewhat inflated. All that means is that you should not accept at face value the proportion of "bad news" cover stories to "good news" cover stories. On the positive side, although the magazine may have an editorial bias that will affect its choice of problems for study, that editorial bias cannot completely lose touch with public opinion, or sales will suffer. So although "problems chosen for cover stories" is not a perfect operationalization of "important domestic problems," it is certainly a defensible one.

Selective Survival. You decide to examine the cover stories, to categorize them, and to use that information to identify the important domestic problems. You go to the library, search through the stacks for the most recent complete volume of *Newsweek* and find the bound volumes that represent 1984. You look through the volumes, and begin writing down the titles of the cover stories. Unfortunately, when you reach November, you discover that all four issues for the month are missing from the bound materials. You have just become aware of one of the three major threats to the internal validity of archival research: **selective survival**. Some records will not last as long as others, either because of natural decay or because of deliberate destruction (or in this case, probably theft).

The advantage you have over most archival researchers, however, is a significant one: You know that the records are missing, because you are dealing with a regular publication. Suppose, instead, that in an attempt to investigate the past history of cheating in your university you have looked through years of back issues of the student newspaper for reports of honor council trials. You discover that between 1940 and 1960 such reports appeared at the rate of roughly six or seven per year. Unfortunately, a pipe burst in the room that was used to house the paper's issues between 1961 and 1970, so all of those issues have turned to mush. Because the honor council reports were issued on an irregular basis, you have no way of estimating how many such reports might have been contained in the issues that are now inaccessible.

Index Numbers. You had been planning merely to count the number of cover stories dealing with important domestic problems, and to report that number (assuming that you had been able to locate all the issues for the year). You now decide to end the survey with the last issue of October, rather than to skip the missing November issues and return with December cover stories, the choice of some of which might have been influenced by the stories that appeared in the November issues you cannot locate. Because you know how many issues there should have been, you can correct for the loss very simply by reporting the percentage of cover stories devoted to domestic problems (now divided by 44). What you have accomplished with this correction is to turn a raw number into an **index number**: a number corrected for base rate.

As simple as this correction for base rate is, it is all too frequently ignored. Suppose you discovered that there were twice as many cases of cheating reported in your school newspaper for last year as for the academic year of 1955–1956. Does that mean that students are more dishonest now, or are at least being caught and prosecuted twice as often? Not if the enrollment of your school has also doubled in the same time period. As another example, how can one radio station in your area boast that it has "the fastest growing audience" in the region, whereas another station claims to have "the biggest share of the market?" Because the two are using different base rates – percentage increase from a low market share for the first, absolute value of the market share for the second. Only when someone compels them to state their claims in terms of the same index numbers will it be possible to determine which might be the best investment of advertising dollars.

Selective Deposit. If the theoretical base rate is known, then it is easy to correct for selective survival by using index numbers. Another threat to the internal validity of archival research designs – **selective deposit** – calls for a different sort of solution. Selective deposit refers to the possibility that some records will be established more fully than others, either because of deliberate administrative action or because of contemporary social custom. In the case of college cheating, for example, it is quite possible that some colleges and universities may be more conscious of their public images than are others. The former would be more likely deliberately to suppress publication of the outcomes of disciplinary hearings, possibly until a widespread scandal overwhelms the administrative tendency toward secrecy.

When you look over the titles of the cover stories for the 44 issues of *Newsweek* that you are still considering for 1984, you notice that two events – the Olympic Games and the presidential election – dominate the news for that year, and you realize that this may be an instance of selective deposit: The editors of the magazine have devoted so much space to these two events that other problems that might have received attention are obscured. Here again, by comparison to someone studying cheating you have a distinct advantage. You know what specific events might have led to the editors' collective decision, and you can check that supposition by comparing the 44 weeks of 1984 to the same 44 weeks for 1983 (or for other years as well). Once you have made this comparison, you could choose either to report the problems identified in years other than the election year, or you could show the difference by reporting data for both 1983 and 1984. Doing the latter could give you an additional clue to what problems are considered important: What categories of stories were reduced to make room for coverage of the Olympics and the election?

The Importance of Interpretation

Category Construction. The data on problems that were the subject of cover stories in the months between January and November of 1983 and 1984 are shown in Table 2.1. Notice that the table does not contain the titles of all 44 cover stories, but rather lists categories of stories, and the percentage of stories devoted to each category. The construction of coding categories in archival (or observational) research is usually guided by the investigator's theory and by some informal rules. The categories should be roughly equivalent in breadth (so that some are not more specific than others) and there should not be more of them than the quotient obtained by dividing the total number of elements to be categorized by 5 (44 divided by 5 is 8+). Finally, once the categories have been constructed, a second person should also do the assignments, to see how well those assignments agree with those of the person who originally developed the categories (you might see how your own classification of the January through October *Newsweek* cover stories agrees with the one shown in the table.

Selective Sampling. The final threat to internal validity in an archival design is **selective sampling**: the possibility that the records chosen for analysis are unrepresentative of the population under study. If we had not

TABLE 2.1 Percentages of Newsweek Cover Stories by Categories, January through October, 1983 and 1984

Category of Cover Story	Jan.-Oct. 1983	Jan.-Oct. 1984
Arms Control, Relations with USSR	9	2
Behavioral or Natural Science	7	4
Domestic Problems in America	25	25
International Relations	32	14
Olympic Games	2	9
Partisan Politics	7	30
Popular Culture	14	14
Unclassifiable	4	2
Total of all categories	100	100

attended to the fact that 1984 included the Olympic Games and a presidential election, we would have erroneously concluded that "partisan politics" might be a significant and enduring national interest. In the 1984 sample 29% of the cover stories dealt with this topic. In 1983, however, only 7% of the stories had to do with partisan politics. Which of these figures is the truly representative one? It is impossible to say with certainty from only the two comparisons given (again, doing your own count for a different year, or even for a different combination of election years and non-election years, would provide the answer).

Notice that even though the two years differ significantly in the attention they pay to partisan politics and the games, they have identical proportions of cover stories devoted to domestic problems (25%). What changes from one year to the next is the coverage of international relations and arms control, not the coverage of domestic problems. Finally, so that you can see what problems the cover stories considered to be important, the titles of the domestic problem covers are shown for the two years in Table 2.2. From these titles, it is clear that drug abuse is one of the important domestic problems, appearing as it does in stories in both years. Another recurring problem is crime (computer fraud and capital punishment one year, child abduction and sexual abuse the next). No doubt you will be able to find others by examining the titles.

As we have seen, archival data can be used to suggest changes in a phenomenon over time, to establish its incidence in various locations, and to discover social conditions correlated with its occurrence. These data have the advantage of high external validity – there is no researcher stand-

TABLE 2.2 Cover Titles for Domestic Problems from Newsweek, January–October, 1983 and January–October, 1984

January–October, 1983	January–October, 1984
Splitting up the family.	Homeless in America.
Portrait of America: The hidden revolution at home and on the job.	Can we keep the skies safe?
Social-security crisis: Who will pay?	Stolen children: What can be done about child abduction?
Cleaning up the mess: The toxic waste threat to America's health.	Tax shelters.
Left out: The human cost of the collapse of industrial America	Sexual abuse: The growing outcry over child molesting.
Race and politics: Chicago's ugly election.	Getting straight: Breaking the grip of drugs and alcohol.
Epidemic. (AIDS)	Closing the door? The angry debate over illegal immigration.
Saving our schools.	The top brass: Can they fight a modern war?
Drugs on the job.	Day care: Who's minding the children?
Computer capers: Trespassing in the information age – pranks or sabotage?	Why teachers fail: How to make them better.
Capital punishment: To die or not to die.	Westmoreland vs. CBS: The media on trial.

ing around with a clipboard, no experimenter directing the subjects' behavior–and can be quite helpful in the generation of hypotheses for testing. But there can be serious limitations in internal validity. Social customs or deliberate actions may affect which data are recorded, records may be destroyed or carelessly maintained, the data to test many hypotheses simply do not exist. Paradoxically, both the principal advantages and the major disadvantages of the method arise from the fact that the data were originally collected for purposes other than social psychological research.

OBSERVATIONAL METHODS: BEHAVIOR IN PUBLIC PLACES

Observational techniques can be distinguished from archival research in two major ways. First, instead of adapting records of past actions, observational methods are used for the collection of data in the present. Second, because this contemporary data collection is almost always performed by the social psychologists who have identified the conceptual hypotheses to be tested, the behavior to be observed can be selected with this goal in mind. There is no need to limit the hypotheses to those that can be tested with the data known to be available.

If observational techniques can be distinguished from archival methods by their reliance on contemporary behavior, they can be differentiated from experimentation primarily by the subject's lack of awareness that he or she is participating in research. The subject does not enter into an explicit contract with the investigator to "participate in an experiment," and with the exception of participant observation–in which the observer is usually present in the open–the subject cannot be certain whether the events happening are natural occurrences or contrived manipulations. True, the subject may become suspicious (is that fragile-looking elderly woman struggling with a large suitcase merely someone's grandmother, or is she someone's experimental confederate?). But suspicion is not the same as certainty, and the remaining element of doubt is sufficient to make the subject's reactions more natural than they might be in the laboratory.

Four Observational Techniques

There are four commonly employed observational techniques: simple observation, participant observation, natural experiments, and field experiments. The first two are more nearly "observational" in character, and the latter two are analogues to the experimental procedures of the laboratory. In **simple observation** the researcher is concealed and records the subject's actions without any interference in the situation. Assessing the level of cheating on an exam from a hidden position such as the projection booth is an example of this sort of observation. At the next level of interference in the natural setting is **participant observation**. Here the investigator might be concealed (we could have a "plant" in the class who would appear to be taking the exam while really recording the behavior of other students) or visible. Obviously, if the observer's presence is known, the fact that observation is taking place will affect the subjects' behavior. This is especially true if the actions that would be taken without the observer are socially undesirable, potentially embarrassing, or illegal. What are proctors of exams for, if not to reduce cheating by their ability to observe its occurrence?

Concealed Participant Observation: The Doomsday Believers

To preclude the inhibiting effects of the observer's presence, social psychologists have resorted to surreptitious observation by someone who appears to be a full participant in the ongoing behavior. This was the case in a classic study of a "doomsday" religious group reported by Festinger, Riecken, and Schachter (1956). Through newspaper accounts, these investigators became aware of a small group of believers who were preparing for the end of the world. The leader (who was given the fictitious name of Marian Keech) of this group, called "the Seekers," had been receiving messages from a planet called Clarion. The messages came to her in the form of automatic writing and warned that on a specific day a cataclysmic flood would destroy the city in which she lived and would spread to create an inland sea from the Arctic Circle to the Gulf of Mexico. In return for her heroic efforts to warn the general public about the impending disaster, Mrs. Keech and her followers were to be saved from the flood by being taking aboard a flying saucer dispatched from Clarion. To prepare for their salvation, most of the believers sold their possessions, left (or were dismissed from) their jobs, and held meetings to determine how they would greet their rescuers from Clarion.

A Test of Theory. For Festinger, Riecken, and Schachter, the Seekers provided a perfect field test of a theory about the behaviors that might follow the disconfirmation of an expectancy. The theory of *cognitive dissonance*, which is described more thoroughly in chapter 5, predicts that a person who is committed to a belief that turns out to be erroneous will be unable to accept the disconfirmation, and instead will interpret it in a manner consistent with the original expectation. To bolster that erroneous interpretation, the person will try to convince others of its validity. But because the Seekers refused to grant press interviews that would have helped them publicize their cause, it was highly unlikely that they would have permitted themselves to be used as sources of data. So the investigators elected to join the group under false pretenses and to conduct their observations from the inside. They participated in the group's meetings, and were on hand when the fateful hour for the rescue came – and went. Four hours after the scheduled time for the rescue, Mrs. Keech received another message, and this one stated that the flood had been averted by heavenly intervention, largely in response to the group's faith and preparations. This message rekindled the group's lagging beliefs, led to a dramatic increase in the attempts by members to recruit new converts, and in both of these ways confirmed the researchers' predictions.

A Methodological Caution.   This study illustrated both some of the possibilities of covert participant observation and some of its difficulties. In order to maintain their "cover" the researchers ran the risk of spuriously enhancing the phenomenon under study. In the words of Festinger, Riecken, and Schachter (1956)

> There is little doubt that the addition of four new people to a fairly small group within ten days had an effect on the state of conviction among the existing members, especially since the four seem to have appeared when public apathy to the belief systems was great (p. 240).

Thus the observer may contribute to the strength of the group's view of the world, even while being careful to avoid becoming an advocate for the group's position. This possibility is greatest in a group with restrictive admission policies, because in such a group mere passive agreement may not be sufficient to maintain credibility. Especially with the dramatic increase in "investigative reporting" and police undercover intelligence work since the 1950s, it is truly challenging for today's concealed participant observer to remain undiscovered.

Ethics of Concealed Participant Observation.   In addition to the methodological problems, concealed participant observation raises serious ethical questions. Whatever else he or she may be doing, the researcher is violating the right to privacy of the group. The behavior under study would not typically be open to the public (or the investigator could have settled for simple observation), but even if it were public some ethical questions would remain. For example, people will participate in demonstrations, engage in public displays of affection, or confide their personal secrets to strangers or coworkers in ways that they would not if they thought that they were contributing to a permanent record by which they could later be identified. Most observational researchers deal with these ethical and methodological problems by selecting a method of *partial concealment*, in which the presence of the observer is made obvious, but the specific behavior to be assessed is not revealed. Partial concealment preserves some of the advantages of observational methods while putting the subjects on notice that their privacy is being invaded.

Natural Experiments

Although they deal with the present, rather than with the past, simple and participant observation resemble archival methods in their reliance on behavior as it occurs without any intervention from the experimenter. When the research objective is the examination of an ongoing social system as it exists normally, outside intervention would only obscure the description. For example, if an evaluation researcher were hired by a corporation to assess the effectiveness of communication among officers at various levels of the business, the last thing the researcher would want to do is change the setting in any significant manner prior to conducting the evaluation. On the contrary, the evaluator would attempt to minimize the effects even of his or her presence, perhaps by beginning to collect the actual data only after having given the corporate officers time to "get back to normal" following the evaluator's first appearance on the scene.

There are, however, numerous questions of social psychological interest that cannot be answered without a manipulation of some form, performed either by the experimenter or by the environment itself. An instance of observational research (outside the laboratory) in which there is a manipulation provided by the environment is called a **natural experiment**, and as it happens, the Festinger, Riecken, and Schachter (1956) study is an illustration of such a natural experiment. True, the behavior was examined through use of concealed participant observation, but the conceptual variable – disconfirmation of expectancy – was manipulated by the natural environment. From the researcher's point of view, this study had an important advantage not found in most other natural experiments, namely a precise date (even the hour) on which the manipulation would take place. It is much more typical for a researcher to make observations before the fact, and then wait months for the natural manipulation (an airplane crash, a criminal indictment, an earthquake) to occur.

If ideal conditions could be maintained, natural experiments might be the social psychologist's dream method. The manipulations performed by the environment (election results, changes in laws such as the drinking age, catastrophic natural disasters) are significantly more powerful and involving than any that could in good conscience be employed in an experimental laboratory. (What experimenter could get away with inducing the amount of stress that accompanies a final examination for which you haven't studied quite enough?) As a result, natural manipulations hold the potential for extremely high internal validity. In addition, because the subjects are "real people" behaving naturally in familiar surroundings where their actions can be recorded unobtrusively, there is also good potential external validity. Unfortunately, with few exceptions (e.g., elections with virtually certain outcomes, the social changes that accompany your first few weeks at college) natural manipulations are unpredictable. They may occur so quickly that a researcher does not have adequate time for preparation (for instance, to administer premeasures), or they may take so long to happen that any changes obtained would be hopelessly confounded by other intervening events. It is virtually impossible to ensure internal validity if you cannot control the occurrence of the manipulation.

Field Experiments

To enhance internal validity while preserving the external validity inherent in research performed in natural settings (with unsuspecting subjects), many social psychologists have turned to the **field experiment**, an observational method in which a manipulation controlled by the experimenter is performed on subjects unaware that they are taking part in research. Although these methods closely resemble the experimental techniques of the laboratory, the fact that the subjects are unaware justifies considering field experiments under the general rubric of observational research. The setting is altered enough to produce the manipulation, but not so much that the subjects become suspicious; behavioral responses to the manipulation are recorded, but as unobtrusively as possible. An excellent example of this method is provided by a study of bystander response to an apparent emergency situation, conducted in the New York subway system by Piliavin, Rodin, and Piliavin (1969).

Drunk in the Subway. This experiment was designed to determine what effects the race (black or white) of a supposed "victim" and the supposed reason for his problem (drunk or ill) would have on the help rendered. There were other conditions involving the behavior of a model, but for now we consider only the four possible conditions arising from variations in the victim's appearance. The experimental team consisted of four persons—the victim, the model, and two observers—and the research was conducted on the old subway cars of the Eighth Avenue A and D trains, because these trains made no stops between 59th and 125th Streets and the cars had a seating arrangement (shown in Fig. 2.1) of two-person seats.

The four members of the team entered the car from different doors, with the victim and the model standing next to the pole in the "critical" end of the car, while the two observers took the seats indicated in the "adjacent" area of the car. Between 59th and 125th Streets there was a period of approximately 7.5 minutes during which any passengers in the critical area were a captive audience for the experiment. About a minute after the train left 59th Street, the victim staggered and collapsed on the floor, remaining in that position either until someone helped him or until the train stopped (when the model helped him out the door).

The victim was a black or white male between the ages of 26 and 35, and was casually dressed. In the "drunk" condition, he smelled of liquor and carried a pint bottle tightly wrapped in a paper bag; in the "ill" condition he

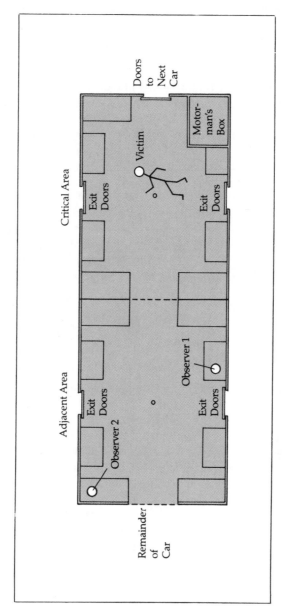

FIGURE 2.1 Diagram of the critical and adjacent areas of the subway car, showing locations of victim, model, and observers (Piliavin, I. M., Rodin, J., and Piliavin, J. A. (1969). Good samaritanism: An underground phenomenon? *Journal of Personality and Social Psychology, 13,* 289–299. Copyright 1969 by the American Psychological Association. Reprinted by permission).

appeared sober and walked with a cane. The observers recorded data as unobtrusively as possible for the entire duration of the ride, and all four team members disembarked at the 125th Street station, waited until other passengers had left the platform, and then went to the other platform to repeat the experiment on a train going in the other direction.

Results of the Study.   The researchers conducted 84 such trials with no intervention by the model, and performed these before an audience that averaged 43 people in the entire car, with an average of 8.5 people in the critical area. The percentage of trials on which the victim received help was truly impressive. Only the black drunk received help in less than 100% of the cases, and on a majority of trials help was provided by more than one passenger. Men were more likely to help than were women, although, as the authors pointed out, the intervention required would have been more difficult for a woman to accomplish. In addition, passengers showed a tendency to help victims of their own race more than victims of the other race.

We return to these results, and to some later research on helping, in chapter 9, but for now it is sufficient to note the high degree of control that can be exerted over a natural setting. Admittedly, few settings provide the kind of captive audience found on a subway, but even public places with free access can be adapted enough to eliminate some of the immense variation that would otherwise occur.

PRECURSORS
TO LABORATORY EXPERIMENTATION

Correlation and Causality

Let us return to the cheating example to look more closely at the kind of information that might be provided by the methods we have considered so far. Suppose that through careful analysis of the academic records of a selected sample of universities (archival research), we might have discovered that the rates for expulsion for cheating fluctuate over the years, increasing during wartime or economic crisis, but decreasing at other times. More importantly, suppose that we have found that the wartime increases contain an extremely high proportion of male students, whereas increases during recession contain roughly equal numbers of males and females. We have identified a *correlation* between expulsion and social conditions: More expulsions are found in the presence of war and recession than in their absence.

Is it fair to say that war and recession cause the increase in cheating? Recall from chapter 1 the criteria for a causal explanation. First, a presumed cause and its presumed effect must be contiguous in time or space, and the observed correlation meets this criterion. Second, the presumed cause must precede the presumed effect in time, and the observed relationship is likely to satisfy this criterion as well. Provided that records can be obtained on a yearly basis, if war or recession truly precedes increases in cheating, then cheating should steadily rise from the beginning of a war or recession through its conclusion. Third, a truly causal statement cannot be made unless other plausible alternatives can be ruled out.

What, exactly, are these alternatives? Logically, there are three possible explanations for the existence of a correlation between two variables. First, variable A (in our example, war or recession) might cause variable B (expulsions for cheating). Second, variable B (expulsions) might cause variable A (war or recession). Admittedly this sounds intuitively implausible, but it is logically no less possible than the first explanation. And third, an unmeasured variable C (a hypothetical construct, like "weakening moral fiber") might have caused both variable A and variable B. In this example, there is no information whatsoever about any of the competing alternative explanations, so it is a mistake to draw a causal inference. There are some instances in which sophisticated statistical techniques (for example, see Kenny, 1979) may permit tests of causal predictions from sets of correlations among variables, but without using these techniques, *we cannot infer causality from correlation,* no matter how intuitively reasonable that inference might seem.

Selecting a Hypothesis

What such archival data would do is permit a speculation about the relationship between social conditions and cheating – a hypothesis that can be tested in later research. Because wars and recessions are accompanied by different amounts of cheating by males and females (assuming that expulsions are a completely accurate measure of actual amounts of cheating), we begin to search for a psychological variable that might account for the correlation. As a first guess, we might suspect that this mediating variable could be pressure to succeed. In wartime, a male student who flunks out will almost certainly find himself in the armed forces, but a female who flunks out will probably not end up in the service. (Notice that this is a post hoc speculation drawn from the correlation, a speculation that depends on the existence of a military draft with exemptions for college students and with differential induction of males and females.) In contrast, during recessions both male and female students need all the education they can obtain to make themselves more attractive to prospective employers.

Because of the dangers of selective deposit and selective survival of archival records, and because we know that post hoc reasoning is not sufficient, we decide to see whether a correlation between pressure to succeed and cheating can be observed in data we collect ourselves. Not wanting to cause a war or recession for research purposes, we choose a conceptual replication such as the natural experiment offered by various examination procedures. Students taking a final exam that accounts for 80% of their course grade should be under more pressure than students taking a final examination that accounts only for 40% of the final grade.

A Natural Manipulation. Suppose we selected two such classes at our university and found through some form of unobtrusive observation that, as expected, there was a higher level of cheating in the 80% class. Have we isolated pressure to succeed as the cause of cheating? No. We have only uncovered another sort of correlation between our dependent variable (the behavior of interest to the researcher – in this case the level of cheating) and the circumstances that might lead to pressure to succeed. We cannot be certain, because there might be numerous other differences between the two classes, such as dislike for the class, hostility toward the professor, and perceived unfairness of having so much ride on a single exam, that could have produced the results without any differences in pressure to succeed.

A Field Experiment in Cheating. Can we find more conclusive evidence if we intervene in the situation and conduct a field experiment? Probably so. We could rule out differences in instructors' reputations and course content by using two sections of our own course in social psychology. We would simply flip a coin at the beginning of the term to determine which class would get the final exam worth 40% and which would get the exam worth 80%. Although this manipulation would be more satisfactory than our earlier attempts, it would still leave something to be desired, this time because of our multiple motives in the situation. We are not merely conducting research; we are also trying to do an effective job of teaching, and we are concerned about avoiding disastrous student evaluations of our courses. As a result, we are likely to find that the final examination is not the only thing that differs between the two classes. If nothing else, students in the two classes might talk to each other, thereby destroying the degree of control we thought we had over the setting. Certainly our manipulation, if effective, could cause a number of intervening events, one or more of which could lead to different levels of cheating. But our conclusions must be guarded in direct proportion to the number of such events the manipulation might have produced. Not surprisingly, the procedures of the laboratory experiment permit us to keep the number of these other possibilities to an absolute minimum.

THE LABORATORY EXPERIMENT

The Factorial Design

In its simplest form the psychological experiment consists of two conditions or treatment groups: an *experimental* group in which some conceptual variable, called the **independent variable**, is manipulated, and a *con-*

trol group in which there is no manipulation of the independent variable. Researchers then compare the scores on the dependent variable achieved by subjects across the two groups, and perform an appropriate statistical test to determine whether the treatment had any measurable effect.

Although laboratory experiments in social psychology can sometimes follow this simple model, they more typically involve (a) multiple treatments based on more than one conceptual variable, (b) absence of a traditional control group, and (c) a consequent necessity for extra precautions against some of the problems of reactivity discussed earlier. Recall that our archival research on cheating suggested that the felt pressure to succeed might have influenced the amount of cheating, a suggestion further corroborated in the observational research conducted in two sections of the same course. Neither of these studies could rule out all of the alternative explanations, especially one based on presumed disliking for the task (greater cheating to show displeasure with having so much of the grade ride on a single test).

The principal advantage of the laboratory experiment is that it permits us to examine the causal influence of more than one factor at a time in what is known as a **factorial design**: a research design in which there are systematic variations in more than one conceptual variable at a time. The design of just such an experiment is presented in Table 2.3, with Factor A (Pressure to Succeed) having two *levels*, or variations, and Factor B (Liking for the Task) also having two levels.

Conducting the Experiment

Creating the Conditions. In conducting such an experiment you might select a task for the subjects to perform that would permit them to cheat if they wanted to, such as having them score their own papers. You would vary the pressure for the subjects to succeed, perhaps by telling half of the subjects that they would be paid for their participation no matter how well they did, while telling the other half of the subjects that their pay would depend entirely on their performance. To manipulate the liking for

TABLE 2.3 Factorial Design of a Hypothetical Experiment to Determine the Effects of Pressure to Succeed and Liking for the Task on Level of Cheating

FACTOR A PRESSURE TO SUCCEED	FACTOR B LIKING FOR THE TASK	
	Level 1: Low Liking	*Level 2: High Liking*
Level 1: Low Pressure	Dull task Unconditional pay	Attractive task Unconditional pay
Level 2: High Pressure	Dull task Conditional pay	Attractive task Conditional pay

the task, half of the subjects in each pressure condition would be permitted to engage in an intrinsically interesting and attractive task, while the other half of the subjects in each pressure condition would be asked to engage in a task known to be dull and boring. As a result, any individual subject would receive one of the four possible treatment combinations: unconditional pay for a dull task, unconditional pay for an attractive task, conditional pay for a dull task, or conditional pay for an attractive task.

Operationalization. In most cases there will be several possible operationalizations of a conceptual variable, and which one will actually be employed depends on a number of considerations. First, a manipulation is chosen that will be appropriate with the other conceptual variables included in the research. In this experiment we hope to manipulate both the pressure to succeed and the attractiveness of the task, so we must choose a manipulation of pressure that is *independent* of the manipulation of attractiveness. For example, this requirement rules out a manipulation of pressure in terms of intelligence testing, because to say that the task is either unreliable or accurate is also to affect the attractiveness manipulation. An otherwise dull task that is a valid test of intelligence has some redeeming value, but an otherwise dull task that measures nothing of importance would be seen as even more worthless than we intend it to be.

After the inappropriate operations have been ruled out, the researcher may evaluate the remaining ones to determine which of them offers the greatest potential difference between conditions while at the same time permitting the subjects to be treated in as similar a manner as possible. If we were to use timing as the manipulation of pressure to succeed, we could not tell the low pressure groups that the test was timed, but emphasize the limited time available in the high pressure groups. This might produce large differences in pressure, but it would do so by making half of the subjects (the two low pressure groups) totally unaware of the importance of time. In contrast, using payment as the manipulation of pressure, we can inform both groups of subjects that they will be paid, and can offer to pay them the same amount of money, basing the entire manipulation on a simple phrase in the instructions: "whether or not," as opposed to "only if" you complete the task. This operationalization will, we hope, lead to large differences in perceived pressure to succeed, even though the instructions given the subjects are almost identical.

Random Assignment. Regardless of the manner in which the conceptual variable is operationalized, the experimental subjects must be randomly assigned to the treatment conditions—by flipping coins, writing the treatment conditions on a set of index cards and shuffling the cards together, or (most frequently) by using a table of random numbers. Why is true random assignment, as opposed to some systematic or haphazard assignment determined by the experimenter, so important? Look closely at the sequence of events in a social psychology experiment. With the exception of a small number of studies in attitude change, there is never any measurement of the dependent variable before the experimental treatments are administered: the subjects are recruited, arrive at the laboratory, are assigned to conditions, and are given instructional manipulations. Only then are the data on the dependent variable collected (for example, level of cheating on a task).

To be sure that the differences obtained between experimental conditions are due entirely to those conditions, we must have made sure that the subject groups began the experiment with no differences on the dependent variable. In the cheating example, an alternative explanation for our findings might have been that more innate cheaters were somehow placed in the Unconditional-Dull condition. The only way to argue against this interpretation (because we did not even attempt to assess individual differences in cheating outside the context of the experiment) is to assign subjects randomly to conditions, and presume that this random assignment will cancel out any relevant individual differences among the subjects. This presumption will occasionally be in error, but without random assignment it cannot even be made.

The Absence of a Control Group. Most social psychological experiments follow a variant of this form, omitting the traditional "control group," because subjects are assumed to be interested problem solvers who can intentionally alter their responses depending on the demand characteristics of the experiment. Experimenter expectancy effects can be reduced to a minimum, but there will always be some demand characteristics, and a no-treatment control group would thus become an "individual differences" group in which any subject's behavior depended on his or her unique perception of what the experimenter was attempting to accomplish.

COMPARISONS AMONG METHODS

Archival, observational, and experimental methods can be compared on a number of dimensions, and these are summarized in Table 2.4. As noted earlier, archival methods are applied to data collected in the past, while all other methods deal with data collected in the present. Also as noted earlier, a major difference between experimentation and all other methods save nonconcealed participant observation is that the subjects are aware (in experimentation) that they are taking part in research. Three other dimensions—the degree of control over the setting, the intrusiveness of the measurement, and the ethical problems raised by the method—deserve more detailed comment.

TABLE 2.4 Comparison of Archival, Observational, and Laboratory Experimental Research Methods

| | | OBSERVATIONAL METHODS | | | | | |
| | | | Participant Observation | | | | |
Dimensions	ARCHIVAL RESEARCH	Simple Observation	Concealed	Non-concealed	Natural Experiments	Field Experiments	LABORATORY EXPERIMENTS
When are the data collected?	Past	Present	Present	Present	Present	Present	Present
Are the subjects aware?	No	No	No	Yes	No	No	Yes
What is the degree of control?	None	None	Low	Low	Low	High	High
How intrusive is the measurement?	Low	Low	Low	Moderate	Low	Low	High
What is the typical internal validity?	Low	Low	Moderate	Moderate	Moderate	Moderate	High
What is the typical external validity?	Moderate	High	High	Moderate	High	High	Low
How great are the ethical problems?	Low	Low	High	Low	Low	Moderate	Moderate

Control Over the Setting

The degree of control over the setting possible in observational research can range from zero (simple observation) to a high amount (a field experiment in a restricted setting). This increasing control carries with it two principal advantages. The first of these deals with the relative frequency of occurrence of behaviors of interest. It has been suggested (Webb et al., 1966) that there may be an inverse relationship between the social significance of a particular behavior and the natural frequency of its occurrence. By increasing the control over the setting, a researcher can devise situations that will produce the behavior of interest more frequently and at a predictable time. No doubt a frequent traveler on the New York subway system would be exposed to occasional fallen drunks, but providing one's own drunk greatly improves the efficiency of the research.

The second advantage to be gained from greater control over the setting is an increase in the internal validity of the research, as Table 2.4 indicates. An immense number of factors other than the variable of interest can influence behavior in a natural setting, so if the researcher can alter the setting to eliminate some of the alternative explanations while maintaining the natural character of the situation, the gain can be substantial. A restricted setting like a subway is ideal for this purpose, but other settings can be altered as well. For example, if you were interested in people's reactions to a lost wallet, you would drop your experimental wallet on a narrow sidewalk that you had further narrowed by a small pile of sand and a barricade, rather than plant the wallet in the middle of a large open plaza where most passersby would not even notice it. You would have maintained the natural quality of the setting, but would have altered it enough to argue against "did not notice" as an explanation for failures to stop and examine the wallet. Of course, as the table indicates, not even a field experiment can match the degree of control (and consequently the degree of internal validity) possible in the laboratory.

Intrusiveness of the Methods

The various methods can also be compared to one another in terms of the degree of intrusiveness of the measurement procedures. In the simple observational study, when the observer is effectively concealed, there should be no contamination of natural behavior. As a result, this method is high in external validity. In natural experiments and field experiments, the researcher may be out in the open, but surreptitious recording of data can still minimize the reactive effects of being observed, especially if the experimental manipulation is powerful enough to capture the subject's attention. The presence of the researcher is a more serious problem in participant observation, regardless of whether the observation is covert or obvious. In concealed observation studies the observer may, as noted earlier, contribute to the effect by the actions he or she takes to establish and maintain a cover. In nonconcealed observation, the researcher's presence is likely to distort the subject's natural reactions. Because there is some contamination in each case, you may wonder why the external validity of concealed participant observation is higher. The reason is that the subjects' awareness that their actions are under scrutiny is presumed to be a more damaging sort of contamination. Real people in natural settings may normally have their behavior affected by the actions of others in the group who have different motives for being there, but they do not normally consider themselves engaged in the act of "being a subject."

Ethical Conduct of Research in Social Psychology

Risks and Benefits. The final dimension on which the methods can be compared is the degree to which they raise ethical questions that must be answered before the research is conducted. Principles of ethical conduct established by the American Psychological Association (Cook, Kimble, Hicks, McGuire, Schoggen, & Smith, 1973) hold that all research in psychology should undergo what is known as a risk/benefit analysis. This is a comparison of the potential benefits to be gained from the research against the potential risks to the participating subjects. Among the possible benefits are the accumulation of scientific knowledge, the solution of particular applied problems, the training of apprentice investigators (through research projects conducted by students), and even the educational value that accrues to an individual participant as a consequence of the "learning by doing" that constitutes serving as a subject in a well designed study. Among the risks for participants are possible embarrassment, anxiety or stress, invasion of privacy, or having one's time wasted to no purpose.

It should be noted that every one of the benefits assumes that the research will be as free from artifacts as possible under the circumstances. If an experimental design is so confounded, or an observational design is so ambiguous, that no useful information can be gained from performing the study (not even badly needed education for a student researcher), then the benefit is zero. And if the benefit is zero, then not even the minimal risk of wasting the subject's time is justified.

Because many of the procedures designed to enhance the impact made by the experimental instructions, to eliminate response biases, or to provide the participants with misleading demand characteristics involve some risk to the subjects, they raise ethical questions that need to be considered. Is the ethically questionable procedure the only appropriate method for studying the behavior of interest? Will a deception be relatively minor or will it establish a situation that could be quite damaging to the participant's self-esteem? In a field experiment, will the manipulations cause the subject to do something illegal or potentially dangerous? Will it leave participants with an erroneous view of the world that will adversely affect their future actions? In an experiment, can the researcher provide a **debriefing** thorough enough to remove or substantially reduce any residual effects of the manipulations? In an observational study, will the participants be informed that their behavior has been noted, and will they be given the opportunity to deny the researcher permission to use those data? Will the subjects be anonymous, or, if names must be taken, will the research records be preserved in a fashion that insures confidentiality? Recognizing that investigators may not be completely objective when it comes to answering these questions about their own research, the ethical principles (as well as regulations of the federal government and some state laws) require that research projects receive external review.

Institutional Review. In a great deal of social psychological research, procedures that are the most methodologically desirable raise the most important ethical questions. Just as investigators have a responsibility to conduct research that is as free from artifacts as possible, they also have an obligation to protect the dignity of the participants who provide the data they gather. Whether or not to employ concealed participant observation, deception, or some other ethically questionable procedure is at first a decision to be made by an individual investigator. But it is neither a decision to be taken lightly nor a decision that is final with the researcher. Once an investigator has decided on a set of procedures, the proposed research should first be reviewed by his or her professional colleagues, then, in many cases, by a university-wide Institutional Review Board constituted according to regulations of the federal government. This broad review applies to all research performed with human participants, regardless of the administrative home of the researcher (e.g., departments of Psychology, Sociology, Communications, Education, Medicine, or even faculty committees or administrative officers who conduct surveys within the university community). Departments that are heavily involved in research with human subjects usually have committees that conduct the initial peer review, whereas other departments or schools (e.g., Economics, English, Business) that only infrequently obtain information directly from individual subjects typically do not have departmental level committees. But their projects, like those of the social science departments, must be subjected to some form of institutional review.

Informed Consent. In an important sense, the research subject is the final reviewer of any study or experiment. Before participating in a project for which he or she has volunteered, a subject must be informed of the potential risks that accompany participation. This does *not* mean that the participant needs to be told of the hypotheses under investigation. Nor does the requirement preclude use of such methods as concealed observation or experimental deception. What it does do is restrict the use of such methods to cases in which the withheld information does not alter the risks to the subjects. To describe an attitude change study as an investigation of interpersonal perception (so the participants will not be alerted to a need to maintain consistency in their attitudes) is an experimental deception, but one with a negligible risk to the subject. By contrast, to lead a participant to believe that he or she may have seriously injured another person (as in the Milgram study of obedience) is to employ a deception that increases the risk of psychological harm to the subject. On the other hand, the very realism of the Milgram experiment is responsible for its profound effect on our thinking about behavior in settings demanding obedience to authority. Had the experimenter informed participants in advance that they would be subjected to a high level of unpleasant stress, the risks to subjects would have diminished, but so too would the potential contribution of the research.

As noted briefly during the discussion of concealed participant observation, this observational technique presents ethical problems that are even more serious than those associated with stressful laboratory experiments. This assertion can now be clarified in terms of **informed consent**. A person who volunteers for a psychological experiment arrives at the research site having made an implicit contract with the researcher. The subject knows, regardless of what the experimenter says, that some portion of his behavior is being observed, recorded, and analyzed. There may or may not be deception, but it is nearly always possible for the subject to grant informed consent at the beginning of the session, and if not then, at the end after the research has been fully explained. But with some of the observational methods, especially concealed participant observation, informed consent cannot be obtained at the beginning and is not typically obtained at the end. People observed in their natural and public behavior do have the advantage of anonymity, but future scientific and philosophical arguments about ethics in research may concentrate more heavily on observational methods than on deception experiments.

No matter where the data are collected, researchers in social psychology have a strong responsibility to protect the welfare of people who participate in their investigations. Researchers should not waste their subjects' time in studies with low internal validity, nor should they employ ethically questionable procedures when ethically preferable and methodologically acceptable alternatives exist. Investigators must keep in mind that they are capable, in their professional lives, of the very same intentional choice of action they assume possible by their subjects. When they employ ethically questionable procedures, it is their responsibility to demonstrate that, procedurally, they could not have done otherwise.

SUMMARY

Social psychological theory and research rest on two fundamental assumptions about human behavior: that underlying regularities can be discovered through statistical methods applied to multiple observations, and that internal processes such as cognition and motivation guide the intentions leading to the actions taken. This possibility of intentional behavior requires that research methods consider subjects to be active problem solvers engaged in a social interaction with the researcher. Consequently, it is important to show that research findings can be repeated when exactly the same procedures are used (**empirical replication**, p. 37), and that theoretical ideas can be validated through a variety of different procedures (**conceptual replication**, p. 38). In pursuit of these goals, we must employ **operational definitions** (p. 3) of the conceptual variables, ensure that the research has as much **internal validity** (p. 40)–freedom from **artifacts** (p. 40)–and **external validity** (p. 40)–generalizability beyond the research setting–as possible.

A major threat to both internal and external validity is that a subject who is aware of participating in research may be "behaving like a subject" instead of "behaving naturally." Subjects who are aware of their participation may try to understand the investigator's purpose, using the **demand characteristics** (p. 43) of the research, or the clues given by the **experimenter's expectancy**, (p. 44) to make these guesses. Participants' responses may also be adversely affected by a variety of **response sets** (p. 45), or by the **evaluation apprehension** (p. 43) that accompanies having one's behavior observed by a psychologist.

The continuing records of a society are its archives, and although these are maintained for other purposes, they can often be put to effective use by social psychology. In using archival data the researcher must guard against three sources of invalidity: The possibility that atypical cases may be drawn through **selective sampling** (p. 49), the chance that either by oversight or intention the items examined were originally **selectively deposited** (p. 48), and the possibility that certain records are better maintained than others (**selective survival**, p. 47).

The observational methods include **simple observation** (p. 51), **participant observation** (p. 52), **natural experiments** (p. 54), and **field experiments** (p. 55). The principal advantage of these methods is their high external validity, derived from the study of subjects who are behaving naturally in familiar settings. To increase the frequency of behaviors for observation, to study unusual situations, and to enhance the internal validity of the research, the observer can increase his or her control over the setting. Even in highly controlled settings, the essential "natural" quality of the situation can be maintained through full or partial concealment of the observer. This increased control enhances the validity of the observational methods, but does so at a cost of increasing the ethical problems that accompany invasion of privacy.

Experimental methods are most valuable for testing particular social psychological theories, because of their high degree of internal validity. Many experiments employ **factorial designs** (p. 60) to rule out alternative explanations while determining whether the manipulated variables interact to produce behavior. Laboratory experiments must be carefully designed to reduce the problems of demand characteristics, evaluation apprehension, and experimenter expectancy to a minimum while still treating the subjects in the most ethical manner possible. Part of the experimenter's responsibility is to obtain the subject's **informed consent** (p. 67) prior to the research, and to conduct a complete **debriefing** (p. 66) that removes or reduces any residual effects of the manipulations.

Research methods can be compared on several dimensions, including the **reactivity** (p. 41) of the measurement techniques, the degree of control over the setting, the internal and external validity, and the ethical problems associated with each method. Unfortunately, many of the procedures that are the most methodologically desirable are also the most ethically questionable. Consequently, before beginning a project the investigator must balance the risks (p. 65) to the participants against the benefits (p. 65) to be gained from conducting the study. Social psychologists, like their subjects, are capable of choices, and their choices of methods need to reflect both methodological sophistication and ethical sensitivity.

SUGGESTED ADDITIONAL READINGS

COOK, S., KIMBLE, G., HICKS, L., McGUIRE, W. J., SCHOGGEN, P., & SMITH, M.B. (1973). *Ethical principles in the conduct of research with human participants*. Washington. DC: American Psychological Association. This report of the APA ad hoc committee on ethical standards for research using human subjects presents summaries of critical incidents, ethical guidelines, and procedures for implementing the guidelines. Read it before conducting your own research.

KIDDER, L. H., & JUDD, C. M. (1986). *Research methods in social relations* (5th ed.). New York: Holt, Rinehart & Winston. This most recent version of a "classic" text on methodology in social psychology describes experimental, quasi-experimental, and survey research designs; presents methods for interviewing and designing questionnaires; and discusses data coding and the communication of research. A thorough introduction to research–don't make up a questionnaire without reading it.

WEBB, E. J., CAMPBELL, D. T., SCHWARTZ, R. D., & SECHREST, L. (1966). *Unobtrusive measures: Nonreactive research in the social sciences*. Chicago: Rand McNally. A thorough but nontechnical discussion of the ways to obtain measures of human behavior, through archival and observational methods, with only minimal awareness by the subjects.

CHAPTER THREE

ELEMENTS
OF
SOCIAL
PERCEPTION

CONTENTS

PREVIEW

A person's social behavior is determined by the physical and social world as the individual perceives it. There are important differences between the perception of objects and the perception of persons, if only because the persons being perceived are, like the perceiver, capable of intentional action. Instead of passively processing all of the information contained in the environment, perceivers actively select bits of information, from which they construct their final percepts. Our impressions of others are formed from descriptions we receive, from the stimulus person's body language, facial expressions, and paralinguistic cues. Although nonverbal cues are less subject to the stimulus person's conscious control than are that person's verbal statements, these nonverbal behaviors are still influenced by socially structured display rules. Six emotions—happiness, surprise, fear, anger, disgust, and sadness—are universally recognized from facial expressions, and such facial expressions may alter the underlying emotion being experienced by the stimulus person. Although perceivers are frequently accurate in their judgments of others, that accuracy is extremely difficult to measure. Recent social psychological research on social perception concentrates more on the process than on the accuracy of the outcome. In the study of that process it is important to remember that the stimulus person can control, through self-presentation, the cues that are made available to the perceiver.

What does it mean to say that someone is an attractive person? Suppose for a moment that we limited the judgment to physical appearance, or restricted it even further to include only facial features. If we asked a hundred people to tell us how attractive a particular individual's facial features were, would we obtain unanimity on the judgments? Probably not. The perceivers making the judgment might agree on the components necessary for a face—two eyes, a nose, a mouth, a chin, two cheeks, a forehead, and perhaps two ears—but there could be disagreement about which particular combinations were attractive and which were not. And this is only considering the standard equipment. If the optional extras, such as hair color and length, presence or absence of moustaches or beards on males, presence or absence of make-up on females, were included, the amount of disagreement would increase.

Now suppose that we were to ask perceivers to make a more inclusive evaluation of attractiveness, considering elements of personality and disposition as well as facial features, our perceivers might no longer agree even on the components that are necessary. Should attractiveness include a pleasing personality, or is beauty only skin deep? Does the overall at-

tractiveness of a physically appealing and socially charming but totally im-
moral person differ from the attractiveness of a less appealing, brusque,
but completely honest person? More important, how do we make judgments regarding the personal characteristics that we cannot observe?
How will those judgments affect our subsequent behavior? All of these
questions are involved in the process of social perception, and we begin
study of the process in this chapter with discussion of the observable features of the environment and other individuals. In chapter 4 we study the
process of social cognition in more detail, as it applies to the inferences
made about the actions of others.

PERSON PERCEPTION AND OBJECT PERCEPTION: A DIFFERENCE IN DEGREE OR A DIFFERENCE IN KIND?

Percepts: The Representations of Objects and People

Recall that social psychology assumes people to have the capability for
choice, and that one aspect of the internal structure required for the exercise of that choice is a representation of the objects, people, and situations
found in the world. As we see in chapter 4, there are numerous different
representations of the external world, and the one specific to an inanimate
object or a person is called a **percept**, defined by Allport (1955) as "a phenomenological experience of the object, that is to say, the way some object
or situation appears to the [perceiver]" (p.23).

You will get a better idea of just how a percept resembles and differs
from other possible internal representations if we take a closer look at the
implications of this definition. First, the fact that a percept is a phenomenological experience of an object implies that your knowledge and understanding of the object are obtained through your senses rather than
through thought or intuition. You can remember a tree, a mountain, or a
river in its absence, but you can only perceive these things through sight,
smell, touch, hearing, or taste. A second implication of the definition is that
there does exist an objectively real world of things and people outside the
perceiver, not merely a fantasy world of inner experience. It should be
noted that this assumes away some important philosophical problems, because a significant amount of philosophical debate has been addressed to
the question of whether there can be a logical proof of the existence of a
world external to the self. Our inattention as psychologists to these problems of importance to philosophers can be justified in part by the different
nature of our task. People behave as though there were an external world,
so the psychologist's duty is to describe the individual social behavior that
occurs within the context of such a widely shared assumption. As a result,

theories of social perception and social cognition, like the people to whom they are applied, assume the existence of a real world outside the mind of the perceiver.

A final implication of the definition is that the perceptual process frequently involves more than a literal translation of the incoming sensation. A series of musical tones with a specific pitch and loudness is perceived as a melody. A tall wooden post with crosspieces at its top will be perceived as a telephone pole whether the perceiver is standing right next to the pole or is looking at it from a block away. An eyewitness account of a crime will tell us something about the objective circumstances, but also something about the perceiver, as well. To say that a percept is the perceiver's experience, the way the object or person *appears* to that person, is to leave open the possibility for two different kinds of deviation from the stimulus array: the perceiver may reach the proper conceptual conclusion even though there is a change in the sensory representation of the incoming stimulus (the case of the telephone pole), or the perceiver may reach an improper conclusion by adding to or subtracting from an unchanging but ambiguous stimulus array (the case of erroneous eyewitness testimony).

Veridicality: Agreement Between Percept and Reality

Both kinds of deviation from the stimulus array assume not only that a real world of objects and people exists outside the perceiver's mind, but also that the true nature of those objects can be ascertained, at least in principle. Obtaining the true description of the telephone pole – height, circumference at various points, composition – is a relatively simple matter. All we need to do is have a number of observers make the necessary measurements and compare their findings. Most probably there will be a very high degree of agreement among these observers about the characteristics of the telephone pole, and we can then assume that this consensus reflects the "true nature" of the object. Note that even in this simple case we should not rely on the judgment of, or measurements made by, a single individual, even though the pole's characteristics, once known, are not expected to change much over time (and certainly they are not expected to change at the pole's instigation). We can then compare your percept of the object with the consensus of the observers, and your percept will be **veridical** if it agrees completely with the objective reality of their description (Allport, 1955).

The determination of veridicality is much more difficult in the case of the social perception of the eyewitness than in the case of the assessment of the pole. For one thing, the pole obligingly stays in one place and submits without protest to the repeated measurements taken by observers. The same is not true either for a person or a situation. A second difference is that the telephone pole does not arouse any special emotion, either in you or in the observers, that might interfere with the perceptual judgments being made. By contrast, a crime victim will have one view of the occurrence, the prosecutor will have a slightly different view, the defendant will have still another view (and a substantial stake in having his or her view prevail), and an eyewitness may have a perception that does not agree completely with any of the other reports. So even if the conditions for observation were optimal, each observer's motives and vantage point could have produced an individual perception of the events. In summary, when the stimulus is a person or a social situation, it is much more difficult to establish the objective standard against which an individual's percept can be compared in order to determine whether the percept is veridical.

The Lens Model of Perception

As we consider the social perception process in more detail, it will become apparent why veridicality is so difficult to establish. The complete process of perception begins with an object in the external world and ends with a phenomenological experience of that object, a meaningful whole or **Gestalt** organized by the perceiver. In an early, but still applicable, model of the perceptual process, Brunswik (1934) likened perception to the focusing of light by a lens, and this lens model is diagrammed in Fig. 3.1. The model

FIGURE 3.1 Brunswik's (1934) lens model of perception (reprinted from Shaver, 1975).

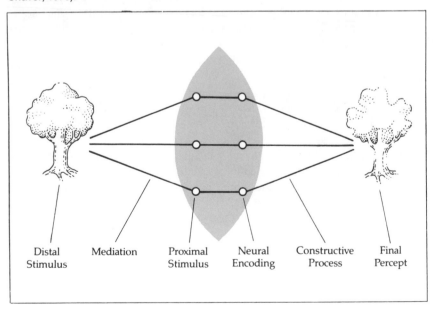

| Distal Stimulus | Mediation | Proximal Stimulus | Neural Encoding | Constructive Process | Final Percept |

was originally proposed to apply to object perception, and contains a probabilistic feature not shown in the figure. It has, however, been applied to instances of social perception as well, by Heider (1958). As a consequence of this adaptation, the lens model can serve as a first point of comparison between object perception and social perception.

The Effective Stimulus. The physical objects and social entities in the external world are referred to as **distal stimuli**, to indicate that they are remote from the perceiver and can be experienced only through the senses. After some appropriate kind of *mediation*–light waves, sound waves, physical contact–a distal stimulus will become represented at the perceiver's peripheral sense organs. The light waves produce an identifiable pattern on the rods and cones of the retina of the eye, the sound waves stimulate a particular pattern of response by various components of the inner ear, and the physical contact gives rise to a certain pattern or response from receptors in the skin that are sensitive to temperature and pressure. In each case, the resulting pattern of stimulation of receptors is called the **proximal stimulus** and is the local (though peripheral) representation of the distal object.

It is generally agreed that the proximal stimulus is a less-than-perfect reproduction of the distal stimulus (see Allport, 1955). Some information is almost necessarily lost, either through selective attention on the part of the perceiver, or through limitations on the information-processing capability of the sense organs. There are sounds we cannot hear (such as the inaudible dog whistle), bands of electromagnetic radiation we cannot see, and sensations to which we habituate over time (you think your perfume or aftershave lotion has lost all of its fragrance until someone you meet pays you a compliment about it). A complex stimulus can easily overwhelm the capacity of the perceiver's senses, with the result that only a fraction of the available information becomes represented as the proximal stimulus.

The Constructive Process. But even the proximal stimulus must undergo further modification before it results in a final percept. As Fig. 3.1 shows, the neural encoding of the proximal stimulus (the parallel lines within the lens) occurs in a relatively faithful manner, with little loss of information, but the encoded stimulus then encounters the interior face of the lens. The encoded stimulus is then evaluated against a background of whatever other neural activity is occurring at the same time–from organic states such as hunger and thirst, from muscle feedback, from the general cognitive activity of the brain–and it is in the context provided by this ongoing activity that the final step in perception takes place.

Although the precise neural mechanisms are only being discovered, the field of activity can include not only present stimulation, but also memories of past events and expectations for the future. Thus, the interpretation of the encoded proximal stimulus can best be considered what Heider (1958) called a **constructive process**, an active interpretation of sensory input influenced by other ongoing activity. It is through the operation of this constructive process that such perceptual phenomena as constancies and organization are thought to occur. More is said about some of the cognitive elements of this process in chapter 4, but for now it is enough to consider the constructive process the sum total of the perceiver's contribution to the process of perception.

As an illustration of the model, suppose that you are listening to recorded music with a group of friends. The sound is available to all of you, as indicated by the lines diverging from the distal stimulus, and it is up to each of you to act as a lens for this sensory experience, focusing it into an individual percept of the music. Just as information is lost between distal stimulus and proximal stimulus, still other changes occur in the final transformation by the constructive process. You may be concentrating on the sheer loudness of the music; one of your friends may be more attuned to the rhythm; and another may be listening primarily to the lyrics. As a result, the percept may differ for each of you, even though the proximal stimulation is the same.

Comparisons Between Object Perception and Social Perception

Nature of the Mediation.   The lens model provides the first opportunity for a comparison between the perception of inanimate objects and the perception of people, and if we begin at the distal end of the process, the first difference we discover may be in the nature of the mediation. Recall that in the case of object perception, mediation typically consists of physical entities—light waves, sound waves, temperatures, pressures, and so forth. In contrast, when the distal stimulus is a social situation or another person, the perceiver's proximal stimulus may not even be derived through firsthand contact with the distal stimulus. Your proximal stimulus of me may well be completely based on a verbal description of me made to you by someone who knows us both (how many of you are taking this particular course in social psychology because the professor was recommended to you by a friend?). Or, one step even further removed, you have social impressions of people for whom the proximal stimulus is an anonymous report in the media (government figures, celebrities, or even the professor you avoid because the course evaluation book panned his teaching). This possibility of mediation by third parties will, of course, increase the likelihood that the proximal stimulus will not be an accurate representation of the distal person. Now the third party's needs, and his or her attitudes toward the stimulus person, are interposed between that distal person and your proximal stimulus of the person. These attitudes cannot help but affect the quality of the mediation.

There is in an additional potential error in mediation of social perception that is largely absent in mediation of object perception, and this error can occur even when the observation is firsthand. In the perception of inanimate objects (or animals presumed incapable of intentional action), what you see is what you get. An oak tree is simply an oak tree, not an elm in disguise; a dog chasing a cat is not doing so in order to prove its superiority, or to impress other dogs that may be watching. There are few hidden meanings in the appearance of inanimate objects, and there are only occasional hidden motives in the behavior of infrahuman animals. This does not assume that the motives behind animal behavior will always be obvious to us (or to others of the species), only that the animals will make no truly intentional attempts to conceal their motivation. But if the distal stimulus is a person, that person's overt behavior may be "only what it seems" or it may be nothing more than a show put on for our benefit. People can, and do, control the social impressions they generate.

Synonymous Mediation or Ambiguous Mediation? When you are perceiving another person, you are as interested in the person's reasons for acting as you are in the actions themselves. In this case, the actions can be considered part of the mediation between you and the real distal stimulus—the reason for acting. If the actions of the stimulus person reflect the distal stimulus unequivocally, those actions would be, in Heider's (1958) terms, **synonymous mediation** for the underlying disposition. The action is a synonym for the disposition. If a person is observed dashing into a burning building at considerable personal risk in order to save people trapped inside, that action rather clearly suggests motives of altruism and helpfulness.

On the other hand, if the actions of a stimulus person could reflect any number of conceivable motives, then there is said to be **ambiguous mediation**. A person who volunteers to take an out-of-town assignment for his or her company over a weekend might have several motives for doing so. The employee might be truly helpful, recognizing that the assignment would cut more deeply into the plans of others; might be trying to ingratiate him or herself with the boss in order to obtain a raise; might be looking for a convenient excuse to "lose" an unattractive weekend date; or might be hoping to get additional experience that would increase his or her future marketability to other companies. As the mediation becomes more ambiguous, the certainty of the proximal stimulus will decrease. Because the stimulus person's reasons for acting are hidden and must be inferred (these inference processes are discussed in more detail in chapter 4), the mediation for social perception may be less than perfect even though the observation has been firsthand.

Complexity of the Stimulus.   A second difference between social perception and object perception is the greater complexity of the social stimulus, and this is first reflected in the proximal stimulus. Obviously the chemical compounds that comprise a person are no more "complex" than those same compounds are in other entities, so at this level there would be no difference in complexity. What people have, that inanimate objects, and infrahuman animals do not have, is a capacity for intentional action that gives rise to an almost infinite number of nuances in behavior. Furthermore, these nuances are more important to us as perceivers than are the subtle variations in stimulus objects that cannot engage in deliberate and persistent actions toward us.

In much the same way, regardless of the faithfulness of the mediation, it is extremely difficult for us to sense all of the potentially relevant dimensions of another person. In the case of object perception, the important qualities are the object's physical properties – size, weight, color, ability for movement – or its uses to us, and there is a small number of such properties that must be kept in mind. Even if some aspects of an object must be ignored to prevent overloading of the perceptual apparatus, the proportion of available information actually processed will remain high.

By contrast, when the distal stimulus is a person, even a complete physical description might overload the senses, and this description would fail to consider the large number of possible reasons the person might have for acting as he or she did. Thus, when our senses establish a proximal stimulus of a person, the proportion of available information that is actually entered into the system will be much lower than in the case of the stimulus object. We simplify our perceptual worlds whether the distal stimuli are objects or people, but that simplification can be much more costly when the distal stimulus is a person.

Role of the Constructive Process.   Assuming that the (limited) proximal stimulus of a person is faithfully encoded into neural transmission, the final difference between the perception of objects and the perception of people is in the part played by the constructive process. Not only does the greater complexity of a person create a greater need for interpretation, our expectations about the person may guide both our search for perceptual information and our use of the information that is obtained. The degree to which our beliefs about a person can produce the very behavior we expect was first formally suggested in Merton's (1948) idea of a self-fulfilling prophecy, and has been extended more recently by Snyder (1984). Let us consider a specific example.

What is the first thing you notice about a stranger? Physical appearance. Before you are close enough to talk, even to exchange perfunctory greetings, you have seen the stimulus person, and have formed a tentative impression based on physical appearance. To what degree will that impression produce expectations that might have a self-confirming nature? In one study to address this question, Snyder, Tanke, and Berscheid (1977) asked male undergraduate students to engage in a telephone conversation with a female undergraduate, ostensibly for the purpose of getting acquainted.

Before the conversation began, each male was given a folder containing biographical information about the female he was to call, and a Polaroid photograph purported to be her snapshot. In fact, although the biographical information had indeed been provided by the target female, the photograph had not. There were 8 different pictures that had been selected on the basis of pretesting from a larger sample of 20. Other undergraduate males had rated these photographs on attractiveness, and those chosen for the research were the four that had received the highest attractiveness ratings and the four that had received the lowest attractiveness ratings. Thus each male received real biographical information, and a false (either attractive or unattractive) picture.

The telephone conversation was unstructured, lasted for 10 minutes, and was conducted through headphones and microphones, so that each participant's voice could be tape recorded on a separate channel. These taped conversations were later rated by undergraduate judges who were unaware of the true nature of the experiment or of the purported attractiveness of the female target (9 people rated the males only, 12 rated the females only). The judges who heard the males considered those males who believed they were talking to attractive females to be more sociable, sexually warm, and outgoing than were the males who believed themselves to be speaking to an unattractive female.

This difference is to be expected; what is much more interesting is the corresponding difference it produced in the telephone behavior of the females. On 17 of 21 adjective rating scales that had been part of the males' stereotype of an attractive female, the naive judges rated the target females more positively if the males thought they were attractive than if the males thought they were unattractive. The same difference was not found in the judges' ratings for other adjectives that had not been part of the male subjects' stereotype regarding attractiveness. In short, the males' expectations had produced precisely the kind of response that the male callers had anticipated.

What this research suggests is that a perceiver's constructive process can go far beyond the mere interpretation of a stimulus array to produce some of the very behaviors that are expected on the basis of the briefest sort of initial encounter. Moreover, even the consensus among naive judges (whose opinion might otherwise have been taken as a standard against which to assess the veridicality of the perceiver's impression) may be spurious. If this had not been an experiment in which we "knew" the truth (by virtue of having provided the pictures), we might have been tempted to compare any perceiver's impression of his telephone partner to the consensus provided by the impressions of the naive judges who rated her voice alone. Because it was an experiment, we know that their impression was no more veridical than was his.

DESCRIPTION OF THE STIMULUS
IN PERSON PERCEPTION

During the constructive process perceptual wholes are actively formed from the diverse attributes of the stimulus person or situation, and in some instances even those attributes are created by the perceiver's expectations. The organizing influence in perception is not typically available to conscious awareness, and operates even on the simplest social stimuli—verbal descriptions of a stimulus person that might be provided by a third party. Does the order in which a perceiver considers various elements of a single stimulus person affect the final impression? Are there some aspects of the stimulus person or situation more important than others in organizing the resulting perception? In short, how does the way in which the stimulus is described affect the perceiver's impression?

The Order of Presentation

Suppose that I described a hypothetical stimulus person to you, and I asked you to write a more inclusive description of that person from the information given. If I tell you that the person is "envious, stubborn, critical, impulsive, industrious, and intelligent," how "happy and sociable" will you believe the person to be? What if I give you the same description, but reverse the order of the adjectives? Will changing the order affect your impression? In one of the first laboratory studies of impression formation, Asch (1946) tried to answer just such questions. His subjects were instructed to form an integrated impression of a stimulus person from limited information provided to them. Half of the subjects received the adjectives in the order just listed, whereas half received the same adjectives in the reverse order. Subjects whose order began with "intelligent" were more likely than the other subjects to see the stimulus person as happy, humorous, sociable, and restrained.

The Primacy Effect.   This apparently greater influence of early information was called the **primacy effect**, and it was explained in terms of word meaning. You will notice that the adjective list contains words that differ in desirability—"intelligent" as opposed to "envious," for example. Asch argued that the words early in the series established an evaluative tone, and that later words were considered in light of this predominant evaluative tone. The meaning of a word like "critical" was thought to be different when interpreted as an attribute of an intelligent person than when interpreted as an attribute of an envious person. In a rough parallel to the behavioral confirmation research showing the importance of an initial impression of attractiveness, it is almost as though the perceiver integrated the remainder of the descriptive adjectives into a context formed from the first word.

A Difference in Importance. An alternative to Asch's suggestion of meaning change as the explanation for primacy effects is the notion that words early in the series are simply given more weight in the impression. Unless you are explicitly told that I am giving you the descriptive adjectives in some random order, you may well believe that I have started with the ones I think are most characteristic of the person. Suppose, for example, that you were given the same list of adjectives, but were instructed to refrain from forming any impression until you had heard the entire series. This procedure should equalize the weights given each adjective, but should not affect shifts in meaning, because each succeeding adjective will still be heard in the context of the ones that have preceded it. Using the same list of adjectives, Luchins (1957) performed this experiment, and found that the primacy effect disappeared. In a similar approach to the problem, Anderson and Hubert (1963) used the same list, but asked subjects to recall all the adjectives before making their judgments about the stimulus person. Their results showed dissipation of the primacy effects in this recall condition, indicating that the primacy effect occurs in part because the perceiver places less weight on the adjectives late in the series. We consider the ways in which information might be combined into a final impression in more detail in chapter 4, during discussion of a weighted averaging model of impression formation.

The Organizing Influence

Central Traits. In the description of a social stimulus, then, the order of presentation of the elements does seem to make a difference. What about the nature of the individual elements? Again, we can begin to answer this question by referring to the classic work of Asch (1946). Just as Asch's Gestalt view of impression formation led him to postulate meaning change as an explanation for primacy, it also suggested to him that some adjectives might exert an organizing influence on those presented with them. A person attempting to form an integrated impression of a stimulus person from a list of descriptive adjectives might consider some of these traits more important than others. In exactly the same way that an almost completely closed circle exerts an organizing influence, leading the perceiver to ignore the small gap in its circumference, these **central traits** might be more powerful than others in organizing the perceiver's impression of a stimulus person.

To test this idea, Asch presented a second group of subjects with a list of traits – "intelligent, skillful, industrious, warm, determined, practical, and cautious" – describing a hypothetical stimulus person. Half of the subjects received the list as it appears here, and half received a list with the word "cold" substituted for the word "warm." All subjects then wrote a brief paragraph describing the person, and completed a series of rating scales identifying other characteristics the person was thought to possess. The results showed that the warm-cold variable did produce substantial differences in the final impressions. The "warm" person was more likely to be seen as generous, happy, and humane, whereas the "cold" person was more likely to be seen as ungenerous, humorless, unhappy, and ruthless. It also appeared that the difference was not simply a matter of a positive description versus a negative description, because both stimulus persons were described by subjects as curious, important, honest, and strong – all positive characteristics.

Warm and Cold People.   At this point you may be about to voice an objection frequently raised against laboratory research in social psychology: "Of course the study worked when the only information the subjects had was that limited amount provided in the written descriptions. Surely that sort of bias wouldn't work if we were evaluating real live people!" Although this kind of criticism is frequently voiced, and occasionally correct, it is wrong in this instance. In an important extension of the Asch study, Kelley (1950) told students in three sections of an introductory psychology course that there would be a guest instructor for an upcoming session. Students were given one of two brief biographical notes describing the guest: one included the statement that the guest was "a rather warm person," whereas the other claimed the guest to be "a rather cold person." The guest then entered and, after a brief introduction by the professor, led the class discussion for 20 minutes. During the discussion, the professor (experimenter) recorded which students initiated conversation with the guest.

After the 20 minutes had passed, all students were asked to rate the guest instructor on a series of adjective rating scales. Scores on these scales replicated the warm-cold personal differences found by Asch (1946), and, more importantly, the behavioral data showed that most of the discussion in class had been initiated by students who had been told that the instructor was warm (if the warm-cold manipulation had not been performed during a single class, would there have been differences in the guest's behavior from the "warm" class to the "cold" one?). Although some later experiments cast doubt on word meaning change as the sole explanation for the operation of central traits, it appears that there are adjectives, such as warm and cold, that do exert substantial organizing influence on the impressions formed of other people.

NONVERBAL MEDIATORS
IN PERSON PERCEPTION

Until now we have been speaking of the stimulus person as he or she might be described by a third party. The stimulus for both the order effects (primacy) and combinatorial effects (central traits) is a list of descriptive adjectives. Although such lists form the core of traditional impression-formation experiments and generalize pretty well to real third-party descriptions, they play a much less important role in firsthand observation. Few people are likely to recite a series of descriptive adjectives if you ask them to say something about themselves. Indeed, research with the Twenty Statements Test (Kuhn & McPartland, 1954) shows that when asked to generate 20 self-descriptions in the space of 12 minutes people typically respond first with social categories—race, gender, name, age, current occupation, or group affiliations. This may be because these concepts are central to the self-concept, or it may simply be that such qualities are relatively "public," and less personally revealing to report than would be descriptive adjectives.

More importantly, even these self-descriptions have to be elicited by rather direct questions from the perceiver, and perceivers usually do not form impressions by asking the stimulus person for a self-description. It is much more likely that the perceiver will just observe the stimulus person's overt behavior, and try to reach conclusions about the person on the basis of appearance, bearing, actions, and communication skills. Trite as it is, much of the "dress for success" advice is consistent with the way perceivers form impressions. An incompetent who dresses for the part he or she hopes to play in an organization will, as time goes by, be discovered to be incompetent. But a competent person who violates the personnel manager's expectations for the appearance of prospective employees may never get the opportunity to demonstrate his or her actual skills.

A stimulus person's actions, as well as that person's appearance, may be communicative—the product of an active attempt to convey a message to the perceiver—or they may simply be expressive of his or her motives, desires, and emotional state. Communicative nonverbal behaviors, like verbal statements, are presumed to be under the stimulus person's conscious control (these aspects of self-presentation are considered in a later section), whereas expressive actions are not designed for the perceiver's benefit. But both sorts of nonverbal behavior will enter into the perceiver's impression.

Kinesic Cues

If your parents patted you on the head when you were a little child, it was probably because the top of your head was as low as they could reach without bending over. But if they continue to pat you on the head when you are 18, that action may be interpreted as evidence that they still consider you a child. All of the body movements readily perceptible to the perceiver are known as **kinesic cues**. Broadly conceived, this category includes both communicative and expressive movements, not only posture, gestures, and tactile communication, but also more specific elements such as facial expressions.

A First Impression.   What sorts of impressions can be conveyed by body position and movement? Let us suppose that you are attending a party at a friend's house, but that aside from your friend you know virtually no one there. You would like to make some new acquaintances, and because you neither want to interrupt an intimate group nor be lost in a large one, you settle for a group of three people. Specifically, assume that there are two potential choices, each group composed of one person of your gender and two of the opposite gender. One of these groups is near the corner of the room, with two of its members facing the wall and only one facing out toward the room, while the other group is arranged in a loose semicircle, sitting on the floor near a coffee table in the center of the room. The fact that they are seated in an open spatial pattern suggests that they are more approachable than is the other group, and this influence of posture on a perceiver's impression has also been shown in research (e.g., Mehrabian, 1968).

Even if the posture of the seated group is not a firm indication of its approachability, other kinesic cues may corroborate your judgment. You may have noticed animated gestures of arms and hands, relatively steady (but not intense) eye contact, and a good deal of smiling. From this information you would guess that the three people would be informal rather than formal (it is difficult to be formal when slouched on the floor), interested in their mutual conversation (a conspicuous absence of furtive glances around to see who has just come in the door), but not intimately engrossed in each other (their eyes are not riveted together, their gestures are animated, and their interpersonal distance is appropriate for the setting (rather than close head-to-head). You might not ordinarily be able to verbalize all of this information, but you would surely be surprised to arrive at the group and discover that they were having a heated argument about capital punishment or abortion.

Nonverbal Leakage.   Why is it that kinesic cues have such high apparent validity? Perhaps the best answer is the one suggested by Goffman (1959) and later elaborated in the work of Ekman (1965): Body language is less susceptible than is verbal language to conscious control by the stimulus person. Words can be chosen carefully to obscure the truth (calling tax increases "revenue enhancements," or calling a first-strike nuclear missile a "peacekeeper), but bodily position and movements are much less easily managed. Some excellent mimes can create almost any emotional expression simply by their bodily movements, but the intentional gestures the rest of us attempt usually look just as staged as they are. Consequently, when there is a discrepancy between the verbal message and the nonverbal cues, the latter tend to take precedence. This discrepancy between the verbal message and the nonverbal message has been described by Ekman (1965) as **nonverbal leakage**, and it can contribute substantially to the perceiver's impression.

Unfortunately, this use of nonverbal cues can have both positive and negative effects. On the positive side, for example, our legal system is constructed to take advantage of nonverbal leakage in its attempt to reach the truth. Juries are instructed to observe the "demeanor" of witnesses in order to make judgments about how credible is the testimony given by those witnesses. In contrast, the possibility for harm from nonverbal leakage is represented in the clinical literature by the *double-bind* hypothesis of the origin of childhood schizophrenia (Bateson, Jackson, Haley, & Weakland, 1956). The parent who tells a child "I love you" while holding the child stiffly away in a manner that says "You disgust me" is putting the child in a double-bind. If the child responds to the verbal message, he or she will be rebuffed; if the child responds to the nonverbal message, the parent will wonder indignantly "How can you say that about me?" The situation is further complicated by the greater perceived validity of the nonverbal message. Not surprisingly, a child receiving double-bind messages is confused, and Bateson and his associates argue that the childhood schizophrenic's characteristic withdrawal from social interaction is just an adaptive response to intolerable emotional inconsistency.

Facial Cues

Even though facial expressions are only one sort of kinesic cue, they deserve special treatment because of their potential importance in the communication of emotion (Ekman & Friesen, 1974; Izard, 1977; Tomkins, 1962). Let us return to your friend's party. You initially guessed from their spatial behavior that the three people sitting on the floor would be interesting and approachable, but that impression had to be confirmed by the facial cues of eye contact and smiling. More importantly, when you join the group, you will study their faces carefully, trying to read from their expressions what effect you are having on them. Once again, it is assumed that the perceiver and the stimulus person share a common nonverbal language. But is this assumption justified? To answer this question, we need to consider two quite different aspects of the communication of emotion.

Encoding and Decoding.   To recall the lens model of perception presented earlier, the emotional expression on another's face is a distal stimulus (of a sort). That expression is transmitted to you through the mediation of light waves (and sound waves, if there is a verbal component to the expression). Once the resulting proximal stimulus has been registered, you begin the constructive process of interpretation. The result will be your percept. But wait a minute: your percept of what? The other person's emotional expression, or that person's presumed internal emotional state? In fact, what you conclude from another person's smile is not merely that the person is smiling, but also that the person is happy. Indeed, the perceptual process of understanding emotion is as much a social inference process as it is a perceptual process, and in this way it is distinct from aspects of social perception that we have considered up to this point. In the preceding discussion we have always assumed that the true distal stimulus was the observable behavior, and that this distal stimulus could be taken as a "given," as a true and correct representation of what it appears to be. In Heider's (1958) terms, the distal stimulus has previously been synonymous with the state it presumably represents. But in the communication of emotion, as well as in more complex social behavior, this need not be the case.

The social inference process that takes place in the understanding of emotional communication is diagrammed in Fig. 3.2; as the diagram indicates, the decoding of a facial expression follows the familiar lens model. The facial expression is an observable distal stimulus, and through the perceptual chain, this stimulus becomes represented in a final percept. That percept, however, is an inference about the stimulus person's underlying emotional state. If you are smiling, I believe you are happy. But because I cannot actually observe your internal state of happiness, I could be mistaken. You could be smiling bravely to mask a great disappointment, and in that case my final percept would not be a veridical reflection of your state. My decoding of the expression has been accurate, but your encoding of your underlying emotional state into a facial expression has led me astray. Because different abilities might be involved in the sending (encoding) and receiving (decoding) of emotional expressions, these two aspects of interpersonal communication are usually considered separately.

Recognition of Posed Emotion. Recognition of facially expressed emotion is a classic problem in person perception, a line of inquiry initiated by Darwin (1872). As investigators have increasingly employed both cross-cultural comparisons and various mathematical scaling models, sophistication in research on the problem has grown tremendously. In the typical study, the decoders are shown either still photographs or videotapes of various encoders who have either been asked to express a particular emotion, or have been induced to do so. The stimulus materials are presented to the decoding subjects in a random order, with instructions to identify the emotion expressed in the photograph or videotape segment. Generally speaking, there are two different kinds of dependent variables measured, depending on the purposes of the research. First, a subject's accuracy can

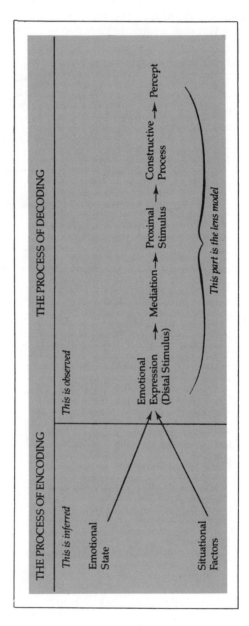

FIGURE 3.2 Encoding and decoding of emotional expressions.

be assessed by comparing his or her identifications with the actual emotion expressed. Second, the kinds of mistakes subjects make can be taken as an indication of emotional expressions that are difficult to distinguish: the more similar the emotional expressions are seen to be, the closer together—in some theoretical representation of the emotions—the underlying emotional states are thought to be.

Early studies of recognition of emotion were almost exclusively concerned with accuracy, and typically found that subjects were not very accurate. As Woodworth (1938) pointed out, however, these studies failed to distinguish errors made on simple judgments from errors made on difficult judgments. In other words, if you had mislabeled anger as "sadness," that error would have been given just the same weight as if you had mislabeled contemplation as "sadness." Woodworth examined the data from several earlier studies, and concluded that emotions could be ordered into a continuum of discrete categories: (a) love, mirth, happiness; (b) surprise, (c) fear and suffering; (d) anger and determination; (e) disgust, and (f) contempt. These categories can be thought of as along a line from left to right, with adjacent categories more likely to be confused than were categories separated by several steps. Using this revised coding scheme, Woodworth found an average accuracy of nearly 80%, and found that judges seldom made errors of more than one category step.

Several years (and a good deal of intervening research) later, Schlosberg (1952) conducted four separate studies in which subjects were asked to rate standard sets of facial photographs on two dimensions—pleasantness-unpleasantness, and attention-rejection—with each dimension measured by a 9-point scale. By an ingenious plotting of the resulting ratings, and through comparisons made to Woodworth's sorting procedure, Schlosberg determined that the facial expressions were really arrayed along the circumference of an oval surface like the one shown in Fig. 3.3.

The longer diameter of this oval is the pleasantness-unpleasantness dimension, whereas the shorter diameter is the the attention-rejection dimension. The real advantage of the oval model was that it accounted for one of the previously most perplexing errors judges made in their category sortings. This error was the confusion of mirth (at one end of Woodworth's bar of categories) with contempt (at the other end of Woodworth's bar of categories). If subjects are rarely wrong by more than a single category, why are they making this mistake of five intervening categories. As Schlosberg plotted the data the answer is obvious: the bar is not really a bar at all, but a closed figure (oval) in which mirth and contempt become adjacent categories. This generally circular conception of facial emotions further improved the prediction of where a single photograph would fall.

Emotional State or Emotional Label? One of the criticisms that has been raised against the two-dimensional generally circular model of emo-

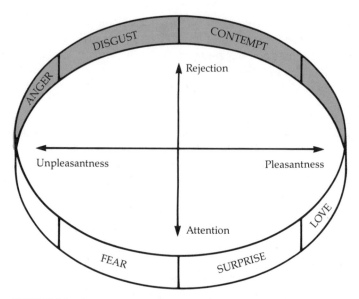

FIGURE 3.3 Schlosberg's (1952) oval classification of facial emotional expressions, characterized by two dimensions of pleasantness-unpleasantness and attention-rejection. Schlosberg, H. (1952). The description of facial expressions in terms of two dimensions. *Journal of Experimental Psychology, 44,* 229–237. Copyright 1952 by the American Psychological Association. Adapted with permission.

tional expressions is that the arrangement of the categories represents only the perceiver's use of language, not his or her "true" perceptions of the similarity of the emotional states described in those linguistic terms. You can see how this criticism might arise if you think of the specific point at which Schlosberg's (1952) model differs from Woodworth's (1938) bar of category labels. Is "love" similar to "contempt?" Few people would answer affirmatively. But is "haughty derisive laughter" similar to "mirth?" Of course. What has changed here, the underlying emotional state, or the label we attach to the state?

It would be tempting to argue that the high degree of similarity in responses to facial emotion across cultures supports the view that it is the emotional states, not the labels, that are similar. The problem with this suggestion is that what might be similar is the semantic properties of emotional labels within languages, not the judgments of the perceivers who speak those different languages. Fortunately, in recent years a data analysis technique called **multidimensional scaling** has been developed that permits an unequivocal answer to the question. Multidimensional scaling (MDS) techniques only require that the subjects judge the *similarity* of the stimuli to be scaled, not that specific linguistic labels be applied to those stimuli. So, for example, in the judgment of facial emotion, subjects can be shown pairs of still photographs, and for each pair indicate "how much alike the two people are feeling."

Testing a Circular Model. Just this experiment was performed by Russell and Bullock (1985), with perceivers who were either adults, or preschoolers incapable of making the sophisticated distinctions among emotional labels that characterize a typical adult's description of emotional states. Obviously, if the two groups of subjects produced similar patterns of judgment, that result would be strong evidence against a linguistic interpretation of the relationships among emotional expressions. But I am getting ahead of the story. You will recall from the discussion of veridicality in perception that one of the problems in person perception is obtaining a consensus among observers against which the judgments of a single perceiver can be compared to determine whether that perceiver's judgments are veridical. The same sort of problem existed in this research. As important as it would be to show that the pattern produced by children matched the pattern produced by adults, it would be even more important to show that both of these patterns obtained from MDS similarity judgments (without linguistic labels) matched the pattern found when adults were asked to use the linguistic labels. Only then could it be argued that the MDS results were a veridical reproduction of the pattern obtained using all of the distinctions inherent in the words that describe emotional states.

Consequently, in the first part of their research Russell and Bullock asked adult subjects to rate 20 facial expressions in terms of two fundamental dimensions obtained in an earlier study. These two dimensions were displeasure–pleasure (a dimension virtually identical to Schlosberg's, 1952, evaluative dimension of pleasantness–unpleasantness), and sleepiness–arousal. This second of Russell's dimensions, while including sleepiness, is very much like Schlosberg's attention–rejection dimension of involvement. Particular emotions like "fear" and "surprise," that have values on the "attention" end of Schlosberg's involvement dimension also have values high on Russell's arousal dimension. Indeed, one of the remarkable aspects of Russell's very recent work is just how much the emotions identified match the patterns initially identified by Woodworth nearly 50 years earlier. Each subject in this first part of the research was shown one randomly selected facial expression, and asked to rate that expression in terms of pleasure and arousal. Three hundred people served as subjects, producing 15 ratings of pleasure and arousal for each photograph, and the two-dimensional space defined by these ratings is shown in Fig. 3.4. As in Schlosberg's case, the array is generally circular, and because there were multiple instances of some emotional expressions, some labels appear twice in the figure.

Scaling of Expressions. The next step in the research was to have both adult and preschool subjects rate the similarity of the emotional expressions without using any linguistic labels. Adult subjects performed this task by rating the pairwise similarity of all possible pairs of the 20 emotional expressions shown in the photographs. Any complete pairwise com-

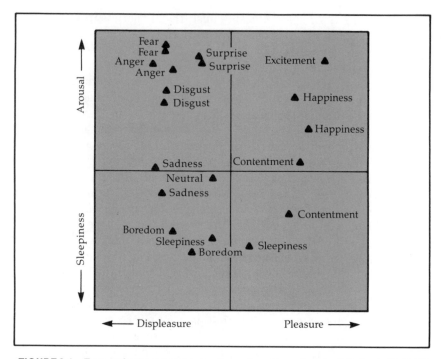

FIGURE 3.4 Twenty facial expressions of emotion. Russell, J.A., & Bullock, M. (1985). Multidimensional scaling of emotional facial expressions: Similarity from preschoolers to adults. *Journal of Personality and Social Psychology, 48,* 1290–1298. Copyright 1985 by the American Psychological Association. Reprinted by permission.

parison of stimuli will require a total number of judgments dictated by the formula $N(N-1)/2$, where N is the number of elements, or in this case, a total of 190 judgments. Adults will do such a task (they may not always enjoy it), but children aged 4 or 5 just would not continue to play such a game. So the similarity judgments for children were obtained by having each child sort the 20 pictures into a specified number of piles.

Universals in Facial Emotion. Regardless of the manner in which the similarity judgments had been obtained, those judgments were subjected to multidimensional scaling analysis. The result of this analysis is a theoretical "space" into which the stimuli can be placed, and this space can have more than two dimensions (it is, after all, multidimensional scaling). The general rule is that the data should be described by as few dimensions as possible, and there are statistical criteria for choosing how many of the resulting dimensions to use in the explanation. In Russell and Bullock's work a two-dimensional "solution" was all that was really needed. The two-dimensional solution for adult subjects is shown in Fig. 3.5, and you can see that it matches quite well the pattern (shown in Fig. 3.4) produced using the linguistic labels. The similarity-judgment patterns for children also very closely resembled the original linguistic label pattern. These results

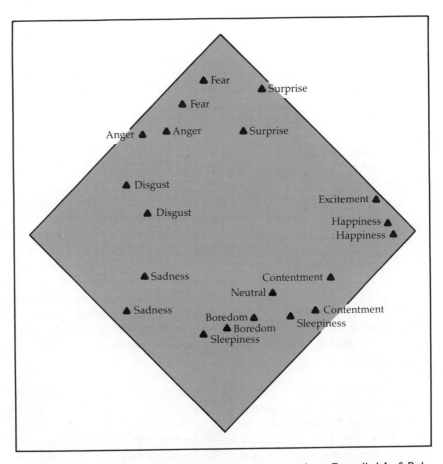

FIGURE 3.5 Multidimensional scaling of 20 facial expressions. Russell, J.A., & Bullock, M. (1985). Multidimensional scaling of emotional facial expressions: Similarity from preschoolers to adults. *Journal of Personality and Social Psychology, 48,* 1290–1298. Copyright 1985 by the American Psychological Association. Reprinted by permission.

together indicate that the consistent judgments of facially expressed emotion obtained through the years (and across cultures) are elementary perceptions not dependent upon skill in the linguistic labeling of emotion.

There are, in fact, six different emotional expressions – happiness, surprise, fear, anger, disgust, and sadness – that are universally recognized across cultures (Ekman & Oster, 1979; Izard, 1971), regardless of whether the stimulus materials are the posed expressions of actors and actresses or the spontaneous expressions of ordinary people experiencing conditions designed to produce certain emotional states (e.g., photographing people who have just been shown the several-day old and rotten remains of an animal near the side of the road). Of these six universally recognized emotions, only "sadness" differs from the general categories outlined by Woodworth (1938). Obviously, there will be individual differences in ability to decode facially expressed emotion (indeed, a review by Hall, 1978, suggests that females in general are better decoders than are males), and just as obviously people can recognize more than six emotional states from facial cues. Nevertheless, the work on recognition of facial emotion supports the view that, at least on the interpretation side, we share a common nonverbal language.

Display Rules
and the Encoding Process

It is clear that perceptions of facial emotion are "stimulus driven: whether the emotion is spontaneous or posed, whether the materials are presented as still photographs or on videotape, and whether the perceivers have the linguistic labels or not, there is remarkable similarity in the judgments of relations between various expressed emotions. But are the emotions expressed "driven" to the same extent by the presence of underlying emotional states? The answer is clearly "no" when the stimulus person is a professional actor on stage, but what about everyday people in natural settings? Is emotional experience sufficient for facial expression, or do social rules for emotional displays govern the overt expression of felt emotions?

Bowlers and Hockey Fans. Research by Kraut and Johnston (1979) suggests that the encoding of facial emotion to a great extent depends on social display rules as well as on underlying felt emotion. In one series of studies Kraut and Johnston observed the facial expressions of bowlers in an attempt to discover whether smiling was the result of an internal state of happiness (for instance, just having made a strike or a spare), or of social engagement with one's bowling partners. If the underlying state alone produces the expressed emotion, then the frequency of smiles should have been greater following strikes and spares than following misses. But the results showed only a weak association between smiling and success, with bowlers smiling 30% of the time after good scores and 23% of the time otherwise. The greatest amount of smiling occurred during social contact between the bowler and his or her companions. Aware of the potential difficulties in the interpretation of these results, the researchers conducted a second study in which the subjects' feeling of emotion might be separated more clearly from the communication of that emotion to others. As before, virtually no association between smiling and score appeared. In fact, out of 116 observations, there were only 4 smiles when bowlers were facing the pins, even though 26 strikes or spares were rolled.

Other studies in the series observed the smiling by fans at a hockey game, and the smiling of pedestrians passing each other on the street either on sunny or rainy days. Again the findings showed smiling only weakly related to external events that might have been expected to produce happiness. Spectators at the hockey game were more likely to smile following events favorable to the home team, and pedestrians were slightly more likely to smile on pleasant days than on dreary ones. But in both cases, a person's involvement in a social unit was a much stronger predictor of smiling than was the impersonal state (winning or sunny).

The Social Unit.   It is possible, of course, that participation in a social unit produces an internal state of happiness, which state is then followed by the smiling. This alternative explanation is less plausible in the case of the bowlers and hockey fans (after all, if you are sufficiently committed to either activity to be participating or watching in person, you ought to care about the actual score) than it is for the pedestrian passersby. Consequently, although each of these studies by itself suffers from some of the problems of internal validity that affect observational research, together they make a strong case for the influence of display rules on the expression of emotion.

Facial Feedback

Thus both true emotion and social display rules can produce facial expressions of emotion, greatly complicating the task of a perceiver whose distal stimulus of interest is the stimulus person's underlying emotional state, rather than that person's overt facial expression. Some intriguing, but still controversial, recent research on facial emotion suggests that the relation between emotional state and encoded expression may be even more complicated: This **facial feedback hypothesis** holds that kinesthetic feedback from the muscles of the face can affect the expressor's underlying emotional state: "I am smiling, so I *must* be happy!"

Whistle a Happy Tune.   Think for a moment about two pieces of advice your parents probably gave you as a child–"whistle if you're afraid," and "put on a happy face." Indeed, both of these admonitions were so widespread that they were the subject of popular songs. Now think about the last time someone suddenly scared you. You screamed. Or at least opened your mouth wide for a sharp intake of breath. Try whistling with your face in that position–or to be more precise, try to scream with your mouth set to whistle. Whistling not only requires concentration, taking your mind off the possible dangers; and requires control, perhaps giving you the feeling that you are in control; it also involves the facial muscles in movements that are antagonistic to expressions of fright. In the same way, the relaxation of the face that accompanies a pleasant smile involves the facial muscles in movements that are antagonistic to those required for sadness or anger.

Experimental Procedures. The possible role of facial feedback in the production of emotion has been investigated in two different ways. In the "muscle-by-muscle" procedure, subjects are asked to contract selected facial muscles, often ostensibly to test some procedure for **electromyography**: the measurement (with surface electrodes) of the minute electrical potentials that initiate contraction of a muscle (e.g., Laird, 1974). What the subjects are actually being asked to do, of course, is, on a muscle by muscle basis, frown, smile, or grimace. By contrast, in the exaggeration/ minimization method (e.g., Lanzetta, Cartwright-Smith, & Kleck, 1976), subjects are shown stimulus materials designed to produce one or another spontaneous emotion (and its corresponding facial expression), and are told that they are to try to "fool" an observer about the intensity of their emotional experience by either exaggerating their facial expression or minimizing it (the well known "poker face).

Typical dependent variables in these studies are self-report scales for the measurement of emotional state, often accompanied by physiological recording of pulse, heart rate, and other indicants of arousal. On all of these dependent variables, subjects' reported emotional states and the physiological indicants of the presence of such states are influenced by the facial emotion expressed. People report being angrier when asked to contract the muscles between the eyebrows and at the corners of the jaw than when asked to raise the corners of their mouths. People asked to minimize their spontaneous emotional expressions show lower levels of arousal than those asked to exaggerate their facial expressions. In short, reported and recorded emotional experience responds to feedback from the emotional expression.

There have been occasional failures to find evidence of facial feedback, but in a recent review article Laird (1984) finds the "box score" for both experimental procedures to be heavily in favor of the existence of facial feedback effects on a wide variety of emotions – anger, happiness, fear, sadness, pain, and humor. More importantly, Laird suggests a reason for some of the failures to replicate the effect: there are substantial individual differences in people's susceptibility to their own facial feedback. Those who do not respond to their own "self-produced" cues to emotion are typically more responsive to the situational cues to emotion, and to other situational information as well. The possibility that an encoded emotion might be further influenced by feedback from the facial expression of that emotion suggests that even in the case of spontaneous emotional expressions there is more to encoding than the perceiver can see.

Paralinguistic Cues

In this description of the elements of social perception, we began the analysis at a distance from the verbal behavior of the stimulus person and have moved steadily closer to that behavior—from the descriptions given by others, through the stimulus person's kinesic cues, to his or her facial expressions. Now we turn to how the stimulus person says what is said, the cues derived from the **paralinguistic** features of verbal behavior. According to an early analysis by Mahl (1957), these include four different dimensions: vocal (loudness and pitch), temporal (rate of speaking, duration of speech segments), verbal-stylistic (dialect, vocabulary peculiarities), and interactive (behavior in a conversation, such as a tendency to interrupt or dominate). The latter two are perhaps the most noticeable to an untrained observer, so we begin with them.

Dialect.   One of the first things that you notice about an unfamiliar person's speech is whether or not the person speaks with an identifiable dialect. Among the more recognizable ones are the clipped and crisp speech of the New Englander, the accent of the Brooklyn New Yorker, and the twang of a Southern drawl. But do these speech characteristics tell the perceiver anything more than the probable origin of the speaker? Hollywood television and movie producers certainly seem to think so. For example, think of the last movie or television show in which the hero was having difficulty with a small-town sheriff. If the sheriff was characterized as a little dull, as willing to bend the law to accommodate the townspeople's wishes, and as openly hostile to people from "outside," he probably also spoke with an identifiable Southern drawl—even in the Pacific Northwest, the setting for the Sylvester Stallone movie "First Blood." Although Labov (1970) has shown that the basic features of various nonstandard dialects of English are structurally and functionally similar, at least the popular wisdom suggests that perceivers still believe in stereotyped views of people based in part on the dialect they speak.

Speaker-State Signals.   Not only the speaker's dialect, but also his or her control over the linguistic interaction will influence the perceiver's impression. What do you think of a person who won't let you get a word in edgewise? You consider the person egocentric and overbearing, more interested in the sound of his or her own voice than in actually communicating. You make an inference about the stimulus person's personality characteristics from verbal assertiveness and from the person's failure to heed your desire to speak. But how do you indicate a desire to be heard? Duncan and Niederehe (1974) suggest that there are at least four specific cues employed by a listener to indicate that the listener wants to take a turn at speaking. Together these constitute the **speaker-state signal** and include (a) a shift in head direction away from pointing directly toward the speaker, (b) an audible inhalation of breath, as a preparation for beginning to speak, (c) the initiation of gesticulation (defined so as to include tensing of the hands, or movement of the hands away from the body), and (d) paralinguistic overloudness.

This last cue needs a little elaboration. In any continued conversation, both the speaker and the listener are participating. The latter is emitting what Yngve (1970) calls *back-channel behaviors*. These include head movements such as nods and shakes, verbalizations such as "m-hm," "yeah," and even short sentences such as "That's right." Ordinarily the back-channel verbalizations are relatively low in intensity and serve the expressive function of indicating that the listener is paying attention, being sympathetic, or agreeing with what speaker is saying. But if a back-channel verbalization is *overloud*, it can serve the communicative purpose of indicating a desire to speak. A "That's right" spoken softly indicates agreement, a louder "That's right" with the "right" a little drawn out may well mean "That's right, *but.* . . ." Given the nature of the cues that form the speaker-state signal, it is not surprising that you infer egocentrism, lack of interpersonal sensitivity, and dominance from a speaker who refuses to yield.

Pitch, Loudness, and Temporal Pattern. Just as an individual's balance between listening and talking can serve as a cue to personality, the pitch, loudness, and rate of a stimulus person's speech can suggest emotional state. Calm and controlled speech may be firm, but every child knows that a shouting parent means business. As the electronic devices for measuring aspects of the acoustic content of speech have become more sophisticated, analysis of that acoustic content has become more important within social perception. An individual's "voiceprint" may reveal his or her emotional state for the same reason that body language may do so. We are not trained in the use of our voices, an speech pattern is a dimension of behavior to which we are not consciously sensitive (unlike, for example, facial expression). As a result, although we may control what we say (the semantic content), and even how loudly we might say it, we do not usually try to control other acoustic properties of speech.

Acoustic Properties and Perception. The combined effects of voice pitch and rate changes on the perceptions formed about a stimulus person have been investigated by Apple, Streeter, and Krauss (1979), in a set of studies that illustrates some of the manipulations now technically feasible. In three different experiments, these researchers asked male and female subjects to listen to tape recordings of male speakers answering two interview questions. One of the questions dealt with college admission quotas designed to favor minority groups, whereas the other asked what the stimulus person would do if he suddenly inherited a large sum of money. All of the speech material was converted to digital signals, which were then reconstructed by a computer system that allowed the experimenter to alter pitch and rate of speech without affecting any other speech characteristics, such as loudness.

In the first of the three experiments, subjects were told that the purpose of the research was to determine how well people could detect lying by judging just from voice qualities. The results showed that lower pitched responses were regarded as more truthful than were higher pitched responses. No significant effects on truthfulness were found as a consequence of changes in speech rate. To guard against the possibility that the "truthfulness" cover story had unnecessarily influenced subjects in the first experiment, a second study was conducted, in which different subjects were simply asked to rate the speakers on a set of rating scales. The resulting ratings revealed that subjects found men speaking in higher pitched voices to be less potent, smaller, and thinner than men speaking in lower pitched voices (keep in mind that the pitch changes were accomplished by computer manipulation of the speakers' original voices). In addition, those speaking at a slower rate were seen as colder, more passive, and those speaking at a higher rate. Finally, in the third study using the same computer-altered tapes, the subjects judged the speakers for such attributes as seriousness, fluency, and persuasiveness. Normal rate speakers were thought most fluent, most persuasive, and least nervous, whereas speakers who were either faster than normal or slower than normal were considered less fluent, less persuasive, and more nervous. Speakers with higher pitch also were judged more nervous and marginally less persuasive.

The researchers noted that their results cannot be generalized to perceptions of female speakers, and they recognized that under normal circumstances the acoustic stimulus received by a perceiver is more complex than the one presented to subjects in their research. Nevertheless, this set of studies does indicate that the acoustic properties of speech can have significant effects on a perceiver's impression. If we are talking about a topic we know well, we speak quickly and without hesitation; if we know our material less well or are under some other stress, our voices rise in pitch. Most probably without even being conscious of it, perceivers are sensitive to these acoustic properties of speech.

ACCURACY IN THE JUDGMENT OF OTHERS

In our everyday social interactions we form impressions of people we meet, guess about their backgrounds and interests, and evaluate their intentions toward us. For the most part, these judgments are correct. We seldom become involved with people who turn out to be completely different from the first impression we form. There are exceptions—"But he didn't *look* like a criminal"—and these can be based on a misleading self-presentation by the stimulus person, or, as we see in chapter 4, on errors in our cognitions about social reality. But when we have sufficient time to make a judgment, we can usually differentiate true praise from ingratiation, tell who will keep our secrets and who will not, and distinguish the person who really believes in honor and justice from the hypocrite who merely talks about them.

Possible Sources of Accuracy

Experience. What sorts of factors contribute to such accuracy in person perception? Surely the combination of cues available to the perceiver aids in the judgment. But are there personal characteristics of the perceiver that might also help? Intuitively, we might identify several possibilities. Suppose that you were asked to choose a person who would be a good roommate for you. First we might expect that your accuracy in such a judgment would increase with your experience. When you first arrived at college you were uncertain what your study habits would be, how you would adapt to the freedom and responsibility that accompany being away from home, and how sharing such a limited space with a stranger would complicate your adaptation to this relatively unfamiliar lifestyle. But after a term or two, you know which of your personal habits are likely to get on a roommate's nerves (and vice versa), you know how much mutual self-disclosure you consider desirable, and you know what proportion of your time you can afford to spend talking and having fun instead of studying. In terms of social perception, your experience has given you a better idea of the behavior to be predicted, or the *criterion*. You now know what behavioral qualities "a good roommate" for you should have.

Intelligence, Empathy, and Similarity. Because the accurate assessment of other people involves some cognitive work, a second factor that might contribute to accuracy in interpersonal judgment would be your overall intelligence. You need to be able to formulate precise questions to ask potential roommates, to recall your own experiences, and to learn from the mistakes of others. It seems reasonable that these abilities should be related to more general intellectual capability. Finally, you ought to be sensitive to the other person's needs and emotions, so that you can put yourself in that person's shoes. After all, how well the two of you get along will depend in part on whether your future roommate can tolerate you. Your ability to place yourself in the other's position is what Mead (1934) called *taking the role of the other*, and we consider this process in more detail in chapter 7. The ability to experience another person's emotional state has been proposed as an operational definition of **empathy** (Stotland, Sherman, & Shaver, 1971), and we return to this concept in the discussion of helping behavior (Chapter 9). We would expect that both your empathy for another person, and your ability to put yourself in his or her place would increase with your similarity to the stimulus person.

Early Research on Accuracy

Thus, our intuitive theories of social psychology would suggest that experience, intelligence, empathy, and personal similarity would all be involved in determining the accuracy of your interpersonal judgment. How could we apply the methods of scientific social psychology to test these presumptions? In the early work on accuracy in interpersonal judgment, investigators simply asked subjects to describe themselves, close friends, and strangers on a number of rating scales, and then compared these descriptions to ones made by the stimulus persons (friends or strangers). The more that other people's descriptions of you matched your self-description, the greater your accuracy in self-rating was presumed to be; the more your description of your friends matched their self-ratings, the greater your accuracy in judging friends was thought to be; and the more your characterization of strangers matched their self-characterization, the greater your accuracy in judging strangers was presumed to be.

It is important to note that in the early studies both a subject's rating and the criterion (whether that was the rating of another or a personality test administered to the other person) were simply taken at face value. There was no consideration of the fallibility or error in the measures involved, no correction for possible social desirability biases (although many of the descriptive terms involved were heavily loaded on social desirability—"generosity," "apathy," "submissiveness). Finally, the subject-friend comparisons (self-perception accuracy and accuracy in judging friends) were, as we see in a moment, statistically inappropriate, because they did not correct for the similarity between the people doing the ratings.

Differential Accuracy. The methodological problems inherent in early research on judgmental accuracy were first noted extensively by Cronbach (1955). As often happens in research, Cronbach's critique demonstrated that before valid answers regarding accuracy in social perception could be obtained, more precise questions would have to be asked. Specifically, Cronbach noted that the global measure of accuracy should really be separated into four relatively independent components. One of these dealt with the perceiver's willingness to use extremes of the scale of judgment (*elevation*); one dealt with the ability to place the stimulus person in the proper rank order among a set of such persons, even though the absolute judgment of each person might be in error (*differential elevation*); and the third represented the perceiver's sensitivity to the distribution of traits in the larger population (*stereotype accuracy*). Only the fourth component, **differential accuracy**, actually reflects a perceiver's ability to estimate correctly how much of a particular trait is possessed by a specific stimulus person. The other three components can contribute to the apparent accuracy of a perceiver, but they do not represent the ability to make absolute judgments of the degree to which a specific stimulus person possesses a certain trait. Thus, Cronbach argued, only differential accuracy should be considered a "pure" accuracy score, and this element of the perceptual judgment is quite difficult to extract independently of the others.

Assumed Similarity. In addition to suggesting that three of the components of global accuracy were of little use in describing a perceiver's social acuity, Cronbach (1955) noted that the actual similarity between a perceiver and a stimulus person could spuriously increase the perceiver's apparent accuracy. If you have no information about the traits of a stimulus person, you might guess that the person would be at least somewhat similar to yourself. Indeed, just such guesses form the basis of the **false-consensus effect**: a tendency for a person to overestimate the proportion of people who agree with his or her own position on an attitude issue, regardless of what that position might be.

In the initial series of four studies dealing with the false consensus effect, Ross, Greene, and House (1977) asked college students to estimate the probability that other students would choose one of two behavioral alternatives (such as pay a traffic ticket by mail or go to court to contest the charge); share the subject's own personal preferences, characteristics, and problems; and wear a sandwich board sign saying "Eat at Joe's" as part of a psychology experiment. In the fourth study in the series, subjects were asked to wear the sandwich board sign themselves, and to estimate the proportion of other students who would have made the decision (to wear it or not to do so) that they, themselves made. Regardless of the task, and regardless of their own position on any issue, the subjects routinely overestimated the commonness of their own judgments, attitudes, or choices.

Estimated and Real Similarity. Obviously, one of the explanations for the false consensus effect is that people tend to talk to those with whom they have many things in common. If they fail to take this self-selection into account, and merely assume that they have sampled a representative group of people, they will overestimate the proportion of individuals who share their position. On the other hand, if they are asked to describe one of their friends, there is likely to be a real, rather than false, consensus in the attributes possessed by the two friends.

To be more specific, suppose that you are given a personality test to measure your assertiveness, and that the same test is given to a friend of yours. Now you are asked to judge how assertive your friend is. The researcher would then have three scores available for analysis: your own assertiveness score from the test—call this score (a); your friend's score on the test (b); and your estimate of your friend's real assertiveness, (c). Using these scores we can define three different variables. The first variable is *accuracy*, in the sense of Cronbach's differential accuracy, and it is defined by the extent to which $c = b$ (further assuming, of course, that what the test actually measures is the assertiveness you were trying to predict). The second variable is the *real similarity* between you and your friend, defined by the extent to which $a = b$. The third variable, called *assumed similarity* by Cronbach, is defined by the extent to which $a = c$.

Aside from possible invalidity of the assertiveness test, the problem is this: If your estimate of your friend's score is largely based on projection from your own level of assertiveness, then your apparent accuracy will increase as the real similarity between you and your friend increases. Even if you are a terrible judge of character (meaning that you have to rely entirely on projection from your own traits), you will appear to be accurate whenever you are judging someone who happens to be quite similar to you! Worse still, assumed similarity cannot even be assessed without reference to a test of the underlying trait being predicted – substantially limiting the meaning of "accuracy" outside the experimental laboratory.

Sending and Receiving Revisited

Although researchers have not entirely abandoned the search for those personal characteristics that will contribute to a perceiver's differential accuracy, most of the recent interest in interpersonal perception has, in large part as a result of Cronbach's (1955) critique, concentrated on the process rather than the outcome. Rather than attempting to catalogue all the personality traits that might make one an excellent judge of others, researchers have sought to discover more about the way in which any perceiver (not just an extremely accurate one) processes the information received about other people. As we noted in the discussion of facial cues, the process of emotional communication involves encoding on the part of the stimulus person and decoding on the part of the perceiver. For the six culturally universal facial expressions, and for a variety of acoustic characteristics, decoding is highly reliable among perceivers. But this can be determined only because in the laboratory studies the *criterion* (e.g., presumed emotional state) can be manipulated by the experimenter. When that criterion changes (as it must in studies of judgmental accuracy) to an enduring personality disposition possessed by a stimulus person outside the laboratory, the task of finding "accurate judges" becomes almost impossible.

THE STIMULUS AS PERSON:
SELF-PRESENTATION

To this point we have concentrated on the elements of social perception, only noting in passing that these might be under the full or partial control of the stimulus person. Implicit in the consideration of nonverbal behavior, and explicit in the idea of nonverbal leakage, is the presumption that such behavior reveals the stimulus person's true emotions, attitudes, and personality. Not surprisingly, research on the detection of deception shows that people can indeed identify deception from nonverbal behavior (Riggio & Friedman, 1983). Although there is evidence that perceivers can even learn to improve their skill at such detection (Zuckerman, Koestner, & Alton, 1984), having a skill is not the same as using it, and this distinction is central to the process of self-presentation.

A Face and a Line

Perhaps the most important difference between stimulus persons and stimulus objects is that the former are not merely inactive collections of attributes. They are, as we have noted before, thinking and feeling beings capable of intentional action who are often engaged in what Goffman (1959) calls **self-presentation**: the creation and maintenance of a public self. In Goffman's view, an encounter between two or more people involves a mutually agreed upon (though often implicit) set of rules that prescribes what behaviors are appropriate for the situation. Of course, different expectations exist for different roles and circumstances. You don't behave the same way with your parents that you do with close friends; but in all cases some of the same rules can be seen to apply.

Each person brings to the encounter what Goffman calls a *line*: a complete pattern of verbal and nonverbal behavior through which one communicates one's view of the situation and the participants (especially oneself). It is important to note that because this line can differ from one setting to the next it cannot be equated with the person's entire repertoire of possible actions. Rather, it is the subset of that behavioral repertoire that the person believes to be appropriate for the circumstances.

A central element of the person's line is called the *face*, defined as the positive social value that the person claims for himself or herself in the interaction. If all the information contributed by participants in the encounter is consistent with the stimulus person's positive social value, the person is said to be "maintaining face." In contrast, if information provided by either the person or by others disconfirms the person's self-worth, then the person is said to be "out of face." Although Goffman does not specifically say so, this process is comparable to the situation described in everyday language as "losing face."

A Mutual Commitment:
The Maintenance of Face

One of the most important rules of interaction is that such encounters involve mutual commitment. Each participant's face becomes a property of the group, and all participants do what they can (within reason) to maintain each other's face. If you doubt this, just try telling someone straight out, with no euphemisms, why you think he or she is the most obnoxious person you have ever met. Perhaps one of the most upsetting features of the student radicals of the 1960s, at least as far as many older people were concerned, was their tendency to describe policies they opposed with profanity, rather than with sophisticated derogatory terms. They were somehow not playing the game properly, not letting other participants "save face." Even in less turbulent times, governmental figures bristle when confronted on state occasions by protesters whose expressions of legitimate concern are out of keeping with the officials' view of the nature of the setting. As we see in chapter 12, however, concentration on the maintenance of face to the exclusion of all else can lead the interactants to erroneous decisions they would not have made if reality had been forced upon them.

In short, there are instances—public debate of issues, psychotherapy, education, friendship—in which the greatest mutual commitment should be to the truth. The maintenance of face is not the goal of interaction, but rather is a necessary condition for its continuation. When you are conversing with close friends, your primary goal is not self-aggrandizement, but the conducting of a relationship in which all of you can express your true feelings, exchange ideas (even on controversial subjects), and only occasionally pat each other on the back. If any incidents threaten the face of a participant, however, a corrective process called *face work* must be initiated and completed if the interaction is to be preserved.

A Closing Word About
the Stimulus in Person Perception

Goffman's (1959) ritual analysis of interaction serves to illustrate two aspects of the crucial difference between a stimulus object and a stimulus person: Properties are selected for presentation by the stimulus person, and observation is a social behavior in which the stimulus person may participate. When the stimulus for perception is an object, even an animate though infrahuman one, nearly all of its properties are accessible to the perceiver. True, mediating conditions may preclude full knowledge (it is difficult to tell the color of an object in the dark), but those conditions are not under the active control of the object itself. By contrast, when the stimulus is a person, there is an active selection of which verbal (and to a lesser extent nonverbal) behaviors to reveal, and that choice depends on the situation. Second, person perception is, by its very nature, an interpersonal phenomenon, governed by many of the same rules and expectations that regulate other forms of social interaction. Which behaviors the stimulus person chooses to emit can have implications for the perceiver, and the impressions the perceiver forms can in the same way affect the stimulus person. The social nature of person perception thus places restrictions and expectations on both participants.

SUMMARY

Virtually all of people's social behavior will be affected by their perception of the social world around them. In social perception, as in object perception, a perceiver's phenomenological experience, the **percept** (p. 73), is not a perfect representation of the **distal stimuli** (p. 76) in the world, although its **veridicality** (p. 74) can be determined through appropriate comparisons. One reason that the percept and distal stimulus may differ is that the perceiver employs a **constructive process** (p. 77) to interpret the incoming stimulation in the context of ongoing physiological and cognitive activity.

The description of the stimulus in person perception has often taken the form of lists of adjectives, and some of these represent **central traits** (p. 82) that exert an organizing influence on the perception. In firsthand observation, of course, descriptive adjectives play a much less important role than do such nonverbal mediators of impressions as the body language of **kinesic cues** (p. 85) and the **paralinguistic cues** (p. 97) that accompany speech. These nonverbal cues can be used as clues to deception in verbal communications, because they are less likely to be under the conscious control of the stimulus person. Nonverbal behavior is, however, subject to socially defined *display rules*.

Among the kinesic cues, the emotional expressions of the face are perhaps the most important, and through the years a number of different techniques, including most recently **multidimensional scaling** (p. 90) have been employed to assess the regularity in perceptions of facial emotion. There are six emotional expressions—happiness, surprise, fear, anger, disgust, sadness—that are universally recognized. Recent studies of facial emotion suggested that the stimulus person's underlying emotional state can be influenced by **facial feedback** (p. 95) from the expression displayed.

Other research indicates that nonverbal signals serve not only to mediate social impressions, but also to regulate interaction through such mechanisms as the **speaker-state signal** (p. 97). Both the social impression function and the social regulation function of nonverbal behavior are affected by the fact that the stimulus person is engaged in an active **self-presentation** (p. 104), controlling the cues the perceiver is permitted to see.

SUGGESTED ADDITIONAL READINGS

ALLPORT, F. H. (1955). *Theories of perception and the concept of structure.* New York: Wiley. An extensive, scholarly discussion of the classic theories of object and social perception. Difficult reading, but well worth the effort if you wish to learn where perceptual theories fit in the larger context of psychological tradition.

SCHNEIDER, D. J., HASTORF, A. H., & ELLSWORTH, P. C. (1979). *Person perception* (2nd ed.). Reading, MA: Addison-Wesley. A short and clearly written introduction to person perception, including recognition of emotion and interpersonal accuracy, among others.

CHAPTER FOUR

SOCIAL COGNITION: CONSTRUCTION OF SOCIAL REALITY

CONTENTS

PREVIEW

The intentional actions that comprise much of a person's social behavior are based on a social reality constructed by the person. Consequently, theoretical explanations for human action rely heavily on the study of social cognition: the gathering, interpreting, and organizing of information about social phenomena. Social perception provides the individual with the data to build or test personal hypotheses about interpersonal behavior, but that data collection process can be compromised by a number of cognitive heuristics and errors. What data are collected are quickly categorized, a simplification process that is a virtual necessity in a complex social environment. But that useful process of categorization can, itself, have negative consequences, represented in the problem of stereotyping. Both cognitive and motivational factors are implicated in the development and perpetuation of stereotypes. When we do attend to the behavior of individual other people, we attempt to explain the actions they have taken, and to predict the ones they will take, by attributing their behavior to underlying personal dispositions. Our impressions of other people will be influenced both by the attributions we make for their actions, and by our own implicit personality theories. These processes of categorization, attribution, and impression formation all contribute to our representation of social reality, and this reality in turn affects our attitudes, self-concept, and exchanges with other people.

An individual's actions toward others to no small degree depend on that person's social perceptions. Friendship, competition, and participation in group activities all require thoughtful, intentional action. Obedience to society's rules of conduct—both formal laws and informal norms—presupposes knowledge of the rules, understanding of the penalties that will follow failure to conform, and a cognitive capacity to distinguish right from wrong. Not surprisingly, most theoretical explanations for social behavior assume that individuals are responding to the world as it appears to them.

In the chapter 3 we focused attention on a principal element of that phenomenological world, another person, and discovered that human beings are complex stimuli whose nonverbal behavior and facial emotional expressions provide information not as easily controlled as is verbal behavior or intentional action. Consequently, we base our judgments of people in part upon what they do and how they do it, as well as on what they say and what others say about them. We look for discrepancies between words and deeds, in an attempt to separate "truth" from self-presentation. In short, we actively seek, interpret, and organize the available information. Frequently this constructive process of interpretation enhances the veridicality of our social perceptions, but in some cases our own thought processes and motives decrease the accuracy of our final impressions. Complete understanding of social perception, and of other aspects of social behavior, thus requires study of *social cognition*: the cognitive processes and structures involved in building the knowledge base for social behavior.

The term social cognition has been applied to a diverse array of topics in social psychology (for example, see Fiske & Taylor, 1984), but we confine its use here to four areas. The first of these identifies some of the cognitive processes involved in the gathering of social information, and contrasts that haphazard procedure with systematic methods of data collection. The second deals with the categorization of social stimuli and sheds new light on an important social problem, that of stereotyping. The third describes the inferences perceivers make about the causes of events, and presents theoretical models of social attribution. The fourth deals with the combination of bits of information into a coherent cognitive structure. The first three areas are primarily concerned with questions of process, whereas the last is primarily a description of cognitive structure. You see that the operative word here is "primarily," because in social cognition the process cannot really be divorced from the structure, any more than a contractor could order the materials for constructing a house without knowing what was called for in the blueprint.

GATHERING INFORMATION

It is your first day as the personnel manager for a new but growing corporation that specializes in the manufacture of computer expansion devices and business software. The previous personnel manager left suddenly and without giving advance notice, and because of your undergraduate background in Psychology the company president asked you to fill in, either until a permanent replacement is found, or, if you do a satisfactory job, until you get the job yourself. Either way, it is clear that the position is one of the steps on your career ladder. You had hoped to have the opportunity for some on-the-job training before having to make any momentous decisions, but that is not to be. As you arrive in the personnel office, you discover a waiting room full of candidates for a position of software development engineer. You wish you had been warned, so that you could have studied the résumés of all of the applicants before interviewing them, but you would make the company look foolish if you asked them all to come back some other day. In short, you are faced with making an important decision on the basis of some very limited social perception information.

Prior to interviewing each candidate you will, of course, take a minute or two to look at the candidate's folder, and during the interview you will ask the obvious questions, hoping to obtain appropriate, but thoughtful answers. Knowing what you know about nonverbal behavior, you will watch closely to make certain that what the candidate communicates through the verbal channel is corroborated through the various nonverbal channels. Is there anything else that social psychology can tell you that will help you make a better choice among the candidates? Not surprisingly, the answer is affirmative, and has to do with a process that is too cognitive to be described accurately as "perceptual," but not sufficiently conscious or contemplative to be thoroughly "cognitive." You are, in the situation given, what Fiske and Taylor (1984) would call a *cognitive miser* – an information processor with limited capabilities who must take strategic shortcuts to achieve an adequate result quickly. Unless you were warned in advance to avoid them, there are two classes of error – salience effects and cognitive heuristics – that might lead you to faulty conclusions.

Salience Effects

The Person in a Cognitive Context. Suppose for a moment that there are five candidates for the position, four of them are of one gender, one is of the other. That one person is a "solo" – obviously different from the other members of the group on a publicly apparent attribute. At first you might think that the person's salience is really a perceptual effect, not a cognitive one. Indeed, the notion of salience owes an intellectual debt to the Gestalt perceptual notion of "figure/ground." And a person's gender is, after all, an inherent characteristic of the person. It is not, however, the attribute of gender per se that leads to the salience (the person would not stand out in the same way if all the other candidates were of like gender), but rather the attribute of gender in the context provided by the other people. And in contrast to the wholly perceptual figure/ground effects, salience effects involve a comparison based on some cognitive characterization of the stimulus person and the surrounding field. Individuals can be salient in a context for a variety of reasons, including being novel (a solo person of that race or gender), being "figural" (contrasting with the background in color, complexity, motion), behaving in an unusual manner compared either to your own past actions or to the current actions of others (try clapping at the "wrong times" at a political rally for a candidate whose position you oppose), or dominating the visual field (sitting at the head of a table).

Consequences of Salience. Whatever the reason that a stimulus person appears salient among a group of others, that salience carries certain consequences, enumerated by Fiske and Taylor (1984). To begin with, the salient person is seen as the principal cause of whatever occurs in the interaction among members of the group. Suppose that on your way into your office – past the waiting room full of candidates – you noticed the candidates talking to each other in subdued tones. Then suppose that every candidate gives you virtually the same answer to your opening question, "What, exactly, do you think you could bring to a position with our firm?" If the thought crosses your mind that the candidates discussed this question in advance, you are most likely to believe that the salient person was "behind it." Furthermore, there is a normal tendency to see people's actions as the product of their underlying personal dispositions, instead of resulting from the constraints of the situation (more about this particular effect later in the section on attribution), and this tendency will be exaggerated for the salient person. Not only the person's causal role, but also his or her personality dispositions, will be exaggerated: a mildly abrasive "solo" will appear obnoxious, a mildly pleasant "solo" will seem the epitome of charm.

The Solution: Get Involved. What can you do to counter this attentionally based error in your judgment of the candidates? Think for a minute about the reason for the error in the first place – you are acting as a cognitive miser, attempting to make an adequate decision in a short amount of time. The problem is not that you are thinking about the candidates, but that you are not really thinking about them enough. So it will come as a relief to you to learn that Borgida and Howard-Pitney (1983) found salience effects to disappear when the perceiver's personal involvement in the judgment was heightened. Take the task as seriously as the company president would expect you to, and you are very likely to avoid salience errors in your judgment.

Problems in Selecting Cases

Salience effects can be reduced to negligible proportions by increasing the perceiver's involvement in the judgment task, but not all of the precognitive influences on social perception can be eliminated so simply. Concentrating on the judgment task will permit you to see the stimulus persons as individuals divorced from their immediate social context. Such concentration, however, will not by itself decrease your tendency to rely on a variety of precognitive devices that simplify (but distort) the process. Indeed, raising the stakes attached to the decision, or decreasing the time you are given to make the decision, may increase the your tendency fall back on these judgmental shortcuts.

Failures of the Intuitive Statistician. Why should this be the case? You will recall from the discussion of research methods in chapter 2 that scientific social psychology places great stock in standardized methods of data collection, and in statistical analysis of those data to identify the underlying regularities in social behavior. As effective as these methods are, they require investments of resources and time that ordinary perceivers are reluctant to devote to the judgment task. Consequently, not only do individual perceivers collect data haphazardly, they also ignore formal statistical principles when making inferences from the information they have gathered. This informality creates problems for the perceiver, because it happens that people are not very effective as intuitive statisticians (Kahneman & Tversky, 1973).

There are a number of ways in which people's intuitive statistical reasoning is faulty. For example, we tend to be more confident about conclusions drawn from small samples than about conclusions drawn from large ones. Hiring the "best" person would be clearer with an applicant pool of 15 people than with 5 or 6 applicants, because you would have a more stable estimate of the "average" applicant in the larger sample. The problem is that without any formal statistical summary of the applicants, you would have to try to hold in your head the individual characteristics of all 15 applicants (and would, therefore, feel more confused about the decision).

Indeed, if the particular individuals you consider are described in a highly vivid way that agrees with your expectations, even providing you with the relevant statistical information may make very little difference in your judgment. In an illustration of this principle, Hamill, Wilson, and Nisbett (1980) had subjects read a popular-magazine account of a

> 43-year-old, obese, friendly, irresponsible, ne'er-do-well woman who had lived in New York City for 16 years, the last 13 of which had been spent on welfare . . . She and her family lived from day to day, eating high-priced cuts of meat and playing the numbers on the days immediately after the welfare check arrived, and eating beans and borrowing money on the days preceding its arrival. (p. 580)

The major experimental manipulation was the provision to subjects of statistical information that clearly showed this woman's life either to be "typical" or "atypical" of welfare recipients. The elements of the story agree with many common stereotypes about welfare recipients, although it is worth noting that the case is in actual fact quite atypical. Subjects who read this vivid case material expressed more highly negative impressions of welfare recipients than did control subjects who did not read the case history. What is more important for our present purposes is that there were only trivial differences between the impressions of subjects who were told that the woman was typical and the impressions of those who were told that she was atypical. The statistical information had virtually no effect on the resulting impressions.

In a sense, we can understand how an extremely vivid case history that confirms all our expectations can overwhelm statistical evidence. Unfortunately, as Kahneman and Tversky's (1973) research among others has shown, the perceiver's tendency to ignore base rate information – the relative frequency with which a behavior occurs – is not limited to such instances. In one of their studies Kahneman and Tversky (1973) had subjects read very brief descriptions of lawyers and engineers. Half of the subjects had been told that the sample from which the descriptions were drawn was composed of 70% lawyers and 30% engineers, the other half had been told that the sample consisted of 30% lawyers and 70% engineers. After reading the descriptions, subjects were asked to estimate the likelihood that each individual described was a either an engineer or a lawyer.

Obviously, careful attention to the base rate would have produced estimates that reflected the 30/70 split in the pool from which the sample had been drawn. But that was true only when subjects were given no specific description before estimating the likelihood. When there was any information at all, the judgments did not properly reflect the base rate. This was true even when the specific information was worthless: "Dick is a 30-year-old man. He is married with children. A man of high ability and high motivation, he promises to be quite successful in his field. He is well liked by his colleagues" (p. 242). By no stretch of the imagination is this an involving or stereotypical description, but it was sufficient to prevent careful attention to the base rate.

Returning to the personnel decision you must make, you are likely to give the applicant's behavior in the interview with you much more weight in your decision than you will give to that applicant's past experience and record. True, the combination of this person's skills and your company's requirements may be unique in the person's employment history, but the fact that the person has never held a previous job for more than a year should still worry you. When two cross-town rivals in basketball meet for their annual contest, it is true, as the announcer says, that "anything can happen." But the most likely outcome is that the team with the poorer record (both overall and in the history of past meetings of the two teams) will lose. Ignoring this kind of base rate information can easily lead to faulty judgments. As Fiske and Taylor (1984) note, there are other ways in which ordinary perceivers are faulty statisticians, but these two examples illustrate the importance of the problem.

Cognitive Heuristics. As a substitute for formal statistical inference, the social perceiver often employs what Tversky and Kahneman (1974) have called judgmental *heuristics*: intuitive (but not necessarily conscious) strategies for simplifying the complex task of social judgment. There are several such heuristics, but three in particular – representativeness, availability, and adjustment – have received the most attention from social psychologists. In social perception the first of these, *representativeness*, is based on a presumed connection between belonging to a particular social category and possessing attributes considered typical of members of the category. Suppose you believe, either on the basis of some personal experience or on the basis of a stereotype in the absence of any such experience, that the best software engineers are quiet, introverted people comfortable with a computer terminal but ill at ease in a social situation.

If one of the candidates fits this description better than the others do, the representativeness heuristic would lead you to conclude that this person might be the best choice. Like the subjects in Kahneman and Tversky's (1973) lawyer-engineer study, you have made a probability judgment (likelihood that the person is an excellent software engineer) on the basis of the presumed relevance to that judgment of certain publicly apparent characteristics. As useful as the representativeness heuristic can be, it does have limitations: at the very least your judgment of the typical instance must be valid, and the stimulus person's behavior must not be determined by the specific situation (the "introversion" may be only uncertainty in the interview setting).

The second major heuristic, *availability*, is also a strategy for estimating probability, except that now the estimate is made on the basis of how easily the relevant events or characteristics can be imagined or recalled. The general idea, of course, is that a frequently encountered event or characteristic will be more easily recalled than will an infrequently encountered one. This heuristic, like representativeness, often produces a reasonable probability estimate, but it, too, can be in error. For example, suppose that one of the questions you ask all of the candidates concerns the security procedures they think would be needed to protect the software they would be developing. To know how to interpret their answers, you must know, at the very least, what poses the greatest security threat to the company's computer system. You do know that the computer facilities are located in a separate building, and that in order to use the computer yourself you need to use a device connected to the telephone lines.

Specifically, would you guess the most danger to security to come from unauthorized access (from computer "hackers") over the telephone, or from the company's own employees? In any other context you might have answered "From hackers," giving paralinguistic cues that showed you thought the question a stupid one. In a discussion of availability, however, you might have been careful enough to realize that although the hackers receive all the publicity, most breaches of computer security are performed by company employees with authorized access to the system.

Because they both deal with probability estimates, representativeness and availability can interact to produce a distorted perception. At the beginning of this example, I noted that four of the candidates were of one gender, and one of the candidates was of the opposite gender. Without looking back, are there four males and one female, or four females and one male? You probably guessed the former, but if you look back, you'll discover that the gender composition of the group was never specified. Your judgment was based on in part on representativeness (males outperform females in mathematical tasks, "engineers" are male) and in part on availability (in films and television programs, if not also in your experience, most of the computer programmers are males). As it happens, in this instance your heuristic guess happens to be correct: male graduates of computer science programs outnumber females by about four to one. The important point is that the heuristics are not always this reliable.

There is one final thing that as a personnel manager you should know before you interview any of the candidates: the possible starting salary for the position. Unfortunately, that is a detail that nobody told you, so when the first interviewee asks you the salary range you have to come up with a number. And that brings us to the *adjustment* heuristic. Whether it is salary levels, numbers of universities in the United States, or the best weekly performance of the New York Stock Exchange, people often are called on to estimate numbers that, with plenty of time and resources, they would prefer to look up. Under the circumstances, however, only an educated guess is possible, and that guess will be influenced by the initial value chosen as an "anchor." You quickly think of your own salary with the company, and your years of experience, but realize that software development engineers are probably in greater demand than are people in other corporate positions. These calculations lead you to a rough number, and you confidently announce it to the candidate. An expression of bewilderment spreads across the candidate's face, and you only later learn to your dismay that your "educated guess" was off by a factor of two. It would have been better to choose the company president as the "anchor" for the salary estimate!

CATEGORIZATION: THE ORGANIZATION OF THE SOCIAL WORLD

As noted in chapter 3, one of the principal differences between social stimuli (people or situations) and inanimate objects lies in the greater complexity of the social world. Even when effective performance of our job (for example, as a personnel manager) depends on thorough consideration of the individual differences among people, we cannot hope to remember every attribute of each person we meet. Our simplification of this complexity begins with the judgmental heuristics employed to gather information, and continues into the creation of cognitive categories in which to store that information.

Category Formation and Criterial Attributes

We notice whether the people we meet are men or women, whether they are friendly or hostile; we place people along scales of height, weight, or physical attractiveness. Cognitive categories are classes of varying size and character: some are mutually exhaustive, some mutually exclusive, others only vaguely defined. Whatever their relationship to one another, the social categories are not merely passive storage devices. Their existence and inclusion rules also shape the social data gathered, in much the same way that a formal scientific theory will lead the social psychologist to look for some phenomena and disregard others.

Recall that when the distal stimulus for perception is another person, the proximal stimulus will represent a smaller proportion of the available information than if the distal stimulus had been an object. Once it has been encoded, this proximal stimulus is subject to even further modification through a constructive process heavily influenced by the perceiver's own needs, motives, and expectations. This interpretation of the stimulus can, as Bruner (1957) suggested, be characterized as an act of *categorization*: through experience, the perceiver learns which stimulus elements are reliably associated with one another, and learns to combine these into meaningful categories. Once the assignment has been made, the perceiver responds to the stimulus person more as a representative of the social category than as a completely unique human being.

Criterial Attributes. In making the category assignment, people obviously find some attributes of the stimulus person more relevant than others. For example, in the 1950s a person's hair length was almost always a good indication of the person's gender: males had short hair and females had long hair. But hair length is not what Bruner would call a **criterial attribute**: a necessary attribute that helps define the boundaries of the category. The criterial attributes for the determination of gender are, of course, the sexual organs, but these are most often hidden from the casual perceiver. So perceivers search for other identifying attributes, such as hair length, and are occasionally reminded (to their embarrassment) that such attributes are not criterial. Some social categories are defined by a single criterial attribute – FBI agent, Democrat, and Lion are categories defined by membership in a formal organization – whereas other categories have multiple criterial attributes. For example, the category "statesman" has behavioral criterial attributes as well as formal ones. A statesman must be a government leader, but not all government leaders are statesmen.

The Prior Entry Effect. In all but the most rigid perceivers the process of categorization is an interchange between the cognitive category and the new information gathered. When a perceiver is confronted by a novel social stimulus or situation, he or she has difficulty distinguishing between the truly criterial attributes and other attributes that may be unique to this particular instance. As an example, suppose that on your first day of college, you attend a large lecture in introductory psychology. The professor arrives late and immediately announces that roughly 25% of the students enrolled will not pass the course. Without so much as a pause for the class's collective gasp, he begins lecturing by reading verbatim from the textbook. The lecture ends with the bell, and the professor quickly departs through a back door in the auditorium.

Because this is your first day of college classes, you need to impose some structure on the experience and to form categories and expectations, including "lecture course," "college professor," "anticipated grades," and "psychology professor." Will all of your lecture classes be so big? Will the professors always use microphones and insist upon being called "Doctor"? Will that matter if they never permit time for questions, or are you not supposed to ask questions in a lecture course? Will the professor always be male; be late; be dressed casually? And will all lecture courses be so darn boring (especially when the subject matter ought to be intrinsically interesting)?

In your attempt to answer these questions, you must distinguish among attributes of the lecture method (independent of the subject and the professor), attributes of the discipline (psychology, independent of the teacher and class size), and attributes of the particular professor. But it will take time and experience with other courses and teachers for you to make all of these distinctions. As a result, at the very beginning of your college career you will be heavily influenced by this one class experience. You have just experienced what Jones and Gerard (1967) call the **prior entry effect**: the early information encountered will contribute more to the *formation* of a category than later, contradictory, information will contribute to change in that category. Should you later take a lecture course that was lively and interesting, that course will be seen as an exception to the rule constructed from this first unfortunate experience. In contrast, if the first lecture you attended had been interesting, that would have formed your category, and the later dull performance would have been seen as an exception.

Social Stereotyping

The prior entry effect and the occasional tendency to confuse noncriterial attributes with criterial ones are relatively minor problems in categorization. Typically, they will be corrected with increasing experience, and even at their worst, they affect only the perceiver. By contrast, the most serious categorization problem, and the one of perennial concern to social psychology, is that of social stereotyping. By one definition, a perceiver engaged in stereotyping believes that any individual who can be placed into a particular cognitive category possesses all of the attributes ever associated with the category (Lippman, 1922). Notice that these do not need to be criterial attributes, but only attributes that for one reason or another are associated with category membership. Thus, unique characteristics mistakenly thought to be criterial can be included in a stereotype, as can the perceiver's wholly unfounded expectations about category members.

Checklist Measures of Stereotyping. Stereotypes have been a theoretical and social problem both because they obscure individual characteristics and because they are frequently, although not necessarily, negative. Because of its social importance in American history, the problem of ethnic stereotyping, and the attitude of racism (to be considered in chapter 6) to which it contributes, have received almost continuous attention from social psychologists. Indeed, the first empirical study of racial stereotyping was performed by Katz and Braly (1933) virtually at the time the discipline was established. Their research incorporated a "checklist" measure of stereotyping that has since been used by numerous other investigators.

The subjects in the research were 100 male undergraduate students at Princeton, and each subject was asked to describe 10 national or ethnic groups – Americans, Chinese, English, Germans, Irish, Italians, Japanese, Jews, Negroes, and Turks – using a list of 84 descriptive adjectives. The subject's task was to select for each national or ethnic group those adjectives he believed to be most characteristic of members of the group. There was an empirical replication of the study (with different numbers of subjects) 18 years later by Gilbert (1951), and again 18 years after that by Karlins, Coffman, and Walters (1969).

Content of the Racial Stereotype. The five traits most frequently ascribed to black people by Katz and Braly's subjects were "superstitious," "lazy," "happy-go-lucky," "ignorant," and "musical." The percentage of Katz and Braly's subjects who considered each of these traits to be most characteristic of Negroes is shown in the first column of Table 4.1. The second column of the table shows the percentages obtained by Gilbert (1951), and the third column presents the percentages found by Karlins and associates (1969). Just looking at these percentages across the three studies, it would appear that social stereotypes ascribed to blacks have faded a great deal over the intervening years. On the five original traits, the percentage endorsement declines through time for four traits, with only "musical" showing an increase in percent endorsement from 1933 to 1969.

Real Change or Raised Consciousness? Can we be certain from the data in Table 4.1 that the pattern has continued during the most recent 18 years (since the data were collected by Karlins, Coffman, and Walters)? Even if the pattern has continued, can we be certain that the change reflects a real diminution in racial and ethnic stereotyping? Unfortunately, the answer to each of these questions is "no." Aside from the obvious possibility that Princeton undergraduates are not representative of the population as a whole, there are two major arguments against such a positive con-

TABLE 4.1 Several Measures of Stereotyping in the Judgment of Negroes

Trait Name	Percentage of Subjects Assigning Each Trait		
	Katz & Braly (1933)	Gilbert (1951)	Karlins, Coffman, & Walters (1969)
Superstitious	84	41	13
Lazy	75	31	26
Happy-go-lucky	38	17	27
Ignorant	38	24	11
Musical	26	33	47
Number of Subjects	100	333	150

Adapted from Karlins, M., Coffman, T. L., and Walters, G. (1969). On the fading of social stereotypes: Studies in three generations of college students. Journal of Personality and Social Psychology, 13, 1–16. Copyright 1969 by the American Psychological Association. Reprinted by permission.

clusion. First, present stereotypes might merely involve traits other than those measured by the researchers. Given a list of 84 trait-descriptive adjectives, this seems an unlikely possibility, but it cannot be ruled out completely.

Second, Karlins and his colleagues reported, as did Gilbert, that their subjects showed resistance when asked to make the necessary judgments, often complaining that it was unfair to categorize people on the basis of their national or ethnic identification. We have all had our "consciousness raised" about the importance of treating each other as individual human beings rather than as instances of some social category. To put it in terms of one of the response biases discussed in chapter 2, we have all become sensitive to the social desirability constraints upon such matters as ethnic and racial judgment. Thus the differences through the years may reflect only a change in willingness to report a stereotype, not a change in the existence of that stereotype.

Individual Belief or Social Consensus? The problem of socially desirable responding is only one of the difficulties inherent in the checklist measure of stereotyping. Several reviews have been critical of the checklist procedure (e.g., Brigham, 1971), and one problem in particular deserves mention. Recall that a stereotype is an assignment by one perceiver to one stimulus person of all of the traits that perceiver associates with the cognitive category into which the stimulus person falls. But in any checklist procedure, the researchers make no attempt either to assess the beliefs of an individual perceiver or to require that a stereotypical trait apply to a majority of stimulus persons. For example, "musical" persists as part of the checklist-determined stereotype of black people, even though there has never been any estimate of the proportion of black people to whom it actually applies, and despite the fact that "musical" has never been endorsed by a majority of perceivers. This lack of contact between the checklist procedure and the beliefs of the individual perceiver was noted by Brigham (1971), who argued for the development of an individualized measure of stereotyping.

Just such a measure has been developed by McCauley and Stitt (1978) and is based on the same mathematical formulation—Bayes' theorem (Feller, 1968)—that guided the work by Kahneman and Tversky (1973) on the judgmental heuristic of representativeness. Without going into any of the mathematical details, Bayes' rule can be used to determine how much a specific piece of information should alter your impression of a stimulus person. To the extent that the bit of information (say, the person's ethnic identification) adds more to your impression than the rule says it should, your opinion will be biased by an ethnic stereotype.

If you had been a subject in McCauley and Stitt's (1978) experiment, you would have been given four trait adjectives shown by Karlins, Coffman, and Walters (1969) to be connected to the social stereotype of Germans: "efficient," "extremely nationalistic," "industrious," and "scientifically minded," and five adjectives irrelevant to the German stereotype. For each of these traits (for example, "efficient"), you would have been asked to estimate four probability values, only two of which are important for present purposes. The first of these is the probability that any person is efficient without considering that person's nationality, stated as "the percent of all the world's people who are efficient" (p. 931). The second was the probability that an efficient person happens to be German, stated as "the percent of efficient people who are German" (p. 931).

The Diagnostic Ratio as a Measure of Stereotyping. Now if you do not consider Germans to be any more or less efficient than other people, these two percentages should be identical, and if the second (percent efficient Germans) is divided by the first (percent efficient people) the quotient should be 1.00. This quotient is called the *diagnostic ratio*, because to the degree that it exceeds 1.00 it is "diagnostic" of your belief that a stimulus person's nationality will affect your judgment of that person's likely efficiency. Indeed, both on an individual level and as a group, the subjects in McCauley and Stitt's experiment showed diagnostic ratios greater than 1.00 for each of the four traits that comprise the German stereotype (efficient = 1.27, extremely nationalistic = 1.59, industrious = 1.14, and scientifically minded = 1.32). By contrast, the diagnostic ratios for the irrelevant adjectives (ignorant, impulsive, pleasure-loving, superstitious, and tradition-loving) were all below 1.00.

If all this study demonstrated was that a diagnostic ratio method could "correctly" (by reference to a presumably flawed checklist procedure) identify elements of a stereotype of an ethnic group, it would not have accomplished a great deal. But it does much more, by providing a trait-specific, and individualized, measure of bias in social judgment. Recall that the original definition of a stereotype (Lippman, 1922) described it as a belief that an individual placed in a social category possesses all of the attributes ever associated with the category. By this definition, if you believed Germans to be industrious, extremely nationalistic, and scientifically minded, but not "efficient," you would not qualify as holding a stereotyped view of Germans. That seems an overly rigid definition for a stereotype.

What the probabilistic measure does, by contrast, is permit us to identify every specific trait you associate more strongly with the members of one national or ethnic group (or gender, for that matter) than with the population as a whole. Furthermore, this trait-specific definition can be constructed for you as an individual, regardless of whether other people share your possibly unique view of the target group. Because of its recent introduction, the diagnostic ratio method cannot be used to determine whether the stereotyped traits that have in the past been associated with black people have truly faded (as the checklist measure suggests that they have). In the future, however, such a measure will provide social psychologists with more precise understanding of the contents and persistence of racial and ethnic stereotypes.

Cognitive Mechanisms in the Production of Stereotypes. Just as the individualized measure of stereotyping has recently provided a new description of the contents of a stereotype, the information-processing ideas on which it is based have recently generated renewed interest in the cognitive processes that are involved in the production of stereotypes. This extensive literature has been reviewed by Hamilton (1981), and by Wilder (1986), and two studies by Hamilton, Dugan, and Trolier (1985) illustrate how some of the cognitive processes we have already considered can contribute to the formation of stereotypes.

As noted earlier, one of the features of the intuitive statistician is a failure to attend to base rates, and a tendency to place too great weight on information that may be atypical. In stereotyping, according to Hamilton and his associates, this tendency is embodied in a principle of *illusory correlation* (Chapman, 1967): An association between two variables or classes of events is assumed by the perceiver, although it is not actually present in the data that form the basis for the judgment. Specifically, if in the experience of a white person, (a) undesirable behavior by others is less frequent than desirable behavior, and (b) interactions with blacks are less frequent than interactions with whites, then an undesirable behavior by a black would, through illusory correlation, be assumed to be representative of all blacks.

To test this idea Hamilton, Dugan, and Trolier (1985) asked subjects to read 39 stimulus sentences, one to a page. Each sentence identified a stimulus person by name, noted that the person was a member either of Group A" or "Group B," and described a behavior that had previously been rated as desirable or undesirable. In each set of 39 sentences, 26 described Group A members (with 18 desirable and 8 undesirable elements), whereas the remaining 13 sentences described Group B members (with 9 desirable and 4 undesirable elements). The sentences had been constructed so that the overall average desirability ratings were the same for Group A members and Group B members, to preclude any preference for one group or another on the basis of overall positivity.

There were several experimental conditions, only three of which are important for our purposes here. In one of these conditions, subjects read only the sentences and then made likeability ratings for the members of the two groups. In a second condition, subjects read the sentences, then were given a summary table showing exactly what the distribution of desirable and undesirable sentences had been for stimulus persons of Group A and Group B, and then made the same likeability ratings. Finally, in the third group, subjects did not read any sentences at all, but made likeability ratings after seeing only the summary table.

If people were good statisticians, there should have been no differences in liking expressed for Groups A and B across these three conditions. But the results showed findings quite similar to those in Kahneman and Tversky's (1973) lawyer–engineer research. When given no specific information (summary table only) subjects expressed no difference in liking for members of Group A and Group B. When given sentences only, subjects expressed a greater preference for members of Group A, and this differential preference was attenuated only slightly in the sentence-plus-table condition. The sentence set was constructed to make the Group B members, and undesirable behaviors, distinctive; the result was an illusory correlation between the two.

We return to the issue of stereotyping in chapter 6, at which time the discussion concentrates on some emotionally charged aspects of intergroup bias. What is important here, however, is that certain kinds of cognitive processes can also contribute to the problem. Subjects, themselves, belonged to neither group, and the group labels carried no extra meaning. Indeed, even the relative proportions of desirable to undesirable statements did not produce any differences (the summary table condition). All that mattered was how that information was obtained. As was the case with salience and the cognitive heuristics, illusory correlation is a problem that arises when the relevant information is given. Keep that in mind as we turn to processes of social inference that require perceivers to go far beyond the information present in the stimulus array.

SOCIAL INFERENCE:
SEARCHING FOR CAUSES OF BEHAVIOR

We are not content merely to observe other people and to place them into one or another cognitive category. In addition, we try to explain their past behavior and to predict their future actions. It is through **attribution processes** that perceivers interpret the actions of other people, and in some cases their own actions as well.

Three Stages of Attribution

Whenever we search for the causes of another person's actions, we are engaging in social attribution. Like cognitive categorization, attribution usually occurs too quickly for us to observe it directly, although computers may soon be used to study some attribution processes as they occur. There is, however, an example of attribution extended through time that, although of limited usefulness in testing theory, does help in our intuitive understanding of the process. This example is a criminal trial, in which a jury (the perceiver) evaluates the behavior of a defendant (the stimulus person) and the circumstances in which that behavior occurred, in order to decide whether to attribute the crime either to the defendant or to circumstances beyond that person's control.

Observation of Action. Suppose we sit in the courtroom and observe the trial of a person accused of murdering an acquaintance by shooting the victim with a pistol. As Shaver (1975) has pointed out, there are three basic stages in the attribution process, as illustrated for this example in Fig. 4.1. The first of these is the observation of action, either firsthand or through the reports of intermediaries who observed the action themselves. The latter mediation by other people (witnesses to the shooting) cannot be considered a perfectly accurate representation of the incident, because the witnesses, as perceivers themselves, will be interpreting the action through the filter of their own personalities, expectations, and personal motives. As we see in chapter 14, the legal system has not in this instance kept pace with the findings of social psychology, because eyewitness testimony remains an extremely strong form of evidence despite research casting serious doubt on its validity. In any case, before there can be an attribution, there must be some observation that can provide information to the perceiver.

Judgment of Intention. The second stage of the attribution process is the judgment of intention. The perceiver must decide that an action was intentionally produced in order for a veridical (valid) attribution to be made. Involuntary reflexes, routine performances of habitual behavior,

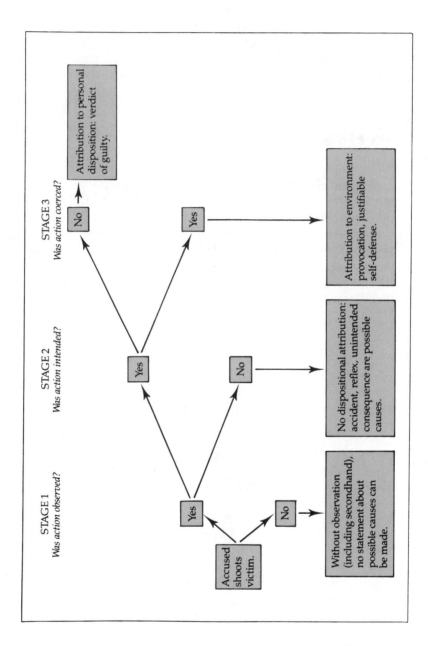

FIGURE 4.1   Stages of the attribution process (adapted from Shaver, 1975).

and accidental occurrences should not tell us much about the stimulus person's reasons for his or her actions. A conviction for murder requires the presence of *mens rea*–guilty mind–as well as the proscribed action of shooting another person. So if the defense attorney can argue convincingly that the shooting was an accident, it cannot have been the product of a guilty mind. In the moral realm as well as in the legal realm, an unintended occurrence reveals nothing to us about the person's motives, because those motives were not translated into intentional actions. All of this is not to suggest that perceivers never make attributions on the basis of accidents, only that such attributions are in error.

Dispositional Attribution. The final link in the chain of inference is the making of a dispositional attribution. Having observed the action (or had it reported) and having decided that the action was intentionally produced, the perceiver must now determine what underlying **personal disposition** (a relatively enduring personality or motivational characteristic of the actor) could have led to the intentional action. In the most elementary sense, this last judgment provides an answer to the question "Why?" For our jury, there are several possibilities. Assuming the report of the incident has been shown to be reliable and that the prosecution has convincingly ruled out an accidental pulling of the trigger, the jury still has some decisions to make. Did the defendant intentionally shoot the victim, but in self-defense? Did the shooting take place when the defendant was in the heat of rage (an "irresistible impulse" in legal terminology)? Did the defendant believe that he or she was simply shooting an invader from Mars (a version of the "insanity defense)? Each of these possibilities would mitigate the criminal responsibility of the defendant, because each involves circumstances normally considered beyond the defendant's control. In the moral realm as well as in the legal realm, various aspects of external coercion can absolve a person of blame even for an admittedly intentional action.

The Analysis of Action

Most of the social attributions we make do not carry the consequences that accompany the attributions made by juries, and most are made so quickly that the elements of the process are never in full view. But perceivers do make attributions of causality, of ability, of responsibility, of emotional state, or of motivation, to mention just a few. Three major theories– by Heider (1958), Jones and Davis (1965) and Jones and McGillis (1976), and Kelley (1967, 1973)–and a number of individual principles attempt to account for the manner in which a perceiver will infer dispositional properties on the basis of observed and intended actions.

Personal and Environmental Forces. Present interest in attribution processes and theory began with the comprehensive and fruitful work of Heider (1958). Trained in the tradition of Gestalt psychology, with its emphasis on the subjective (phenomenological) experience of the person, Heider tried to construct a **naive psychology** of attribution that would describe how we, as naive perceivers not trained in formal methods of psychology, try to identify the causes of human actions. In Heider's model the perceiver tries to enumerate the factors that would be logically necessary for action to occur. The perceiver takes the stimulus person's actions "at face value," and deduces what factors must have been present in order for the event being accounted for to have occurred.

For example, consider the action "building a brick wall." For this action to be completed successfully, the actor must have had the intention to build the wall (nobody does that sort of thing by accident) and must have exerted energy to complete the task (picking up the bricks, "buttering" them with mortar, and placing them in the wall requires quite a bit of effort). In addition, the mason's ability must have been sufficient to overcome the inherent task difficulty: Only if the actor's personal force exceeds the opposing environmental force can the actor accomplish the task.

The relationships among the various factors logically necessary for the production of action can be diagrammed as shown in Fig. 4.2. The components can be grouped under the general headings of *personal force* and *environmental force*, with personal force first subdivided into ability and the general motivational component Heider called *trying*. As previously noted, ability combines with task difficulty to determine the possibility of action, the state Heider refers to as *can*. The general motivational factor of trying is further subdivided into the components of *intention* (which represents a direction for the action) and *exertion* (which represents the drive needed to accomplish the task), and these, in the presence of *can* produce the action. According to Heider's theory, the greater the personal force contributing to the production of an effect, the greater the actor's responsibility for the occurrence of that effect.

Tests of the Levels of Responsibility. The idea that a person should be held more accountable as his or her contribution to the event increases was first tested by Shaw and Sulzer (1964). These investigators had subjects read 40 short vignettes describing the production of an outcome the valence of which was either positive or negative. Within the valence conditions the intensity was varied so that half of the outcomes were mildly intense, the other half quite intense. The last variable built into the stories was the presumed degree of the stimulus person's contribution to the outcome. There were five such "levels," with names provided by Sulzer (1971) as follows: association (no causal connection between stimulus person and occurrence), causality (causal production, including pure "accident), foreseeability (causal production coupled with the belief the stimulus per-

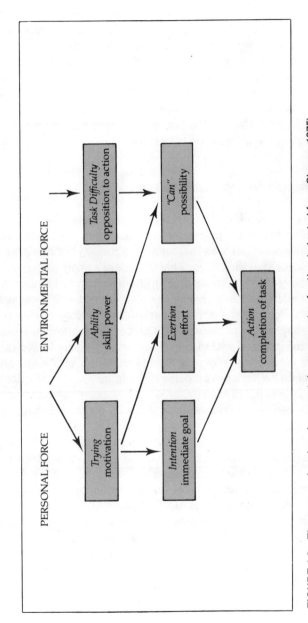

FIGURE 4.2 The personal and environmental components of action (adapted from Shaver, 1975).

son should have been able to anticipate the occurrence), intentionality (true personal causality, including intention and exertion), and justifiability (intentionality with external coercion).

If Heider's view of personal accountability is correct, the responsibility assigned to the stimulus person should increase from association through intentionality, and then decline at the level of justifiability. This is precisely what Shaw and Sulzer (1964) found, and the same basic pattern of attribution has been obtained by other investigators as well, with a diverse array of subjects, including adults and children (Fincham & Jaspars, 1979), and even including hospitalized schizophrenic patients (Shaver et al., 1984). Indeed, the "levels" research has produced some of the most stable findings in the attribution literature.

Correspondence of Inference

It is easy to see how Heider's (1958) principles could be invoked after the fact of an action to state what must have been necessary for the action to occur. As descriptive as this "naive psychology" is, however, it is not a complete account of the action. That is, Heider's analysis does not explicitly say how the reason behind an actor's intention can be identified. Did the bricklayer undertake the arduous task of building a wall because that was his or her job? Because the wall was part of the bricklayer's own mountain cabin? Or perhaps because the wall was part of a neighborhood community center to be constructed with donated materials by people working at their own trades without any monetary compensation. For the perceiver, getting an answer to "What are you doing?" (building a wall, the intention) is not the same as getting an answer to "Why?" (because the community needs a recreation center, the reason behind the intentional action).

This inquiry into underlying motives is the subject of Jones and Davis's (1965) *correspondent inference theory* of attribution. Every action that a person might take is conceived of as a choice between alternatives (even if that choice is limited to "building the wall" and "doing nothing"). Which choice the actor makes can, according to the theory, reveal that person's underlying dispositions. For example, let us suppose that you have two choices right now: continuing to read your assignment in this book, or beginning to read a best-selling novel. Each of those choices has certain effects for you. Continuing to read this book will have the effects of (a) finishing the assignment, (b) tiring your eyes, and (c) helping you prepare for the exam. Alternatively, beginning a best-selling novel will have the effects of (a) making you sound well read in your informal conversations with your friends, (b) tiring your eyes, and (c) giving you some needed recreation.

Noncommon Effects.   Notice that one of these effects, (b) tiring your eyes, is common to both choices. This effect is of no attributional value: Because it is produced by both choices, it cannot serve as a reason for choosing between the two choices. By contrast, the remaining two effects of each choice are unique to the choice made. So it is those **noncommon effects** that the perceiver uses to infer your reasons for making one choice as opposed to another. Take a closer look at these noncommon effects. You can prepare for an exam by reading the material, by organizing and studying the notes you take during lectures, or by discussing the subject with other students in the class. By contrast, if the assignment was to read this chapter, there is only one way you can complete that assignment, so a perceiver who knew of the noncommon effects would most probably conclude that your reason for reading was to finish the assignment. Turning to the other choice, there are, again, numerous ways to hold your attention and interest, only one of which is reading a best-selling novel. There are also multiple ways to sound well read to your friends, but probably fewer of those than ways to hold your attention. So a perceiver of your choice to read the novel, knowing the noncommon effects, might conclude that your reason was to sound well read to your friends. How certain might the perceiver be in each of these instances? That is the specific question answered by correspondent inference theory.

Assumed Desirability. According to the theory, the perceiver examines the effects produced by an action, and compares those to the effects that would be produced by any alternative to the action taken. Then, considering the noncommon effects only, the perceiver determines first, how many noncommon effects there are, and next, what the **assumed desirability** of those effects might be. The result is illustrated in Fig. 4.3. When the number of noncommon effects is very large, any attribution made by a perceiver is going to be ambiguous, as indicated by the first row of Figure 4-3. In contrast, when the number of noncommon effects is low, the perceiver

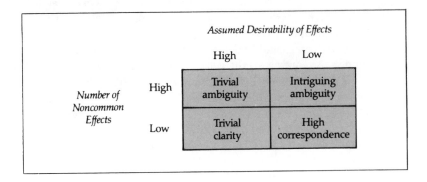

FIGURE 4.3 The determination of correspondence of inference from the number and assumed desirability of the noncommon effects of action (adapted from Jones and Davis, 1965, p. 229).

can be relatively certain of the reasons for the choice, as indicated by the second row of the figure.

When the noncommon effects are assumed to be highly desirable for the class of people to which the actor belongs, the perceiver only learns that any such person placed in the situation would have done the same thing. Consequently, the left column of the figure indicates that the perceiver's information gain is "trivial" from the actor's production of highly desirable effects. In contrast, when the assumed desirability of the noncommon effects is low, then the perceiver will believe the actor made the particular choice because of some "intriguing" personal disposition. It should be noted that the "assumed desirability" specified by the theory is not the general sort of "social desirability" discussed in the section on response biases in chapter 2. Rather "assumed desirability" is specific to the particular class of people to which the actor belongs. Behaviors that are highly desirable for "professors" may not be nearly so desirable for other people.

The conjunction of low number of noncommon effects and low assumed desirability of those effects is the condition Jones and Davis (1965) refer to as high **correspondence of inference**. This means that the perceiver's inference about the actor is most likely to correspond to the underlying personal disposition that actually prompted the choice by the actor. High correspondence is thus a measure of the perceiver's certainty about the causal role of a particular motivation behind action. A politician up for reelection who argues for decreases in Social Security benefits before an audience of retired people will be thought to be speaking from strong conviction, an instance of high correspondence of inference.

The Structure of Attributional Inference

Notice that both in Heider's (1958) naive psychology and in correspondent inference theory there is one critical question that is assumed to have been settled before the perceiver's analysis begins. That question is whether the actor should be seen as the cause of the event, or whether, alternatively, the event should be seen as the product of forces external to (and not under the control of) the actor. But if an actor did not cause the occurrence, it does not make sense to wonder about his or her intentions and exertion, or to wonder which underlying disposition might have given rise to that intention and exertion. This inquiry into possible causes of events is the subject of Kelley's (1967, 1973) attribution theory, which, like correspondent inference theory, builds on Heider's previous work.

The Principle of Covariation. Kelley's theory embodies the analogy I have repeatedly made between social perception and social psychological research: His ideal perceiver is likened to a "naive scientist" conducting a series of perceptual experiments. Just as the social psychologist infers the causes of social phenomena on the basis of underlying regularities across multiple instances, the perceiver utilizes a principle of **covariation**: an effect will be attributed to the presumed cause that is present when the effect is present and absent when effect is absent.

Suppose, for example, that you have an internal feeling of pleasure when you see a new film with a group of friends right after your last examination of the term. To what will you attribute this feeling of pleasure? Specifically, will you attribute your reaction to the film (what Kelley calls the *entity*), or will you attribute your reaction to the circumstances of good friends and the end of an exam period (referred to as *time and modality*) under which the film was seen? Just as the social psychologist will attempt to verify a particular theory by testing it under a variety of conditions, Kelley argues that the perceiver will sample various entities and times and compare his or her reactions with those of other *persons* in order to arrive at an attribution.

The theory can be summarized in terms of the three-dimensional solid shown in Fig. 4.4. One dimension represents the entities, in this case the film you saw, and two other films (other film #1, other film #2). The sec-

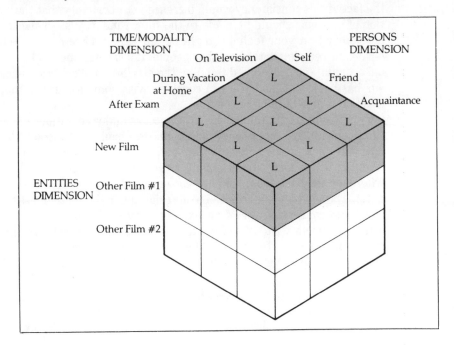

FIGURE 4.4 Attributional data table representing an attribution of likeability (L) to an entity (New Film) by all observers under all circumstances (adapted from the 1967 *Nebraska Symposium on Motivation,* ed. David Levine by permission of the University of Nebraska Press. Copyright © 1967 by the University of Nebraska Press.)

ond dimension (time/modality) represents the various circumstances under which it is possible to see the film (after the exam, at home during vacation, and later on television). The third dimension of the model (persons) includes both you (self) and others (friend, acquaintance) with whom you might compare reactions.

Attributional Criteria.   Not only does the theory suggest the dimensions along which you look for covariation, it also identifies **attributional criteria** that can be used to measure the covariation. To begin with, your reaction to the film must be *distinctive* from your reactions to other films you may have seen. If you are a film buff, liking virtually all the films you see, (bad ones as well as good ones), your reaction to this film is not distinctive. But if there are some films you do not enjoy and if your reaction to this one is somehow special, then the criterion of distinctiveness has been met, and you can move on to another dimension.

The second attributional question you ask yourself is "Was it just because exams were finally over, or would I feel the same way about the film under different circumstances?" If your reaction to the film remains *consistent* whether you see it at home during vacation, or even on television, the fact of this consistency would increase your certainty that the attribution of pleasure should be made to the film. Finally, just to check on the possibility that your feelings might be unique for some reason, you compare your reaction to that of other people. If a close friend, and even a casual acquaintance, also liked the film, the attributional criterion of *consensus* has been met, and you can conclude with some assurance that your reaction is attributable to the film.

Thus an attribution to the entity occurs under conditions of high distinctiveness, high consistency, and high consensus. By contrast, the attribution is made to the person (a "film buff") under conditions of low distinctiveness (likes many films equally well), high consistency (likes them wherever they are seen), and low consensus (likes films that other people hate). The effects on attributions of variations in distinctiveness, consistency, and consensus were first examined by McArthur (1972), who presented subjects with sets of sentences containing the relevant information. For example, to adapt an illustration later suggested by Jaspars, Hewstone, and Fincham (1983),

1. John laughs at the comedian, but does not laugh at other comedians. (Distinctiveness.)
2. In the past, John has almost always laughed at the same comedian. (Consistency.)
3. Almost everyone else who hears the comedian laughs at him. (Consensus.)

This particular set should produce a strong attribution to the comedian, and McArthur's research found that sets of sentences embodying high distinctiveness, high consistency, and high consensus did exactly that. Indeed, Elig and Frieze (1975) found evidence for the importance of these three factors in subjects' free-response explanations for the occurrence of a variety of events. Although Jaspars, Hewstone, and Fincham (1983) and others have pointed out several theoretical qualifications that may be necessary, the general idea that people employ covariation information in their causal attributions still enjoys broad empirical support.

Causal Schemata

Of course, for the principle of covariation to be employed, it must be possible for you to consider multiple entities, to observe your reactions in multiple circumstances, and to examine the opinions of multiple other people. But such multiple observations are not always possible. There may only be one entity to examine, and even if there are multiple entities, it is not always possible either to view those entities or actions under a variety of different circumstances. Nor is it always possible to ask any other people what they think about the action or event to be explained. Obviously perceivers still make attributions from single observations, but how do they go about it?

According to Kelley's (1967, 1973) theory, people faced with making an attribution from single instances of behavior rely on knowledge structures that help "fill in" for the covariation data that would otherwise be gathered. These constructions are a form of **cognitive schema**: a relatively enduring structure that represents organized knowledge about a concept, person, or process. Although such cognitive schemata can be modified by experience, they frequently act as templates for perception and knowledge. The schemata discussed in Kelley's theory summarize the perceiver's notions about an important process: the way in which potential causes can combine to produce events. For this reason, they are known as *causal schemata*. As an example of a simple cognitive schema, suppose I ask you what is necessary to make ice. Obviously water and cold. But how, exactly do the water and cold combine? Each is what Kelley would call a *necessary cause*: it is impossible to make ice without water, or to make ice without cold. So from the fact of an ice cube you can infer with certainty that both of these multiple necessary causes were present.

Multiple Sufficient Causes. Some social phenomena take the form of multiple necessary causes—it is impossible to have a "married couple" without both a bride and a groom—but many more follow a schema called *multiple sufficient causes*. This latter kind of schema is illustrated in Fig. 4.5, which identifies two different possible causes of a recommendation for promotion of one of your company's employees. Most businesses and government organizations actively discourage romantic relationships among

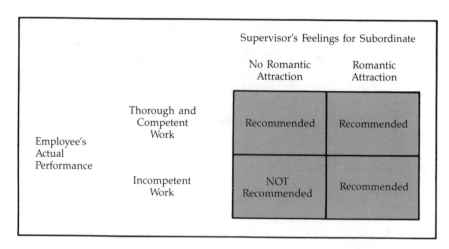

FIGURE 4.5 Multiple sufficient causes for a recommendation for promotion.

coworkers, especially when one is the supervisor of the other. Whatever the morality of the situation may be, the prohibition makes good attributional sense. Suppose that you were asked to review a recommendation for promotion made on behalf of one of the company's employees by that person's immediate supervisor. Just for the sake of argument, also assume that you know either that the supervisor has no romantic feelings toward the employee, or that the supervisor is romantically involved with the subordinate. Finally, suppose that the subordinate's actual job performance is either thorough and competent or is incompetent.

The Principle of Discounting. The "event" that you are to explain is the recommendation for promotion, and this event has multiple sufficient causes. The recommendation could have been made on the basis of the employee's job performance regardless of the supervisor's feelings (the top row in the diagram), or it could have been made on the basis of the supervisor's romantic attraction toward the employee regardless of that person's actual performance (the right-hand column in the diagram). Each cause is by itself sufficient, and there are multiple such causes. Part of the point of your review is to ensure that recommendations for promotion reflect real job performance. Unfortunately, you cannot determine, on the basis of the information contained in the recommendation, exactly which of the three combinations of multiple sufficient causes produced the recommendation.

Because of this uncertainty, Kelley's theory (1973) argues that you will *discount* the contribution of one sufficient cause when you discover that another sufficient cause is also present. Even in the top row of the diagram, representing excellent performance by the employee, the recommendation will not have the force in the presence of romantic attraction that it would have in the absence of such attraction. Thus your cognitive schema for how multiple sufficient causes combine will influence your perception of the letter of recommendation, to the detriment of a really thorough and competent employee.

The Principle of Augmentation. Although quite a few events of interest to social psychology can be explained in terms of multiple sufficient causes, there are others that need to include an additional principle. To change the example of a recommended promotion slightly, let us assume that the supervisor has no romantic attraction for the employee. There might still be other causes of the recommendation besides the employee's thorough and competent work. It would also be reasonable to consider the employee's length of service, "loyalty" to the company, or the difficulty of the tasks that the employee has performed so admirably.

But wait a minute. The last of these – an especially onerous and difficult task – is not really one of the multiple sufficient causes of the recommendation for promotion. Indeed, it is better thought of as an obstacle to the thorough and competent job performance. How can it be entered into the perceiver's reckoning of the employee's ability? According to Kelley's (1973) theory, those causes thought to facilitate production of effects will be *augmented* if the effects occur despite the presence of an obstacle. A person able to do thorough and competent work on a very tedious task under great time pressure will rightfully be considered more highly than a person able to do the same level of work on routine matters that do not demand any additional commitment. Augmentation, like discounting, is thus a fundamental component of the cognitive schemata that guide attributions for single instances of behavior with multiple possible causes.

Actors and Observers

To this point our discussion has taken the perspective of an observer attempting to explain the actions of another person. But what about an attributional account of your own actions? Would it follow the same general principles? The answer is affirmative, but with an important qualification. Recall the three stages of attribution: observation of action, judgment of intention, and dispositional attribution. At each of these stages, you should have more information about your own behavior than you would be expected to have about the actions of another. You should be attending to the situational constraints on your actions, you should know whether your behavior is intended, and you should know whether those intentions have arisen from a momentary whim or from an enduring personal disposition. In addition, you should also know more about your own past history, personal goals, and capabilities than you would about those of anyone else.

A Pervasive Tendency. Imagine for a moment that you are a member of your school's debating team, and that the statement to be debated this year is "Terrorism is a legitimate form of political expression for those who cannot otherwise attract attention to their causes." You have been assigned by your debating coach to argue the affirmative case, and you do so, even though your personal opinion is the exact opposite of the one expressed in the resolution. Because you are a proficient debater, you present a good case for the resolution. Now a social psychologist approaches you and asks you to identify the reasons for your persuasive arguments. Somewhat chagrined, you say that you do not really believe the position, that you had no choice as to which side to argue, and that your actions should be attributed entirely to the requirements of the situation. The social psychologist will accept your explanation, but it is quite likely that a member of the audience would not. Perhaps thinking that you could have either "leaked" your own real position, or refused to argue the affirmative side in the first place, an observer of your behavior may decide that you are personally in favor of terrorism. A good deal of such "attitude attribution" research based generally on correspondent inference theory has been conducted (see a review by Jones, 1979). With only a few exceptions it leads to the conclusion first suggested by Jones and Nisbett (1972) that there is a "pervasive tendency for actors to attribute their actions to situational requirements, whereas observers tend to attribute the same actions to stable personal dispositions" (p. 80).

The Fundamental Attribution Error. Why is it that, even when an individual clearly has no choice about an action to be taken, perceivers will attribute the action at least in part to the underlying dispositions of the actor? On an intuitive level, perhaps the best answer to this question is an analogy to one of the Gestalt principles of perception. In order to deal with the complexity of the environment, the perceiver will organize the incoming information and will isolate the part that is to be *figure* (the portion attended to, perceived, and dealt with) from the *ground* provided by the remainder of the sensory input. For the actor in a situation, the environmental constraints on behavior constitute the figure, because the actor's energies must be directed toward overcoming any barriers the environment erects. For the observer, however, the actor's behavior is the figure, because it is that behavior, rather than the constraints upon it, that has the greatest importance for the observer.

Building on this general idea, Heider (1958) first noted that the actor's behavior has "such salient properties that it tends to engulf the total field" (p. 54). If this sounds very much like some of the categorization and salience effects we considered earlier, it should. As perceivers, we regard persons as the sources of actions, so action is salient to us. Additionally, we know that people's intentional actions often arise from their enduring dispositions, so we categorize any action as dispositional, ignoring the base rate of situational influence – a base rate we could have derived from our own experience. Overattribution of actions to a stimulus person's dispositions, the *fundamental attribution error* (Ross, 1977), is presumed to arise from perspective differences and cognitive categorization processes. There are, however, several important sources of error in attribution that are not so easily ascribed to variations in viewpoint, and our discussion of attribution concludes with some of these errors.

Other Errors in Attribution

Credit for Success, Blame for Failure. Think for a moment of the way you might describe your performance on a difficult examination, and assume that your description is an attempt to be accurate, rather than an attempt at self-presentation (Chapter 3). You know you studied hard for the exam, and that when you try hard, your grades are usually satisfactory to you. Now suppose that you learn you have done very well on the test. Quite probably you will attribute your success to internal causes – ability or effort – and you will be proud of your accomplishments. In contrast, suppose that you have done very poorly on the examination. In this case you will attribute the causes of your failure externally, to the difficulty of the exam, the capricious grading practices of the instructor, or the student two seats away whose incessant coughing during the exam destroyed your concentration.

Notice that your work was the same in both cases, but your explanation changes with a difference in the outcome. With constant effort and ability on your part, you have taken more credit for success than you are willing to accept blame for failure. Obviously, under the circumstances described in the example, your taking credit makes more objective sense, but several studies involving artificially created success and failure have obtained similar results. In these studies (reviewed by Weary & Arkin, 1981), subjects often are asked to solve problems that are, unbeknownst to them, unsolvable. Then half of the subjects are told that they have succeeded, whereas the other half are told that they have failed. Some controversy remains regarding the degree of motivation present in the attributions, and the precise form (self-presentation to an experimenter vs. self-enhancement even though nobody would learn of the outcome) that such a motivational distortion might take. But it is clear that people take more credit for success and less blame for failure than the objective circumstances would warrant. This issue is treated more fully in the discussion of achievement motivation in chapter 10.

COMBINATION OF INFORMATION: IMPRESSION FORMATION

As social cognition progresses from the gathering of information, through the categorization of that material, to the attribution of personal characteristics, the perceiver's own cognitive structure has an increasing effect on the substance of the judgments to be made. In this final section of the chapter the emphasis is more directly on the structure itself, specifically on the perceiver's schemata for what personality traits might be mutually associated.

Implicit Personality Theory

In the same way that information gathering, categorization, and attribution take place against the background of the perceiver's socialization, experience, and motivation, the formation of a final impression takes place against a set of expectations the perceiver holds about the behavior and personality traits of other people. How much variability in personality should be expected from a person who possesses a particular set of core traits? What personality traits "go together?" Is the relationship between two or more traits reflexive—if an unpredictable person is thought to be dangerous, is a dangerous person also considered unpredictable? This set of expectations about which personality traits will be mutually associated is referred to as the perceiver's **implicit personality theory** (Bruner & Taguiri, 1954). An implicit personality theory differs from what I have called an implicit theory of social psychology, because the implicit personality theory is concerned only with the covariation among personality traits, rather than with the covariation between social behaviors and all the personal/situational determinants of those behaviors. In addition, although it resembles a stereotype in leading the perceiver to ignore relevant individual differences, an implicit personality theory operates at the trait-to-trait level, rather than at the social category-to-trait level.

Some of these distinctions will be clarified by describing ways in which implicit personality theories can be measured. Suppose that you were interested in measuring the implicit personality theories held by some of your friends. You can either give each person a "standard" list of trait words to evaluate, or you can ask each person to generate as many descriptive adjectives as he or she can. Whichever method you use to produce the list of descriptive traits, you next need to have each of your friends indicate the degree to which one trait word might be associated with the other. For example, you could ask "How much do you think 'warm' goes with 'likable?' With 'friendly?' With 'open?'" and continue this pairing for every trait that appears on the list. You can imagine that this process would be quite time-consuming, because as was the case with the multidimensional scaling described in chapter 3, there will be $N(N$-$1)/2$ possible pairs. Fortunately, there are three procedures that can be used to reach the same end much more efficiently.

Correlational Methods. The first general method substitutes a correlation between the trait ratings for the direct paired comparisons of all traits, but it employs a standard set of descriptive traits. You would provide each of your friends with the same list of stimulus persons (people all your friends would know equally well, such as some of your professors, some of your mutual acquaintances, or even some public figures whom all of you know only by reputation). Then you would ask each of your friends to rate each of these stimulus persons on every one of the standard list of descriptive traits (this procedure, and other methods of measuring implicit personality theory, are described in detail in the Methodological Appendix). Thus, you would have one rating on each adjective for each of the several stimulus persons in the set.

You will remember from the discussion of accuracy in social judgment in chapter 3 that true "accuracy" is really the degree to which a perceiver is able to identify the degree to which different stimulus persons possess varying amounts of all traits. In other words, true accuracy occurs when the particular values for all descriptive trait words are determined entirely by the personal characteristics of the stimulus person. By contrast, an implicit personality theory is an identified pattern of trait responses produced by the perceiver, regardless of the individual characteristics of the stimulus persons described. If one of your friends describes a close acquaintance by saying that the person is both "warm" and "likable," that may very well reflect the perceiver's accurate judgment of the stimulus person. If, however, the same perceiver also claims that a celebrity he or she has never met is also "warm and likable," then it begins to look as though a positive correlation between "warm" and "likable" is part of the perceiver's implicit personality theory. It is just such patterns across stimulus persons that are identified by the correlational method of studying implicit personality theory.

The Trait Implication Method. The intercorrelations necessary to identify elements of an implicit personality theory often are gathered in the manner just described, but they also may be collected through the trait implication method of investigating implicit personality theory (Bruner, Shapiro, & Taguiri, 1958). In this method, instead of presenting your subjects with a set of particular stimulus persons—politician, professor, acquaintance, and friend—you would just use an unidentified person. Rather than ask your subjects to rate this unknown person on a series of descriptive adjectives, you would measure the extent to which the presence of one trait (called the *cue trait* by Warr & Knapper, 1968) would imply the presence of another trait (called the *response trait*). For example, you would say to the subject, "A person is warm. To what extent is that person also likely to be open?"

The trait implication method increases the structure inherent in the subject's task, and provides somewhat more precise information than does the correlational method. If two traits (or any two variables) are correlated, it may be that trait A "causes" trait B, or it may be that trait B "causes" trait A, or it may merely be that the two are together "caused" by a third trait that has not been measured. As you will remember from chapter 2, one of the difficulties with correlational research is that such research cannot determine with confidence which of these possibilities actually occurred.

But the trait implication method does enable the researcher to identify which explanation is correct. For example, Warr and Knapper (1968) have found that a cue trait of "cynicism" will imply (among other things) a response trait of "precision," but that the reverse is not true. In short, your knowledge that a person is cynical may cause you to evaluate that person as precise, but your knowledge that a person is precise tells you nothing about whether the person is also cynical. For this reason, the trait implication method is preferable if you are interested in the *structural relationships* among elements of an implicit personality theory.

The Peer Nomination Method. The third traditional method for measuring implicit personality theory is the peer nomination method used by Passini and Norman (1966) in their demonstration of just how generalized some aspects of implicit personality theory can be. Peer nomination proceeds in the opposite direction from the correlational or trait implication methods. Instead of being given stimulus persons to be described by specified descriptive adjectives, the subjects are provided with the adjectives and asked to nominate stimulus persons who represent each pole of the dimension (such as "active-passive") involved.

For example, in a group of six subjects, each subject would be asked to identify secretly to the experimenter one third of the group (two persons, excluding the subject) who best represent the "active" end of the scale, and two persons who best represent the "passive" end of the scale. This nomination procedure would be followed for every rating dimension included in the research. You can imagine that deciding who are the two most active people and the most passive people in a group would be – by comparison to some of the other rating methods – a relatively simple task. This would be especially true for people who knew each other well, and might not be too difficult even for casual acquaintances, provided that they had had some previous interaction with one another.

Five General Factors. Before beginning their study, Passini and Norman (1966) reviewed previous research using the peer nomination method. They noted that factor analyses of the ratings obtained in these studies showed a remarkable consistency, even though the participants in one investigation had known each other well for as long as 3 years, whereas subjects in another study had been acquainted only for a few days. In either case, a factor analysis revealed five major clusters of ratings: (a) extraversion (talkativeness, openness), (b) agreeableness, (c) conscientiousness, (d) emotional stability, and (e) degree of culture (refinement, artistic sensitivity, degree of poise).

From this similarity of factor structure, Passini and Norman concluded that the important variable was not the length of interaction among members of the peer group, but rather the fact of interaction. To test this idea they performed a peer nomination study on the first day of an experimental psychology class, before the students had engaged in any interaction whatsoever. Passini and Norman naturally predicted that under these circumstances the regularity in the ratings would disappear. The results were a surprise. The same five-factor structure was found in the ratings made by these unacquainted subjects. Apparently the peer nomination procedure (at least with the adjectives typically used) calls into play a cognitive schema for "interacting person," rather than reflecting any true characteristics of the participants themselves.

Prototypes: The Structure of Implicit Personality Theory

A Hierarchical Organization.   Throughout our discussion of implicit personality theory it has become increasingly clear that these expectations about the covariation among traits bear a strong resemblance to both the behavioral expectations that constitute stereotypes and the notions about the production of events that constitute causal schemata. All that remains is to demonstrate that, as a form of cognitive schema, an implicit personality theory influences impression formation. As an example, let us consider one of the five general factors in implicit personality theory (the "cultured person"), showing how that factor can be represented as a cognitive schema.

What is it that makes a person cultured? An appreciation of the arts, breadth of contact with the world, savoir faire, a taste for fine food and vintage wine are qualities that immediately come to mind, and no doubt you can think of more. But are all of these characteristics equivalent, or do some represent higher levels of abstraction? In other words, do the characteristics exist only as a set of correlated elements, or can they be placed into a meaningful cognitive structure?

Drawing on recent work in cognitive psychology, Cantor and Mischel (1979) suggested that our impressions of others can be organized into structured hierarchies, an their example for the cultured person appears in Fig. 4.6. The traditional implicit personality theory factor "cultured per-

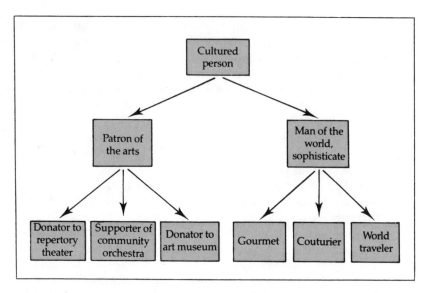

FIGURE 4.6   Three-level structure for the prototype of a cultured person (adapted from Cantor, N., and Mischel, W. Prototypes in person perception. In L. Berkowitz, ed., *Advances in experimental social psychology,* vol. 12. New York: Academic Press, 1979. Reprinted with permission).

son" appears as the superordinate category. At the middle level of abstraction this category is divided into "patron of the arts" and "man of the world, sophisticate." At the subordinate level of abstraction, threepossible descriptions appear for each of the middle-level categories. It should be noted that the middle-level and subordinate-level descriptions are only a few of those that might be possible.

Richness and Differentiation.   In their research, Cantor and Mischel (1979) asked subjects to think of attributes that would be associated with each description of a person. For example, you would be asked to name as many attributes as you could for "a cultured person," for "a donator to the repertory theater," for a "patron of the arts," and so forth, without being told the place of each of these descriptions in the hierarchy. As the level of abstraction decreased (from superordinate category to middle level to subordinate element), the average number of attributes assigned increased. Thus the *richness* of the description was greater for the lower level elements in the schema. But the price for this degree of richness was a loss of *differentiation*: a donator to the theater and a donator to the museum, for example, shared a many common attributes. In contrast, the superordinate category of "cultured person" shared almost no attributes with other superordinate categories (such as "emotionally disturbed person") also derived from the Passini and Norman (1966) general factors in implicit personality.

Thus, it appears that the general factors may constitute what Cantor and Mischel (1979) call *prototypes*: central, clear exemplars of kinds of persons. These prototypes are hierarchically organized, and like other cognitive schemata, direct the perceiver's use of social information. There are, of course, wide individual differences in the use of such schemata, and particular stimulus persons do not fit the prototypical descriptions any more exactly than they fit the popular stereotypes for behavior. But in the formation of social impressions without complete information, these cognitive structures can play an important role.

Information Integration Theory: Combination of Traits

Ever since Asch's (1946) pioneering study of the formation of social impressions from descriptive adjectives, social psychologists have tried to specify just how these adjectives might be combined into final perceptions. We have seen that this process is influenced by the manner in which data are gathered, by aspects of the categorization process, and by implicit personality theory. Yet none of these processes can account for the order-of-presentation effects discussed in chapter 3, or for the creation of impressions based on the incoming information instead of on the preexisting schemata of the perceiver. One theory that does accomplish these tasks is the **information integration theory** of impression formation (Anderson, 1968, 1974; Kaplan, 1975).

Possible Combinatorial Principles. The core of information integration theory is a mathematical model of the impression formation process, and before describing this model it is useful to consider some of the alternatives. Suppose that we reconsider Asch's (1946) original descriptive adjectives—warm (or cold), intelligent, skillful, practical, cautious—and ask how these might be combined into a final impression. We have already seen, from Asch's work, and from the later work of Kelley (1950), that the perceiver's final impression differs depending on whether we use the word "warm" or the word "cold." The entire group of adjectives presented to the subject is called the *set*, and each adjective is an *element* of that set. An important distinction can be drawn between possible models of impression formation on the basis of the way these elements are thought to combine.

If, as Asch (1946) suggested, the central trait alters the final impression by changing the meaning of every other element of the set, then there are at least two different ways in which this might occur. First, there might be change in the connotative meaning: "Intelligence" paired with "warm" might be considered a different sort of ability from "intelligence" paired with "cold." Alternatively, the central trait might alter the overall evaluative tone of the remainder of the series. For purposes of illustration, we shall consider only the latter possibility here. If the central trait changed the evaluative tone of every other element, then the most appropriate model would be one that specified a *multiplicative* relationship among elements of the set:

$$\text{Impression} = \frac{\text{Positivity of}}{\text{Central Trait}} \times \frac{\text{Positivity of Every}}{\text{Other Element}}$$

For example, "cautious" multiplied by "warm" might appear to the perceiver to be twice as positive as "cautious" multiplied by "cold." This multiplicative relationship would, of course, have to told for every element of the adjective set.

On the other hand, if changing the central trait alters the final impression without necessarily changing the meaning of every other element in the set, then a different sort of model would be more appropriate. One such alternative would be a *linear* model that predicts a final impression determined by the simple addition of stimulus elements:

$$\text{Impression} = \text{Sum of the Elements.}$$

For example, the noncentral elements might be added together (intelligent + skillful + practical + cautious) to create a sum representing the impression, and this sum would be increased by adding "warm" or decreased by adding "cold."

A Weighted Averaging Model. As this example indicates, however, simple addition of elements is not a complete description of the process. How can we take into account the dramatic effect of the central trait on the overall impression, especially as compared to the smaller individual effects of the other elements? We can provide for this discrepancy by building into the model the possibility that the perceiver might give different weights to the different stimulus elements. In other words, we can consider each adjective to possess two characteristics. First, the adjective will have a *scale value* (a numerical score indicating the adjective's positivity or likableness). Second, each will also have its own *weight* (some numerical estimate of the adjective's contribution to the overall impression).

Intuitively, it is simplest to think of an adjective's weight as representing the proportion that the adjective contributes to the final impression, and this can be accomplished by requiring that the weights sum to 1.00. Considering both an element's scale value and weight, and requiring that the sum of the weights be 1.00, the weighted averaging model of information integration holds that the

$$\text{Impression} = \sum s_i W_i$$

where s_i = scale value of the ith adjective in the set and W_i = a normalized weight for the ith adjective (which weight is created by dividing the weight for the particular adjective by the sum of all the weights).

This weighted averaging model of information integration has been used successfully to account for the influence that central traits exert on impression formation, to account for the kind of primacy effects (adjectives early in a list have more weight than adjectives later in a list) discussed in chapter 3, and for the opposite, *recency*, effects, that also occasionally occur. The overall dependent variable in the model is, of course, a measure of the likableness of the stimulus person (the sum of the products of the likability reflected in an adjective times its weight). Although there is some question about the degree to which the likableness of a stimulus person is specifically linked to the perceiver's actual behavior toward that stimulus person, the information integration theory is still an important mathematical representation of some of the cognitive structure that has been the subject of this chapter.

Social Cognition and Behavior

We have examined the gathering of social data, the categorization of individuals, the attribution processes that aid in our understanding of their behavior, and the principles according to which information is organized into final impressions. This active construction of the social reality to which a person then responds can simplify the perceptual task, but it can also lead to various kinds of distortion and error. Perceivers possess distinctive personalities of their own, heuristics to simplify the data collection, a tendency to stereotype, a number of schemata that fill in for missing information, and personal motives that can affect judgment. It will be valuable in subsequent chapters to remember that a person's social behavior is determined by that person's own construction of social reality. Our first step in the exploration of the relationship between cognitive structures and behavior is the study of social attitudes, to which we turn next.

SUMMARY

Social-psychological explanations of human action rely heavily upon the study of social cognition: the gathering, interpreting, and organizing of information about other people and events. In our attempt to deal with the complexity of the social world, we rely on cognitive heuristics, categorization, and schemata. In our unsystematic gathering of social information, we can be overly influenced by an individual's social *salience* (p. 112), and can place too much reliance on a variety of *cognitive heuristics* (p. 115).

When categorizing people we sort them into classes according to their **criterial attributes** (p. 118), but may occasionally engage in social *stereotyping* (p. 119), the extent of which can be measured by checklist (p. 120) or individualized, trait-specific (p. 122) methods. When we search for the causes of the behavior of others we employ various sorts of **attribution processes**. We engage in a naive analysis of action (p. 127), evaluating the personal and environmental contributors to behavior. When we know the **noncommon effects** (p. 131) and **assumed desirability** (p. 131) of an action, we strive for **correspondence of inference** (p. 132) – the certainty that a performed action represents the underlying personal disposition of the actor. To understand the proper source of an internal state, we can employ **attributional criteria** (p. 134) – distinctiveness, consistency, and consensus – attributing the state to those things with which it covaries. If only a single observation is possible, we rely on a variety of **cognitive schemata** (p. 135) to fill in for the missing information. Finally, our impressions of other people will be affected by our **implicit personality theories** (p. 140), our sets of expectations about which traits will be mutually associated. These theories can be measured with correlational methods (p. 141), and can be thought of as hierarchical structures or *prototypes* (p. 143). The actual traits that contribute to our impressions of others can be described by a weighted averaging model of **information integration** (p. 145).

SUGGESTED ADDITIONAL READINGS

FISKE, S. T., & TAYLOR, S. E. (1984). *Social cognition*. Reading, MA: Addison-Wesley. This readable book contains a wealth of information about all forms of social cognition—attention, inference, attribution. It contains a chapter on methods of studying social cognition that is a must for any student planning research in the area. Highly recommended.

HEIDER, F. (1958). *The psychology of interpersonal relations*. New York: Wiley. This scholarly classic is the foundation for present attribution theory. As numerous subsequent experimental studies have demonstrated, this "naive psychology" of perception, motivation, desire, and duty is common sense at its sophisticated best. It is difficult reading, but will be rewarding for the reader with enough time to appreciate its depth.

CHAPTER FIVE

ATTITUDE ORGANIZATION AND COGNITIVE CONSISTENCY

CONTENTS

PREVIEW

An attitude is a predisposition to behave in a favorable or unfavorable manner toward a particular class of social objects. Social attitudes are organized and interrelated, having both a horizontal structure and a vertical structure. These complex attitudes can be described by syllogistic models that emphasize the logical and probabilistic connections among elements, and by the principle of cognitive consistency. Three major cognitive consistency theories are considered. Balance theory describes the relations between attitude objects in terms of liking and unit formation, and balance principles can also apply to interpersonal behavior. Congruity theory is a special case of balance theory, but it suggests that proportional change in evaluations will follow the creation of incongruity. Cognitive dissonance theory has received the most research attention, in part because of its ability to make predictions that are counter to established views of reinforcement. The dissonance theory position, namely that dissonance is unpleasant and motivates attitude change, has been challenged by two other explanations–incentive theory and self-perception theory. The research flowing from this controversy serves as an excellent example of development in any science, with theoretical advances going hand in hand with methodological improvements.

How do you feel about military spending? Do you think that women or minorities should be given an affirmative preference in hiring and promotion in order to make up for past discrimination? If the local school board informed you that your child would have to be bussed out of your neighborhood to attend school across town, what would you do? All these questions, and a great many others of social importance, involve your attitudes toward various social objects–people, issues, institutions. If a single concept has dominated social psychology through most of its existence, that concept is the social attitude. Although there have been a number of definitions of the concept through the years (for example, see a recent review by McGuire, 1985), many of these can be summarized by saying that an **attitude** is an organized predisposition to respond in a favorable or unfavorable manner toward a specified class of social objects.

Three Components: Cognitive, Affective, and Behavioral

A closer look at this definition shows why social psychologists have typically considered an attitude to have a cognitive component, an affective component, and a behavioral component. To begin with, an attitude is an organized cognitive structure much like the schemata, prototypes, and stereotypes we have discussed in previous chapters (Chapters 3 and 4). A person's world is represented by a set of cognitive categories, and at least one such category exists for every class of social objects of importance to the person. But the cognitive component of an attitude is more than the category into which the attitude object would be placed; it also includes a set of beliefs about the characteristics of the attitude object.

For example, consider the attitude object "rock singer." The criterial attributes for membership in this category might be stated as making a living from recordings and concert performances with a particular sort of musical accompaniment. The cognitive component of your attitude toward any rock singer would also include your noncriterial beliefs about that performer. How does he or she stand on the issues of the day? How much does he or she make from royalties on records and videos? What is he or she really like as a person? Your answers to these questions, and your other beliefs about rock singers, will certainly influence your attitude, even though they do not serve as criterial attributes for the category.

If the cognitive component of an attitude is the sum total of all you believe about the attitude object, the affective component is the sum total of your feelings about the object. Your values, your emotions, and your experience will all lead you to evaluate aspects of your social world in positive or negative terms, and this evaluation will be of paramount importance in your attitudes. Do you feel that the rock singer's positions on questions of politics or personal style are good ones or bad ones? Do you feel that his or her royalties on record and video sales are fair, insufficient, or exorbitant? Would you like the singer as a person? These evaluative judgments predispose you to act in a generally favorable or unfavorable manner toward the attitude object, and some social psychologists consider evaluation to be the essential component of an attitude (e.g., Fishbein & Ajzen, 1975).

Finally, the social attitude contains a behavioral component—the "predisposition to respond"—that reflects both your beliefs about the object and the evaluative judgments you have made about the object. If your overall evaluation of rock singers is positive (given what you believe to be true about them), we would expect you to engage in actions, such as attending concerts and buying everything from tour t-shirts to laser disks, that would be consistent with this evaluative judgment. In contrast, if your attitude is a negative one, then we would expect you to refrain from these favorable actions and perhaps to take some unfavorable actions. It should be emphasized that the behavioral component of an attitude is regarded as only a general *predisposition* to engage in favorable or unfavorable behavior, not as a specific set of actions that will always occur regardless of the circumstances.

The Structural Properties
of an Attitude

There are two quite different senses in which an attitude is an organized predisposition to behave in a favorable or an unfavorable manner toward a set of social objects. First, an individual social attitude is, itself, an organized entity: the cognitive, evaluative, and behavioral components are interrelated, with the former two combining to produce the latter. Second, these individual attitudes do not exist in isolation from one another; on the contrary, they are as highly interconnected as were the other cognitive structures considered in chapter 4. In short, if we know a person's attitude on one issue, we can rather reliably predict his or her position on quite a few related questions.

In an ideal world, we might hope to develop some sophisticated measurement devices that would enable us to create a map of an individual's attitude structure, much as a cartographer creates a map of a highway system. But attitudes, unlike highways, are not directly observable. So we must construct models of attitude organization and test these models for their explanatory and predictive value. The particular models of attitude organization presented in this chapter include two **probabilogical** models that concentrate on the logical structure of an attitude and the probabilistic relationships that hold among attitude elements, and the **cognitive consistency** models that emphasize the individual's need to conform his or her attitudes to publicly observable behavior. The probabilogical models discussed include the syllogistic model initially described by McGuire (1960) and later elaborated by Jones and Gerard (1967), and the information-processing model described by Fishbein and Ajzen (1975). The cognitive consistency models include the theories of balance (Heider, 1958), congruity (Osgood & Tannenbaum, 1955), and cognitive dissonance (Festinger, 1957).

PROBABILOGICAL MODELS OF ATTITUDE ORGANIZATION

You will recall that at several places in chapter 4 the social perceiver was compared to a "naive scientist"—a seeker after truth whose inferences were based on a combination of logical reasoning and an intuitive sense of the laws of probability. You will also remember that most of those comparisons were unfavorable to the naive perceiver. The scientific researcher collects data systematically, the perceiver does so haphazardly. The scientist uses formal statistics to identify the underlying regularities in human social behavior, the perceiver can fail to pay attention to the statistical base rates. The scientist's formal theories are corrected by disconfirming instances, the perceiver's implicit personality theory, cognitive schemata, and informal theories of social behavior are not sufficiently responsive to contradictory information.

If people are such ineffective users of formal logic and probability theory, why in the world would attitude theorists construct models explicitly based on the assumption that human cognitive processes generally conform to the dictates of formal logic and probability theory? There are at least two different ways in which this question can be answered. The first of these has to do with the relative proportion of errors to correct judgments. Despite the occasionally serious errors, most of the naive perceiver's judgments are reasonably accurate. Multiple necessary causes are rarely confused with multiple sufficient causes, cognitive categories remain stable over time, and even the judgmental heuristics function in much the same manner in most perceivers. So the perceiver's cognitive processes do possess an internal logic, even if that internal logic is imperfect. And the perceiver's inferences about other people's personalities and reasons for acting do respond to a version of probability, even if there are fairly regular departures from the judgments that would be made on the basis of formal probability theory. Specifically, for example, a perceiver may err in the judgment of a facial emotion because his or her constructive processes adversely affected the information processing. Nevertheless, across perceivers, and even cross-culturally, there is widespread agreement on the underlying emotional state represented by particular facial expressions.

The second answer to the question has to do with the nature of the phenomenon to be accounted for. In social perception the emphasis is on a comparison between the phenomenological experience of the perceiver and the "real" distal stimulus as "we know it to be." That is, there is a more or less objective criterion against which the perceiver's impression can be compared to determine its "accuracy." Consequently, in the study of the cognitive processes involved in person perception, attention is quite naturally focused on those instances in which the perceiver makes mistakes. By contrast, in the study of attitude organization, there is no comparable "objective" criterion. Why?

Think again about the definition of an attitude—a cognitive component, an affective component, and a behavioral component. It is, of course, quite reasonable to suggest checking the veridicality of a person's beliefs about an attitude object. Regardless of one's attitude toward raising the drinking age as a means of reducing traffic fatalities, there is a known number of alcohol-related traffic deaths each year. There is, however, no comparable objective criterion for judging a person's evaluation of changing the drinking age as a means of reducing that number of fatalities (as opposed, for example, to raising the age at which people can obtain driver's licenses). Reasonable people could legitimately be expected to disagree about which of those solutions would be better. Consequently, the theoretical questions of interest deal with the internal organization of the person's attitudes, whatever their content, rather than with comparisons of that content to the "objective" truth. And that focus leads to a concentration on the "probabilogical" character of attitudes, not on errors.

THE SYLLOGISTIC MODEL

The **syllogistic model** of attitude structure initially suggested by McGuire (1960) and later elaborated by Jones and Gerard (1967) and Bem (1970) provides an explanation of how the cognitive and affective components of an attitude might combine to produce a behavioral predisposition. The syllogism is a form of logical reasoning in which two premises are related to each other in such a way that they logically imply a conclusion.

Premises and Conclusions

The Belief Premise.   The minor premise, which appears first in an attitude syllogism, is the **belief premise**. Just what is a belief? You will recall from the discussion in chapter 4 of cognitive categorization that categories are formed on the basis of the criterial, or defining, attributes of the objects concerned. For example, biological gender is the criterial attribute in the formation of the two categories "male," and "female." But there are other attributes (appearance, personality characteristics, behavior) that are more or less reliably associated with gender, even though they are not criterial. These attributes constitute our beliefs about "masculine" and "feminine" characteristics. In short, according to Jones and Gerard (1967) a belief is a statement of the noncriterial attributes of an object. This definition of a belief in terms of the process of categorization suggests that the belief premise in an attitude syllogism corresponds quite well to what we have previously called the cognitive component of an attitude.

The Evaluative Premise.   The major premise, which appears second in an attitude syllogism, is the value or **evaluative premise**. This evaluative premise states the person's affective or emotional reaction to the characteristic mentioned in the belief premise. A positive value motivates the individual to approach or praise the object, but a negative value motivates the person to avoid or denigrate the object. Those objects that have both some positive and some negative characteristics produce correspondingly ambivalent behavioral predispositions. Just as the belief premise of an attitude syllogism represents the cognitive component, the evaluative premise of a syllogism represents the affective component.

The Attitudinal Conclusion.   The combination of the belief premise with the evaluative premise produces the attitudinal conclusion. This conclusion itself is a positive or negative evaluation of the attitude object, and it is presumed that such an evaluation will produce the predisposition toward favorable or unfavorable behavior:

Minor premise (belief):	Defense creates jobs.
Major premise (evaluation):	Creating jobs is good.
Conclusion:	Defense spending is good.

The minor premise is stated first and contains two elements: the subject is the attitude entity in question, and the predicate is a characterization of that entity, or a statement of the entity's effects. The predicate of this belief premise is called the *middle term*, because it appears again as the subject of the evaluative or major premise. The predicate of this major (evaluative) premise is typically a claim that the middle term is either good or bad.

Horizontal Structure

The middle term provides the link between belief and evaluation that is necessary for these two premises to imply the attitudinal conclusion. In an important sense, the middle term is the reason for the final conclusion, and the fact that this reason disappears from the conclusion strengthens the analogy between the syllogistic model and other views of an attitude. As we see in chapter 6, it is often difficult to infer an attitude from an individual's overt behavior. Even when the attitude itself is relatively obvious, the person's reasons for holding that attitude may not be available to us.

For example, if we know that an individual has written to a congressional representative asking for an increase in the appropriations for the Department of Defense, we can be fairly certain that the writer has a positive attitude toward defense spending. But why does the writer favor defense spending? Is it because of a belief that such spending creates jobs, or a belief that such expenditures enhance national prestige, or that they prevent war? Obviously, there are multiple possibilities for the middle terms, so we cannot infer reliably which reason applies just from the demonstrated existence of the attitude.

Another way to describe the multiple possibilities for the middle term is to say that the final attitudinal conclusion might be the result of any number of individual syllogisms. Consider the following:

Defense spending creates jobs.	Defense spending prevents war.
Creating jobs is good.	Preventing war is good.

Therefore, Defense spending is good.

These two syllogisms differ only in their middle terms (creation of jobs or prevention of war), and both lead to exactly the same attitudinal conclusion, a positive evaluation of defense spending. They are two different reasons for holding the same attitude, even though they are relatively independent of each other. Such parallel syllogisms leading to the same attitudinal conclusion form the **horizontal structure** of the attitude, and the greater the number of such syllogisms, the greater the support for the attitudinal conclusion.

Vertical Structure

But where did the ideas in each of these horizontally arranged syllogisms come from? Certainly we were not born thinking that defense spending creates jobs and prevents war, so there must be more than these premises to the attitude. Considering the origins of a belief or of an evaluation leads us to the idea of the **vertical structure** of the attitude. Take, for example, the evaluative premise "preventing war is good." This premise might itself be the conclusion of a prior syllogism:

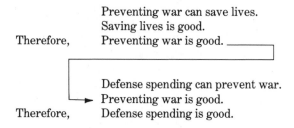

	Preventing war can save lives.
	Saving lives is good.
Therefore,	Preventing war is good.

	Defense spending can prevent war.
	Preventing war is good.
Therefore,	Defense spending is good.

In this case the conclusion of one syllogism has become the evaluative premise of a later syllogism, and this relationship is the basis for the vertical structure of an attitude. This vertical structure can be thought of as a form of cognitive "past history" leading to a recent conclusion (the last one in the long vertical chain). As the amount of history involved in an attitude increases, change becomes more difficult.

Degrees of Belief

To this point we have considered only the "logical" portion of the "probabilolgical" model of attitude structure. The elements of all the syllogisms shown have been connected to one another by the rules of logic, and each premise has been stated without any qualification (even "preventing war can save lives" does not say how many such lives will be preserved). But what if the person's beliefs and evaluations are not stated in these unqualified terms? Can predictions still be made from the model? The answer to this question is affirmative, and depends on the "probability" portion of the model.

Combinations of Probabilities.   Consider an alternative version of the defense spending issue. Suppose, for example, that a person held the belief that increased defense spending by the United States would lead the Soviet Union to strike first, rather than attempting to match the defense buildup dollar for dollar. On the assumption that a preemptive nuclear first strike by the Soviets would be bad, this complete view could be expressed in terms of the following syllogism

> A. Defense spending will produce a Soviet first strike.
> B. A Soviet first strike is bad.
> C. Defense spending is bad.

As usual, the minor (belief) premise is stated first, the major (evaluative) premise is stated second, and the attitudinal conclusion is last. This time, however, each element of the syllogism is labeled with a capital letter to make its later identification simpler.

To begin with the minor premise, the belief stated in (A) is a matter of conjecture and, as such, is open to question. Suppose that the person whose attitude is described by the conclusion (C) recognizes the controversial nature of (A) and so really thinks that there is only a 40% chance that defense spending will produce a Soviet first strike. In other words, the person believes the probability of defense spending's creating a Soviet first strike to be .40, and in the language of the theory this subjective probability estimate is denoted $p(A)$. Now, because defense spending will either produce a Soviet first strike or not, the probability that it will *not* do so is $1.00 - p(A)$ or .60. This latter probability is called "the probability of not-A" and is denoted $p(A')$.

Turning to the major premise, virtually no Americans would disagree with the assertion that a Soviet first strike would be a bad thing, so for the stimulus person this premise has a truth value of $p(B) = 1.00$. Finally, to examine the attitudinal conclusion it is necessary to recall a principle from the horizontal structure of an attitude: the syllogism under consideration at the moment may not contain the only reason for the expressed attitudinal conclusion. In this example, the possibility of producing a Soviet first strike is the only reason given for "defense spending is bad." It may not, however, be the only reason possible. In short, there is some probability that the person will consider defense spending bad for other reasons. In terms of the probabilogical model outlined by McGuire (1960), this other probability is denoted $p(K)$, and for illustration let us assume that this value is .30.

A Final Value for the Attitude.   Taking all of these probabilities into account, it is possible to attach a numerical value to the final attitude that defense spending is bad. That final probability value is, according to McGuire (1960),

$$p(C) = p(A)p(B) + p(K),$$

where $p(C)$ is the likelihood that person will believe defense spending to be bad, $p(A)$ is the probability that the person will believe defense spending likely to produce a Soviet first strike, $p(B)$ is the subjective probability (in this example, unity) that such a first strike will be bad, and $p(K)$ is the subjective probability that defense spending will be bad for reasons entirely independent of the production of a first strike. Substituting numbers for the general probability values produces

$$p(\text{defense spending is bad}) = .70 = (.40)(1.00) + (.30).$$

The equation shows how a final number can be achieved, but it may have suggested a question to many of you. Suppose the probability for "other reasons" had been .80 instead of .30. Would not that have caused the equation to add up to more than 1.00 (an outcome that probability theory (would) preclude)? The answer is that $p(K)$ cannot ever exceed $1-[p(A)p(B)]$, because $p(K)$ represents *all* reasons other than a Soviet first strike for concluding that defense spending is bad.

THE INFORMATION-PROCESSING MODEL

Multiple Attributes

This necessity in McGuire's (1960) probabilogical model of dichotomizing the attributes associated with the attitude object represents a limitation in the amount of information that the model can consider at one time. That is, if a person's beliefs about defense spending must be divided into (a) those associated with a Soviet first strike, and (b) all others, then we cannot examine, on an individual basis, the elements that make up these other reasons. To do so we would need a model that could take into account the multiple attributes that an attitude object might possess.

Beliefs and Evaluations

Let us consider a model proposed by Fishbein and Ajzen (1975) to account for the manner in which a person processes information about an attitude object. Although the terms are stated in a slightly different fashion, this model contains components that are roughly equivalent to those specified by the tripartite division of an attitude into cognitive, affective, and behavioral components. The theory's essential cognitive element is the *belief*, an assertion that the attitude object possesses some characteristic. It is fair to think of this belief in terms we have used before: a subjective judgment that the attitude object possesses particular criterial or noncriterial attributes. Each of these beliefs is multiplied by an *evaluation*, a positive or negative judgment about the particular attribute in question. Thus the theory takes into account multiple attributes possessed by an attitude object, with each of those attributes separately evaluated.

The beliefs and evaluations combine to produce an overall affective response to the object. This general predisposition is the attitude, and it is important to note that it represents only affect, not probable behavior. The attitude then gives rise to specific response tendencies, called **behavioral intentions**. These are actions that the person might take toward the attitude object. For example, the question "How do you feel about women in the professions?" is directed toward a general predisposition, whereas the question "Will you select a female dentist?" deals with a behavioral intention. The **information-processing model** thus suggests a sequence of judgment, with beliefs and their evaluations leading to an attitude that, in turn, produces behavioral intentions, with these culminating in behavior.

The Scaling of an Attitude

Belief Strength. With the exception of the behavioral intention, the concepts used in Fishbein and Ajzen's (1975) theory are nearly the same as those used in other approaches to attitude organization. But unlike the traditional tripartite conception of an attitude, the information-processing theory enables us to identify the precise contribution that each of the multiple attributes makes to the overall attitude. To begin with, if a belief is an assertion that the attitude object possesses a particular attribute, then **belief strength** can be measured by determining the subjective probability that the attitude object actually possesses the characteristic in question.

For example, for the belief "Politician X has integrity," we can assess belief strength by asking the attitude holder to estimate the probability that Politician X really possesses the characteristic of integrity. Note that this, like the probability judgments in McGuire's (1960) probabilogical model, is fundamentally a social perception judgment from the perspective of the attitude holder, not an objective assessment of the politician's true characteristics, so the judgment is open to influence by all of the errors in social perception discussed in chapters 3 and 4. For some individuals who would agree with the statement "Politician X has integrity," the probability estimate might be low (say, .20), whereas for others who would agree it would be high (say, .90). These differences in belief strength would permit us to distinguish between people who otherwise would appear to be similar in their overall beliefs.

Expectancy and Value. Having obtained the set of characteristics the attitude object is thought to possess (each one expressed as a subjective probability), it is a simple matter to get the attitude holder to tell us how good or bad he or she considers each characteristic (such as "integrity") to be. Once we have obtained the evaluation of the characteristic, and know the subjective probability estimate that the attitude object possesses that characteristic, then we can determine the overall attitude. In the information-processing model, the attitude (A) toward a stimulus object is determined by the beliefs (b_i) about which characteristics are associated with the object, and the evaluations (e_i) of those characteristics, as shown in the formula

$$A = \sum_{i=1}^{n} b_i e_i.$$

There are n characteristics associated with the attitude object, and the overall attitude is determined by multiplying the evaluation of each of these characteristics by the subjective probability that the attitude object possesses the characteristic, and then summing the products.

You will notice that this means of computing an attitude is very much like the computation of a social impression using the information integration theory (Chapter Four). Both involve a *value* placed on individual elements, and an *expectancy* (either the subjective probability that an object possesses an element or the normalized weight that an element carries), and the two are combined across all elements to produce the attitude or the final impression. Thus both constitute **expectancy-value models**, respectively of attitude organization and impression formation.

Place of the Model

In their presentation of the theory, Fishbein and Ajzen (1975) report a number of experimental tests of the information-processing model. They also discuss refinements of the probability estimation technique that attempt to broaden the model to include phenomena of impression formation, attribution, and attitude change, as well as attitude organization. Consideration of these extensions is beyond the scope of this book; for our purposes it is sufficient to note that the model improves upon the initial syllogistic conception by showing exactly how beliefs and evaluations may be combined into a final attitude. Each belief × evaluation product can be regarded as one element in the horizontal structure of the attitude. Thus,

"Politician X is consistent, and consistency is good;" "Politician X is mentally healthy, and mental health is good;" and "Politician X is not merely an opportunist, and having principles is good" are three separate belief ×evaluation premises leading to the attitudinal conclusion "Politician X is good." The advantage of the information-processing approach is that the subjective probability estimates and scaled evaluations can give a more precise notion of the strength of each of these syllogisms, and of the final attitudinal conclusion.

THE PRINCIPLE OF COGNITIVE CONSISTENCY

The probabilogical models of attitude organization describe the structure of an existing attitude, but neither supplies an organizing principle to account for dynamic change in that structure. For example, suppose that a person believes defense spending is good, and that providing unemployment benefits for people who have been the victims of difficult economic times is also good. We know that these two conclusions can serve as the evaluative premises for additional syllogisms, such as

Senator Smith votes for defense spending.	Senator Smith votes for unemployment benefits.
Defense spending is good.	Unemployment benefits are good.
Senator Smith is good.	Senator Smith is good.

In the terms we have used so far, these two syllogisms would simply represent two different aspects of the horizontal structure of a favorable attitude toward Senator Smith. But in a world of limited resources it may not always be possible to accomplish all of the objectives a person might consider worthy. Suppose that the good senator votes for defense spending but not for unemployment benefits. The conclusion of one syllogism thus becomes inconsistent with the conclusion of the other, and the two can no longer be regarded as part of the same horizontal structure. They must be considered different (and conflicting) attitudes toward the same social object (Senator Smith). It is clear that we need some additional explanatory device to account for the structural changes that may take place, and that device is the principle of cognitive consistency.

COGNITIVE CONSISTENCY

Notwithstanding that consistency is the hobgoblin of small minds, the principle of cognitive consistency holds that "the person tends to behave in ways that minimize the internal inconsistency among his interpersonal relations, among his intrapersonal cognitions, or among his beliefs, feelings, and actions" (McGuire, 1966, p. 1). It is important to note that although the principle is usually referred to as one of cognitive consistency, it presumably applies not only to cognitions held by a single person, but also to the relationships between those cognitions and various sorts of interpersonal behaviors. In addition, the principle is both a description of attitude structure (attitudes will be organized in a manner that promotes and maintains consistency), and an assertion of a motivational force (reduction of inconsistency) that can affect behavior.

RELATIONS AMONG COGNITIVE ELEMENTS

Consistency theory has occupied much of social psychology's interest, and researchers have developed six main theoretical positions in the general consistency framework. Only three of these—balance theory, congruity theory, and dissonance theory—are presented here. Two of the others are very similar to the probabilogical models previously discussed, because they deal with logical consistency in the structure of thought (McGuire, 1968), and with psychological implication (Abelson, 1968), minimizing the motivational aspects of inconsistency. The final theoretical position (Rosenberg, 1968) is really more of an extension of existing theory than it is a distinct alternative.

Regardless of the particular terms it uses, each of the three theories to be presented here attempts to specify the antecedents and consequences of various relations among cognitive elements. A cognitive element can be a belief, a value, an attitude, or the cognitive representation of a behavior. So, "capitalism is not an appropriate economic system for underdeveloped countries," "justice," "consumer protection is good," and "I am getting soaked standing here in the rain" are all examples of cognitive elements. What sorts of relationships exist among such elements?

All three of the theories specify variations on three basic relations. As a first possibility, two or more elements may be consistent with one another, a state referred to in balance theory as *balance*, in congruity theory as *congruence*, and in dissonance theory as *consonance*. An example of two consistent cognitive elements would be "I like my wife" and "I am doing something nice for her." The second possibility is that the two elements would be inconsistent with each other: "I like my wife" but "I am shouting at her." This inconsistency is referred to as *imbalance* (balance theory), as *incongruity* (congruity theory), or as *dissonance* (dissonance theory). A final possibility recognized by each model is that the two elements may have nothing whatsoever to do with one another: "I like my wife" and "Today is July 13." Each of the three theories assumes that these unrelated elements do not enter into the determination of consistency. Each theory further assumes that consistency is a desired state, and that inconsistency is sufficiently unpleasant to serve as a motive for change in one or the other inconsistent element. So much for what the theories have in common. Now let us consider in more detail some of the differences among them.

BALANCE THEORY

Liking and Unit Formation

Balance theory is primarily an *inter*personal theory of consistency, and its most complete description has been given by Heider (1958)—in the same book that provides much of the foundation for attribution theory (Chapter 4)! The particular interpersonal processes with which balance theory is concerned are what Heider called *sentiments*—positive and negative feelings between people. What leads people to like, or to dislike, each other? One of the answers Heider suggested (which has since been confirmed in any number of research studies) is that we like those people with whom we have some association (members of our families, people who share our attitudes and values, people whom we benefit, and so forth). The tie can be based on kinship, formal organization, similarity, actions, or a number of other possibilities, just so long as the individuals involved for a unit. In other words, **unit formation** between a person (p) and another person (o) will lead to *liking* between p and o. This relationship is designated as follows: $pUo \rightarrow pLo$, where both unit formation (U) and liking (L) are considered to be positive relations.

Denial of Unit Formation.　Just as the positive relation of unit formation (U) leads to liking (L), the negative relation of denial of unit formation ($\sim$U) leads to disliking ($\sim$L). But as Cartwright and Harary (1956) have noted, there is an additional complication, because these two characterizations of unit formation do not exhaust the alternatives. Consider the relations of cooperation and competition as examples. You come to like a person with whom you cooperate to achieve a mutually desired goal ($pUo \rightarrow pLo$). By the same token, you quickly come to dislike a person with whom you are in competition for scarce resources ($p \sim Uo \rightarrow p \sim Lo$).

What about a person you meet for the first time, with no thoughts of cooperation or competition? Certainly it would be wrong to assume that you would form an immediate bond with the person, or to assume that you would immediately deny unit formation. When you meet a person for the first time, you don't know whether the relationship will be positive or negative until you have had at least some opportunity to get acquainted. In short, there may be some instances of interaction for which unit formation is irrelevant. Perhaps the best solution, suggested by the breadth of the unit-formation concept and supported by research on interpersonal attraction (that is considered in chapter 9) is to assume that first encounters ought to be described as cases of positive unit formation. After all, the two of you are together in the same place, you do begin the conversation by discussing topics familiar to you both, and there are some fairly strong social constraints against the expression of instant dislike.

The Determination of Balance or Imbalance.   Thus we see that according to balance theory, two possible relations exist between individuals: liking and unit formation. Each of these relations can have a positive sign (L or U) or a negative sign (~L or ~U). How do we determine whether a particular relationship is balanced or not? Imagine that each relation is preceded by the numeral 1, and that this numeral 1 assumes the sign (+ or −) associated with the relation. Thus U and L would each be +1, and ~U and ~L would be − 1. Then simply multiply the numbers together. If the final product carries a positive sign, the relationship is considered balanced; if the final product is negative, the relationship is imbalanced. This computational procedure is illustrated in Table 5.1 for a *dyad* (a two-person group). As the table shows, balance is achieved when the signs of the two relations are the same.

Antipathy and Change.   It is important to notice that only one of the two balanced states described in Table 5.1 represents an active association between the two people (*p*U*o* with *p*L*o*). The other balanced state represents both antipathy (*p* ~ L*o*) and denial of a relationship (*p* ~ U*o*). The two states are equally balanced in Heider's system, but we would like to think that the former, active, association is more probable.

The motivational aspect of balance theory predicts that the imbalanced states will be resolved by changing the sign of one of the two rela-

TABLE 5.1 Computation of Balance Within a Dyad

Numerical Value Attached to Each Relation

Unit Formation: U = +1 ~U = −1 Liking: L = ~1 L = −1		
Balanced States	*Represented as*	*Multiplication*
1. You like a person with whom you are associated.	*p*L*o* and *p*U*o*	+1 × +1 = +1
2. You dislike a person with whom you are not associated.	*p* L*o* and *p* ~ U*o*	−1 × −1 = +1
Imbalanced States		
1. You dislike a person with whom you are associated.	*p* ~ L*o* but *p*U*o*	−1 × +1 = −1
2. You like a person with whom you are not associated.	*p*L*o*, but *p* ~ U*o*	+1 × −1 = −1

Note: *Whenever the product of the multiplication is positive, the state is considered balanced; whenever the product is negative, the state is considered imbalanced.*

tions. Which sign undergoes change may be determined by the ease of change. Suppose that you are employed in a job where one of your close coworkers is exceedingly difficult to like (pUo, but $p \sim$Lo). Do you change jobs, thereby dissolving the unit that the two of you had formed, or do you learn to like the person for his or her few positive qualities? Obviously the resolution you select will depend on such things as the other rewards you get from your job, the ease of finding another position, how close your association with the person must be, and just how objectionable he or she really is.

Degrees of Balance and Imbalance

This example serves to illustrate not only the possible resolutions of a state of imbalance, but also a major disadvantage of the theory as it was originally stated by Heider (1958). The two relations – unit formation and liking – are both *dichotomous* variables: each relation has only two values (unit formation or denial of unit; liking or disliking). Unfortunately, as Cartwright and Harary (1956) have pointed out, the psychological world is not that simple. Your coworker may not be totally unredeemable, but may just have a few upsetting quirks, and the extent to which the job requires that you interact may vary. You may be part of a production team that must spend the entire day together; you might only have to deal with one another on an occasional basis; or you might simply work in the same general location. How badly you will need to learn to like the other person will thus depend on the degree of unit formation and liking as well as on the direction of each relation.

More Than a Dichotomy. Although some later reformulations of balance theory continued the all-or-nothing character of the liking and unit formation relations, other extensions of the theory (e.g., Wiest, 1965) have specified degrees for each relation. How might differences in degree be reflected in our example of the coworker? To begin with positive unit formation, you might have infrequent contact ($+1$), regular necessary contact ($+2$), or close contact on a daily basis ($+3$). There could be degrees of denial of unit formation as well, but I omit them to keep the example from becoming too complicated. As for liking, your opinion of the coworker could vary from a belief that he or she was really a terrific person ($+3$), through a judgment that the person was slightly unpleasant (-1), to a judgment that the person was really obnoxious (-3), with other judgments at the intervening scale values. The signed value of the unit-formation relation would be multiplied by the signed value of the liking relation to determine the strength of the balance or imbalance. As before, the sign of this product determines whether the whole system is balanced or not. Using degrees of balance and imbalance it would be possible to represent the fact that constant interaction with a wonderful person is preferable to occasional contact with a mildly attractive person, even though by sign alone both relations would be balanced.

Resolution of Imbalance. Scaling the degrees of liking and unit formation not only gives us more insight into balanced relationships, it also suggests which element is most likely to be changed if the relationship is imbalanced. Suppose you have constant interaction with a slightly unpleasant persón (a total imbalance of -3). Or, as an alternative, suppose you have only occasional contact with a truly obnoxious person (again, a total imbalance of -3). Even though the total imbalance is the same, we would expect a resolution of the imbalance in different ways. In the first case, we would guess that your opinion would change. The constant interaction is dictated by the requirements of your job, and the amount of imbalance is not sufficient for you to seek employment elsewhere. In the second case, it is your opinion of the person that is the more fixed. Although you cannot find any redeeming qualities in a truly obnoxious person, you can arrange your movements at work so that you seldom run across the person. In each of these cases, imbalance is resolved through change in the weaker relation. This sort of prediction will recur in the discussion of congruity theory.

Intrapersonal Balance

Although balance theory was originally formulated in *inter*personal terms, it can be applied to problems of *intra*personal consistency as well. The internal state, attitude, opinion, or belief, or even an external object connected with the self, is identified by the term, x, and it, too, is part of liking and unit formation relations. For example, "I give a televised lecture an am pleased with my performance," might be represented by

$$p[U = +3]x \text{ and } p[L = +3]x = +9$$

where I am person p, the lecture is x, the strength of the unit formation is based on the obvious connection between my lectures and me, and the strength of the liking relation reflects my pleasure with my performance. Now suppose that instead of being entirely satisfied with my lecture, I believed it was not up to my usual standards:

$$p[U = +3]x \text{ but } p[\sim L = -1]x = -3.$$

Which of the two relations will be changed? I cannot retract my public performance–it is there on videotape, ready for instant replay at any moment–so to remove the imbalance I simply change my private opinion.

In this example, change in my internal belief follows directly from the principle that the weaker relation will be the one to change, but what happens if I hated my performance ($\sim$L = -3)? The two relations are now equally polarized, or equally displaced from zero. Even so, we might expect that the liking relation would be the one to change, because the public unit-formation relation ought still to be more difficult to alter. Balance theory, however, does not contain any conceptual distinctions that could be used to justify this assumption. So we are left without a satisfactory answer to the question of which of two equally polarized relations – one public, one private – will be the more likely to change. Just this question has formed the basis for a large amount of research conducted within the framework of cognitive dissonance theory, and we shall return to the problem of inconsistency between word and deed in the later section on this theory.

Balance in a Triad

The inclusion in the relationship of an object or internal entity, x, represents a broadening of balance theory from its original concern with interpersonal relationships to intrapersonal relations. Up to now we have considered relationships with only two elements, either two people (p and o) or a single person and an entity (p and x). The final aspect of balance theory to be considered is the further generalization to a *triad* consisting of two persons and an entity. This structure is known, not surprisingly, as the **p-o-x triad**, and it has received a great deal of conceptual attention, as indicated in a recent review by Insko (1984).

Computation of Balance.   The balanced triad is probably best illustrated with a simple example. Suppose that a friend of mine watched me give my lecture on television. Two possible outcomes of this triad (me, my friend, and my lecture) are shown in Fig. 5.1. Because these outcomes are considered from my friend's point of view, he is referred to as p. I would be the other person in the triad (o), and my lecture would be the object (x). In the first triad shown in the figure, we see that my friend likes both me and the lecture, with which I have formed a unit. In the second triad, my friend likes me but dislikes the lecture. The first triad is balanced, because each relation has a positive sign, and the multiplication of three positives produces a positive. The second triad is imbalanced, because the product of two positives and a negative is a negative.

Limitations of the Example.   As you might guess, the two triads presented in Fig. 5.1 oversimplify the relations involved in several ways. First, we have omitted my liking or disliking for the lecture, and included in the diagrams only that I am connected to it. This makes the diagrams less cluttered, but it does so at the cost of assuming that I positively value

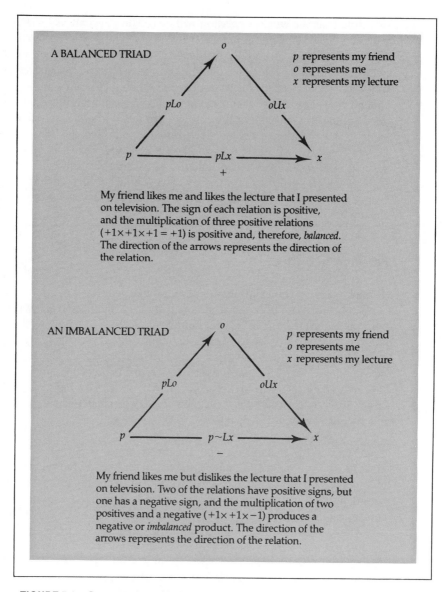

A BALANCED TRIAD

p represents my friend
o represents me
x represents my lecture

My friend likes me and likes the lecture that I presented on television. The sign of each relation is positive, and the multiplication of three positive relations $(+1 \times +1 \times +1 = +1)$ is positive and, therefore, *balanced*. The direction of the arrows represents the direction of the relation.

AN IMBALANCED TRIAD

p represents my friend
o represents me
x represents my lecture

My friend likes me but dislikes the lecture that I presented on television. Two of the relations have positive signs, but one has a negative sign, and the multiplication of two positives and a negative $(+1 \times +1 \times -1)$ produces a negative or *imbalanced* product. The direction of the arrows represents the direction of the relation.

FIGURE 5.1   Computation of balance in a triad.

anything I am connected to. Interestingly enough, purposeful violation of this assumption is one of the interpersonal techniques we employ to differentiate our honest friends from people who merely flatter us because they have something to gain (Jones, 1964). One of the things that a true friend ought to do is tell us when we have made fools of ourselves. Therefore, if we wish to determine how discerning a person is, we might make a statement we know to be preposterous (in balance theory terms, $p\text{U}x$ but p

~Lx). By the multiplication rule, the resulting sign of this combination of relations is negative. Now suppose that a person compliments me on the statement. What must I think of this person, in order for the triad (me, the other person, and my statement) to be balanced? I must evaluate this person negatively in order for the final product of the multiplication to be positive. In short, I like my true friends not only because they compliment me when they should, but also because they do not tell me how great I am when I do something stupid.

A second way in which the diagram of the triads oversimplifies the situation is that it omits the degrees of liking and disliking that were discussed earlier. My friend is characterized as liking me, but the diagram does not indicate the strength of this bond. In a similar manner, the degree of unit formation between me and my lecture is not specified, nor is the extent to which my friend likes the lecture. If we wished to complicate matters, we could include degrees of liking and unit formation, but balance would still be determined by the sign of the multiplicative product, regardless of its strength. And, just as the weaker element in a dyadic relationship would be the one to change, the weakest element in a triadic relationship would be the most likely to change in order to restore balance.

CONGRUITY THEORY

Elements of the Theory

Sources and Objects. In some respects, the **congruity theory** of cognitive consistency, developed by Osgood and Tannenbaum (1955), can be regarded as a cross between the probabilogical models and balance theory. According to Tannenbaum (1968), the congruity model was originally formulated as a specific explanation for the attitude change that occurs when a *source* (*S*) is connected to a particular attitude *object* (*O*). This is a somewhat narrower goal than that of balance theory, because it deals only with two elements, both external to the person whose attitude is being characterized. But by focusing on this narrower goal, congruity theory attempted to build in some of the measurement precision that characterizes the probabilogical models.

Examples of sources would be newspapers, television commentators, experts in a profession, the person next door, books, your friends, and so forth. In short, sources consist of documents, publications, and people. Attitude objects can include things, people, legislative proposals, social conditions, or in some cases, entities that otherwise would be considered sources. For example, if a newspaper such as the *New York Times* makes an editorial comment about a candidate for Congress, the newspaper is the source and the candidate is the object. But if the candidate issues a public statement denouncing the editorial, he or she becomes the source and the paper becomes the object. It is probably simplest to think of sources as the makers of statements about objects.

Bonds: Associative and Dissociative. All the statements that sources can make about objects are grouped into two classes, according to whether the statement implies a positive connection (known as an **associative bond**) or a negative connection (a **dissociative bond**). These bonds are equivalent to the unit formation relation in balance theory, with the associative bond corresponding to U and the dissociative bond corresponding to ~U. Thus the dissociative bond is the denial of a connection, rather than the absence of a connection. Associative and dissociative bonds can be verbal statements or overt actions. As in the case of the original formulation of balance theory (Heider, 1958), there is no distinction made concerning the degree of association or dissociation. For example, if a friend of your says that she thinks a particular musical group is good, she is expressing an associative bond between her and the group. The *bond* would be characterized in exactly the same way if she had said the group was "okay" or "terrific." or had said nothing but had purchased their latest recording. As long as her description of the group, or her other behavior, indicates a positive connection—regardless of its degree—the congruity model would say she has an associative bond with the group.

The final element of congruity theory is the *evaluation* placed on both the source and the object by the person whose attitude is being considered. This evaluation component of congruity theory was derived from Osgood's other work on the semantic meaning of concepts (Osgood, Suci, & Tannenbaum, 1957). In this work Osgood and his associates used a *semantic differential* scaling technique (discussed more fully in the Methodological Appendix) that asks subjects to rate concepts on a set of 7-point scales (usually from $+3$ to -3). The semantic differential technique is content free, so it can easily be applied to a variety of concepts. Congruity theory takes advantage of this methodological capability by assuming that both the sources of statements and the objects of those statements can be described by their positions on the 7-point evaluative scale.

A Leftist's View of Sources and Objects. Evaluations of sources and objects can be illustrated by the material in Table 5.2, and from the nature of the evaluations you can tell that the person holding these attitudes is a confirmed leftist. The United States Labor Party, a source,and the issue of government control of industry, an object, both receive very high evaluations. In contrast, the John Birch Society, a source, and the object of racial segregation both receive very negative evaluations. It is important to emphasize that all the evaluations shown in the table represent the opinions of the one individual whose attitudes are being considered. Other people might have quite different evaluations of both the sources and the objects listed in the table. Also, for purposes of this example, we must assume that

TABLE 5.2 Possible Scale Positions of Some Sources and Objects as Judged by a Confirmed Leftist

Scale Position	Sources	Objects	Scale Position
+3	U.S. Labor Party	Government control of industry	+3
+2	Socialist Party	National health insurance	+2
+1	Democratic Party	Election reform	+1
0	Common Cause		
−1	Republican Party	Continuation of tax advantages	−1
−2	American Independent Party	Multinational companies	−2
−3	John Birch Society	Racial segregation	−3

the person has made evaluations of sources on purely partisan grounds, so that Common Cause, an explicitly nonpartisan group, receives a score of 0. In fact, it might be difficult to find an organization engaged in political activity of any kind toward which most people have no evaluative reaction whatsoever. This reality is recognized in the list of objects, though not in the list of sources, by the omission of an element at the zero point on the scale.

Resolution of Incongruity: Proportional Change

How is incongruity created and resolved? Suppose that our leftist learns that the Socialist Party (with a positive scale position of +2) has advocated the continuation of certain tax advantages (an object with a negative scale position of −1). This associative bond between a source of one sign and an object of the opposite sign will create incongruity, as would an associative bond between two elements of like sign but different scale positions. Both the sign of the source and object and the degree of *polarization* (the scale position, as a displacement from zero) of each will enter into the creation of incongruity. Notice that this is different from balance theory. Balance theory (even the modification that includes degrees of balance) defines imbalance only in terms of the *signs* of the elements. But here, to avoid incongruity, not only must the signs be the same; the scale positions must also be the same.

By considering both the sign and the scale position, congruity theory has formalized the idea that the weaker of the two elements (the one with a scale position closer to zero) will change more in the resolution of the incongruity. To resolve incongruity, the individual must make some alteration to the evaluation of each element involved in the incongruous relationship, and the change in each element will be inversely proportional to its original scale position.

The point of equilibrium after the resolution of the incongruity arising from the advocacy of tax advantages by the Socialist Party is shown in Fig. 5.2. The Socialist Party had an original scale position of +2 (two units away from zero), whereas the tax advantages had an initial position of −1 (one unit away from zero). Because it was twice as polarized to begin with, the Socialist Party will change only half as much in the resolution of the incongruity. The total incongruity is three evaluative units, so the Socialist Party will move through one of these, while the issue of tax advantages will move through two units of the three, with the result that both the source and the object will attain a new scale value of +1.

COGNITIVE DISSONANCE THEORY

The theory of **cognitive dissonance**, originally proposed by Festinger (1957), and later extended by Brehm and Cohen (1962), Aronson (1969), and Wicklund and Brehm (1976), has generated more research, and controversy, than any of the other cognitive consistency theories. Dissonance theory's impact on social psychology arises not from its conceptual sophistication—in many respects it is less thoroughly, and less formally, specified than either balance theory or congruity theory—but from its ability to make nonobvious predictions, and from the methodological advances that have been made as a consequence of some of its theoretical arguments. In this last section of the chapter we consider a common dissonance-arousing experimental technique, the elements of the theory, and some of the research performed to test dissonance predictions. Where appropriate, I also mention some of the criticisms that have been leveled at the theory and at the research flowing from it.

FIGURE 5.2   Change in scale positions of Socialist Party and tax advantages necessary to resolve incongruity.

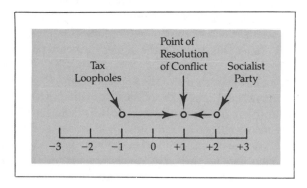

An Alternative to Reinforcement

If there is a single, fundamental principle of psychology that seems to apply in the behavior of almost every organism, it is the principle of **reinforcement**. As you know, the principle of reinforcement states that behavior that leads to rewards (or to the reduction of pain) is more likely to recur than is behavior that does not lead to these desirable outcomes. Rewards are supposed to increase the frequency, duration, and intensity of the rewarded behavior. This general principle is an explicit or implicit feature of most psychological theories, including a number of social exchange theories discussed in chapter 8.

One of the reasons that cognitive dissonance theory has had such an effect on social psychology is that the first major test of the theory by Festinger and Carlsmith (1959) appeared to contradict this time-honored principle of reinforcement. The purpose of the experiment was to investigate some of the conditions under which an individual's attitude might be changed by inducing the person to behave in a manner contrary to his or her existing attitude. Although the correlation between attitude and behavior is far from perfect, you can still appreciate what a novel idea it was to suggest that people can easily be induced to change their attitudes by engaging in counterattitudinal actions.

Forced Compliance: Lying for a Lot or a Little. Suppose that you had been a subject in the Festinger and Carlsmith research. You would have arrived at the experimental laboratory and would have been seated in a small room in front of a table. On this table would be the apparatus, an elevated platform with several rows of round holes, each hole containing a round peg. Your task would have been to turn each peg one-quarter turn to the right. When you had finished doing this for the first row, you would continue to the next row, and as soon as you had completed the last row you would begin all over again. This dreadfully dull task would have continued for about 20 minutes. Finally, the experimenter would have told you to stop, and would have explained that the research was designed to test the effect of prior instructions on performance of a motor task. Because you were in the control group, you did not receive any instructions, but the next subject to be run (who was now sitting in the waiting room) was supposed to be told that the peg-turning task was interesting and enjoyable.

The experimenter would then have continued by telling you (and here comes the manipulation) that the assistant who was supposed to say how enjoyable the task was had not showed up. Rather than dismiss the waiting subject, the experimenter would wonder whether you would be willing to give the necessary instructions. In half of the cases the experimenter would offer to pay you $1 for your help; in the other half, he would offer you $20 (remember, this was the late 1950s, when $20 was a great deal of money). He would say that the choice of whether to help or not was strictly up to you, but that he would be grateful if you would decide to help him.

From your perspective, this is an unusual situation, and you decide to help the experimenter out of his predicament. It is difficult to argue that you have a positive attitude toward the task; rather, you agree to help in spite of your negative feelings about the task. What you do not know is that the same request is being made of every subject (with a payment of $1 to half of the people and $20 to the other half). Although permitting you to maintain an *illusion of free choice*, the experimenter has actually forced you to comply with his request. Not surprisingly, this experimental paradigm is known as the **forced compliance** technique, and it is a common occurrence in research on cognitive dissonance.

Counterattitudinal Advocacy and Insufficient Justification. So you agree to tell the next subject how interesting and enjoyable you found the peg-turning task. You go out into the waiting room, discover a person sitting there ready to take part in the experiment, and you give your speech about the task. In terms of the theory, that speech is an instance of **counterattitudinal advocacy**. Most probably your own attitude is that the task is boring, yet you have now told another person (who is actually an accomplice of the experimenter) how interesting it is. What will happen to your attitude under these circumstances? The prediction from reinforcement theory is that the more you have been paid to perform this service, the more your attitude will change in favor of the task.

Interestingly enough, the prediction from dissonance theory is just the opposite: There should be more attitude change in the $1 condition than in the $20 condition. The reasoning goes like this. You believe the task to have been dreeadfully dull, but you have just made a public claim that it was interesting. Knowledge of these two facts creates cognitive dissonance, a negative drive state that arises whenever an individual simultaneously holds two cognitions (ideas, beliefs, opinions, attitudes, representations of behavior) that are opposite one another. Dissonance is unpleasant, and must be reduced. You feel uncomfortable because you lied about the character of the task, and you begin searching for some justification for your behavior. In the $20 condition, the payment alone constitutes sufficient justification (remember, this is 1958): The cognition "I got a bundle for doing it" is so consistent with having described the task as interesting that "I didn't really like the task myself" is greatly outweighed. But in the $1 condition, the payment is an **insufficient justification** for the counterattitudinal advocacy, so dissonance must be reduced by some other means. What is left? Changing your attitude about the task is the only possibility: "I wasn't really lying, because in retrospect I think that the task did have some useful scientific value, and for that reason alone I feel that it was interesting and enjoyable."

The results of the experiment confirmed Festinger and Carlsmith's predictions on the basis of dissonance theory. After delivering the "instructions" to the waiting person, the subject was asked to describe his own participation in the study. One of the questions on this written evaluation form asked how interesting the task had been, and here the $1 group described the task as significantly more interesting than did the subjects in the $20 or control groups (in the latter there was no payment and no delivery of instructions to a waiting "subject"). These findings understandably created quite a reaction, and we shall return to some of the controversy after a description of dissonance theory.

The Formal Theory

Elements and Relations.   As the name of the theory implies, the basic units in cognitive dissonance theory are *cognitive elements*. These can be ideas, attitudes, beliefs, values, representations of past behavior, or expectations about future events. For purposes of comparison, the elements involved in dissonance theory are not as precisely specified as those involved in congruity or balance theories. This fact makes the testing of dissonance predictions slightly more difficult, but also permits a broader application of the theoretical ideas.

There are three possible relationships between these cognitive elements: *consonance, dissonance,* and *irrelevance.* Two cognitive elements are said to be consonant with one another if one of the elements implies the other. Thus "It is raining" and "I am carrying my umbrella" are consonant elements, as are "I really enjoy playing tennis," and "I am describing the game in glowing terms to my friends." In both of these pairs, each element implies the other, so each pair is consonant.

Violation of Expectancy.   In contrast to this pretty cognitive picture, two cognitive elements are dissonant whenever one implies the opposite of the other. The cognitions presumably held by Festinger and Carlsmith's subjects are a perfect illustration of dissonance. It is safe to assume that the subject's real impression is "I thought that task was exceedingly dull," but his verbal statement "The task is really quite interesting" is exactly opposite what the first one would imply. Festinger (1957) described this relation of dissonance by stating that one element implies the *obverse* of the other. The difficulty with using this term from formal logic to describe dissonance is that the state of dissonance – like imbalance but unlike the probabilogical syllogisms discussed at the beginning of the chapter – deals not so much with formal implication as with psychological expectation. Indeed, Brehm and Cohen (1962), and later Aronson (1969), point out that dissonance can best be conceived of as a *violation of expectancy.* We expect that people will behave in accordance with their attitudes, or at least will not behave in direct contradiction of them. When that expectancy is violated, dissonance is created.

Finally, it is possible for cognitive elements to have no psychological implications for one another, and these elements are said to be in a relation of irrelevance. "This was a very dull task" and "I am six feet tall" are cognitive elements that are irrelevant to one another.

The Magnitude of Dissonance

As suggested by the example from Festinger and Carlsmith's study, dissonance can be reduced by the presence of suitable cognitions other than the two involved in the relation of dissonance. Disliking the task is dissonant with saying that it was great, but being paid a large amount of money for the statement virtually eliminates the cognitive problems. According to the theory, both the number, and the importance of the other cognitions will affect the magnitude of dissonance

$$\text{Magnitude} = \frac{\text{Importance} \times \text{Number of Dissonant Cognitions}}{\text{Importance} \times \text{Number of Consonant Cognitions}}.$$

Although its operational meaning is not well specified in dissonance theory, the concept of importance has the same effect on the degree of consistency or inconsistency that the scale value of a source or object has in congruity theory and the same effect that the degree of liking or unit formation has in balance theory.

You will notice that the estimation of the magnitude of dissonance is much less precise than the estimation of incongruity, and it is also less precise than the procedures for the estimation of imbalance. For example, without any specification of the units involved (and dissonance theory does not suggest what those units might be), it is virtually impossible to tell whether the number of dissonant cognitions is more or less influential in producing dissonance than is the importance of those cognitions. We can well imagine that a large amount of dissonance can be generated by a single extremely important cognition, such as "the world has not ended" for Mrs. Keech and the group of Seekers described in chapter 2. But how many cognitions of less individual importance would be necessary to create the same magnitude of dissonance? There is no way to know for certain.

Four Ways to Reduce Dissonance

Although the theory is not entirely clear on the determination of the magnitude of dissonance, it is quite clear on the motivating properties of that unpleasant cognitive state. In passing, it is interesting to note that "reducing the unpleasantness" of dissonance is essentially a hedonistic principle, just like the principle of reinforcement. "Avoiding pain" is the other side of the "seeking pleasure" coin. Yet dissonance theory has made its mark on social psychology in large measure because of its apparent contradictions of reinforcement theory predictions.

In a typical dissonance study an individual is induced to engage in some behavior (which produces a *behavioral element*) that is inconsistent with his or her private opinion (which I call the *evaluative element*). Whether the dissonance created arises from counterattitudinal advocacy, from foregoing some attractive alternatives to take one other opportunity, or from having one's expectancy violated, there are four ways to reduce the dissonance. These are (a) change the behavioral element, (b) change the evaluative element, (c) add elements consonant with the behavioral element, and (d) change the importance of either the consonant or dissonant elements. The first of these modes of reduction is the least likely. Your behavior is public, and people would think you were strange if you tried to deny performing actions that everyone observed. In experimental situations, as opposed to real-life situations, changes in importance are also not very likely. In our everyday lives we can (and often do) forget about our inconsistencies, but in the laboratory setting we are constantly reminded of them. Next most probable is the addition of elements consonant with the attitude-discrepant behavior, but again, the experimental situations are expressly designed to minimize or eliminate this alternative.

What is left? Only change in the evaluative element. When the structure of an experiment or the constraints inherent in social settings outside the laboratory preclude other modes of dissonance reduction, people will change their private attitudes to make those attitude agree with their overt behavior. Let us now take a closer look at some of the research, and some of the controversy, that has been generated by the theory of cognitive dissonance.

An Example
of the Evolution of a Concept

In the development of any scientific discipline, refinements in theory go hand in hand with advances in methodology. When theories are relatively crude, simple experiments can be devised to test their differing predictions. But as theories become more complex and attempt to deal with alternative explanations for the data, new instruments and techniques must be developed that will accommodate the more sophisticated predictions. In social psychology, this interplay between competing theories and the creation of new methods is best illustrated by some of the research flowing from the theory of cognitive dissonance. This is true not because the theory itself is so conceptually sophisticated (balance theory is more so), but rather because the large volume of dissonance research has been interesting and controversial, leading investigators of other persuasions to try to disconfirm dissonance theory. In many ways, the experiment by Festinger and Carlsmith (1959) began the controversy, so it is instructive to examine some of the research based directly or indirectly on that study. Recall that the dissonance theory explanation of the outcome is that the small payment constituted insufficient justification for the positive description, so the resulting dissonance produced internal attitude change. There have, however, been two major alternative explanations, one provided by incentive theory, and one provided by self-perception theory.

Incentive Theory.   **Incentive theory** is based on the principle of reinforcement, and it holds that the more a person is paid to advocate a particular position, the more the internal attitude should change in the direction advocated (Elms, 1967; Elms & Janis, 1965; Janis, 1968; Janis & Gilmore, 1965; Rosenberg, 1965, 1968). Festinger and Carlsmith's findings directly contradicted this prediction, so the incentive theorists were faced with having to deal with these results. Their first response (Janis & Gilmore, 1965; Rosenberg, 1965) was to suggest that there were artifacts in Festinger and Carlsmith's procedure and in the procedure of other dissonance researchers (Cohen, 1962) that rendered the findings meaningless.

Evaluation Apprehension.   The first criticism raised by incentive theorists was that the $20 payment was "inappropriate" – an amount so high that it would have raised the suspicions of even the most trusting subjects. That position was argued best by Rosenberg (1965), who suggested that any experimental subject approaches an interaction with a professional psychologist with a certain amount of evaluation apprehension (the fear, discussed in chapter 2, that the psychologist will discover his or her emotional weaknesses and immaturities). Evaluation apprehension can contaminate research findings, because subjects will presumably avoid revealing anything damaging about themselves. Given this background, subjects who are (effectively) offered $20 to change their attitudes will resist, if only to show the experimenter that they cannot be "bought" (remember, in 1985 dollars this would have been a payment of some $70).

To test this idea Rosenberg repeated the Cohen (1962) experiment (that had, to be fair, used much lower payments than had Festinger and Carlsmith – only ranging as high as $2.50. In his study, Cohen (1962) had asked subjects to write an essay favoring police intervention in a campus demonstration, and had found, as did Festinger and Carlsmith (1959), that there was greater attitude change with smaller payments for writing the essay. In his replication of this procedure, Rosenberg (1965) arranged for the dissonance arousal part of the study to be divorced from the attitude measurement portion. When the subject arrived for the experiment, he found Rosenberg either busily writing or talking to "another student."

Rosenberg then explained that he was running late, and as an afterthought suggested that the subject might occupy his time by participating for pay in "another little experiment" unrelated to Rosenberg's own research.

When the subjects reported to this other experiment (as all but three did), they were given Cohen's procedure word for word, except that the issue of a university's denial of permission for its football team to take part in a postseason game was substituted for the issue of police intervention into a campus disturbance. After each subject had written an essay on why the university was justified (counterattitudinal advocacy as a consequence of the forced compliance technique), the "experiment" was concluded and the subject was sent back to Rosenberg's office. There the subject's attitudes on a number of issues, including participation in the postseason game, were assessed, and the true nature of the experiment was explained.

The results of this study confirmed incentive theory predictions: The more the subjects were paid for their counterattitudinal essays, the more likely they were to state that the university had been justified in prohibiting the team's participation in the postseason game. Thus Rosenberg concluded that with the artifact of evaluation apprehension removed, payment for writing counterattitudinal essays would produce results consistent with incentive theory, rather than results supporting dissonance theory.

The Possibility of Suspicion. Two other experiments by incentive theorists (Elms & Janis, 1965; Janis & Gilmore, 1965) were performed in response to the "inappropriateness" of the $20 payment in Festinger and Carlsmith's original study. In both of these either a large payment or a small payment was made, but these payments were offered by either one of two different institutional sponsors. When the attitude research had a positively valued sponsor, the large payment produced greater attitude change; when the research apparently had shady purposes, the small payment produced the greater change. This was a less direct attack on the question than was Rosenberg's research, but it led to the same conclusion: dissonance effects will be obtained for a large payment only when the subjects are suspicious of the experimenter's motives. Thus the incentive theory raised some important questions about the validity of Festinger and Carlsmith's, as well as Cohen's, results.

Self-Perception Theory. **Self-perception theory** (Bem, 1965, 1972) took a quite different position, agreeing with the results of dissonance studies, but disagreeing with the theoretical explanation for those findings. You will recall that a fundamental assumption of any cognitive consistency theory (be it balance, congruity, or dissonance) is that cognitive inconsistency has motivating properties. Inconsistency is considered to be unpleasant, and all the consistency theories presume that people will reorganize their cognitive worlds to remove that unpleasant inconsistency.

Thus, a motivational state is thought to intervene between counter-attitudinal advocacy and the final expression of private attitudes. It is important to note that there is usually no direct measurement of the existence of this internal motivation in dissonance studies, although research by Brehm, Back, and Bogdanoff (1964), and Zanna and Cooper (1974) among others, suggests that such motivation is present. Nevertheless, without direct evidence of motivation, many dissonance studies can be reinterpreted in self-perception theory terms.

Such a reinterpretation goes like this: even after you have taken part in Festinger and Carlsmith's boring task, your attitude toward that task is vague and uncrystallized. It surely wasn't the most interesting thing you have done, but it wasn't the worst, either. If you now tell another subject (for a payment of $20) that the task was interesting, you will see that action as a product of the external reward, rather than as the result of your internal attitude. If, however, you perform the same service for only $1, the payment by itself is not powerful enough to get you to lie, so you will think your attitude toward the task cannot be all that negative. When the experimenter then asks you to indicate your "true attitude" you observe your behavior in much the same way that another person would observe you, and look for the external variables that might be controlling your actions. In effect, you are asking yourself, "What must my attitude have been, in order for me to describe the task as enjoyable for such a large (small) reward?" Thus, the only difference between the self-perception explanation and the dissonance explanation is that self-perception does *not* postulate the existence of an internal motivating state.

Interpersonal Simulations.   In order to demonstrate that no internal motivation is required, Bem (1965) introduced the the technique of **interpersonal simulation**: If a presumably noninvolved observer of a persuasive communication can reproduce the results obtained with an involved target of that communication, then internal motivation would not be required to account for the findings. You will notice that this procedure is very much like the comparison (discussed in chapter 4) between the attributions made by observers and those made by the actors whose behavior is to be explained. The difference is that here, the recipient of the persuasive message (the actual dissonance experimental subject) is behaving like an observer instead of behaving like an actor. The social constraints on behavior that constitute the forced compliance technique are specifically *hidden* from the subject, making his or her actions the "figure" for self-attribution.

If there is no motivation involved in the attitude change that accompanies forced compliance, then "real" dissonance subjects should produce results that are identical to those of simulating subjects, because all of these people are, in an important sense, only observers. Like Rosenberg, Bem replicated the Cohen experiment on essay-writing, but included only simulating subjects. There were three experimental conditions: a Control condition in which there was no mention of any money paid to Cohen's subjects; a $1 condition, in which it was stated that Cohen's subjects were paid $1 to write their essays; and a $.50 condition, in which the pay to Cohen's subjects was described as $.50. These conditions corresponded to Cohen's actual control, $1, and $.50 conditions. The prediction was that the simulating subjects would make estimates of final attitudes that were the same as the actual attitudes expressed by Cohen's subjects.

The simulation appeared to be a resounding success. Cohen had found significantly more attitude change in the $.50 condition than in the $1 condition, and some evidence that even this latter group had changed away from the attitudes expressed in the Control condition. The simulating subjects in Bem's (1965) study reproduced this pattern exactly. Because Bem's subjects were merely responding to written descriptions of the behavior of others, rather than writing the essays themselves, they could not possibly be experiencing cognitive dissonance.

Dissonance Theorists' Reactions to the Alternatives. It was now the dissonance theorists' turn to cry "Artifact!" In the first of several responses to the incentive and self-perception theory alternatives, Carlsmith, Collins, and Helmreich (1966) pointed out that the essay-writing task employed by Janis and Gilmore (1965) and Elms and Janis (1965) was not really comparable to the face-to-face deception required of subjects in the original Festinger and Carlsmith (1959) research. The degree of personal commitment inherent in writing an anonymous essay is simply not as high as that involved in taking a public stance that conflicts with your private beliefs. In effect, this argument held that the counterattitudinal actions required by the two incentive studies were of such low importance that no measurable dissonance was aroused.

To test this idea, Carlsmith, Collins, and Helmreich (1966) had subjects either write essays or engage in face-to-face deception for one of three levels of payment—$.50, $1, or $5. The results showed the predicted interaction between nature of the task and level of payment. When the task was writing an essay that described a boring procedure as fun and interesting, the more subjects were paid for their essays the more favorable their attitudes became; but when the task was face-to-face deception of another subject by describing the same task as fun and interesting, the more subjects were paid the less their private attitudes changed. In short, incentive findings were obtained for essay writing, but dissonance findings were obtained for face-to-face deception.

Balanced Replication. In the second major dissonance response to the incentive theory work, Linder, Cooper, and Jones (1967) argued that Rosenberg's (1965) two-experiment design obscured the role of commitment in the production of dissonance. These investigators pointed out that for dissonance effects to occur, the subject must know the amount of money contingent upon performance of the counterattitudinal behavior at the time he or she decides whether or not to participate. If you have already agreed to an unpleasant task and I offer to pay you for accomplishing it, you will evaluate it more highly the more I pay you (an incentive effect). But if the amount of the reward is made a part of your decision, then the principle of insufficient justification should take over. Linder, Cooper, and Jones argued that subjects in Rosenberg's experiment committed themselves to participate in the "other little experiment" by announcing that they would wait for Rosenberg to finish his work, and further by walking to another part of the building where the "other experiment" was being conducted. These actions constituted a decision to participate regardless of the rewards involved, so naturally those rewards produced incentive effects.

In a standard procedure for artifact discovery, Linder, Cooper, and Jones included one complete set of conditions that exactly paralleled Rosenberg's conditions. They then included a second set of conditions designed to remove the artifact: subjects in these groups were specifically told not to decide whether to participate in the "other experiment" until *after* they had heard all that the experimenter had to say (obviously including the amount of money). This design is known as a **balanced replication**: a design involving both those conditions that are thought to include the artifact and parallel conditions that are thought to have eliminated the artifact. The results supported the predictions. In the No-choice conditions, in which subjects had been sent to the "other experiment" incentive effects were obtained; but in the Free Decision conditions, in which subjects waited to decide whether to participate until after they had heard the amounts of money involved, dissonance effects were obtained.

Not only did the dissonance theorists point out artifacts in the incentive research, they also identified artifacts in the interpersonal simulations (Jones, Linder, Kiesler, Zanna, & Brehm, 1968; Piliavin, Piliavin, Loewenton, McCauley, & Hammond, 1969). Specifically, these investigators noted that one aspect of the information available to a "real" subject that is unavailable to a simulating subject is that "real" subject's initial attitude on the topic in question. Both these sets of researchers conducted balanced replications of Bem's simulations in which results similar to Bem's were obtained when the simulating subjects had no information about the "real" subject's initial attitudes. When such information was provided, however, the simulators made predictions that differed from the results obtained from involved subjects. It appeared, as Piliavin and her associates noted, that Bem's simulators had made the right answers for the wrong reasons.

Extensions and Reinterpretations.   At this stage in the development of the controversy, most of the researchers involved reached the conclusion I hope you have also reached: Dissonance theory can account for some of the results, incentive theory can account for some of the results, and self-perception theory can account for some of the results. Furthermore, it became clear that the theorists of different persuasions were much more effective in convincing themselves than in convincing each other. Reviews of the literature by incentive theorists concluded that the findings on the whole supported incentive theory; extensions of the dissonance work found evidence consistent with dissonance theory, provided that the subject felt personally responsible for making the choices involved; and replies by the self-perception theorists took issue with criticisms that had been leveled at the interpersonal simulations. All these extensions and reinterpretations helped to clarify the *limiting conditions* (Chapter 1) under which one theory as opposed to another might provide the best account of the data obtained. In so doing, they all helped to reveal just how complex were the phenomena that had seemed so simple immediately following the Festinger and Carlsmith (1959) experiment.

Recent Attempts at Resolution. The trend toward clarification and integration of various theoretical viewpoints has continued in recent research. With regard to the long-standing dissonance-incentive controversy, Gerard, Conolley, and Wilhelmy (1974) have argued that depending on the degree of justification for engaging in counterattitudinal behavior, both dissonance and incentive effects are possible. When there is insufficient justification, dissonance effects will be obtained; when the justification is sufficient, and appropriate, no attitude change will occur at all; when the justification is too great, incentive effects will be obtained. In short, if I pay you either too little (dissonance) or too much (incentive) to perform a behavior that runs counter to your initial position on the topic, your attitude toward the topic will become more favorable. It remains to be seen whether this attempted integration will withstand the test of future research and criticism.

With regard to the self-perception–dissonance controversy, research by Taylor (1975) suggests that the self-perception explanation may be limited to cases in which the person is either unsure of or not strongly committed to his or her initial attitudes. On the other hand, research in an area that has become known as **oversufficient justification**–extrinsic payment for *pro*attitudinal action (Nisbett & Valins, 1971)–shows support for the self-perception approach. Oversufficient justification is discussed more thoroughly in chapter 7, so for now it is enough to note that when one is paid to do something one would have done otherwise, no dissonance could possibly occur. But the self-perception analysis for this circumstance is the same as the one for the case of insufficient justification. A person who is receiving a large external payment for engaging in a proattitudinal behavior should evaluate his or her action and conclude that the payment, not any intrinsic interest, is the true cause of the action. The self-perception explanation for insufficient justification gains credence because its principles apply without modification in these two divergent instances.

Finally, with regard to the presence or absence of arousal resulting from cognitive dissonance, reviews of research on whether dissonance has drivelike properties (e.g., Wicklund & Brehm, 1976; Zanna & Cooper, 1974) do point to the existence of some form of motivational state. In a paper reporting two separate studies, Croyle and Cooper (1983) attempted to provide physiological evidence for the existence of arousal from dissonance. Undergraduate students were asked told that the university was considering banning alcohol from the campus in light of changes in the relevant state laws. All subjects had been given an attitude survey earlier in the semester, and those chosen for participation in the research had expressed initial attitudes against the ban. In a proattitudinal condition, subjects were permitted to write essays consonant with their private views. There were two counterattitudinal conditions, one of which provided the subjects with virtually no choice about whether to continue, and the other of which—the high-choice dissonance-arousal condition—provided subjects with several reminders that their continued participation was strictly up to them. The results of this first experiment showed attitude change only in the high-choice condition.

In the second experiment, different undergraduate students were connected to physiological recording equipment as part of a study of "the impact of simple mental and physical tasks on heart rate and electrical activity of the skin" (p. 786). After two filler tasks to allow the subjects time to adjust to the recording apparatus, subjects were again asked to write essays having to do with banning alcohol. Although in this second study there was not differential attitude change, writing a counterattitudinal essay under conditions of high choice did produce the greatest physiological arousal.

The Path from Arousal to Attitude Change.   There are some obvious problems with the Croyle and Cooper (1983) studies, not the least of which is a failure to find attitude change simultaneously with physiological arousal. Nevertheless, the research does provide both important evidence and a method that others could use in the future. Part of that future is outlined in a recent summary of the current status of dissonance theory by Cooper and Fazio (1984).

Incorporating the qualifications that have become necessary since Festinger and Carlsmith's (1959) original study, Cooper and Fazio (1984) present a sequential model that includes four elements critical for attitude change from cognitive dissonance. The first of these is *consequences*. The person's behavior must produce consequences that the individual considers aversive. Nonaversive or trivial inconsistencies will not be sufficient to lead to dissonance. The second element is personal *responsibility*. If the actor comes to believe that he or she could not have foreseen the aversive consequences, or is not responsible for their occurrence (i.e., by virtue of having had no choice in the action), then no dissonance will result. This requirement for personal responsibility is, of course, the dissonance theory response to much of the early incentive theory research.

If responsibility is accepted for the aversive consequences, then the third element will be *dissonance arousal*. The generalized arousal produced at this stage must be correctly identified. If it is considered positive rather than negative, or if it is attributed to an external source, then there will be little in the way of what Cooper and Fazio (1984) call *dissonance motivation*. That motivation, based on arousal tied to acceptance of personal responsibility for aversive consequences, is what finally produces the *outcomes*. These may include either a weakening of the link between responsibility acceptance and dissonance arousal, or attitude change. The third and fourth element show the substantial impact that the attributional approach (which began with self-perception theory) has had on the conceptualization of dissonance.

It should be emphasized that the controversy between dissonance theory, incentive theory, and self-perception theory is important not so much because one of the explanations is "correct" whereas the other two are "in error." Rather, the controversy is extremely valuable as an example of the development of method and theory in social psychology, or, for that matter, in any scientific discipline. What begins as a simple statement (that is, dissonance will be produced whenever one cognitive element implies the opposite of another) becomes, through continuous refinement, a more complex but more accurate statement (dissonance will be created whenever a person can be made to feel personally responsible for having chosen actions that are counter to his or her existing opinions). Along the way, new methods are developed (evaluation apprehension reduction techniques, interpersonal simulations, more widespread use of balanced replications), new pitfalls are discovered, and new areas of research grow out of attempts to resolve theoretical controversy. Perhaps the greatest compliment that can be paid to the theory of cognitive dissonance is the recognition of its extensive role in this continuing process.

SUMMARY

Traditionally, an attitude is regarded as consisting of a cognitive component, an affective component, and a behavioral component. Major attitude organization theories can be grouped into two general classes, those dealing with the logical structure of the attitude, and those concentrating on the maintenance of consistency among aspects of this structure. Among the former **probabilogical** models (p. 154) are ones that conceive of an attitude as the conclusion of a syllogism (p. 156), and ones that consider the attitude to be the sum of a set of beliefs, with each belief weighted by an evaluation (p. 160). The syllogistic models indicate that attitudes have both a **horizontal structure** (p. 158) and a **vertical structure** (p. 158), and these structural characteristics have implications for the difficulty of producing attitude change. The information-processing view of an attitude combines **belief strength** (p. 161) with evaluations to produce attitudes, which generalized predispositions, in turn, produce **behavioral intentions** (p. 161) that lead to action.

Among the cognitive consistency theories of attitude organization, **balance theory** (p. 165) was originally developed to apply to *inter*personal relationships, but can be used to describe intrapersonal phenomena as well. The cognitive elements involved in the theory can be associated with each other in either or both of two ways: the *relations* of liking (p. 165), and **unit formation** (p. 165). Whether the relationship is a dyadic or a triadic one, balance is determined by a *multiplicative rule*: the positive or negative signs of all relations involved in any system are multiplied together, and if the sign of the product is positive the system is balanced (p. 166). The **congruity theory** (p. 171) can be regarded as a special case of balance theory, in which cognitive elements consisting of *sources* and *objects* (p. 171) are joined together either in **associative bonds** (p. 172) or **dissociative bonds** (p. 172). The only determinant of incongruity is *discrepancy in scale position*, so the resolution of this inconsistency will involve *proportional change* (p. 173) by each element.

Cognitive dissonance theory (p. 174) is a strictly interpersonal consistency theory, the elements of which are *propositions* reflecting a person's view of the social world and his or her own behavior. These propositions can be *consonant, dissonant* (p. 177), or *irrelevant* to one another. The *magnitude* (p. 178) of dissonance will increase as the number and importance of dissonant cognitions increases. Dissonance research has frequently employed **forced compliance** (p. 176) to induce subjects to make **counterattitudinal** public statements (p. 176), and these are presumed to produce an internal, unpleasant state of dissonance that needs to be *reduced* (p. 178). Dissonance theory has been involved in a theoretical controversy with **incentive theory** (p. 180), and **self-perception theory** (p. 181), both of which provide alternative explanations for many of the results obtained in dissonance research. This controversy has contributed to methodological advances that transcend the attitude area, and to theoretical refinements.

SUGGESTED ADDITIONAL READINGS

McGuire, W. J. (1985). Attitudes and attitude change. In G. Lindzey & E. Aronson (Eds.), *Handbook of social psychology* (3rd ed., Vol. 2, pp. 233–346). New York: Random House. This comprehensive recent view of the area of attitude organization and change discusses numerous models of the structure of attitudes, and proposes a guiding model for categorizing processes of attitude change. Very technical reading for beginners.

Petty, R. E., & Cacioppo, J. T. (1981). *Attitudes and persuasion: Classic and contemporary approaches.* Dubuque, IA: W. C. Brown. This review considers several different approaches to the study of attitude organization and change, including conditioning, message-learning, judgmental, motivational, attributional, and self-persuasion approaches. Written for undergraduates who may already have had a course in social psychology, this book is less difficult than the McGuire chapter, but still contains detailed descriptions of all the important models. An excellent introduction to the wide range of attitude theories.

CHAPTER SIX

PERSUASION
AND
ATTITUDE CHANGE

CONTENTS

PREVIEW

Although a variety of situational variables can diminish the relationship between a person's attitudes and his or her behavior, that relationship is still strong enough to warrant the attention devoted in social psychology to attitude measurement and the study of persuasion. The fact that prejudice and discrimination still exist in contemporary society indicates just how difficult some attitudes are to alter. A persuasive attempt can be regarded as including a source, a message, a recipient, and in examining the consequences of persuasion it is important to distinguish between public compliance and private acceptance. Sources of resistance to attitude change include the complexity of the structure of the target attitude, the functions that holding particular attitudes may serve, and discrepancy between the individual's existing attitude and the persuasive communication. Attitude change can be facilitated by communicator credibility and other characteristics of the persuasive appeal, and by the active participation of the target person in the process of change. Attempts to alter attitudes, whether in the laboratory or in the real social world, involve ethical issues to which social psychologists should attend.

Think for a moment of all the money spent in a year in the attempt to measure and change attitudes. Politicians take extensive opinion polls on controversial issues; corporations spend millions of dollars on market research and advertising; even in your everyday dealings with other people you try to determine what your friends think about matters that are important to you. What justifies all this interest? The belief that attitudes are related to behavior, and that changes in attitudes will lead to changes in actions. The politician wants to know how your judgment of his or her record will translate into contributions and votes. The corporation hopes that establishing a positive image for its products will increase sales. And if your friends hold you in high esteem, they will treat you well. Although the correlation between attitude and action is less than perfect, it is still strong enough to justify much of the effort devoted to the study of persuasion.

In addition to the presumed influence of attitudes on behavior, there is another reason that the study of attitude change has played an important role in social psychology. Throughout the history of the discipline social psychologists have been interested in solving social problems, and in this area, too, attitude change can be a precursor of behavior change. You will remember from chapter 1 that one of the early tests of Lewin's field theory involved changing people's attitudes about serving beef hearts, sweetbreads, and kidneys in order to conserve meat for the American troops involved in World War II. This social issue, and more contemporary topics such as energy conservation, aid for victims of crime, or nuclear disarmament, provide researchers with the opportunity to test their theories on topics that are highly involving to their subjects. Conducting such tests can contribute to the solution of the problem, at the same time that it tests the generality of the sophisticated models of attitude organization that are usually developed from research on less emotional issues. One such problem that has received a great deal of attention from social psychology is the attitude of racial bias. For this reason, and also because it illustrates some of the difficulties inherent in attempts at persuasion, a description of that attitude serves as a backdrop for the general discussion of attitude change.

THE ATTITUDE OF RACISM

Definitions of Racial Bias

Racial bias is usually referred to in any of several ways—as discrimination, stereotyping, prejudice, or racism—and it is important to distinguish among these terms. *Stereotyping* is the word traditionally used to describe the cognitive component of an attitude of racial bias, and some of the antecedents of this faulty cognitive processing were discussed in chapter 4. *Discrimination* is the traditional label for racially motivated behavior by an individual or group, and I use this term in the same way.

Problems in designation arise, however, in the search for a term to describe the affective component of racial bias, as well as for the attitude as a whole. Social psychologists have traditionally used the word *prejudice* to represent the entire attitude (e.g., Allport, 1954/1958), but for several reasons the term *racism* may be preferable. First, as Jones (1972) points out, "Few people would call someone who commented that a talented black individual is 'a credit to his race' a prejudiced person. Yet most black people consider that comment insulting rather than complimentary, and view its speaker as racist. The comment seems to be based on the assumption that the talented person is unusual among his race—unusual in the sense that he is talented" (p. 72). In short, *racism* is, psychologically, more inclusive term than is *prejudice*, and the overall attitude ought to be described in terms that are as inclusive as possible. Second, racism generalizes to the actions of groups and organizations much more appropriately than does prejudice. The latter is usually defined to include a strongly negative emotional reaction toward the target group (Allport, 1958; Jones, 1972), and it is difficult to characterize an organization as "emotional." Particularly where an official government policy is involved, such as South Africa's apartheid, is concerned, "prejudice" does not capture the essence of the policy. Finally, *racism* as a descriptive term has become the model for terms describing biased attitudes toward other groups ("sexism," and "ageism" are examples). For these reasons I use *racism* to refer to the overall attitude of racial bias, and the term *prejudice* to describe the affective component of that attitude.

Prejudice

The Presence of Emotion.   The research on stereotyping (Gilbert, 1951; Karlins, Coffman, & Walters, 1969; Katz & Braly, 1933) that was reported in chapter 4 suggested that there has been some fading of racial stereotypes during the last 30 years. Nevertheless, there are still many individuals who show stereotyping, and this often is accompanied by strong emotional reactions of prejudice. Some of these feelings have been identified by Harding, Kutner, Proshansky, and Chein (1969): "On the positive side they include such feelings as admiration, sympathy, and 'closeness' or identification; on the negative side they include contempt, fear, envy, and 'distance' or alienation" (p. 4).

The extremes that are possible in these feelings can be illustrated by excerpts from an interview that was part of an extensive project to assess white and black attitudes (Campbell, 1971). The largest single study in this project was a survey of 2,945 white and 2,814 black residents of 15 major American cities. The survey was conducted in early 1968, and many of its questions dealt with the riots that occurred in several inner-city ghettos during the summers of 1966 and 1967. As one way of summarizing the contrasts present in the attitudes of white people toward these disturbances (and toward black people in general), Campbell presented the verbatim answers of two respondents to several of the interview questions. One of these sets of answers is reproduced here, and it indicates quite dramatically the intense emotions that can accompany racial bias.

What do you think was the main cause of these disturbances?

"Nigger agitators. Martin Luther King and Rap Brown, and that black bastard [Stokely] Carmichael."

Have the disturbances helped or hurt the cause of Negro rights?

"Hurt. Whites are starting to wise up what a danger these people can be. They are going to be tough from now on. People are fed up with giving in and giving them everything their little black hearts want."

What do you think the city government could do to keep a disturbance from breaking out here?

"Ship them all back to Africa. Lock up all the agitators and show them we mean business."*

---

*(From Campbell, A. (1971). *White attitudes toward black people*, Ann Arbor, MI: Institute for Social Research. Used with permission of the publisher.)

Emotional Response in the Laboratory. Admittedly, this person's responses were chosen by Campbell to represent an extreme viewpoint, and even though in recent years there has been a movement away from racial tolerance, it is doubtful that many people would express their emotional reactions quite this directly to an interviewer. There is, however, a strong emotional component of prejudice, as indicated in laboratory studies comparing the physiological reactions to black people that are exhibited by racially biased and unbiased subjects. The general method can be illustrated by the work of Porier and Lott (1967).

Because describing an experiment as a study of "prejudice" would heighten still further the social constraints against expressing bias, this study was explained to subjects (white male undergraduates at a border-state university) as an investigation of emotional reactions to various stimulus words. When each subject arrived at the laboratory for testing, he was met by a white experimenter who told him about the study and then attached a set of recording electrodes to each of the subject's hands. The subject was led to believe that both sets of electrodes measured the galvanic skin response (GSR), an index of emotionality that involves sending a minute electric current along the surface of the skin. When there is moisture on the palm (sweating palms indicate emotional arousal), this current travels with less resistance than when the palm is dry.

One set of electrodes was, in fact, the GSR apparatus described, but the other set was not connected to the recording equipment, and had been placed on the subject's arm only so that at various points in the procedure an assistant could "adjust" it. For half of the adjustments for each subject the assistant was white, but for the other half of the adjustments the assistant was black.

Whether the measure is used to assess racial bias or to determine whether someone is "telling the truth," physiological measuring devices such as the GSR and the polygraph are likely to create some of the emotional response that they then measure. When the doctor takes your blood pressure in the campus infirmary, the readings are likely to be elevated from your "normal" pressure just because of the surroundings, and because you are anxious about what the doctor is likely to tell you. To try to correct for this kind of problem, Porier and Lott (1967) constructed a measure of the relative emotionality produced by the two kinds of "assistants." This measure of relative emotionality, called the *GSR bias*, was obtained by subtracting each subject's GSR scores in the presence of white assistants from the same subject's scores in the presence of black assistants. Obviously, on this measure, a positive score indicates greater emotionality in the presence of black assistants.

The results of the study showed greater emotionality (positive GSR bias) for only 32 of the 60 subjects, approximating the 50–50 split that would be expected by chance. Like much of the stereotyping research reported in chapter 4, this finding by itself suggests that there may have been a lessening of racial prejudice. Even in the absence of overall GSR bias, however, there was a much greater positive bias on the part of those subjects who had received high scores on a previously administered test of racial prejudice. Thus, although there was no appreciable difference across all of the subjects, emotional reactions to the procedure clearly occurred on the part of highly prejudiced individuals.

Socialization and Emotional Reactions.   Both the interview excerpts from survey research and the studies of physiological arousal indicate that there is a strong emotional component to the attitude of racism. What might be the sources of these negative emotions? The first contributing factor might be the socialization experiences of the prejudiced person. In an extended discussion of the process of socialization, Jones and Gerard (1967) distinguish between **effect dependence**, the fact that nearly all the child's rewards and punishments are mediated by the parents, and **information dependence**, the fact that a child's knowledge about the social world is derived largely from the information provided by the parents.

Both sorts of dependence can be involved in the development of prejudice. For the first few years of your life – typically until you enter school – nearly all of your rewards and punishments are controlled by your parents. It is, of course, not necessary that parents employ direct physical punishment in order to teach racial bias, any more than it is necessary for them to employ physical punishment to teach you to stop chasing the cat. Saying that it is "not nice" to play with children of another race may be just as effective. Not only do parents have control over the outcomes their young children obtain, they are, in addition, the principal source of social information. This control, like the direct provision of rewards and punishments, is virtually exclusive during the first two or three years of life, but then other socializing influences (preschools, television, peers) enter the picture.

It is important to remember, however, that parents have substantial control over which other influences are present. Does the child attend a preschool that is integrated, or one that is not? Are the television programs the children are permitted to watch sensitive to the issue of race ("Sesame Street," "The Electric Company"), or are they all white ("Batman," "Superman")? Are friendships with children from other racial and ethnic groups encouraged or discouraged? Not until a child enters the public schools does a parent's control over the available social information diminish appreciably, and even then the parent remains one of the major sources. Given this background, it is not surprising that a majority of college students in one study (Allport & Kramer, 1946) reported that their racial attitudes were influenced by the attitudes of their parents, and that the racial attitudes of adults differ according to region of birth (Campbell, 1971), with attitudes toward blacks becoming more favorable from the South, through Middle Atlantic, Midwest, and New England, to the West.

Competition and Frustration. Although information dependence, effect dependence, and socialization processes could certainly influence beliefs about ethnic minorities, they do not seem powerful enough to account for the even stronger emotions that are all too often expressed "I don't think we have anything in common" is not at all the same as "Lock them up to show we mean business." Although there is virtually no experimental evidence to support their claims, a number of social psychologists (Allport, 1954; Harding et al., 1969; Pettigrew, 1971) give frustration the primary role.

The original **frustration-aggression hypothesis** was advanced by Dollard, Doob, Miller, Mowrer, and Sears (1939). It maintained that all aggression is the product of frustration, and that frustration inevitably causes aggression. As we see in chapter 10, this relatively unsophisticated view of aggression has undergone substantial modification. But the essential principle remains intact: Aggression is the product of events in the situation, and not the result of any inherent aggressive instincts (see Freud, 1933; Lorenz, 1966, for the alternative viewpoint). Applied to racial violence, such as lynching, the argument goes like this: Life in America has always carried with it some frustration – in interpersonal relations between lovers or spouses, in relations between employers and their bosses, in the virtual certainty that few people's achievements will live up to the goals set by the American Dream. All of this frustration cries out for release through aggression, as evidenced by our everyday language ("control yourself," "don't take it out on me"), our love of institutionalized violence (everything from football, wrestling, and roller derby to the size of the military establishment), and our nostalgia about the "good old days, when the only law was a fast gun." But, ironically, this pent-up aggression usually cannot be directed at the source of the frustration.

Differential Power and Deserving Victims. Inherent in the idea of frustration is the notion of a power differential between the frustrating agent and the person being frustrated. You can't ordinarily tell your boss "where to go," no matter how much you might like to. If you push far enough, your lover will leave you; your spouse will sue for divorce. But no matter how far short of the American Dream you fall, you cannot stop advertisers from trying to sell you still more. What must happen? Your aggression will typically be *displaced* onto a convenient person or object with still less power than you have, so that no retaliation is possible. Everyone is looking for a suitable victim, and for a large number of reasons, black people have filled that role quite well (Jones, 1972).

Blacks began their history in this country as victims, and their color has made them much more readily identifiable than members of any other minority group. A great deal of the social interaction between whites and blacks has emphasized this role, from the foot-shuffling obsequious black of early Hollywood movies, right through the implicit assumption of many white liberal participants in the civil rights movement in the 1960s that the Southern rural blacks could not take care of their own problems without outside help from concerned whites. Each of these views of black people may or may not have been an accurate reflection of social reality at its time, but regardless of its accuracy, each contributed to maintenance of the belief that blacks are victims. And as potential victims, blacks are a suitable outlet for frustration.

GENERAL ISSUES IN ATTITUDE CHANGE

Affect and Complexity

Despite the attention that the attitude of racism has received from social psychologists, there is still more to be learned about its origins and effects. Regardless of whether socialization, differences in beliefs, competition, or frustration, is ultimately implicated as the principal source of prejudice, the discussion of racism makes one crucial point very clear: In the "real world" outside the experimental laboratory, social attitudes involve emotions to a much greater extent than you might think from a quick reading of the research on attitude organization. Not only are real social attitudes composed of the complex structures suggested by probabilogical and consistency models, they also serve psychological functions for the people who hold them, and this fact will make attitude change more difficult to bring about.

Real or Apparent Change?

Both the complexity and the emotional content of many attitudes toward real social objects suggest that producing true attitude change can be a very difficult task. This task is complicated by the problem of identifying such change when it does occur, that is, distinguishing true change in the internal structure of an attitude (called *private acceptance*) from mere conformity in overt behavior (called *public compliance*). The former, of course, is the desired outcome for techniques of attitude change. Let us consider a specific example.

Suppose that I am in the business of making candy bars, and that these candy bars are always sold in opaque wrappers. Even though I must print the weight of the enclosed bar on the wrapper, I have discovered that I can make every fifth bar smaller, thereby cheating some of the customers and saving myself a lot of money. Now suppose that you represent a consumer group, and by weighing my candy bars you have found out what I am doing. What will you do about it? One possibility is to threaten to bring legal action if you catch me shortchanging customers again. That would produce compliance – I would stop shortchanging as long as you were watching me – but not private acceptance (I might go right back to my old ways the moment you stopped watching). How can you lead me to private acceptance of your viewpoint?

Compliance: Agreement Only in Public. One answer is suggested by Kelman's (1961) analysis of processes of attitude change. Considering attitude change attempts in the broader perspective of social influence, Kelman argued that at least three different outcomes could be distinguished: compliance, identification, and internalization. In Kelman's terms, **compliance** is the observable change in behavior in the direction advocated by the influencing agent, and is therefore equivalent to the public compliance referred to previously. Compliance takes place as as result of threatened punishment or promised reward, and behavior so affected may revert back to its original form once the punishing or rewarding agent leaves the scene. Your threats have not changed my attitude toward my customers; all they have accomplished is to make me want to keep from getting caught.

Identification: The Role of Self-Image. In contrast to compliance, identification and internalization are both aspects of private acceptance. They differ in the motivation presumed to account for that private acceptance. **Identification** is private acceptance based on a "satisfying self-defining relationship" (Kelman, 1961, p. 63) between the target person (me) and the change agent (you). To the extent that my self-image depends on having you think of me as a respected businessman, you may be able to influence me to identify with your requests. Note that I privately accept your view not because I have considered it and think it to be morally correct, but rather because I now think of giving full portions as "good business." I have identified with your notion of what a "respected businessman" should be, and if I do not privately accept your request that I not cheat my customers, I will lose an important part of my identity. Kelman uses the process of identification to account for the formation of attitudes in children who are socialized by their parents, and for attitude change that occurs in more extreme socialization experiences as well. For example, a new recruit in the armed forces will adopt a great many attitudes held by the military establishment through identification, because his or her self-image is so dependent upon the relationship to the group.

Internalization: Congruence with Values. The other sort of private acceptance, **internalization**, is based on the target person's belief that the position advocated is "congruent with his value system" (Kelman, 1961, p. 65). Here private acceptance comes about not because of the instrumental value of the attitude, but because holding that attitude is a valuable end in itself. If I believe that it is morally and ethically correct for business people to deal with their customers in a forthright and honest way, then I will deal with my own customers according to those principles. The basis for judgment will be my own value system, not the views of of the consuming public. Although the process of internalization has quite a rational sound to it, it may not be entirely a rational process. Suppose that my own values held, for some reason, that one should cheat one's customers as much as possible. We would like to think of this as an irrational view of business practices, but any attitude consistent with this orientation would be adopted through a process of internalization. It does not matter what my customers think about the issue—I will shortchange or not depending on my own values.

In summary, compliance is superficial behavior change "because I have to," identification is private acceptance that occurs "because it is expected of me," and internalization is private acceptance "because it is right." To induce compliance in a target person, the change agent must identify the threats and rewards, limit the behavioral choices, and constantly engage in surveillance to ensure that there will be no backsliding. To induce identification, the change agent needs to make salient to the target person the role expectations for his or her behavior, and to make it attractive for the target person to live up to those expectations. Because this is an internal change, no surveillance is required as long as the role expectations remain clear and attractive. To induce internalization, the change agent must convince the target person that the behavior is value relevant, and this task will be simplest when the change agent shares the target person's value system. Again, because the change is an internal one, no surveillance is necessary (unless, of course, there is some later contrary change in the target person's value structure). Thus, real attitude change can be distinguished from apparent change by whether or not surveillance is required, and by whether or not external rewards/punishments are involved. Within the domain of private acceptance, identification and internalization can be distinguished from each other by whether the change agent's influence attempts are stated in terms, respectively, of role expectations or basic values.

The Functions of Attitudes

Attitudes toward dull and boring experimental tasks, and even those toward one position or another on a matter of current university controversy, do not have the strong affective component that is found in many naturally occurring attitudes. When the object is to change a person's attitude toward a real social object, it becomes important to consider the function that the attitude may serve for its holder. Perhaps the most comprehensive theory of the psychological functions of attitudes was developed by Katz and his associates (e.g., Katz & Kahn, 1966; Katz & Stotland, 1959).

The Instrumental Function. To begin with, people will develop positive attitudes toward people and objects that make their achievement of desired goals easier, and will develop negative attitudes toward people and objects that frustrate the achievement of those goals. This is the **instrumental function** of an attitude, and it is similar to to Kelman's (1961) idea of identification. Each formulation depends on the fact that holding the attitude has some end besides itself. If the candy-making businessman has a positive attitude toward his customers, that attitude will help increase his sales (that is, will have some instrumental value) quite apart from the ethical, moral, or value justification for being pleasant. The instrumental function is, for a privately accepted attitude, what superficial compliance is for overt behavior: Each helps the individual attain desired goals, and neither is an end in itself.

The Value-Expressive Function. Although some attitudes serve instrumental purposes, others are developed because they are consistent with, and expressive of, their broader value system. This is the **value-expressive function** of an attitude. A person who places high value on human life, compared to someone who places a lesser value on life, will be more likely to develop attitudes against capital punishment, and in favor of medical and food aid to people in underdeveloped countries. This functional category is roughly equivalent to private acceptance through Kelman's (1961) process of internalization, because its defining characteristic is congruence with the person's value system.

The Knowledge Function. People will develop attitudes that bring structure to their social worlds. This is the **knowledge function** of an attitude, and at first it sounds very much like the instrumental function. After all, "bringing structure to one's world" suggests that the attitude is not an end in itself, but rather is an objective for reaching a goal. At a very literal level this is true, but there is a critical difference. Instrumental attitudes are held for the purpose of advancing one's position with people and forces outside the self, but knowledge attitudes are held in order to reduce the cognitive work for the self. The knowledge function is, therefore, internal in a fashion that instrumental attitudes are not.

Knowledge-function attitudes simplify a person's experience, provide organizing principles, and guide information gathering on topics of importance tance to the person. This function is for the domain of attitudes what the organizing principles of social cognition are for the domain of social perceptions. Another way to describe these attitudes is to compare them to the attributions that a person makes for the causes of the actions of other people. For example, the attribution "He is an evil person" is at once a categorization of the person's actions, an implicit evaluation of those behaviors, and a good predictor of the attributor's future responses toward the actor. In the same way that the usually valuable process of social cognition may have occasional negative side effects, so the knowledge function of an attitude can place too stringent limits on behavior. Thus, stereotypes that limit actions toward members of the identified class can be thought of as part of knowledge-function attitudes.

The Ego-Defensive Function. Finally, people may develop attitudes that have the effect of shielding them from conscious recognition of their own inadequacies and failings. This is the **ego-defensive function** of an attitude. An excellent example of this function is the attitude of racism, which can have any number of ego-defensive expressions. These could include "I wouldn't have so much trouble getting a job if *they* weren't given preferential treatment," or "I don't have anything to do with them because you can't trust them to be fair with you." Ego-defensive attitudes deny or distort reality in order to protect the person holding them from having to admit some of his or her own negative characteristics.

Implications for Attitude Change

The major contribution to our understanding of attitude change that is provided by the functional approach is the specification of some of the conditions under which attitudes might change. For example, an instrumental attitude can be altered simply by changing the reinforcements (rewards or punishments) associated with holding that attitude, and a knowledge attitude can be altered by correcting misinformation about the world. A value-expressive attitude that is inconsistent with the person's value system could be changed by pointing out the inconsistency, and a consistent value-expressive attitude might be altered by rational discussion of the entire value system. But the arguments against a strongly held ego-defensive attitude are themselves likely to be misinterpreted, distorted, or denied. It is unlikely that we can reduce people's racism by convincing them that the problem is really their own inadequacy, so instead of dealing only with the attitude, we must try to deal with the circumstances that have produced the inadequacy in the first place.

In short, the functional theory of attitudes suggests that before we can accurately predict the difficulty of changing a particular attitude, we must know the function the attitude serves for the individual. This is, as we have seen, an intuitively pleasing formulation. But well articulated measures of the various functions do not exist, and the research based on the approach has not produced clear-cut findings. Indeed, it would be very difficult to identify people whose attitudes serve ego-defensive functions, because the more successfully the attitudes work, the less defensive the person will appear on the surface. Despite these difficulties, the functional theory of attitudes can suggest some of the reasons for resistance to attitude change.

The Structure of Persuasive Communication

To this point we have been concentrating on the characteristics of the target of a persuasive attempt–noting that many attitudes contain strong emotional components, suggesting that there may be three general outcomes of a persuasive attempt, and discovering that which psychological function is served by an attitude may affect the likelihood of change. The target person is obviously an important part of persuasive communication, but he or she is not the only part. The classical analysis of persuasion outlined by Lasswell (1948), and recently extended by McGuire (1985), incorporates other crucial parts as well, and is shown in Fig. 6.1. As the diagram indicates, the elements of a persuasive communication include the *source, message, channel, receiver,* and *target*. Each of these is illustrated using the example of your attempt to get me to return to putting a full portion in all of my candy bars. You are the source of the persuasive communication, the message of which is a request to me to return to making all the bars the weight they are supposed to be. Your communication in this example takes the form of a petition, although other alternatives (such as the threat of legal action) are obvious alternatives. I am the receiver of this message, but the specific target of the message is that behavior of mine that you wish to influence.

Mediating and Dependent Variables

In his version of the model of communication structure, McGuire (1985) argued that the five elements of the communication could be considered independent variables (Chapter 1), things that an experimenter (or a communicator) might vary in order to make as persuasive a case as possible. For example, in terms of the congruity theory discussed in chapter 5, a more polarized positive source would have a greater positive effect on the resulting evaluation of an object than would a less polarized positive source.

FIGURE 6.1 Components of the structure of a communication. Adapted from McGuire, W. J. (1985). Attitudes and attitude change. In G. Lindzey & E. Aronson (Eds.), *Handbook of social psychology* (3rd ed., Vol. 2, pp. 233–346). New York: Random House. (Diagram in his article is Table 1 on page 259. Reprinted by permission.)

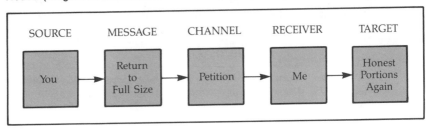

As another example, if the ultimate target is change in an attitude held for ego-defensive reasons, then the message ought to be couched in terms that will help bolster the receiver's self-esteem, and the channel should be as private as possible, so as not to keep the receiver's personal stake in consistency as low as it can be.

But as the functional theory of attitudes, and the distinctions among compliance, identification, and internalization suggest, the very same independent variable may have different effects, depending on the nature of the beliefs, opinions, or evaluations that are attacked in the persuasive communication. To take the various dependent variables into account, McGuire (1985) identified 12 mediating processes and dependent variables that also ought to be considered in the general model of persuasion. These are shown in Table 6.1, and I have grouped them into four categories that help to summarize what is thought to occur at the time of each mediating step. There are, as McGuire (1985) points out, numerous mediators between the production of a persuasive communication by the source and the performance by the recipient of behavior that indicates that change in attitude has occurred. The ones presented here comprise a reasonably exhaustive list, but not the only possible such list.

Before you can attempt to change a person's attitude, you have to have his or her attention, so the first two steps outlined by McGuire (1985) involve exposing the recipient to the communication and attempting to make certain that the person attends to what is being said or done. But attention alone is not sufficient to produce attitude change. The recipient must process the communication, which processing specifically includes the development of liking for the message, the comprehension of the message, the generation of cognitions related to the message, the acquisition of whatever skills are needed to accomplish the change, and finally agreeing with the communication (this is capitalized in the Table, because it is the single step that represents attitude change as we have described it previously. The memory step is testimony to the fact that few changed attitudes can be translated into altered behavior immediately. Rather, there must be some storing of the changed attitude, and then retrieval of that

TABLE 6.1 Mediating and Dependent Variables in Persuasion

ATTENTION	PROCESSING	MEMORY	ACTION
1. Exposure	3. Liking	8. Storing	10. Decision making
2. Attention	4. Comprehension	9. Retrieval	11. Action
	5. Related thought		12. Consolidation
	6. Acquiring skills		
	7. AGREEING		

Note: Adapted from McGuire, W. J. (1985). Attitudes and attitude change. In G. Lindzey & E. Aronson (Eds.), *Handbook of social psychology* (3rd ed., Vol. 2, pp. 233–346). New York: Random House. (Diagram in his article is Table 1 on page 259. Reprinted by permission.)

changed material when it is appropriate. The object of changing attitudes is, as noted earlier, to change behavior, so the last three steps are making decisions that agree with the changed attitude, acting according to those decisions, and consolidating that new behavior into one's self-image and attitude structure.

Not all of these steps apply to every persuasive attempt, nor is the order invariant across attempts. Let us return to the example of my candy making one last time. Certainly you do need to expose me to your communication, you need to get me to pay attention, I need to understand what you want me to do, and I need to act accordingly. In short, only steps 1, 2, 4, 10, and 11 are absolutely critical for compliance in Kelman's (1961) sense. I do not need to like what you say, to generate any related cognitions, to acquire any skills, or to undergo some form of internal attitude change. If we're talking about compliance, then your surveillance will remind me to "do what's right," so no storage or retrieval is needed, and because all you have achieved is compliance, there will be no consolidation. Alternatively, if what you achieve is internalization, rather than compliance, all of the steps (with the possible exception in this example of #6 – I already have the requisite skills) will be necessary.

Attitudes are organized predispositions to behave in a favorable or unfavorable manner toward a specified social object, and many naturally occurring attitudes carry with them an emotional component that makes changing them quite difficult. Even attitudes without strong emotional overtones can be hard to alter if the nature of the persuasive appeal is out of keeping with the function that the attitude serves for the person who holds it. Not only must that function be considered, but also the elements of the actual process of persuasion (both the independent variables of source, message, channel, recipient, and target, and the various mediating and dependent variables) need to be taken into account by students of attitude change and by those who construct persuasive appeals. we will need to keep these things in mind as we consider the sources of resistance to, and facilitation of, attitude change.

SOURCES OF RESISTANCE TO ATTITUDE CHANGE

Resistance Arising from Discrepancy

Most of the resistance to persuasive communications, and thereby to attitude change, occurs within the set of mediating variables having to do with processing of the information, most specifically with related thought. The whole idea behind any of the consistency theories discussed in chapter 5 is, of course, that the related – and inconsistent – cognitions will produce attitude change. There, however, pressure toward change arises because the inconsistent behavioral element cannot simply be dismissed or disregarded. But presenting a person with a persuasive communication is not the same as actually getting that person to engage in a counterattitudinal action. A persuasive attempt can be rejected or ignored, in part depending on the relationship between the message and the person's existing attitude structure, and that process embodies the first source of resistance to be considered here—discrepancy between the message and the person's existing position on the issue.

For example, suppose that you are a social science major and are asked to participate in a debate with two other students, one a humanities major and one a natural science major. Each of you is trying to persuade the audience that his or her approach should be adopted by everyone, and that the other two areas of inquiry should be discarded altogether. It is reasonable to expect that the members of the audience will be relatively committed to their own positions, but it is possible that the way in which you state your case might have some bearing on the outcome of the debate. The winner is decided by a vote of the audience, so in order to win, you need to hold all your social science majors in line, while changing the opinions of a number of other people. You are in the fortunate position of having more in common with each of the other areas than they have with each other. Should you try to convert a few from each other area, or should you aim your message at one group alone?

The answer depends on the discrepancy between the position you advocate and the original position of the hearers. If you assert that "Chemistry is nonsense," you may win friends among the humanities majors, but you will make some confirmed enemies among the natural science students, and you may even lose the support of the biologically oriented psychologists. The ways in which people react to attitude statements such as this one can be described in terms of the **social judgment theory** of attitude change first elaborated by Sherif and Hovland (1961). The essential principle of social judgment theory is that an individual's own position on an issue will influence his or her perception of attitude statements about that issue. This fundamental assumption can be seen in a wide variety of social judgment theories (e.g., Eiser & Stroebe, 1972; Upshaw, 1969), but we concentrate on the version proposed by Sherif and Hovland (1961).

Latitudes of Acceptance, Rejection, and Noncommitment. As an example, imagine a scale of attitudes toward a specific natural science (chemistry) that runs from one extreme (highly favorable) to the other (highly unfavorable). Both the "own positions" of members of your audience and the scale values of possible persuasive messages could be located on this dimension. A senior chemistry major planning graduate work in the discipline should have a very favorable "own position," a student planning graduate work in biology might be expected to have a moderate position "own position" on chemistry, and a student who almost didn't get into graduate school in English because he or she had flunked chemistry would have a highly unfavorable "own position." Just as members of the audience can be located on the scale, so can the possible messages you might use in an attempt to persuade people to your position.

Social judgment theory proposes that an individual's evaluation of a message will depend on the discrepancy between the recipient's own position and the scale position of the message. The idea is represented in three zones or *latitudes* thought to surround an individual's own position. These are (a) the **latitude of acceptance**, which encloses all the messages that might be accepted by the recipient, even though they do not coincide exactly with his or her own position, (b) the **latitude of rejection**, which encloses all of the messages that will be rejected out of hand, and (c) the **latitude of noncommitment**, which encloses all the remaining possible messages. Examples of these latitudes are shown in Fig. 6.2 for an ardent chemistry major (whose own position is F), and for a biology major (whose own position is D). The latitudes shown have all been set arbitrarily, to illu-

FIGURE 6.2 Assimilation and contrast in acceptance of persuasive communications.

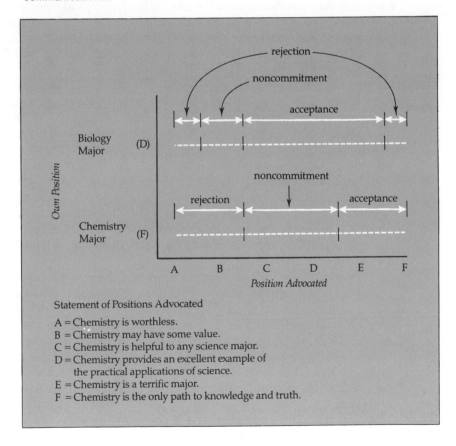

Statement of Positions Advocated

A = Chemistry is worthless.
B = Chemistry may have some value.
C = Chemistry is helpful to any science major.
D = Chemistry provides an excellent example of
    the practical applications of science.
E = Chemistry is a terrific major.
F = Chemistry is the only path to knowledge and truth.

strate that they may differ for different people. In practice, however, the latitudes can be established empirically, by having an individual accept or reject each of a series of statements that cover the entire range of the scale.

Consider first the judgments of the ardent chemistry major. She really believes that chemistry is the only path to knowledge and truth (F), but can also accept the idea that chemistry may be just a terrific major field (E). She is not terribly concerned about whether chemical research produces practical benefits (D), and hasn't thought too much about the field's potential for other science majors (C), so these messages fall into her latitude of noncommitment. She must, of course, reject the notion that chemistry has "some value" (B), because that statement would be perceived as suggesting that there were instances in which it would have no value, and she must also reject the assertion that chemistry is worthless (A).

The biology major takes the position that chemistry has significant practical applications (D), and can also accept either the idea that chemistry can be a terrific major (E) or the argument that it is useful for any science major (C). He has no particular commitment about the assertion that chemistry may have some value (he thinks that it does, and is not sensitive to the other interpretation of the statement). But he cannot accept either the notion that chemistry is worthless (A) or the claim that it is the only true path to knowledge (F). Thus, each student's opinion of the statements in this series will depend on his or her own position.

Assimilation, Contrast, and the Perception of Discrepancy. Social judgment theory was originally derived from classical psychophysical methods, in which subjects are to give psychologically based descriptions of various physical stimuli. For example, suppose that you are asked to estimate the heaviness of a series of lifted weights by comparing each weight in the series to a *standard*, or anchor, weight. Your judgments of the heaviness of all of the weights will be affected by the weight of the standard. Weights that are close to the standard will be *assimilated* to its value (judged closer than they really are), whereas weights that are distant from the standard will be *contrasted* with its value (judged to be even farther away than they are).

In attitude issues, as opposed to psychophysical judgments, the standard is your initial position on the issue. Messages that are close to your own position (that is, messages that fall into your latitude of acceptance) will be assimilated to your view. Consequently, the assimilated messages will produce only the slightest attitude change, because you mistakenly believe that they are only alternative ways to state your position. Messages that fall in your latitude of rejection will be contrasted with your view, and will be seen as further away from your position than they really are. Contrasted messages will exert no pressure toward attitude change. Messages that fall into your latitude of noncommitment are the only ones that have any chance of producing significant attitude change. So, to return to the example of the debate, social judgment theory would have you direct your comments toward those humanities majors and natural science majors who have some interest in social science, in an attempt to change a few minds in each category without losing any of your own following.

Notice that when the discrepant cognitive element is a persuasive message directed at you by a communicator, your response is to ignore the substance of the communication. This response is obviously quite different from what happens when the discrepant cognitive element is one of your own behaviors (produced through forced compliance). Those discrepant actions, as we saw in chapter 5, do produce attitude change, either by creating dissonance that must be resolved, or by causing you to re-evaluate your self-conception.

Personal Reference Scales. Although there is a body of research that generally supports the social judgment theory view of persuasive communication, the approach is not without its critics. Perhaps the most important objection raised is that people who have extreme positions on any attitude topic are also very likely to be more personally involved in the subject than are people who have moderate positions with large latitudes of noncommitment. To recall material from chapters 3 and 4, our social world is organized by a variety of cognitive categories and schemata. When we approach an unfamiliar person, or an unfamiliar attitude issue, our categorization of the person or issue is a simple one. As we become more familiar with the person, or as we learn the nuances of the issue, our cognitive category becomes more *differentiated*—we see finer shades of personality or meaning. Thus increased involvement with an attitude issue may change the nature of the scale used to make the judgments.

Suppose, for example, that you were interested in having two people rate a candidate for public office. You might state the candidate's party affiliation, and then describe his or her position on one major issue, such as the budget deficit. Then you would ask the subject to say whether the candidate was a conservative Republican, a moderate Republican, a liberal Republican, a conservative Democrat, a moderate Democrat, or a liberal Democrat. Further assume that one of your subjects was very heavily involved in politics, but the other was only an occasional (and straight-ticket) voter. For the politically involved person, able to distinguish among candidates by their stands on a variety of issues, you have provided neither enough information nor enough response categories. What is the candidate's position on defense spending? On a constitutional amendment to ban abortion? On federal aid to victims of crime? On the control of access to handguns? The politically involved individual would like to know answers to these questions before making a rating, and would be unhappy trying to fit his or her answer into the six categories you have provided. But for the straight-ticket voter, the candidate would fall into one of two categories with no loss of meaning. A Republican is a Republican and a Democrat is a Democrat; the shadings of position within party would be lost on such a person. It is important to note that not only do these individualized judgment scales (called **personal reference scales** by Upshaw, 1969) of the two subjects differ from one another, they also differ from the six response categories you have provided. So the rating of the candidate that you actually obtain may show either a contrast effect or an assimilation effect only because of a difference in personal reference scales between the two subjects.

Unlimited Response Languages. In one approach to increasing the precision of predictions derived from social judgment theory, Upshaw (1969) reported a series of experiments to demonstrate how an individual's personal reference scale can be measured using an **unlimited response language**. For example, Upshaw asked subjects to indicate their moral outrage at a number of criminal offenses by placing into a small bucket an amount of sand equivalent to their degree of censure. The sand was then weighed to obtain a measure of censure independent of any pre-existing cognitive categories. Inclusion of involvement as a separate factor in social judgment, and the use of unlimited response languages, have permitted better tests of the social judgment theory's predictions about the relationship between the discrepancy of a message and its persuasive impact. Particularly when involvement is also considered, the greatest attitude change does seem to follow communications of moderate discrepancy (Sherif & Sherif, 1969). One review of the social judgment literature (Eiser & Stroebe, 1972) concluded that on balance there was substantial support for the notion that an individual's own position and involvement will affect his or her perception of a persuasive communication, and a later review (Petty & Cacioppo, 1981), although noting some difficulties with the theory, nevertheless describes it as an ambitious attempt to account for some central phenomena in attitude change.

Resistance Arising from Restrictions on Freedom

Resistance to persuasive communications that arises from assimilation-contrast depends on the discrepancy between one's own position and the one advocated in the communication. Surprisingly, resistance to persuasion may also occur when the position advocated is identical to the recipient's initial position, and this resistance will be engendered by the forcefulness of the persuasive appeal. Suppose, for example, that you are planning to spend your spring break from classes at one of the popular Florida resorts. That is your initial position on the issue, and is the choice you would make if I said nothing to you, or even if I said "Do you want to go to Florida for spring break?" But what if I said, "This year you have absolutely no choice. You *must* go to Florida for spring break." You might then reply, "Nuts to you—I am going skiing in Utah instead!"

Psychological Reactance. What is happening here? In one sense I am just strongly advocating a position that you already hold, so you should simply agree with me. But in another sense, I am suggesting that the decision is not really yours to make, but that you are required to do what I want you to do. This threatened reduction in your freedom to make your own decisions is the essential element in what Brehm (1966) has called **psychological reactance**. Reactance is a negative motivational state (presumed to be unpleasant) specifically directed toward restoring a lost decision freedom. In our example, I have not attacked your attitude position (indeed, I have agreed with it), but I have severely restricted your freedom to make whatever choice of vacation spot you might want to make. The only way you can restore your threatened freedom is to change away from the position I have advocated, even though that is cutting off your nose to spite your face. Reactance theory argues that you cannot afford to let me continue to think that I can make all of your choices for you.

The Magnitude of Reactance. The amount of psychological reactance produced by a threat to your freedom to choose will depend on the number of freedoms threatened (greater reactance accompanies threat to more freedoms), on the future implications of the threat (greater reactance occurs when the threat carries with it the promise of future threats to come), and on the source of the threat (greater reactance against a personal, as opposed to impersonal, threat). Thus the greatest reactance should be produced by a personal restriction of many freedoms that implies that similar restrictions will be forthcoming in the future.

But even with impersonal and immediate restrictions, some reactance is likely. Suppose that you approach a vending machine on a hot day and stand there for a moment trying to decide whether to choose a sugar-free soft drink (your normal favorite) or a soft drink with sugar added to it. You finally decide to try something different, insert your money, and press the button. Then a little light comes on that tells you "Make another selection, please," forcing you to choose your normally preferred drink. Do you hit the machine for restricting your freedom to choose as you wish? Whether you do so or not, you will surely feel frustration.

Restriction of Freedom or Frustration? Not only does this example illustrate some basic reactance principles, it also suggests one of the problems with testing for reactance in the experimental laboratory. One description of the vending machine's "behavior" is that it has restricted your freedom of choice. Unfortunately, there is another description: it has frustrated your goal-directed actions. And, as theorists from Dollard, Doob, Miller, Mowrer, and Sears (1939) onward have suggested, frustration can lead to aggression. So one of the problems in reactance research has been to design experimental settings that would induce reactance without also producing frustration in the subjects.

One of the early studies testing reactance theory predictions for attitude change was conducted by Sensenig and Brehm (1968). In this experiment, reactance was produced by implied (rather than explicit) threats to freedom, and a number of additional measures were collected to rule out the alternative explanation in terms of frustration. Subjects were asked to indicate their attitudes on a number of issues, and then were told that they would be asked to write essays supporting one side or another for five of these attitude issues. The female subjects were run in pairs, and each member of the pair was led to believe that (a) the other person would make the choices for both of them as to which side of the issue to support, and (b) her own preferences would be taken into account before the decision was made.

In a Low Implied Threat condition, the subjects were informed that the other person would make the choice only on the first one of the five issues, whereas in a High Implied Threat condition the other person was to make all five choices. In both of these conditions, reactance was induced by a note delivered to the subject (ostensibly coming from the other subject) that said "I've decided that we will both agree [disagree] with [the attitude issue in question]." This note was prepared by the experimenter, and it agreed with the subject's initial position on the one (or five) attitude issues. Yet it appeared to come from the other woman (who could not be expected to know the subject's position), so it seemed to make the decision without taking into account the subject's preferences. Before writing her first essay, each subject was asked to indicate her actual feelings on the issue (the first issue was always the question of federal aid to private colleges), and this indication of "actual feeling" could then be compared to the subject's previously measured position on the issue. The experimental procedure concluded with the collection of this dependent variable, so in neither of the conditions were any essays written.

Superficially, the reactance-induction note does not seem like a very important restriction of freedom—especially when that restriction is confined to the first essay to be written. The results confirmed this impression, showing no difference between the Low Implied Threat condition and a Control condition in which the subject's preferences had actually been taken into account. There was, however, a significant difference between the High Implied Threat condition and these other two conditions, with subjects in the High Threat condition changing their expressed opinions about the issue of federal aid to private colleges away from their original views.

Reactance Makes Directional Predictions. In the case of this experiment, as opposed to the case of the vending-machine example, it is difficult to argue that the same outcome could have come about as a result of frustration. For one thing, the idea of frustration does not make a directional prediction: There is no reason to believe that a frustrated subject should change away from her initial position, rather than reassert that position even more strongly than before. Another argument against frustration is based on the subject's evaluations of the other subject (who had presumably performed the restriction of freedom). In this situation, a subject frustrated enough to change her attitude should have been frustrated enough to derogate the person she considered responsible. But there were no significant differences across conditions in either the rated likability or competence of the other subject, so it seems unlikely that any frustration was produced by the induction of reactance.

Reactance theory predictions have been successfully confirmed in a number of different experimental settings, and many of these studies are reported in books by Brehm (1966), Wicklund (1974), and Brehm and Brehm (1981). On the basis of reactance findings, especially in the area of attitude change, we can conclude that not only moderate discrepancy from the initial position of the recipient, but also moderation in the influence attempt is necessary to avoid resistance to a persuasive message.

Resistance Arising from Advance Warning

Inoculation Against Counterpropaganda.   Suppose that, following the advice of social judgment and reactance theories, you have carefully constructed a communication of moderate forcefulness that falls in the recipient's latitude of noncommitment. You have obtained the recipient's agreement (in the sense of internalization) that your position is the valid one, and may even have induced the person to act according to this new view of the attitude object. How can you make this change a relatively permanent one, so that the recipient will not change to a different position as soon as another persuasive communicator comes along?

One answer to this question is suggested by a theory of **inoculation** proposed by McGuire (1964). Based on an analogy to medicine, and on research that has found two-sided presentations of issues to be more effective than one-sided presentations, inoculation theory argues that a weak dose of possible counterarguments can immunize the hearer against much of the effect that those counterarguments (later presented forcefully) might have. If at the time that you initially change the person's attitudes you also try to deal with some of the objections against your position, the change you produce in the recipient is more likely to withstand later attack.

Refute the Counterarguments.   Suppose that you belong to a national organization for owners of firearms, and that I am trying to convince you to support a complete ban on possession of any handguns – target pistols, antiques, pistols for protection, or Saturday-night specials. To give me even a remote chance of success initially, we must assume that you are not a highly committed member of this organization, and that you harbor some doubts about its position on this issue. Nevertheless, my proposal is still moderately discrepant from your view. Further, we will assume that I make my case in a way that does not threaten your freedom to believe what you wish. My message will probably include several elements, such as the statistics on the numbers of murders committed with guns not by "criminals" but by husbands and wives whose arguments get out of control; public statements by conservative big-city mayors and police chiefs in favor of outlawing the possession of handguns; and arguments in support of the idea that handguns have no value for recreation. If my message is a convincing one, and is followed by some actions on your part that indicate your acceptance of my view, I might be tempted to stop there.

But inoculation theory indicates that I should include some additional elements in the message – specifically, some points from the "other side." Fortunately for me, your organization's public position is so well known that I can construct, and then refute, a weakened version of the later counterpropaganda to which I know you will be exposed. For example, I can say, "Now they will tell you that with guns outlawed, only outlaws will have guns. Why do you suppose that the police chiefs (who, after all, are supposed to deal with all of those outlaws) are not worried about that? And because you are much more likely to be shot by a member of your family than by an outlaw, a complete ban on handguns will actually reduce your chances of getting shot, even if the outlaws still carry guns. Besides, you are proficient enough with your rifle so that you could easily use it against an intruder, without the risk of shooting yourself that a handgun carries." There are, of course, other aspects to the position of your organization, and I should try to deal with those in a similar manner.

An Example of Inoculation.   How well does inoculation work? As of this writing, no researcher has actually attempted the difficult sort of persuasive communication and inoculation illustrated in the example, but the theory has received support in a variety of other contexts. The first experiment demonstrating the effectiveness of inoculation was conducted by McGuire and Papageorgis (1961). These investigators first identified a set of what they called *cultural truisms*, beliefs that are so widely shared that a person would not ever have heard them attacked, and might even think that they were immune from attack. The examples used included "It is a good idea to brush your teeth after every meal," "The effects of penicillin have been, almost without exception, of great benefit to mankind," and "Everyone should get a yearly chest X-ray to detect signs of TB at an early age." It should be noted that this latter issue would not even be considered a truism today, because the medical risk from repeated X-ray exposure is now estimated to be higher than the risk of contracting tuberculosis.

The experiment involved two separate sessions, a "defense" session followed by an "attack" session. The subject's final attitudes were measured at the conclusion of the attack session. There were two sorts of defenses provided at the opening: the *supportive* defenses consisted of additional arguments in favor of the position taken by the truism, whereas the *refutational* defenses briefly mentioned, and then refuted, some of the arguments that might be raised against the truisms. In the second session each truism was restated, and then attacked in detail. The results on the attitude measures showed that the refutational defenses were more successful at inoculating the subjects against the later counterarguments than the supportive defenses had been. The effectiveness of inoculation against future counterarguments has been demonstrated in a number of other studies as well, and the success of the technique indicates that resistance to persuasion can be induced in the process of establishing the initial attitude. Whether this presents advantages or difficulties for the changer of attitudes depends, of course, on whether you are the change agent doing the inoculating, or the one having to persuade a person whose previous inoculation makes your task more challenging.

SOURCES OF FACILITATION

Characteristics of the Source

Are highly credible people more influential than communicators with lower credibility? Is a message that presents both sides of a controversial issue more effective or less effective than a message that presents only one side of the issue? Does frightening a recipient by pointing out the disastrous consequences of his or her present attitude make the person more or less susceptible to the new position advocated? What happens to the effectiveness of a persuasive communication over time? Research designed to provide answers to these and other similar questions began in earnest near the end of World War II in what was to become the Yale Communication and Attitude Change Program, under the direction of Carl Hovland.

The Yale Program. The Yale Program produced four volumes of research reports (Hovland, 1957; Hovland, Janis, & Kelley, 1953; Hovland & Rosenberg, 1960; Sherif & Hovland, 1961) that addressed, respectively, the order of presentation of material, communicator **credibility**, cognitive consistency, and social judgment (assimilation and contrast). In part because of the sheer volume of research and in part because of the stature of many of the social psychologists associated at various times with the program, it was thought that the program's findings had adequately answered many of the important questions. It is, however, instructive to re-examine some of these findings in light of today's more sophisticated methods of experimentation and analysis.

For example, several investigators attached to the program (e.g., Hovland & Weiss, 1951) found evidence of a "sleeper" effect – the tendency of some communications to produce more attitude change after a time delay of up to a month than they produced immediately after their delivery. This experiment is a good example, because it illustrates the approach of the program, because it deals with two of the issues (credibility and the sleeper effect) that many people had until recently considered resolved by the program's research, and because it had achieved the status of a classic study, being widely reported, reprinted, and uncritically discussed in textbooks. But its conclusions are suspect, as both Fishbein and Ajzen (1975) and Gillig and Greenwald (1974) have noted.

A Re-Examination of Communicator Credibility. The Hovland and Weiss (1951) experiment was designed to determine the effects on persuasion of having either a high credibility source or a low credibility source take either an affirmative or a negative position on an issue of contemporary interest. There were four different issues: should antihistamine drugs continue to be sold without a doctor's prescription; can a practicable atomic powered submarine be built at the present time; is the steel industry to blame for the current shortage of steel; and as a result of television, will there be a decrease in the number of movie theaters in operation by 1955? Each subject read a statement about each of the four issues. The two variables of interest (credibility and position on the issue) were arranged in a factorial design so that a subject would receive a different treatment combination on each issue. In other words, across the four issues, a subject would receive two affirmative arguments (one from a high credibility source, one from a low credibility source) and two negative arguments (one from each kind of source). This is, by the way, an excellent model for an experimental design.

A few days before the experiment was conducted, all the subjects were asked to indicate their positions on the four issues, and their rating of the eight sources later to be used as high or low credibility communicators. (In both cases, the relevant issues or sources had been carefully embedded in a larger list of possibilities.) In the experimental session the subjects were exposed to a booklet containing the persuasive communications on the four topics. After subjects had read the communications, their attitudes were again measured. Finally, there was a third assessment of attitudes on the issues four weeks after the experimental session, in order to test for a sleeper effect.

Hovland and Weiss (1951) presented the results in terms of the percentage of net opinion change in the direction advocated by the communication. That is, for each issue, a certain percentage of subjects changed from their own original position away from the position advocated in the communication, a second percentage of the subjects maintained their initial position, and a certain percentage changed away from their original position toward the position advocated in the communication. The *net opinion change* was the percentage changing toward the communication minus the percentage changing away from the position of the communication. Over four different issues, this net percentage opinion change was 23.0% for high credibility sources, but only 6.6% for low credibility sources, and this difference was interpreted as evidence for the greater effectiveness of the high credibility sources.

Trustworthiness and Expertise. Unfortunately, as Fishbein and Ajzen (1975) pointed out, there was significant net opinion change on only two of the four issues (atomic submarines and the steel shortage), and the differences obtained on these two measures were so great as to boost the overall average to such a point that it, too, became significant. Some of the difficulties in the research can be illustrated by considering the issue that produced the greatest difference: the feasibility of atomic submarines. Most attitude change researchers have suggested that credibility involves at least two different dimensions, trustworthiness, and expertise. People will think you are credible if you know what you are talking about, either through experience or training, and if they think that you have nothing to gain personally by advocating the position you take.

For the atomic submarine issue, the high credibility source was Dr. Robert Oppenheimer, a well known physicist, whereas the low credibility source was *Pravda*, the official newspaper of the Soviet Communist Party. We would probably agree that both trustworthiness differences and expertise differences contributed to the subjects' varying impressions of these two sources, but only trustworthiness was used to establish that the credibility manipulation had been successful. Worse still, the low credibility source carried strong political overtones (remember that those were the Cold War days between the Soviet Union and the United States). These confounding factors make it very difficult to determine whether the final results on net opinion change were due to change in the subjects' actual attitudes, to differential perception of the messages (what Fishbein and Ajzen, 1975, called *reception* and what McGuire's analysis of the communication process in Table 6.1 might consider attention, liking, or related thought), or to a differential willingness to admit to having been influenced by one source or the other.

One final aspect of the research that deserves comment is the fact that the results on the follow-up were interpreted as evidence for the sleeper effect. After 4 weeks, the net opinion change in the high credibility groups dropped from 23.0% to 12.3%, whereas that in the low credibility groups increased from 6.6% to 14.0%. In short, after a period of 4 weeks, net opinion change was approximately the same in the two credibility conditions. The sleeper effect has always been defined as the increase in persuasive power of a message (usually from an untrustworthy source) over a long period of time. But as Gillig and Greenwald (1974) noted, the evidence used by Hovland and Weiss (1951), and by others who have obtained favorable results, was a statistical interaction between credibility and time. The concept of an interaction, in this instance, involves *both* the slight increase in the low credibility condition and the greater decrease in the high credibility condition. In short, although the conceptual definition of the effect involves only the rise in one group, the evidence taken as showing the effect mistakenly included the decrease in the other group as well.

Current Status of the Findings.   Recent critiques of the Hovland and Weiss (1951) study, and of others in the Yale Program, dramatically illustrate the developments in method that have occurred since the 1950s. What began as simple questions about the characteristics of persuasive communications have become complex questions about the circumstances that produce one effect rather than another. Although the procedures of individual studies have become suspect, many of the Program's findings have first been questioned, and then subsequently reaffirmed. The review by Fishbein and Ajzen (1975) certainly casts doubt on the Hovland and Weiss (1951) analysis of communicator credibility, but still more recent work (which takes into account the methodological criticisms) has obtained differences based on credibility, at least for issues that do not engender great personal involvement (e.g., Birnbaum & Stegner, 1979). In much the same way, the findings for the sleeper effect have been questioned (Gillig & Greenwald, 1974), but later reaffirmed in research incorporating all of the required methodological and statistical controls (e.g., Gruder et al., 1978).

Thus research on attitude change, like research on attitude organization, has undergone continued refinement, made possible by increasingly sophisticated methods. "Are highly credible communicators more effective than communicators of lower credibility?" has been prefaced by "Why" and by "When." In the same way, researchers now ask "Under what circumstances will highly threatening fear communications be more effective than moderately threatening ones, and when will these effects be reversed," "When will presenting one side first benefit that side and when will it benefit the other advocate," and, even more importantly, "How do these message and source characteristics *interact* to produce or inhibit attitude change?" As of this writing, the major contribution of the research on characteristics of the communication is not the conclusive answers obtained, but the complexity that has been revealed in the initial questions. It remains the task of future research to establish what aspects of the communication always increase the probability of attitude change.

Facilitation Arising
from the Participation of the Recipient

In contrast to questions about the nature and presentation of the communication, questions about the effects on attitude change of participation by the recipient have frequently led to highly replicable findings. For example, the idea that public advocacy of an attitude will lead to change in the direction advocated is a consistent result in most research. As we saw in chapter 5, there is still some theoretical controversy about the reason for this experimental outcome (in terms of dissonance, incentive, or self-perception theory), but there is widespread agreement on the empirical generalization that advocacy leads to attitude change. Effective as it is, counterattitudinal advocacy is not the only sort of participation possible by the communication recipient. For our purposes it is useful to distinguish among three levels of recipient contribution: no participation, induced participation, and informed participation.

No Participation

Classical Conditioning. To begin with an approach familiar to every introductory psychology student, there is evidence that attitudes, like other social behaviors, can be formed through processes of classical conditioning. The basic idea of classical (or Pavlovian) conditioning is that an initially neutral stimulus will become endowed with positive or negative properties through repeated association with other stimuli that are inherently positive or negative. (The evening news could be a neutral stimulus to the viewer, unless it is associated with eating dinner, at which point it would become positive.)

In one of the early studies of the classical conditioning of attitudes, Lott and Lott (1960) had groups of third- and fifth-grade children play a noncompetitive board game. Each play group was composed of three children from the same classroom who had not previously chosen each other as friends on a questionnaire collected in class. Therefore, at the beginning of the experiment, it was assumed that the children had approximately neutral attitudes toward each other. During the course of the play, some of the children in each group were rewarded for their successes at the game, while other children in the same group were not rewarded for success. Different numbers of children (zero, one, two, or three) were rewarded in different groups, so that the play of the game would not appear to have been rigged. At the conclusion of the day, all the children were given another questionnaire, which asked them to select from the members of the class two children with whom they would like to take an imaginary vacation. Children who had been in the rewarded play groups were more likely to select the other members of that group than were children who had been in groups not rewarded for success. Thus the presence or absence of reward produced differences in the friendship choice—we prefer associates who are part of a positive experience we have shared with them.

Mere Exposure. Not only is it possible for attitudes to be classically conditioned, it is also possible for favorableness toward an attitude object to increase simply with repeated presentation of the object, with no reward at all. In a series of experiments, Zajonc (1968) found that the rated "favorability" of various stimuli (nonsense words, photographs of faces, and even Chinese-like pictograms) increased with repeated presentation. No matter what the stimulus was, the more frequently it was presented (up to a maximum of 25 times), the more favorably it was evaluated. Zajonc referred to this phenomenon as the *mere exposure* effect, and suggested that it might serve as a confounding factor in studies that attempt to show attitude change through various conditioning procedures. After all, in any conditioning technique, the attitude object is repeatedly paired with the positive or negative stimulus that serves as a reward or punishment. How much of the conditioning effect is due to the presence of that reward or punishment, and how much is based simply on repeated presentation? This question has not yet been answered satisfactorily, but a number of different studies have explored the characteristics of the mere exposure effect.

One of the conclusions from this research (much of which is reviewed by Harrison, 1977) is that there are limits to the mere exposure effect. For example, imagine eating your favorite food. Pleasant? Now imagine eating absolutely nothing else for a month. Still pleasant? In a first modification of the mere exposure idea, Berlyne (1970) suggested that a two-factor theory would provide a better explanation of the results. The two factors thought to be involved were a "learning" factor and a "satiation" factor, with the two together determining the attitude toward the object. Repeated presentations were thought to facilitate learning in the early stages of exposure to a novel stimulus; that learning is considered pleasurable, and attitudes toward the object become more positive. As the presentation wears on, after the stimulus has been learned well, further presentation produces boredom. Thus, the two-factor theory argues that Zajonc's findings represented only the first phase of mere exposure. His stimuli were complex and unusual, so they might have required even more than 25 trials to be learned. Consequently, the argument goes, all of his ratings of increased favorableness occurred prior to satiation. Later research has generally supported a two-factor theory, replicating the early-stage increase in favorableness, even in the absence of significant learning.

Induced Participation

In an important sense, of course, any participation by a recipient in activities designed to change his or her attitudes can be thought of as induced participation. Cases in which we voluntarily seek to alter our attitudes, such as embarking upon psychotherapy, occur only occasionally. For our purposes, however, the category of induced participation will be restricted to those instances in which there is deliberate concealment of the goal of attitude change.

Forced Compliance. The most familiar experimental example of induced attitude change is the forced compliance technique employed in studies of cognitive dissonance. The success of changing attitudes with this procedure depends not only on concealing the goal of attitude change, but also upon establishing in the subject's mind the illusion of having been personally responsible for the decisions that are made. When these decisions lead to negative consequences, dissonance is presumably aroused, and this dissonance leads to attitude change. There are other explanations for the effects of forced compliance, but as noted earlier, the important point for present purposes is that counterattitudinal advocacy produces attitude change.

The Foot-in-the-Door Technique. One of the ways in which the forced compliance procedure differs from processes of attitude change in the real social world is that only a single experimental trial is run for any given attitude. The request from the experimenter is an all-or-nothing affair. In contrast, most attempts to produce attitude change in the real world involve gradual and repeated requests that ultimately lead to performance of what would previously have been a counterattitudinal action.

Suppose I own an automobile dealership and the only models I can get from the factory have automatic transmission and factory air conditioning. Let's also suppose that you are interested in a new car, but that you have always considered automatic transmission and air conditioning frivolous and wasteful. Do I tell you the whole story of my offerings in a newspaper advertisement, so that the only people who will respond are ones who want exactly what I have to sell? Certainly not. I talk of "stupendous savings," of my dealership's "care for its customers," and of its "excellent service facilities." Because those are things that every car buyer would like, you may decide to visit me. You don't know it yet, but you have taken the initial step toward counterattitudinal action. My first task is not to convince you to buy a particular car, but simply to get my foot in the door (or, more appropriately for this example, to get your foot into my door).

Do I hit you with the full package when you arrive at my showroom? Again, certainly not. I try to ascertain your likes and dislikes, show you features of the car, and try to discover how you feel about various accessories. When I learn that you don't want the only thing I have, I don't mention the equipment you dislike. I try to get you to take a test drive. If you agree to do so, then I suggest that we have enough in common that we ought to "talk a little business." (You are getting more and more committed with every action.) You may now agree to talk with me, just to find out how much your old car is worth, and that gives my my last needed opportunity. If I can make you an offer that is sufficiently better than you might have expected, then I will have sold you something you initially did not want. The process has been a gradual one, with your commitment increasing slightly at each successive level of the interchange. I will be more successful at getting you to accede to my final large request to sign on the dotted line if I have previously been able to get you to agree to smaller requests along the way.

The foot-in-the-door technique was introduced by Freedman and Fraser (1966), and it was soon touted as an excellent example of the potential practical application of social psychological knowledge. Whether the concern was blood donation, conservation of energy, or support for one or another national policy, the technique – if it had worked as advertised – would have given individuals and groups an important tool in their attempts to change public attitudes and behavior. Unfortunately, even a review that finds overall support for the technique (DeJong, 1979) notes numerous failures to replicate Freedman and Fraser's research, and a study that is not included in this review (Foss & Dempsey, 1979) again failed to confirm the presence of the effect.

It may be, as Foss and Dempsey (1979) note, that verbal agreement to engage in a behavior cannot be taken as evidence for the likelihood of actual behavioral compliance, especially when the final request is for an action about which the subject was initially hesitant. In short, my sales pitch to you may have been successful as much because it was what you really wanted (you just needed coaxing) as because it was a gradual approach of increasing commitment.

Informed Participation: Group Discussion

The final category includes all of those attitude change procedures in which there is full and informed involvement by the recipient. On of the earliest examples of this approach, the *group discussion method* developed by Lewin (1958) and his students was described in chapter 1. The basic idea is that many of an individual's attitudes are reinforced and maintained by the social groups to which he or she belongs (in the structure of persuasion, this would involve both related cognitions and acquiring skills). Fraternities and sororities typically differ regarding the relative importance of various campus activities, corporations often share certain attitudes, and political parties have formal platforms that justify their positions on issues they consider important. To one degree or another, these organizational views will be reflected in the attitudes of the members, so if it is possible to change the entire group's position (perhaps through group discussion) then the individual attitudes will follow.

The first step in achieving attitude change through discussion is the **unfreezing** of the group's initial position on the issue. This is followed by **moving** the group to a new attitude, and the process is concluded by **refreezing** the group attitude at the new location. Unfreezing can be accomplished by presenting new information, or by pointing out how the new position would be in the group's interest. For example, the purpose of a political party is to field candidates who can win elections. Suppose that time after time a party's candidates lose, and the public opinion polls indicate that there are aspects of the party's platform that the electorate simply will not support. This information alone would be sufficient to unfreeze the party's position, and discussions at party conventions might reveal a new position to which the party could move. Formal adoption of this change in position would refreeze the platform at the new value, and members who placed the party high in their personal priorities would change their own attitudes to agree with the new position. (Members who could not support the change would probably leave the party.)

The specific effects that groups can have on the attitudes of their members are discussed more fully in chapter 12, but for our purposes here it is enough to note that these effects can be substantial. In one of the first studies of group participation in decision making, Coch and French (1948) compared the attitudes toward new working conditions of employees who had been permitted to have either full participation, representative participation, or no participation in the design of the changes to be implemented. Not surprisingly, the resulting attitudes were most positive when the employees had full participation in designing the new conditions, but even the representative participation group showed positive change. In passing, it is worth noting that this idea of employee participation in the design of working conditions—first exported to Japan and only recently imported again—has dramatically influenced the production methods in a variety of manufacturing industries.

Attitudes and Behavior

Prejudice and Discrimination. We began this chapter by noting that the expenditure of time and money in the attempt to change attitudes is justified by the presumption that an individual's attitudes will lead to actions consonant with those attitudes. To what extent is this presumption justified? This question has been of interest to social psychology ever since the first studies of prejudice and discrimination (LaPiere, 1934). To obtain an estimate of the racial attitudes of a restaurant proprietor, the researchers called the restaurant on the telephone, identified themselves as members of a minority group, and then asked for a reservation for dinner. To assess the behavior, members of the minority group would then simply appear at the restaurant unannounced and see if they would be seated.

In a later review of this research, Dillehay (1973) has noted some important limitations of the method, but the technique does identify factors that can affect the relationship between an attitude and behavior. From the proprietor's viewpoint, the demands of the immediate social situation (a tradition of courtesy to customers, an unwillingness to create a scene over a small group of people) might have been sufficient to depress discriminatory behavior. If larger numbers of people had been involved, or it there had been some reason for the proprietor to think that serving this one group carried strong implications for the future, the response might well have been different. After all, during the civil rights movement of the 1960s, numerous restaurants, city recreation areas, and even some public schools, closed down entirely rather than integrate their facilities.

Just a Predisposition?   Despite the differences in behavior that have been obtained in studies comparing people with positive racial attitudes to people with racist attitudes, several reviews of the attitude literature remain skeptical about the power of attitudes to affect behavior. In one comprehensive review, Wicker (1969) found that at best a measured attitude accounted for roughly 25% of the variation observed in actual behavior. And in the words of McGuire (1985), the "low correlations between attitudes and behaviors have been the scandal of the field for a half century" (p. 251).

So why study attitude change at all? For at least two different reasons. First, it is an important psychological phenomenon in its own right, regardless of its implications for behavior. To argue that the only justification for research on attitude change is that such change will lead to more positive interpersonal behavior is a specific version of the general argument that the only justification for accumulating social psychological knowledge is the social-engineering benefit that might accompany such knowledge. This view denies the general principle that guides most scientific research: More knowledge is better, whether it has an immediate practical application or not. So even though the correlations between attitudes and behavior might be a "scandal," those low correlations will not cause social psychologists to lose interest in the topic of attitude change.

The second reason to study attitude change is the very practical truth that although the correlations between attitudes and behaviors are low, they are larger than the correlations between anything else and behavior. So although there is plenty of variability in action that remains unexplained if you know a person's attitude, at least some of the variability *is* explained. Not surprisingly, one of the recent developments in the study of attitude change is the attempt to increase the predictive value of knowing a person's social attitudes. That is one of the major goals behind McGuire's (1985) list of the elements of persuasion: Several of the steps — storing, retrieving, decision making — are interposed between attitude change (agreeing) and overt behavior (action). If the influence of external factors can be held to a minimum at each of these intervening steps, then attitude change ought to be a better predictor of behavior change.

Work in this direction has recently built on Fishbein and Ajzen's idea of the behavioral intention (discussed in chapter 5). You will recall that a behavioral intention is a precise statement of a planned action toward an attitude object, rather than a global evaluation of the object. Any behavioral intention is thought to be determined by two principal factors: the person's attitude toward the object (which attitude is composed of the summed products of beliefs times evaluations), and a subjective norm. This *subjective norm*, in turn, consists of the person's "normative beliefs" (the person's expectation that important reference people or groups endorse performing the behavior) and "motivation to comply" (a measure of the individual's interest in living up to the expectations held by each of the individuals or groups).

The two-component (attitude and subjective norm) formulation has led researchers to refine their attitude measures, and to concentrate on factors within the immediate social environment that might mitigate the attitude-behavior relationship. For example, in a 2-year study of 244 married women's attitudes toward use of oral contraceptives and toward having children, Davidson and Jaccard (1979) were able to identify situational factors that reduced the correlation between attitude and behavior. These included (a) increases in the time interval between the measurement of the attitude and the performance of the behavior, (b) the intervention of events (such as becoming pregnant after intercourse without contraception) not entirely under volitional control, and (c) changes in the perceived normative environment.

Other studies have pointed to additional variables that moderate the attitude-behavior relationship. When an attitude is formed by direct contact with the attitude object, rather than through second-hand information, the correlation between the measured attitude and subsequent behavior increases (Fazio & Zanna, 1978). When the individual takes personal responsibility for actions (Schwartz, 1977), and carefully monitors his or her own behavior (Snyder & Tanke, 1976), the correlation between attitude and behavior increases. Perhaps most important, the application of new statistical techniques (e.g., Kahle & Berman, 1979) to attitude measurement has permitted better assessment of the initial attitudes, with attendant increases in the attitude-behavior correlation. None of the resulting correlations is a perfect one, and social psychology still has much to learn about the relationship between attitude and behavior. Nevertheless, it is still fair to conclude with Kahle and Berman (1979) that "for the politicians, theologians, and alcoholism therapists who may be interested in knowing whether their efforts to change attitudes will help them to achieve their ultimate goals of changing behaviors, the answer appears to be yes" (p. 320).

ETHICAL ISSUES IN ATTITUDE CHANGE

In many of the experiments discussed in this and the preceding chapter, researchers have deliberately concealed the fact that their goal was to change the subject's attitudes. This concealment, like other forms of experimental deception (discussed more fully in chapter 2), raises ethical questions. Just how serious are the risks to the subjects, and do the potential benefits of the research outweigh these risks? Unfortunately, as noted earlier, it is often difficult to achieve both of these goals within the context of a single experiment. Using materials of very little importance to subjects would certainly help protect the self-esteem of a person who happened to be persuaded to change his or her opinion, but would such research have sufficient external validity to warrant taking the subject's time?

Informed Consent and Mundane Realism. Obtaining the subject's informed consent prior to the research, by describing the experiment in detail before the subject makes the decision to participate, will reduce the risk, but may also enhance the demand characteristics. And if the informed consent is not based on complete information, the act of obtaining consent may be in actuality a kind of forced compliance procedure; the subject might then be more dramatically affected by any adverse effects of the experiment, believing that he or she had been warned and had freely chosen to suffer the consequences anyway. In the vast majority of attitude change (and other) research, experimenters are conscientious about their responsibilities to their subjects. These standards are high, and should remain so, but some additional observations may help us keep our perspective.

Unlike other forms of experimental deception, the deliberate attempt to produce attitude change has innumerable counterparts in the everyday world. The extent to which the task an experimental subject performs is equivalent to what the subject might do in the real world outside the laboratory is the mundane realism (Aronson & Carlsmith, 1968) of the experiment, and in attitude change research this mundane realism is usually quite high. The merchant who lures you into a store with the promise of great bargains may be trying to get you to purchase something more expensive. The advertiser who claims that his or her products will make you more attractive and self-assured is concerned with your attitude toward buying, not with your attitude toward yourself. The politician who accuses opponents of association with undesirable people or unpopular causes is not merely informing the public, but is trying to get your vote. The list could go on and on. We are continually bombarded by persuasive messages that play on our desires, our uncertainties, and our fears. So to be subjected to attitude change attempts in experiments is hardly a novel experience. Indeed, some of the comparisons between the real social world and the laboratory suggest that we might have greater cause for ethical concern in the former.

Issue Importance and Debriefing. The first such comparison deals with the importance of the attitudes and behaviors in question. It is difficult to imagine that many subjects suffered psychological damage from writing an essay favoring police intervention in a campus disturbance (Cohen, 1962), supporting a governing board's decision to forbid a post-season football game (Rosenberg, 1965), or favoring the continuation of a ban against campus appearances by radical speakers (Linder, Cooper, & Jones, 1967). Even when the behavior was performed outside a laboratory setting, placing a 3-inch sign in one's window (Freedman & Fraser, 1966) does not seem terribly important. In contrast, attitude changes in everyday life lead us to consequences of much greater magnitude. The unwary buyer who is sold something he or she cannot really afford, the cosmetic purchaser who buys something that may be harmful either personally or to the environment, and the voter who helps contribute to a candidate's landslide election victory may all live to regret their changed attitudes.

A second difference between laboratory studies of attitude change and attempts at persuasion in the real world is the presence (in the former) of a debriefing. When laboratory experiments carry risk to the subjects, a careful debriefing designed to minimize those risks is given at the conclusion of the study. For example, in any of the forced compliance research in which the action called for was the face-to-face deception of another person (e.g., Carlsmith, Collins, & Helmreich, 1966; Festinger & Carlsmith, 1959), the subject's self-esteem may be threatened by the realization that he or she can be induced to lie for (in some cases) very little justification. But the debriefing tries to minimize the threat contained in this realization by emphasizing that the subject's behavior should be attributed to the overwhelming power of the situation, rather than to some inherent character failing. By contrast, attitude manipulation techniques in the real social world never include a debriefing. Indeed, one of the purposes behind the federal rules requiring a three-day "cooling-off period" during which time an expensive installment purchase can be returned for full credit is to provide the opportunity for the purchaser to discover on his or her own how much the decision to buy might have been influenced by hidden situational pressures.

It is not my purpose here either to minimize the ethical questions raised by attitude change research by comparing them favorably to the ethical problems found in real-world attempts to change attitudes. But the prevalence of everyday persuasion, and the importance of the attitudes involved, suggest that we should maintain a certain degree of perspective. Perhaps more ethical concern should be directed at the pressures toward attitude change that are so common in our society.

SUMMARY

The attitude of racism, like many other attitudes toward real social objects, has a strong emotional component (p. 194) that makes it very difficult to change. Such attitudes may be developed during socialization because of the child's **effect dependence** and **information dependence** (p. 196) on the parents, and they may also be derived from competition or frustration (p. 197).

When we speak of modifying a person's attitudes, we must distinguish between public **compliance** (p. 199) with a persuasive appeal and private acceptance that can come about either through **identification** (p. 199) or **internalization** (p. 199). We must also recognize that an individual's attitudes can serve several psychological functions, such as expressing a person's values (p. 201), bringing order to social knowledge (p. 201), or helping to maintain ego defenses (p. 202).

A person will be reluctant to change attitudes that serve ego defensive functions, that have numerous horizontal or vertical connections, or that are consistent with the person's other cognitions. In addition, the process of persuasion can be affected by a number of variables associated with the source of the communication (p. 203), the message itself and the channel through which it comes (p. 203), the characteristics of the recipient (p. 203), or the specific target of change (p. 203). An attitude change attempt that advocates a position highly discrepant from the recipient's original position will have less chance of success than a communication of moderate discrepancy (p. 205). A communication that restricts the recipient's freedom to believe as he or she chooses will create **reactance** (p. 211) that will lead to rejection of the influence attempt, and the success of an attack on an attitude may depend on whether the recipient has previously been **inoculated** (p. 215) against such attacks.

Sources of facilitation of attitude change include the characteristics of the communication and the participation of the recipient. There is reason to believe that attitudes can be changed through classical conditioning (p. 219), through **mere exposure** (p. 220), with no active participation on the part of the recipient. Attitudes can also be altered through the induced participation that accompanies *forced compliance* (p. 221), and the *foot-in-the-door effect* (p. 221), or through the full and informed participation found in *group discussion* (p. 222) of attitude issues. Whether the attempts to change attitudes occur in the laboratory or in everyday life, they involve ethical questions that we need to consider as researchers, and as citizens.

SUGGESTED ADDITIONAL READINGS

EAGLY, A. H., & CHAIKIN, S. (1984). Cognitive theories of persuasion. In L. Berkowitz (Ed.), *Advances in experimental social psychology* (Vol. 17, pp. 267-359). New York: Academic Press. This detailed chapter, written for a professional audience, describes process theories, such as attribution, and combinatorial theories, such as the probabilogical models, of attitude change. Very technical, but an excellent overview of the cognitive processes that are involved in attitude change.

ZIMBARDO, P. G., EBBESEN, E. B., & MASLACH, C. (1977). *Influencing attitudes and changing behavior* (2nd ed.). Reading, MA: Addison-Wesley. This updated and expanded book is still a highly readable introduction to issues in attitude organization and change.

CHAPTER SEVEN

THE SELF

CONTENTS

PREVIEW

The self forms the transition between the intrapersonal processes of social perception, social cognition, and attitude organization and the volitional activity initiated by the person toward the social world. Social psychological study of the self illuminates a conflict between forces toward accuracy – in self-perception, self-evaluation, and self-disclosure – and forces toward distortion in the same areas. Individuals possess multiple constructions of a social self, derived in part from the opinions and expectations of other people. This idea is represented both in the notion of the looking-glass self and in the concept of role conflict. The process of self-evaluation involves reference groups, social comparisons with other individuals, the notion of oneself as distinctive. Labels provided by the surrounding environment can affect the subjective experience of emotion, the persistence of attitudes, and the degree of motivation to succeed at various tasks. The development of self-esteem involves comparisons between a person's real self and ideal self, and this comparison can also be influenced by personal and situational factors beyond the individual's immediate control (such as socialization, race, gender, and attractiveness). Finally, the interchange between the forces toward accuracy and the forces toward distortion can be seen in the public behavior of the self, both in everyday self-presentation and in the unusual circumstances of objective self-awareness and deindividuation.

Engaging in meditation, playing handball, and asking your neighbor for an opinion on your new automobile all have something in common. Each of these activities can serve to reveal to you a different aspect of your self. But there is more to the **self** than inner experience, observable abilities, and material possessions. It also includes such elements as social perceptions, attitudes, personality characteristics, motives, and emotions. In short, the self often is considered to be the totality of answers to the question, "Who am I?"

At the outset it should be noted that there are two very different sorts of answers to this question: "I am what I *have*" and "I am what I *do*." Not only material possessions, but also a physical presence, cognitions about oneself and other elements of the social world, and attitudes are components of the self. Indeed, it is impossible to think of a "self" that has none of these material and intangible constituents. As necessary as they are, the components of the self are not sufficient for its complete definition. Recall from chapter 2 one of the fundamental assumptions of theory and research in social psychology: people make choices among behavioral alternatives on the basis of their internal representations of people and events. The self is the agent that makes these considered choices. This is such a critical element of selfhood that we have a number of ways to describe a person who seems temporarily to have lost the capacity to do so: "She lost control of herself," or "He's going off to find himself." But there can also be too much of a good thing, as in "He's only out for himself."

Because the self both "is," and "does," it has played a prominent role in a wide variety of social and psychological theories. Psychologists interested in personality dynamics have concentrated on the conscious determinants of the self (e.g., Jourard, 1964; Maslow, 1961), whereas more traditional clinical theorists have emphasized unconscious or irrational forces involved in the development of the self (e.g., Freud, 1933, Jung, 1953). For their part, social psychologists have been preoccupied with the idea of self-evaluation (Bem, 1972; Duval & Wicklund, 1972; Festinger, 1954; Jones & Nisbett, 1972; Schachter, 1964) and the resulting self-concept or self-esteem (e.g., Janis & Field, 1959; Ziller, 1973). Finally, sociologists have explored the social context for the individual self (Cooley, 1902; Goffman, 1959; Mead, 1934).

Accuracy versus Distortion

Unfortunately, this extensive interest in the self has not been reflected in a unified body of theory. Indeed, even on a topic as fundamental as the conceptual status of the self it is possible to find recent disagreement (e.g., Gergen, 1984, as opposed to Kihlstrom & Cantor, 1984). There is, however, one recurrent theme that is most important for our purposes: the conflict between pressures toward accuracy and pressures toward distortion, both in the acquisition of knowledge about the self and in the public behavior of the self. Social psychology's particular concern is the joint influence of personal and situational factors on individual behavior, and both of these kinds of factors play a part in the conflict between accuracy and distortion.

Let's consider an example. Suppose you are attempting to evaluate yourself to determine whether you have a real chance of developing a close relationship with an attractive person of the opposite sex. Put very simply, you want to find out if you are "good enough" to be regarded as a worthy partner. So you ask your friends for their opinions. What sort of information do you really want, and what sort are they likely to give you? You would like them to tell you if they think you have no chance at all, so you won't make a fool of yourself by attempting the impossible. But at the same time, you would relish at least a few compliments. What your friends tell you may depend in part on the attractiveness of the intended partner, in part on your actual social stimulus value, and in part on their desire to retain your friendship. They will probably tell you if they think you have no chance with the person, but even under these circumstances, they may refrain from being "brutally frank" about your shortcomings. Thus, situational and personal factors are involved in your search for information, and in the provision of that information by your friends. In each case, there is some conflict between pressures toward accuracy and pressures toward distortion.

The Social Self

The discussion in this chapter is limited to the social self, emphasizing the uniquely social features of (a) the process of self-evaluation, and (b) the public behavior of the self. Those aspects of the self that are more closely associated with personality development (such as self-actualization) and with clinical applications of self theory (such as irrational determinants of the self, or the apparent changes in the self-concept that accompany emotional disorder) are omitted. Such omissions would be lamentable in a volume devoted entirely to the self, but they are justified for an introductory text in social psychology.

THE SELF AS CONTENT AND PROCESS

The Me

One of the earliest descriptions of the self that is of interest to social psychologists is the characterization suggested by William James (e.g., 1892). Making a point that remains vital today, James distinguished between the self as an object of reflection (called the **Me**) and the self as a conscious agent (called the **I**). The me consists of the sum total of all that a person can call his or her own, and is divided into three categories: the constituents of the Me, the emotions to which those constituents may give rise, and the actions that result from those emotions. The category of *constituents*, in turn, includes the material self, the spiritual self, and the several social selves. These three aspects of the self are illustrated in Fig. 7.1. You have only a single material self, and it includes your body, your home, and other material possessions (such as that car you so proudly displayed to your neighbor). In the same way, you have only a single spiritual self. It consists of all of your psychological faculties and dispositions, such as personality traits, verbal skills, attitudes, social perceptions, and that inner experience you seek through meditation.

Multiple Social Selves.   In contrast, you are presumed to have multiple social selves, one for each person who carries an image of you in his or

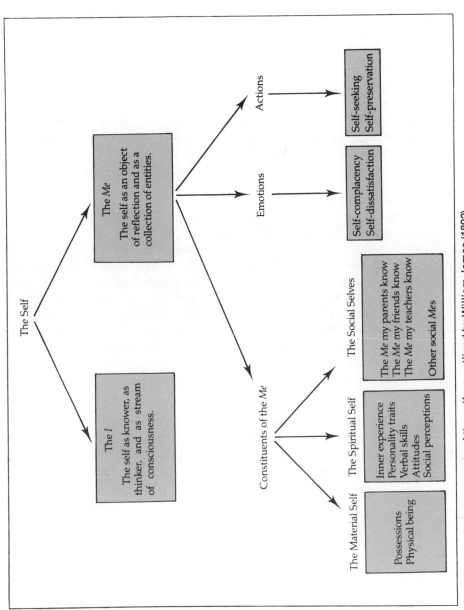

FIGURE 7.1 The components of the self, as outlined by William James (1892).

her mind. This suggests that you might have hundreds of social selves, but James (1892) points out that for all practical purposes, the number can be reduced to one social self for each class or group of people who recognize you as an individual. Thus you have one social self that you reveal to your close friends, another that you present to your parents, and a different one that you offer to your instructors. This is not to say that you are a different person around each of these groups of people, but rather to suggest that the elements of your self that are disclosed in each situation may be different.

The material self, the spiritual self, and the social selves complete the constituents of the Me. The second aspect of the Me is the *emotions* to which these constituents give rise, and James believed those to fall into two broad classes, *self-complacency* (such as pride, self-confidence, or arrogance), and *self-dissatisfaction* (such as humility or despair). These arise when the Me is evaluated, either by your own I, or by other people whose opinions are important to you. In many cases the nature of the emotion (positive or negative) will depend as much on the circumstances of the evaluation as on the characteristic being judged. For example, if you have much of your self invested in material possessions, you will be happy when they are becoming more valuable, but will be sad if they are lost. If you are concentrating on your spiritual self, you might be pleased with your keen sense of smell when you walk into the florist's, but you would be unhappy if your home were located downwind from a paper mill. Finally, if all of the people around you are singing your praises, (positively evaluating your social selves), you cannot hear enough; but if no one has a good word to say, it is easy to hear too much.

Self-Preservation and Self-Seeking. The third component of the Me consists of the *actions* that can be produced by the constituents of the Me, either directly, or indirectly through the emotions. There are two general classes of actions: self-preservation and self-seeking. The first set is directed toward maintenance of the self as it exists in the present, and these actions of self-preservation include physical responses (startle reactions, bodily self-defense) and social behaviors designed to protect the integrity of your spiritual or social selves. If, for example, you suffer a heavy blow to your self-esteem through an unpleasant interchange with another person, you may need to spend some recuperative time alone (to "pull yourself together") before returning to social activities. As we see in chapter 13, this is one of the functions of the state known as "privacy." The second set of actions, self-seeking, consists of behaviors designed to provide for the future rather than merely to maintain the status quo. As the name suggests, self-seeking may not always be a purely rational process. We return to this point later.

The I

If the Me is the sum total of the content of the self, then the I is the ongo-ing process of consciousness. It is the pure ego, the knower, the thinker, or as James describes it, the organized stream of consciousness. Because the I is a process rather than a collection of elements, it is more difficult to de-scribe in concrete terms than is the Me. Although the I can reflect upon the contents of consciousness, it is not simply the aggregate of those contents. Although it can be regarded as directing the purposeful behavior that we call "making choices," it is not the same thing as the actions that are taken. Nor is it considered (in James', 1892 words) "an unchanging metaphysical entity like the Soul, or a principle like the transcendental Ego" (p. 215) that exists apart from space and time. The I participates in causation of behav-ior and in the evaluation of the Me, but it is not thought to be a causal force apart from consciousness. Rather the I *is* the dynamic process of conscious-ness, the awareness of self, and of individuality.

Role Conflict

Multiple Elements of the Self.   There are two aspects of James's anal-ysis of the self that are most important from our perspective: the idea of multiple social selves, and the description of actions taken for the benefit of the self. These are, respectively, the self as content and the self as process. To begin with the content, it is important not to take James's description too literally. Do you really become a completely different person when the situational or interpersonal context changes? Of course not (unless you are a true multiple personality, probably in need of therapy). It is not that your "fun-loving, carefree self" disappears when you go to talk to your professor about your marginal performance on an examination, it is just that such a lighthearted approach is just not appropriate or relevant in the context. The content of your self is better thought of as arranged in numerous clus-ters of related attributes and skills. Your friends see one cluster, your pro-fessor sees another, and different, cluster. A single element may be pres-ent in more than one cluster (you would like for both your friends and your professor to think of you as "intelligent") or a single element may be spe-cific to only one cluster (those elements that collectively comprise "sibling" will only be relevant when the family relationship, itself, is part of the stim-ulus for your behavior).

Competing Expectations.   Despite the fact that the various clusters are all part of the same overall self, there will be occasions on which the clusters will get in each other's way. For example, your friends may ask you to spend the weekend sailing with them, but you have an assignment due Monday, and you have just received a letter from your parents wondering when you will have enough free time to come home for a weekend. Part of your overall self-concept is based on a positive evaluation by your friends of the cluster that you reveal to them, but your self-concept is also boosted by the positive opinions of your instructors and parents. Yet in this situation it is impossible for you to live up to everyone's expectations.

You are suffering from a variant of what Gross, Mason, and McEachern (1957) call **role conflict**: the existence of incompatible expectations for your behavior that are the result of different roles that you occupy. Technically speaking, the **role** is a set of expectations held by perceivers for the behavior of a person who fulfills a particular social function. So the roles of "friend," "student," and "child" are really in the eye of the beholder, not specific to you as an individual. Very similar expectations would hold for anyone who happened to be filling the role at the time. What you have done, however, is reveal to each of these different perceivers that cluster of your attributes that is most appropriate for the specific role expectations. In an important sense, a role is a cognitive schema (see chapter 4), so although it provides a structure into which you need to fit, it also can be modified somewhat by your behavior: If you are not quite the student that others are, the professor will not be surprised to discover you haven't done the assignment (he or she still won't approve). So the more closely you have tailored the various clusters of your self to fit the existing role expectations, the greater the role conflict that you will suffer when those expectations are in conflict with one another. To resolve this conflict, you must choose one set of expectations to follow, and because of this choice, other roles and expectations may be distorted. For example, you might rationalize your choice of sailing with your friends on the grounds that "I am in college to make lifelong friendships, as well as to do homework. Besides, my parents can't really want to see me again so soon—I went home just a couple of months ago." This kind of rationalization is, of course, just like the distortion that accompanies the reduction of cognitive inconsistency from counterattitudinal advocacy (Chapter 5), except that the source of the inconsistency is "built in" to the various clusters of your social self, rather than being induced by an external agent.

Actions of the Self.   The kind of conflict that occurs between accuracy and distortion in the perception of aspects of your social self can also be seen in the actions you take. Consider, for example, what is involved in self-preservation. To protect your self, you should have accurate information about impending threats and about ways to minimize those dangers. How much preparation is really necessary to pass a difficult required course? What balance between academic work and extracurricular activities is appropriate for your occupational and personal goals? Are you likely to find a particular social relationship rewarding, or will it be too stressful? In each of these instances, the goal of self-protection would best be served by accurate information. But in each case, self-seeking or self-enhancement would be better served by a distortion of reality. Given the best possible circumstances, you would like to think it easy to pass the course, to believe that you can handle an extensive extracurricular life while maintaining a high academic average, and to have a degree of self-assurance that would permit you to gain from almost any relationship. When your goal is self-seeking, you may emphasize your strengths, minimize your weaknesses, strive to achieve beyond your capacity, and overestimate the extent to which fortune will smile upon you. In this opposition between self-preservation and self-seeking, we can see the beginning of the conflict between accuracy and distortion in self-knowledge and self-expression.

Symbolic Interactionism

Taking the Role of the Other. Whether the multiple aspects of the self are regarded as true multiple social selves, as James (1892) would argue, or simply as clusters of attributes that differ depending on the social surroundings, it is still important to suggest how these relationships with other people affect our self-concept. Early interest in this problem can be traced to the origin (Cooley, 1902) of the sociological tradition that has become known as **symbolic interactionism** (Mead, 1934; Stryker, 1983). This approach describes social encounters in terms of their *meaning* and their *value*. People exist in a symbolic, as well as a physical, environment where even physical objects assume importance because of their social meaning. A building is not significant to us because of its physical characteristics—walls, floor, roof, doors, windows—but because of its function as a gathering place for people. Similarly, the importance of a social interaction is derived not from the physical fact of the encounter, but from the meaning it holds for the participants. Was the meeting a business transaction, an exchange of pleasantries among casual acquaintances, or an angry debate between partisans for different political causes? In addition to its social meaning, an encounter or interaction has a particular value to the participants (and to observers). This value is usually phrased in positive or negative terms. For example, a conservationist may agree with a campground developer that construction of buildings in a wilderness area has a social meaning of "increased public use of the area." For the developer this would be a good thing; for the conservationist, it might be a bad thing.

Until now the description of meanings and values sounds very much like the information-processing view of an attitude (Chapter 5), in which the attitude is the summed products of beliefs about the object times the evaluation of each of those beliefs. There is, however, an important difference. Unlike the information-processing theory of attitude organization, symbolic interactionism describes a specific interpersonal process thought to account for the shared meanings, and for many of the values as well. The "interaction" in symbolic interactionism refers specifically to the fact that people do communicate with each other, thereby providing the opportunity for meanings to be learned and for values to be exchanged. Because we share a common language and have the ability for symbolic thought, we can (at least in principle) put aside our own concerns to look at the world from the point of view of other perceivers. Certainly we do not do this all of the time (as the actor-observer differences in attribution discussed in chapter 4 indicate), or even often enough, but as Mead (1934) put it, we are able to take the role of the other. We can empathize with the feelings and attitudes of others by symbolically stepping into each other's shoes.

The Looking-Glass Self. The ability to take the role of another person has an important implication for the development of the self-concept. When I take another's view of the social world, one of the things that I will see is, obviously, my self. Not surprisingly, Cooley (1902) described the resulting picture as a **looking-glass self** with three major components. The first component is our social meaning; our imagination of our appearance to the other person, and that person's estimate of our behavior and motives. The second component is our social value; our imagination of the evaluative judgment that the other person would make about the behavior he or she sees. The third component is some form of self-feeling (such as pride or shame) that arises from what we believe the other person's evaluation of us to be. Here our emotions arise not from our own evaluation of our social selves, but from the evaluation that we believe is being made by the perceiver. In keeping with the notion of a multiplicity of clusters of "selves," Cooley (1902) points out that the looking glass is not a "mere mechanical reflection" (p. 152), because it will differ depending on whose view we take. The great surgeon who takes pride in a professional reputation for technical brilliance might feel shame should his or her patients discover that some of this expertise has been gained at their risk. The looking glass can be tarnished by self-preservation and self-seeking; and the intriguing question "What does he really think of me?" is made even more intriguing by the relative infrequency with which it is asked.

THE PROCESS OF SELF-EVALUATION

The assertion that the self we present differs depending upon the audience, and the idea that we can learn of that audience's expectations through interaction, together have provided much of the foundation for social psychological study of the self. But these two ideas still leave some crucial questions unanswered. Whose opinions are the most valuable, and for what purposes? When do we desire accurate information, and when do we want to be misled? How do we assess our attitudes and emotions? What consequences does all of this self-assessment have for our self-esteem? In this section of the chapter, we examine some recent formulations that suggest answers to these questions.

Perhaps nothing is more basic to self-evaluation than comparison of the self with other people. Through such comparison we obtain estimates of our abilities, confirmation for our opinions, and judgments of our self-worth. This principle of comparison is inherent in the ideas of James (1892) and the symbolic interactionists, and it can be seen in a wide variety of other social evaluation theories (summarized by Pettigrew, 1967). For our purposes, the most important of these theories are the *reference group* theory of Hyman (1942), the *social comparison* theory of Festinger (1954), and the *cognitive labeling* theory of Schachter (1964). The first deals with the choice of comparison groups, the second concentrates on the selection of individual comparison persons within a group, and the third shows how social factors can influence even private experiences such as emotions.

Reference Groups

Normative and Comparison Functions. According to reference group theory (Hyman, 1942, later extended by Kelley, 1952, and by Merton, 1957), a **reference group** is any group that a person uses as a standard for self-evaluation or attitude formation, regardless of whether it is also a membership group for the person doing the comparing. For example, you may compare your attitudes toward getting high grades with the attitudes held by members of a particular fraternity or sorority, even though you do not belong to such a group yourself. If you use the group as an example of what your attitudes ought to be, then it is serving as a *positive* reference group; if you use it as an example of what your attitudes should not be, then it is serving as a *negative* reference group. In either case the group is serving what Kelley (1952) called the **comparison function:** The group does not attempt to set, or enforce, rules for your behavior, but only serves as a standard you choose for comparison.

But a reference group may perform another function as well—what Kelley called the **normative function**—especially if you have or desire membership in the group. In this case the group establishes rules for your actions (group norms) and enforces your adherence to these rules by providing appropriate rewards and punishments. If you actually belong to a fraternity or sorority, the evaluations that other members make of you as a person may well depend upon your expressed agreement with the group's attitudes toward study habits, social life, and participation in school activities. The fewer outside sources of self-evaluation you have, the more you will need to conform to the group's requirements.

The Bennington Study. As Pettigrew (1967) notes, most of the research on aspects of reference groups has concentrated on the normative function of such groups. The best known of these studies is the large-scale investigation of attitudes toward public affairs among students at Bennington College (Newcomb, 1943). The study was begun in 1934 and lasted for 4 years (Newcomb, 1978). During this time over 600 students participated in a variety of measures, some dealing with presidential preferences, some with political attitudes (such as those toward unemployment, rights of organized labor, and welfare payments) made salient by the New Deal policies of the federal government, and some with mutual friendship choices and ratings of prestige. Most of the students, all females, had come from urban, politically conservative families of high socioeconomic standing, and Newcomb was interested in determining what changes in attitudes might develop as a consequence of the students' exposure to a liberal and politically active faculty.

In terms of the theory, the membership group consisted of the entire student body, but there were at least three major possibilities for reference groups: family and friends at home, the faculty, or other students at the college. Within this last category were the campus leaders (who were, for the most part, quite liberal), the majority of the other students (who typically became more liberal from their freshman year to their senior year), and a small minority of students who maintained their conservatism throughout the four years of college. Support for the reference group analysis is provided by the fact that the most liberal students identified strongly with the liberal elements of the community, whereas students who remained conservative identified with their families and underestimated the degree of liberalism present in the college environment. In addition, the normative aspects of the situation were apparent in the interview responses of conservatives, many of whom noted their isolation from the larger social system of the campus community.

In the normative and comparison functions of a reference group we can see the conflicting pressures toward accuracy and distortion. When a reference group serves only a comparison function, you can be relatively honest with yourself about your position and that of the group (except for the usual social desirability constraints). But when the reference group also has normative power over you, differences between its opinion and your own may have detrimental effects on your self-interest. As a result, you may misjudge the group's position (the case of the conservative Bennington students who dramatically underestimated the liberalism of the college environment), or you may find it necessary to shift your opinion so it more closely matches that of the group. In terms of Kelman's (1961) three processes of opinion change (Chapter 5), change that follows comparison with a reference group would most probably be identification, whereas change that occurs through normative pressure would be compliance (we shall return to these distinctions in chapter 12, in the discussion of the power that a group can exercise over individual decisions).

Social Comparison Among Individuals

Reference group theory is useful for describing comparisons with identifiable groups of people, but it does not attempt to deal with the numerous comparisons that we make with other individuals. This is the province of Festinger's (1954) **social comparison theory**. Although the complete statement of social comparison theory is quite detailed (see, for example, a description of the social comparison of abilities by Darley & Goethals, 1980), for our purposes it can be summarized into three fundamental propositions: (a) people have a drive to evaluate their opinions and abilities; (b) in the absence of "objective" bases for comparison, this need can be satisfied by "social" comparison with other people; and (c) such social comparisons will, when possible, be made with similar others. Let us take a closer look at each of these propositions.

Two Kinds of Evaluation. What does it mean to say that people have a drive to evaluate their opinions and abilities? The two key words in this proposition are "drive" and "evaluate." Although motivational theorists differ regarding the precise meaning of the term *drive*, they concur that drivelike states can be inferred from actions that follow deprivation. If we make you go without food for a week, you will behave as if you had a "hunger drive." You will seek food, perform various tasks to try to obtain it, and devour any food you happen to get. In the general theoretical terms discussed in chapter 2, your hunger drive is a hypothetical construct that is inferred as the motive behind the underlying regularities we observe in your actions. In a similar manner, if we deprive you of information about your opinions and abilities, you will behave as if you had a drive to acquire that knowledge. The minute you acquire a new skill, you will want to find out how your ability compares with that of others who possess the skill. As soon as a new means of travel is invented—be it swamp buggy, airboat, or snowmobile—someone will hold races to see who can drive it the fastest. The same thing is true, although not so obviously, for opinions. We want to determine where our opinions fit with those of other people, and we want to see what others think of us for holding one opinion or another. Thus it is appropriate to postulate the existence of a drive for the evaluation of abilities and opinions.

But what about the evaluation? You may have noticed that the examples involved two different sorts of evaluation. Although Festinger (1954) used the term to mean "find the location of," a number of other writers have pointed out that it could also mean "place a value upon." For example, you may discover that your tennis-playing ability is located at the high end of the scale (there are few people you cannot beat), but how much this discovery adds to your self-esteem will depend on the value you place on being good at tennis. The distinction between "location" and "valuation" senses of "evaluate" arises because we value some opinions more than others, and because we prize great ability. For example, if we use some test of mechanical aptitude to determine that 95% of the people have more aptitude than you do, we have not merely provided you with information about your location. None of us wants to think that he or she is among the worst 5% at anything, so the test outcome will be damaging to your self-esteem.

Objective versus Social Comparison. The second basic proposition of social comparison theory is that when a person cannot obtain information about opinions and abilities from objective sources, he or she will gather it from other people. To set the stage for the two sorts of comparison, Festinger first distinguishes between *physical reality* and *social reality*. Physical reality is an objective world of space and time, containing objects whose characteristics can be specified with relative certainty. This physical reality is equivalent to the physical environment in symbolic interactionist theory. In contrast to this objective world, social reality (analagous to the symbolic environment) consists of an interpersonal world of subjective judgments.

The critical difference between an objective comparison and a social comparison is that the former can be tested against physical reality, whereas the latter cannot. This does not necessarily mean that the appropriate physical tests will always be made. To illustrate the difference, suppose that I am approached by a shady character who offers to sell me a "diamond" for zircon prices. I do not have to rely on his word alone, but can rub the stone across a piece of glass, safe in the knowledge that only a real diamond will make a scratch in the glass. My opinion that the stone is a diamond can be tested against objective physical reality. In contrast, many of our social opinions rest entirely on the judgments of others. Suppose, for example, that I believe people's privacy should be respected by the police and the government, no matter who the people in question might be. There is no physical test I can perform to decide whether this opinion is "correct" either in the sense of agreeing with universal ethical principles, or in the sense of being so positively valued that holding the belief will enhance my self-esteem. These latter judgments must be made through social comparison with other people.

The Importance of Similarity. The third fundamental assumption of social comparison theory is that people most often will choose similar others for purposes of evaluation. Why should I choose a similar other? Intuitively, we might think that such a choice would serve both evaluative goals. Suppose that I want to find the location of one of my political opinions—that the government should respect a person's privacy—and I compare myself with extremists at both ends of the political spectrum. If I discover that anarchists also want privacy (so their bomb factories won't be discovered) and law-and-order radical rightists want privacy (so the meetings of their vigilante group won't be disturbed), does that really tell me anything new about my belief's location or correctness? Probably not. And if my purpose were self-aggrandizement for holding a correct opinion, it certainly would not improve my self-image to be associated with either comparison group. Similar others provide me with a more precise estimate of where in the spectrum my opinion falls. In addition, because they share my values, they are more likely to commend me for the opinions I do hold.

There are, however, several difficulties with this notion of similarity. To begin with, the original statement of social comparison theory (Festinger, 1954) was not explicit about what sort of similarity might be involved. At first, we might think that the important similarity would be on the opinion or ability in question. But this creates the logical difficulty of conducting a social comparison (to determine similarity) before conducting a social comparison (to assess your own position). As a consequence, a number of writers have noted that the similarity must be on attributes related to the object of comparison. Even this modification may not be sufficient, because opinions are correlated with one another, and the same is true for abilities. And the closer the calibrating opinion or ability is to the target opinion or ability, the more likely the logical problem will arise on the related attributes as well.

Furthermore, considering some of the principles of social attribution outlined in chapter 4, there may be times when, as Darley and Goethals (1980) suggest, we can learn more by comparing with others who are *dissimilar*. Suppose that I check my views on privacy against those of people whose political attitudes differ substantially from mine without being radical in one direction or the other. Further, suppose that these new comparisons persons agree with me on the issue of privacy, even though we disagree on taxes and defense spending. What have I learned? From the attributional perspective, I am attempting to locate the cause of my high regard for privacy (the *entity*, in Kelley's, 1967, terms) either internally – my own unique background and views – or externally – privacy is something valued by all people. Comparing my opinion to those of various radicals does not provide me with useful information, because they differ from me in too many ways. But comparison with extremely similar people might not be helpful either, because we could be sharing the same biases. If, however, I discover that a moderately discrepant person agrees with me, then I have achieved consensus, and can be more certain that the entity is to be desired on its own merits by most people.

Unidirectional Drive Upward.   When the issue is the social comparison of opinions, both the traditional and attributional versions of the theory suggest that the major objective is the reduction of uncertainty, the location of one's position in the marketplace of ideas. An interesting complication arises in the choice of a comparison other when the question is one of ability, rather than opinion. Festinger (1954) states that there is a "unidirectional drive upward" in the case of abilities that virtually disappears in the case of opinions. In short, we like to see ourselves as constantly improving. Because we place a high value on good performance, it might not always be best to choose a similar other for comparison: If the selection was too similar, and if there is competition, you might lose. Do you really want to know your where your true ability lies? Enough to risk being defeated at an activity you value? It is highly unlikely that the uncertainty reduction comprising comparison will be continued at the expense of self-esteem.

Information and Motivation. What does all of this tell us about the factors that might lead to the choice of a comparison other? Perhaps the most general conclusion is that both informational and motivational goals are involved in the choice. On balance, the research in social comparison justifies Festinger's (1954) original assumption that people have a drive to evaluate their opinions and abilities. It also justifies the distinction between the two senses of evaluate, and it provides evidence that similar others are involved in a preponderance of the comparison choices. For abilities, this selection of similar others is especially likely when the question to be answered is "What can I do with the ability?" rather than "How much of the ability do I possess?" Apparently we do evaluate constituents of our social selves through comparison with other people, and these evaluations show the twin pressures toward accuracy and distortion that are present in other aspects of self-knowledge.

Assessment of Emotional States

The James-Lange Peripheral Theory of Emotion. Of all the aspects of your social self, intense emotional experience would seem to be the most subjective and private. The joy of giving birth, the profound grief at the death of a loved one, the contentment with a life well spent—these emotions are very difficult to convey to other people who have not shared the same circumstances. Yet many emotional states can be verbally described, and shared, through literature, drama, and conversation. Furthermore, an extension of social comparison theory suggests that the labels provided by others can be combined with internal physiological arousal to produce, not merely communicate, the subjective experience of emotion (Schachter, 1964). We take a closer look at this theory after briefly considering some alternative positions on the origin of emotion.

Let us take fear as an example of an emotion to be understood. In terms of self-assessment, how do you know when you are afraid? The first answer to this question to have substantial impact on psychological interest in emotion was proposed by James and Lange (1922). They suggested that the subjective experience of emotion was the consequence of visceral changes and feedback from skeletal muscles. You have the experience of fear because you are running from that large brown bear that just stood up in the middle of your hiking trail. The threat from the bear not only produces running behavior, it also produces visceral changes – a surge of adrenalin, increases in heart rate and respiration – that are interpreted as the emotional experience of fear. Thus emotion is the result of feedback to the brain from peripheral organs in the body. This position is an all-inclusive version of the "facial feedback" hypothesis described in chapter 3. The difference is that the latter holds only that some emotional experiences may be directed, or intensified by feedback from facial skeletal muscles (saying nothing about the need for internal visceral arousal).

Cannon's Central Theory of Emotion. The peripheral theory requires two fundamental assumptions. First, there must be a different pattern of physiological arousal for every different emotion. Second, any visceral arousal must be accompanied by some emotional experience. Both of these assumptions are necessary for a one-to-one correspondence between the arousal/feedback pair and the subjective experience of emotion, but an early critique by Cannon (1927) seemed to undercut both assumptions.

On the basis of experimental and surgical evidence, Cannon (1927) raised five different objections to the peripheral theory, three of which are considered most important. These are, first, that the artificial arousal of the visceral changes associated with emotion (for example, by the administration of drugs), does not produce equally strong "emotional" experiences. Second, that when visceral changes occur naturally, they take place too slowly to account for the almost instantaneous onset of some emotions. And third, that the viscera are relatively insensitive structures, not likely to be capable of producing the shades of emotion that are often common. In a later review, however, Zillmann (1978) has pointed out that Cannon's criticisms would be devastating only to an absolutist peripheral theory, not to the moderate version presented by James and Lange (1922).

Although it now appears that some of Cannon's criticisms of the peripheral theory were overdrawn, his alternative theory still has contributed its part to our understanding of emotion. According to this alternative theory, both the visceral changes and the subjective experience of emotion are produced by activation of a part of the central nervous system, specifically the thalamus. In our example, the external stimulus (the bear) activates particular structures in the brain, and this activation leads to both the overt behavior (running) and the internal changes (visceral arousal and the subjective experience of fear). Because it attributes emotional experience to changes in the brain, Cannon's theory is known as a *central* theory of emotion. The important contribution made by this notion is that mental structures are implicated in the experience of emotional states.

The Social Psychology of Emotion

Having central structures involved in the production of emotion is not, however, the same as having cognitive processes involved. As Leventhal (1974) has pointed out, Cannon's central theory only described the neurophysiology of emotion, not the psychology of emotion, and certainly not the *social* psychology of emotion. It remained for Schachter (1964) and his associates to describe how social phenomena might affect emotional experience, and the first studies in this series (Schachter, 1959) can be thought of as extensions of social comparison theory. The same factors that give rise to the drive for social comparison—uncertainty about an opinion or ability, coupled with a reason to try to reduce that uncertainty—might also produce attempts to compare emotional experiences.

To test this idea, Schachter (1959) performed an experiment in which groups of five to eight female undergraduates were brought into a laboratory containing an impressive array of electrical hardware. The subjects were met by an experimenter who introduced himself as "Dr. Gregor Zilstein, of the Medical School's Department of Neurology and Psychiatry." As if this introduction alone were not frightening enough, "Zilstein," who was wearing a white lab coat with a stethoscope drooping out of one pocket, then described the experiment as a study of the physiological effects of electric shock. He explained that although this intense series of shocks would be quite painful, it would produce no permanent tissue damage. This introduction concluded, "Zilstein" went on to say that the subjects would have to wait for a few moments while he finished setting up and calibrating the equipment. Each subject was given the option of waiting alone or waiting together with other female undergraduate students, but there were two different descriptions of these other students. In the Same-State condition, the other students were described as waiting for the same experiment, while in the Different-State condition, the students were described as waiting to talk with their professors.

Social Comparison and Self-Esteem Again. The prediction from social comparison theory is that there would be a stronger preference toward waiting with others when those others were similar to the subject, in short, when they were also waiting to take part in the experiment. It is doubtful that you will learn just how frightened you should be of Dr. Zilstein and his shock machine if you are sitting in a room with people who are there for an entirely different purpose. The data supported the prediction, with stronger preferences indicated in the Same-State condition than in the Different-State condition. The dependent variable of interest was the subject's choice of where to wait, so the experiment was terminated as soon as these choices had been made (no subjects were actually given electric shocks). Because the experiment did not include observation of the subjects while they were waiting, it cannot conclusively establish that the desire for social comparison of emotional states led to the choices, but later research has ruled out most of the other possible explanations.

The social comparison of emotions, like the social comparisons of abilities, is limited by the constraints of maintaining self-esteem. You may be interested in the reactions of other people when you are trying to decide how afraid you should be, but the results of this social comparison will have only minor effects on your self-esteem. If you find that others are fearful too, your apprehensions will be justified. If you find that others are not frightened, you will reduce your own level of fear. Only if you continue to be afraid in the absence of objective danger will your emotional state have implications for your self-esteem. But what if the social comparison is not so safe? In an important limitation of the tendency toward social comparison, Sarnoff and Zimbardo (1961) found that people who were anticipating an embarrassing task (sucking on nipples from baby bottles) actively avoided social comparison. When we are confronted with the threat of embarrassment, we prefer to wait alone, or with others who can serve as a distraction.

Cognitive Labeling of Emotion. In Schachter's (1959) first series of experiments, the emotion (fear) was induced by the threatening situation. All that social comparison with other subjects could provide was an estimate of the degree of fear that was justified. The next step in the research attempted to show that the quality of an emotion, not just its degree, could be affected by comparison with other people. The original experiment by Schachter and Singer (1962) illustrates this approach.

In this study subjects were injected with epinephrine (adrenaline), which produces some heart palpitations, hand tremor, rapid breathing, and a warm feeling of flushing. All the subjects had been led to believe that the injection was an experimental vitamin supplement ("suproxin"), but some (the Informed group) had been told to expect these side effects as a result of the injection. When the symptoms did occur, this informed group would have an appropriate label for their subjective feelings. A second group of subjects (the Ignorant group) was given the injection with no prior warning about the symptoms to follow, and a third (Misinformed) group was told that "suproxin" should produce side effects of numbness, itching, and slight headache (all obviously inappropriate to explain the symptoms actually induced). This Misinformed group was included as a control against later emotional differences based solely on physiological introspection, and a second control group was given an injection of saline solution and no prior instructions.

A 3- to 5-minute delay usually occurs before the onset of symptoms after an injection of epinephrine (this, of course, was one of Cannon's objections to the body-reaction theory of emotion), and during this time the subject was joined by an experimental confederate. The confederate had been trained to act in either an angry manner or in a euphoric manner. Thus, for subjects without an adequate explanation for their impending symptoms, the actions of the confederate could provide an appropriate cognitive label.

The results of the study showed that the subjects without a prior explanation for their arousal (the Ignorant and Misinformed groups) adopted the label provided by the confederate's behavior, whereas the Informed subjects did not. These and other findings led Schachter (1964) to propose a **cognitive labeling theory** of emotion, in which both physiological arousal and cognitive elements are required for the subjective experience of emotional states. The physiological component contributes some generalized arousal, and the cognitive component translates that arousal into what the person recognizes as an emotional state. Just how external stimuli create physiological arousal is not spelled out clearly in the theory (all of the emotion theories are relatively vague on this point). Although aspects of the Schachter and Singer (1962) study are quite controversial, there is strong support for the notion that social cognitions play a crucial role in the subjective experience of emotion. Indeed, as Gergen (1984) points out, Schachter's ideas made these cognitive processes not only independent of physiological arousal, but more important than that arousal in generating emotional experience.

Misattribution of Emotion. That emotion consists of two independent components, arousal and cognition, raises some intriguing questions. Can people make mistaken estimates of the degree of their arousal? The success of such techniques as acupuncture and hypnosis in producing anesthesia might depend on this sort of misattribution. Can people be induced to misattribute the source of their arousal, and might this kind of misattribution serve therapeutic purposes? Research based on the cognitive labeling approach indicates that the best answer to all of these questions is a qualified yes.

First consider judgments of the degree of physiological arousal. In a technique that has since become known as the *false feedback* method, Valins (1966) showed slides of female nudes to undergraduate males who had been wired with dummy electrodes. These electrodes ostensibly measured the subject's heart rate, and the resulting heart rate was played back to the subject over a loudspeaker. On a randomly selected few of the slides, the programmed heart rate either increased or decreased appreciably. Attractiveness ratings of the nudes were obtained as the slides were shown, and at the conclusion of the study the subjects were told that they could take a few of the slides with them as a reward for participating in the research. On both the attractiveness ratings and the slide choices made at the end of the study, there was a definite preference for those slides on which there had been a presumed heart rate change, regardless of whether that change had been an increase or a decrease.

Apparently people can be misled into believing that they have been emotionally aroused by a stimulus. Interestingly enough, the reverse also seems to be true. For example, in a similar false heart-rate feedback study, Valins and Ray (1967) showed slides of snakes and the word "shock" to people who had admitted being afraid of snakes. Presentation of the word "shock" was accompanied by a mild shock to the fingers and by a change in the programmed heart rate. Presentation of the snake slides was not accompanied by any change in heart rate (or by shock). After several trials of this procedure, experimental subjects who had been told that the heartbeat was their own were able to approach a small boa constrictor more closely than were control subjects who had been told that the heartbeat was not their own. The experimental subjects may well have observed their own (presumed) arousal, noted that there was no arousal accompanying presentation of the "feared" snakes, and concluded that they must not be as frightened of the animals as they had originally thought. This explanation should sound familiar, because it is, for emotions, the same kind of self-perception argument that Bem (1972) offered for the self-perception of attitudes (Chapter 5).

Next, let us turn to misattribution of the source of arousal. In an early study of this sort, Nisbett and Schachter (1966) gave subjects a placebo pill and then administered an increasingly intense series of electric shocks. Half of the subjects had been led to expect some autonomic arousal as a side effect of the pill, and these subjects showed a much greater shock tolerance before reporting pain. The major contribution of this research was to apply the misattribution paradigm to a natural emotion of general concern. Few of us will ever be in a position to listen to an amplified version of our heartbeat while viewing either attractive or frightening stimuli. Even if we are conscious of our heart rate, we have not programmed it to vary in order to change our emotional experiences. But all of us suffer pain now and then, and for many of us that experience may be as much in our heads as in our bodies. The results of Nisbett and Schachter's experiment make us wonder to what extent aspirin and other pain relievers can act as placebos that rely for their effectiveness on our belief that they will relieve pain.

The potential therapeutic benefit from induced cognitive misattribution of the source of arousal is perhaps best illustrated in the work of Storms and Nisbett (1970). These investigators attacked a common problem that appears tailor-made for a solution with misattribution therapy—insomnia. What happens when you are tense and think you will have difficulty getting to sleep? You know that you need the rest, but you are afraid that you will not be able to sleep. You lie down and try to take your mind off your problems, but the harder you try, the more wide awake you become. Confirming your worst fears, you are not able to get to sleep. But what if you could attribute your sleeplessness to some emotionally irrelevant external stimulus?

To answer this question Storms and Nisbett (1970) gave insomniac subjects a placebo pill that was described as producing alertness, high temperature, and heart rate increases. Because all these physiological symptoms typically accompany insomnia, subjects receiving the pill could readily attribute their arousal to the drug, rather than to the fears and worries that had previously been keeping them awake. As anticipated, the subjects reported being able to get to sleep earlier on nights when they had taken the pill than on nights when they had not. Later research has suggested that the placebo pill is probably not necessary, and can be replaced by misattribution to social factors that the insomniac can control.

There is, however, an important caveat that must be entered regarding "therapeutic misattribution." Think for a moment about the experimental technique. What is actually involved? The subject arrives with a self-identified problem, and the researcher explicitly deceives the subject into thinking that the "true cause" of the symptom is something other than what the subject initially believed it to be. In the discussion of the ethical difficulties associated with research (Chapter 2), the presence of deception in experimentation was held to be justified for the knowledge to be gained, providing that (a) the risks to the subjects were minimal, (b) there was an implicit contract between the subject and researcher, at least part of which suggested that experimenters cannot always be completely above-board with their subjects, and (c) there was a debriefing following the procedure.

Now contrast this description with the description of therapy. The only person whose knowledge really matters is the client, and the risks to that person should be zero (first, do no harm). The implicit contract—and in many cases the explicit contract as well—requires that the therapist be truthful. Even if these provisions were violated by "therapeutic misattribution," there could be no debriefing without jeopardizing the effectiveness of the treatment. In short, the process of induced misattribution is of substantial theoretical value, but the ethical difficulties it presents may prevent it from becoming much of a contender as therapy.

Self-Perception of Attitudes

All of the forms of misattribution of emotion rely on an external stimulus to provide the person with an explanation for internal feelings that would otherwise be either undefined or defined in a way harmful to the person. As previously noted, this reliance on an external view of the self is very similar to the process Bem (1972) postulated for the development and change of social attitudes. We may base some of our attitudes on those held by reference groups that are important to us, and we may evaluate the location and social value of other attitudes through social comparison. But these processes often may be supplemented, especially when attitudes are not well formed, by observation of the self and its actions.

You will recall that the basic premise of Bem's approach is that people do observe both their own behavior and the situational context in which it occurs in much the same way that they might observe the behavior of another person. There are obvious limits on the match between these two processes, as the divergent perception of actors and observers, discussed in chapter 4, indicates. But within these limits, the self infers its attitude toward a particular object on the basis of internal feelings and external rewards or punishments. Because Bem's theory was discussed in detail in chapter 5, all that needs to be done here is to place it in the larger framework of the self-evaluation principles we have just considered (looking-glass self, social comparison, cognitive labeling).

In many ways, Bem's self-perception approach is quite similar to other views of self-evaluation, but there is one critical difference: the focus is on one's own behavior rather than on the cues provided by the actions of others. This difference can be seen first in the notion of the looking-glass self, which has us taking the role of significant other people and evaluating ourselves as we guess they might evaluate us. This is not direct self-observation, but observation through the eyes of another. Next, social comparison describes ways in which we learn about and judge our opinions and abilities by means of explicit references to the opinions and abilities of others. Certainly some evaluation of the self follows social comparison, but the principal source of information is the behavior of other people. Finally, cognitive labeling theory concentrates on the emotional labels suggested by the external environment. There is much more emphasis on internal states (such as physiological arousal) in cognitive labeling theory than in either symbolic interactionism or social comparison, but the major role is still given to the externally based label. Thus, although all the self-evaluation theories discuss some form of interchange between the self and the social environment, self-perception theory can be distinguished from the rest by its more exclusive concern with the direct observation of one's own behavior.

Self-Perception of Motivation

Oversufficient Justification.   One aspect of this self-observation that has received increasing attention in recent years is the self-perception of motivation to engage in a variety of tasks. This area of research has obvious implications for performance in school and on the job, and builds on the principle of oversufficient justification discussed in chapter 5. You will remember that self-perception theory and the theory of cognitive dissonance make virtually identical predictions for attitude change among individuals who perform actions counter to their existing attitudes. The less the external payment for the action (insufficient justification), the greater the attitude change. Dissonance theory accounts for these results by reference to an internal motivational state, whereas self-perception theory merely assumes that the person is taking into account the internal attitude and the external constraints in the same way that a noninvolved observer might. In the case of a large extrinsic payment for *pro*attitudinal behavior, however, it is the self-perception theory that makes the nonobvious prediction: The more you pay a person to do what he or she would do anyway, the less favorable toward that activity will become his or her private attitude.

One of the first experiments to test this idea was reported by Lepper, Greene, and Nisbett (1973). These researchers first gave nursery-school children the opportunity to play with felt-tipped pens and high-quality drawing paper, to determine their level of intrinsic interest in these materials. They then assigned the children who met a criterion of intrinsic interest to one of three experimental conditions. In the Expected Reward condition, the children were told that they would receive "Good Player" awards for drawing pictures in a later play session. No instructions were given to children in either of the other conditions in advance of the play session, but after the session the Unexpected Reward children who drew with the materials did receive "Good Player" awards; in the Control condition no awards were given.

ᵣ Several days later, the researchers allowed the children in all conditions to use the drawing materials as part of a free-play session, and the amount of time they spent drawing was observed and recorded. As would be expected from the notion of oversufficient justification, children in the Expected Reward condition actually engaged in less free play with the materials than did children in either other condition. This basic finding has been replicated and extended in later research, and it raises serious questions about the entire practice of providing extrinsic rewards for activities, such as schoolwork, that have the development of intrinsic interest as one of their primary objectives. In a later book, Lepper and Greene (1978) do not go so far as to suggest that extrinsic academic rewards (such as smiling faces, gold stars, or – more to your level – grades) be done away with in order to enhance intrinsic interest. But the future implications of this work for the educational process could be profound.

Cognitive Evaluation Theory. In a slightly different approach to the self-perception of emotion, Deci and his associates (e.g., Deci & Ryan, 1980) have suggested that the changes in intrinsic interest come about not because of oversufficient justification, but rather for two other reasons. First, building on the naive psychology of Heider (1958) described in chapter 4, Deci and Ryan argue that one of the critical effects of a reward is to shift the locus of causality from internal to external. If you do something because you like to, that is an internal reason; if you do it because I pay you handsomely for doing so, that is an external reason. To this notion of locus of causality, Deci's **cognitive evaluation theory** adds the assumption that people strive for competence in their activities. Anything that provides *information* about competence (even if that thing is a reward) will enhance intrinsic motivation. Alternatively, if an extrinsic reward does not add to the individual's knowledge about his or her capabilities, it will be seen as an attempt to *control* behavior, and will consequently reduce intrinsic motivation. Because money is typically considered to be an incentive for behavior, people are especially likely to see monetary rewards as controlling rather than as informational. The fact that this view of motivation, like the oversufficient justification view, has received substantial empirical support suggests that business practices and educational practices might benefit from analysis based on principles of self-perception.

THE DEVELOPMENT OF SELF-ESTEEM

Successes and Pretensions

The self-perception analysis of motivation brings us closer to that all-important personal estimate of worthiness, *self-esteem*. Indeed, a major study of self-esteem (Coopersmith, 1967) defined the term as a set of self-evaluative attitudes. Whether the evaluative behavior involves modeling an attitude after one held by a positive reference group, comparing ability with a similar (but slightly better-off) other, avoiding excessive fear by obtaining appropriate emotional labels for threatening situations, or weighing the relative contributions of internal and external sources of an attitude, the ultimate goal is the same: protection or enhancement of self-esteem.

Just as the topic of evaluation of the social self must begin with the ideas of James (1892), so a discussion of self-esteem must begin with his definition:

$$\text{Self-esteem} = \frac{\text{Successes}}{\text{Pretensions}}$$

According to this definition, what you think of yourself will depend on the degree to which your actual successes coincide with the goals and aspirations you set for yourself. The first thing to notice about this definition is that your "pretensions" can be considered internal standards over which you have substantial control, both in the selection of which aspects you consider important, and in the level of performance you expect to attain on each of those aspects.

Level of Aspiration. Suppose that I ask you to tell me something you are proud of, and you reply, "I can almost always break 90 when I play golf." What is involved in this assertion of self-esteem? To begin with, you have chosen to tell me about your athletic ability (rather than your musical talent or your interpersonal skills), and this choice reflects the importance to you of the general arena of athletics. Within this arena, you have further confined your pretensions to a single game, rather than asserting that you have equal competence in other sports as well. Finally, you have set a numerical score of 90 as your **level of aspiration**: that standard of performance that will determine whether your self-evaluation is positive or negative (Lewin, Dembo, Festinger, & Sears, 1944). If you obtain a score lower than 90, you will be pleased with yourself; if you do not break 90, you will be unhappy with your game. The choice of athletics, the choice of golf, and the score of 90 are all standards for evaluation that you set for yourself.

Once you have set these standards, you evaluate your performance against that set of standards, and it is in this judgment of "success" that many of the self-evaluation theories come into play. If your chosen ability were tennis rather than golf, there would be no standard such as a score of 90 against which to judge your success. Your achievements in tennis must be gauged against the play of various opponents, through a process of social comparison. In the same way, if what you value is your ability to keep cool when others around you are losing their heads, you will need to do some social comparison of emotional state. And if you derive much of your self-esteem from thinking that you are an intellectually independent person, you will need to evaluate the extent to which your attitudes are determined by internal, as opposed to external, forces. Among the social evaluation theories previously considered, only reference group theory might be more appropriate for establishing pretensions than for evaluating successes.

One final feature of the definition deserves comment. Because self-esteem is a ratio of successes to pretensions, you can raise your overall level of self-esteem either by increasing your successes, or by decreasing your pretensions. If you and I play a round of golf together, and your goal is to break 90, while my goal is to lose fewer than a dozen balls in the ponds and the rough, I can play much, much worse than you do and still feel more success at the end of the round. My pretensions are so much lower that it takes very little success to keep me happy. Unfortunately, one of the most difficult tasks in the maintenance of self-esteem is the setting of realistic aspirations. Particularly in the case of abilities, there is that "unidirectional drive upward" with which to contend.

Real Self and Ideal Self. The explicit comparison between actual ability, performance, or personality and the internal standards of aspiration can be seen in many of the recent descriptions of self-esteem. Some of these measures are verbal, some are nonverbal; some ask the subject to make a direct comparison of success to pretensions, other simply assume that individual pretensions can be equated with more general societal expectations for "good" characteristics.

The wide range of measurement possibilities can be illustrated by two of the scales. The first of these, developed by Bills, Vance, and McLean (1951), is perhaps the most literal translation of James's (1892) ideas. It asks the subject to answer three questions about each of 49 self-descriptive traits: how often the trait is characteristic of him or her, how often he or she would like for it to be so, and how he or she feels about possessing the characteristic. The first of these is the measure of successes (called the **real self**), the second is the measure of pretensions (called the **ideal self**), and the third is a measure of the importance of the trait in question. The person's self-esteem is defined as an inverse function of the discrepancy between the real self and the ideal self, a definition quite similar to James's conception of self-esteem.

One of the difficulties that would plague the Bills, Vance, and McLean measure (or any other measure of self-esteem that involves descriptive adjectives) is that people are likely to be concerned about the impression they are making on the experimenter by the responses they give. Worse still, there is the chance that such impression management objectives could change the measured self-esteem in either direction from what it would be if there were no such complications. Some people might inflate their real self, hoping to convince the experimenter that they were everything they claimed was important, while other people might artificially lower either their real self or their ideal self in a show of false modesty. Indeed, some recent research by Jones and his associates (e.g., Jones & Pittman, 1982) shows, among other things, that people will *self-handicap*—expressly choosing to perform potentially difficult tasks under less than ideal conditions. That way, these external obstacles provide (in attributional terms) a nonthreatening explanation for failure and an augmentation of any success that might be achieved.

Recognizing the limitations of many verbal measures, Ziller (1973) developed a nonobvious measure of self-esteem. In one form of this scale, the subject is presented with a horizontal row of six circles and is asked to indicate which circle corresponds to the self and which circles correspond to significant other people (such as "someone who is flunking," or "the strongest person you know"). The crucial measure of self-esteem is how far to the left the subject places himself or herself, on the grounds that in our culture there is a "norm of hierarchical ordering of social objects in a horizontal line from left to right" (Ziller, 1973, p. 11). In the case of this measure, successes are represented by the placement of the self, and pretensions are considered to be implicit in the ordering from left to right.

External Factors Influencing Self-Esteem

Socialization Experiences.   Although we have concentrated on the relationship between success and pretensions as a major determinant of self-esteem, other influences on self-esteem are largely outside the control of the person. These begin in childhood with the actions of the parents and continue into adulthood with the responses of peers and significant reference persons. In an extensive study of preadolescent children aged 10 to 12, Coopersmith (1967) found three separate factors leading to the development of high self-esteem: (a) parental acceptance of the children, (b) clearly defined and enforced limits on behavior, but (c)respect for individual action within those limits. The parents of children with high self-esteem were themselves "active, poised, and relatively self-assured individuals who recognize the significance of childbearing and believe they can cope with the increased duties and responsibilities it entails" (Coopersmith, 1967, p. 237). The sort of parents we have, and the way they deal with us as children, are profound influences on our later self-esteem over which we obviously have no personal control.

Distinctiveness. You will recall from chapter 4 the extent to which perceivers simplify their social environments, forming cognitive categories into which they place other people. This categorization of others is accompanied by a variety of perceptual effects, including salience: individuals who stand out from their social background are regarded differently from those who blend into the background. Applying the same principle to self-perception, McGuire, McGuire, & Winton (1979) have argued that a person's self-concept will be unduly influenced by those personal characteristics on which the person is *distinctive*. These do not need to be unique personality traits, however, because even a person's gender will be distinctive to the extent that members of the opposite gender predominate in his or her family.

In order to discover what people believe to be distinctive about themselves, McGuire and his colleagues ask subjects to "tell us about yourself," a question that elicits the person's *spontaneous self-concept*. This spontaneous self-description is then coded to reveal the categories used by the person. This method is obviously similar to the Twenty Statements Test (Kuhn & McPartland, 1954), but it has two advantages over that measure. First, the spontaneous self-concept technique is less leading. You are less likely to respond with social categories under the relatively vague instructions to "tell us about yourself" than if we ask you to respond by naming a set number of descriptive statements. Thus, if you do give us a spontaneous self-concept replete with social categories, we can be more certain that those categories were included because they were important to you, not because you believed they were important to us. The second advantage of the spontaneous technique is that the *negation self-concept*, your opinion of what sort of person you are not is less artificially obtained, simply by asking you to "tell us what you are not."

Race and Gender. Some of the attributes over which we have no control are our physical characteristics—race, gender, attractiveness—yet these qualities may be not only distinctive to us, but also important in the judgments that others make about us. One of the earliest demonstrations of how these biosocial attributes can affect self-esteem was the classic study of Clark and Clark (1947), which showed that black children chose a white doll and rejected a black doll when asked to select the one that was nice, or the one with which they would like to play. Because the children were aware of both the color of the doll and their own skin color, the investigators made a convincing case that this culturally approved choice nevertheless constituted a denial of self-worth. There is some recent evidence that these preferences have begun to change, but there are still occasional studies that show results very much like those obtained by Clark and Clark (1947). Part of this effect, of course, may just be due to distinctiveness, because race is mentioned in spontaneous self-concepts to the extent that one's own race is in the minority in the social milieu.

Another biosocial attribute that can have lasting effects on self-esteem is gender, with conditions favoring higher self-esteem for males. At first you might think "Of course, traditional sex roles for women have always been of lower prestige than the roles prescribed for men, so women develop lower self-esteem as a consequence of this difference in role expectation." But some of the influences on a woman's self-esteem are more subtle than that. Remember that self-esteem is defined as the ratio of successes to pretensions, so that successes are supposed to have a positive effect on self-worth. But there are two different judgments involved in the determination of a "success." First, there is the question of whether the behavioral outcome was truly a success, in the sense that objective observers (not just you) would consider it to be one. Second, there is a determination of the causes for that success, and a number of studies indicate that this attribution of causes is made differently depending upon whether the person doing the performance is a man or a woman.

For example, Deaux and Emswiller (1974) asked subjects to explain the success of a stimulus person on a perceptual task of identifying familiar objects shown as part of a confusing background. This stimulus person was described as being either male or female, and the objects were either traditionally male-oriented (such as a wrench or a tire jack), or traditionally female-oriented (such as a mop or a double-boiler). It was implied that male stimulus persons should do better on the male-oriented materials and female stimulus persons should excel on the female-oriented materials. The results showed that when the female succeeded at the male-oriented task, her performance was attributed to luck, whereas male success at the female-oriented task was attributed to ability. What is most interesting for our purposes is that these evaluations were the same whether they were made by male or female subjects. Later studies suggest that the gender orientation of the task may play a larger part than first thought, but one recent review of research in sex roles (Spence, Deaux, & Helmreich, 1985) still concludes that on nonfeminine tasks male success is attributed to ability, while female success is attributed to effort or luck. This difference obtains whether the performance is one's own or that of someone else, and such attributions cannot help but have deleterious consequences on the self-esteem of females.

Physical Attractiveness. Finally, it is important to note that your physical attractiveness will have a substantial effect on your self-esteem, especially to the degree that your self-impression is based on the opinions of others (the looking-glass self). The effect of physical attractiveness begins early in socialization and continues into adulthood, as pointed out in an extensive review by Berscheid and Walster (1974b). Differences in attractiveness among preschool children affect the way in which the children judge each other, with unattractive children considered by their peers to be more aggressive and antisocial (defined as "fighting a lot," "hitting and yelling at the teacher," and "saying angry things").

This tendency to equate physical unattractiveness with antisocial behavior can also be seen in the evaluations of children made by adults (Dion, 1972). In this study, college females evaluated the reported misbehavior of a 7-year-old child. The descriptions were ostensibly based on daily reports of elementary school teachers, and related an incident that was either mild or serious. Attached to each report was a picture of the child, and four different sorts of pictures were used—attractive or unattractive boys and girls. When the transgression was mild (such as stepping on the tail of a sleeping dog), subjects did not differentially evaluate offenders of differing attractiveness. But when the transgression was serious (such as throwing sharp stones at a dog, which cut one of its legs), that transgression was excused as a result of temporary mood for attractive children (of both sexes), but was condemned as a product of antisocial character for unattractive children.

Unfortunately, there is also other research that confirms the existence of a stereotype that "what is beautiful is good." Support for this general proposition has been obtained in a wide variety of settings, including the evaluation of intellectual potential by teachers, evaluations of criminal guilt, and dating choice. There are some limits to this stereotype, especially when the beauty itself is used part of a criminal endeavor (e.g., Sigall & Ostrove, 1975), but its broad area of application cannot help but limit the self-esteem of people who, through no fault of their own, do not possess much physical attractiveness.

THE PUBLIC SELF: MASK OR REALITY?

In the broadest sense, of course, any of your behavior that is observed by another person is a public expression of your self. The clothes you wear, your posture and body language, your words and how you say them, the actions you perform and those you refuse to take—these are some of the cues that other people will use to try to determine what you are "really like."

Their impressions of you are formed according to the same principles of social perception and social cognition (Chapters 3 and 4) that apply to your understanding of others. In this section, however, the emphasis is on the control you choose to exert over the information your actions convey. Are the different clusters of your attributes merely masks that you wear on different occasions? Or do they all reveal something of the "real you?" What factors affect your honest disclosure to other people? What are the consequences of making you self-conscious, or of making you anonymous? In trying to answer some of these questions, it will be necessary to distinguish between the normal circumstances of everyday interaction and the extreme pressures on the social self that are inherent in some less frequent situations.

Concealment and Disclosure in Daily Interaction

Whether it is in the evaluation of an ability, the assessment of an emotion, or the development of self-esteem, the social context plays an important role in the characteristics of the self. As we have noted throughout this chapter, the search for the social self is influenced at times by a desire for accurate self-appraisal and at times for a desire for self-enhancement. This conflict can also be seen in the public behavior of the self, and is represented in the distinction between self-presentation and self-disclosure.

Self-Presentation. Initially defined by Goffman (1959) as the creation and maintenance of a public self, self-presentation occurs in what Goffman argues is a highly structured and ritualized interaction. As noted in chapter 3, each participant in an interaction brings to it a *line* (a view of the situation and the people involved), a central element of which is the **face** (the positive social value the person claims for himself or herself). This face is essentially a public expression of self-worth, and it is enhanced both by what is revealed and by what is withheld. Making an analogy to the theater, Goffman suggests that each participant is engaged in a performance designed as much for its effects on the audience as it is for honest and open expression of the self. This is not to say that the person is consciously aware of or hypocritical about his or her performance or face – in fact, the person may really come to believe in the front that is being presented (like the politician who is to busy being a legislator to notice a few campaign irregularities here and there).

Because an individual's face is a public expression, the person has a vested interest in maintaining and enhancing that face. The same is true of all the participants in an interaction, and there is an implicit rule of reciprocity: you help protect and maintain my face and I will do the same for you, so that neither of us will suffer a loss of face in the interaction. Continuation of an encounter depends on mutual acceptance of this social contract, as indicated by the nature of the corrective process (what Goffman calls the "interchange") that follows a blunder.

For example, suppose that you and I are discussing a mutual acquaintance, and I suggest that the person is so obnoxious that only equally unpleasant people could stand him. As it happens, you have some of the same reservations about the person that I do, but despite those reservations, you have agreed to take an apartment with the person for the summer. The first step in the interchange is the *challenge*, in which the blunder is brought to the offender's attention (you inform me somewhat icily of your plans). The second step is the *offering*, in which the offender has the opportunity to correct the error (I try to recover by saying that of course I didn't mean you, that you will probably be very good for the person. Next (if the interaction is to continue), there is your *acceptance* of my offering, followed by my *thanks* for your graciously letting me recover my face. Unless my original statement was made maliciously (for example, I knew of your plans and was just trying to tar you with the same brush I used on the other person), the interchange has a distinct "We're all in this together; let's make the best of a bad situation" character about it.

Self-Monitoring of Expressive Behavior. As valuable as this mutual commitment is in maintaining an interaction, it is not all that is happening when two or more people get together. Regardless of the ties the participants may have to each other, each also has his or her own objectives for the interaction. Furthermore, there are wide individual differences in the degree to which people are conscious of, and highly involved in, the public impression they make. This intuitively sensible idea has been confirmed in a program of research by Snyder and his associates (e.g., reviewed by Snyder, 1979). The notion of individual differences in impression management is as old as James's suggestion that there are multiple social selves, and self-monitoring research is based on a test that measures these individual differences.

The Self-Monitoring Scale consists of 25 true–false items that assess (a) concern with appropriateness of self-presentation ("At parties and social gatherings, I do not attempt to do or say things that others will like"), (b) use of social comparison information in deciding how to behave, (c) ability to control and modify one's self-presentation ("I can look anyone in the eye and tell a lie [if for the right end]"), (d) use of this ability in particular situations, and (e) the extent to which expressive behavior is tailored to meet the demands of the situation. High scorers on this self-monitoring scale are thought to see themselves as adaptive people who match their actions to the requirements of the situation, while low-scoring people are thought to see themselves as principled individuals who claim a high degree of congruence between their private attitudes and their public behavior.

In an important sense, self-monitoring can be thought of as part of the process of self-presentation. And the idea behind the scale is that some individuals will be more facile at that process than will others. Specifically, for example, a person who is incapable of "reading" the requirements of the situation will, obviously, have difficulty conforming to those requirements (except purely by accident should his or her personal characteristics happen to match those demanded by the situation). But knowing what the situational demands are is not the same as responding to those demands, so the self-monitoring scale also assesses willingness to become what the situation requires. A high self-monitor is high on both of these aspects of self-presentation.

Symbolic Self-Completion. But there is more to self-presentation than process alone. There is also content. Here the question is not on how information gets communicated to the other participants in an interaction, but rather on what information about the self is presented. A recent theory of **symbolic self-completion** (Wicklund & Gollwitzer, 1982) suggests that a substantial portion of this self-presentational content will be determined not by the presenter's strengths, but by his or her weaknesses.

Recall the notion of psychological tension built into Lewin's field theory (briefly described in chapter 1, discussed in detail in chapter 11). The waiter was able to remember all of the orders until they had been paid for; tasks that are interrupted are recalled more effectively than tasks that are completed – the very incompleteness generates a psychological tension that is resolved only when the act has been finished. The theory of symbolic self-completion combines this notion of psychological tension with the idea, taken from symbolic interactionism, that we live in a symbolic environment. The result is the prediction that people who are insecure about their social selves (people who, in other terms, might have quite a discrepancy between their ideal self and real self) will need to present themselves as more complete than they really are. They will substitute symbolic self-completion for real self-completion. In their book, Wicklund and Gollwitzer find symbolic self-completion among nations insecure of their historical past, universities able to buy high-powered faculty members (but not tradition), and individuals who busily go out and "have fun" to keep from admitting how lonely they really are. Wicklund and Gollwitzer also cite the results of a variety of experiments to demonstrate that the less secure people are about their status, abilities, or possessions, the more frequently those aspects of their social selves appear in their self-presentations. It seems that those who are "number two" really do have to try harder.

Self-Disclosure. At this point in the description of the everyday interaction of the self with others, it is useful to point out that the forces toward distortion do not reign supreme. Not all social encounters consist of the interchange between role occupants described in Goffman's (1959) view of self-presentation. Many times people (even high self-monitors) will just do what they believe to be right, regardless of the consequences. And although we will tolerate a certain amount of "puffery" in an initial meeting, we want close friends who are sufficiently self-confident that they do not need to remind us continually of how good, or how important, they are. What we want from close friends—and even from new acquaintances, although to a lesser degree—is some insight into the person behind the presentation. And this person is most likely to be revealed through the process of *self-disclosure.*

Not only is self-disclosure an important source of information to the recipient, it is also considered psychologically healthy for the discloser. Drawing on his experience as a clinical practitioner, Jourard (1964) pointed out that much of psychotherapy consists of listening sympathetically to intimate revelations that the client may not have disclosed to anyone else. To share your self honestly with another human being is to admit your fears and desires, and consequently to know yourself. In contrast, to play a role, or to hide your real self from others is to create for yourself the continual stress of being what Goffman would call "on stage." According to Jourard (1964), this stress is "subtle and unrecognized, but none the less effective in producing not only the assorted patterns of unhealthy personality which psychiatry talks about, but also the wide array of physical ills that have come to be recognized as the province of psychosomatic medicine" (p. 33).

Interaction as a Relationship. It should be noted, however, that even Jourard does not encourage us to disclose all our intimate secrets to everyone we meet. Healthy personality only requires complete self-disclosure to at least one other *significant* person—a close friend, a marriage partner, a parent, or a therapist. But there can also be too much of a good thing. We are embarrassed by someone who describes his or her psychological or medical problems in excessive detail, and we find ourselves wondering whether the person is obtaining some unhealthy gratification from recounting these troubles. Some recent experimental work in self-disclosure lends support to this idea, indicating that too much disclosure, as well as too little, might be related to faulty psychological adjustment (e.g., Chaikin, Derlega, Bayma, & Shaw, 1975).

What governs the degree of self-disclosure? First consider some of the consistent findings. In a series of studies Jourard (1971) reported that (a) females disclose more to each other than do males, (b) women tend to receive more disclosure than do men, and (c) regardless of gender, the amount of information revealed is highly correlated with the amount received. This last phenomenon, designated the **dyadic effect** by Jourard (1964), is perhaps the most consistent result obtained in self-disclosure research. What do these effects have in common? They all illustrate that the process of self-disclosure, like the process of self-presentation, depends upon the existence of a social relationship between the two parties involved. Whether the conversation is between an experimenter and a subject, one good friend and another, or even between passing strangers, self-disclosure implies the same sort of mutual commitment found in the maintenance of face.

Myth and Reality. At this point it is difficult to say with any assurance just how much of everyday social interaction is myth, and how much is reality. What is most intriguing is that both seem to require reciprocity and commitment. If you create a social blunder that threatens your face, only my commitment to continuation of the interaction leads me to help you restore your position in the ritual. But if we are to get to know one another better, our pursuit of that goal requires some honest self-disclosure. A great deal of our interpersonal behavior is specified by the roles we play, and as we see in the next section, those roles can have powerful effects on our actions that would not occur if we were "just pretending." But just as much of our behavior can be characterized in role terms, we see in the discussion of friendship in chapter 9 that changes in the depth of a relationship probably will not occur in the absence of self-disclosure. Strangers become acquaintances, and acquaintances become friends, through mutual sharing of aspirations and anxieties, through the revelation of an increasing amount of previously concealed material. Friendship develops by adding reality without completely destroying myth.

Unusual Situations for the Self

The everyday interaction of the self is, as we have seen, a mixture of role and real self. Even in the most superficial self-presentation, the individual must focus enough attention on his or her true characteristics to ensure that undesirable information does not inadvertently slip out. Similarly, even in the most real and honest self-disclosure, a person must have some minimal awareness of the role requirements in order to direct that self-disclosure toward good friends (or possibly complete strangers), rather than toward casual acquaintances. Thus, in most circumstances, people achieve some degree of balance between self-awareness and role awareness. But there can be other instances in which self-consciousness can be increased to an uncomfortable level (giving a report to a large class, meeting your steady date's parents for the first time, participating in some forms of encounter groups), and cases in which individuality can be all but destroyed (being in mass demonstrations, working in an office that has rows of identical desks almost as far as the eye can see, going to prison). What happens to public behavior of the self under these circumstances?

Objective Self-Awareness. First, let us consider the case of increased attention to the self. Suppose your superior in a business organization asks you to make a presentation to the executive council and board of directors. You have been working on this project for a year, and in truth you know the project better than anyone else in the company. Just to be safe, you prepare voluminous notes, all of the necessary "visuals," and you time the presentation in front of a mirror. When the time comes, however, you still cannot help but be nervous. You are afraid you will say something stupid, or boring, or worse, and you don't know whether you will make it through to the end of your talk.

According to a theory of **objective self-awareness** (Duval & Wicklund, 1972), your discomfort is the result of a heightened recognition of your self as a social object. In a sense, you join the audience, and evaluate your own performance as you are giving it. This idea of objective self-awareness is obviously an extension of the symbolic interactionists' conception of the looking-glass self, except that there is one added ingredient. In the case of the looking-glass self, your emotional reaction of pride or shame is based on your imagination of the evaluations of other people; in the case of objective self-awareness what is important is your own evaluation of yourself. Other people are not even necessary. In fact, many of the studies of objective self-awareness have simply used the presence or absence of a mirror as the experimental manipulation.

Dispositional Differences in Self-Consciousness. Why should your own response to your self be a critical one? After all, you are thought to have control over the level of your pretensions, and other people have at least some favorable things to say about you. There might be several reasons. First, you know your shortcomings much better than the outside observers of your behavior do (there are some aspects of your self that you do not disclose even to your close friends). Second, although you have control over your pretensions, your private aspirations for your self may follow Festinger's (1954) principle of unidirectional drive upwards. The pretensions you announce to the public are modest enough so that you have an excellent chance of achieving them, but you might privately have hoped to do even better. Third, nobody is perfect. If you are realistic about yourself, you will always be able to find some part of your behavior that could be improved. Normally you put such flaws in proper perspective to maintain your self-esteem, but when your attention is forced on your self as a social object, this balancing is more difficult to accomplish. As a consequence of your self-focused attention, you are likely to be excessively self-critical, taking more of the blame for negative occurrences, and expressing a lower self-esteem, than you would otherwise.

In addition to the effects produced by external evaluations of your performance, there is a dispositional variable—*public* versus *private self-consciousness*—that will have parallel effects on your emotional reactions. Specifically, when all of those eyes are watching you perform, will you be thinking about your public self-presentation ("How well is this going over?"), or will you be thinking about your own internal states ("What can I do to get a better grip on my nervousness?")? In an important extension of the notion of self-focused attention, Fenigstein, Scheier, and Buss (1975) developed a Self-Consciousness Scale that measures social anxiety and distinguishes individuals whose predominant self-focus is public from those whose predominant self-focus is private. The public self-consciousness subscale contains items such as "I'm concerned about the way I present myself," whereas the private self-consciousness subscale contains items such as "I'm generally attentive to my inner feelings."

Although the two subscales measure distinct aspects of self-focus, scores on the two scales are usually positively (though weakly) correlated in the aggregate. It is possible, however, to identify individuals who are high in one kind of self-consciousness but low in the other, and there are some clear behavioral differences between these two sets of people. Those who are high on public self-consciousness are much more likely to adjust their behavior to conform to the requirements of the situation, whereas the actions of people high on private self-consciousness are likely to remain more consistent from one setting to another (Carver & Scheier, 1981).

These behavioral differences sound very much like the ones found between people who are, respectively, either high or low in self-monitoring (Snyder, 1979). The parallel between public-private self-consciousness and self-monitoring has been noted by Carver and Scheier (1981), among others, but the somewhat surprising finding is that scores on the Self-Consciousness Scale typically bear little relation to scores on the Self-Monitoring Scale. According to Carver and Scheier (1981) there are both methodological and theoretical reasons why the two constructs might not be as closely related as it would first appear, but these are beyond the scope of the present chapter. What is important for our purposes is Carver and Scheier's (1981) integrative speculation that one construct refers to choice of behavioral standards, whereas the other refers to utilization of those standards, once obtained. Specifically, self-monitoring may refer to a person's preferred source of information about what is correct in the situation (external standards for the high self-monitor, personal standards for the low self-monitor), whereas self-consciousness should predict the extent to which the standards are internalized (greater responsiveness to external standards by publicly self-conscious people, greater responsiveness to internal standards by privately self-conscious individuals).

Anonymity and Deindividuation

Whatever relationship may ultimately be established between self-consciousness and self-monitoring, it is clear that both constructs, like the notion of objective self-awareness, depend on conscious attention to the self. And, as heightened self-attention may make you overly critical, reduced self-focus may prevent you from being self-critical enough. This possibility has guided theory about group behavior ever since LeBon (1895) argued that a person might entirely lose "conscious personality" in a crowd, causing action "in utter contradiction with his character and habits" (p. 34). By contrast, the effects of anonymity on the behavior of individuals has received much less attention, with Zimbardo (1970) able to conclude that only three earlier accounts dealt with the phenomenon that has come to be known as **deindividuation**. As described by Zimbardo, the process of deindividuation consists of a decreased concern for social evaluation (either self-evaluation or evaluation of the self by other people).

This change can be characterized as a loss of identity, individuality, or distinctiveness, and it is reflected in *lowered restraints* against inappropriate behavior (especially of a negative or hostile form). Some of the possible antecedents of deindividuation might include anonymity, the diffusion of responsibility for action among members of a large group, and altered states of consciousness produced by drugs, stress, or lack of sleep (Zimbardo, 1970).

The actions that follow deindividuation are not only irrational, impulsive, and atypical for the person involved, they must also be *auto-reinforcing*, in the sense that they are not under the control of discriminative stimuli in the environment. The behavior, once begun, carries through to a conclusion on the basis of its own momentum. An excellent example of an auto-reinforcing behavior, cited by Zimbardo (1970), and based on an account by the undersea explorer Jacques Cousteau, is the "dance of death" of killer sharks that have surrounded a passive victim. The sharks circle for hours, until one of them takes the first bite. Then all the sharks attack in a fury until there is virtually nothing left of the victim; if one of the sharks is injured in the melee, it, too, becomes a victim.

Deindividuation in a Simulated Prison. Deindividuation among humans rarely produces behavior that approaches this extreme, although some inner-city riots in the late 1960s, many of the lynchings of blacks in the Old South, and some of the actions of political terrorists have had a similar mindless quality to them. More frequently, deindividuation leads to the performance of actions that would otherwise be inhibited – to a lack of restraint, rather than a complete loss of control. This difference can be seen in many of the studies reporrted by Zimbardo (1970), and in the research reported by Haney, Banks, and Zimbardo (1973). This investigation deserves detailed comment for three reasons. First, it illustrates the occurrence of undesirable behavior without complete loss of control. More important, it shows that deindividuation can be the consequence not only of anonymity, but also of the normal performance of a social role. Finally , because of its subject matter, it has implications for social policy.

The subjects in this study were undergraduate males who had volunteered for a 2-week psychological study, for which they were to be paid $15 per day. Participants were informed at the outset that the research was a simulation of a prison environment, and they were prescreened on a variety of psychological tests in order to exclude any individuals who might have had problems that would have been exacerbated by their taking part in the study. Half of the 24 subjects who passed the prescreening were randomly assigned to be "prisoners," and the other half were assigned to be "guards." Only nine prisoners and nine guards took part at any one time; the remainder were on standby in case they were needed.

The nine subjects who were to be the first prisoners were arrested at their homes by the local police, and were transported without explanation to the city jail, where they were fingerprinted, blindfolded, and placed in holding cells. They were then taken by the experimenters from the jail to the simulated prison, constructed in the basement of one of the academic buildings. Upon their arrival at the "prison," the prisoners were searched, stripped naked, deloused, and issued uniforms that were designed to humiliate them still further. The uniform consisted of a hospital gown worn without underwear (to make the prisoners feel emasculated), a cap made from a nylon stocking (to remove any individuality of hair style), a heavy chain locked around one ankle (to serve as a constant reminder of the oppressiveness of the environment), and a pair of flip-flop sandals.

The individuality of the guards was also reduced, by providing them with khaki uniforms, nightsticks borrowed from the local police, and reflecting sunglasses that prevented anyone from seeing their eyes. The guards worked three at a time in rotating 8-hour shifts, and they were given no special training for their roles. The were just told to do what was "necessary to maintain law and order" in the prison environment. There was no prearranged schedule of operation, so the three guards on duty at any time had complete authority to establish rules of conduct, kinds of activities that would be permitted, times at which these activities could take place, and punishments for infractions of rules or for displays of "improper attitude."

Chronology of the Simulation. The first full day passed uneventfully, with the guards beginning to exercise their authority, but on the second day there was a rebellion. The prisoners barricaded themselves in their cells, removed their caps, and taunted the guards. The guards responded by calling in everyone who was off duty, and putting down the rebellion by force. Realizing that they could not all continue to serve 24-hour shifts, the guards resorted to psychological tactics to break the prisoners' solidarity. They arbitrarily dispensed special privileges to some prisoners, and as the days passed, they became increasingly capricious in their administration of the prison, often refusing requests by the prisoners even to go to the bathroom. During the same time, the prisoners were becoming more and more accepting of their total helplessness.

By the sixth day of the study, it had become apparent that not only were the guards and prisoners virtually living their randomly assigned roles, but so were the prison superintendent (Zimbardo), the prisoners' relatives (who had been permitted the opportunity to visit), a former prison chaplain who had been invited to evaluate the validity of the simulation, and even by an attorney requested through the chaplain by some of the prisoners. The simulation was terminated at this point, and a series of encounter groups was conducted, first among the guards, then among the prisoners, and finally including all participants in the study. The purpose of these sessions was to try to deal with the changes in themselves that the participants had observed during the course of the simulation. The relationship of master to slave dehumanizes both, although in different ways: the guards became part of an oppressive social system, and the prisoners became that system's unprotesting victims.

Simulation, Ethics, and Social Policy. This prison simulation raises some profound ethical and social questions, precisely because of its apparent success in producing deindividuation. Ever since the early stages of research in social psychology, concerned people have disagreed over the ethical justification for various experimental and observational procedures. Many of these problems were discussed in chapter 2, but a recurring concern has been the use of deception to create a powerful impact on the subjects in research. It has been argued that role-playing is an ineffective tool for producing sufficient realism (indeed, some of the controversy between incentive and dissonance theories, discussed in chapter 5, dealt with precisely this issue).

So the preponderance of opinion at the time that Zimbardo and his colleagues conducted their simulation, few social psychologists would have predicted the extremes in behavior that were actually observed. There was no deception in the prison simulation—all participants knew in advance what was planned—but nobody was prepared for the powerful effects on all participants that the roles would have. In retrospect, it is clear that Zimbardo should have stayed apart from the day-to-day operation of the prison, and it is tempting to suggest that the research borders on the unethical by virtue of the effects it had on those who took part. We would not, however, have been concerned about the ethics of the procedure *in advance*. It is the very success of the simulation that now gives us pause.

This success of the simulation also raises serious questions of social policy. There is ample anecdotal evidence to support the assertion that particular roles and situations can deindividuate and dehumanize the people involved in them. But because the evidence is primarily anecdotal, it can be dismissed as specific either to the individuals or to the times. The results of this simulation, however, like the results of Milgram's destructive obedience research (discussed in chapter 1), refuse to go away. Remember that the participants were randomly assigned to their roles of prisoner or guard, precluding any self-selection of a role congruent with personal characteristics. Moreover, none of the personality tests administered in the preliminary screening predicted the extent of the effects observed or the individual differences that emerged in behavior (especially among the guards). Finally, the whole enterprise had been billed in advance as research, a situation (unlike a real prison) that any participant could have left at any point during the simulation. All these factors work against the effectiveness of the procedure. Its results suggest how truly awesome the deindividuating effects of a real prison – or, for that matter, any total institution in which a person becomes his or her role – might be.

SUMMARY

The self consists of social perceptions, attitudes, personality characteristics, motives, material possessions, and conscious experience. But the aspect of the self most important to social psychologists is the way in which that self produces behavior that responds to and affects the social environment. We have what can be regarded as multiple social selves (p. 234), each slightly different and each relating to a different group of other people. We learn to evaluate our social selves in part by considering the impressions we make on others (the **looking-glass self**, p. 240), and our public behavior may depend on the balance between the roles we play and the elements of self that remain constant across situations. In public behavior, as well as in the course of acquisition of knowledge about the self, there is a recurrent conflict between pressures toward accuracy and pressures toward distortion.

The process of self-evaluation includes choice of **reference groups** (p. 241) that may set standards for our behavior. These groups may simply provide us with models of appropriate action (the **comparison function**, p. 241), or they may administer rewards and punishments designed to enforce their standards (the **normative function**, p. 241. On an individual, rather than group, level, we attempt to evaluate our opinions and abilities by engaging in **social comparison** (p. 243) with similar others. These comparisons enable us to find the location of our beliefs and abilities, and provide self-validation that can enhance self-esteem. In much the same way, we may assess our emotional states by means of the **cognitive labels** (p. 250) provided by the social context. Particularly in novel situations, our judgments about the degree to which we are physiologically aroused or about the source of that arousal may be susceptible to influence by the social cues available to us. In some cases, experimentally induced *misattribution* (p. 250) of emotional arousal may have therapeutic value.

The impressions that we have of our self-worth, designated by the term *self-esteem* (p. 255), will depend on circumstances both within and beyond our control. One critical aspect of self-esteem is the degree to which our successes in life correspond to the pretensions (p. 255) we set for ourselves, and this component of self-esteem can be measured by a comparison between the **ideal self** (p. 257), and the **real self** (p. 257). We have control over our pretensions, and can raise our self-esteem either by increasing our successes or by decreasing the goals we set. There are, however, significant contributors to *self-esteem* (or lack thereof) that are beyond our direct control, including the child-rearing practices of our parents (p. 257) and various of our biosocial attributes (p. 258), such as race, gender, and attractiveness.

The conflict between accuracy and distortion is also represented in the public behavior of the self by the opposing processes of *self-presentation* (p. 261) and *self-disclosure* (p. 263). Self-presentation as a process occurs in a ritualized interaction in which the major element is the role taken (p. 262) by each participant and maintained by the mutual commitment of members of the group. This process may be affected by individual differences in *self-monitoring* (p. 262). In addition, some of the content of self-presentation may arise from a need to compensate for our weaknesses through **symbolic self-completion** (p. 263). By contrast to self-presentation, honest self-disclosure involves the admission of desires and failings, and the ability to disclose those to at least one other significant person may be needed for a healthy personality (p. 264). In extreme circumstances **objective self-awareness** (p. 266) can lead to exaggerated self-criticism, whereas **deindividuation** (p. 268) can produce a variety of socially undesirable or inappropriate responses.

SUGGESTED ADDITIONAL READINGS

GERGEN, K. J. (1984). Theory of the self: Impasse and evolution. In L. Berkowitz (Ed.), *Advances in experimental social psychology* (Vol. 17, pp. 49-115). New York: Academic Press. This chapter is written for the professional audience, and takes a controversial position on the nature of the concept of self. But it also provides a stimulating overview of the self in a social context. Difficult, but rewarding.

WEGNER, D. M., & VALLACHER, R. R. (Eds.). (1980). *The self in social psychology.* New York: Oxford. This book of readings contains chapters on self-awareness, motivation, emotion, thought and memory, self-disclosure, and others. Broad coverage, but written for the undergraduate student. A recommended first supplement.

CHAPTER EIGHT

REINFORCEMENT AND FAIRNESS IN SOCIAL EXCHANGE

CONTENTS

PREVIEW

This chapter completes the shift from the study of processes that occur within a single individual to investigation of processes that take place in an interaction between two or more individuals. Much of this interpersonal behavior is guided by the principle of reinforcement, which can be seen in social learning theory, exchange theory, and equity theory. Social learning theory suggests that novel social behavior can be learned through the observation of models and then maintained by various sorts of reinforcement. The desire to maximize one's own outcomes is a fundamental element in social exchange theory, which indicates that these outcomes can be evaluated according to a comparison level based on prior experience. the fact that the other participant's outcomes will also determine satisfaction with a relationship is reflected in the principles of relative deprivation, distributive justice, and equity. Equity theory suggests what actions will be taken by a person who believes that his or her rewards are either too great or too small in comparison to those of others in the situation.

As noted in several places to this point, social psychology is the scientific study of the social behavior of the individual person. Nearly all of the material contained in the first seven chapters has dealt with psychological factors within the individual that influence social actions. We have examined social perception and social cognition (Chapters 3 and 4), describing cues that might be used in the formation of impressions, and in the perceiver's own active construction of the social world and the people in it. Next, we considered another aspect of the individual, social attitudes, outlining the components and organization of attitudes and suggesting how they might be changed (Chapters 5 and 6). Finally, we began the transition to interpersonal behavior by describing the individual's evaluation and presentation of his or her social self (Chapter 7).

Recall that one of the fundamental assumptions of social psychology is that observable social behavior is driven by internal cognitive and motivational processes. Given this assumption, it is not surprising that the majority of theories described in the early chapters have been intrapersonal in nature. The integration of perceptual information and the making of dispositional attributions, the formation of attitudes and the maintenance of cognitive consistency, the social comparison of abilities and the cognitive labeling of emotion—all involve processes within a single individual. There is very little truly interpersonal content in any of these theories, and the social benefits (gains or losses) that may accompany the various intrapersonal phenomena are of less importance than the manner in which each internal process is presumed to function. For example, the theory of cognitive dissonance assumes that dissonance is unpleasant and consonance is pleasant, but the major task of the theory is to describe how dissonance can be aroused, and once aroused, reduced.

REWARDS AND SOCIAL LEARNING

Now, however, our focus shifts from the individual to the interpersonal, so the social benefits and costs of action become paramount. The topics described in the remainder of the book all involve social exchange among participants: helping and attraction (Chapter 9), competition and aggression (Chapter 10), interpersonal influence (Chapter 11), group processes (Chapter 12), environmental effects on social behavior (Chapter 13), and the social context provided by the legal system (Chapter 14). These social exchanges are best described in terms of the rewards achieved and the costs incurred by participants in the exchange. To provide a conceptual framework for the remaining material the present chapter discusses a number of theories based on the general idea of reward and cost. Because it is intended to be an overview of principles in social exchange, this chapter concentrates on a single body of theory more exclusively than have preceding chapters.

The Principle of Reinforcement

The Hedonistic Calculus.   As suggested in chapter 2, many of the origins of social psychology can be traced to the philosophy of earlier times, and nowhere is this more true than in the case of social exchange. One of the first explanations of human behavior held that people were motivated to seek pleasure and to avoid pain. In Western philosophy, this principle was represented in the views of Bentham (1789/1879), who devised what he called a **hedonistic calculus** for analyzing pleasure and pain. Bentham recognized that pleasure and pain could have different sources, but he argued that all of these could be characterized with respect to a number of dimensions such as duration, intensity, certainty, and extent (participation of more than one individual). People could also differ individually in what they found pleasurable or painful, but the behavioral prediction remained the same: people should act in ways that will maximize their pleasure and minimize their pain.

The Law of Effect.   This doctrine of hedonism was first formally expressed in psychology in the **law of effect** proposed by Thorndike (1898). According to Thorndike, any behavior that led to pleasure would be "stamped in," whereas any behavior that led to pain would be "stamped out." Behaviors that consistently produced pleasurable consequences would thus be more likely to occur among the future actions of the individual. In this way the *effect* of an action might actually serve as the cause of future behavior.

Let's consider a concrete example. Suppose that you are a student in my class, and that early in the term you ask a very perceptive question. If my immediate response is to commend you for your insight (and then to give a satisfactory answer to the question), the frequency with which you ask questions in class would presumably increase. The theory assumes that the commendation is pleasurable to you, ant that achieving that pleasurable effect will increase the chances of your asking questions in the future. Thorndike would not claim that you "expected" future commendations, only that this one commendation had helped "stamp in" your question-asking behavior. Because the effect was observable and the relevant future actions would also be observable, it was claimed that no intervening cognitive processes needed to be assumed to exist (a claim with which most social psychologists would, of course, disagree).

Modern Behaviorism.   Concentration on observable actions and effects is the hallmark of Skinner's (1953) **behaviorism**, but Skinner has taken the argument one step further. He refers to the law of effect as the principle of *reinforcement,* and defines a positive reinforcer as any stimulus that increases the probability of an action that it follows. A negative reinforcer is a stimulus whose withdrawal increases the probability of the behavior that it follows (the provision of something unpleasant is called *punishment*). Notice that this is a dramatic shift in emphasis from the early doctrine of hedonism. Where Bentham proposed ways to distinguish one subjective experience of pleasure or pain from another such experience, Skinner defined pleasure (positive or negative reinforcement) or pain (punishment) solely in terms of its effects on behavior. My commendation for your asking perceptive questions is considered positively reinforcing only if the frequency of your questions increases.

A number of writers (e.g., Gergen, 1969; Sahakian, 1974) have noted some major conceptual difficulties with this approach. Foremost among the difficulties is the circular character of such a strict definition of reinforcement. What is a positive reinforcer? Any stimulus that leads to an increase in the probability of the behavior it follows. And why does the probability of an action increase? Because that action has been positively reinforced. Apart from observing its effects, there is no way to tell whether a stimulus will be a positive reinforcer. This circularity is of only minor importance when one is dealing with animal subjects over which one has virtually complete control, but it presents substantial difficulties when dealing with people. You can give your experimental pigeon almost any isolated stimulus, observe the bird's behavior, and be relatively certain that any change in the pigeon's actions is a direct result of the stimulus change you have made. So the question "What is positively reinforcing?" is easy to answer through well-controlled experiments. But if your subject is a human being, you simply do not have sufficient control over that person's environment (nor would we hope you could ever achieve such control) to be sure that the subject's changes are the consequence of your manipulation, or the result of some uncontrolled environmental event, or even the product of a change in the subject's willingness to cooperate in the research. Under these circumstances, it would seem necessary to include the person's human qualities and capacities in the reinforcement equation. This task has fallen to social learning theory, to which we now turn.

Social Learning Theory

Expectancy and Value. Beginning with your earliest experiences as an infant and continuing through your development into adulthood (and beyond), other people try to influence your social behavior. Your parents try to socialize you by teaching you which interpersonal behaviors are appropriate, which are forbidden, and which may be approved in some circumstances but proscribed in others. In order to get along with your peers you may have to learn an entirely different set of social rules, and even after you have achieved adulthood you may need to alter your actions in response to increased responsibilities or a changing social climate. In short, through most of your life you will literally be learning how to behave. How can we account for this **social learning**?

If the behavior is one that you have performed before and the only change involves the rate at which you emit the action, a modified reinforcement position is sufficient. But even here, social learning theories shy away from the extreme form of behaviorism exemplified in Skinner's (1953) views. For example, the social learning theory of Rotter (1954) includes a nonobservable *expectancy* about the likelihood of reinforcement and a nonobservable *value* that each incentive is presumed to have. A business executive's willingness to take a risk for his or her company will depend on both the probability of success and on the size of the profit or loss that might obtain. Thus interpersonal behavior, like social impression formation (the weighted averaging model described chapter 4) and attitude organization (the information-processing model described in chapter 5) is affected by the multiplicative combination of a probability times a scale value. The higher the value of the incentive and the more certain the expectancy that this positive reinforcement will be forthcoming, the greater the probability of the action. Here the observable characteristics of the reward are less important than the actor's subjective estimates of value and expectancy. This view takes into account some of the complexity of social behavior, but it shares with more behavioristic analyses one major deficiency: it cannot adequately account for the emergence of novel social behaviors (Bandura & Walters, 1963).

The Importance of Imitation. Some of your social behavior can be learned while you are doing it (the principle behind on-the-job training), and some can be learned through what Skinner would call *successive approximations* (for instance, the transition from a skateboard to surfing to windsurfing)). But a great deal of your interpersonal behavior is learned through *imitation* of various models, rather than through direct trial and error. The social learning theory of Bandura and Walters (1963), later extended by Bandura (e.g., 1973), gives imitation the predominant role. Novel social behaviors are first learned through the observation of models, with multiple models who behave consistently producing the greatest amount of imitation (Fehrenbach, Miller, & Thelen, 1979). Newly learned behaviors are then either strengthened through positive reinforcement or weakened through the absence of reward (or occasionally through punishment). This sequence of events can be used to explain the acquisition of deviant (socially undesirable) actions as well as the learning of conforming (socially approved) ones.

The Informational Value of Reinforcement. Although Bandura and Walters (1963) emphasize the role of imitation in the production of novel responses, their social learning theory also rests heavily on the principle of reinforcement. Once a new response occurs in a person's repertoire, its future prevalence will be determined largely by the reinforcement that it receives. Any behavior that receives positive or negative reinforcement (as contrasted with behavior that receives punishment) will be more likely to recur in the future. Consistent with findings from animal studies of reinforcement schedules, social behaviors that receive only partial, or **intermittent reinforcement** will show greater increases in strength and greater resistance to extinction than will social behaviors that receive continuous reinforcement. Bandura and Walters illustrate the importance of intermittent reinforcement with the example of a whining, demanding child: sometimes the parents ignore the unpleasantness, but occasionally they respond to the child's request. Unfortunately for the parents, this teaches the child that whining succeeds.

In Bandura and Walters's (1963) view, reinforcement can have informational value in addition to its motivational properties for maintaining interpersonal behavior. When I commend you for asking perceptive questions in class, I am not only boosting your ego (the motivational function of reinforcement), I am also showing you and the other members of the class that such behavior is socially acceptable (the informational function). Indeed, as far as the other students are concerned, information about what I expect in the classroom is the thing of value in my commendation of your speaking out. If you are rewarded, then it is safe for them, too, to ask questions; if you are punished, then they had better refrain from making the same mistakes. Thus **vicarious reinforcement**, as well as direct reward or punishment, can play a part in social learning. Indeed, if the distinction between the control value and the informational value of reward made in Deci's cognitive evaluation theory (discussed in chapter 7) is as important as it seems to be, vicarious reinforcement may in many instances be even more effective than direct reinforcement in the development and maintenance of social behavior.

Most of the research accomplished within the framework of social learning theory concentrates on the behavior of children, because it is during childhood that the vast majority of social learning occurs. But it would be a mistake to conclude that imitation ceases after a person reaches adulthood. (Consider, for example, the amount that advertisers spend on product endorsements made by famous people whose choices we are expected to imitate.) And it would also be a mistake to think that the effects of social reinforcers become substantially less pronounced as we get older. We are all susceptible to a little flattery here and there, and we become increasingly aware of the social costs incurred (and the rewards derived) from our relationships with other people. If there is any apparent change from childhood, it is that as adults, our imitation of others and our search for social rewards becomes more deliberate. This more or less conscious weighing of the social alternatives is at the heart of several theories of interaction.

EXCHANGE THEORY

The fundamental assumption of various theories of social **exchange** is that in their interpersonal relations as well as in their own lives people will seek to maximize their pleasure and minimize their pain. We form friendships on the basis of mutual trust and support, we avoid social entanglements that we might be too costly, and we join groups that will provide us with personal rewards. The principles of social exchange are most easily described when only two people (a dyad) are involved, so our discussion of social exchange will concentrate on the theory of dyadic interaction developed by Kelley and Thibaut (1978). This theory draws upon the principle of reinforcement, and upon aspects of economics and sociology, and it suggests that each participant brings to an interaction a *repertoire* of possible behaviors that could be performed. The pleasure or pain experienced by each participant will thus jointly depend on his or her own actions and the actions of the other person. The theory diagrams the interactional possibilities in the form of a matrix, which can be used to illustrate some of the relationships that are possible. In addition, the theory suggests how each participant might evaluate his or her rewards from the interaction.

The Interaction Matrix

Suppose that I am your employer, and that you have been working for me long enough to think that it might be time for a raise in your salary, especially because you have just completed a major piece of work that is important to me and the company. We meet in the hallway one day, and each of us has a number of behavioral possibilities. For my part, I can choose to say something about your work or I can ignore it; I can give you a pleasant greeting and ask about your family, or I can merely grunt as I walk by. Your repertoire will be a bit more limited. If you are really interested in a raise, you can neither be openly hostile nor obsequious. You might just say hello, you could ask my advice on a problem, or you could come right out and ask me for a raise. Some of these possibilities are diagrammed in the **interaction matrix** shown in Fig. 8.1.

In the diagram, I am person A (the Superior), and you are person B (the Employee). My behaviors are referred to as a_1 (Cheery Greeting), a_2 (Compliment on Work), and a_3 through a_n (the complete set of remaining actions that I could take in the situation). Your alternatives are b_1 (Request Advice), b_2 (Request Raise), and b_3 through b_k (the complete set of remaining actions that you could take). The final subscripts are different

FIGURE 8.1 The matrix of interaction possibilities (adapted from Thibaut and Kelley, 1959, p. 14).

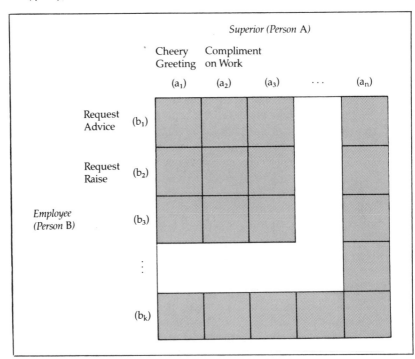

(a_n as opposed to b_k) to indicate that the number of alternatives open to one participant in an interaction may not be the same as the number available to the other. Each cell of the resulting matrix represents a specific interaction outcome. For example, in cell a_1b_1 I could give you a Cheery Greeting and you could Request Advice; in cell a_1b_2 you could think that my good humor made me approachable for a raise.

Costs and Rewards.   Let us take a closer look at just the first two possible actions for each of us (the four interaction cells a_1b_1, a_1b_2, a_2b_1, a_2b_2). Exchange theory assumes that each action, whether it be one of yours or one of mine, carries a certain cost to produce and a reward that follows it. The cost of an action will include the time and physical effort involved in performing the action, the social cost that might accrue as a result of the action, and the benefits that were foregone by not doing something else. The physical cost to one person will remain virtually unchanged regardless of the behavior of the other participant, but the social cost may change as a consequence of the other's action. For example, I expend the same amount of physical effort, and take the same amount of time, to compliment you on your work, whether you respond by asking for advice or by asking for a raise. But the social cost to me is much greater in the latter case. I have committed myself to a high evaluation of your worth to the company, and I am thus in a bad position to argue that you do not deserve the raise you request. Costs of a behavior may change over time, because of physical fatigue or its social analogue: your request for advice may be a pleasant consultation the first time or two, but if you keep it up, I will soon think it a nuisance.

Just as every action has some cost, each also leads to some reward. Unlike the costs, the rewards are almost entirely determined by the behavior of the other person. There is some intrinsic reward—no matter whether I give a pleasant greeting or a compliment, I can enhance my self-esteem by thinking of myself as a forthright and pleasant executive—but the effects of this self-administered pat on the back can be dramatically outweighed by your behavior. I will be rewarded by your asking for advice, but your request for a raise will ruin my pleasant mood. Rewards can change over time, usually decreasing with the repetition of an action. For me to compliment you once indicates that I have been paying close attention to your work, whereas for me to repeat my congratulations every time we meet suggests to you that I am routinely doling out praise that is relatively independent of anyone's actual performance.

Goodness of Outcomes.   Exchange theory assumes that both costs and rewards can be quantified in terms of whatever units of measurement are appropriate for the relationship, and there are scaling procedures that can be used toward this end. To illustrate the computations that can be performed on the scaled costs and rewards, assume for the moment that my complimenting you might cost me 5 such units if all you did was ask for advice, but 25 units if you asked me for a raise. In the same way, if you were asking advice you might obtain a reward of 6 from my cheery greeting, but you might get a reward of 10 units from my compliment.

In each behavioral instance, the cost of producing the action is subtracted from the reward obtained in order to arrive at the **goodness of outcome,** the net profit from the action taken. A complete set of hypothetical rewards, costs, and resulting profits is shown in Fig. 8.2 for the four interaction possibilities. In each cell the numbers above the diagonal refer to the outcomes for person A (in this example, the Superior), whereas the numbers below the diagonal line in each cell refer to the outcomes of the Employee (person B). So, for example, in cell a_2b_2 the cost to the Superior of providing the compliment is 25 units, the reward is −5 units, so the total goodness of outcome (reward minus cost) is a negative 30 units. In this instance the social costs to the Superior are increased by the behavior of the Employee: The same compliment costs the supervisor only 5 units in cell a_2b_1, where the employee only requests advice. It should be noted that the costs (C), rewards (R), and profits (P) shown in the diagram have been arbitrarily set for purposes of illustration.

Evaluation of Outcomes

Choices of Behavior. People given choices of what behaviors to perform will seek pleasure and avoid pain. That assumption guides all

FIGURE 8.2   Rewards (R), costs (C), and profits (P) in a hypothetical interaction between an employee and a superior.

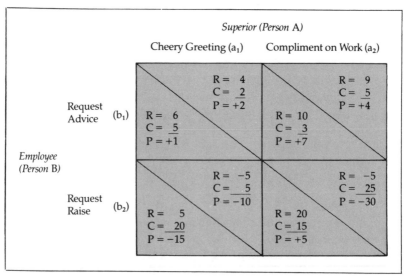

reinforcement-related explanations of social behavior, and Thibaut and Kelley's theory is no exception. Although participants in an interaction are unlikely to perform the computations just outlined, they do have a general idea of which actions cost the most to produce, and they also informally gauge their profits from an encounter. Each participant will "sample" from the alternatives, trying to gain the most personal profit, although we shall see in a later section that only actions involving true interdependence and sustained mutual profit are likely to continue for the long term. A traditionally behavioristic analysis would simply end here, satisfied that a description of the actions chosen would be a sufficient explanation of the interaction. But the exchange theory goes one step further to suggest how the participants might feel about their relative outcomes.

Two Different Standards. According to Thibaut and Kelley (1959), there are two different standards against which a person can evaluate the outcomes (profits or losses) from a relationship. The first of these standards is the **comparison level** (CL), defined as the average value of all of the outcomes known to the person, each outcome weighted by its momentary salience. In the course of your experience you have participated in a wide variety of relationships, with parents, friends, co-workers, teachers, and numerous other people. The exchange theory asserts that you ought to be able to quantify the outcomes obtained from these relationships and use that average value as a standard against which to compare the outcomes you are receiving from the present relationship.

The phrase "each weighted by its momentary salience" indicates that when you are judging a relationship, you will base the comparison level only on the experiences you consider relevant. For example, your interactions with professors would properly be compared to experiences with teachers (and perhaps with other authority figures), but might not be compared to interactions with good friends. The comparison level can change over time, as your general level of outcomes improves or declines, and it can be specific to the sort of situation as well as to the people involved. Singing songs around a campfire on a beautiful evening in the mountains may not be comparable to singing in other places and at other times.

The second standard against which outcomes can be evaluated is called the **comparison level for alternatives** (abbreviated CL_{alt}), and is defined as the level of outcomes prevailing in the best currently available alternative to the present relationship. Here the standard for comparison is not a weighted average of other salient possibilities, but rather is simply the level that could be attained in any alternative to the present relationship, regardless of whether that alternative was the same sort of experience. These "other relationships" include solitude, as well as interactions with people other than the participants in the present situation. When you are sitting in a lecture hall on a sunny spring day, the CL may well be based on other lectures, but the CL_{alt} may be going to the beach. Thus, you might be unhappy in the middle of a lecture that by a different standard would ordinarily have been considered quite good.

The Nature of the Relationship: Attraction and Dependence. Your satisfaction with a relationship–indeed, the very nature of that relationship–will depend on the relative positions of the two comparison levels and your outcomes, as shown in Table 8.1. When your outcomes are better than both your comparison level (CL) and your comparison level for alternatives (CL_{alt}), we might describe your attitude toward the relationship as one of Contentment. This will be a stable interaction, not only because it will be seen as positive (above CL), but also because it is better than anything else currently available (above CL_{alt}). In the next possibility shown, your outcomes are higher than CL but lower than CL_{alt}, and this interaction can be characterized as one of Pleasure. You will enjoy the relationship, but it will be unstable, because of the other attractive possibilities. Whenever your outcomes exceed the comparison level (CL), as they do in both Contentment and Pleasure, Thibaut and Kelley say that the result will be *attraction* to the relationship.

The next bond is not so pleasant. When your outcomes are below your CL but still above your CL_{alt}, Thibaut and Kelley (1959) assert that you will feel *dependence* upon the relationship. It does not live up to your expectations, but it is much better than whatever else you might do. For example, this is the kind of situation confronting a person who does not like his or her job. The person cannot be happy with it, but even as bad as it is, it is better than no job at all (or than other worse jobs that might be open). It should be noted that this condition of dependence is quite stable, and cannot be explained by a simple reinforcement theory that considers only the

TABLE 8.1 Nature of the Bond to a Relationship as a Function of the Comparison Level (CL), the Comparison Level for Alternatives (CL_{alt}), and the Goodness of Outcomes

	NATURE OF THE BOND TO THE RELATIONSHIP			
	Attraction			
↑ Goodness of Outcomes	*Contentment (Stable)*	*Pleasure (Unstable)*	*Dependence (Stable)*	*Dissatisfaction (Unstable)*
	Outcomes	CL_{alt}	CL	CL,CL_{alt}
		Outcomes	Outcomes	
	CL,CL_{alt}	CL	CL_{alt}	Outcomes

Note: *Adapted from Thibaut and Kelley, 1959, pp. 24–25, and Swensen, 1973, pp. 228–229.*

outcomes presently being experienced. These outcomes are negative, and by themselves ought to lead to dissolution of the relationship. They do not do so only because the other alternatives are even worse. But to take into account those other alternatives requires a cognitive mechanism not found in the extreme behaviorism of some reinforcement theories (such as Skinner's). Thus, the idea of the comparison level of alternatives, like the idea of the informational value of vicarious reinforcement found in social learning theory, is a significant addition to the basic principle that people will try to maximize their own gain. They will, but they will also try to minimize their losses.

The last possibility shown in Table 8.1 is what may be called Dissatisfaction. In this case the interaction is highly unstable (indeed, it is about to be ended), because the person finds that the outcomes from the relationship are far below both his or her comparison level and comparison level for alternatives. There is no attraction to the relationship, and no dependence on it, so it will be terminated quickly. Because of the possibility of moving from one relationship to the best available alternative, the CL_{alt} is considered the *zero* point in the matrix description of interaction. As the proportion of cells with negative outcomes increases, the likelihood of termination of the interaction also increases.

Interdependence: Power Within a Relationship

Suppose that the relationship continues, because each participant's average outcomes exceed the CL_{alt} available to each person. Does this mean that the interactants have no preferences among the possible mutual activities? Most certainly not. In any interaction some joint activities (cells in the interaction matrix) will be preferable to others. How each person's preferences get realized will reflect the both the kind of power each person possesses, and the relative balance of power between the two participants.

Every relationship involves the mutual exercise of power over the outcomes experienced by each participant. The revised version of exchange theory (Kelley & Thibaut, 1978) describes three different elements of the total amount of control present in a relationship. The first of these, called **reflexive control**, represents the person's ability to alter his or her own outcomes by changing from one action to another. Reflexive control can be thought of as the person's preferences, assuming "other things equal." Imagine yourself and a date trying to decide whether to go to a concert or a movie. The movie might be less expensive, but it will be available for a longer period of time. After discussing the advantages and disadvantages of each choice, your date says, "I *really* don't care. I will be happy to do whichever you prefer. So just decide which would be more fun for you." Assuming, of course, that you have reason to believe your date means what he or she has just said, then your choice will be an exercise in reflexive control. You will select the choice that provides you with a preferable outcome, regardless of what implications that alternative might have for your date's outcomes, or for the future of your interaction together.

From your perspective, this "interaction" is really more like having company while you do something you enjoy. Your date has left the matter entirely up to you, and does not seem to have a preference of his or her own. True *interdependence* in a relationship, however, requires more. Suppose that after the discussion of the two possibilities, your date expressed a strong preference for going to the concert, but still left the choice up to you. Now further suppose that you didn't really care which activity provided the two of you with an evening's entertainment. In the words of the theory, you are indifferent to the choice. In such circumstances, you would have what is called **fate control** over your date: His or her outcomes would be entirely dependent on your choice. If you selected the concert, your date's outcomes would be greater than if you selected the movie. The notion of fate control assumes that you are impervious to your date's entreaties, because it requires that you be indifferent to your date's behavioral choices.

Such indifference is rarely achieved, because most continuing relationships will include *mutual* fate control: There will be some times when your date receives differential outcomes because of your following a whim, and times when your outcomes depend entirely on his or her behaving according to to the same sort of whim. But in Thibaut and Kelley's (1959) original analysis, this repeated exercise of mutual fate control will evolve (if the relationship is to last) into the third kind of power, **mutual behavior control**. You can have fate control over your date only if you are indifferent to his or her actions, and your date can have fate control over you only by maintaining a similar detachment from your behavior. But after successive exchanges of behavior, each of you will come to lose the indifference required for fate control. In short, what the other person does will matter to you, and will partially dictate your own behavioral choices. The essence of interaction is mutual commitment, a quality achieved by attending to, not by ignoring, each other's actions and outcomes.

Thus, in a continuing interaction, exchange theory argues that each participant's outcomes in a particular interaction cell will be dictated in part by aspects of independence and in part by true *inter*dependence. For example, reflexive control is that portion of the outcome produced by one's own preferences, all other things (including the other person's behavior) presumed to be equal. In contrast, mutual behavior control is that portion of the outcome produced by the joint choices, with each person's choice taking into account what the action will mean for the self. If you have a distinct preference for concerts over movies, you can exercise reflexive control and satisfy the preference whether or not your date chooses to accompany you. But that enjoyment can be enhanced if your date shares your enthusiasm for concerts, and accompanies you willingly. Thus the final goodness of outcome that would be expressed in an interaction matrix consists of the sum of the components based on both independence and interdependence.

Correspondence of Outcomes

With the possible components of each outcome, and the ways in which outcomes are evaluated by participants, in mind, let us return to the Employee–Superior example to examine how one person's outcomes might compare to the outcomes achieved by the other participant in the interaction. The Compliment–Advice cell of Fig. 8.2 represents a profit for both the Employee and the Superior, whereas the Greeting–Raise cell (a_1b_2) represents a substantial loss for each participant. In each of these cases, the outcomes achieved by the Employee correspond to the outcomes achieved by the Superior, and although the actual values are much less, the same correspondence can be seen in the Greeting–Advice cell (a_1b_1).

Imagine, for a moment, that the interaction matrix were extended to include a large number of behaviors by each of the participants. We could then examine all the cells of the matrix to determine how the profits of one person were related to the profits of the other. If over a broad range of behaviors the two participants either gain together or lose together, the relationship would be described as one of high **correspondence of outcomes**: the gains of one participant are accompanied by gains by the other. High correspondence of outcomes can be seen in helping relationships that call for reciprocation of favors, and in friendship development and romantic attraction. We return to these situations in chapter 9.

Mixed-Motive Games. But what about the one exceptional cell in Fig. 8.2? In this Compliment–Raise cell (a_2b_2), the Employee gains, but the Superior loses. If the matrix were extended and the large majority of cells followed this pattern, we would say that the relationship was characterized by a very low correspondence of outcomes. Indeed, with this many outcomes below CL_{alt}, the Superior would very likely break off the interaction and retreat to his or her private office. In the language of game theory (Luce & Raiffa, 1957), low correspondence of outcomes is at best a **mixed-motive game**: a game in which the most favorable outcome for one person is also the riskiest. In such a game, each participant must choose between maximizing immediate gain and minimizing long-term losses, and each person's gains will to some degree be made at the other person's expense. When there is perfect noncorrespondence of outcomes, the situation is best described as a **zero-sum game**: whatever gains one person achieves are obtained at the expense of the other participant.

To illustrate the difference, consider the case of a star NBA basketball player. No matter how well that individual can play, he cannot beat the other team singlehandedly. Therefore he depends on the cooperation of his four teammates, and to receive their cooperation he must be a "team player" at least some of the time. So within his own team, his situation is a mixed-motive game. He can make those fantastic plays that have earned him his reputation as a star only if his teammates will pass him the ball at the critical moment. In order to compete (be the best player on his own team), he must also cooperate. Although the star player has mixed motives toward his teammates, his motives toward the opposition are purely competitive, because, as any number of famous coaches can tell you, there can be only one winning team. Athletic contests, like poker games and many social relationships, are zero-sum games. There is a winner whose victory is achieved at the expense of those who lose. These competitive social relationships are discussed more fully in chapter 10.

Extensions of Reinforcement. By assuming that costs, rewards, and the resulting outcomes can be quantified and held in memory, exchange theory adds to the principle of reinforcement and permits us to describe the course of a relationship, assess each participant's attraction to and dependence upon the relationship, and describe interactions as primarily cooperative or competitive. Unfortunately, there is one gap in the exchange model. The standards (CL and CL_{alt}) a person uses to assess his or her satisfaction with a relationship are both internal to the person doing the evaluation. This does not make the exchange theory any less interpersonal, because the outcomes being evaluated are produced by interaction, and because the states of satisfaction and dependence produce consequences that are themselves interpersonal.

In some cases, however, the fact that the standards are entirely internal can reduce the predictive value of the theory. For example, if your outcomes exceed your CL and your CL_{alt} you ought to be content. But what if the other person involved in the interaction is receiving even greater rewards from it than you are? Will surpassing your own standards be sufficient for happiness? Probably not. You may well be dissatisfied because you think that, pleasant as the interaction is, you are not benefiting from it nearly as much as is the other person. In short, one of the elements in your judgment of satisfaction is a social comparison of your outcomes with the outcomes of the other participant(s), and exchange theory makes no provision for this comparison. Such judgments are the subject matter for the theories to which we now turn.

FAIRNESS IN SOCIAL EXCHANGE

A common observation among professors is that there are only two categories of students who complain about their grades on examinations—those who flunk and those who just missed getting an A. Indeed, the latter group is usually more vocal. It is easy to understand the position of the students who have failed, because failing grades among college students are below both CL (or they never would have been admitted) and CL_{alt} (or they would flunk out). But most exchange theories have difficulty accounting for the strong reactions of the other dissatisfied students. Even though grade averages continue to rise in most colleges and universities, a grade of B is not yet a "bad" grade, so what is the basis for the complaint?

Procedural Justice

If the examinations have all been essay questions, and if early in the term the complaining student had stated some opinions that (the student learned later) contradicted the strong views of the professor, then the student might well wonder whether the procedures used to arrive at the final grade were fair. In an extensive analysis of procedural justice, Thibaut and Walker (1975) noted that perceived fairness of an outcome can be affected by aspects of the process of dispute resolution. The procedural solution usually adopted in our society involves the mediation of the dispute by a third party (a labor arbitrator, a judge, or, in the case of our example, a grade-review committee). At least three factors can be involved in the choice dispute resolution through the mediation by a third party: urgent time pressure to reach a solution of the dispute; extremely low correspondence of outcomes among the parties (the mixed-motive or zero-sum games described earlier); and the presence of a standard against which the outcome can be gauged. This standard may be a physical one or it may be one established through social comparison (Chapter 7).

The research of Thibaut and Walker was specifically directed at the resolution of disputes through legal processes, and is discussed in more detail in chapter 14. Nevertheless, at least one of their findings has broad implications outside the courtroom. In a variety of experimental contexts, the procedure that the subjects considered to be the most fair had the least participation by the third-party mediator. No matter how much they might have disagreed with each other, disputants seemed reluctant to relinquish control over the process of dispute resolution by giving complete authority to a third party. As Thibaut and Walker note, this finding constitutes a resounding vote of confidence in the adversary system. For our purposes here, however, it also suggests that perceived fairness in a social exchange will depend to no small degree on the control that the participants have over the course of that exchange.

The Principle of Distributive Justice

Relative Deprivation. Even if a student complaining about a high "B" were satisfied with the process through which grades had been assigned, he or she might still be unhappy with the outcome. If you were to question such a student, the first explanation you might get for dissatisfaction would be the damage done to the student's chances for admission to graduate school. A bit of the unidirectional drive upward also enters into the student's social comparison of abilities. But if you probed a little further, you might discover that part of the student's objection is based on the fact that his or her grade was worse than that of a friend who was taking another professor's section of the same course. The two friends had studied together and had achieved virtually the same numerical score on the exam. But in the other section that score translated into a "low A," instead of a "high B." Thus the complaining student (a) *wants* an A, (b) *perceives* that another student has an A, (c) feels *entitled* to an A, (d) thinks it is *feasible* to obtain an A, and (e) does not see the failure to obtain an A as his or her own *fault*, meeting all of the preconditions for a feeling of relative deprivation (Crosby, 1976). Regardless of how fair the procedures might have been in this particular class, the fact that students in another section have received better grades for the same numerical scores will rankle.

This social comparison of rewards and effort first came to the attention of social psychologists in a large scale study by Stouffer, Suchman, DeVinney, Starr, & Williams (1949). These investigators reported that men in the Army Air Corps were much less satisfied with opportunities for promotion than were men in the Military Police. What is surprising is that promotions in the Air Corps were extremely fast, whereas promotions in the Military Police were very slow. Why should the Air Corps troops have been unhappy with objectively better outcomes? Stouffer and his colleagues attributed this inconsistency to what they termed **relative deprivation**. In the Air Corps, people who knew that others were being promoted quickly knew that such promotion was possible and felt entitled to it. Those who (in their view) through no fault of their own failed to achieve early promotion felt deprived relative to others in the unit, and this relative deprivation was expressed as resentment. It was not a man's objective standing, but rather his standing in relation to his peers that was important.

Profits and Investments.   At another level, the issue can be drawn in terms of the fairness with which the available rewards are dispensed. But what is meant by "fairness?" According to Homans (1961), the principal criterion for determining the fairness of a distribution of rewards ought to be the *investments* made by each party in an interaction. In his elaboration of the idea of relative deprivation, Homans argued that **distributive justice** would obtain in a relationship between two people (A and B) when

$$\frac{\text{A's profits}}{\text{A's investments}} = \frac{\text{B's profits}}{\text{B's investments}}.$$

A person's investments include age, experience, education, interpersonal skills, and active contributions to the interaction. Profits are determined by subtracting costs (time, money, effort, and so forth) from rewards, just as in the case of Thibaut and Kelley's (1959) exchange theory. Notice that the person's costs are not necessarily the same as his or her investments. If you and I spend an hour talking about social psychology, I may feel that distributive justice requires my profits to be greater than yours. The cost to each of us (say, in time) is the same, but my investments in social psychology are greater than yours, and those greater investments need to be compensated by higher rewards in order for distributive justice to prevail.

The principle of distributive justice has been extended to include relationships between more than two parties (Homans, 1961), such as a triad consisting of an employer and two employees. The two workers compare their investments in the company against the salaries they are paid to see whether they are being treated fairly. In this case, the difference between costs and investments becomes even clearer. For example, each worker may spend exactly the same time and effort to produce the same amount of the company's product. But the worker with seniority will be dissatisfied if his or her investment of previous years is not reflected in salary.

In cases of distributive injustice, it is clear that the party who feels unfairly treated will be dissatisfied with the relationship, but as Adams (1965) points out, the principle of distributive justice makes few predictions about the behavior that might be undertaken in order to remedy the injustice. To make such predictions, Adams combined the principle of distributive justice with some features of cognitive dissonance theory (Festinger, 1957, discussed in chapter 5) to develop what he called an *equity theory* of social exchange.

Equity Theory

Definitions of Equity.   Whereas the principle of distributive justice concentrates on a condition of equality between two participants in a social exchange, Adams (1965) and later writers (e.g., see a review by Walster, Walster, & Berscheid, 1978) have focused on the antecedents and consequences of inequity. In his initial discussion of **equity theory**, Adams adapted the formula of Homans (1961), suggesting that a condition of equity between participants in an interaction obtains when each person's outcomes are proportional to his or her inputs:

$$\frac{A\text{'s outcomes}}{A\text{'s inputs}} = \frac{B\text{'s outcomes}}{B\text{'s inputs}}.$$

To the extent that one person's ratio of outcomes to inputs exceeds that of the other person, both participants are supposed to feel inequitably treated (but of course the "overpaid" person is less likely to complain than is the "underpaid" person).

How does the formula work? Consider a brief example. If you are comparing a grade you have received with the grade received on the same examination by a good friend of yours, you will know how much work each of you put into studying for the examination, and you will also have some idea of how well each of you would have done on the basis of native ability in the subject, regardless of how much you had prepared. These two inputs, native ability and study time, are both positive. If by some scaling method the sum of your two inputs is 2 and the sum of your friend's two inputs is 4, then for equity to be maintained, your friend's outcomes would have to be twice as good as yours.

There is, however, a difficulty with this definitional formula. It does not apply as shown if there is a mixture of positive and negative inputs and outcomes. Suppose, for example, that you are comparing your outcome on the examination with a person who not only did not study for the exam, but in addition spent the night before the exam at an all-night beer party. This person's native ability (on a good day) might have been slightly positive, but under the circumstances the person's input "sum" would add to a negative 4. Further suppose that you did not do at all well on the exam. You expected to receive a B, but were distressed to discover that the actual grade was a D–. Given your expectation you would certainly consider this a negative outcome, say a –10. Now, what would the other person's score have been for this situation to be equitable according to the original Adams formula? Your –10 divided by 2 is –5, so the other person's –4 input would have to be divided into a +20 to make the same ratio of –5. But wait a minute. Could you possibly consider it equitable, in any sense of that word, for a person who intentionally avoided studying to perform better on an exam than you did after having put a great deal into preparation for the test? Certainly not.

In order to deal with settings like this one, Walster, Berscheid, and Walster (1976) made three changes in the definition. First, returning to Homans's (1961) notion of profits, the numerator of each fraction was changed by subtracting each person's inputs from his or her outcomes, producing either $[O_A - I_A]$ or $[O_B - I_B]$. Next, in the divisor each person's inputs were taken as an absolute value, eliminating the sign associated with the input (producing either $[I_A]$ or $[I_B]$. And finally, to preserve the sign, although it is no longer attached to the input, Walster, Berscheid, and Walster added an exponent for the input (k_A, or k_B) that represented the comparison between each person's profits and inputs. The final result is the definitional formula:

$$\frac{\text{Outcomes}_A - \text{Inputs}_A}{(|\text{Inputs}_A|)^{k_A}} = \frac{\text{Outcomes}_B - \text{Inputs}_B}{(|\text{Inputs}_B|)^{k_B}}.$$

The exponent, k, is constructed by multiplying the *sign* removed from each person's inputs times the *sign* of the profits (outcomes minus inputs) for that person. Thus, in the example, your exponent would be negative (your input is 2, with a positive sign; your profits are the outcome of -10 minus your input of 2 for a total of -12, with a negative sign). The result of such a negative exponent applied to the inputs is to cause those inputs to be moved to the numerator of the fraction and multiplied by the profits, whereas inputs with a positive exponent remain in the denominator of the fraction. Thus, to complete the example, your profits (-12) would be multiplied by the absolute value of your inputs (2) to produce a final number of -24. The other person's profits (20 minus -4, or 24) would be multiplied (because the exponent is -1 for that person as well) by the absolute value of his or her inputs (4) to produce a final number of $+96$. This difference between your -24 and the other person's $+96$ much better illustrates the psychological inequity you will feel to have that person do so much better than you did, even though you worked hard and the other person did not.

Recognition and Relevance. Not only is it important to distinguish positive inputs from negative ones, as the revised definitional formula does, it is also important to distinguish among kinds of inputs, regardless of their sign. Whereas Homans (1961) treated all investments in the same terms, regardless of whether or not they were *recognized* by the participants and whether they were, or were not, considered *relevant* to the exchange, Adams (1965) pointed out that inputs could differ on precisely these two grounds. Any attribute–experience, race, gender, possession of certain tools, interpersonal skills, seniority–that is recognized by either party in an interaction has the potential to become an input. But some of these inputs will be relevant to the exchange at hand, whereas some will not. The perception of inequity may depend as much on the degree of agreement about the relevance of an input as it does on the actual value of the input or profit.

For example, many industries used to discriminate against blacks and other minorities in terms of hiring, salary, and promotion. Passage of the civil rights laws and issuance of later governmental regulations on affirmative action then changed the balance by suggesting that there be preferential treatment for minorities in order to redress past injustices. This policy works reasonably well when there is full employment, but what happens in a recession? If an employer follows the customary rule of "last hired, first fired," minority workers will believe that they are being inequitably treated, but if the employer tries to maintain the level of minority employees, the workers with seniority will feel inequitably treated. The issue is not whether layoffs are necessary in hard economic times, but rather whether "being a victim of past discrimination" is a relevant input.

Workers with seniority claim, of course, that seniority alone is the relevant input, whereas minority workers argue that past discrimination is also relevant.

Consequences of Inequity. In addition to distinguishing between relevant and irrelevant inputs, Adams (1965) outlined the behavioral consequences of perceived inequity. When you receive profits (outcomes minus inputs) that are proportionally too small for your inputs, you will experience a psychological tension (usually labeled *anger*) and this tension will lead you to try to reduce the inequity. Similar tension (*guilt*) will be aroused if the rewards you receive are proportionally too great for your inputs, although in this case the tension will be mitigated somewhat by the pleasure of maximizing your own outcomes. If this use of an internal tension to account for a person's reactions to a situation in the environment—the combination of profits and inputs leading to inequity—sounds familiar to you, it should. Adams patterned his model after cognitive dissonance (Festinger, 1957), and as we saw in chapter 5, dissonance is a hypothesized internal state presumed to have motivating properties.

How can an internal tension arising from inequity be resolved? Adams (1965) suggests several possibilities: (a) changing your own inputs or outcomes, (b) acting on the other person to channge his or her inputs or outcomes, (c) choosing a different person for comparison, (d) cognitively distorting your inputs or outcomes, or those of the other person, and (e) leaving the field altogether.

The Case of Underpayment. Let us consider how each of these mechanisms might work in the case of underpayment. Suppose that you are working for me. You compare your salary with that of some of my other employees, and this comparison suggests to you that you are being treated unfairly. The first alternative is for you to reduce your inputs, by producing less work on the job, by increasing your absenteeism, or even by sabotaging some of the products to which you have unrestricted access. Next you might try to increase your outcomes, by padding your expense account, or by pilfering from my supplies. It is interesting to note in this connection that the large majority of shoplifting is done by employees of the businesses affected. The business response to losses of this kind is often to try to "hire only honest people," frequently by extensive pre-employment polygraph testing of job candidates. Yet if the stealing is a disgruntled but otherwise honest employee's attempt to restore equity, no amount of pre-employment screening will help, because the perceived inequity arises only after the employee has been on the job. If you cannot alter your own inputs or outcomes, you might try to get the comparison person(s) to restore equity by working harder.

If none of the behavioral alternatives succeeds in redressing the balance, you might distort either your own inputs or outcomes, or the inputs or outcomes of the others. For example, you might be able to convince yourself that although your salary may not be high enough, you could not easily find another job that provided you with such pleasant working conditions. If these tactics fail, you might search for a different comparison group (but Adams suggests that this is a very difficult alternative to select). Finally, your last resort is to remove yourself from the inequitable situation by finding a job in which you feel fairly compensated.

There is good reason to believe that people will take direct action to increase their rewards if they are being underpaid. As an example, in 1975 the firefighters of Kansas City, Missouri, went out on strike, demanding to have their salary scale equated with the salaries paid to police officers in the same city. This example and frequent laboratory demonstrations are consistent with the equity theory, but do we really need the concept of equity to explain them? Why not simply say that underpayment creates dissonance (or even "anger"), and it is this state, rather than a tension presumed to arise from inequity, that accounts for the reactions. What we have here is another case in which two theories make exactly the same prediction. Is the second theory really necessary?

The Case of Overpayment. You may remember from chapter 5 that this is the same sort of question that arose in the initial stages of the controversy between dissonance theory and self-perception theory for the case of insufficient justification. People who performed counterattitudinal actions for small rewards could have changed their attitudes in order to reduce dissonance, or they could have taken into account their own behavior (as well as their vague internal reactions to the task) and perceived their attitudes to be more positive than we would expect them to be. In this controversy, the explanatory value of self-perception theory became clearest in the case of oversufficient justification, which presumably should have produced no cognitive dissonance. The same is true for equity theory. In the case of underpayment, both dissonance and inequity might lead to attempts to redress the imbalance. But overpayment should create only inequity, not dissonance. Because we would need a concept similar to inequity in order to account for the reduction of imbalance generated by overpayment, it is more parsimonious to let the same concept apply to the situation of underpayment as well.

In part because the concept of equity applies more convincingly to cases in which the person is better off than those with whom he or she compares, most of the research conducted within the equity framework has dealt with overpayment (Walster, Berscheid, & Walster, 1976). To use a typical illustration, suppose that you were asked to work with a partner on a task for which the two of you were to receive a monetary reward. The amount of the reward would depend on the total amount of work completed by the two of you together, although you were to work independently on the task. After you have completed your part of the task, and without reuniting you with your partner, the experimenter informs you of how much you have contributed to the team effort. Specifically, you are told either that you have provided 65% of the team's total production, or 35%, with the remainder in each instance being provided by your partner. Then the experimenter tells you that you have been chosen randomly to divide the team's earnings ($2.05) between you and your partner. The crucial question is, how much do you take for yourself?

When Leventhal and Michaels (1969) actually performed such an experiment, they discovered that subjects would allocate earnings in proportion to their own perceived inputs (their proportional contribution to the outcome). Subjects who thought they had contributed only 35% of the outcome took less of the reward for themselves than did subjects who believed that they had contributed 65% of the outcome. Thus the subjects attempted to make their rewards consistent with their inputs, as equity theory would predict. There is some controversy over whether the results of such *reward allocation* studies reflect a drive toward equity (proportional pay) or a desire for equality (Shapiro, 1975), but predictions from equity theory have been supported in a number of different contexts as well. For example, when subjects are overpaid for a task, they try to work harder than if they have been fairly paid or underpaid (Adams & Jacobsen, 1964). This is an adjustment of inputs rather than outcomes, but the purpose is still the maintenance of equity.

Equity and Exploitation. In all of the examples considered so far, both the person who is evaluating the equity of the relationship and the person chosen for comparison purposes have had their outcomes determined by some third party. This is obviously the case in most business organizations, where only a few people have the power to set their own salaries. The remainder of the workers and managers compare their compensation with that of their fellows. It is also the case in most experimental settings. If the dependent variable is reward allocation, the experimenter arbitrarily establishes each subject's inputs, and if the dependent variable is alteration of inputs, the experimenter establishes the rewards provided (in order to produce conditions of underpayment or overpayment). Finally, the equity model originally proposed by Adams (1965) also emphasizes the case in which one recipient of benefits compares those rewards with the outcomes of another recipient.

Recently, however, the equity model has been extended to include other cases in which the person that Walster, Berscheid, and Walster (1976) call the "scrutineer" has produced the outcomes of the other (comparison) person. Included in this category are instances in which the scrutineer is an exploiter and the other person is exploited (the harm-doer and the victim), and instances in which the scrutineer is a helper and the other person is a recipient of that help. Consider, for example, the harm-doer and the victim. The theory holds that a harm-doer will feel tension from producing the harm, and that this tension will lead to an attempt to restore equity. This attempt can take the form of compensation (returning the victim to his or her previctimization state, or providing restitution for the victim's losses), or it can take the psychological tack of reducing the victim's inputs by asserting that for some reason the victim deserved to suffer. We return to a more detailed consideration of such attempts at equity restoration in the discussions of altruism and helping behavior (Chapter 9) and social psychological processes involved in the law (Chapter 14). For now it is sufficient to note that equity theory makes the same predictions about the removal of inequity, regardless of whether that inequity was brought about by the actions of the person doing the evaluating or by some third party.

A Further Refinement of Reinforcement

Equity theory represents a further step in the application of reinforcement principles to social interaction. It assumes, as do social learning theory and exchange theory, that people will try to maximize their outcomes. But whereas social learning theory asserts that people will imitate success, and exchange theory proposes that people will evaluate their own outcomes against internal standards (CL and CL_{alt}), equity theory suggests that the successes of other people will enter into the calculation of satisfaction with one's own outcomes. There is some disagreement about whether equity theory might involve internal standards as well as external ones (Austin & Susmilch, 1974; Messé & Lane, 1974), but the principal focus of the theory does require comparison of one's own profits with the profits of others.

Whereas Thibaut and Kelley's (1959) model shows how a relationship might develop in order to maximize the rewards of both participants, equity theory concentrates on the possible consequences of a failure to achieve parity. Like the notion of relative deprivation and the principle of distributive justice, equity theory argues that people will be dissatisfied if they believe they are being treated unfairly. But equity theory identifies in greater detail the specific actions that might be taken in order to bring the situation into (at least) psychological balance, regardless of the original source of the injustice.

The theories discussed in this chapter all deal with the development, maintenance, and evaluation of interpersonal interaction, whether that interaction is a helping relationship, a friendship, an adversary relationship, or the search for individual goals through group membership. These principles of social exchange, occasionally combined with elements of the cognitive theories we have studied in earlier chapters, provide the framework that undergirds much of the material in chapters to follow.

SUMMARY

Interpersonal behavior can be characterized as a social **exchange** (p. 281) between people, and these social exchanges typically involve both rewards and costs to the participants. A fundamental assumption of all theories of interpersonal behavior is that on balance, a person will perform those actions that produce the greatest rewards at the least cost. Social behavior that leads to positive *reinforcement* (p. 277) will be strengthened, whereas social behavior that leads to punishment will be weakened. The three theories described in this chapter deal with the development, maintenance, and evaluation of such social behavior.

Social learning theory (p. 279) suggests that novel social behavior is first learned through *imitation* (p. 280) of the actions taken by models. The reinforcement received by a model serves as information to the person about which behaviors are acceptable and appropriate for the circumstances. Once a novel action has been acquired through imitation, its strength will depend on the reinforcement it receives and on whether that reinforcement is administered according to an **intermittent** schedule (p. 280) or a continuous one.

The theory of social **exchange** (p. 281) assumes that each participant in a dyadic interaction brings to the interchange a repertoire of possible actions, and that the goodness of each person's outcomes will be determined jointly by the behaviors of both parties. During the formation of a relationship, the participants will sample the cells of the **interaction matrix** (p. 282) and the **goodness of the outcomes** (p. 284) for each participant will be evaluated against two different standards. These are the **comparison level** (p. 285) and the **comparison level for alternatives** (p. 285). The relative value of the person's outcomes, the comparison level, and the comparison level for alternatives will determine both the person's *attraction* to the relationship and his or her *dependence* (p. 286) on it. Across all cells of the interaction matrix, the correlation between the losses and gains of one person and those of the other is known as the **correspondence of outcomes** (p. 289) within the interaction. Low correspondence of outcomes produces competition, whereas high correspondence of outcomes produces cooperation.

The principles of **relative deprivation** (p. 292) and **distributive justice** (p. 292) and the theory of **equity** (p. 293) all suggest that a person's satisfaction with the outcomes received will depend in part upon the the outcomes received by relevant comparison persons. When an individual believes that the ratio of his or her profits to inputs is unequal to the same ratio for a comparison person, the perceived underpayment or overpayment will lead to corrective action designed to reduce the inequity (p. 296). To restore equity, an individual may directly change his or her inputs or outcomes (or those of the comparison person), may engage in psychological distortion of the various inputs and outcomes, or may leave the field. Although equity theory is most clearly relevant to business relationships, it also applies to cases of exploitation and helping behavior.

SUGGESTED ADDITIONAL READINGS

BANDURA, A., & WALTERS, R. J. (1963). *Social learning and personality development.* New York: Holt, Rinehart, & Winston. This short book contains a complete statement of the authors' version of social learning theory.

KELLEY, H. H., & THIBAUT, J. W. (1978). *Interpersonal relations: A theory of interdependence.* New York: Wiley. For the most part this is a technical description of a detailed, matrix-based, theory of interaction, a sequel to the Thibaut and Kelley (1959) exchange theory. The introductory chapter, however, is an overview of the theory that is certainly accessible to undergraduate students.

WALSTER, E. H., WALSTER, G. W., & BERSCHEID, E. (1978). *Equity: Theory and research.* Boston: Allyn & Bacon. This book was written for undergraduates, and does an excellent job of stating and illustrating the formal propositions of equity theory. For advanced students, an extensive appendix describes the derivation of the alternative to Adams's definitional formula.

CHAPTER NINE

POSITIVE FORMS OF SOCIAL BEHAVIOR

CONTENTS

PREVIEW

In this chapter we consider two principal forms of positive social behavior, helping and interpersonal attraction. Objective altruism is limited to instances in which a voluntary action actually benefits the recipient without providing any external rewards to the helpful person. The occurrence of objective altruism can be influenced by social norms, by the presence of helpful models in the situation, and by internal states of the helper, such as guilt or the need to restore equity. In emergency situations, the decision to intervene can be affected by social comparison with others and by the costs and rewards involved in taking direct action. Attraction toward another person typically involves an attitude of favorability toward the other, mutual dependence, and a commitment to care about the other's desires and needs. Antecedents of attraction include propinquity, similarity of attitudes and interests, and personal qualities of the stimulus person.

Perhaps no personal qualities are considered more "human" than the ability to care for others and the self-sacrifice that such caring often entails. A passing stranger rushes into a burning building to save a person trapped inside. People who have little money of their own contribute to innumerable charitable organizations. Entire communities pull together to rebuild after a disaster. But positive social behavior is not limited to helping. Good friends share adventures, joys, and sorrows. Lovers become passionately devoted to each other. Our history and literature are filled with examples like these, but only recently have social psychologists begun to study altruism and interpersonal attraction in earnest. This may be because much social psychological research has been problem-oriented, concentrating on topics such as prejudice, competition, and conformity, rather than on more positive social behavior.

Some Common Themes. In this chapter we consider two primary forms of positive behavior, helping and interpersonal attraction. You will notice common themes in our discussion of both topics. First, there is a common thread of theory – reward, cost, reinforcement – running through both areas. In the case of altruistic action reinforcement is a theoretical problem that needs to be addressed, because "altruism" ought to be action not motivated by desire for personal gain. A typical solution to this problem involves defining altruistic action "objectively" in terms of observable criteria that rule out externally provided gain but do permit internal increases in self-esteem that might accompany performance of a helpful action. In general terms, the absence of reward is the rule, and occasional reinforcement is the exception. For interpersonal attraction, this relation is reversed. Some form of reinforcement is the preferred explanation for much of interpersonal attraction, although instances occasionally occur in which costs, not rewards, produce increased liking.

The second common theme in the discussion of the two topics is the emphasis on an interchange between the people involved. As noted in chapter 8, our emphasis has now shifted from a focus on the individual person's cognitive structure to consideration of that person's dealings with other people. Until now we have been attempting to explain social behavior in terms of two different sets of factors: the personal characteristics of the individual, and the characteristics of the situation in which that individual's actions occur. To these we must now add a third source of influence, the relationship between the person whose actions we seek to understand and the person who is the beneficiary or target of those actions. In the case of helping behavior, the influence of the relationship between the two can be seen in work on the social responsibility norm, a norm that requires us to help those who are dependent upon us. In the case of attraction, the mutual interchange and disclosure that leads to friendship is an excellent example of the influence of the relationship between two people.

Behavioral and Theoretical Complexity.   One final note about the material in this chapter and succeeding ones: As the behavior we study becomes more complex and interpersonal, the task of explanation must change. The phenomena to be understood are more complex, involving the effects of the relationship between two or more people as well as the situational factors and personal characteristics of each participating individual. But there is a limit to the number of unknowns that can be involved in the scientific enterprise. Consequently, many of the theoretical accounts are less detailed than those we have considered earlier, such as the social cognition theories (Chapter 4) and the attitude organization theories (Chapter 5). In large measure, this difference reflects the domain of behavior covered by the theory. A theory with a restricted range of application can be more specific in describing the behavior of interest without exceeding our ability to follow is explanations. But a theory that attempts to deal with a wide range of action must keep its explanatory principles simple or risk losing its audience through misunderstanding.

As a result of the decrease in complexity, you will notice a change in the nature of the theoretical disagreements. Arguments over applicability of an approach to an entire area of behavior will replace controversy over the particular methods that might be employed in testing theoretical propositions. For example, you will recall from chapter 5 that the controversy among dissonance theory, incentive theory, and self-perception theory over the proper explanation for insufficient justification effects was quite narrowly drawn. Slight changes in experimental procedures were all that was necessary to produce results more favorable to one account than to others. You will not see this sort of disagreement regarding interpersonal processes. Where a theory appears inadequate, critics of one theoretical approach will point to a whole class of behaviors inadequately explained, not to a specific set of experimental operations that are presumed to be in error. Ultimately, the theories describing interpersonal behavior will be refined, and these refinements will narrow the range of possible disagreement. At this writing, however, breadth of explanatory power is necessarily more important than conceptual precision in the accounts of interpersonal behavior, and you should keep this distinction in mind as you read.

ALTRUISM AND HELPING BEHAVIOR

THE PROBLEM OF DEFINITION

Motives and Self-Sacrifice

In common usage, the term *altruism* usually refers to intentional, self-sacrificing behavior that benefits other people. We can all think of actions we would describe as altruistic – the missionary who is devoted to improving the living conditions in a primitive society, the country doctor who maintains a practice for the good of the community though barely able to cover expenses, the passerby who intervenes in an emergency at considerable personal risk – and most of these examples are consistent with the popular definition. But illustrations of a concept do not constitute the sort of operational definition (Chapter 2) required for scientific research.

For example, consider the idea that altruistic behavior must be self-sacrificing in light of the principles of reinforcement and exchange discussed in chapter 8. As Rosenhan (1972) and later writers as well (Krebs & Miller, 1985) have noted, altruistic action presents a paradox for reinforcement theory, because by definition such behavior would appear to have costs that exceed the rewards reaped. Perhaps people might occasionally engage in actions of this kind, but how could we account for an entire lifetime of altruism? There are three possible explanations, but each would have an important limitation. First, altruism could simply be the exception that proves the rule of reinforcement. Our continued self-seeking can be justified on the grounds that occasionally we do give something for nothing. This explanation sounds plausible, but it fails to tell us anything about why altruism occurs. A second possibility is to assume that lifelong altruists are not in touch with the rewards and costs of their behavior. But this lack of contact with reality would make altruists so abnormal that their behavior would be of little interest to social psychologists, who, after all, presume to deal with the interpersonal behavior of a majority of people. Finally, lifelong altruists could really be pursuing goals they find rewarding. In this instance, their rewards would outweigh their personal costs; it is just that their system of costs and rewards differs from that of most people. This final explanation leaves the principle of reinforcement intact, but it does so at the expense of part of the definition of altruism. The self-sacrifice is gone.

If the problem of self-sacrifice were not troublesome enough, there is also difficulty in establishing objective criteria for distinguishing between altruistic and nonaltruistic action. Suppose we adopt a criterion based on the motives behind the action. Then we would say that a philanthropist who donated $1 million to charity in order to achieve a tax reduction was not altruistic, whereas a poor person who gave $10 to the same charity was altruistic because the latter's motives were pure. This sounds fine at first, but what about the effects of the action? There is no doubt that the philanthropist's donation will accomplish more good than the poor person's donation will. And what about the case of a person who intervenes in an accident with pure motives of helpfulness, but inadvertently prevents the victim from receiving professionally trained help? Will we judge such a person as altruistic, even though the actions had negative consequences? Probably not. At this point we are ready to admit that we would like to consider some actions altruistic (or not) because of the motives behind them and regardless of their consequences, although considering others altruistic because of their consequences and regardless of the motives behind them. In our everyday lives this solution is probably widely adopted, but its internal inconsistency keeps it from being very useful for research.

Objective Altruism

Because the choice of whether to consider motives, or only effects, is an individual value judgment not based on any objectively specifiable criteria, it is not surprising that social psychologists interested in positive social behavior have either defined the object of study as *helping behavior* rather than altruism (Latané & Darley, 1970), or have side-stepped some of the conceptual problems by concentrating exclusively on observable criteria (Macaulay & Berkowitz, 1970; Wispé, 1972). We adopt the latter approach, and distinguish **objective altruism** both from helping behavior and from the subjective altruism based on individual value judgments of motives and effects.

Researchers generally agree that what we are calling objective altruism must been three different tests. First, the action must be voluntary rather than coerced by social pressure. Second, it may produce no external rewards for the actor. Self-administered pats on the back are permitted, and there is no requirement for self-sacrifice. Third, it must actually benefit the recipient. Good intentions are necessary (or the action would not have been voluntary), but they alone are not sufficient. When defined according to these three criteria, objective altruism can be regarded as a special case of helping behavior. Only the third criterion, actual benefit, is required for an act to be helpful, but the other two are needed before that helpful action can be considered a case of objective altruism.

Altruism and Reinforcement

How does this objective altruism square with the principle of reinforcement and with social exchange theories? To begin with, it does not contradict the principle of reinforcement, because it does permit internal, self-administered rewards that might outweigh the costs of action. Such internal motives as sincere concern for others, empathy with a suffering victim, or even a desire to avoid the guilt that would follow a failure to help can all lead to behavior that would be objectively altruistic. Although it does not contradict the principle of reinforcement, objective altruism does exclude the rewards that might be gained through social exchange. Thus, aiding a good friend (who might be expected to return the favor) would be helping, but not objective altruism. Performing the same actions for strangers (with whom no future relationship is contemplated) would qualify as objective altruism.

When we compare the definition of objective altruism to the common usage of the term, we discover that scientific precision has been achieved at the expense of some of the richness of the term. Objective altruism, like its common-language counterpart, assumes that altruistic actions are intentional (rather than accidental) and reflect the actor's character. External rewards are precluded by both definitions, although objective altruism does not require self-sacrifice. The greatest difference between the two concepts is in the way they deal with internal motives. Objective altruism concentrates on results, assuming that the absence of social pressure and external reward will be sufficient to ensure that the actor's motives were pure. But this definition in terms of outcomes makes it impossible for us to consider objectively altruistic any actions—even those of heroic proportions—that fail in the attempt. Although this restriction is necessary to avoid subjective value judgments about the purity of a person's motives, it does diminish the intuitive appeal of the idea. Perhaps after greater experience in the study of positive social behavior, social psychologists will be able to extend their operational definitions to encompass some of the additional judgments implicit in the intuitive idea of altruism.

Having outlined the criteria for objective altruism, we now turn to some of the personal and situational factors that influence its occurrence. For ease of presentation, we distinguish between normal circumstances in which help might be rendered and the special case of bystander intervention in emergency situations. In the absence of an emergency, objective altruism will be affected by a number of factors, including cultural prescriptions, situational variables, and personal characteristics of the actor. As examples of these factors we consider, respectively, the norms of reciprocity and social responsibility, the situational factor of modeling, and several important internal motives. Other factors that might affect objective altruism include parental socialization practices, cognitive developmental processes, and sociobiological influences (Krebs & Miller, 1985), but a complete review of these is beyond the scope of this chapter. As a result, our discussion is restricted to those variables that have received the greatest research attention from social psychologists.

OBJECTIVE ALTRUISM IN NONEMERGENCY SITUATIONS

The Effects of Norms

Even the theories of social interaction that assume that people will try to maximize their outcomes do not suggest that interaction can be sustained through reward seeking alone. If you recall the example of the Employee and the Superior that was used in chapter 8 to illustrate some of the concepts in Thibaut and Kelley's (1959; Kelley & Thibaut, 1978) exchange theory, you will remember that positive outcomes were obtained by both participants only if the Employee did not ask for a raise when meeting the boss in the hallway. Continuation of their informal interaction depended on the Employee's tacit acceptance of a particular social rule: Do not ask for a raise during a casual conversation. This rule, which specified the expected or appropriate behavior for a particular interactional setting, is simply one example of a social **norm**. In its most general sense, the norm serves as a guide for action, no matter who the participants in the interchange might be. For example, whether you are a mail clerk or an executive vice-president, a brief encounter in the hallway with the boss is neither the time nor the place to request an increase in salary.

Reciprocity. Several writers, notably Gouldner (1960), and Homans (1961) have argued that the most fundamental rule of social interaction is the norm of **reciprocity**. Interaction, after all, is the mutual exchange of rewards, and will not continue if one party does all the giving and the other does all the receiving. In his analysis of the reciprocity norm, Gouldner (1960) argued that it establishes at least two "minimal demands: (1) [sic] people should help those who have helped them, and (2) [sic] people should not injure those who have helped them" (p. 171). The reciprocity norm creates an obligation for repayment that must be satisfied if the interaction is to continue. In addition to these positive demands, the reciprocity norm also suggests that it is fair to retaliate for evils and injustices that one has received, provided that retaliation is commensurate with the gravity of the offense.

Evidence for the existence of a reciprocity norm comes from our own social experience (as represented in the admonition to "do unto others as you would have them do unto you," or in the justification "an eye for an eye . . .") and from a number of research studies. For example, Staub and Sherk (1970) gave pairs of children an opportunity to interact with each other while listening to a tape-recorded story. One child in each pair had previously received several pieces of candy that could be shared with the other as the two listened to the story. Later in the experiment the pairs of children were asked to make drawings, but were provided only one crayon, and this was given to the child who had not previously received the candy from the experimenter. The results showed a strong reciprocity effect. The more candy the second child had received from his or her peer, the more often he or she shared the crayon; if the first child had been blatantly selfish with the candy, the second reciprocated by being selfish with the crayon. So reciprocity was involved both in the positive action of sharing and in the retaliatory action of denial. In a similar matching of reciprocation, Pruitt (1968) found that college undergraduates gave more to a partner in an experimental game when they had previously received a great deal from the partner, and when the partner's previous gift amounted to a greater percentage of his or her resources. The norm of reciprocity demands not only repayment in kind, but also repayment in degree.

Social Responsibility.   There are two limitations to the norm of reciprocity. First, because reciprocity is defined as an aspect of an ongoing exchange, its obligations lead only to helping behavior, not to objective altruism. You help your friend either because you owed him or her a favor, or because you expect reciprocation in the future. But people do help strangers, and our cultural values imply that these cases should also be influenced by normative pressures. Second, reciprocity is possible only when the people involved in an interaction have roughly equivalent capabilities, power, and access to appropriate rewards or punishments. But in many social relationships—especially, for example, the relationship between parents and children—the participants differ greatly in power and resources. Are there not norms that also govern these situations?

The difficulties posed to normative explanations by objective altruism and differential resources were remedied in part by Berkowitz and Daniels (1963), who extended the concept of reciprocity to encompass any dependent other, not just others who happen to be in exchange relationships with the benefactor. This extension of reciprocity is called the **social responsibility norm**, and it holds that people should help anyone in a dependent position. Not only does the social responsibility norm take the obligation to render assistance outside the bounds of an ongoing relationship, it also generalizes the normative account to cases in which the participants have differential power.

Evidence for the existence of a social responsibility norm was obtained by Berkowitz and Daniels (1963), in two experiments that became models for this sort of research. In studies purportedly investigating supervisory skills, subjects were asked to serve as workers whose task was to construct paper boxes for a peer described as a "supervisor." Although there were no external rewards available for the subjects serving as workers, it was possible that the supervisor might earn a prize. The supervisor's dependency on the subject was manipulated by convincing subjects that the supervisor's chances of winning the prize depended either a great deal (High Dependency) or very little (Low Dependency) on the productivity of the worker.

Of the two studies, the second was the more convincing. There the dependency manipulation was combined in a factorial design with the timing of when the supervisor was to find out about the employee's performance (either Immediately over a month Later). Notice that the High Dependency–Later condition satisfies all the criteria for objective altruism. There are no external rewards for the subject; there is no possibility of a social exchange; the worker is in a position to benefit the supervisor; and there is no social pressure (apart from the pressure implicit in the fact that the experimenter knew about the worker's performance immediately, a point to which return later). What happened? The High Dependent supervisor received more help than the Low Dependent one, and this was true even when the supervisor would not find out until much later just how much the worker had done.

These results would appear to rule out nearly all the explanations for the objective altruism displayed, except for adherence to the norm of social responsibility. There was, however, the methodological problem presented by the experimenter's knowledge of the subject's performance. This might have constituted social pressure to help, or at least might have led the subject to expect approval from the experimenter. A later study by Berkowitz, Klanderman, and Harris (1964) ruled out these alternatives by convincing subjects that even the experimenter would not see the worker's output until a month or so later. The results of this study confirmed those found earlier; more help was given to the dependent other, suggesting the operation of a social responsibility norm.

Is a Normative Explanation Sufficient? There is, as the research indicates, experimental support for the notion of reciprocity in helping, and for the idea that objective altruism can be influenced by the social responsibility norm. In addition, Schwartz (1977) has taken a more general normative approach to objective altruism, arguing that the benefactor's acceptance of personal responsibility for the dependent other is a crucial link in the chain leading toward the provision of help. But a normative approach to objective altruism cannot by itself be a sufficient explanation for the behavior. In the experiments by Berkowitz and his associates, and in other "normative" research as well, the norm is made salient by the experimental design. Subjects are explicitly given the responsibility for another person, a person who has either helped them in the past (in research on reciprocity) or who will have no relationship whatsoever with them (in studies on social responsibility). Most of the subjects in these conditions then behave helpfully (whether they are returning a favor or responding to an obvious dependency). From this observable behavior the investigators infer the existence of a particular norm for helpfulness. But in the much more complex world outside the experimental laboratory, social responsibility, or even reciprocity, may not be uppermost in our minds. It is, of course, impossible in such a research procedure to know how much, or even whether, the relevant norm was actually in the benefactor's consciousness prior to his or her performance of the behavior dictated by the experimental conditions. To be fair, it should be noted that those who study normative influences on helping behavior describe the manipulations as ways to make the relevant norm "salient" in the setting. But even this description makes it clear that situational cues must of necessity play some role in bringing the norms to our conscious attention, so that they may guide our helping behavior.

Effects of the Situation

In discussing social learning theory (Chapter 8) we noted that a great deal of learning occurs without benefit of direct reward or punishment. Reinforcements delivered to one person (a *model*) have informational value to other people, who learn vicariously what actions are desired. The salesperson who plants an accomplice to express appreciation for a product, the politician who brings along an entourage of enthusiastic supporters, and the evangelist who concludes a presentation with the dramatic conversion of several members of the audience are all relying on models to influence the reactions of the remaining observers. Given the effectiveness of modeling in situations like these, it is not surprising that a number of experimental studies of helping have found that the presence of a model can increase the prevalence of objective altruism. What is more interesting is the wide variety of modeling effects. Let us take a closer look at some of this research.

Positive and Negative Models. In an early series of studies conducted outside the laboratory, Bryan and Test (1967) found increased helping in two different situations in which there was a helpful model. The first study measured the willingness of motorists to stop and help a woman whose automobile appeared disabled. There were two experimental conditions: In the Model condition, the motorists had just driven past another disabled vehicle whose driver was receiving help; in the No Model condition no good example was provided. The woman whose car appeared disabled and the driver and "helper" in the Model condition were all confederates of the experimenter. As expected, more help was rendered in the

Model condition. The second study involved donations to a Salvation Army kettle in a shopping center, and found similar effects for the presence of a helpful model.

Apparently observation of a helpful will increase the likelihood of helping. But what accounts for this effect? Is it that the model's actions make the social responsibility norm more salient, or that they merely suggest courses of behavior that the observer might not otherwise have considered? The available experimental evidence indicates that both explanations may be partially correct. For example, in a study by Macaulay (1970), college students were given the opportunity to make donations as they passed a table set up in the student union building. The donations were tabulated after a model had loudly announced to the person sitting at the table that she either would or would not make a donation. No matter what the model said, there were more donations immediately after her speech than in control periods when no model was present. The fact that donations increased even when the model stated that she would not donate suggests that her refusal made other passersby conscious of their own social responsibility to help. The study also included a manipulation of the legitimacy of the charity involved – either a starvation relief agency or a political committee – but there were no differences based on the legitimacy of the charity. Yet the social responsibility norm would predict differences based on the validity of the appeal.

Legitimacy of the Cause.   In another experiment that varied the behavior of a model and the legitimacy of the cause, Wagner and Wheeler (1969) arranged for Navy enlisted men and recruits to overhear a model's being asked to donate to a fund. The worthiness of the cause was varied by describing the fund as necessary either to fly in the immediate family of a serviceman who was dying or to augment the funds of a local club for enlisted personnel. The subjects in the Positive model condition overheard the model agreeing to donate, whereas those in the Negative model condition overheard the model refusing to give anything. The subjects were then asked to make a donation of their own. Results showed that, compared to a control condition in which the subjects were asked to make their own contributions before they had heard the model's response, more money was donated in the Positive conditions, and less money was donated in the Negative conditions.

Whereas Macaulay (1970) had obtained increased donation after a negative model, this study found decreased donation after a negative model. The two studies were alike, however, in that the presumed worthiness of the cause had no effect whatsoever on the amount given. These results suggest that there must be more to helping than a norm of social responsibility (or there would have been greater help given to worthy causes), and that there must be more than the specific actions of a model (otherwise negative models should produce consistent failures to help). In short, we might do well also to consider the potential effects of individual differences within observers. How do people interpret a situation requiring assistance, and how do their own personal characteristics enter into the decision of whether to help?

Effects of Internal States

Guilt.   The popular literature is filled with examples of how guilt can affect human behavior. We read of parents who try to use their children's guilt about the inevitable and normal childhood transgressions to control the children's future behavior, and we suspect that psychotherapists spend a great deal of time with adults who had this experience as children. When we learn of obvious mistakes made by a criminal we had considered clever, we wonder whether that person might unconsciously have wanted to be caught and punished. Even when positive social behavior is concerned, guilt may play a causal role: We expect harm-doers to want to provide restitution to their victims, and we wonder whether at least part of a philanthropist's large donations to charity might be guilt over possession of wealth in the midst of poverty. As it happens, a substantial amount of research indicates that guilt can motivate helping behavior.

Restoration of Equity.   Much of this research has been conducted within the framework of equity theory (Walster, Walster, & Berscheid, 1978), with the clearest application of the theory being the case in which the helper is a former harm-doer trying to square accounts with a recipient who has been his or her victim. As Walster, Walster, and Berscheid note, a harm doer may have either of two mutually exclusive reactions to a person harmed. First, the exploiter might justify his or her own behavior and the victim's suffering—thereby restoring psychological equity—by convincing himself or herself that the victim deserved to suffer. The second possible reaction is one of compensation, providing the victim with rewards or help that will restore equity.

Although it can be regarded as an example of the restoration of equity, much of the research on derogation of victims has been conceptualized as demonstrating the *need to believe in a just world*, where people get what they deserve, or deserve what they get (Lerner & Miller, 1978; Lerner & Simmons, 1966). This self-protective need produces a distortion in attribution, by which a perceiver holds a victim responsible for his or her own suffering. The attribution can take one of two forms, either a claim that the victim made some behavioral error that led to the victimization ("behavioral fault") or a claim that despite behavioral innocence the victim is the kind of person who just deserved to suffer ("characterological fault"). There are instances in which an attribution of behavioral fault is justified, such as the case of a person who leaves his or her car running while stepping into the convenience store for a moment, only to return and find the automobile stolen. The defensive attribution of characterological fault, however, is almost universally an error, because it is based on the fact of victimization, not on any of the victim's intentional actions. Surely there are "bad people" in the world, but we discover who they are by watching them hurt others, not by watching them get hurt.

Suppose that instead of restoring psychological equity by derogating his or her victim, the harm-doer chooses compensation. How does equity theory account for this choice? The theory assumes that the harm-doer feels two different sorts of distress upon hurting another person (Walster, Walster, & Berscheid, 1978). The first of these is called **retaliation distress**—the simple fear that the victim, or some outside agent—will restore equity to the relationship not by helping the victim, but by punishing the harm-doer. The second sort of distress is called **self-concept distress** and arises from the inconsistency between the harm-doer's behavior and his or her presumed internalized values prescribing fairness and equity. Self-concept distress is probably the least likely of the two when the harm has been intentional (or the harm-doer presumably would have refrained from the action), but if there really is "honor among thieves" then self-concept distress may not be completely foreign even to criminal offenders. It is fair to say that self-concept distress is roughly equivalent to the state we have been calling guilt. In the absence of any potential for the victim (or others) to retaliate, a choice of compensation will be attributed to guilt; in the presence of retaliatory capability, compensation will be attributed to retaliation distress, on the assumption that the latter is more threatening than guilt. A harm-doer has very little control over the actions that others might take in order to restore equity, but he or she does have at least nominal control over the recriminations directed at the self. Any assistance rendered a victim by a harm-doer is, of course, helping behavior rather than objective altruism. Whether the motive is restoration of a tarnished self-concept or insurance against threatened retaliation, the harm-doer definitely gains from providing compensation.

The Problem of Generality. Before the results of research on various aspects of guilt are generalized to the case of the robber baron who must contribute to charity in order to salve his conscience, two notes of caution are in order. First, because guilt is an internal state that cannot be measured directly, there is always the chance that the experiments have produced results for some reason other than guilt. For example, many of the studies have involved public behavior of the subject (public at least to the extent that the experimenter knows about it), the internal state leading to helping might be shame, rather than guilt. Or there might be no internal state at all. This is the same problem of measurement that arises in connection with the inference of any intervening variable (the drive for cognitive consistency thought to produce attitude change is a prime example). The only solution to the problem is to conduct a wide variety of studies that will rule out other plausible alternatives, a solution that may already have been achieved for the role of guilt in producing helping (Freedman, 1970).

The second note of caution is based on an important difference between the experimental procedures for inducing guilt and the presumed causes of guilt outside the laboratory. In all of the experimental studies, it has been necessary to mislead subjects into behaving contrary to their moral codes. If experimenters do this with too heavy a hand, people will feel so coerced that they will not develop any guilt. But with too little inducement, subjects will just follow their moral codes, also preventing guilt. When subjects are successfully induced to behave contrary to their moral codes, they may well develop an internal reaction that can plausibly be called guilt. In real life, however, people who voluntarily cause others to suffer may not experience any guilt. Even if such harm-doers later express remorse over their actions, these admissions are complicated by the fact that it is socially desirable to tell an interviewer, or a judge, that one feels guilty for actions known to be disapproved.

Personal Responsibility for Helpful Action

We have seen that social norms of reciprocity and social responsibility do not always appear to produce helping, that similar performances by models may have quite different effects, and that internal states may also lead to helping. Equity and exchange theories can account for much of this behavior, but there is nothing to explain unless an individual provider of aid takes the sort of intentional action needed to translate good motives into altruistic behavior. Recent work in nonemergency helping has begun to explore the factors that lead individuals to accept personal responsibility for helpful action. In a sense, personal responsibility can be regarded as yet another internal state, but because of its critical role it deserves special attention.

A model developed by Schwartz (1977) suggests that two factors interact to determine whether the cultural and situational pressures toward help-giving will in fact result in helpful action. First, you must be aware of the consequences your actions might have for a person in need. If you believe that nothing you do will make a difference, or if you remain ignorant of how your behavior might contribute to benefits received by others, it is unlikely that the situational pressures will affect your actions. Awareness of consequences can activate what Schwartz considers to be **personal norms**–expectations for one's own behavior in a given situation, as opposed to the societal expectations inherent in more general norms.

Notice that the operative word here is *can*. Whether the awareness of consequences actually culminates in altruistic action depends on the second factor, what Schwartz calls **responsibility denial**. Responsibility denial is the individual tendency to rationalize away responsibility for the consequences of behavior. These two factors interact to produce altruistic action, with help likely to be rendered only by persons who are aware of the consequences and have little in the way of responsibility denial. The model assumes that individual differences occur on both factors, and that aspects of the situation may also affect the outcome (you could be high on awareness, low on denial, and still not have the technical expertise to help). In an extensive program of research, Schwartz has found support for the interactive model, although some limitations of the approach have been noted (Krebs & Miller, 1985; Zuckerman & Reis, 1978).

Finally, it is important to note that helping behavior can be the consequence not only of negative internal states such as guilt, but also of positive feelings such as happiness, empathy with the person in need of help, or personal similarity to the intended beneficiary. Although Schwartz has not specifically made the suggestion, it seems reasonable to say that many of these effects might also be mediated by an increased sense of personal responsibility toward others, including the particular beneficiary. Such personal responsibility for action is a critical element in the provision of aid. Not everyone who recognizes the existence of a social responsibility norm will behave according to its dictates. Not everyone who is placed in a situation demanding some helpful intervention will respond accordingly. And not everyone who feels guilt will translate that internal state into restoration of equity. Only when the social norms, situational factors, and individual characteristics combine in a particular manner within one specific decision maker will aid be provided. The major contribution of Schwartz's two-factor model is its representation–within the individual person–of general cultural norms, specific elements of the situation, and internal states of the potential helper.

OBJECTIVE ALTRUISM IN EMERGENCIES

The Failure to Act

Intervention in an emergency situation should be slightly simpler to explain than is nonemergency helping, if only because the need for quick action ought to preclude consideration of some of the long-term consequences of the action. But even in emergencies, the reasons for acting or for failing to act are not as obvious as they might seem. For example, let us look at one widely reported failure to intervene (Latané & Darley, 1970; Rosenthal, 1964). In the early hours of a March morning, a young woman returned from her job, parked her car in a lot near her apartment building, and started walking the short distance to the front door. A man who had been standing in the parking lot suddenly attacked her, stabbing her with a knife. The woman screamed for help, some lights went on in the building, a man called out, and the attacker got in his car and drove away. Then the lights in the building went out and the attacker returned to stab her again. Lights went on again, windows were opened, and the attacker drove off. By now the woman had managed to crawl to the doorway of the building, but the attacker returned a third time, fatally stabbed her, and drove away. The entire sequence of events took more than a half hour and was observed by 38 witnesses (Rosenthal, 1964), but not a single person directly intervened (one apparently did call the police, but too late).

What makes this tragic incident important for our purposes here is, unfortunately, not that it happened at all—similar murders occur with alarming regularity; nor is it particularly noteworthy that the murder took place in New York City, because incidents like this one can be found in most major cities, and in smaller towns as well. What is important for us is that this incident marked the beginning of serious inquiry into why virtually none of the bystanders took even the minimal action of notifying the police. In interviews with psychologists, sociologists, and psychiatrists, Rosenthal (1964) obtained a variety of explanations for the witnesses' failure to intervene, but a consistent theme was apathy, presumably the result of the depersonalizing influence of living in a large city. This explanation has the ring of intuitive plausibility, but as Latané and Darley (1970) point out, it may not be a correct interpretation: "The 38 witnesses . . . did not merely look at the scene once and then ignore it. Instead they continued to stare out of their windows at what was going on. Caught, fascinated, distressed, unwilling to act but unable to turn away, their behavior was neither helpful nor heroic; but it was not indifferent or apathetic either" (p. 4).

Diffusion of Responsibility

Rather than attempting to answer the general question, "What leads people to help others in emergencies?" Latané and Darley (1970) and other social psychologists who have studied bystander intervention have tried to identify particular characteristics of emergency situations that either promote or inhibit intervention. The first of these experiments (Darley & Latané, 1968) was designed to determine the effects on helping of the number of bystanders who witnessed an incident. Remember that one of the internal states thought to influence helping in a nonemergency situation is an acceptance of personal responsibility for the victim (Schwartz, 1977). When there are numerous witnesses to an even, this personal responsibility becomes *diffused* among the witnesses, with the possible result that none of them will take any action. If you are alone with a person who suddenly collapses, you know that if help is to be rendered, you will have to be the one to do it. But if you and a number of your friends are all present, the responsibility is diffused among you all, and this may make each of you individually less likely to help.

An Epileptic Seizure.   To test this idea, Darley and Latané (1968) had male and female undergraduates at New York University overhear what they thought was an epileptic seizure suffered by one participant in a discussion of personal problems. The subjects had been told that the purpose of the research was to discuss the sorts of problems faced by students who were adjusting to college and to life in the city. Ostensibly to preserve subjects' anonymity, but really to remove the obviously responsible experimenter from the situation, the subjects were told that they would have the opportunity to talk about their experiences with other students, but that the experimenter would not listen to this initial discussion. Each subject was placed in a room alone, and was given a pair of earphones through which the instructions were delivered and the subject could hear the statements of other participants. Subjects were to take turns talking, with a mechanical switch allowing each person's microphone to be on for a period of 2 minutes, during which time all other microphones would be off. This was done so that when the "seizure" occurred, the subjects would be unable simply to discuss it with one another prior to deciding what to do.

The future victim spoke first and said that he found it difficult to adjust to New York City and to his studies. Then, with obvious embarrassment, he admitted that he was prone to seizures, especially when he was under pressure. Other participants (including the real subject) then took their turns presenting their problems, and finally the switching apparatus returned to the victim. This time, after making a few relatively calm comments, the victim became increasingly incoherent, spluttering that he was having a seizure, and asking for help. After about 70 seconds, the victim seemed to have suffered a complete breakdown.

Number of Bystanders.   Although the incident in this experiment was mild by comparison, the witnessing subject was placed in a position analogous to that of the witnesses of the murder described earlier. The subject was confronted with a clear behavioral choice – to intervene or not to intervene – and was isolated from other witnesses so that there could be no discussion of the matter. There were three experimental conditions. In all of these only one naive subject was run at a time (speeches of the other participants, including the victim, had been tape-recorded), but from that subject's point of view there were either Two people (the subject and the victim), Three people (subject, victim, one other), or Six people (subject, victim, four others) taking part in the experiment.

If the idea of diffusion of responsibility is correct, then the proportion of witnesses helping the victim should have decreased as the group size increased from Two to Six, and the results confirmed this expectation. When only the subject and victim were present, 85% of subjects reported the emergency to the experimenter before the end of the seizure. When the apparent group size was Three, this proportion decreased to 62%, and when the apparent group consisted of Six, there was a dramatic decrease in reporting to 31%. Not only did a greater proportion of subjects report the incident in the Two condition, those who responded did so more quickly (an average of 52 seconds) than did subjects in the Three condition (93 seconds) or the Six condition (166 seconds). Thus, increased group size, and presumably more greatly diffused responsibility, led to a decrease in an individual's tendency to intervene and help.

As Latané and Darley (1970) have noted, these percentages only represent the likelihood that a *particular* bystander will intervene, not the likelihood that the victim will receive help. The results from the Two conditions, in which there is a single bystander, can be transformed to constitute create "as if" groups. When this transformation is calculated, it shows that the victim is equally likely to receive help in all conditions, but that help will be rendered more quickly when there are few bystanders. In real emergencies, where time is often very short, the additional delay created in larger groups can be disastrous for a victim.

A Decision Process Model of Intervention

Noticing the Event.   To account for some of the bystander intervention effects, Latané and Darley (1970) proposed a decision making model of the process that incorporates elements of exchange theory (Chapter 8) and social comparison theory (Chapter 7). The model is outlined in Fig. 9.1, and shows that there are five basic steps leading to an intervention in an emergency situation. The first of these is to notice that something is wrong, and this is not as trivial a step as it might seem. For example, remember how you felt the first time you drove into a large city during the morning rush hour. You were probably so intent on staying in the proper lane of traffic, and on avoiding accidents, that you noticed very little except for the other cars near you. Had there been some sort of an incident on a sidewalk, or in the entrance to a building, you would have missed it completely. The more familiar the surroundings, and the less you need to "tune them out" because they are noisy or unpleasant, the more likely you will be to notice an incident that might call for intervention.

What is an Emergency?   After noticing something amiss, the observer must define that occurrence as an emergency. A series of studies by Shotland and Huston (1979) suggests some of the factors that will enter into this critical judgment. In the first study, subjects were asked simply to list those events they had witnessed, heard about, or or just imagined that they considered emergencies. Then a second group of subjects was

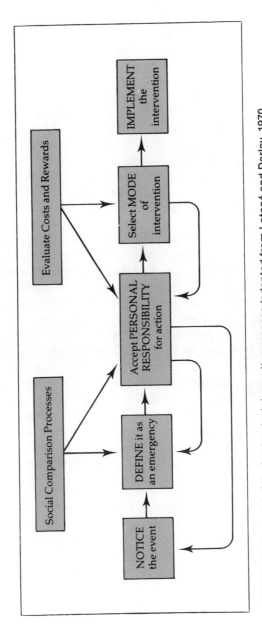

FIGURE 9.1 A model of the bystander intervention process (adapted from Latané and Darley, 1970, pp. 31–36).

asked to characterize the 96 problem situations identified in the first study, in order to determine the common features of an emergency. The results showed that people distinguish among definite emergencies (such as a cut artery with profuse bleeding), events that may be emergencies (a person who is lost in the woods and shouting for help), and problems that are probably not emergencies (opening a car door too hard and chipping paint off of the adjacent car) on the basis of three major dimensions. First, there is the fact that the actual harm or threat of harm will worsen with the passage of time. Second, no easy solution to the problem is immediately available. Third, the victim cannot be expected to take care of the problem alone; some outside help is required. Other findings from the series of studies showed a remarkable degree of agreement about what constituted real emergencies, that these problem situations were usually the result of accidents, and that help was more likely to be rendered for real emergencies than for other kinds of problem situations.

Of course, some problem situations may be emergencies even though they are not as obvious as a cut artery, a house ablaze with its occupants screaming for help, or a child who has swallowed poison or a razor blade (the three most obvious emergencies from Shotland and Huston's research). When there is some doubt about the nature of the problem or the need for immediate action, the decision process model asserts that the uncertainty will be resolved through social comparison, because there are few objective standards available. Are the child's screams you hear from inside a house an indication of real pain, or just frustration at the actions of a sibling? Does the smoke coming from the rear of a building indicate that the structure is on fire, or merely that someone is burning trash? For that matter, is the automobile parked on the side of the road disabled, or are its occupants just waiting to rob the first person who stops to help? In any of these cases, what should you do? If you are alone when confronted by such possible emergencies, you will have to decide for yourself, but if there are other people around you will probably study their reactions to determine what your own should be. In short, you will engage in social comparison to reach a definition of the situation.

Personal Responsibility for Action. If you decide that you are witnessing a real emergency, the next step in the process is the acceptance of personal responsibility for whatever action might be necessary. This step, like its counterpart in nonemergency helping, will be affected both by social comparison and by your evaluation of the costs and rewards connected with intervention. If you have the technical competence to deal with the problem, you will be more likely to intervene than if you do not know what to do (Schwartz & Clausen, 1970), and you will be more likely to take responsibility if others are unable to help (Bickman, 1971). But how can you judge your ability against that of a group of strangers? Only through social comparison. Even if you determine that you can help, the social costs of intervention—which may range from merely making a fool of yourself through making the situation worse to getting sued, injured, or killed for your trouble—may keep you from taking personal responsibility for action. Indeed, as Fig. 9.1 illustrates, Latané and Darley (1970) suggest that your desire to avoid personal responsibility may cycle the decision process backward, getting you to change your definition of the event, or even leading you to pretend that you didn't notice that the event was happening.

After you have accepted personal responsibility for action, you must still decide which course of action to take. You have committed yourself to becoming involved; the only question is to what degree. Should you intervene directly in the emergency, doing what you can for the victim yourself? Or should you take the indirect course of notifying the proper authorities? Although direct intervention is the more obvious choice, it also has the greater social cost, and this may lead you to cycle back one step, avoiding personal responsibility by leaving the situation "to the experts." Once you have decided that you will intervene, either directly or indirectly, the last step in the process, implementing that decision, follows rather naturally.

Ambiguity, Social Comparison, and Costs/Rewards. The decision process model is useful primarily in explaining instances of potential emergencies, in which the situation is ambiguous. In such circumstances, the need for extensive social comparison may inhibit intervention. When you are looking at the reactions of others (and they are observing your reactions), you want to be certain of the situation before committing yourself to an action that may prove inappropriate. We are taught to respond unemotionally—to look before we leap—and we hesitate to do something that others will think foolish. The more bystanders there are in an ambiguous situation, the more a person will hesitate.

The importance of ambiguity in mediating the inhibitory effect of a larger number of bystanders is illustrated in two experiments by Clark and Word (1974). In these two studies, the researchers found that more help was given a technician who had apparently suffered a severe electrical shock in full view of the subject (no ambiguity) than when it had occurred out of the subject's view (some ambiguity). More important, the subjects were run either alone or in pairs, and this difference in group size affected helping (less help from the pairs) only when the situation was ambiguous. The social constraints against intervention in an ambiguous situation should be even more powerful in larger groups.

In contrast, when the need for intervention is clear, the first two steps of the decision process model (and, consequently, much of the social comparison) will be omitted. Indeed, when the situation is an obvious emergency in which no specialized skills are required for intervention, doing nothing is the inappropriate behavior. Thus in these settings the major influence on the choice of whether or not to intervene will be the costs to the potential helper. In determining these costs, people take into account both the magnitude of the cost and the likelihood that the cost will be incurred (Lynch & Cohen, 1978). For example, it is not surprising to learn that people will be more likely to help people of the same race than people of another race (West, Whitney, & Schmedler, 1975), or that females will be helped more often and more quickly than will males (Latané & Darley, 1970; West, Whitney, & Schmedler, 1975).

In a less obvious example of the cost of helping, Piliavin and Piliavin (1972) found that a bloody victim will receive less help than a nonbloody one. Intuitively, we would have expected precisely the opposite result, on the grounds that a bloody victim would more obviously need help. But this greater need creates higher potential costs for the helper: more opportunity inadvertently to make the situation worse, more commitment of time and resources to get the victim to a hospital, the fear that whoever caused the victim to bleed may return and attack the helper as well. These results indicate that in some cases, the people who need help the most may be the least likely to receive aid, because of the costs to potential helpers.

Bystander Intervention as Objective Altruism

The fact that costs incurred by the potential helper may influence the decision to intervene, or the kind of action (direct or indirect) taken, does not eliminate bystander intervention from the class of objectively altruistic actions. Such intervention is still voluntary action that helps the victim and earns no external reward, so it still satisfies all the criteria for objective altruism. But it is also the result of a decision, and this decision may be influenced by the costs to the potential helper, by the ambiguity of the situation, and by the number and reactions of other witnesses to the incident.

Let us return to the 38 observers of the murder. It is easy to imagine that many of the witnesses at first considered the incident to be a lover's quarrel, failing to define the situation as an emergency. It may also have been true that just as the observers might have been ready to accept personal responsibility for calling the police, the assailant drove off and the emergency was over. When the attacker returned, it is possible that the passage of time justified the assumption that somebody had surely called the police. Then the emergency apparently ended again. When it began for a third time, people might have been so committed to inaction that they could not at that late time notify the police ("Why didn't you call sooner?"). Their decision process had cycled from one step to another without ever leading to an acceptance of personal responsibility for intervention, with tragic consequences for the victim.

In the years since this tragedy, two widespread social changes may have made bystander intervention in similar settings more likely. Thanks to the women's movement and victim's rights organizations, many of us have come to believe that violence between lovers, or even within a marriage, is still violence demanding some kind of intervention. Additionally, the police in many communities have helped to organize "neighborhood watch" programs that among other things lead participants to notice what is going on in the neighborhood, be ready to define incidents as emergencies, and systematize who is to call the police. There are still no external rewards for helping, but some of the social costs of intervention may have been reduced. Perhaps these changes, and a thorough understanding of the nature of the decision process, will keep us all from becoming trapped in a cycle of indecision should we ever be faced with a similar occurrence.

INTERPERSONAL ATTRACTION

As we have seen, a substantial amount of helping behavior, and all of objective altruism, are independent of the external rewards so prevalent in other forms of social exchange. This contrasts with the case of interpersonal attraction, a form of positive social behavior that is heavily dependent upon mutual reward. Indeed, as you will recall from chapter 8, one definition of attraction to a relationship, and presumably to the other people in that relationship, requires that that the outcomes received surpass both the comparison level (the average of the past outcomes) and the comparison level for alternatives (the best available alternative to the current interaction). Thus, although reward is excluded from objective altruism, it is practically essential for interpersonal attraction.

AN ATTITUDE OF FAVORABILITY

What does it mean to say that you are attracted to a person? Think of some of the words that could be used to describe a relationship between two people: respect, admiration, friendship, liking, love. Can these be used interchangeably? Does the use of one necessitate the use of others? Occasionally so, but much of the time probably not. For example, you can respect a professor whom you do not like; you can develop a friendship with a person whose faults you cannot admire; you can like a person for a long time without that liking's becoming love. Each descriptive word has a slightly different meaning, and often these differences are important. But each word also represents a favorable, or positive, evaluation of the target person. In order to recognize some of the complexity of interpersonal attraction and simultaneously to provide a conceptual definition that is clear enough to serve as the foundation for research, many social psychologists have considered **attraction** to be an attitude of favorability toward the target person (Berscheid, 1985; Berscheid & Walster, 1969, 1978; Huston & Levinger, 1978).

Let us consider this attitude of favorability in terms we have used earlier (Chapters 5 and 6). Compared to other attitudes, interpersonal attraction is probably less cognitive and more emotional, with more clearly identifiable behavioral cconsequences. The cognitive component of your attraction toward another might include your perception of the other's competence, your estimate that many of the person's beliefs are similar to yours, and your judgment of the person's ability to provide you with social rewards. As we see in the next section, the affective or emotional component has recently been considered in its own right, but for now that component might include the value you place on qualities the person possesses, the pleasure you receive from rewards actually provided, and some indefinable "chemistry" of immediate liking. The behavioral component could include your willingness to help the other person, the words you use to describe him or her to someone else, and the amount of time you choose to spend together. Because attraction is a positive social behavior, its existence is more easily documented (indeed, we may tend to overestimate its prevalence) than is the existence of socially undesirable attitudes. People will try to show positive actions, but conceal negative feelings.

As prevalent as the phenomena of interpersonal attraction may be, there is an important limitation in the way attraction has typically been measured by social psychologists: duration. Most of the measures gathered in laboratory research on attraction are taken during a single experimental session rather than repeated over a long period of time. In addition, most of the relationships that have been investigated are themselves of short duration: first impressions, casual friendships, or short-term dating relationships. Indeed, Huston (1974) estimated that perhaps 80% of the social psychological research available at that time consisted of single-session studies of short-term relationships. There are several exceptions to this rule, such as Newcomb's (1961) study of the development of acquaintance and friendship in a college dormitory, and Altman and Taylor's (1973) research on the changes that occur in self-disclosure over a time period of more than a year, but even these studies might more properly be considered to cover the formative stages of a relationship than to cover its maintenance through time.

Only recently has there been intensive study of close relationships that persist through time (e.g., Kelley et al., 1983). These relationships typically involve a dyad composed of opposite-sex partners, with the two people being highly interdependent. According to Berscheid and Peplau (1983), this interdependence is indicated by the fact that the individuals have frequent impact on each other over a wide variety of activities for a relatively long duration of time, with each encounter having a strong effect on the two partners. It is important to note, however, that the scientific study of close relationships is truly "emerging" at the present time, so most of the interpersonal attraction research is still accurately described by Berscheid (1985) as being conducted "outside the context of ongoing relationships" (p. 417).

EMOTION AND COMMITMENT

Once the study of interpersonal attraction moves from virtually exclusive concentration on relationships of short duration to investigation of the course of naturally occurring relationships that exist through time, the conceptualization of attraction as an attitude will need a corresponding expansion (Berscheid, 1985). Specifically, a greater role will most probably be given to emotion, and to the mutual commitment arising from interdependence. Think about some of the relationships you know well. Suppose I asked you to describe your attachment to your parents, or to a romantic partner you have known for a long time. Chances are slim that you would voluntarily characterize either relationship with a check on a single bipolar adjective scale running from "like completely" to "dislike completely." Certainly you could make such a characterization if I asked you to do so, but it would not have been your first choice at an explanation. What you would do, if you believed that I really wanted to know, is tell me things about the target(s) that you like, and things that you don't like. You would recount the moments of extreme happiness and the occasional bitter arguments. Moreover, you would use many of the descriptive adjectives noted above—respect, admiration, liking, love—in a truly multidimensional account of the relationship. Implicit in this description is an underlying commitment to the relationship over time, regardless of the day-to-day variations.

Notice the differences between this account and a description based entirely on an attitude of favorability. As conceptualized in chapters 5 and 6, attitudes are presumed to be relatively stable cognitive structures that can be changed only with some difficulty. They certainly would not be expected to fluctuate from day to day, let alone from hour to hour. Furthermore, attitudes, once organized, are expected to be internally consistent. Indeed, maintaining that very consistency is the point behind balance, congruity, and dissonance theories: make a person aware of inconsistencies between attitude and action, and the attitude will change to restore equilibrium. In contrast, the positive and negative characteristics of ongoing relationships successfully coexist without the same pressure toward resolution at one or the other end of the hedonic scale. We would expect a relationship characterized by continual bickering and unpleasantness not to last, but we are just as pessimistic about the chances for a relationship in which no disagreement ever surfaces.

Whereas attitudes are unidimensional, stable, and internally consistent, emotions are inherently multidimensional and variable, with no presumption of internal consistency. At the very least, emotional experience has been described since Schachter's (1964) cognitive labeling theory (Chapter 8) as comprising both cognitive and physiological elements, and other recent descriptions of emotion (e.g., Plutchik, 1980) involve even more distinct elements. A person's present attitude is presumed to tell you not only how the person will behave toward the attitude object right now, but also in the future; knowing a person's present emotional state tells you only how the person is likely to behave immediately toward the object of emotion. Holding contradictory attitudes toward an object or person is thought to motivate change, having disparate emotions toward a person is only thought to reflect the realities of interpersonal behavior.

The idea that interpersonal attraction involves strong emotions, and a commitment to the continuation of the relationship that transcends momentary feelings, is as recent an addition to the literature as is the study of ongoing, close relationships. Consequently, much of the existing social psychological research on interpersonal attraction is best regarded as a "snapshot" taken at a particular point in time. It is an accurate statement of what is well-known now, but it cannot adequately capture some of the changes that are bound to occur just out of the camera's field of view. You need to keep this caution in mind as we consider the measurement, and antecedents, of interpersonal attraction.

THE MEASUREMENT OF ATTRACTION

Friendship Choice

Both because it has served as the model for a number of other measurement procedures and because it demonstrates some of the difficulties encountered in the study of interpersonal attraction, the topic of friendship choice deserves more detailed comment. One of the earliest attempts to assess interpersonal attraction by means of friendship choice was the *sociometric* method developed by Moreno (1934).

Constructing a Sociogram. To illustrate the method, imagine that you are in a small class with eight other people you know but do not know very well. I ask each of you to write down the names of no more than two other people (the number listed can change, and two is used here only to simplify the example) with whom you would like to become good friends. Then I collect the papers, assign a number to each of you, and construct a diagram known as a sociogram based on your responses. Such a **sociogram** is shown in Fig. 9.2, with each arrow indicating a friendship choice. The sociogram shows that person #1 wrote down the names of person #2 and person #3; that person #2 reciprocated person #1's choice and in addition chose person #5; person #3 also reciprocated person #1's choice and in addition selected person #5; the remaining choices can be described in similar

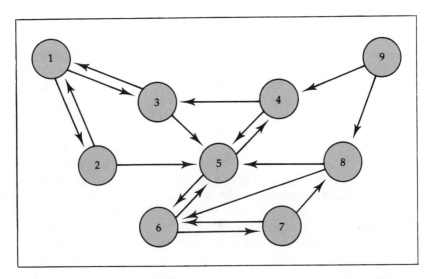

FIGURE 9.2   A sociogram of friendship choice (adapted from Moreno, 1934, p. 32).

terms. As the diagram indicates, person #5 is the most popular (the "star"), with a total of five choices (because of the limit on choices that could be made, we do not know how many of those five would actually be reciprocated). Person #9, in contrast, is somewhat of an outcast (the "isolate"), being chosen for friendship by nobody else in the group. The choices used to construct a sociogram can be spontaneous and virtually unlimited, or they can be inferences made by the investigator from interviews conducted with the subjects (rather than explicit choices made by the subjects themselves), or they can be direct answers to a restricted set of questions, as in our example.

Complications with the Method.   When the choices are responses to direct questions, which specific questions are asked will make quite a difference. Suppose that instead of asking you to pick the two people you would like to have as good friends, I asked you to pick the two people you would most like to have on your team if I were to split the nine of you into three groups competing for a single prize. You might choose for teammates the two most uncompromising and fiercely competitive people in the class, but most probably you would not select these same people to be your good friends. Indeed, a consistent finding in the study of leadership in small groups is that the people selected for task leadership are not often chosen to maintain the emotional needs of the group (Bales, 1958; Gibb, 1969; Halpin, 1966). We return to this issue in chapter 12; for now it is sufficient to note that the results of a sociogram will depend on the questions asked.

In much the same way that the precise questions asked can influence the outcome of a sociogram, some of the questions that are not asked can affect the degree to which that sociogram–or some other measure of attraction–reflects the subject's interpersonal reality (Berscheid, 1985). If you know a person's friendship choices within a defined sociogram, do you know who that person's actual friends are likely to be? Just asking this question suggests the answer: no. To assume otherwise is, in exchange theory terms, to confuse the comparison level for alternatives (CL_{alt}) with the comparison level (CL). The most attractive individual in this group of nine may be better than nobody (this is the question I have implicitly asked), but that individual may still not be up to your standards for a true friend. Furthermore, as Berscheid (1985) notes, your expressed attraction toward another person is only one of the determinants of actual friendship, with such factors as physical proximity, similarity of interests, and your own personal qualities also affecting the process of friendship choice. In short, "attraction is neither necessary nor sufficient for affiliation to occur" (p. 442), so investigators using the sociometric method need (a) to consider the person's social network as it exists outside the laboratory, and (b) to ask a variety of questions in the sociometric interview. In this way the researchers can attempt to obtain a more complete picture of a person's actual structure of friends.

Attitude Scaling Approaches

The goal of differentiating one kind of attraction from another is also present to some degree in attitude scaling approaches to interpersonal attraction, although most of these studies tend to concentrate more on the antecedents and consequences of attraction than on the diversity of ways in which individuals may become involved with one another. Two examples illustrate the attitude scaling approach. The first of these is the work of Byrne (1961, 1971) and his associates, which deals with the relation between attitude similarity and liking; the second is the research on love conducted by Rubin (1970, 1973).

The major finding from Byrne's program of research–that attraction will increase as a direct function of attitude similarity–is discussed more fully at a later point. The scales used to measure liking in this research, however, are drawn directly from sociometric studies. One of these scales asks the subject to judge how much he or she would like to have the stimulus person as a work partner (the task-oriented choice), whereas another scale asks the person to indicate how much he or she likes the stimulus person (the friendship choice). These two ratings are embedded in a short series of other scales that include estimates of the stimulus person's morality, intelligence, personal adjustment, and knowledge of current events. The entire inventory is known as the Interpersonal Judgment Scale (Byrne, 1971). In most cases, interpersonal attraction is simply considered to be the sum of the scores on the work-partner and liking scales (Byrne, 1971), although all of the ratings have occasionally been used to indicate attraction.

Needing and Giving. Especially because attraction has so frequently been regarded as an attitude of favorability, it is easy to conceive of attitude measurement techniques to assess liking, but it is much more difficult to imagine how love could be translated into the unemotional and objective terms of an attitude scale. Yet the study of this romantic bond is just what Rubin (1970; 1973) attempted. In analyzing the treatment of romantic love (as opposed, for example, to the love of a parent for a child) in philosophy and literature, Rubin identified two common themes, needing, and giving. Romantic love is usually thought to involve physical or emotional need represented in a strong attachment to the object person, and to involve an altruistic caring for that person's own needs.

In a standard attitude scaling procedure, Rubin constructed a large number of attitude statements relating to liking and loving and administered these items to a group of judges who were instructed to sort them into liking, caring, and needing categories based on their content. Items that were consistently sorted in the appropriate categories were further refined by having 182 dating couples at the University of Michigan complete both the liking and loving items as they would apply (a) to their dating partner, and (b) to a same-sex close friend. Rubin found that for the liking items, there was not much difference between the total scores for liking of friend and liking of romantic partner, but for the loving items the totals for partners far exceeded those for friends. These results, and further analyses of the correlations among the various items, suggested that the two scales did in fact measure two different aspects of attraction.

Liking and Loving. In later work, Rubin (1974) reported further refinement of the liking and loving scales, such that each scale now consists of nine items. The liking scale contains items related to liking, admiration, and respect for the object person, and judgments of that person's maturity, personal adjustment, and personal responsibility. In contrast, the loving scale consists of items relating to caring and need. Examples of these latter items are "I would do almost anything for ____," "I would forgive ____ for practically anything," and "It would be hard for me to get along without ____." For each item on either the liking or loving scale, the subject is asked to say how much the statement is true for the stimulus person in question (e.g., a romantic partner or an opposite-sex close friend). A score of 1 is given for each item that is not at all true for the stimulus person in question; with a score of 9 given for an assertion that the item is definitely true for the person in question. Thus, for the total of nine items in each scale, the possible scores range from a low of 9 to a high of 81.

The data presented by Rubin (1974) suggest that on such 9-item scales, the average liking scores for friends and partners would be approximately 60. Love scores for partners would be about 65, whereas love scores for friends would be closer to 40. Later research (Dermer & Pyszczynski, 1978) supports the distinction between liking and loving, indicating that attitudinal research can at least account for these different dimensions of attraction, although maintaining the overall view of attraction as an attitude of favorability.

Although Rubin's work has served as a model for attitudinal study of interpersonal attraction, it does suffer from some of the problems that are common to the attitudinal approach. First, with regard to the duration of the relationships investigated, the initial items were validated on a sample of subjects who can best be described as in the early phases of a romantic relationship. Would married couples celebrating a 25th anniversary answer the questions the same way? Perhaps, but as a relationship progresses some of the important questions may change. As an obvious example, a person who has seriously contemplated his or her own death and the death of a partner would be less likely to agree with the statement "It would be hard for me to get along without ____" than would a young person for whom that sort of tragedy is not yet a cloud on the horizon.

Second, with regard to the different varieties of interpersonal attraction, the two dimensions of liking and loving are a definite improvement over a unidimensional conception, but even they cannot do justice to the complexity of the relationships involved. The "loving" scale was never intended to apply to the love that a parent might have for a child, and indeed, it does not. For example, many parents might think that complete agreement with the statement "I would do almost anything for ____" would reflect an attitude likely to produce a child incapable of standing on his or her own. Indeed, the specific objective of the "Toughlove" program designed to help parents cope with their delinquent older children is to make parental support and encouragement contingent on acceptable behavior by the child. The attitude scaling approach is a good beginning to the study of interpersonal attraction, but it is only a beginning, and much still remains to be learned.

SOME ANTECEDENTS OF ATTRACTION

The Influence of Rewards

Whether interpersonal attraction is considered merely an attitude of favorability or a more complex form of social interdependence involving emotion and mutual commitment, its initial development can be predicted by principles of exchange theory (Chapter 8) and cognitive consistency theory (Chapter 5). As an alternative to theory-based predictions, we might try to make guesses based on the popular wisdom about attraction, but the inconsistency inherent in that "wisdom" would make this a difficult task. For example, consider the potentially important environmental variable of *propinquity*, or physical closeness. Does attraction increase with physical separation ("absence makes the heart grow fonder"), or does separation cause a decrease in attachment ("out of sight, out of mind")? The popular wisdom permits both predictions, but on the grounds that physical proximity is usually necessary for the provision of rewards, exchange theory suggests that propinquity would be a necessary condition for the development and maintenance of attraction.

In much the same way, we might guess that the interpersonal variable of *similarity* should influence attraction. But as initially noted in chapter 1, the popular wisdom makes contradictory predictions. Does attraction increase with similarity ("birds of a feather flock together"), or are attraction and similarity negatively related ("opposites attract")? Here several of the theories we have considered would lead to the expectation that similarity should increase attraction. Balance theory argues that you should have positive feelings for those with whom you agree, social comparison theory (Chapter 7) suggests that similar others will reward you with comparisons that are likely to be both more meaningful and more ego-enhancing, and exchange theory implies that similar others may be able to provide you with a wider range of rewarding interactions.

Finally, the ideas of exchange theory suggest that certain personal qualities of the target person ought to be related to the development of attraction. Specifically, you should prefer people who want to reward you and are capable of doing so. One of the best predictors of a person's desire to give you social rewards should be the person's attitude toward you, so exchange theories predict that you should be more attracted to people who express liking for you than to people who do not think highly of you. As far as capacity to bestow rewards is concerned, in any culture that places a high value on good looks, physically attractive people should have more to give; in any culture that values success, competent people should be better able to deliver. So, in contemporary American society, at least, competent and physically attractive people will be liked more than incompetent and unattractive people. Exchange and reinforcement theorists do not argue that this preference is morally correct, only that it is highly likely.

All these factors assume, to one degree or another, that interpersonal attraction is strongly influenced by received rewards. Indeed, the relationship between each factor and interpersonal attraction can be regarded as an aspect of the general rule that rewards increase attraction. A considerable amount of experimental evidence supports this general rule (e.g., see reviews by Berscheid, 1985; Berscheid & Walster, 1978; Byrne, 1971), and compared to the inconsistency of commonsense statements about attraction, the general rule is a decided improvement. Of course, when the phenomenon under investigation is multifaceted, as is interpersonal attraction, there will be exceptions to any general rule. In many of these cases, however, the guidance of theory is a valuable aid in understanding why the exception has occurred.

We now consider propinquity, similarity, and personal qualities in more detail, showing some of the ways in which these variables influence attraction, but also pointing out some of the exceptional cases. It should be noted that these variables do not exhaust the list of contributors to attraction, although they are the ones that have received the most attention from social psychologists. You should also remember that the effects of these variables have been demonstrated predominantly in relationships that are in the formative stages, not in relationships that have alredy been established for a long period of time. (For a more complete discussion of the phenomena of interpersonal attraction, see Berscheid & Walster, 1978, or the much more technical review by Berscheid, 1985. For a thorough discussion of close relationships, see Kelley, et al., 1983, a book recently devoted entirely to that topic.

Propinquity

Housing Patterns and Friendship. Advertisements for long-distance telephone calls notwithstanding, the best way to give and receive rewards through social interaction is in person. Therefore, physical proximity, and the opportunity for interaction it provides, will have substantial impact on the development of liking. This has been illustrated in a classic study of housing patterns and friendship conducted at the Massachusetts Institute of Technology by Festinger, Schachter, and Back (1950). The university maintained a housing project for married students that consisted of 17 two-story buildings, with each building divided into 10 apartments as diagrammed in Fig. 9.3. For the most part, students who were assigned to live in the project did not know each other in advance, and more importantly, they were assigned to apartments in the project as space became available, so they had no choice about which apartment they occupied.

To determine the effect of living in the project on friendship choices, participation in the governing body of the project, and a variety of other attitudes, the researchers conducted extensive interviews with residents of the project. These interviews were conducted after the tenants had lived in the project for some time, and one of the first questions asked each couple was which three other couples they saw socially most frequently. Proximity was measured in functional units rather than in terms of actual physical distance, with the units based on doors passed and stairways climbed in order to reach other apartments. Thus, next-door neighbors on the same floor were counted as a single unit apart, even though the distance between apartment #3 and apartment #4 was almost twice that between #3 and #2, as shown in Fig. 9.3.

The results showed that next-door neighbors on the same floor were

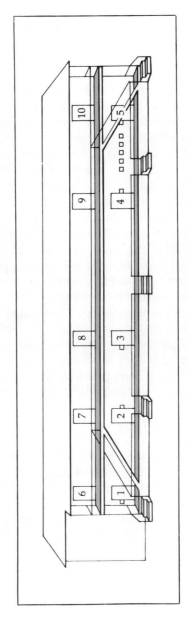

FIGURE 9.3 A Westgate West residential unit (adapted from Festinger, Schachter, and Back, 1950, p. 36).

named as good friends 41% of the time, whereas people two units away on the same floor were named only 22% of the time, and people the farthest away on the same floor were named only 10% of the time. Overall, residents living on the same floor were more likely to be friends than residents living on different floors, and close friends were seldom found in different buildings.

Proximity and Attraction. Why does proximity lead to attraction in this case? Think about what it is like to move into a new building. You give your new neighbors every benefit of the doubt, overlooking their faults so that the interaction made necessary by your close proximity will not be unpleasant. This sort of anticipatory avoidance of the dissonance that would be produced by the cognitions "I have to live here" and "I hate my neighbors" has been demonstrated in a study by Darley and Berscheid (1967), who found that subjects evaluated a stimulus person with whom they expected to interact more favorably than a stimulus person with whom no interaction was anticipated. Close proximity also leads to familiarity with each other's habits and preferences, and familiarity alone can lead to greater liking. Within the limits of novelty and interest, learning more about others who reside close by is likely to be a positive experience, in the same way that "mere exposure" (discussed in chapter 7) to an attitude object initially enhances the opinion of that object. Not only are we familiar with people who live nearby, we cannot help but be aware of many features of their lives: when they go to work, what sorts of friends they already have, the kinds of parties they give, and (in many apartment buildings and dormitories) even what they say to each other in ostensible privacy. As a result, their behavior is more predictable, and we are less likely to offend them inadvertently and more likely to learn in which ways their attitudes are similar to our own. Finally, once a relationship is established, the interaction forced by proximity may lead us to ignore minor difficulties that might lessen liking.

As powerful as proximity is in the development of attraction, it has significant limitations. If your new neighbors have a barking dog that keeps you awake at night, no amount of pleasant interaction during the day will produce unqualified liking. These are situational limitations on the effects of propinquity, but there may be personal limitations as well. For example, Wrightsman and Cook (1965) examined the personality characteristics of initially prejudiced white subjects who were given prolonged positive contact with blacks in a work setting. These investigators found that subjects whose attitudes did not change in a more positive direction were lower in self-esteem, and had more negative views of people in general, than did subjects whose attitudes did become less prejudiced. People need to like themselves and to maintain open minds toward others in order to avail themselves of the opportunities for wider contact that proximity may provide.

Finally, the frustrations often found in close relationships, especially relationships that persist through time, may become so great that even an initially favorable evaluation is insufficient to guarantee harmony and mutual reward. Considering the exceptions to the rule that propinquity leads to liking, it may be more appropriate to suggest that proximity enhances whatever emotional tone predominates, whether that is attraction or repulsion. Enhancement of our initial tendency to give others the benefit of the doubt may encourage the development of a relationship, but when faults can no longer be overlooked, proximity may magnify unpleasantness into hatred. Eloquent testimony to this aspect of proximity is, unfortunately, provided by the high proportion of homicides committed by a member of the victim's immediate family.

Similarity

If propinquity is often regarded as an essential condition for the development of attraction (on the grounds that important interpersonal rewards can only be exchanged in person), similarity is often cited as a reason that such rewards are forthcoming. Attitude similarity contributes to balance, and thus to a relation of liking. Similar others provide us with the best social comparison—both the most accurate and the most likely to be self-enhancing. The interaction matrix of two similar people will have more possibility for mutual reward, and hence, a higher correspondence of outcomes. Similar people will be more likely to believe that the same factors are relevant in the determination of equity, and they may judge outcomes by comparison levels constructed from equivalent past experiences. For these reasons and others, it has long been acknowledged that similarity will lead to attraction, and an extensive program of research by Byrne (1961, 1971) and his associates illustrates how the relation between similarity and attraction has been investigated in the laboratory.

An Experimental Example. Suppose that you were a subject in one of these experiments. Early in the school term, you would have been given a standardized attitude scale (Byrne, 1971) to obtain your opinions on 26 different issues, including school activities, political parties, religious beliefs, and sexual customs. Some weeks later, you would be asked to serve as a subject in a study of interpersonal judgment, and your task would be to make a number of judgments about a person, basing those perceptions on limited information consisting of the person's answers to the same 26-item attitude scale. You might learn about the person's attitudes by reading what was purported to be his or her answer sheet, by listening to a tape recording in which the person described his or her answers, by watching a sound film of the person's responses, or even by being present when the person was being interviewed by the experimenter. No matter what the stimulus mode, you would learn just how much this *bogus stranger's* attitudes agreed with your own. Then you would be asked to use the Interpersonal Judgment Scale mentioned earlier to estimate the person's knowledge of current events, intelligence, morality, and personal adjustment, and to indicate how much you liked the person as an individual and as a work partner. The ratings on these last two scales would be added together to determine your attraction toward the person. What sort of ratings would you make?

If you were responding the way most subjects in these experiments did, you would indicate more attraction toward people who were similar to you. Indeed, most of Byrne's research shows that attraction increases as a direct function of the proportion of agreement: the higher the percentage of statements on which the bogus stranger agrees with you, the more attraction you express toward that person. This relationship has been fund to hold across modes of stimulus presentation and across a wide variety of subject populations, including hospitalized surgical and psychiatric patients, primary and secondary school children, clerical workers, and participants in federal job-training programs.

The Law of Attraction?   In an attempt to account for this rather consistent finding, Byrne has proposed (e.g., 1971) a **law of attraction**, which states that attraction toward some object or person, X, is a positive linear function of the proportion of reinforcements received (or possibly even anticipated) from X. This explanation of interpersonal attraction in terms of reinforcement assumes that similarity, by itself, is positively reinforcing, an assumption that has been confirmed in much of Byrne's work.

Has the attitude similarity-attraction research really produced a "law" of attraction based on positive reinforcement, or are there still significant exceptions that limit the domain of the principle? Critics of Byrne's approach would point out that (a) the experimental work itself is missing a crucial control, (b) the task does not generalize well to situations outside the laboratory, (c) there are cases in which similarity appears to be unpleasant and difference is pleasant, and (d) on the more general question, there is a sizable body of research that conflicts with the hypothesized relationship between positive reinforcement and attraction. Let us consider each of these objections in turn.

The most recent criticism raised against the "law of attraction" is that "in this entire line of research, and it certainly is considerable, an adequate control or baseline condition has never been included" (Rosenbaum, 1986, p. 1157). Let us return to the experimental situation. Suppose that you are shown an attitude scale purported to represent the views of another student at your university. You discover that your views agree with those of the bogus stranger on 13 (or 7, or 10, or 16, or 19, or 22) of the items. Then, in the complete absence of any other information about the person, you make ratings on the Interpersonal Judgment Scale, and the results show that as the number of agreed-upon attitudes increases, your expressed "attraction" (the numerical sum of the scores on the liking and desirability as work partner items) toward the bogus stranger also increases. So what is the problem?

According to Rosenbaum (1986) the trouble is that there is no experimental condition in which you are asked to make Interpersonal Judgment Scale ratings of the bogus stranger in the absence of any information whatsoever. There is, in short, no no-attitude control group. Think for a moment of the other students you know at your school. Now restrict that sample to the subset of people who took the same initial attitude scale that you did (in other words, everyone else who registered for introductory Psychology in the same term you were in the class). Now, what do you know about the bogus stranger, even without seeing any attitude scale? You know that the person is a college student (or in the same occupational setting that you are in), that the person attends the same institution you attend, and that the person has made at least some of the same course choices you have made. Now, how many attitudes is such a person likely to have in common with you? Probably quite a few. And how much are you apt to like the person upon first meeting? Given the other similarities in your current status, the chances are very good that you will like each other. Indeed, Rosenbaum (1986) reports an experiment containing a no-attitude control condition in which the sum of the two liking items from the Interpersonal Judgment Scale is 9.70 (out of the 14 possible). This compares to a score of 9.89 in a condition of attitude similarity (agreement on 10 of 12 possible attitude items) and a score of 8.00 in a condition of attitude dissimilarity (disagreement on the same 10 of 12 attitude statements). What these data suggest is not that agreement leads to attraction (by comparison to no information at all), but that disagreement leads to repulsion.

Other critics of the law of attraction note (Murstein, 1971) that the restricted experimental paradigm may not generalize well. When you meet a person for the first time, you do not administer an attitude scale before you make any attempts to be friendly. You may assume quite a degree of common ground, if the two of you are similar in other respects, but the person's real attitudes on crucial issues may not become obvious until the relationship has progressed quite far. We approach a new relationship cautiously, revealing a little of ourselves at a time, and expecting reciprocal self-disclosure. Gradually this reciprocal disclosure broadens (including a wider variety of issues) and deepens (including increasingly intimate details), enabling us to penetrate each other's masks and defenses (Altman & Taylor, 1973). But the process can be short-circuited at any time, and the depth of agreement may be more important than the simple proportion of agreement. If you disagree with another person about the moral justification for war, or the value of human life, extensive agreement about superficial issues may not be sufficient to maintain the relationship.

Complementarity in Attraction.   Quite apart from questions about the similarity-attraction paradigm and its generality, there is some doubt as to whether similarity per se is always rewarding. For example, consider similarity of personality rather than attitude. In long-term relationships, this sort of similarity might turn out to be uninteresting. As Winch (1958) suggested in his detailed study of the personality characteristics and personal needs of 25 married couples, strong relationships may be built on **complementarity**. On such important dimensions as dominance–submission and nurturance–receptivity, Winch found that the needs of one spouse often complemented those of the other. Although support for the specific idea of need complementarity has not frequently been obtained in other research, a more general notion of complementarity is still accepted in the analysis of ongoing relationships. Whether the discussion concerns traditional marital roles (Peplau, 1983) or situation-specific actions (Levinger, 1983), the principle of complementarity recognizes that in close relationships, as in business, some specialization is desirable, provided that each partner's choice of specialty meshes with the other's choice to facilitate the couple's achievement of mutually desired goals.

In other research involving personality similarity, Novak and Lerner (1968) have shown that subjects find it threatening to learn that they are personally similar to a person who is mentally unstable, and research by Shaver (1970) and Schroeder and Linder (1976) shows that personality similarity to a stimulus person who actually causes harm to another person can also be threatening. You don't want to think that you could make the same mistakes, so similarity that could lead to negative outcomes is unpleasant.

It should be noted that the research on complementarity presents difficulties only for the specific issue of similarity-attraction, not for the larger principle that explains attraction in terms of positive reinforcement. The reinforcement theorist could easily argue that whenever similarity leads to rewards (as mediated, for example, by shared attitudes), it will lead to attraction, but that whenever similarity leads to punishment (such as boredom or threat), it will reduce attraction. Thus the larger principle of reinforcement can accommodate both cases of similarity-attraction and cases in which attraction is increased by personal differences. This resolves some of the specific problems, but the general issue still remains: Does attraction only follow positive reinforcement, or are there instances in which pain and suffering lead to greater attraction?

Suffering

Many of the studies conducted to test cognitive dissonance theory (Chapter 5) suggest that there will indeed be times when interpersonal attraction will be enhanced by suffering. Particularly relevant are the experiments that have dealt with the severity of an initiation to a group and subsequent attraction toward that group (Aronson & Mills, 1959; Gerard & Matthewson, 1966).

In the first of these studies, Aronson and Mills (1959) asked female undergraduates to volunteer to participate in a group discussion of the psychology of sex. Each subject was tested individually, and there were three conditions: a Severe initiation condition, a Mild initiation condition, and a No-initiation control. In all three conditions the subjects listened to a dull discussion on the reproductive habits of animals, and then rated the topic and the participants in the discussion. In the control condition, the subjects heard the discussion (actually a tape recording) without any prior "test." But in the two initiation conditions, subject were told that they would first have to pass a screening test, ostensibly to ensure that they would not be too shy to participate in the discussion. In the Severe initiation condition, this screening test required the subjects to read aloud (to the male experimenter) a rather explicit passage from a contemporary novel and a list of 12 obscene words. In the Mild initiation condition, the subject had to read aloud a number of words related to sex that were not obscene.

Subjects in the Severe initiation condition expressed the most positive feelings toward the dull group discussion and its participants. These results supported the prediction from dissonance theory, but conflict with the principle of reinforcement. There were, however, a number of alternative explanations for the findings, such as the relief the Severe initiation subjects might have felt at the end of the initiation. Many of these alternatives were ruled out in Gerard and Matthewson's (1966) conceptual replication. These investigators employed a short series of either mild or painful electric shocks for the initiations, changed the topic of the discussion group from sexual behavior to cheating in college, and had some subjects evaluate the discussion without thinking that it was a group they would later join. The results of this experiment replicated those of Aronson and Mills (1959), with higher ratings of the discussion obtained when there had been a severe initiation.

These experiments, and others in the cognitive dissonance tradition, show that in some cases suffering can lead to positive evaluations and attraction. Such results pose a problem for reinforcement theories of attraction, which assume that liking will increase with the rewards obtained from a relationship. To be fair to the reinforcement position, the attraction expressed toward a group is not likely to be identical to the liking shown for an individual. In addition, the punishment in the initiation studies was administered by a third party (the experimenter) rather than by the object of attraction. Despite these obvious differences, the research on severity of initiation combines with issues of complementarity, generalizability, and experimental control to suggest that it is premature to claim that a true *law* of attraction has been identified.

Personal Qualities of the Stimulus Person

Physical Attractiveness. From the viewpoint of reinforcement or exchange theory, propinquity makes reward possible, similarity makes it more likely, and some of the personal characteristics of the stimulus person set limits on how much reward is available. For example, consider physical attractiveness. A number of experiments reviewed by Berscheid and Walster (1974) indicate that people do equate attractiveness with positive aspects of character and behavior—what is beautiful is good. In one such study, Dion, Berscheid, and Walster (1972) found that physically attractive people were expected to be more sensitive, kind, strong, poised, modest, sociable, outgoing, and sexually responsive than were less physically attractive individuals. This stereotype held for both male and female stimulus persons, and did not differ between female and male subjects. Later research has suggested that some negative characteristics, such as vanity and egotism, may also be associated with physical attractiveness, but even this study replicated many of the positive qualities of the stereotype (Dermer & Thiel, 1975).

The relationship between physical attractiveness and ability to bestow interpersonal rewards can be illustrated in a number of ways. In a study of how a woman's appearance might be related to her marriage choice, Elder (1969) found that women who married above their working-class origins were, on the average, prettier as adolescents than those who did not marry above their original level. Studies of satisfaction with partners who have been provided by computer dating services have indicated that physical attractiveness is the most important determinant of desire to date the partner again (e.g., Brislin & Lewis, 1968), and research by Berscheid, Dion, Walster, and Walster (1971) extended this analysis to the active choice of a dating partner.

These investigators found evidence for a **matching principle**: People tended to select dates whose attractiveness was similar to their own. Apparently physical attractiveness not only signifies how much social reward might be available, but it also indicates how likely it is that such rewards will be forthcoming. We prefer attractive people to unattractive ones, but we also expect attractive people to be more discriminating, themselves. Thus the preference for more attractive individuals is moderated by a fear of being rejected. Exactly these results have been found for the dating preferences of male students by Huston (1973) and females by Shanteau and Nagy (1979). It is in many respects unflattering to learn that many of our dating choices are dictated by such a "superficial" characteristic as physical attractiveness, so we are likely to conclude that the principle might have had some merit when it was first proposed over 15 years ago, but that it would not apply with equal force in the more enlightened present. Unfortunately, we would be mistaken in that conclusion. A much more recent study by Folkes (1982), using participants in a metropolitan dating service as subjects, still found support for the matching principle, even though the subjects were not college students (mean age was 36) and had already received information about each other's education, occupation, and personality characteristics.

Competence. In the same way that we prefer physically attractive people to people who are unattractive, we prefer people who are competent to those who are incompetent (Spence & Helmreich, 1972). But here again, some moderation of the preference occurs. We like those who are competent enough to reward us, but people who are perfect might have nothing to do with us. You can probably think of a classmate who seems to breeze through school with high grades although spending more time on extracurricular activities than on studies. You might even be able to bring yourself to like such a person—if only he or she would make a mistake now and then.

The humanizing influence of making a mistake has been demonstrated in an experiment by Aronson, Willerman, and Floyd (1966). These investigators had subjects listen to a tape recording of what was purported to be a preliminary session for choosing a person to represent the university in a nationally televised quiz program for college students. In fact, there were two different tapes, one in which the person appeared to be extremely competent (answering 92% of the very difficult questions correctly) and one in which he appeared to be incompetent (answering only 30% correctly). For half of the subjects within each of these competence conditions, the end of the questions ended the tape, and those subjects then completed a number of rating scales to describe the stimulus person. For the other half of the subjects in each competence condition, the tape continued. The interviewer was heard to offer the candidate a cup of coffee, there was the sound of confusion, and the candidate was heard lamenting that he had spilled coffee all over his new suit. At the conclusion of this incident the tape ended, and the subjects made their ratings of the stimulus person. Overall, the competent person was seen as more attractive than the incompetent one, but more importantly, he was judged even more attractive when he spilled coffee on himself than when he did not. In contrast, the incompetent stimulus person was seen as even less attractive when the accident came after his poor performance.

The research on competence, like that on physical attractiveness, can easily be interpreted in terms of reinforcement. All that is necessary is to assume that the actual reward value of a stimulus person is a combination of what rewards that person has to offer and how likely it is that you will be the recipient. The highly competent but human person won't hold your own minor failings against you. This view of actual reward as the product of the magnitude of the incentive and the probability that the incentive will be forthcoming is implicit in most reinforcement theories relating to human behavior, and is explicit in the social learning theory of Rotter (1954) and other approaches based on his formulation. You will notice that this combination of value and expectancy is conceptually similar both to the information integration theory of impression formation (Anderson, 1974) described in chapter 4 and the information-processing view of attitude organization (Fishbein & Ajzen, 1975) discussed in chapter 5. Despite the limitations that need to be placed on specific reinforcement-based principles such as the "law of attraction," the general idea of reinforcement can account for attraction to physically attractive people, as well as for the dating choice of partners who match and for the attraction expressed toward highly competent, but human, people. As the reward value of a person (the magnitude of the incentives he or she has to offer times the likelihood that they will be offered) increases, so does your attraction to that person.

Arousal and Attraction

You may recall from chapter 7 that several theories of emotion give an important role to the cognitive labels that are provided for the physiological arousal that is experienced. In most circumstances the label and the arousal are clearly intertwined, but it is possible for arousal to occur without an appropriate cognitive label. Where there is ambiguity about the nature of the emotional experience, the label may be provided by cues in the situation, and this may lead to misattribution of the emotion. Some investigators have suggested that this cognitive labeling view of emotion should lead us to wonder, especially in the case of romantic attraction, just how much of passion depends on the target person and how much depends on other aspects of the situation (Berscheid & Walster, 1974a; Carducci, Cozby, & Ward, 1974).

Imagine that you are on a first date with an attractive person, on your way to a concert to be followed by a small party. You have been looking forward to the date with anticipation, but also with some apprehension about making a good impression. The concert involves several of your favorite performers, and many of your good friends will be at the party. During the evening you will be trying to guess whether your date is having a good time, and you will be evaluating your own feelings as well. Let's examine the things that might be contributing to your own state of physiological arousal. There will be the apprehension about the impression you are creating, the pleasure of the concert, the company of your friends, and of course the attraction you feel toward your date. But will each of these be separately identified and properly labeled? Or will all of the sources of arousal be combined and mistakenly attributed to the most salient feature of the situation – your date?

In their discussion of romantic love, Berscheid and Walster (1974a) suggest that misattribution is sometimes the more likely outcome, and some experimental evidence supports this interpretation. For example, Brehm, Gatz, Goethals, McCrimmon, and Ward (1970) found that even a wholly irrelevant source of emotional arousal might be attributed erroneously to the attractiveness of a potential date. In this study, male undergraduates were led to believe that they would later receive a series of electric shocks and then were interviewed by an attractive female student. Compared to a control group that had received no threat, the threatened subjects rated the woman as more attractive and expressed a greater interest in dating her. There have been important failures to replicate this kind of misattribution of arousal (Kenrick, Cialdini, & Linder, 1979), and at this writing the possibility that fear may be misattributed as love must be regarded as just that – an intriguing possibility not yet conclusively demonstrated. Some indirect support for the idea comes, as we see in chapter 10, from the fact that similar misattribution of arousal can enhance aggressive tendencies.

At this point it may be appropriate to ask again, "What leads to interpersonal attraction?" We have seen that the best answer is "Usually propinquity, sometimes similarity, some personal characteristics, and usually (but not always) reinforcement." Do not be discouraged by the close resemblance between this answer and the popular wisdom "Birds of a feather flock together; but sometimes opposites attract." Social psychologists may not yet have discovered a great wealth of counterintuitive findings about interpersonal attraction, but they have even at this point identified many of the conditions under which different features of the commonsense analysis seem to apply. In addition, the experimental research on interpersonal attraction can be placed in the context of existing theory (especially exchange theory), leading to predictions that could not be made on the basis of common sense alone. Perhaps most importantly, the very recent attempts to include emotion as well as attitudes, and to investigate ongoing long-term relationships, promise to contribute to our future understanding of attraction as one more aspect of positive social behavior.

SUMMARY

The scientific study of positive social action requires an operational definition of terms dealing with observable antecedents and consequences, rather than with the motives leading to action. By this sort of definition, *helping behavior* (p. 307) is any action that benefits another person, and **objective altruism** (p. 307) is a special case of helping behavior. Not only must objective altruism benefit the recipient, it must also be a voluntary action that earns no external rewards for the actor.

Where no emergency exists, helping behavior can be produced in response to social norms, the presence of models in the situation, and internal feeling states within the helper. The norm of **reciprocity** (p. 309) is fundamental to social exchange and leads to helping behavior, whereas the **social responsibility norm** (p. 310) does not depend on exchange and can lead to objectively altruistic action. Helpful models (p. 312) may contribute to objective altruism by making the social responsibility norm more salient, but modeling effects may also be mediated by a variety of internal states (p. 314) including **personal norms** and **responsibility denial** (p. 316). The failure to intervene in emergency situations has sometimes been attributed to the apathy of the bystanders, but it may be more appropriate to view the act of intervention as the final step in a *decision process* (p. 320) that is influenced by social comparison and evaluation of the costs and rewards associated with various kinds of intervention.

Interpersonal **attraction** (p. 325) has traditionally been defined as an attitude of favorability toward an object person, and most of the existing social psychological research on attraction has been based on this definition. But attraction is a complex phenomenon, reflected in dimensions such as respect, liking, friendship, and the needing and giving that are characteristic of love. Although attraction is a positive social behavior, the study of long-term intimate relationships has only recently been possible, so much of the research on attraction consists of single measurements of attraction taken among relative strangers. Liking can be assessed through **sociograms** (p. 328) of friendship choices, and through a variety of social, behavioral, and physiological measures, as well as through traditional forms of attitude measurement.

Among the antecedents of interpersonal attraction are *propinquity* (p. 334), similarity (p. 337), and some of the personal characteristics of the stimulus person. Other things being equal, people will become attracted to others with whom they come into frequent contact, to people whose attitudes are similar to their own, and to those whose personal characteristics suggest both the capability and willingness to provide them with rewards. All these factors assume that liking will increase with the exchange of benefits, and a tentative **law of attraction** (p. 338) has been proposed that asserts that attraction will increase as a positive linear function of the proportion of rewards provided. There are, however, several important limitations to this principle. For example, in long-term relationships **complementarity** (p. 340) in some form may be as important as similarity. By charting the course of the general rule of reinforcement enhancing attraction, and by noting exceptions to the rule, scientific study of interpersonal attraction can lead to better understanding of the affective ties between individuals.

SUGGESTED ADDITIONAL READINGS

BERSCHEID, E. (1985). Interpersonal attraction. In G. Lindzey & E. Aronson (Eds.), *Handbook of social psychology* (3rd ed., Vol. 2, pp. 413-484.). New York: Random House. Although this chapter is intended for a professional audience, it is still accessible to interested undergraduates. A good overview of theories and research on interpersonal attraction, and a minimum of jargon.

BERSCHEID, E., & WALSTER, E. H. (1978). *Interpersonal attraction* (2nd ed.). Reading, MA: Addison-Wesley. This short book is a very good introduction to a variety of topics in interpersonal attraction. Highly readable and recommended.

KREBS, D. L., & MILLER, D. T. (1985). Altruism and aggression. In G. Lindzey & E. Aronson (Eds.), *Handbook of social psychology* (3rd ed., Vol. 2, pp. 413-484.). New York: Random House. This extensive chapter reviews research in nonemergency helping and bystander intervention into emergencies, putting both of these positive social behaviors into a conceptual context that is also used to explain aggression. A bit technical, but well worth the effort.

LATANÉ, B., & DARLEY, J. M. (1970). *The unresponsive bystander: Why won't he help?* New York: Appleton-Century-Crofts. This influential book is often regarded as having launched social psychological study of helping in emergencies. Although it is basically a research report, it is written in a manner designed for nontechnical readers.

CHAPTER TEN

COMPETITION AND AGGRESSION

CONTENTS

PREVIEW

Competition and aggression, like altruism and interpersonal attraction, involve social exchange in which the individual's decisions have substantial effects on the welfare of others. Competition can be studied in the laboratory through use of experimental games, such as the Prisoner's Dilemma game and the trucking game. These studies point to the importance of communication, power of the participants, and characteristics of the bargaining situation as determinants of competition. Many of the principles discovered in this research can then be generalized to instances of bargaining and negotiation in the real world outside the laboratory. Whether accomplishment of a goal requires negotiation or not, persistence in the face of possible failure is affected by individual differences in achievement motivation. Achievement strivings can be thought of as the result of motives to approach success and to avoid failure, and the attributions a person makes for the causes of success and failure can influence both motives and behavior. Some theoretical explanations of aggression, especially those of Freud and Lorenz, also propose the importance of internal motives. But aggression can also be instigated and maintained by external factors, such as frustration, the transfer of arousal from other sources, or the social learning that has established violence as an effective means for dealing with problems.

Not all social behavior is as positive as the altruism and attraction we have just considered. Indeed, the lessons of history and the contemporary records of crime indicate that a vast amount of antisocial behavior has always been, and currently is, present in human society. Assassination, kidnaping, and unprovoked terrorist attacks on innocent victims have become all too popular as methods for drawing attention to political grievances. The Federal Bureau of Investigation's Uniform Crime Reports for 1984 recorded more than 685,000 aggravated assaults, more than 485,000 robberies, over 84,000 forcible rapes, and more than 18,600 murders (U. S. Department of Justice, 1985). On the average, this is the equivalent of a violent crime every 25 seconds for every day in the year. Even worse, these figures only reflect crimes reported to the police, and most studies of victimization place the actual number of offenses at roughly double the numbers shown in the Uniform Crime Reports.

But aggression and violent crime are not the only examples of antisocial action: Some corporations make huge payments to agents of foreign governments in order to ensure their competitive position; others engage in economic or "white-collar" crime that costs the country millions of dollars a year; the effects of economic and social competition can be seen in everything from the actions of a politician who uses his or her position for personal financial gain to the behavior of a student who cheats on an examination in order to improve a grade.

It would seem that competition, like aggression, might have predominantly negative effects on society. But is this necessarily true? Aren't there times when competition benefits society, and when aggression is encouraged? What exactly do we mean by competition and aggression? What social and personal factors lead to the occurrence of competition? Of aggression? Can any of the theories of social psychology discussed earlier (especially in chapter 8) shed light on these phenomena? The purpose of this chapter is to suggest answers to some of these questions. We begin with a definition of competition, then consider situational factors that enhance competition (reward structure, presence of threat) and individual differences in competitive desires (such as achievement motivation). Next we define aggression, examine internal predispositions toward aggression, and describe situational factors that contribute to its expression. We conclude with a discussion of the effects of witnessing aggression—the problem of filmed and televised violence.

The Definition of Competition

When we speak of competition or aggression, we are confronted by definitional problems quite different from those encountered in the description of positive social behavior. You will remember that the common usage of the term *altruism* included an element of self-sacrifice that could not be represented in any operational manner satisfactory for the needs of social science. In a sense, the common term was a bit too specific. In contrast, the normal usage of *competition* and *aggression* encompasses too many different meanings; the terms are not precise enough. For example, to say that two parties are in competition for scarce resources usually means that each is actively trying to get more than an equal share, at the other's expense. But to say that there is stiff competition for prestigious jobs after graduation only means that there are too many highly qualified applicants for the number of openings. No direct confrontation among applicants is implied, and the final outcome is under the control of third parties (the personnel officers) rather than under the control of either competitor. Stretching the definition even further, some businesses claim that their prices are "competitive," meaning only that they are no higher than usual, not that they are substantially lower.

Correspondence of Outcomes

Most social psychologists would restrict the meaning of the word *competition* to a variation of its first usage, requiring that (a) one person's gains be achieved at the other's expense, and (b) the outcomes be determined primarily by the actions of the competing parties. Such a definition can be stated most precisely in terms of Thibaut and Kelley's (1959; Kelley & Thibaut, 1978) exchange theory. You will recall from chapter 8 that an interaction between two or more people can be described by the degree of correspondence of outcomes for the participants. In a dyad, if one person's profitable choices also provide good outcomes for the other, there is high correspondence of outcomes. Alternatively, if one's most profitable choices provide bad outcomes for the other, then there is low correspondence of outcomes. **Competition** thus occurs whenever all participants strive to achieve their individual goals in an interaction characterized by low correspondence of outcomes.

Zero-Sum and Nonzero-Sum Games. The definition of competition in terms of correspondence of outcomes encompasses cases in which there are multiple winners with varying degrees of success and cases in which there is only one winner and one loser. In a winner-take-all contest, there is a perfect negative correspondence of outcomes: When you match wits with a confidence man, every dollar he gains is a dollar you have lost, and the interaction as a whole has a **zero-sum** (his gains minus your losses equals zero). In the other sort of competitive interaction, the correspondence of outcomes is low, but not perfectly negative. For example, in automobile races, professional tennis and golf tournaments, and college classes, rewards await the several people who finish at the top of the group. But because these rewards (prize money or high grades) do not come directly from the "losers," the interaction as a whole has a **nonzero-sum**. Strong competition can obviously occur in both situations.

Factors Contributing to Competition. Why do some people seem to have a relentless drive for competition, even if their achievements must be obtained at others' expense? When does the legitimate and beneficial competition inherent in so many relationships become destructive exploitation? How do differences in power and resources among competing parties influence the process? Perhaps most important, how should social psychology attempt to answer these questions?

Given the prevalence of competition in our society, it might seem appropriate to assess the personalities of successful individuals, to observe the frequent negotiating sessions between management and labor, or to assess the process through which special interest and minority groups try to influence policy. But because of the complexity of the social world, the difficulty of inferring causality from events not under the direct control of the investigators, and the natural reluctance of many successful negotiators to have their methods examined, the great majority of research on competition involves experimental analogues of the competition found in the outside world.

EXPERIMENTAL METHODS FOR THE STUDY OF COMPETITION

The Prisoner's Dilemma

One of the first requirements for conducting research on competition is an appropriate dependent variable, one that represents the essential elements of the phenomenon, can be measured easily, yet is responsive to variations in experimental procedure. If you were brought into a laboratory and asked to take part in something resembling a television game show in which monetary prizes were given, and it was made clear that the questions to be asked would be a good indication of your basic intelligence, virtually no experimental manipulations would lessen either your desire to win or your anxiety over losing. In order to test the effects of various theoretical variables, a good experimental task must moderate these incentives and reactions by becoming a more distant abstraction from normal competitive situations. Social psychologists have found one such abstraction in a situation originally described as part of game theory (a branch of decision-making theory)–the **Prisoner's Dilemma Game** (Luce & Raiffa, 1957).

Suppose that you and a co-conspirator are taken into custody by the police on suspicion of having committed a crime, for example, an armed robbery. The prosecutor is certain that you have committed the crime, but knows that because of a complication with the evidence it will be impossible to obtain a conviction without a confession from at least one of you. The two of you are led to separate interrogation rooms, where the prosecutor points out to each of you (alone) that you have two alternatives: either you can confess to the armed robbery, or you can refuse to confess. Then the prosecutor outlines the possible consequences. If both of you confess, you will both be convicted, and the prosecution will recommend moderately harsh sentences for you both. If neither of you confesses to the armed robbery, you both will still be convicted of illegal possession of a firearm, which carries a shorter sentence than the minimum for robbery. If one of you confesses when the other does not, however, the one who confesses will be permitted to plea bargain to an even lesser charge, whereas the one who refused to confess will not only get convicted, but will also receive the longest possible sentence.

These consequences, represented in months of possible sentence, are shown in Fig. 10.1 and Fig. 10.2. Fig. 10.1 is a verbal description of the sen-

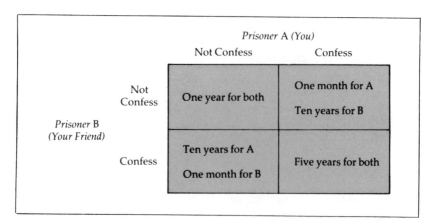

FIGURE 10.1 Verbal description of the Prisoner's Dilemma (after Luce and Raiffa, 1957).

tences that might be imposed for the various outcomes, and Fig. 10.2 is a numerical representation of those sentences, showing the number of months that will be taken away from your life of freedom.

A Mixed-Motive Game. The Prisoner's Dilemma is one sort of **mixed-motive game.** In those cells where you and your co-conspirator make the same choice (either not to confess or to confess), your outcomes are identical. In the two cells where the two of you reach different decisions, there is a low correspondence of outcomes: One of you will receive a harsh penalty whereas the other will get away with what amounts to a slap on the wrist. What action should you take? The answer to this question will depend on a number of factors, including how much you trust your co-

FIGURE 10.2 Numerical representation of the Prisoner's Dilemma, scaled in months of imprisonment (after Luce and Raiffa, 1957).

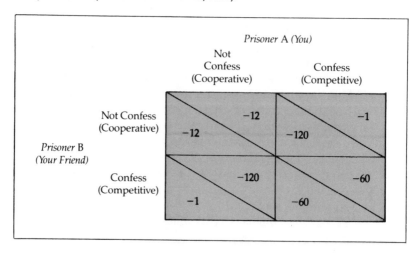

conspirator, how cooperative a person you are, the particular characteristics of the payoffs involved (how long all the sentences are), and whether you have only a single opportunity to make the choice, or whether (as in much experimental research) you experience repeated plays of the game.

As indicated in Fig. 10.2, the cooperative choice in the Prisoner's Dilemma Game is to remain firm and not confess. This may sound confusing at first, because in most cases, we describe a prisoner who is helping the prosecutor as "cooperative." But this is society's view, not the view of the co-conspirator. From that person's perspective, the not-confess choice is the truly cooperative one. Not only does that choice open up the opportunity for both of you to prove that there is honor among thieves (and get away with moderately light sentences), it also demonstrates that you trust your co-conspirator not to take advantage of the situation by turning state's evidence and helping to put you away for a long time. In contrast, the choice to confess is actually the competitive choice, because from the co-conspirator's viewpoint, a 5-year sentence for each of you would be better than a 10-year sentence served alone.

All the outcomes in the original example of the Prisoner's Dilemma are negative, but the essential structure of the game does not require this to be true. That fundamental structure is shown in Fig. 10.3, in which letters have been substituted for the numerical payoffs. If both participants make the cooperative (C or C') choice, they will both receive a payoff of S; if both make the competitive choice (traditionally labeled D or D' to stand for defecting), they both will receive a payoff of T; if their choices differ, the one making the competitive choice will receive a payoff of R, whereas the other will receive a payoff of U. The essential character of the dilemma will be preserved in any payoff matrix were the inequality

$$R > S > T > U$$

FIGURE 10.3 Schematic representation of the general payoff matrix for the Prisoner's Dilemma.

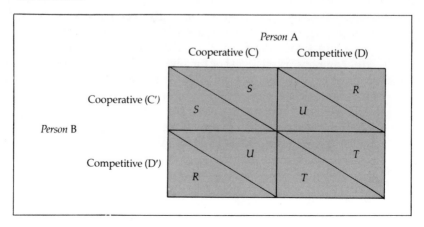

holds true. This means that the psychological quality of the dilemma will be the same whether all of the payoffs are negative (as in the original example), all are positive (with the defecting partner winning disproportionately the most), or a mixture of positive and negative outcomes. In research, these payoffs can represent either points gained or money earned on every trial of the game. Especially in the all-positive form, the game represents a wide variety of competitive situations—businesses exchanging market information, athletes playing for themselves rather than for their teams—in which conflict occurs between achievement of individual objectives and achievement of the highest mutual profit.

Cooperation or Competition?   Suppose that you were serving as a subject in a study of competition using the Prisoner's Dilemma Game. You would be shown the complete payoff matrix (the psychological force of the dilemma arises because of your knowledge that each of you has the opportunity to "win big" at the other's expense). Then you would be asked to make a choice (either C or D) on a number of trials that could range from a single play to several hundred plays, with the usual number being between 25 and 50. In most studies, you would never see your opponent, who would be described to you by the experimenter. In fact, you would typically be playing against a standard or *programmed* opponent, because the experimenter would be interested in your reactions to a standard performance by your ostensible rival. Your choice and the opponent's choice are made simultaneously, and on any trial your dilemma is to decide whether you should make the cooperative (C) response in the hope that your opponent will do the same (thus maximizing the *joint profit* achieved by the two of you), or whether instead you should make the competitive, defecting (D) choice in the hope that you can exploit your opponent and maximize your own outcomes. Extensive research with the Prisoner's Dilemma Game (see reviews by Apfelbaum, 1974; Oskamp, 1972) has suggested several factors that affect whether you choose to cooperate or compete.

Relative Payoffs.   Not too surprisingly, changing the relative values of the payoffs can affect the degree of cooperation. Suppose that you were engaged in a cooperative project with another person in your company. After having worked together for several weeks on this project, the two of you turn in your report to one of the company vice-presidents. Impressed with the work, the vice-president interviews each of you separately to try to determine whether there were any differences in the level of contribution. If the vice-president merely wants to make certain that a bonus to be split between the two of you is shared in an equitable fashion, there will be less pressure on you to take more of the credit for yourself than if the reward for the project is to be a major promotion, but only for one person. In the first case, your expected gain from competing is so close to your expected gain from cooperating that exploiting your partner would literally not be worth the trouble. In the second case there is a substantial difference between what could be obtained through cooperation and what might be obtained through claiming more credit than you really deserve. The fact that the values in a payoff matrix will influence the level of cooperation has been shown experimentally through comparisons between the Prisoner's Dilemma and other games (for example, see research by Enzle, Hansen, & Lowe, 1975; Gallo & McClintock, 1965), and it is reasonable to believe that the relative size of payoffs would have the same effects in a conflict structured along the lines of the Prisoner's Dilemma.

Characteristics of Competitors. With the exception of gender (females tend to be more cooperative than males), few individual differences have been found to exert strong influence over the long-term play of experimental games. Much more important are the transient motives that competitors bring to the contest, or have instilled in them when they arrive. For example, Deutsch (1960) found that subjects who were asked to take an interest in their opponent's welfare cooperated to a much greater extent than did subject who were told either to beat their opponent or to win as much as possible for themselves. Because these cooperative, competitive, or "individualistic" motives affect competition, and because people frequently assume that their opponents will behave in the way that they, themselves, do (Messé & Sivacek, 1979), it is clear that a competitor's motives and expectations can affect the outcome of a competitive setting.

Not only will your own motives and your guesses about the other's motives influence the play, the opponent's apparent characteristics will also affect the outcome. Imagine that you are about to play some kind of game – chess, tennis, horseshoes – against a single opponent. If you both view the contest as just a game, you will play to win, but you will not try to exploit the other person just to achieve this end. If, however, your opponent has an inflated ego, you may try a little harder to bring the person into touch with reality, and if he or she appears to be weak, you may try to take advantage of this weakness. On a broader scale, how many times have you heard national leaders suggest that safety lies in strength ("force is all they understand," "cuts in defense spending will be interpreted as a sign of weakness")? Will people actually put up strong defenses against potentially threatening opponents, and will they also take advantage of the weak? Experimental evidence from Prisoner's Dilemma research suggests affirmative answers to both of these questions. Subjects in one study (Marlowe, Gergen, & Doob, 1966) played against an opponent who was either self-effacing or egotistical, and believed that they would (or would not) interact with the opponent following play of the game. The highest levels of competitive behavior occurred when subjects either expected to see the egotist or expected not to have to confront the self-effacing person.

Opponent's Strategy. A programmed opponent can take one of three basic strategies in repeated plays of the Prisoner's Dilemma game. The first is unconditional cooperation, the second is unconditional competition; there can, of course, be various proportional mixtures of the two. What is important is that they are preplanned and continue as programmed regardless of the behavior of the real subject. The third general class is the **contingent strategy**, in which the programmed opponent's choice on any given trial is determined by the subject's choice on the preceding trial. This contingent strategy produces by far the highest levels of cooperation (Nemeth, 1972), perhaps because it permits a form of implicit communication between the players. In the usual Prisoner's Dilemma game, experimenters allow no communication during play, so the contingent strategy might be a way of restoring this usual element of bargaining.

Communication and Power in Bargaining

Although there are times when there is no open discussion between competing parties, much of competition in the real social world typically involves some formal communication between the players. This communication may not always be honest (bluffing and deceit are all too common), but it is nonetheless present in the situation. So the Prisoner's Dilemma game requirement that there be no formal communication to some degree limits the applicability of the technique. Another limitation of the Prisoner's Dilemma format is that the parties are of equal power; the best and worst outcomes for each party are matched. Finally, the Prisoner's Dilemma denies either participant the opportunity to "opt out" of the interaction and attempt to achieve his or her goals individually. In order to increase the generalizability of bargaining research, investigators have developed a number of experimental games that permit communication, differential power, and individual action. Foremost among these is the Trucking game originated by Deutsch and Krauss (1960).

The Trucking Game. The Trucking game is a mixed-motive game for two players, each of whom assumes the role of a trucking company (Acme or Bolt) that is paid to move cargo from a point of origin to a destination. In the original version of the game, each player completing a trip received a payment of 60¢ minus the "operating expenses" for the trip (which expenses were determined principally by the time taken to complete the journey). The game is electrically operated, so that the timing is automatic. A road map (shown in Fig. 10.4) is provided to the subjects. As you can see from the diagram, there are two possible routes that each player might take. The main route, represented by the solid line, is constructed so that the middle third is one lane. If both trucks are to use this main road, one must wait at the entrance while the other passes through the one-lane sec-

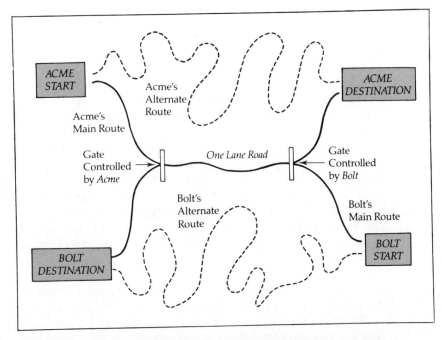

FIGURE 10.4   The road map for the Trucking game (adapted from Deutsch, M. and Krauss, R. M. (1960). The effect of threat on interpersonal bargaining. *Journal of Abnormal and Social Psychology 61*, 183. Copyright 1960 by the American Psychological Association. Reprinted by permission.

tion. The time involved in using the main road is such that the trucker who passes through immediately will earn a profit of 15¢ (60¢ payment minus 45¢ operating expenses), while the trucker who waits will earn nothing. In addition to the main route, each company has unrestricted access to an alternate route (the dotted lines on the diagram), but this alternate route is so much longer that its use results in an operating loss of 10¢ for the trial. The optimal strategy in the game is, of course, cooperative alternation on the main road, with one party earning profit on one trial and the other earning profit on the next trial. Such a cooperative strategy would produce average winnings (over the 20 trials of the game) of $1.50 per person.

Effects of Threat.   In the first experiment using the Trucking game, Deutsch and Krauss (1960) were interested in the influence of threat on the level of cooperation. The presence of threat was made possible by the gates shown at each end of the one-way section of the main route. If a gate was operable (this was up to the experimenter), the player who controlled it could choose to close the gate, permitting his or her own truck to pass through, but preventing the other person's truck from doing so. There were three experimental conditions. In the No Threat condition, neither gate was operable; in the Unilateral Threat condition, only Acme's gate was operable; in the Bilateral Threat condition both gates could be used.

Now consider the power of each person to punish the other. In the No Threat condition, neither player had the potential to punish the other without also losing, and this correspondence of outcomes was even more direct than in the Prisoner's Dilemma game. In the Unilateral Threat condition, Acme is endowed with an additional source of power, quite apart from the ability to block the opponent's truck with his or her own. Finally, in the Bilateral Threat condition, both participants have this capability. The subjects in the first experiment were female employees of the Bell Telephone Company (remember that females are typically more cooperative than males in mixed-motive games). Pairs of subjects played 20 trials against each other (not against a programmed opponent), neither member of the pair knew who the other was, and no communication was permitted. How do you think these variations would affect the process of cooperation or competition?

The effects of threat were striking. In the No Threat condition, mutual accommodation emerged without formal communication, such that the average winnings were slightly over $1 for each subject (out of a possible $1.50). In the Unilateral Threat condition, both players lost money, with the more powerful Acme losing an average of $1.19, and the weaker Bolt losing an average of $2.87. In the Bilateral Threat condition – contrary to the popular belief that two equally strong adversaries will not have to use their power – the losses to both sides were even greater, with the average loss for both being $4.38! (None of the losses incurred by the subjects was actually collected by the experimenter.) It is important to note that these outcomes are substantially worse than the $2 loss that would have accompanied consistent use of the alternate route.

Threat and Communication. What could explain this apparent attempt to hurt the opponent – even to the extent of hurting oneself in the process? One possibility is that the external threat was an attempt at implicit communication, much like use of a contingent strategy in the Prisoner's Dilemma game: "I am willing to suffer substantial losses myself, just to make sure you understand how serious I am." To evaluate the use of threat as communication, Deutsch and Krauss (1962) replicated the original study, but this time permitted formal communication between the two competitors. Interestingly enough, the greatest amount of such communication occurred in the No Threat condition, less occurred in the Unilateral Threat condition, and the Bilateral Threat condition the two participants hardly spoke to each other. The large losses incurred in this last condition thus appear to be the result of injury inflicted for punishment's sake, not for the sake of communication.

A slightly different outcome was obtained in a more recent study (Smith & Anderson, 1975) that included both a manipulation of threat availability and a manipulation of possibility for communication. This research also employed a version of the Trucking game, but changed the payoffs to higher monetary incentives the value of which was randomly varied across trials to preclude discovery of the "obvious" strategy of alternation. The results showed that when no formal communication was permitted, the presence of threat did improve the level of cooperation. But when full communication was allowed, the presence of threat *decreased* the likelihood of cooperation. Thus, threat may serve as part of the implicit communication between competing parties, but if there is already full communication, threat may just get in the way of settlement of the dispute.

Socially Relevant Science

Imagine for a moment that these results could be generalized to interpersonal or even international conflict (as many researchers in the area have argued). Such findings would suggest that the huge nuclear stockpiles maintained by the United States and the Soviet Union, which once served as an implicit communication of power, might with increasingly direct communication only inhibit cooperation, possibly leading to aggression. But can the findings from laboratory studies of cooperation and competition be generalized to this degree? There are arguments on both sides of the question. For example, Nemeth (1972) has argued that the limited communication inherent in the Prisoner's Dilemma game makes it difficult to generalize beyond the walls of the laboratory. But this objection cannot apply to versions of the Trucking in which communication is permitted, and sometimes even encouraged. Another limitation is that experimental studies typically involve pairs of subjects engaged in a temporary relationship, rather than groups of societies involved in numerous and long-lasting relationships. On the other hand, one recent study has found that groups of subjects (even when those were two-person groups) are less likely to cooperate in a Prisoner's Dilemma game than are individuals (McCallum et al., 1985). If reluctance to cooperate really does increase with the size of the group on each side, then all of the factors that act to reduce cooperation in an ordinary experimental bargaining game will be even more important obstacles to settlement of real conflicts outside the laboratory.

Although we must consider the usual reservations about the artificiality of the experimental setting, it is apparent that the participating subjects find the bargaining situation quite ego-involving. Furthermore, the personal characteristics of the participants are much less of a problem than they might be in other studies, because the college students who serve as subjects will go on after graduation to become the negotiators, government officials, and diplomats of the future. More importantly, the experimental techniques do capture some of the essential elements of conflict in the outside world. It is fair to say, on balance, that many social psychologists share Deutsch's (1969) view that although laboratory studies of cooperation and competition must be generalized with care, they still represent socially relevant science.

ACHIEVEMENT MOTIVATION AND COMPETITION

Throughout this chapter I have argued that competition can best be thought of as an interaction in which there is low correspondence between the outcomes of the two participants. Various structural features of the interaction—such as the nature of the payoffs to both parties, the temporary motives of each participant, the ease of communication, and the distribution of power—will affect the degree of competition. But these alone cannot account for the diversity in responses in competitive situations. For example, consider the realm of academic accomplishment. The external situation, composed of your professors' expectations, the scarcity of places in graduate and professional schools, the competition for jobs upon graduation, and the institution's own requirements for maintenance of good academic standing, is the same for nearly all students. Yet reactions to these external pressures differ greatly. Some of you elect to pursue membership in Phi Beta Kappa, some of you are more concerned with the breadth and depth of your education than with the grades you happen to obtain, and some of you may decide to drop out of college altogether. Only a relatively enduring personality or motivational variable can account for these differences, and the need for achievement is such a variable. Our treatment of competition will, therefore, conclude with a discussion of achievement motivation.

Measurement of Achievement Needs

In his comprehensive theory of personality, Murray (1938) argued that behavior could be explained by describing both the individual's relatively enduring predispositions to action (called *needs*) and the situational factors (called by the general name of environmental *press*) that might facilitate or inhibit the expression of one or more of those needs. In many ways this was a very social description of personality, and the measuring instrument that Murray (1938) developed to assess personal needs involved judgment of social stimuli. This instrument, the Thematic Apperception Test (TAT) consists of a series of 20 pictures of ambiguous situations, such as a picture of a college-age youth sitting at a desk with a book open before him. Rather than concentrating on the book, the youth is resting his head on his hand as he gazes out at the viewer. The TAT is based on the presumption that a person's fantasy life will reveal important characteristics about personality, so the person who is being tested is asked to make up a story about each of the 20 pictures. The person is usually given from 3 to 5 minutes to write down a short story, and each story is to describe such things as (a) what has led up to the situation depicted, (b) what is wanted, (c) by whom, and (d) what will happen in the future. The content of the stories thus produced is later analyzed to determine which needs predominate.

The Motive to Approach Success. When the goal is the measurement of achievement motivation alone, only 4 of the 20 pictures are typically used (McClelland, Atkinson, Clark, & Lowell, 1953), and each story is scored for a number of different aspects of achievement motivation. For example, a story receives one point if the entire theme is achievement-oriented, another point for an apparent state of need, an additional point for the anticipation of success in obtaining the desired goal, and still additional points for mentioning aspects of the social environment that would either be aids or obstacles to completion of the objective. Using the content coding categories outlined by McClelland et al. (1953), a researcher might give as much as 15 points to a story high in all aspects of achievement motivation. This scoring system is described in detail in a manual by Atkinson (1958). Anyone interested in measuring achievement motivation using the TAT must first establish reliability as a scorer by comparing his or her scoring of a standard set of stories to the scores presented in the manuals for those same stories. Raters following the prescribed methods can usually obtain quite high levels of reliability, and the validity of the scoring system (the degree to which the actual behavior of high scorers differs from the behavior of low scorers) also seems to be good (see Weiner, 1972, for a review).

It is important to note that the content analysis of stories written about the four TAT pictures will reveal only the subject's interest in successful achievement, what Atkinson (1958) has called the *motive to approach success* (abbreviated M_S). According to this later version of achievement theory, a person's tendency to approach an achievement-oriented task will be determined by the motive to approach success; the probability of obtaining success [$P(S)$] on a specific task; and the positive incentive value that such success would have (I_S), thought to be inversely proportional to the probability of success.

The Motive to Avoid Failure. But there is more to the attempting of tasks than the certainty of success: there is also the possibility of failure. When you are about to make an oral report to a very important class, you hope to do a good job (the desire to achieve success), but you are also anxious about making a fool of yourself (what Atkinson calls the *motive to avoid failure*, abbreviated M_{AF}). This motive to avoid failure cannot be measured from the achievement imagery found in the TAT responses, so it must be obtained in a different fashion. Traditionally, achievement researchers have used the Mandler–Sarason (1952) Test Anxiety Questionnaire (TAQ) to estimate the motive to avoid failure, because it deals with anxiety in what most people would consider an achievement-related situation. More recently, however, Mehrabian (1969) has developed an objective scale of achievement motivation that measures both the motive to achieve success and thee motive to avoid failure, and it may be used instead of the combination of TAT and TAQ.

The tendency to avoid achievement-related situations is considered to be a function of the enduring motive to avoid failure (M_{AF}), the probability of failure at the specific task (which, of course, is unity minus the probability of success), and the incentive value of failure. Just as the incentive value for success varies inversely with the probability of success, the incentive value of failure varies inversely with the probability of failure (or positively with the probability of success). In short, the more likely you are to succeed at a task, (the higher $P(S)$), the less reward you will achieve for succeeding, and the more pain you will suffer for failing. You cannot gain much credit for accomplishing an easy task, but should you fail at such a task you will be roundly denounced as incompetent.

Resultant Achievement Motivation. Achievement theory thus argues that your overall tendency to approach a task will depend on the probability of success, and upon what Atkinson calls **resultant achievement motivation**: the strength of your motive to achieve success minus the strength of your motive to avoid failure ($M_S - M_{AF}$). If you are very high on the motive to achieve success and very low on the motive to avoid failure, your resultant achievement motivation will be quite high (a positive number). If you are high on both motives, or low on both, your resultant achievement motivation will be at an intermediate level (a numerical value near zero). Finally, if your motive to achieve success is low and your motive to avoid failure is high, your resultant achievement motivation will be low (a negative number).

How do these various tendencies become expressed in action? The theory states that the tendency to undertake any task related to achievement (T_A) will be the product of resultant achievement motivation ($M_S - M_{AF}$) times the relevant probability estimates (because the incentive values are the inverse of the probability values, they cancel out of the final equation):

$$T_A = (M_S - M_{AF}) \times [P(S)] \times [1 - P(S)].$$

Thus, both the personal factor of resultant achievement motivation and the environmental factor of task difficulty jointly determine the tendency to undertake an achievement-related task. M_S and M_{AF} are usually computed in *standard scores* (or **z-scores**) that seldom differ from zero by more than three points ($+3$ to -3). As a result, the value of resultant achievement motivation will generally vary between an extreme high of $6 [+3 - (-3) = 6]$ and an extreme low of $-6 [-3 - (+3) = -6]$.

Choice of Achievement Tasks.   Let us consider an example of just how this formula might predict the choice of an achievement-related task. Suppose that you are about to select a college major, and you have narrowed the choice to two alternatives. Both subjects are equally interesting to you, but your family expects you to do graduate work, and you realize you will have to keep your grades up in order to gain entrance to graduate or professional school. Assume that getting good grades would be relatively easy in one subject (the probability of success would be high) but more difficult in the other. Further, assume that your resultant achievement motivation is high $(M_S > M_{AF})$. Because of the way in which resultant achievement motivation combines with the probability of success, the theory predicts that people who are high in achievement motivation will choose tasks of intermediate difficulty over tasks that are either very easy or very difficult.

The tendency of people in whom $M_S > M_{AF}$ to select intermediate-difficulty tasks has been demonstrated in a number of experiments, but what about the people who are low in resultant achievement motivation? The theory predicts that these people will generally try to avoid achievement situations altogether (the overall "approach" tendency is negative). When such situations cannot be avoided, the ones of intermediate difficulty will be the most threatening. Easy tasks will permit success, and extremely difficult tasks will provide a ready excuse for the anticipated failure. To return to the example, if you are high in resultant achievement motivation $(M_S > M_{AF})$, you will choose the moderately difficult major, but if you are low in resultant achievement motivation $(M_S < M_{AF})$, you will choose the easy major. Further, if the choice were between the moderately difficult one and an extremely difficult major, those in whom $M_S > M_{AF}$ would again select the task of intermediate difficulty, whereas those in whom $M_S < M_{AF}$ would now choose the extremely difficult major.

This general prediction has, in fact, been confirmed in two studies of occupational choice (Mahone, 1960; Morris, 1966), which found that students for whom $M_S > M_{AF}$ had occupational preferences that corresponded to their level of competence, whereas students in whom $M_S < M_{AF}$ often held occupational preferences that were more likely to be either too easy or too difficult when compared to their actual level of competence.

Persistence in Achievement Settings.   There is substantial support for the achievement theory prediction that people high in resultant achievement motivation prefer tasks of intermediate or moderate difficulty, but apart from the two studies of occupational choice, the evidence is less clear that people who are low in achievement motivation will choose tasks that are either too difficult or too easy. Although this aspect of the theory remains to be confirmed in a convincing manner, social psychologists generally agree (Atkinson, 1964; Weiner, 1974) that there are important behavioral differences between people who are high in resultant achievement motivation and people who are low. Highs initiate achievement-related activities, lows are forced into them; highs work at such tasks more diligently than do lows; and highs will persist even when confronted by failure, whereas lows are only too willing to stop at the first lack of success.

Let us illustrate how these differences might be related to competition by examining the idea of persistence in the face of failure. We hold in high admiration those who succeed against all odds, and in the popular wisdom, a "true competitor" is a person who keeps on trying as hard as possible, even though he or she is not always successful. No matter whether the competition is limited to the play of an experimental game, broadened to include other interactions in which there is a low correspondence of outcomes, or generalized to economic competition on a grand scale, some losses will always be mixed in with the wins. The critical question for sustained competition is not "What leads people to engage in competition?" but "How do the people who persist after failure differ from those who resign after the slightest setback?"

Perceiving the Causes of Success and Failure

Recent work begun by Weiner and his associates (Weiner, 1974; Weiner et al., 1972; Weiner, Russell, & Lerman, 1978) suggests that the attributions a person makes for the causes of successes and failures will dramatically affect persistence on achievement-related tasks. Consider a specific example: Suppose that you have just received a grade on a midterm examination. Depending on your prior expectations, your comparisons with other students in the class, and perhaps questions of equity, this midterm examination score will be either a success or a failure for you. To what might you attribute that success or failure? More important, how will that attribution be reflected in your further work in the course? What will be the behavioral consequences of your attribution?

Locus of Control. To answer such questions, Weiner and his colleagues constructed an attributional model of achievement motivation that builds on Heider's (1958) attribution theory and upon a Rotter's (1966) distinction between internal and external locus of control of reinforcement. You will recall from chapter 8 that social learning theory argues that people's social behavior is shaped by the reinforcements they receive. One of the difficulties confronting social learning theory is that not everyone seems equally responsive to such reinforcements. Given the same reinforcement, one person's behavior might change, whereas another person's might show no appreciable effect. Rotter (1966) suggested that these individual differences reflected variations in what he called "generalized expectancies" for locus of control of reinforcements: some people will perceive a link between their own actions and the reinforcements they receive ("internals"), whereas other people will almost fatalistically be resigned to thinking that nothing they do will affect what happens to them ("externals"). Social reinforcements should be much more effective for internals than for externals.

To assess these individual differences Rotter (1966) and his colleagues developed the Internal-External Control of Reinforcement Scale (usually abbreviated I-E Scale), consisting of 23 pairs of items, such as

6. a. Without the right breaks one cannot be an effective leader. (E)
   b. Capable people who fail to become leaders have not taken advantage of their opportunities. (I)
23. a. Sometimes I can't understand how teachers arrive at the grades they give. (E)
    b. There is a direct connection between how hard I study and the grades I get. (I)

Each pair of items consists of one statement indicative of external control (designated here by an E), and one statement indicative of internal control (designated by an I), and subjects are asked to indicate which member of each pair is more true for them. There are actually 29 pairs, six of which are filler items designed to make the purposes of the test less obvious, and the I and E do not, of course, appear on the form given to subjects. The person's score on the test is the number of external items endorsed, and in a number of studies summarized by Lefcourt (1976), the average score for college undergraduates is roughly 9.

Over the years several different versions of the locus of control scale have been developed. Some of these have specific purposes such as measurement of perceived personal responsibility for intellectual achievements (Crandall, Katkovsky, & Crandall, 1965), whereas others incorporate control expectations from a variety of domains, such as socio-political, interpersonal, and achievement (Paulhus, 1983). The locus is quite extensive (for example, see reviews by Lefcourt, 1976; 1981), and most of that work is beyond the scope of the present chapter.

What is important for our purposes here is a relationship between locus of control and achievement motivation noted by Weiner et al. (1972). Specifically, Weiner and his associates examined the control attributions of people who were high or low in achievement motivation. Rather than employ the Rotter (1966) scale that contains items of varying content,

Weiner and his colleagues used the Crandall, Katkovsky, and Crandall (1965) Intellectual Achievement Responsibility (IAR) Questionnaire, which concentrates on achievement settings. This questionnaire produces two subscales, one representing the positive outcomes for which the person takes credit, and one representing the negative outcomes for which the person takes blame. What Weiner and his associates found in several experiments was that individuals high in achievement motivation would typically internalize the responsibility for their successes and externalize the responsibility for their failures, whereas people low in achievement motivation would do precisely the reverse.

The Attributional Model. This consistent pattern of differential attributions for performance has obvious implications for a person's willingness to persist in the face of an initial failure, and so the locus of control concept, as well as Heider's (1958) distinctions among effort, ability, task difficulty, and luck, were built into Weiner's attributional model of achievement motivation. A revised version of this attributional model, as it would apply to your examination performance, is shown in Table 10.1. Beginning at the left of the diagram, you will notice the four causes of success or failure – ability, effort, luck, and task difficulty – found in Heider's (1958) attribution theory (discussed more fully in chapter 4). Other possible causes, such as your mood or health at the time of the exam and the chance that you are the teacher's pet or enemy do exist, but these are not considered to be as important as the first four causes.

The Causal Dimensions. According to the attributional model, the presumed causes of success and failure can be described by various combinations of three underlying theoretical dimensions. The first of these is *stability*: Is the cause an enduring one, or one that varies from time to time and situation to situation? Task difficulty is a stable cause, constant within the task no matter who might be attempting it, but your own effort is a variable cause that can change from one exam to the next. The second dimension is *locus* of causality (the updated version of locus of control): Is the cause presumed to be internal to the person or present in the external environment? Ability and effort are internal, task difficulty and luck are external. The third dimension is *intentionality*: Is the cause under intentional control of a person, or is it not? Your effort is intentionally exerted, but your ability is not regarded as being under your volitional control. (Of course you can intentionally "act stupid," but it is less plausible to think that you could intentionally augment your ability.) Bias on the part of the teacher might also be considered intentional, although external to you.

The four causes originally identified by Heider (1958) are usually characterized in terms of the first two dimensions, stability and locus of causality. Ability happens to be stable and internal, effort is variable and internal; task difficulty is stable but external, and luck is variable and ex-

TABLE 10.1 The Midterm Exam: An Attributional Model of Achievement Motivation

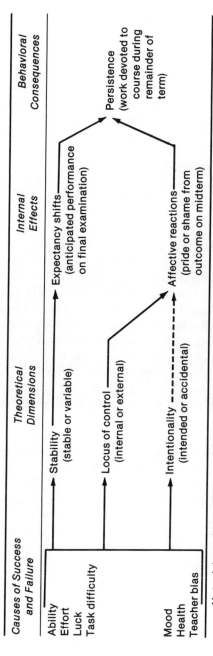

Causes of Success and Failure	Theoretical Dimensions	Internal Effects	Behavioral Consequences
Ability Effort Luck Task difficulty	Stability (stable or variable)	Expectancy shifts (anticipated performance on final examination)	Persistence (work devoted to course during remainder of term)
	Locus of control (internal or external)		
Mood Health Teacher bias	Intentionality (intended or accidental)	Affective reactions (pride or shame from outcome on midterm)	

Note: Adapted from Weiner, B., Russell, D., and Lerman, D. Affective consequences of causal ascriptions. In J. H. Harvey, W. Ickes, and R. F. Kidd (eds.). *New directions in attribution research.* Vol. 2. Hillsdale, NJ: Lawrence Erlbaum Associates, 1978. Reprinted with permission.

ternal. These dimensions, however, are independent. That is, knowing that a cause is stable does not tell us whether it is internal or external. Suppose that a student you know continually obtains high grades (a stable performance). Without knowing what sort of courses this person has taken (the usual selection, or nothing but known "easy" courses), you cannot with any certainty attribute the success to ability. The third dimension, intentionality, is not independent from the other two, because an intentionally produced cause must be internal to you (or to some other person, such as the teacher). It does not make sense to argue that the task intentionally selected you as a victim for its difficulty, while becoming simpler for everyone else.

Internal and Observable Effects. Continuing with the diagram, the first consequences of your attribution for success and failure are internal effects. If you decide that your performance was due to ability, your expectations about future performance will not shift very much. Only if you attribute a failure to a lack of effort can you convince yourself that next time you will do better. Not only will the attribution made affect your expectations for future performance, it will also affect your self-esteem. If you have succeeded because of high ability and hard work, you will understandably feel proud of yourself. The solid arrows in the diagram indicate that expectancy shifts are predominantly the consequence of variations in stability, whereas the extent of affective reaction is determined by changes in the locus of causality dimension (although pride and shame are also partially influenced by whether the cause was intended or not).

Finally, your persistence in the task—how hard you study, how intensely you concentrate, how carefully you take notes—is determined by the joint action of expectancy shifts and affective reactions. If you are upset by your midterm performance, and believe that it reflects a lack of motivation rather than a lack of ability, then you will try harder on the final exam. If you are pleased with the midterm performance, but not certain that your success is stable, the theory again argues that you will try harder on the final exam.

There does seem, however, to be an exception to this prediction. Research by Berglas and Jones (1978) among others shows that sometimes the combination of good, but unstable, initial performance can lead people to engage in self-handicapping. If you have succeeded the first time you attempt a task, people are likely to expect you to continue that good performance. But if you are uncertain about the correct attribution for the performance, you may not feel confident that you can live up to these expectations. To protect your self-esteem from future failure, Berglas and Jones (1978) argue that you will intentionally do something to impair your second performance (e.g., fail to study until the last minute, engage in some form of substance abuse prior to the test). That way, if you succeed, you will feel great about having overcome these additional obstacles; if you fail you will have a ready explanation that does not require you to think of the earlier success as a fluke.

Attribution and Achievement Motivation.   How are all of these effects related to achievement motivation? In two different ways. First, the attributional analysis makes it clear that an important component of the tendency to approach an achievement task, the probability of success at the task [$P(S)$] has to be evaluated from the perspective of the actor. Certainly it is true that in many of the studies of achievement motivation the experimenter has artificially manipulated that probability, thus ensuring objective differences in probability across experimental conditions. But in the real social world, your impression of the likelihood of success is substantially more important than the objective probability value. If you believe your chances for success are low because you have made some faulty attribution for the causes of the outcome (or because you routinely attribute failure internally and success externally), our insistence that the probability is really higher than you think it to be will fall on deaf ears. In a sense, the attributional model of achievement motivation brings to the subject of task performance what the social cognition approach to behavior has brought us before (Chapter 4): the notion that actions, in order to be understood, must be considered from the viewpoint of the actor.

Not only do attributions influence achievement motivation, the reverse is also true, and this is the second relationship between the two. As noted earlier, in a number of research studies (e.g., 1974), Weiner and his colleagues have demonstrated that people who are high in resultant achievement motivation attribute success internally, more specifically to ability, but attribute failure (if internally at all) to lack of effort. In rather direct contrast, people who are low in achievement motivation attribute failure internally to lack of ability, but attribute success externally to good luck (or at least not to an internal disposition). In short, highly achievement-motivated people see themselves as causing their successes and consider their failures to be from lack of trying—leading them to try even harder in the face of occasional setbacks. People whose achievement motivation is low see their failures as caused by a lack of ability that cannot be changed, so they avoid achievement tasks in order to preserve what self-esteem they can still maintain. Because most achievement tasks contain elements of both ability and effort, these errors in causal attribution tend to become self-fulfilling.

Achievement Motivation in Women: Fear of Success?

The vast majority of research on achievement motivation has employed male subjects, primarily because the TAT-TAQ technique for measuring achievement motivation has proved unreliable with females. In an attempt to account for this difficulty, Horner (1972) argued that although achievement, ambition, and competitiveness may be desirable for males (that is, may have a positive incentive value), the same characteristics may be widely perceived as being undesirable or unfeminine for females. Consequently, whereas the congruence between achievement and role expectations leads to a desire for success among males, the inconsistency between achievement and traditional role expectations for females leads them to fear success. It is important to note that this is not the same as a desire for failure, which would preclude attempts at success; rather, it is a fear that increases as the probability of success increases: Potentially highly successful women should suffer more from fear of success than should women who never attempt to achieve.

Success in Medical School. To test for the existence of the fear of success, Horner (1972) described a number of ambiguous situations to female and male subjects and asked them to describe what was happening and what would happen in the future. The crucial situation described a stimulus person who placed at the top of a medical school class after final examinations for the first term. The stimulus person was identified by name (Anne or John) and the pronouns used in the story further reinforced the sexual identification of the stimulus person. Male subjects received a version containing only John, whereas female subjects received a version containing only Anne. The stories written in response to the situation were coded for fear of success if they contained any of several themes. These themes (and examples of them) were (a) negative consequences of success (loss of a valued male friend), (b) future activities away from success (becoming a housewife after completing medical school), (c) direct expression of conflict about success or denial of responsibility for achieving success (the grades were just good luck), or (d) bizarre or inappropriate responses ("Anne" was really a code name for a nonexistent person).

The results of this part of Horner's research showed that 65.5% of the female subjects wrote stories showing fear of success in response to the cue name Anne, whereas only 9.1% of the male subjects wrote fear-of-success stories in response to the cue name John. Horner interpreted these findings, and the results from a second experimental session involving the completion of a number of tasks as confirming the existence of a motive to avoid success.

Fear of Gender-Inappropriate Success. Not surprisingly, these results generated a great deal of interest. They served the conceptual function of explaining why traditional measures of achievement motivation might not apply to females, at the same time that they suggested that the prevailing role expectations for women might be having quite detrimental effects on them. Unfortunately, the balance of research conducted since

Horner's original study indicates that although the idea had merit, it oversimplified the situation. Critics soon pointed out a number of difficulties in Horner's work, not the least of which was that Anne's success was in one of the most male-dominated professions. Indeed, when other researchers gave the Anne cue to male subjects, well over half of the subjects also wrote stories showing fear of success imagery (e.g., Monahan, Kuhn, & Shaver, 1974).

These results, coupled with the fact that males are not supposed to suffer from fear of success produced by conflicting role expectations, suggest that the stimulus story, not the enduring personality characteristics of the subjects, produced the data Horner obtained. In a comprehensive review of the fear of success literature, Zuckerman and Wheeler (1975) illustrate other methodological problems with Horner's study, discuss the consistencies in subsequent work, and present alternative measures of the fear of success. Their conclusion, and that of later reviewers as well (Spence, Deaux, & Helmreich, 1985) is that what people (both males and females) really fear is *gender-inappropriate success*. This conclusion does not solve the original problem, namely that traditional achievement measurement techniques have low reliability for females, and that difficulty remains a limitation of the theory of achievement motivation. Despite this problem, the attributional analysis of achievement does indicate one important way in which high achievement motivation, reflected in persistence in the face of failure, might affect willingness to engage in sustained competition. We now turn from this pursuit of one's own goals to the intentional injury of other people – the topic of aggression.

THE DEFINITION OF AGGRESSION

If anything, our everyday uses of the word *aggression* are even more confusing than such uses of the word *competition*. We describe the physical attack by one person against another as aggression unless the attacker is in a role (soldier, police officer, professional boxer) in which physical attacks against selected other people are sanctioned. We describe an especially hard-hitting football player as aggressive, but we use the same label for a salesperson who is assertively promoting a product. We often refuse to take some actions by saying that to do so would "do violence to" our moral principles, and nations sometimes describe the self-interested economic policies of their adversaries as acts of aggression. It would be tempting to assert that the concept of aggression is really quite clear; that it is only our everyday language that is imprecise. But there are important contradictions even in the scientific definitions offered for the concept of aggression (see discussions of the concept by Bandura, 1973; Kaufmann, 1970; Krebs & Miller, 1985).

Aggression as an Instinct

More often than not, these contradictions reflect differences in theoretical approach rather than disagreements about which behaviors should be called aggressive. For example, researchers continue to debate whether aggression is primarily instinctive or primarily a response to cultural, situational, and personal influences. On one side of this issue are Freud (1933, 1950) and the ethologgists (scientists who study animal social behavior in its natural setting), such as Lorenz (1966); on the other side are most social psychologists. Freud traced aggressive impulses to a death instinct (called *Thanatos*), the aim of which is to destroy life. This death instinct is presumably manifest in self-destructive behavior (of which suicide would be the most extreme version), and in aggression directed outward toward other people. From a slightly different perspective, Lorenz argues that aggression among members of the same species (*intraspecific* aggression) serves evolutionary purposes. Intraspecific aggression, properly regulated by rituals and inhibitions developed over time, disperses the population to take maximum advantage of the available food, and encourages selective breeding among the most hardy. Thus, although Freud and Lorenz might disagree on the precise function of aggression, both argue that it is an instinctual drive that is virtually immune from the influence of culture or situation.

Aggression as a Response to Frustration

In rather direct contrast to this view is the extreme environmentalist position initially proposed by Dollard, Doob, Miller, Mowrer, and Sears (1939). This now classic work argued that aggression was always the consequence of *frustration*, which was defined as interference with a goal-directed response. As Kaufmann (1970) has noted, Dollard et al. did not specifically state whether this proposed relationship between frustration and aggression was supposed to be innate or learned, but the occurrence of aggression was, in their model, quite clearly attributed to conditions in the external environment, not to aggressive instincts within the person.

Later discussions by social psychologists have suggested that frustration need not always lead to aggression (Berkowitz, 1962); that aggression can be either an intentional action (Berkowitz, 1975) or not necessarily intentional (Buss, 1961); and that which actions are designated as aggressive may depend as much on the value judgments of the observers as on the nature of the action (Bandura, 1973). In a very recent review of the concept, Krebs and Miller (1985) argue that biological factors (along with cultural requirements and prohibitions) contribute to the "enduring characteristics of people" that interact with features of the situation to make aggression more likely or less likely. Despite all of these differences of opinion (which we consider in more detail later), all these theorists place little stock in an aggressive instinct such as the one central to Freudian theory.

Three Qualifications on a Definition

Perhaps the only common element in all of the various definitions of aggression is the idea of injury to the target. The injury may be physical or psychological; the attempt at injury may be successful or unsuccessful; the target may be a person or an inanimate object; the source of the attempt at injury may be an aggressive instinct or an environmental frustration; the attempt may be guided by intent or it may not; and the aggressor may or may not be in close proximity to the target. Obviously, a definition this general would be of little use to us, so some additional conditions must be imposed. First, because our interest is human social behavior, let us restrict the class of targets to persons. Second, to rule out the possibility of aggression-by-accident, let us side with those (e.g., Bandura, 1973; Berkowitz, 1975; Kaufmann, 1970) who argue that aggression must be intentional. Third, let us distinguish between injury to the self and injury to others by restricting aggression to the latter circumstances.

These three restrictions are sufficient for our purposes, and leave us with a definition of **aggression** as intentional action directed toward the injury of another person. This definition is not very different from the original one proposed by Dollard and his colleagues (1939)–"a response having for its goal the injury of a living organism" (p. 11)–even though we have considered some of the arguments raised in the intervening years. Such a definition permits us to describe as aggressive those actions that produce psychological injury as well as those that produce physical injury, and those actions that fail in the attempt as well as the ones that succeed. In this latter respect, the definition of aggression differs from the definition proposed in chapter 9 for objective altruism. To recall Heider's (1958) distinction between ambiguous mediation and synonymous mediation (Chapter 3), an aggressive act is likely to be synonymous with an aggressive intention. In contrast, the specific intention giving rise to a helpful action is ambiguous: It may be altruism, but it may also be self-interest or ingratiation. Thus, only those actions that produce benefit for the recipient and no external rewards for the benefactor could qualify as objectively altruistic. In the present case, the actor's intentions are clear from the actions, even though those actions may not be successful in inflicting harm because of the superior power of the target person or fortunate intervention by a third party.

Consequences for the Aggressor

Finally, although the definition of aggression is stated in terms of injury to the target, aggressive actions are not without consequences for the actor. Whether we presume the action to be instinctive or learned, we can argue that aggression involves rewards to the actor. If aggression is really the discharge of an accumulated instinctual drive, according to Freudian theory such a release of tension would be pleasurable. On the other hand, if aggression is regarded as having at least some causes that are external to the person (such as frustrations), the social learning that would have to be involved would include some rewards that have accompanied previous performances of aggressive behavior.

In either case, it is reasonable to suggest that aggression, like competition, can be seen as an example of social exchange. The aggressor and the target are in an interaction in which each one's outcomes are determined by the joint behavior of the two. For example, whether an aggressive action succeeds in producing injury to the target person will depend on the particular form of aggression chosen by the attacker and on the defenses against that attack that are mounted by the target. The situation involves a low correspondence of outcomes, but because the target's costs may far exceed the aggressor's rewards, the interaction as a whole has a nonzero (usually negative) sum. In this way at least, and perhaps in others as well, aggression and competition can be seen in the same light.

INSTIGATION AND MAINTENANCE OF AGGRESSION

Although the problem of aggression is as old as recorded history, the scientific study of aggression is a relatively recent development. This scientific interest may be attributable as much to the emergence of competing theories of aggression as to the social consequences of the problem. Is aggression innate, or learned? How can it be controlled and reduced? What role, if any, does society play in fostering aggression, and can society itself survive if aggression is permitted to grow unchecked? These questions deal with the presumed source of instigation to aggression. Our definition of aggression as intentional action directed toward the injury of another person identifies the immediate or proximate cause of an aggressive action as the actor's intention to produce harm. Thus the social and scientific question becomes "What was the source of the intention; what *instigated* the aggression?"

Beginning with Freud's (1933) suggestion that aggression is only an interpersonal manifestation of an individual death instinct, and continuing through some recent theories that hold aggression to be a joint product of cognitive and motivational factors (Kaufmann, 1970; Tannenbaum &

Zillmann, 1975), researchers have provided widely differing answers to this question. These theories can be grouped into three categories defined by the presumed source(s) of instigation: pressures internal to the person, conditions in the environment, and a combination of the two. We shall briefly consider these three categories of theory, and then examine a single social problem—televised violence—to suggest which sort of theory best accommodates the available experimental evidence.

Theories of Internal Instigation

Freud's Instinctive Theory. Freud was the first to suggest psychological factors in aggressive behavior, and in his early work he considered aggression to be a response to the thwarting of the person's pursuit of pleasure or avoidance of pain. Confronted with the problem of explaining sadism and self-destructive behavior, Freud (1933, 1950) later postulated the existence of a death instinct (Thanatos), which opposed the life instinct (Eros) and tried to reduce the organism to its inanimate state. Both actions of self-destruction (as minor as nail biting and as serious as suicide) and acts of aggression directed at others were thought to be manifestations of this death instinct.

In this view, the death instinct is a constant source of aggressive impulses. Many of these can be **displaced** onto nonhuman targets (an example would be the hunting of animals for sport), and others can be **sublimated**, or channeled into socially acceptable activities (everything from contact sports to merciless political satire). But substitutes cannot be satisfactory indefinitely; eventually the death instinct will be discharged in an overt act of aggression. This model of aggressive instinct often has been described by an analogy to the hydraulic system of a reservoir. Thanatos is an underground spring feeding a small stream of aggressive impulses, but this stream is dammed up by societal prohibitions against the expression of aggression. Some socially acceptable spillways in the dam permit a portion of the pressure to be relieved, but eventually the stream will flood over the dam in periodic discharges of aggression.

Lorenz's Instinctive Theory. A similar "hydraulic" theory of human aggression has been advanced by Lorenz (1966), based on extensive study of aggression among infrahuman animals in their natural settings. Lorenz shares with Freud the position that human aggression is innate rather than learned, but he attributes such aggressiveness to an aberration in the evolutionary process of natural selection. According to Lorenz's theory, human beings, like their infrahuman counterparts, are endowed with an instinct for fighting that serves to disperse the population (thus providing for better utilization of resources) and to ensure mating only among the most hardy. But unlike other animals, human beings are not naturally endowed with lethal weapons (fangs, claws, crushing strength). Consequently, humans have never developed the instinctive inhibitions against killing that are thought to be practically universal among the lower animals. Throughout most of human history, this lack of inhibitions against killing presented no problems, but when humans developed a technology capable of producing a tremendous variety of weapons that were lethal even at a great distance, the inevitable result was a dramatic increase in aggression, violence, and war.

Although Lorenz's position and similar generalizations from animal behavior by others have gained wide popular appeal, they have been met with skepticism in the scientific community. A collection of papers edited by Montagu (1968) is especially critical of Lorenz's observations of animal behavior, and his generalizations to human, and the vast majority of research by social scientists contradicts a purely instinctual position (Bandura, 1973; Berkowitz, 1975).

For example, consider the idea of territoriality. One of the evolutionary purposes usually thought to be served by intraspecies aggression is the distribution of the population across the available resources–the establishment and maintenance of territoriality (Altman, 1975; Johnson, 1972; Klopfer, 1969). People build fences and personalize their homes and offices, and they defend their neighborhoods against what they perceive to be intrusions from outsiders. But even when reactions to intruders are sudden and violent, is the simple presence of the intruders the cause of the reaction (as it would be among animals), or is it the symbolic value of the intrusion that leads to the reaction? The small town that is openly hostile to anyone who tries to settle there may still be friendly to outsiders who just come to visit; the discomfort you feel when someone you don't know well stands too close to you arises not because the resources (such as oxygen) have become restricted, but because the social meaning of the intrusion causes embarrassment or fright. Extensive experimental research on crowding (discussed in chapter 13) has indicated that whether social density is pleasant or unpleasant will depend on the situation. Under some circumstances, it appears, increased density can even enhance pleasure (for example, compare a crowded party or dance floor with one that is underpopulated). The general conclusion to be drawn from these examples is that direct generalization from animal to human behavior is tenuous even when an issue as basic as territoriality is concerned. This suggests that other potential sources of instigation to aggression found among animals should be generalized to humans with even greater caution.

Theories of External Instigation

The Frustration-Aggression Hypothesis. As noted earlier, the **frustration–aggression hypothesis** first proposed by Dollard et al. (1939)

is the foremost example of a purely environmentalist or external theory of the instigation of aggression. The original version of the hypothesis avoided taking a position on whether the proposed relationship was instinctive or learned, but it did argue that (a) frustration always leads to aggression, and (b) aggression is always the consequence of frustration. In other words, frustration will produce only aggression – not coping behavior, not withdrawal, not tearful helplessness – and aggression can be brought about only by frustration, not by pain, not by deprivation, not by anticipated reward. As you can imagine, this is a highly restrictive interpretation causes of aggression, and in a later paper Miller (1941) modified the position considerably. Miller still maintained that frustration was the only antecedent of aggression, but he suggested that such frustration would lead to the instigation of aggression, not necessarily to an overt aggressive act. This modification of the original hypothesis made it possible for features of the situation to prevent the occurrence of an aggressive act, even though the instigation to aggression may be present.

Aversive Events and Cues to Aggression. Recently, the frustration–aggression hypothesis has been extended further in a reformulation by Berkowitz (1969). Since the publication of the original hypothesis, a large amount of experimental research had been performed to explore various aspects of the presumed relationship between frustration and aggression. In reviewing that literature, Berkowitz (1969) concluded that two additional modifications of the hypothesis were warranted. First, the antecedents of aggression should be expanded to a general class of *aversive events*, of which frustration is only one. Research with animals had indicated that aggressive responses could be brought about by pain, even when external cues were largely absent (Scott, 1966), and by other aversive events such as hunger (predatory aggression) and a need for territorial defense (Moyer, 1967). Second, Miller's (1941) modification was extended slightly to incorporate all of the aggressive cues present in the situation. Some of these relevant cues might enhance aggression, whereas others might inhibit its expression. The function of aggressive cues can be seen in the finding by Berkowitz and Geen (1967) that subjects showed more aggression against a target person who resembled the victim in an aggressive film than against a target person who did not resemble the victim, even when the only resemblance was the first names of the two people.

This reformulation of the frustration–aggression hypothesis thus holds that a variety of aversive events can create an instigation to aggression, conceived of as a state of emotional arousal or a readiness to engage in aggressive behavior. It is important to note that although this readiness is an internal state, it is nearly always the direct product of some aversive stimulus in the external environment. Thus, in contrast to the instinctive theories, the reformulation still places most of the sources of instigation outside the person.

The Role of Cognition. Although this reformulation can account for a high proportion of the data on aggression, there is reason to believe that at least some internal factors must also be considered. For example, Burnstein and Worchel (1962) found less aggression against a person who kept interrupting a group discussion if that person appeared to be hard of hearing (wore a hearing aid) than if he did not. In the latter case, the interruptions seemed arbitrary and were followed by aggression, whereas in the former case the interruptions were understandable. What differed across these two conditions was the subject's internal interpretation of the reasons for the blocking of the group's goal, and this influence of cognitive factors has been obtained in later research as well (e.g., Dyck & Rule, 1978). In addition to the influence of cognitive factors on aggression, wide individual differences in reactions to situational frustration occur, and these also suggest that internal variables may play a part in the response to instigation. We now turn to theories that explicitly encompass both internal and external sources of instigation to aggression.

Combinatorial Theories

Excitation-Transfer Theory. In Berkowitz's reformulation of the frustration–aggression hypothesis, aversive events in the environment are thought to produce a state of readiness to be aggressive (instigation), with an aggressive response occurring if the situational cues suggest that aggression is appropriate. The internal arousal is thus relatively specific to both the aversive events and the aggressive response. But you will recall from the discussion of the cognitive labeling theory of emotion (Chapter 7) and from some of the research on misattribution of arousal and attraction (Chapter 9), that the subjective experience of emotion may not be specific to a single identifiable state of physiological arousal. Indeed, there is strong evidence that arousal from one source can be mistaken, under the proper circumstances, for a different sort of emotion. Does this mean that other sources of arousal (besides aversive events) may contribute to the instigation to aggression? In their **excitation-transfer theory** of aggression, Tannenbaum and Zillmann (1975) argue for an affirmative answer to this question.

Specifically, the theory holds that once an aversive event has created an instigation to aggression, increasing the person's arousal by other means will enhance the aggressive response. In a typical experiment, a subject will first be angered by a confederate who insults the subject's intelligence. This aversive event presumably produces the initial instigation to aggression. Then, in a second phase of the experiment, the subject is exposed to a film or videotape that has either Aggressive or Nonaggressive (erotic or humorous) Content. Finally, the aggressive response is measured by permitting the subject to deliver electric shocks to a confederate (who does not actually receive the shocks) as punishment for mistakes in what is purported to be a learning task (this latter portion of the research is typical of most studies of aggression in the laboratory).

Results from a number of different experiments have indicated that the greatest aggressive reactions are produced in the Aggressive Content conditions, but that overt aggression is greater in the Nonaggressive Content conditions than in nonarousal control conditions (Tannenbaum & Zillmann, 1975). These results indicate that nonaggressive content can energize an existing aggressive response, increasing the intensity of that response. Even more strikingly, shows that cognitive factors can enhance aggression several days after the initial instigation—long after the initial arousal should have been dissipated.

Sexual Arousal and Aggression. One of the objections traditionally raised against unrestricted distribution of pornography is that because the sexual arousal derived from pornography has a hostile content, pornography will increase the viewer's likelihood of engaging in sexual aggression. In 1970, the report of the President's Commission on Obscenity and Pornography (Wilson & Goldstein, 1973) concluded that there was no evidence of a relationship between exposure to erotica and subsequent sexual aggression. But criticisms of that report (e.g., Dienstbier, 1977) and the implications of both cognitive labeling theory and excitation–transfer theory have led researchers to reopen this question.

In a procedure that combines traditional methods for measuring aggression with those of excitation–transfer research, studies of the effects of erotica on aggression typically take the following form (e.g., Baron & Bell, 1977; Malamuth & Donnerstein, 1982): The subject is brought into an experimental laboratory and is provided with some reason for interacting with another person (a male or female experimental confederate) who either insults the subject or does not do so (the presence or absence of instigation to aggression). Then the subject is asked to view some stimulus materials (slides, videotapes, or segments of movies) that either do or do not have sexually arousing content. Finally, under the guise of studying physiological arousal based on "unpleasant stimuli," the subject is given the opportunity to provide electric shocks of varying intensities to the confederate (or, occasionally, to another person whom the subject has not previously seen). Dependent variables can be the duration of the shock administered, the apparent average intensity (of course, no shocks are actually delivered, and the presumed recipient of them is an experimental assistant), or some combination of the two. In more recent work such as that reported by Malamuth and Donnerstein (1982) various indications of sexual arousal are assessed physiologically (often using blood pressure, occasionally using penile tumescence, as the measure).

Effects of Aggressive Erotica.   Why did the President's Commission find no influence of pornography on aggression? Perhaps the most important reason, suggested by Malamuth and Donnerstein (1982), is that when that research was conducted there simply was not the level of aggressive pornography available that there is today. Not only is the sheer volume of aggressive pornography much greater now than it was 15 years ago, its actual content increasingly implies that the (female) victims somehow "enjoy" their victimization. The danger posed by this implication is dramatically illustrated in research reported by Donnerstein and Berkowitz (1981), and Malamuth and Donnerstein (1982). In the study by Donnerstein and Berkowitz (1981), subjects were shown a neutral film, an erotic film of a young couple making love, or a film depicting a woman's being violently sexually assaulted by two men. There were two versions of this last film, one in which the woman was shown to be suffering throughout her victimization, and one in which she was shown as becoming a willing victim. When the victim did not seem to suffer, the aggressive pornography film enhanced aggression in both angered and nonangered subjects. When the victim did suffer, the aggressive film enhanced aggression among angered, but not among nonangered, subjects. Thus the effects of erotica on aggression depend in part on the presence of instigation to aggression, in part on the kind of erotica viewed following the instigation, and in part on the victim's presumed suffering.

To summarize, the findings from studies of sexual arousal and aggression support two fundamental conclusions. First, an interaction does occur between sexual arousal and aggression, as would be predicted by excitation–transfer and cognitive labeling theories. Second, the nature of this relationship between sexual arousal and aggression depends on factors that might be involved in the misattribution that is thought to occur. Specifically, (a) exposure to mildly arousing sexual material actually reduces later aggression (Baron & Bell, 1977), (b) exposure to *non*aggressive pornography will increase later aggression toward females only if subjects have been angered (Donnerstein & Berkowitz, 1981), (c) exposure to aggressive pornography, especially that which implies that in some sense the female victim "liked it," will enhance later aggression against females even among subjects who have *not* been instigated to aggression by being angered, and (d) virtually no sort of pornography increases the aggression by male subjects against male targets. The more easily one source of arousal can be confused with another, the more likely subsequent aggression is to occur.

Social Learning Theory.   There is a common thread in the major external and combinatorial theories: Each assumes that aggressive actions are specific responses to the instigation provided by aversive events of one sort or another. This view is the essential ingredient of the strictly external theories, and it can be seen, though to a lesser degree, in excitation–transfer theory as well. But is instigation always necessary for aggression? The research on aggressive pornography would suggest not. Even in the absence of specific instigation to aggression, people viewing sexual violence in which the victim participates respond aggressively toward a female target.

Moreover, there are numerous examples of social aggression outside the laboratory for which no immediate instigation is at all obvious. Is it reasonable to argue that that the purse snatcher who pushes a victim to the ground was instigated to aggression? What about the juvenile gang that sets a drunk on fire "just for kicks?" Or the professional killer who murders for hire? Or, for that matter, what about armies engaged in battle? It strains credibility to argue that in all these cases a specific instigation to aggression has occurred, or even to argue that in the absence of an aversive event, aggression is the result of innate instincts toward death or population dispersal. It is much more plausible to suggest that although aggression may be a response to the push of aversive instigation, it may also be a response to the pull of rewards anticipated for its successful completion. Aggression may thus be an *instrumental activity* as well as a hostile response to thwarting.

Because it includes both the likelihood of instigation from aversive events and the possibility of aggression in order to achieve anticipated rewards, the social learning analysis of aggression outlined by Bandura (1973) is the most comprehensive of the aggression theories. You will recall from chapter 8 that social learning theory asserts that imitation and vicarious reinforcement, as well as the more direct attainment of desired goals, will influence social behavior. In contrast to the strict environmentalist view of reinforcement maintained by Skinner (1953) and other behaviorists, social learning theory includes emotional states and cognitive functions such as anticipation and expectancy within its broad framework of explanatory principles. Especially important are the cognitive representations of the reinforcement contingencies that will accompany anticipated actions: "If I behave aggressively in this situation, will I get away with it?" Indeed, in one of the studies reported by Malamuth and Donnerstein (1982), a question that asked male subjects whether they would rape a woman if they thought they could get away with it successfully distinguished between individuals who had positive physiological reactions and those who had negative reactions to a rape scene with a suffering victim. The assumption that cognitive representations of the contingencies exist is inherent in many of society's attempts to control aggressive behavior, ranging all the way from the parent's threats against an errant child to the legal threats of punishment for criminal behavior.

As noted previously, Berkowitz (1969) pointed out the importance of the cues in the situation for determining the scope of the aggressive response. But his reformulation of frustration–aggression theory was limited to two response options: aggression versus nonaggression. In contrast, Bandura's (1973) social learning model not only extends the possible sources of instigation, it also suggests that depending on the individual's social learning history and the stimulus features of the situation an instigation can lead to behavior as diverse as dependency, withdrawal, constructive problem solving, or outright aggression. Finally, Bandura reviews a great deal of research that indicates how changes in stimulus and reinforcement conditions can transform aggression into other, more socially desirable, responses. The social learning approach is especially relevant for the social policy question we now consider: the effects of televised violence.

Theory and Practice: The Issue of Televised Violence

Television has practically become a way of life in America. Most adults get their news from television; a home is more likely to have a television than to have any other electrical appliance; counting summer vacations and weekends, children spend more time in front of television sets than they spend in school (Liebert, Neale, & Davidson, 1973). Both the advertisers who pay for commercial programs and the creators of children's programs on noncommercial television obviously believe that television can have significant effects on behavior, and the research evidence supports this belief.

What concerns us here is the effect that televised violence may have on the actions of people who view such violence. Is the immediate and in-depth coverage of terrorist activities likely to contribute to increases in these antisocial actions? Do crime-oriented programs encourage criminal actions, or teach people how to become more successful criminals? Does the violence exhibited even by the heroes of these shows, and by the "good guys" in children's cartoons teach the lesson that violence is not only an accepted means of resolving conflict, but the preferred solution? In recent years questions such as these have become of increasing concern to the television industry, to regulatory agencies, to researchers, and to the public.

In conceptual terms, all these questions can be reduced to a central issue: whether the observation of televised aggression (apart from any sexual content of that aggression) increase or decrease the subsequent level of aggression displayed by the viewer. This issue has implications for theory as well as for social policy, because the various theories of aggression can be show to make opposing predictions. On the one hand, there is the prediction from the instinctive approaches that observation of aggression will serve as a vicarious outlet for impulses that otherwise would be manifest in overt behavior. On the other hand, there is the position of the social learning theories that observation of violence will teach aggression as a way of resolving conflict and obtaining satisfaction, thereby increasing the probability of future aggression by the viewers.

The Catharsis Hypothesis. The suggestion that observed aggression will decrease overt aggression is known as the **catharsis hypothesis**, and it assumes a reservoir model of aggression. The catharsis hypothesis was first formally advanced in the original frustration–aggression doctrine (Dollard et al., 1939), but it was derived from earlier Freudian theory. Although the frustration–aggression hypothesis assumes that all instigation to aggression is external to the person, whereas the instinctive theories of Freud and Lorenz assume that instigation is internal, the source of the instigation is not the critical element of catharsis. The point is that whatever the presumed source of instigation, that instigation will create a reservoir of aggressive impulses that will need to be reduced. This reduction can occur through displacement, sublimation, or through the vicarious experience of observing aggression and violence (catharsis).

The best evidence for the catharsis hypothesis comes from an extensive field study by Feshbach and Singer (1971). These investigators used as subjects over 400 preadolescent and adolescent boys who were living either in college preparatory boarding schools or in public institutions for homeless boys. Within each sort of institution, half of the boys were randomly assigned to watch programs high in aggressive content, whereas the other half of the boys were assigned to watch programs low in aggressive content. All of the boys were required to watch at least 6 hours of television per week for 6 weeks, and during this time they were rated on aggressiveness by the house staff, using a behavior rating scale devised by the investigators. Consistent with the catharsis hypothesis, in the public institutions the level of aggressiveness declined among boys watching the aggressive material but increased among boys watching the nonaggressive material. In the private boarding schools the reverse pattern of results appeared, but here the differences were not statistically significant.

On balance, these results supported the catharsis hypothesis, with a television diet of aggressive content leading to decreased expressed aggression among boys in the public homes. Although Feshbach and Singer had taken what methodological precautions they could, problems often appear in a field experiment. For example, the boys in the nonaggressive conditions demanded to be permitted to see "Batman," even though its content was considered aggressive. The ratings of aggressiveness were made by house staff, who could not help but know each boy's experimental condition, so the fact that the catharsis findings were obtained only among the public-home boys (for whom violence might stereotypically have been considered more of a problem) is unsettling. Most important, there was some evidence that the aggressive programs were universally preferred, suggesting that the boys in the nonaggressive condition might have been frustrated by not being able to see programs they would otherwise have watched.

Unfortunately, several field studies reported by Liebert, Neale, and Davidson (1973), and by Parke, Berkowitz, Leyens, West, and Sebastian (1977) found increased aggression among juvenile delinquents who watched violent movies. These findings, and the research described earlier on the effects of aggressive pornography, provide little comfort to the catharsis position. It still seems fair to conclude, with an extensive review by Geen and Quanty (1977), that at present there is no convincing evidence in favor of catharsis.

Social Learning and Increased Aggression. Critics of the research on televised violence have made two important points: too much of the research is conducted in experimental settings, and it is often impossible to control for a great number of other social factors that might lead to aggression. Although these criticisms are well taken, there is still sufficient grounds to believe that exposure to televised violence will enhance later aggression. Thinking about the theories of aggression, it is easy to see why this might be the case. First, suppose that the viewer (especially a child) is instigated to aggression before watching the program. In terms of Berkowitz's (1969) reformulation of the frustration–aggression doctrine, the televised violence would serve as an aggressive cue establishing the appropriateness of releasing the aggressive impulses. In addition, the excitation-transfer theory of Tannenbaum and Zillmann (1975) suggests that the excitement of the program itself may be be misattributed to a desire to behave aggressively. Because we do not regard the program as the source of this arousal, we have no available label for the subjective feeling, and may mistakenly consider it part of our anger at having been instigated to aggression.

But what if there is no prior instigation to aggression? The social learning viewpoint taken by Bandura (1973) predicts that observation of televised violence will still increase subsequent aggression. Recall that this model postulates two different reasons for aggressive action: the aversive events described by many other theories, and the use of aggression as a means of obtaining rewards in the absence of aversive instigation. Let us concentrate on the latter reason for aggression. A detailed analysis of the content of television programs conducted by Larsen (1968) found that violent methods were the single most widely employed means of reaching desired goals, and as Malamuth and Donnerstein (1982) note, this use of violence has increased in frequency while at the same time being applied to new settings (i.e., sexual activity).

The social learning theory analysis thus argues that with or without prior instigation, televised violence is likely to increase subsequent aggression, and the great preponderance of research evidence confirms this prediction. Included in this supporting evidence is a huge study undertaken by the United States Surgeon General (reported by Cater & Strickland, 1975), which contains seven volumes of reports by researchers using a variety of experimental and nonexperimental procedures and an extensive array of dependent variables. The research with aggressive erotica provides the most recent, and extremely troubling, evidence of the negative consequences that can follow exposure to violent material.

A Concluding Comment

In this chapter we have seen that competition and aggression, like the positive social behaviors of altruism and attraction, can be influenced by both situational factors and personal characteristics. Competition can be increased by changing the payoffs for success, by suggesting individualistic goals, or by altering the apparent characteristics of the opponent. But over the long term, an individual's participation in competition may also be affected by his or her level of resultant achievement motivation. Aggression can reliably be instigated by aversive events, but it can also be the learned solution to the problem of obtaining one's own ends.

If competition and aggression are like the positive social behaviors in their dependence on both personal and situational factors, they are unlike altruism and attraction in their characterization by society. We foster competition among children by training them to be self-sufficient, we further encourage competition by rewarding good performance in school, and competition is presumed to be an essential element of our economic system. In these and other ways we label competition as positive and healthy, and we profess to be surprised when our children seem uncaring for the welfare of others, when students cheat on examinations in order to maintain high grade averages, and when businesses engage in illegal activities and campaign contributions. We discourage individual aggression through socialization and a legal system that punishes violence, asserting all the while that there must be better ways of resolving interpersonal conflicts. Yet at the same time we do little to restrict the contradictory lessons taught by television and we insist that our armed forces must be the most powerful in the world.

We began this chapter by pointing out the confusion in common language definitions of competition and aggression. After some refinements of the terms, we were in a position to see what situational and personal factors might affect these two behaviors, at least in the context of scientific research. When we wonder how many of these research findings might be applied in the real social world, we face a different confusion—one of inconsistent social attitudes toward competition and aggression. Easy generalization from research to interpersonal behaviors of competition and aggression may well require the resolution of these attitudinal inconsistencies.

SUMMARY

People are said to be in **competition** (p. 352) if their interaction is characterized by a low correspondence of outcomes and if each party to the interaction is striving to achieve individual goals. The process of competition may be studied in the laboratory in a variety of **mixed-motive games** (p. 354), such as the Prisoner's Dilemma Game or the Trucking game. Research with these and other experimental games has demonstrated that competition can be increased by changes in the structure of the game, by the opponents' strategy, or by the personal characteristics of the players. Cooperation will be enhanced if the parties are allowed to communicate with each other (p. 358), provided that this communication is used for coordination rather than for transmission of threats.

Among the personal factors that may affect an individual's willingness to engage in sustained competition is his or her level of **resultant achievement motivation** (p. 364). Both a motive to achieve success, traditionally measured by pictures selected from the Thematic Apperception Test (TAT), and a motive to avoid failure, usually measured by the Test Anxiety Questionnaire (TAQ), enter into this resultant achievement motivation. People in whom the resultant level is high will tend to choose tasks of intermediate difficulty and will attribute their success to internal causes. The *attributions* (p. 368) that an individual makes for the occurrence of success and failure will affect pride, shame, and expectations for future performance. A persistent problem is that the measurement of achievement motivation has been unreliable for women. Although it has been suggested that this problem arises because of *fear of success* (p. 371), a better explanation is that both males and females fear success that is gender-inappropriate.

Human **aggression** (p. 375) can be defined as intentional action directed toward the injury of another person, and theories of the origin of aggression can be distinguished from one another on the basis of whether they view the source of instigation as inherent in the person, as coming from the external environment, or as the result of some combination of the two. Foremost among the internal theories are the instinctive theories (p. 377) of Freud and Lorenz; the principal external theory is the **frustration–aggression hypothesis** (p. 378); an important combinatorial theory argues that the excitation from one source of arousal might be transferred (p. 380) to later aggression. The most inclusive explanation is provided by *social learning theory* (p. 382), which covers aggression committed for instrumental purposes as well as in response to aversive events. In recent years controversy has arisen over the role of pornography (p. 382) and televised violence (p. 384) in the creation and amplification of aggressive impulses. It was first thought that televised violence might provide **catharsis** (p. 385) for aggressive impulses that would otherwise be expressed in socially destructive ways. But on balance the recent evidence cent evidence indicates that aggressive pornography will contribute to later aggression, and that televised violence with no sexual content whatsoever can do the same thing.

SUGGESTED ADDITIONAL READINGS

APFELBAUM, E. (1974). On conflicts and bargaining. In L. Berkowitz (Ed.), *Advances in experimental social psychology* (Vol. 7, pp. 103-156). New York: Academic Press. A review of research using mixed-motive games that takes into account the social nature of such interactions. A bit technical at times, but a thorough review.

BANDURA, A. (1973). *Aggression: A social learning analysis.* Englewood Cliffs, NJ: Prentice-Hall. This is an extensive review of theory and research on aggression, concentrating on the social learning position, but with coverage of the major alternatives as well.

MALAMUTH, N. M., & DONNERSTEIN, E. (1982). The effects of aggressive-pornographic mass media stimuli. In L. Berkowitz (Ed.), *Advances in experimental social psychology* (Vol. 15, pp. 103-136). New York: Academic Press. Although written for a professional audience, this chapter is quite accessible to undergraduates. An excellent summary of research on a significant social problem.

CHAPTER ELEVEN

SOCIAL
INFLUENCE

CONTENTS

PREVIEW

The social influence of one individual over another, or of a group over an individual, can be represented in the forces and vectors of Lewin's field theory of social behavior. The sources of social power include the previous socialization of the target person and the characteristics of the influencing agent; many of these depend on social exchange and reinforcement. Counterforces of opposition and avoidance reduce the usable power of the influencing agent. Two major sources of individual social influence are the interpersonal style of Machiavellianism and the power conferred upon legitimate authorities. Groups can exert informational social influence over their members through processes of social comparison, and can exert normative social influence in order to obtain conformity from members. The readiness of an individual to accept social influence is often determined by that person's uncertainty about a correct response or by his or her expectation of personal gain through compliance. Because the social influence process is an interchange between individuals, it is often possible for a consistent minority to alter the position of the majority.

Of all the topics of interest to scientific social psychology, social influence perhaps best matches intuitive conceptions of what the subject matter of the discipline ought to be. We may not be attuned to the accuracy or error of our social perceptions, we may not be conscious of all the factors shaping our social attitudes and self-concept, and we may not reflect upon the degree to which our own actions might help or harm other people. Yet we are usually aware of attempts by others to influence our actions, and of our own attempts to change the behavior of other people. From an intuitive point of view, this process of mutual influence is the real stuff of social behavior: we plead, bargain, and threaten in order to have our views prevail; we resist those who attempt to change our behavior; and the society passes laws to keep this mutual influence within acceptable bounds.

Social influence, like competition and aggression, may be a positive phenomenon or a negative one, depending on the circumstances of influence and on the value system of the person making the judgment. Suppose, for example, that a new high technology manufacturing plant is planned for vacant land near a park. Representatives of labor and business will seek approval of the local governing body, whereas residents who fear that the park will be destroyed will argue against such approval. Each side will see its own efforts as legitimate attempts to exert influence for the betterment of the community, and will think the other group's efforts unjustified and improper. From the standpoint of scientific social psychology, both groups are engaged in a process of social influence. Their ultimate goals may be contradictory, but the means they employ to achieve those goals may be identical.

In this chapter we take a closer look at the process of social influence. We begin with some broad questions about the process, distinguishing between power and influence, illustrating some of the bases of social power, and recalling a distinction drawn in chapter 6 between public compliance and private acceptance. In the next section, we discuss ways in which one individual may exert influence over another, noting the role played by personal factors such as Machiavellianism and by situational variables such as direct orders. Then we turn to the issue of individual conformity with group opinion, showing how this conformity may arise from either informational or normative pressures. Finally, we consider social influence as an interaction, discussing the possible role of an active minority in bringing about social change.

AN OVERVIEW OF POWER AND INFLUENCE

Let us suppose that your professor has announced that there will be an important examination early next week. You know that you need time to study, and as late as Friday afternoon you intend to spend most of the weekend in the library, preparing for the test and catching up on your other work. If you actually did spend a great deal of time studying, we might say either that the professor had power over you or that the professor had influenced your behavior. But now imagine that late on Friday evening some of your close friends decide to take a really special weekend trip, leaving early Saturday morning and returning late Sunday night. They urge you to come along, and against your better judgment you decide to do so. In this case, it is clear that the professor has exerted very little influence on your actions, but what can we say about the professor's power? Is the power less because there was no influence, or will the power just be implemented in a different way (by punishing you with a bad grade for your poor performance on the test)?

Social Power is a Capacity. Although some theorists concerned with organizational decision making equate power with influence, social psychologists more typically distinguish between the two (e.g., Cartwright, 1959; Schopler, 1965; Thibaut & Kelley, 1959). In terms of our example, decision theory would say that in the second case the professor had no power (you went on the weekend trip anyway), whereas the social psychological theories would argue that what had changed was the professor's influence, not his or her power. In keeping with the latter perspective, we define **social power** as the capacity of a person or group to affect the behavior of another person or group. Implicit in this idea of capacity to affect behavior is the qualification "other things being equal." Under normal circumstances, you would probably have spent the weekend studying, and you might even have been able to disregard distractions of an ordinary sort. Only the prospect of an uncommonly attractive distraction kept the professor's power from affecting your action over the weekend (and you realize that this power may result in later unpleasantness).

Social Influence is an Outcome. In contrast to power, **social influence** can be defined as the attitudinal or behavioral change brought about by the application of social power. Although such change is often correlated with the power of the influencing agent, the relationship between power and influence is nonsymmetrical: power is a prerequisite for the occurrence of direct social influence, but a lack of influence does not necessarily imply a lack of power. If the professor had no social power, he or she could not influence you to spend the weekend studying, even under the most favorable of conditions. But the fact that you choose not to comply does not diminish the professor's social power, it only indicates that there are still more powerful agents influencing you to do otherwise.

Field Theory:
A Representation of Influence

The Life Space. The distinction between power and influence can best be illustrated in terms of Lewin's (1942, 1951) **field theory** of social behavior, which holds that the social person exists in a field of forces that affect his or her actions. This total field of environmental factors and personal desires is called the **life space**, and a simple diagram of a life space is shown in part A of Fig. 11.1. The large ellipse represents the life space, whereas the small circle represents the person (P). The area outside the circle but within the ellipse represents the subjective or phenomenological environment; that is, the environment as it is perceived by the person. At any moment in time, the person's behavior is a joint function of his or her own desires, goals, and abilities and the pressures and constraints the person perceives in the environment. In terms of the theory, behavior (b) is a function of the person (P) and the environment (E), or

$$b = f(P, E).$$

This is not, of course, a true mathematical expression, but rather a convenient way to represent a functional relationship. This relationship should be quite familiar to you now, because throughout the book it has been emphasized that situational and personal factors jointly produce social behavior. Indeed, among the behavioral sciences, social psychology is unique for its concentration on the combination of these two classes of factors.

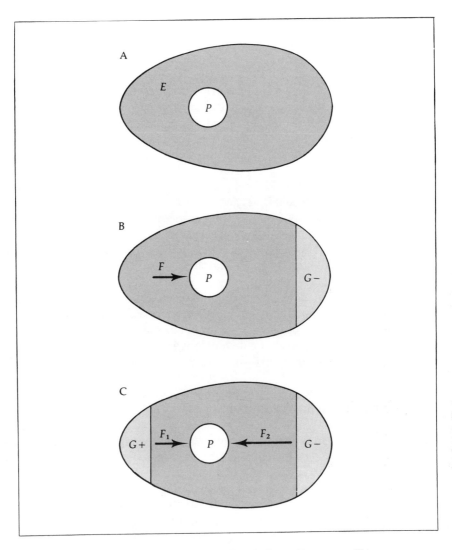

FIGURE 11.1 Diagrams of the life space. Part A shows the person (P) surrounded by the social environment (E). B shows the force (F) exerted by the professor to induce the student (P) to approach the negatively valued goal (G −) of studying for the examination. C shows the force (F_1) exerted by the professor on the student (P) and the opposing force (F_2) exerted by the student's friends to approach the positively valued goal (G +) of taking the weekend trip with them (adapted from Lewin, 1946).

Forces and Vectors. The example of a student who chooses not to study is shown in parts B and C of Fig. 11.1. Part B is a diagram of the situation as it existed until late Friday afternoon, with the student fully intending to approach the negatively valued goal of spending the weekend in the library, because of the force (F_1) exerted by the professor. This force is a *vector*, which has both a direction and a magnitude. In the absence of other outside influences, the force would have been sufficient to overcome the negative value of the goal. But as part C shows, the situation is complicated by the invitation from friends to take a weekend trip. The trip is a positive goal that the student would approach on his or her own, and there is the added force (F_2) provided by the urging of friends. Because the second force is greater than the first, and in the opposite direction, the student will take the trip (and perhaps pay the consequences on the day of the test).

In terms of field theory, an individual's power can be thought of as his or her force vector (F_1 is the power of the professor, F_2 is the power of the friends). The social influence is the *resultant* of all the forces acting upon the person. In this situation, because F_2 is much greater than F_1 and in the opposite direction, the resultant is a vector directed toward the positively valued goal, with a value equal to $F_1 - F_2$. The professor's power (represented by F_1) is not diminished by the actions of the student; it is only overcome by the more powerful force exerted by the student's friends. This conception of power and influence in terms of forces and their resultant, respectively, will be useful to us in our later discussion of the factors that contribute to the power of individuals over each other and the power of groups over their members.

Sources of Social Power

If we continue for a moment with the example of a student's taking a weekend trip instead of studying for an examination, we can identify some of the important sources of social power. In an analysis based on field theory, French and Raven (1959) distinguished among five different kinds of power: reward, coercive, legitimate, referent, and expert power. For purposes of illustration, these are usually described separately, but any single powerful agent is likely to derive power from more than one source at a time.

Exchange of Rewards and Punishments.   Reward power and coercive power are based on aspects of social exchange (described in chapter 8) that we have considered before. I have reward power over you if I can govern either the likelihood that you will receive rewards or the size of the rewards you obtain. **Reward power** is nothing more or less than my ability to provide you with positive reinforcements or with outcomes that, in terms of Thibaut and Kelley's (1959) exchange theory, would be above both your comparison level (CL_{alt}) and your comparison level for alternatives (CL_{alt}). In contrast, **coercive power** is based on the fact that I can provide you with aversive stimuli, or with outcomes that would be below your CL. (In the next section we consider what might happen if these punishments are also below your CL_{alt}.

The ability to bestow social rewards depends on a variety of factors, one of which is the physical attractiveness of the influencing agent. You will recall from chapter 9 the "beautiful is good" stereotype, thought to arise at least in part from the greater reward value of attractive people. The relationship between attractiveness and successful influence is illustrated in a study by Dion and Stein (1978). These investigators had fifth- and sixth-grade children try to influence a same-sex or opposite-sex peer to eat some unappetizing crackers (billed as health food). Successful influence attempts were to be rewarded by payments to the influencers, and the influence targets were aware of this contingency. Attractive boys and girls were more successful in their influencing attempts than were less attractive boys and girls, with the greatest success experienced by attractive girls attempting to influence boys. Moreover, these girls were most successful even though by all of the ratings of their actual behavior (by investigators) they had been trying less hard to accomplish the influence.

Previous Socialization. **Legitimate power** is derived from the previous socialization of the person upon whom such power is to be used. If you have been taught that your elders, your professors, your supervisors have the right to ask you to perform certain tasks for them, then they have legitimate claims to power over you. Legitimacy often combines with reward and coercive power. We respect the responsibility of the police officers to enforce the laws (even though we may disagree with a particular application of those laws), but we would not respect attempts by vigilante groups to punish violations of the same laws. The limitations on legitimate power include the nature and extent of your socialization, as well as the degree to which the powerful agent represents the class of individuals whom you endow with legitimate power. Just as we would think it improper for vigilante groups to police traffic laws, we might think it improper for duly constituted authorities to enforce laws that regulate private morality. People will disagree more about the sorts of behaviors that can be regulated than about the kinds of agents who might be justified in exercising legitimate power.

Characteristics of the Influencing Agent. **Referent power** is derived from a desire for identification with the powerful agent. Here identification is defined as it was in the discussion of Kelman's (1961) three processes of attitude change (Chapter 6): acceptance of influence in order to ensure a satisfying self-defining relationship. Those whom you desire to emulate will have referent power over you. Doing their bidding will make a positive contribution to your self-concept. Finally, **expert power** rests on the fact that the powerful person has skills or knowledge that you lack or need. If you believe that such a person is acting in good faith and being truthful, you will follow his or her recommendations for your activities.

In our example, the professor can be seen to possess reward power (the ability to give you a good grade on the test), coercive power (the ability to flunk you), and legitimate power (his or her giving of tests and your taking them is part of the educational enterprise). To the extent that the test is seen as the professor's way of measuring your knowledge of the material, he or she may have expert power. And to the extent that being thought of as a conscientious student is important to you, the professor may also have some degree of referent power. In contrast, your friends can only exert reward power (the pleasure of the journey and of their company), and some referent power (you want to be thought of as a reliable friend).

With all the different sources of power available to the professor, why did you decide to take the trip with your friends? The answer is, of course, that what finally determines your decision is the total amount of force that each party is able to bring to bear on you, not the variety of sources contributing to that power. There will be cases in which the source of the influencing agent's power will affect the amount of power he or she can wield (rewards obviously generate less resistance than punishments, so fewer rewards are needed to create the same amount of power), but even here the crucial variable is the total amount of power possessed by the influencing agent.

Counterforces to Social Influence

The analysis of power in terms of forces brought to bear upon the target person can be extended to include that person's tendency to resist or avoid the intended influence. We now briefly consider four different counterforces available to the target person: inertia, resistance, avoidance, and opposition. All four of these counterforces will have the effect of reducing the level of influence (the actual change in attitude or behavior), and the last two also limit the amount of power the influencing agent is willing to exercise (as opposed to the amount the agent possesses). The power the influencing agent is willing to exercise is called **usable power**, and later we see why it this is typically a smaller amount than the total power available to the influencing agent.

Inertia and Resistance. Only rarely does someone pressure to do something you were about to do anyway, and in such a case the restriction of your behavioral freedom might generate psychological reactance (discussed more fully in chapter 6). In most instances of social influence, the influencing agent's goal is to change your attitude or behavior from what it would have been without intervention. The first source of force against influence will simply be the *inertia* in your normal actions. You get accustomed to a particular way of perceiving the social environment, to a set of social attitudes, or to a pattern of interpersonal behavior, and it requires a special effort to change away from that routine. You may not even claim that your way is the best way, only that it is comfortable for you. This behavioral inertia is a nonspecific sort of resistance to social influence: It will act as a counterforce to any influence attempt, no matter what the direction of the applied force.

In contrast to the nonspecific character of inertia, *resistance* is a counterforce specifically induced by the nature of the influence attempt. Resistance, like reactance, is a response to a threatened freedom. But it is produced by an attempt to change your actions from what they would have been without influence, rather than an attempt to require you to do what you were already about to do. What would it mean to change in the direction advocated by the powerful person? By accepting influence, you not only change your behavior, you also imply that future influence attempts by the same powerful agent will be successful. You sacrifice a certain amount of personal freedom, and the greater the threatened freedom, the greater the resistance. Suppose that two people ask you to change one of your behaviors; one of the influencing agents is a person you will never see again, whereas the other is a person with whom you interact on a regular basis. Both requests will produce the same degree of counterforce from inertia, but the second will produce the greater resistance. Thus, resistance is the social-influence counterpart of reactance.

Avoidance and Opposition. A third response to the influence attempt is to leave the situation entirely. This *avoidance* response is not so much a true counterforce to the influence attempt as it is a demonstration that the powerful person cannot even force you to subject yourself to continued pressure. The avoidance response in social influence corresponds to the response in a conflict situation of "leaving the field" (Lewin, 1933).

Finally, the most direct counterforce to an influence attempt is direct *opposition*: the exercise of power by the target person against the would-be influencing agent. In terms of our earlier example, avoidance of the professor's power might be accomplished by a psychologically induced trip to the university infirmary on the day of the examination, whereas opposition might be shown by negativistic and argumentative behavior in class—you may still flunk, but you will succeed in ruining the class for everyone else. (Please do not take this particular illustration too literally!)

Usable Power. The avoidance and opposition responses and their effect on the usable power of the powerful person can be shown more clearly in terms of Thibaut and Kelley's (1959) exchange theory. According to this theory, social power is defined as the range of outcomes through which one participant in the interaction can move the other. This definition makes more specific our earlier characterization of social power as a capacity to affect the social behavior of another person or group. If I can give you both highly positive outcomes and highly negative ones, my power over you is greater than it would be if the range of outcomes were smaller. But there is a limit to my willingness to exercise this power to control your outcomes, and two different factors contribute to the limit. First, if I provide you with outcomes that are consistently below your comparison level for alternatives ($CL_{alt.}$), you will avoid my power by leaving the situation. Thus my usable power is restricted to the range of outcomes through which I can move you and still stay above your $CL_{alt.}$.

There is a second restriction on my power, and this corresponds to the counterforce of opposition. In most of the discussion so far, we have assumed that the powerful agent is indifferent to the actions of the target of influence. Certainly that agent would find compliance by the target person more satisfying than defiance, but other than this difference in satisfaction, we have assumed that the target person has little opportunity to affect the outcomes of the powerful agent. In most social relationships, however, that is not the case. The agent and the target person are in a relationship that has either proven valuable to both in the past, or promises to do so in the future, so each has a range of outcomes through which he or she can move the other. The higher the correspondence of those joint outcomes, the less usable power the influencing agent possesses. If by giving you punishment for noncompliance I substantially lower my own outcomes, I will be careful about issuing threats I may not like to carry out. Only in the case of low correspondence of outcomes (e.g., indifference or competition) will the influencing agent's own outcomes permit a broad range of threats, and in this case the influencing agent's power is still limited to the amount of punishment you will accept before leaving the relationship entirely.

Compliance or Acceptance?

The final distinction that should be drawn before moving on to deal with the factors that affect power and influence is the distinction made earlier (Chapter 6) between public compliance and private acceptance. As the poet Ferlinghetti has asserted, "Just because you have silenced a man does not mean you have changed his mind." The target of social influence may publicly comply with the influence attempt, all the time intending privately to find a way to sabotage the influencing agent's wishes. Although the definition of social influence is broad enough to include attitude change, most research has concentrated on public conformity rather than private acceptance, because the dependent variables have been behavioral changes rather than changes in private attitudes or opinions. In the destructive obedience research of Milgram (1963), for example, the principal research question was "How many subjects will administer the most severe shock?" (a question of behavioral conformity), rather than "How many subjects will come to believe that giving severe shocks is a proper thing to do?" (a question of private acceptance).

This is not to say that private acceptance is unimportant to social influence. From the exchange theory perspective, continuance of the interaction depends on the internal satisfaction of the less powerful person (unless, of course, there is dependence upon a relationship that consistently provides outcomes below CL but above CL_{alt}). Variations in bases of social power also ought to affect private acceptance in different ways. Legitimate power should produce more private acceptance than power deemed illegitimate; rewards ought to produce a greater probability of private acceptance, whereas coercion ought to engender compliance alone; the effectiveness of both referent power and expert power depends entirely on private acceptance.

Informational and Normative Social Influence. Deutsch and Gerard (1955) used the designation **informational social influence** to describe social power that produces private acceptance, in order to reflect the fact that such power achieves its ends by providing the target person with the information needed to make a wise decision individually. In contrast to this benign persuasion is the group or individual pressure brought to bear on a target person in an attempt to induce a change in behavior in order to gain rewards or avoid punishments. This sort of pressure is called **normative social influence** (Deutsch & Gerard, 1955) to denote that it achieves success through the imposition of norms on the target person, with the implication that sanctions could follow failure to adhere to those norms.

Both forms of social influence are related to concepts that we have considered in earlier chapters. Specifically, you will recall that in chapter 7 I outlined Kelley's (1952) distinction between the two sorts of self-evaluation functions that can be served by a reference group–the comparison function and the normative function. If a group (or an individual reference person) merely provides an example that you are free to emulate or not, that group or person is serving the comparison function. If in addition the group (or person) establishes rules for your behavior and enforces those rules with sanctions, then it is also serving a normative function. (This function is most often seen in membership groups.)

As it is possible to distinguish informational from normative attempts at influence, it is also possible to describe the behavioral outcomes in terms of Kelman's (1961) three processes of attitude change: compliance, identification, and internalization (discussed more fully in chapter 6). We have already seen that referent power is based on the target person's identification with the influencing agent, and that expert power achieves its success through internalization of the expert's recommendations. Normative social influence is most likely to produce compliance without private acceptance, whereas informational social influence is most likely to produce some form of private acceptance. Whether this will be identification or internalization may well depend on the basis of the influencing agent's power.

A Summary of Social Influence Processes. So far we have characterized the process of social influence, described the bases of power, and outlined the possible responses to influence attempts. In addition, we have recalled material from earlier chapters on the role that different kinds of groups might play in social influence, and have reiterated a distinction among three kinds of attitude change. The way in which all these aspects of social influence might be interrelated is summarized in Table 11.1. Thus, for the case of "persuasion," we see that informational social influence is exerted by groups or individuals serving the comparison function. These are reference groups or individuals who derive their power from expertise, the legitimacy of their position, or their ability to serve as examples (referents) for the target person. The solid arrows in the table indicate that in this process of informational social influence expert and legitimate power will most frequently produce private acceptance through internalization, whereas referent power will most often produce the same private acceptance, but through a process of identification.

In contrast, the "pressure" of normative social influence will be exerted by groups or individuals who serve the normative function. If the influencing agent is a reference group, it will most typically also be a membership group, or if the agent is an individual, it will probably be someone in a stable relationship with the target person. These influence agents derive their power primarily from the rewards they dispense and the punish-

TABLE 11.1 Classification of Social-Influence Process Showing the Conceptual Differences Between "Persuasion" (Informational Social Influence) and "Pressure" (Normative Social Influence)

Characteristic	Conceptual Terms Used to Describe the Characteristic				
Influence process (Deutsch & Gerard, 1955)	Informational social influence			Normative social influence	
Function of the reference individual or group (Kelley, 1952)	Comparison function			Normative function	
Base of power (French & Raven, 1959)	Expert	Legitimate	Reference	Reward	Coercive
Process of change (Kelman, 1961)	Internalization	Internalization	Identification	Compliance	Compliance

ments they threaten to administer. The solid arrows in the table indicate that such tactics are most likely to produce overt compliance without private acceptance. Over the long term (indicated by the dotted arrows), the chance is that rewards will lead to identification and that compliance with threats might (through dissonance reduction) eventually have the same end.

The relationships outlined in Table 11.1 are not intended to exhaust the possible combinations of nature of influence, source of power, and character of response to the influence attempt. Indeed, we have already noted that the bases of power themselves seldom appear in pure form. The table does identify conceptual similarities between aspects of social influence and related material considered in earlier chapters, and it does show that influence is composed of a number of dimensions: the nature of the influencing agent, the source of that agent's power, and the nature of the response. In this respect, our view of social influence draws on a number of other formulations (e.g., Gamson, 1968; Stricker, Messick, & Jackson, 1970) that describe social influence as a multidimensional concept. The final resultant pressure on the target person can still be represented by the familiar single force vector, just so we keep in mind that a variety of different components contribute to that vector, and that the target person has a repertoire of possible responses to the influence attempt. Unfortunately, much of the research on conformity and social influence—with its stress on the dependent variable of behavioral compliance—necessarily oversimplifies the process.

THE INFLUENCE
OF ONE INDIVIDUAL OVER ANOTHER

Machiavellianism:
Influence as an Interpersonal Style

Having discussed some of the complexities in the social influence process, let us now turn to the process in action. Our first concern is the people who seem able to wield social power not by virtue of their legitimate position or expertise, but entirely without any trappings of office. Can extremely successful manipulators be distinguished from other people? What tactics do they employ? In one kind of answer to these questions, Christie and his associates (reported in Christie & Geis, 1970) looked for an individual difference variable that might discriminate between people who were successful at manipulation, regardless of the circumstances, and people who were not. They began by studying historical treatments of social power and influence including two works by Niccolo Machiavelli: *The Prince* and the *Discourses*. In *The Prince*, Machiavelli (1532/1952) not only gave advice about tactics of social influence, he also made a number of specific statements about the nature of humanity. On the assumption that people who would follow Machiavelli's advice about social influence might also share his views of human nature, Christie and his colleagues collected a wide variety of statements from *The Prince* and added some others of their own in a first attempt to measure individual differences in manipulativeness, or **Machiavellianism.** Examples of the statements used are "the best way to handle people is to tell them what they want to hear," and "it is hard to get ahead without cutting corners here and there."

Construction of a Machiavellianism Scale. Christie and his associates edited the complete set of statements and reversed some of the wordings (for example, Machiavelli's views on the prevalence of cowardice became "most men are brave) to guard against the *acquiescence* response set. In answering questionnaires, people (some more than others) tend to agree with the items as worded, no matter what the content might be. Under these circumstances, if all items were worded in the same direction, the final score would be inflated by the tendency to agree. The researchers then presented the edited statements in a Likert format (degrees of agreement and disagreement, as discussed more fully in the Methodological Appendix) to undergraduate students at three universities. As a result of this pretesting, a final sample of 20 items, half worded in the positive direction and half worded in the negative direction, was selected as the most discriminating.

Selecting items that will discriminate people high in Machiavellianism from people who are low on the trait is only the beginning. Not surprisingly, many of the Machiavellianism items are very low in social desirability (or very high, if reverse-worded). How is this confounding influence of social desirability to be removed? The solution that Christie and his associates adopted first paired each Machiavellianism item with another item irrelevant to Machiavellianism that was *matched* in social desirability to the Machiavellianism-keyed item, and asked subjects to choose which of the two was "most like them." In theory, then, a subject would have no reason (on the basis of social desirability) to endorse one as opposed to the other, so the selection presumably would reflect Machiavellianism. This kind of scale, consisting of pairs of statements, only one of which is to be endorsed, is known as a **forced-choice scale.**

Unfortunately, when forced to choose between two equally undesirable self-characterizations, many subjects just refused to make the choice and left the item blank. To deal with this problem the investigators next included a "buffer" item, the social desirability value of which was opposite that of the Machiavellianism-keyed item and its matched item. Then, within each triad of items, subjects were asked to say which item was most like them and which item was least like them. A person who was concerned about social desirability could, in a triad containing undesirable Machiavellianism and matched items, say that the buffer item was most like him or her. Then the measurement of Machiavellianism turned on which of the two remaining items was claimed to be "least like" the subject: A low Mach would say that the Machiavellianism item was "least like," whereas a high Mach would say that the matched item was "least like." This final version of the scale, consisting of the 20 triads, is known as the Mach-V, because it is the fifth version of the scale.

What are Machiavellians Like?   What sort of person scores high on the final version of the Machiavellianism scale? First, let us see what personal characteristics do not seem related to Machiavellianism. Studies reported by Christie and Geis (1970) indicate no correlation between Machiavellianism and IQ; data from Wrightsman and Cook (1965) show no important correlations between Machiavellianism and racial attitudes; a national survey conducted in 1963 by the National Opinion Research Corporation (Christie & Geis, 1970) found no correlation between Machiavellianism and political party or candidate preference; Christie and Geis (1970) report few significant relationships between Machiavellianism and personality measures such as achievement motivation, anxiety, or authoritarianism (a recent bibliography of Machiavellianism research has been compiled by Hanson & Vleeming, 1982).

These results suggest that Machiavellianism is better regarded as an *interpersonal style* than as an enduring personality trait, and other research confirms this interpretation. For example, Exline, Thibaut, Hickey, and Gumpert (1970) had subjects participate in a series of decision tasks with an experimental confederate. In the middle of the series, the experimenter was called out of the room, ostensibly for a long-distance telephone call. In his absence, the confederate looked at the answers for the remaining tasks with such a flourish that it implicated the subject in his cheating. The experimenter then returned, the series of tasks was completed, and the experimenter expressed amazement at the success of the pair, first implicitly and then explicitly accusing them of cheating. The dependent variable of interest to us is the amount of eye contact maintained by the subject with the experimenter, both during the accusation and in the subsequent two minutes. Compared to low Machiavellians, the high Machiavellianism subjects actually increased their eye contact with the experimenter right after the formal accusation. After being confronted with an instance of unethical behavior, it is the high Mach, as well as the honest person, who can look you in the eye and deny the charges.

What Social Conditions Favor Machiavellians?   This experiment, and a large number of others reported by Christie and Geis (1970), establish the high Mach as a manipulator of other people, suggesting both aspects of disposition and characteristics of the situation that permit the person to make the most of opportunities that present themselves. The principal dispositional difference between the high and low scorer is that high Machs show much greater emotional detachment in the interpersonal situation. They are oriented toward cognitions – rules of the game, rational solutions to problems – rather than toward the persons who may be taking part in the interaction. They initiate and control the structure of the interaction, setting limits, defining goals, recommending procedures; whereas the low Machs accept and follow the structure established by others. Not surprisingly, high Machs are quite resistant to sheer social pressure. They can be persuaded by rational arguments (informational social influence) just as easily as can low Machs, but they are much less susceptible to normative social influence attempted by others in the situation.

High machs are best able to take advantage of their substantial emotional detachment in interactions that provide advantages for them at the expense of the low Mach. The "best" situation, from the standpoint of the high Mach, is one that (a) involves *face-to-face interaction*, (b) has some latitude for improvisation, and (c) offers the possibility for the high Mach to *arouse irrelevant affect* in the other participants. Machiavellianism is, as we have seen, less of a personality trait than an interpersonal style, and it is a style that cannot be effective except in person. There cannot be fixed structure for the interaction, and there cannot be sufficient time for the other participants to reflect on the situation before taking action. The interaction must be face-to-face so that the high Mach can concentrate on strategy whereas the low Mach gets personally involved with the participants; there must be enough flexibility in the rules so that the high Mach can tailor new ones to suit his or her purposes; and there must be the potential for playing on the emotions of the other people who are likely to be taking their own positions seriously. High Machs cannot be wedded to ideological commitments of their own, for then they would be unable to make the necessary compromises (it is not surprising that Machiavellianism is unrelated to political preferences), and they must be well enough adjusted so that personal problems do not complicate their goals for the interaction. Given these limits on disposition and situation, the high Mach can be an extremely successful agent of social influence, even in the absence of any obvious source of social power.

Direct Influence:
Obedience to Authority

A vast amount of social influence among individuals takes place in the context of giving and following orders. Obviously, the armed forces depend on the "chain of command" for everything from the completion of routine clerical tasks to successful performance in battle, but a similar relationship between supervisor and subordinate can be found in any stable organization. In most cases, the orders are not stated directly, but they still rest on a tacit agreement that the supervisor's status provides the legitimacy for exercise of social influence. The boss may say to an assistant "Will you please prepare this report for me," the department chairman may ask a new assistant professor, "Do you think you could teach Introductory Psychology next term," or your apartment manager may ask politely if it is possible for you to keep your parties just a bit more quiet. But no matter how pleasantly the request is phrased, it contains an implicit threat. An employee who hopes to continue to receive salary increases will not often disregard requests from his or her employer. A professor who hopes to maintain the esteem of colleagues will not refuse to carry a fair share of the teaching responsibilities. A tenant who wishes to stay in the apartment complex will not take the manager's advice too lightly.

The Danger of Uncritical Acceptance of Influence. This sort of individualized normative social influence depends both on the provision of appropriate rewards for compliance and on the threat of punishment for failure to comply. It also depends on the target person's belief that the influence attempt is justified and that the influencing agent is acting within the bounds of legitimate authority. The smooth operation of any structured organization requires acceptance by subordinates of legitimate directives issued by their supervisors. But the process of individual normative social influence is so prevalent that its uncritical acceptance may have disastrous consequences. In 1971, a platoon of American soldiers under the command of Lt. William Calley murdered 22 Vietnamese men, women, and children in the village of My Lai. The participating soldiers asserted that they had been ordered to shoot, and in his subsequent trial Lt. Calley argued that he, too, had been following orders. In 1973, it was disclosed that the acting director of the Federal Bureau of Investigation, L. Patrick Gray, had destroyed papers that might have proven politically embarrassing to the Nixon administration. In 1975, a Senate committee revealed that the Central Intelligence Agency had attempted several times in preceding years to assassinate Cuba's leader, Fidel Castro. These are not isolated instances, only well known ones, and they can tell us something about the process of individual normative social influence.

These examples hold three common threads that are relevant for our purposes. First, people who did not originate the idea for each action were nevertheless involved in the action – in an important sense they were following orders. Second, it has been virtually impossible to pinpoint the responsibility for initiating each action. Lt. Calley is the only one to have been convicted of a crime, or otherwise to be held personally responsible in a formal proceeding, and there is some reason to think that at least the *climate* leading to his order to shoot was the responsibility of his military and civilian superiors. Third, the disclosure of each event was accompanied by a public outcry sufficient to indicate a general lack of approval for the action that had been taken. Thus, doubt about the legitimacy of the actions occurred after the fact, but at the time of compliance the various subordinates did not consider the requests made of them to be illegitimate. It would be tempting to condemn the participants in these incidents, attributing the occurrence in each case to some flaws in the character of the people involved, but to do so would be to deny the power of the situation and the degree to which all of us are likely to do what is asked of us.

Destructive Obedience. The experiments on destructive obedience conducted by Milgram (1963) are perhaps the most convincing demonstration of this tendency to follow orders. A massacre of people considered to be "the enemy" can be attributed to the conditions under which a guerrilla war must be fought; the mistakes of an appointed official can be thought of as misguided loyalty; and the excesses of an agency might be attributable to overzealous performance of its legitimate mandate. Whether any of these reasons serves as a sufficient excuse for the action taken is a personal value judgment. For our purposes here, the critical point is that these attributions to the specific circumstances suggest that only in rare cases will people succumb to destructive individualized social influence. The major contribution of Milgram's research is to demonstrate just how prevalent such influence can be.

You will recall from chapter 1 that subjects in Milgram's (1963) first experiment participated individually with an experimental confederate in what was described as a learning study. The subject was always chosen to "teach" the confederate a series of paired associates by administering an increasing level of electric shock for every successive failure during testing. The situation was purposely contrived so that the subject would be placed in the position of following orders from the experimenter to continue giving these shocks long after they had obviously become intolerably painful to the learner. The dependent variable was the point on the shock scale at which the subject adamantly refused to proceed, even after prodding by the experimenter. Contrary to all advance predictions, fully 60% of the subjects continued with the procedure until they were administering the maximum shock to an unresponsive learner. For these subjects, the experimenter's attempted influence was highly successful.

The Power of the Situation. How are these findings to be explained? First, let us consider the obvious sources of power over the subject that were available to the experimenter. Coercive power must be ruled out, because no subject was ever threatened with punishment for failure to comply. Reward power is also an unlikely explanation, because it was repeatedly stated that the subject's payment for participation was for simply showing up at the laboratory, not for any actions he or she might take during the experiment. It is doubtful that the experimenter was a positive referent for many of the subjects, in view of what he was asking them to do. In later versions of the research, Milgram (1965) moved from the psychology laboratory at Yale to a run-down brownstone building in Bridgeport, Connecticut. Compliance was somewhat lower in that setting than in the Yale laboratory, although a majority of subjects still complied. This argues against an explanation in terms of legitimate and expert power, leaving us with the impression that none of the bases of power alone provides a convincing explanation for the effect.

In other changes, Milgram substituted a variety of different victim behaviors and altered the proximity of the experimenter to the subject and the subject to the victim. All of these variations affected the dependent variable (percent compliance) to some degree. Compliance decreased when the experimenter gave his instructions over the telephone instead of in person, and decreased still further when the instructions were delivered by a tape recorder with no experimenter present. Subject compliance also decreased when the victim was brought into the room with the subject, and still further when the subject was required to hold the victim's hand on a shock plate in order to administer punishment. Even in this last condition, however, over 30% of the subjects followed instructions to the bitter end.

As Milgram (1965) has noted, the destructive obedience paradigm is an excellent example of the analysis of social influence in terms of the forces brought to bear on the subject's actions. An internal restraining force against injuring another person does exist, and this is enhanced by the immediacy of the victim. Opposing this force toward morality is the force exerted by the experimenter and the situation. Contributing to this force might be at least some legitimacy inherent in the research process (no matter what the setting), the experimenter's willingness to accept the responsibility for the outcome, and the experimenter's immediacy to the subject.

Influence Outside the Laboratory. One might perceive all these factors as specific to the experimental setting, but before we become complacent, let us see how they generalize to the real world. There we do not often deal with experimenters, but we do interact with people in positions of legitimate authority, we recognize that the responsibility for an action lies with the person who ordered the action performed, and we are all too willing to leave decision making to "the experts," who presumably have more information than is available to us. From the child who says to a parent "All right, if you say so," in a tone that clearly indicates who will be at fault if there is trouble, to the congressional representative who argues that the president should be allowed to make important decisions "because he has all the information," people serve as the instruments of legitimate authority and are only too pleased to shift to others the responsibility even for their own actions. It is certainly true that questioning every attempt at legitimate social influence would be detrimental to society. But a failure to recognize the power of the situation, and a wholly uncritical acceptance of all individualized normative social influence may be equally dangerous. A reasonable compromise can be reached only if we attend to the situation in which that influence occurs and consider the forces affecting our actions.

Selling, Buying, and Giving

Observe the Professionals. As important as direct orders, explicit or implied, are in everyday life, they do not exhaust the varieties of individual social influence. Nor do they stand as the only example of the power of the situation to affect human behavior. How many of us brag that we never purchase anything unless it is "on sale," but do so little comparison shopping that we have no idea what the item's "real" price might be? For that matter, how many of us have bought something we truly didn't want, or agreed to do something we really didn't want to do, only because we couldn't find a convenient way to refuse? What is each of these examples? An instance of successful social influence. External forces have been applied to change the resultant vector from what it would have been without the outside influence.

Many of the common techniques of social influence outside the laboratory have recently been described in a fascinating book by Cialdini (1985), who used his training as a social psychologist in an attempt to understand why "All my life I've been a patsy. For as long as I can recall, I've been an easy mark for the pitches of peddlers, fund raisers, and operators of one sort or another" (p. i). What Cialdini did, in addition to a great deal of experimental research on compliance, was engage in participant observation among compliance professionals. He answered newspaper advertisements for sales traineeships, and in a similar fashion penetrated advertising, public relations, and fund raising agencies in order to study their techniques of social influence. In short, he became an aspiring compliance professional, and learned from the experts.

Automatic Responding. As noted in chapter 8, a great deal of our social behavior is learned according to principles of social learning theory, and much of what is learned involves informal rules of social exchange. The point that Cialdini (1985) makes is that a great deal of this material is overlearned to such a degree that it becomes automatic, and an effective "compliance professional" will take advantage of this overlearning to produce immediate compliance, rather than thoughtful consideration of the requests that are being made.

One example Cialdini cites to illustrate the point describes a fundraising technique—the giving away of flowers—familiar to most people who have been through any major airport. As you walk through the airport lobby, loaded down with your suitcases and late for your plane, a member of a religious sect approaches you, steps in your path, and either gives you a flower or pins it on your coat. You are not permitted to give the flower back, even if you do not want it. Then the sect member asks you for a donation to support the group's religious and humanitarian activities. "This benefactor-before-beggar strategy has been wildly successful for the Hare Krishna Society, producing large-scale economic gains and funding the ownership of temples, businesses, houses, and property in 108 centers in the United States and abroad" (Cialdini, 1985, p. 23).

How does this tactic, and its merchandising equivalent, the "free sample" or the "free estimate" work? By engaging a principle of reciprocation, a fundamental element of any social exchange. We enjoy most those interactions in which there is a high correspondence of outcomes. We learn to rely on others to help us do the things we cannot do alone, expecting all the time to "return the favor." Our helpfulness in nonemergency situations will be strongly influenced by the norms of reciprocity and social responsibility. We believe that exchanges are equitable if each person's outcomes are proportional to his or her inputs, and even when it harms our own interest, we restore equity by giving away enough of our own assets to make the situation "fair." The common element in all of these situations is the achieving of some kind of interpersonal balance through reciprocal exchange. This "reciprocation rule" ordinarily serves us quite well, but it can be made to work against us if we respond to a contrived setting in an overlearned way, without thinking of the consequence, and without realizing that the entire relationship has been forced upon us.

Six Weapons of Influence. According to Cialdini (1985) there are six general psychological principles that can be used to produce virtually automatic compliance. Reciprocation is one that we have discussed in a number of different contexts, such as the providing of help and the determination of fairness in social exchange. Others that have also been discussed previously include *authority, liking, consistency,* and *social proof.* Milgram's (1963) research alone is eloquent testimony to the power of authority. What about liking? We will comply more readily with those who like us than with those who do not, and this principle can be turned against us. When was the last time you picked a new blazer off a rack in a clothing store, only to have the salesperson say "I'm sorry, but that really looks terrible on you?" On the contrary, what the salesperson says is positive, something that confirms your taste or, even better, suggests that he or she shares your taste (remember similarity and attraction?). So liking, like reciprocation, can lead to the unwitting acceptance of influence.

As for consistency, if a "compliance professional" can get you to make a public commitment to attitudes of one sort or another, it will be simpler to sell you a product consistent with that commitment than if no public expression was obtained. Concerned about your health? (Who isn't?) Try to maintain a vigorous life even though you have to spend a good deal of time studying? (Of course.) Find it easier to give yourself a good workout when there are like-minded people engaging in activity at the same time? (Yes, I do.) Good, then you need a year's membership in the Superfit Spa. (Oops.)

The principle of social proof has several variants. First is that large numbers of people cannot be wrong. A product that is "best selling" or "fastest growing" must be good, or all of those people would have stopped buying it. Sometimes it is not how many people believe in a product or an idea, but who the people are, the attitude change technique of prestige suggestion. Still another possibility is the *strength* of commitment among the true believers, such as the intensity of the beliefs of the doomsday group described in chapter 2. Each participant's conviction that the world was, indeed, going to end, was reinforced by the conviction of the other members. We see more of the principle of social proof in the discussion of group processes in chapter 12.

The last "weapon of influence" Cialdini describes is the principle of *scarcity*. Things that are truly rare are prized for their very distinctiveness. Collectors of everything from comic books to antique automobiles know that the sale value of an item will increase as it becomes less common. Knowing this general rule, we are susceptible to the claims of a compliance professional who can convince us that this will be our "last opportunity" to do or buy something, either because the product is being discontinued or because it is becoming unavailable in our area. People who would not ordinarily be interested in borrowing a recording by a particular musical group, much less buying one of the group's records, will nonetheless pay twice the price of an album to attend the group's "last concert tour." Cialdini suggests that one explanation for scarcity effects is psychological reactance (Chapter 6): behavioral freedoms that are threatened become more valuable.

Whether the weapon of influence is authority, reciprocation, liking, consistency, social proof, or scarcity, it is typically wielded by a single individual against another individual. The influence professional is successful not because he or she has the real backing of other people, but because the situation has been structured to make it very difficult for the (unwitting) target person to do anything else. Certainly it is true that in social proof the names of others are invoked to provide legitimacy to the claims, and in scarcity the presence of others is noted to increase the felt competition for the diminishing resources. Even in these latter two cases, the group itself does not apply the pressure. It is to this more direct group-based influence that we now turn.

GROUP INFLUENCE OVER THE INDIVIDUAL

Conformity

Much of our social behavior is influenced not only by the other individuals in our lives, but also by the social groups that are important to us. A **social group** is more than a statistical aggregate (such as people over 40, college graduates, or two-car families); it is a collectivity that has psychological implications for the individual. As Kiesler and Kiesler (1969) have noted, a group will have this effect only if the person (a) is aware of the other members of the group, (b) either defines himself or herself as a member of the group, or would like to do so, and (c) feels that the group is emotionally or cognitively personally significant. Because the reference group serves as a standard for self-evaluation, its effects are achieved principally through informational social influence. When the reference group is also a membership group, its effects may then be accomplished through normative social influence. It should be emphasized that in many real social groups these distinctions will be blurred: Reference groups often double as membership groups, serving both the normative and the comparison function.

A Definition of Conformity.   According to one accepted definition, **conformity** is a change in belief or behavior toward a group as a result of real or imagined group pressure (Kiesler & Kiesler, 1969). Let us see how this definition compares with terms used to describe other forms of social influence. To begin with, conformity is a kind of influence (change). Conformity in belief corresponds to private acceptance (probably based on identification, rather than internalization); conformity in behavior corresponds to public compliance. Finally, the distinction between real pressure and imagined pressure reflects the difference between normative and informational social influence. Thus conformity is a more inclusive term than most used so far in this chapter, because it applies to any sort of influence by a group on an individual, as long as the change in the individual's position is in the direction of the group's position.

Other Responses to Pressure.   But acceptance of influence is not the only possible response to group pressure. At least two other responses have received attention: independence and anticonformity. In terms of the counterforces to influence outlined earlier in the chapter, **independence** could encompass the counterforces of inertia and resistance (the target person could steadfastly maintain his or her own position despite the group pressure), or it could be reflected in avoidance (the target person could leave the sphere of influence of the group). The other response, **anticonformity** (action in direct opposition to the group norms), corresponds to the individual counterforce of opposition, and would be reflected in an active attempt to sabotage the group's objectives. As in the case of individual social influence, the response to an instance of group pressure will depend on the balance of forces present in the situation. If the group is highly attractive to the target person, if it has the capability of helping that person achieve his or her own goals, or if the person has few alternative relationships, the pressure to conform will have a substantial effect. If, on the other hand, the group has little attraction for the individual, the usable power it can exert will diminish. We now examine more closely both informational and normative social influence as they might be exerted by a group on an individual.

Group Informational Social Influence

Sherif's Study of Autokinetic Effects. Sherif's (1936) pioneering research on the formation of social norms for perceptual judgments was described in detail in chapter 1. You will recall that Sherif employed the autokinetic effect—the perceptual illusion that occurs when a person views a point of light in a darkened room—to study convergence in judgment. In a first series of trials, subjects privately estimated how much the light appeared to move; in a second series of trials, these judgments were announced out loud and the several subjects converged on a common norm for perceived movement. In the final stage of the experiment, subjects once again made private judgments, but these remained close to the norms established in the second phase of the research. Despite its expressed concern with norms, this research actually typifies the process of informational social influence: the group simply defined the perceptual situation for the individual, and sanctions were not even implied for failure to adhere to the group standards.

Social Reality and Social Comparison. Imagine that you had been a subject in this experiment, and suppose you believe the point of light to be moving around through an arc of more than a foot (this sort of estimate would be much higher than average). You have never been in a situation precisely like the experimental setting, and you are quite uncertain about most of your answers. There are no objective standards against which you can evaluate your perceptual experience. In the second set of trials the responses of other subjects permit you to judge your own perceptions through social comparison processes (discussed in chapter 7). You have no reason to doubt the report of the other subjects, but you learn that they are quite different from your own. These other reports constitute the **social reality** (Festinger, 1950) of the situation, and it makes you uncomfortable to express an opinion that differs so greatly from this consensus.

According to social comparison theory, this dependency on the prevailing social reality will exert pressure on you to change at least your public report of your perceptual experience, if not the experience itself. The fact that in the third session of the experiment your privately reported judgments still follow the previously established norm indicates that the informational social influence has produced private acceptance as well as public compliance. You have changed your view of the phenomenon not because the group was explicitly threatening you with punishment for your errors, but because you have used the group opinion to define the situation for you.

Norm Transmission Through Information.   The informational social influence present in Sherif's research differs from that found in the real social world in one respect. The group standard did not exist prior to the public judgments made by all subjects. Strictly speaking, only the subjects whose initial public pronouncements differed from the later group consensus actually conformed to that consensus. Those whose initial judgments were near the later norm did not actually change their beliefs, and no group pressure to change was ever exerted on them. In most cases of comparison with a group outside the laboratory, however, the group has an existing position on the issue in advance of the comparison by the target individual. The particular target person may be ignorant of the group's stand, but at least the position is not in the process of development at the time of comparison. This characteristic limits the external validity of Sherif's research to cases of consensus formation, but a later study with the autokinetic effect extends the findings to a pre-existing norm.

In this study of norm transmission (Jacobs & Campbell, 1961), subjects were placed in the autokinetic situation in groups of four. Each group member made public judgments of the degree of movement for 30 trials. At the conclusion of the first block of 30 trials, one subject in the group was replaced by a new subject, and then the group made another 30 judgments. Then a second experienced group member was replaced by a naive subject, and this process of judgment and replacement of the most experienced member continue for a total of 11 blocks of 30 trials each. Thus, by the end of the fourth block of trials, all the subjects present during the first block had been replaced.

For each new replacement, the first series of 30 trials consisted of a comparison between his or her own perceptions and the previously established norm for the group—just the sort of situation that might prevail in the real social world. There were two experimental conditions in the research. In the Control condition, the very first group consisted of four naive subjects, but in the Arbitrary Norm condition, the very first group consisted of three experimental confederates and one naive subject. The confederates had been instructed to make extreme judgments of movement, averaging 16 inches of movement per trial. Not surprisingly, the first naive subject placed in with the three confederates also made estimates that were extreme (more than 14 inches per trial on the average). In short, this subject conformed to the group's pre-established norm.

What is more interesting than the naive subject's conformity to the arbitrary norm is that this norm was transmitted to later replacement subjects, even after all the confederates had been replaced. Each new replacement in the Arbitrary Norm condition made judgments less extreme than those made by the previous replacement, but until the seventh trial block (long after all confederates had departed), the judgments in the Arbitrary Norm condition were more extreme than those in the Control condition. The arbitrary norm had been successfully transmitted to several generations of naive subjects.

This experiment is more than an illustration of informational social influence. It also serves as a model for too many organizations, bureaucracies, and informal social groups. Laws are left on the books long after the function they originally served is no longer needed; bureaucracies insist that certain procedures must be followed because in their memory "it has always been done that way;" informal groups cling to "traditions" that have become outmoded. In most of these instances the original procedures and judgments were–unlike those in the experiment–not arbitrary. But they nevertheless impede social change that might be highly constructive. People begin to feel comfortable with rules they have privately accepted, and cognitive consistency needs preclude any dramatic shifts in belief just to accommodate newcomers. Informational social influence may not be as effective as normative social influence in producing immediate public compliance, but its long-term effects may be much stronger.

A Step Toward Normative Influence

The Asch Experiment.   The research by Sherif (1936) and by Jacobs and Campbell (1961) shows how informational social influence can produce both compliance and acceptance when the stimulus situation is ambiguous. No normative pressure is needed, because the information provided by the group defines the situation for the target person. But what happens when the group judgment quite clearly differs from objective reality as perceived by the target person? In order to answer this question, Asch (1951) conducted what has become a classic study of social influence.

Imagine for a moment that you were a subject in such an experiment. You would arrive at the laboratory to find eight other subjects (all of whom are actually confederates) already seated in chairs that had been arranged in a semicircle in front of a blackboard. You would take the only vacant seat, the second one from the end of the semicircle. After appropriate introductions, the experimenter would describe the task as one of visual discrimination and would show you a sample of the stimulus materials. These would be vertical lines drawn on large pieces of cardboard. Two pieces of cardboard would be placed on the chalk rail of the blackboard one at a time, one containing the *standard* line (from 2 inches long to 10 inches long) and one containing as set of three *comparison* lines (one the same length as the standard, one longer, and one shorter). Your task in the experiment would be to say which of the comparison lines was equal in length to the standard. Unlike estimation of movement in the autokinetic situation, this judgment task is unambiguous, and if you were to do the task in private you would make virtually no errors.

Ostensibly so that the experimenter could keep track of the judgments, all of you would be asked to state your decisions aloud, beginning with the person at the other end of the semicircle from you. Thus, by the time it was your turn, you would have heard the judgments of seven of the eight other people. In a typical experiment there would be 18 such trials, and on 6 of these (the Neutral trials) all other people would report decisions that agreed with your perceptual experience. On the other 12 trials (the Critical trials), however, every other subject would report what seemed to you to be the wrong choice. The question is, how will you respond when confronted by a unanimous majority whose opinion differs so widely from your perceptual experience?

Factors Contributing to Conformity. Research through the years with variants of this procedure has demonstrated that the answer to this question depends on a number of factors. Even with a judgment as unambiguous as the one in Asch's (1951) original study, errors were made on approximately one third of the critical trials, and not surprisingly, greater ambiguity of the task enhances conformity (Allen, 1965). Asch found extensive individual differences, with some subjects remaining independent on almost all critical trials and other subjects yielding on nearly all. The independent subjects (those who conformed less than half of the time) were either quite confident of their responses, or withdrawn and nervous. The yielding subjects (who conformed on more than half of the trials) most frequently distorted their judgment (actively considered the possibility that the majority was wrong, but adopted its position as a way to resolve their own uncertainty), sometimes distorted their action (knowing quite well that the majority was wrong, but conforming only to go along with the group), and infrequently distorted their perception (thinking that the majority was factually correct).

In a review of conformity research, Allen (1965) shows that greater conformity occurs when subjects respond publicly rather than privately, when the group is attractive to the subjects, when the group members are similar to one another (in gender, ability), and when the issue in question is relatively unimportant to the individual under pressure. These four factors can be seen as contributing to the forces impinging on the target person. The force of the group is increased by its attractiveness, cohesiveness, similarity among members, and demand for public responses. The resistance available to the target person will depend on his or her certainty (largely a function of the ambiguity of the task), and willingness to take a stand on an issue of principle (importance).

Unanimity of the Majority. One aspect of the situation that has received a great deal of attention is the nature of the majority. The available research evidence suggests that unanimity among the majority is much more important than its sheer size. In his initial series of studies, Asch (1951) found that a unanimous majority of 16 was no more effective in producing conformity than was a unanimous majority of three. With very few exceptions, subsequent research confirms the finding that conformity does not increase with the size of the majority as long as that majority consists of at least three people (Allen, 1965). In contrast to the marginal effects of changes in group size beyond three, changes in the unanimity of the majority have profound effects on conformity. Again, in the initial series of studies Asch found that errors dropped from 32% to 5% with the addition of a single confederate who agreed with the naive subject against the majority.

Social Support for Nonconformity.   There are at least two things that you learn when one other member of the group agrees with you against the majority. First, you discover that the group does not punish those who contradict its majority position. As we see in chapter 12, fear of being rejected from a group can be a powerful contributor to conformity, so learning that dissent is tolerated removes an important threat. Second, you obtain much-needed support for your construction of social reality. In at least one case, your private judgment matches that of another person.

In the Asch (1951) study, these two aspects of social support were confounded, but they have been examined separately in a program of research by Allen and his associates (1975). Some of these studies have dealt with judgments about physical entities, whereas others have required subjects to provide information or state their opinions on a variety of issues. In a typical study, the subject is faced with a unanimous majority, or has the social support provided by a single dissenter who either agrees with the subject or takes a position more extreme than that taken by the majority. The presence of a dissenter has the greatest effect on nonconformity by the subject when the judgments to be made are physical ones, and a dissenter who agrees with the subject reduces conformity more than does one who takes a third position. But in all cases, people are more independent if they do not have to stand alone to be so.

SOCIAL INFLUENCE AND SOCIAL CHANGE

The Readiness to Accept Influence

Uncertainty and Personal Advantage.   We have seen that an individual's social power, or that of a group, can be derived from a variety of sources, that the application of this power may induce a number of counterforces, and that the response to attempted influence may range from resistance and anticonformity through public compliance to private acceptance. Across all the examples and the research, two basic factors contribute to the target person's final willingness to accept social influence. These are uncertainty, about the correct, or appropriate response, and the personal advantage that might be gained by compliance. Any single instance of social influence need not involve both factors, indeed, the former is more typical of informational social influence, whereas the latter is more characteristic of normative social influence.

The Response to Individual Pressure. Let us consider first the influence of one individual over another. In an interaction between a high Mach and a low Mach, the high's wishes will usually prevail, and this can be described in terms of uncertainty. For the high Mach, the latitude for improvisation represents an opportunity to structure the situation to his or her own advantage, but for the low, this flexibility increases uncertainty about what responses might be appropriate. The high's concentration on cognitions leads the person to discard personal feelings as irrelevant to the task at hand, but such feelings and emotional involvements complicate the low Mach's social decisions.

In an interaction between a compliance professional and an unsuspecting target person, the role of uncertainty is slightly different. To begin with, the target person is responding with what might best be described as a misplaced certainty. Only after you have given the solicitor more than you would otherwise have donated do you begin to question whether you have done the right thing for you. True, the weapons of social proof and scarcity represent attempts by the compliance professional to eliminate uncertainty by reference either to the opinions of a near-unanimous majority or to the intrinsic value of an object about to become scarce. So your initial uncertainty about the value of the objects involved will definitely increase the likelihood of your compliance. But most of the techniques of the compliance professional can be regarded as involving uncertainty only from the viewpoint of an outside observer. The compliance professional knows what the real situation is, whereas the target of influence does not. Perhaps lack of awareness of the true constraints built into the situation is just the extreme of uncertainty.

When the interaction is between a legitimate authority and a target person, uncertainty and personal advantage will both contribute to the willingness to accept influence. Milgram's (1963) subjects, and their counterparts in the real social world, do as they are told unless they become convinced that it would be morally wrong to do so. In their uncertainty about their responsibilities in the situation, they rely on the judgment of the expert and the legitimacy of his or her authority. If our dealings with compliance professionals are characterized by our unwittingly granting permission to the professional to define the situation, our dealings with authorities can be regarded as involving a conscious decision to do the same. Most of the previous social learning of Milgram's subjects taught them that it is more costly to disobey the requests of legitimate authority than to comply with those requests, and if there is any doubt at all, they will be more likely to comply, letting the authority take the risks and the responsibility.

The Response to Group Pressure.   Uncertainty and personal advantage can also be seen in the individual's response to group pressure. In the autokinetic situation, we seen an excellent example of the effects of uncertainty. Here the group defines the situation for the individual; to reduce perceptual ambiguity, the person engages in social comparison (that outside the laboratory has proven quite helpful) and shifts his or her judgments to agree with the discovered consensus. In the Asch situation, there is no question about the perceptual judgment, but there is a high degree of confusion regarding the "correct" response in the situation. Although individual differences in perceptual acuity are commonplace, finding yourself a minority of one cannot help but shake your confidence. In this instance there is comfort in being wrong with others instead of correct alone. The Asch situation is a group version of the contrived situation employed by the influence professional, with a crucial difference. Participation in the Asch situation is followed by a debriefing that explains just how structured the setting really was.

Because of frequent extremes in its manifestation, the term *conformity* has acquired pejorative connotations. When we hear of people who conform, we often get a mental picture of the subjugation of individual wills to the arbitrary whims of a powerful authority. We would do well to remember that although some conformity may indeed be mindless, much of the acceptance of social influence may be the result of active processes – social comparison to reduce uncertainty and a desire to maximize outcomes – that in other circumstances would lead to effective individuality. In addition, if there were no conformity at all, and no obedience to legitimate authority, anarchy and chaos might make thoughtful individual action impossible.

Contingency in Interaction

As noted at several points in the chapter, one way to conceive of the process of social influence is to ask what the target person would have done without influence from others, and to compare that to his or her actions following intervention by the influencing agent. But it is unlikely that this intervention will produce a completely changed target person. Some actions will still be the result of the person's own wishes. In addition, because of the target person's ability to resist, avoid, or oppose influence, the powerful agent's behavior may itself be affected by the actions of the target. The two parties must be regarded as participating in an ongoing interaction in which each one's actions are partly determined by his or her own goals, and partly determined by the actions of the other. The relative social influence exerted by one party on another can be described in terms of a model of interaction proposed by Jones and Gerard (1967).

Limited Interpersonal Contact. If we imagine two parties to an interaction, in this case an influencing agent and a target person, and consider that each party may (or may not) have a *plan* for the interaction and may (or may not) alter this grand design in response to the actions of the other, then four kinds of interaction are possible. These four types are shown in Fig. 11.2 as they might progress through time. Both the actions of the influencing agent and those of the target person are shown, with arrows indicating whether those behaviors are produced by one's own internal plan, the actions of the other person, or some combination of the two. The first type of interaction, which Jones and Gerard (1967) called **pseudocontingency**, is the limiting case of social interaction. Pseudocontingency is illustrated by actors following a script, or by two young children engaged in "parallel play"–using the same playground equipment or selection of toys, but not attending to what the other is doing. Each participant's response (R) is determined entirely by his or her own internal plan, with no consideration for the other's behavior. In terms of social influence, of course, this type represents no influence at all.

The second type, called **asymmetric contingency**, is typical of the interaction between the compliance professional and the target person. The agent's actions are determined by this plan alone, by the ultimate objective of changing the target's behavior. In contrast, the unwitting target's actions are determined entirely by the influencing agent and the situation that person has constructed. In such a setting, the agent succeeds only because the target person is unaware of the plan and the structure it has imposed. There are other instances of asymmetric contingency in which the targets are aware of the influencing agent's plan, but are powerless to resist it. This extreme form of social influence is found in concentration camps, some prisons, and occasional mental hospitals. Influencing agents in these settings have virtually complete control over the behavior of the target persons, and there are few limits on their power.

Responding to the Other Party. The third case, **reactive contingency**, can best be illustrated by such things as panics, anarchy, or responses to political terrorism. The influencing agent may have started the interaction with a plan, but after the target person's first response, all either of them can do is quite literally react to the other's earlier behavior. For example, a government might issue stiff curfew regulations in order to prevent demonstrations, but then people would demonstrate against the curfew, the demonstrators would be jailed, there would be riots against the incarceration of peaceful demonstrators, troops would be called out to

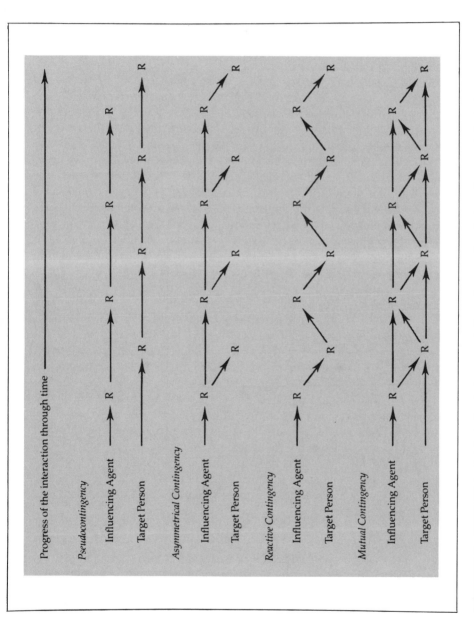

FIGURE 11.2 Contingency of interaction between an influencing agent and a target person (adapted from Jones and Gerard, 1967).

disperse the rioting crowds, and pretty soon the situation is out of the control of either party to the interaction. This is the logical extreme of social influence, because neither party is able to follow any sort of internal plan for the interaction.

Finally, there is **mutual contingency**, in which each party's actions are partly the result of his or her plan and partly the result of the other's actions. This last category is thought to typify true interaction and may be the most prevalent form of social influence. The influencing agent has a plan for the interaction, and in some important ways this agent's influence attempts affect the behavior of the target person. Yet the target person, too, has a plan for the interaction, and his or her compliance, acceptance, or resistance will affect the subsequent behavior of the influencing agent. This type of reciprocal influence is found in nearly all ongoing relationships, from friendship to formal negotiations between nations. Indeed, the recent analysis of close relationships by Kelley et al. (1983) includes a model of the interchange between partners that can be regarded as an elaborated version of mutual contingency.

Active Minorities and Social Change

The fact that so much social influence takes the form of mutual contingency makes explicit what has been a implicit assumption throughout this chapter: The process of social influence is an interactive, reciprocal exchange. The very prevalence of this reciprocation is what puts us at a disadvantage when dealing with compliance professionals. We believe that we are engaged in the usual reciprocal exchange, with all of the normal rules applying, when in fact the situation is not really as it appears to us. Only in these instances and some extreme forms of social control is there an almost total lack of correspondence between the outcomes of the target person and those of the influencing agent. More typically, the positive correspondence of outcomes between influencing agent and target restricts the influencing agent's freedom of action and usable power. Moreover, in a great deal of interaction the would be influencing agent must change some of his or her subsequent actions to accommodate the target person's desires. Failure to do so risks alienating the target to such a degree that he or she will have no alternatives except dramatic opposition. The result can be seen in such events as inner-city riots, prison uprisings, and political terrorism that, from the view of their perpetrators, may be the only rational solution left (Gamson, 1968).

Violence for the sake of a cause may be the final step in a target person's attempt to mitigate the power of an overbearing influencing agent, but precisely because social influence is a reciprocal process, this last step is usually unnecessary. Most of the social influence literature takes the perspective of the influencing agent, examining conformity by the minority to the wishes of the majority. But there are some notable exceptions, such as Cialdini's (1985) description of the weapons of influence and Moscovici's (1985) review of research showing how a minority can influence the majority. For example, recall the Jacobs and Campbell (1961) study of the transmission of an arbitrary norm in the autokinetic situation. That study showed that when the first generation of subjects was three fourths composed of confederates who made extreme judgments, it took six additional generations to bring the "movement" estimates back to the level obtained throughout among control subjects. Every replacement subject in the arbitrary norm condition was influenced by the prevailing norm. But another way to look at this result—and, indeed, another way to look at the results of any social influence experiment—is to examine the failures to produce change. Specifically, each new replacement moved the entire group a little farther in the direction of reality, exerting a *minority influence* on the perceptual judgments of the majority. A number of recent studies have confirmed this finding, showing that a determined and consistent minority can cause the majority to question its own position.

This interchange between majority and minority, or between influencing agent and target person, is not limited to social influence. It is also at the core of social change. In the exchange among people, or between people and social institutions, no party to the interaction can adhere completely to his or her own plan, oblivious to the behavior of the other participants. The mutual contingency of social influence will eventually produce changes in the powerful agent as well as changes in the target of influence.

SUMMARY

In an interaction between an influencing agent and the person who is the target of that influence, **social power** (p. 393) is the influencing agent's capacity to produce change, whereas **social influence** (p. 394) is the actual attitudinal or behavioral consequence of the influence attempt. An influencing agent may derive power from any of five different sources: ability to reward, or punish, the target person; legitimate and accepted authority; the target person's desire to emulate the influence agent; or the agent's expertise. No matter what its source, the influencing agent's theoretical capacity to produce change will be restricted by the correspondence of his or her outcomes with those of the target, and by that person's alternative relationships to a smaller range of **usable power** (p. 398). The process of persuasion, or **informational social influence** (p. 401), is most likely to lead to private acceptance, in the form either of identification or internalization. In contrast, the social pressure inherent in **normative social influence** (p. 401) will probably lead to public compliance without private acceptance.

Some behavioral changes in targets can be produced by change agents who have no obvious sources of social power. People who are high in

Machiavellianism (p. 404) excel in interactions that are face-to-face, involve latitude for improvisation, and provide the opportunity to inject irrelevant affect into the exchange. If the high Mach's power comes from his or her interpersonal style, the power of the *compliance professional* (p. 410) derives from the way that person structures the social exchange. Even in the absence of differences in interpersonal style or willful misuse of the situation, the role relationship between a supervisor and a subordinate can dictate compliance by the subordinate. Research on destructive obedience (p. 408) illustrates just how far this tendency to follow orders may extend.

A **social group** (p. 412) is a collectivity that has psychological implications for the person. Like the individual influencing agent, groups can exert either informational or normative social influence over their members. Research with the autokinetic effect shows how the **social reality** (p. 414) established by a group can affect an individual's judgments, even when this social reality is an arbitrary and erroneous one. Although it does not contain the explicit rewards and punishments usual in normative social influence, the Asch situation demonstrate's the group's power to produce public compliance, at least as long as the majority opinion is unanimous (p. 417).

A target person who is uncertain about the correct course of action, or who finds it to his or her personal advantage to comply will more readily accept social influence, regardless of the objective facts. But as the characterization of influence in terms of **mutual contingency** (p. 423) makes clear, the interchange between agent and target is a reciprocal one. Not only can the target restrict a group's usable power, he or she may also exert a *minority influence* (p. 423) on the group's judgment through consistency and determination.

SUGGESTED ADDITIONAL READINGS

CHRISTIE, R., & GEIS, F. L. (1970). *Studies in Machiavellianism.* New York: Academic Press. This book reports the development of the Machiavellianism scale, and contains numerous experimental studies on the characteristics of the high Mach. An interesting and readable book that provides a very good model for construction of any scale of interpersonal style.

CIALDINI, R. B. (1985). *Influence: Science and practice.* Glenview, IL: Scott-Foresman. This witty and entertaining book combines the author's experience as an aspiring "compliance professional" with a thorough grounding in research to describe the weapons of influence often used on unsuspecting targets. Each chapter concludes with a suggested defense against the weapon described. Highly recommended.

MOSCOVICI, S. (1985). Social influence and conformity. In G. Lindzey & E. Aronson (Eds.), *Handbook of social psychology* (3rd ed., Vol. 2, pp. 347-412). New York: Random House. This review of research on conformity and social influence builds on the idea that influence involves a reciprocal exchange between the agent and the target. Intended for a professional audience, but an especially comprehensive picture of social influence research conducted in Europe.

CHAPTER TWELVE

THE INDIVIDUAL
AND
THE GROUP

CONTENTS

PREVIEW

In their everyday lives, individuals participate as members of social groups. In order for a group to accomplish its goals, and thereby to fulfill some of the goals of individual members, communication must occur within the group. A formally organized group will have a specific communication network, and this will affect an individual's satisfaction with his or her participation. Two dimensions of this participation are group locomotion and group maintenance. Whether a group is formally organized or not, it is likely to have a leader, whose effectiveness will depend on his or her personal characteristics and on the nature of the situation affecting the group's performance. An individual's socialization as a new group member follows a particular pattern, with the person's commitment to the group changing over time; the attraction that members feel toward a group will produce pressures toward uniformity of opinion, especially on matters of critical importance to the group. In some cases this pressure can lead to the development of groupthink, a denial of reality that invites bad group decisions.

At the beginning of this book, *social psychology* was defined as the study of the personal and situational factors that influence the social behavior of the individual. In keeping with this definition, I have used the individual person as the unit of analysis, examining social perceptions, attitudes, self-concept, and social motives before turning to interactions with other people. Even the definition of a social group as a collectivity with psychological implications for the individual (Chapter 11) is consistent with this level of analysis. I have, of course, referred to social groups throughout the book, whenever their influence on the individual was clear. Thus, we have seen that reference groups can serve as sources of self-evaluation, that deindividuation can accompany the anonymity of being just one among many, and that groups can exert conformity pressures on their members. Now in order to show the individual's place in the group, the perspective shifts to that of the group itself.

The numerical range of the social group logically extends from the dyad through the organization and nation to the human group as a whole, and a new set of problems for study appears at every level. There are, however, some common elements. Whatever the size of the group, its members must be able to communicate with each other, and often this interchange takes place according to some formalized communication structure. Again, almost regardless of the size of the group, there will be a recognized leader. The leader may have been elected or appointed to a position in the formal structure of the group, or may simply have emerged from among those people present during the formative stages of the group. In either case, he or she will be more than just another member. Finally, whether the group's purposes include the completion of specific goals, the maintenance of a group or national identity, or merely the pursuit of mutual enjoyment and satisfaction, the group will need to make decisions that will affect its future.

Not surprisingly, a review of group research by Zander (1979) notes that these three topics – communication, leadership, and decision making – have been among the few to hold the attention of the scientific community for over 30 years. The limited scope of the chapter requires omission of some material of interest, such as the formation of coalitions among members of a group (Komorita, 1984) or intergroup relations (Stephan, 1985). Instead, we must concentrate on the individual's actions and role within a social group.

COMMUNICATION WITHIN THE GROUP

The Structure of Communication

What factors may contribute to a disgruntled citizen's complaint that "big government just doesn't listen to ordinary people any more"? Or to an unhappy industrial worker's assertion that an impending strike is the result of a "failure of communication between the employees and the management of the company"? Or even to a student's belief that his or her university treats the student "like a number, not like a person"? In part, these complaints may be traced to the sheer size of the institution involved, and they may also serve as rationalizations for intended actions against the organization or institution. But the complaints may also reflect the actual structure of communication within the organization. Direct, face-to-face contact with decision makers, if possible at all, will require penetration of several layers of administrative bureaucracy. At any point along the way, a complaint may be misunderstood, unsatisfactorily answered by someone without the authority necessary to provide relief, or arbitrarily discarded.

Communication Networks. Small groups in which most of the participants are of equal status initially are quite different from formal organizations, but even in these groups the structure of communication can have important social consequences. For example, suppose that you and four other people are brought together in a laboratory setting and asked to solve a number of simple problems. Each of you would be given part of the information needed to solve the problem, and the experimental variable would be the manner in which the five of you were permitted to exchange and consolidate the various elements. Some of the possible communication patterns are shown in Fig. 12.1. Each solid line represents a two-way communication link between two people, and each pattern, or **communication network** has been given a descriptive name, as indicated in the figure.

Let us take a closer look at the flow of communication within each network. Suppose that you took the position of person *s* in each network. In the chain and the circle, you could communicate directly with two other people (*r* and *t*), but in the Y or the wheel you could communicate directly only with person *r*. In any network, your *distance* from other participants will be defined as the number of steps required for communication. Direct communication entails only one step, indirect communication requires an additional step for each intervening person. So although your distance from *t* in the chain is a value of 1, your distance from *p* in the same chain is a value of 3 (*s* to *r*, *r* to *q*, *q* to *p*) steps. The circle network immediately ap-

FIGURE 12.1   Some possible communication networks among five people. A: the chain. B: the circle. C: the Y. D: two equivalent representations of the wheel. (Adapted from Leavitt, H. J. (1951). Some effects of certain communication patterns on group performance. *Journal of Abnormal and Social Psychology 46,* 38–50. Copyright 1951 by the American Psychological Association. Reprinted by permission.)

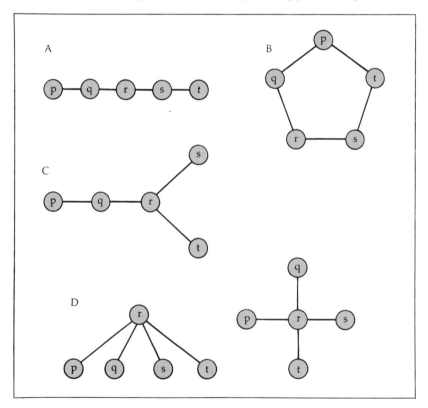

pears to be leaderless, with no one position having an advantage, whereas the wheel obviously gives a substantial advantage to person r. This intuitive impression is borne out when the importance of each position is computed according to a method suggested by Bavelas (1950), based on the distances involved for each position.

Relative Centrality. In the chain network, the distance from s (your position) to p is 3, from s to q is 2, from s to r is 1, and from s to t is 1, for a summed distance of 7. Computations of this sort can be made for each of the five positions, and the grand total of all the distances involved in the chain network is 40 (totals of 7 each for s and q; 10 each for p and t; and 6 for r). To determine the importance of each position in the chain, simply divide the total of the distances (40) by the sum for the position. The result is the **relative centrality** of the position, and in a five-element chain these values are 4.0 for each end, 5.7 for the next interior position from each end, and 6.7 for the center position. The relative centrality values for the chain will confirm your intuitive impressions from sitting on the side of a long table during a formal dinner: The person in the middle is literally the center of the conversation. Comparable computations can be made for any of the other networks as well, and these show that position r's advantage is even greater in the Y (a value of 7.2) and the wheel (a value of 8.0) than in the chain.

In the same way that positions within a network can be compared for relative centrality, different networks can be compared to one another for centrality of organization by using the difference between the most advantaged and least advantaged positions. Thus, in the circle (the least centralized network), every position has a relative centrality of 5.0, so the difference from most to least advantaged is zero. In the chain, the difference between position r and the "worst" position (on either end) is $6.7 - 4.0 = 2.7$. The next most centralized network is the Y, and there the difference between r and p is $7.2 - 4.0 = 3.2$. Finally, the most centralized network is the wheel, with a difference between r and any other position being $8.0 - 4.6 = 3.4$.

Social Consequences of Structure. What are the social consequences of the structure of communication within a small group? To answer this question, Leavitt (1951) conducted an experiment in which five-person groups, arranged as wheels, chains, or circles, tried to solve a problem. Each person was given a card upon which had been printed five symbols. Only one of the five symbols appeared on all five cards, and the group's task was to determine which symbol was common to all participants. The subjects were forced to communicate with each other through written messages that were relayed by the experimenter (so that the experimenter could control the structure of the network). The participants indicated their choices of the correct symbol by closing switches that illuminated lights on a panel monitored by the experimenter. Incorrect choices could thus be counted. The task was completed when all five participants made the correct choice. At the conclusion of this task, subjects were asked whether their group had a leader, and if so, what position that leader occupied in the network. Subjects were also asked how their morale had been during the task.

These and other dependent variables were nearly always ordered according to the centrality either of the networks or the centrality of the individual's position within the network. For example, the group's efficiency in completing the task increased from circle to chain, to the Y, with the wheel being the most efficient. Although the more centralized networks were more efficient, subjects in them found the experience less pleasant, reporting the highest morale in the circle, less in the chain, still less in the Y, and the least in the wheel. Within networks, subjects who occupied more central positions enjoyed the task the most and were most consistently nominated as the leader. Subjects who occupied the peripheral positions were the least happy, and were almost never nominated as leader.

Since this original study by Leavitt (1951), a great deal of research has been conducted on the characteristics of various communication networks. Much of this literature has been reviewed by Collins and Raven (1969), who concluded that many of Leavitt's findings remain valid. Inconsistencies can be found from one experiment to another, but in general the efficiency of a group increases, and the group members' morale decreases, with increasing centralization of the structure of communication. Considering each position within a network, rather than the network as a whole, the occupants of relatively central positions like the task more and are nominated more frequently for leadership roles than are the occupants of more peripheral positions.

Social Structure in an Intact Group. It is important to notice that in nearly all of the research on communication networks, the structure of the group has been imposed by the experimenters. This has two ramifications. First, the results from experimental work with communication networks probably generalizes better to formally organized groups, whose internal communications proceed through "channels," than to informal social groups. Second, there is some chance that the experimental research overestimates both the efficiency differences across various communication structures and the corresponding morale differences. Why? Because in the research subjects were necessarily randomly assigned to various communication structures, but in the real social world people have some choice about their positions in such structures. No doubt you know people who want to be the center of attention, and others who are more comfortable being left alone; you know people who are highly efficient, and others who cannot seem to get organized. Especially in an informal group, but even in a formal organization, people may gravitate toward positions in the structure that correspond to their own predilections. A true "workaholic" might be most comfortable, and most efficient, in a peripheral position that provided enough information to get the job done but not so much that it caused interruptions.

Despite its possible limitations, experimental work on communication structure was, until very recently, the only available method. Traditional statistical techniques were inadequate to describe the complexity inherent in the interaction among members of an intact social group. With the development of a new method of analysis, known as *individual differences multidimensional scaling* (Carroll & Chang, 1970), it has become possible for social psychologists to examine the structural dimensions of ongoing groups. In one such study (Forgas, 1978), the participants were faculty members, research students, and support staff in a university laboratory. Each participant was asked to describe all the others on a set of 22 bipolar adjective scales and asked to estimate how similar to one another were members of all possible pairs of the 16 people in the group. These similarity judgments formed the basis for the multidimensional scaling, and researchers could then use the bipolar adjectives to give labels to the dimensions obtained in the scaling procedure. These procedures can be thought of as a more complex version of the sociometric method (Moreno, 1934) described in chapter 9. The major difference is that sociometric methods can describe a group on only a single dimension at a time, a serious limitation in the study of an ongoing group.

The multidimensional scaling revealed three structural dimensions on which individuals in the group could be placed. These were sociability (friendliness, warmth, humor), creativity (being creative, critical, and quick), and competence (dominance, intelligence, and articulateness). The faculty members were clustered into a generally competent and creative subgroup, the support staff into a subgroup characterized primarily by sociability, and the students into a more heterogeneous cluster that was high in competence but low in sociability. For our purposes here, the results are most important for their demonstration of how a newly developed analysis technique enables researchers to examine an intact group. Many of the descriptions obtained certainly agree with our intuitive expectations for members of a small academic group. But without multidimensional scaling or a comparable statistical procedure, these particular intuitions would have been impossible to test.

The Nature of Communication

As we have seen, the structure of communication can affect both efficiency and satisfaction, certainly in experimental groups and most probably in formally organized groups as well. Given the prevalence of formal groups in our society, these two aspects of group performance deserve further attention. It is generally agreed that a member's participation in a group can be described by the two relatively independent dimensions of **group locomotion**, or progress toward the group goal (Festinger, 1950), and **group maintenance**, the facilitation of pleasant interaction among group members (Thibaut & Kelley, 1959). Indeed, in the three-dimensional characterization found by Forgas (1978), the sociability dimension is equivalent to group maintenance, whereas the competence and creativity dimensions can be seen as aspects of group locomotion for a group whose product is ideas.

Any group not organized purely for social purposes will have some sort of task to perform–a committee reaching a decision, a work group completing a product, or a group of friends organizing a party. Although group success requires concerted task effort by members, that task-directed behavior can proceed smoothly only if the members of the group remain amicable. People whose feelings are consistently ignored will not remain productive contributors.

Interaction Process Analysis. How can we tell whether a particular action by a group member is a contribution primarily to the task achievement or to the social maintenance of a group? In the first attempt to deal with this problem, Bales (1950) developed an objective interaction scoring system known as **Interaction Process Analysis** (IPA). He began with the basic distinction between task achievement and social maintenance, and suggested that each of these dimensions might find expression in two different ways in a group. First, in order to achieve the group's goal, the members will need to share relevant information: some people will ask questions, others will give answers. Second, although group success will require mutual cooperation and good feeling, a scoring system should provide for disruption as well: the social process may contain both positive and negative elements. These divisions produce four different classes of behavior, and Bales then outlined three more specific elements for each class, for a total of the 12 interaction categories shown in Table 12.1.

To illustrate how the categories can be employed to assess the nature of an interaction, let us consider an example drawn from research on small-group communication. Suppose you bring a group of subjects together in a room equipped with one-way vision screens so that you can observe the discussion without actually being present in the same room. So that all your groups will be discussing the same issues, you might provide them with a standard case to discuss, such as the one used by Schachter (1951) and others. The case describes the life history of a fictitious juvenile delinquent named Johnny Rocco, and the case ends with Johnny about to be sentenced for a minor crime. The group's task is to take the role of the juvenile authorities and decide which of several possible punishments should be imposed. After making the appropriate introductions, you leave the group

TABLE 12.1 The Scoring Categories of Interaction Process Analysis

Social-emotional area		
	Positive reactions	1. *Shows solidarity:* gives reward, help
		2. *Shows tension release:* jokes, laughs
		3. *Agrees:* accepts, complies, concurs
Task area		
	Answers	4. *Gives suggestion:* direction, not command
		5. *Gives opinion:* expresses feeling, evaluates
		6. *Gives information:* repeats, clarifies
		7. *Asks for information*
	Questions	8. *Asks for opinion*
		9. *Asks for suggestion*
Social-emotional area		
	Negative reactions	10. *Disagrees:* rejects, resists compliance
		11. *Shows tension:* withdraws from field
		12. *Shows antagonism:* asserts self, deflates others

Note: *Adapted from Bales (1950).*

alone to discuss the case and arrive at a decision about the penalty. While the group is engaged in its task, you and your assistants try to code everything that is communicated (verbally or nonverbally) into the appropriate Bales category.

As it happens, one person starts off by saying "I think the guy should get the book thrown at him" (Table 12.1, category 5), and another person nods her agreement (category 3). A third person says that he thinks such a punishment would be too harsh (category 10), while a fourth asserts that any punishment at all would be a "dumb idea" (category 12). A fifth person then says that both arguments have some merit (category 1), and suggests (category 4) that before any more discussion takes place it might be a good idea to see just which punishment each person would select. This is done, and the discussion then continues as you and your assistants code everything the participants communicate. When you are through, you will have a profile for the group showing what proportion of the discussion occurred in each of the 12 categories, and (if you have been keeping separate records for each participant) you will also have such a profile for each individual.

Group Maintenance. In one of the early applications of Interaction Process Analysis, Bales (1955) found that category 5 (gives opinion) was the most prevalent in groups discussing human relations problems, with a total of over 30% of the communicative acts falling in this category. Category 6 (giving information) was the next most frequent, at nearly 18%, closely followed by category 3 (shows agreement) at 16%. None of the remaining categories received more than 8%. If we consider the four major divisions, rather than the 12 categories, the results showed that 56% of the group's time was spent in problem-solving action—the "answers" class—and an additional 26% was devoted to group maintenance activity—the "positive reactions" class. The remainder of the time was split between questions (7%) and negative reactions (11%), with most of the latter representing disagreement. Even in a highly task-oriented group whose members do not anticipate any future interaction, a fair proportion of the time is devoted to keeping things running smoothly. And though some disagreement naturally occurs, little tension and virtually no open antagonism take place.

Emergent Leadership. The Interaction Process Analysis scores for members of a group can also be used to examine a phenomenon called **emergent leadership**. At the beginning of an experimental session (or, for that matter, the beginning of a jury deliberation) the group is leaderless. No one is appointed to be in charge, and because there is full communication among the participants, no built-in structural bias favors any individual member. Nevertheless, by the conclusion of the experimental session, two different sorts of leaders seem to have emerged. In most groups, one person seemed to take charge of the task, contribute a great deal to the discussion, and be recognized as having the best ideas. Bales (1955) refers to this kind of leader as the *task specialist.* In addition, a different person typically showed the greatest amount of agreement, tension release, and solidarity. This *social-emotional specialist* was usually the best liked, even though his or her contributions to the task were undistinguished. Just as there are two dimensions to the group process—efficiency and morale—there seem to be different people in each group whose specialty is one dimension or the other. As we see in the next section, this finding has also been obtained in groups with formal leadership structures, suggesting that both efficiency and morale will be influenced by the predilections of the individuals involved as well as by the communication structure within the group or organization.

In the years since the introduction of IPA, its scoring has been refined (Borgatta, 1962) and other coding systems have been developed to measure different aspects of group process. Despite these additions, the original version of Interaction Process Analysis remains a popular method for assessing group dynamics. More recently, Bales (1970) has reported an extensive series of studies founded on IPA that lead to a theoretical model of the relationship between an individual's personality characteristics and the mode of participation. The IPA scoring technique, together with its methodological and theoretical extensions, illustrates both the contributions that a person might make to the group and some of the effects on the individual that might follow group participation. Thus the content of the communication within a group, as well as the structure through which that communication occurs, can affect the group's efficiency and morale.

GROUP LEADERSHIP

Leader Characteristics

Personality Traits. What makes a good leader of a group? Is it charisma, interpersonal skill, or just being in the right place at the right time? Does the nature of the group make any difference? Will someone who is an excellent leader of a small group also be an outstanding head of a large formal organization? Are some corporate "headhunters" correct to think that a successful manager of one kind of business can manage any other business equally well? These questions have concerned voters and personnel managers, as well as social psychologists, for years, and the first studies of leadership perhaps naively began collecting evidence on the personality traits of successful leaders. In a review of this evidence, Gibb (1969) reports early research showing that leaders, as compared to followers, tended to be taller, more interpersonally attractive, more intelligent, more self-confident, better adjusted, and more dominant. Yet, as Gibb points out, the most striking thing about all these presumed correlates of leadership is how little importance they seem to have from one situation to another. Of all the traits, only intelligence is consistently associated with leadership, and even here the relationship must be qualified. The overall correlations are usually low, and although task leaders tend to be more intelligent than their followers, the same differential does not appear to hold for social–emotional leaders. It also appears that leaders cannot exceed their followers in intelligence by too wide a margin, or they lose their effectiveness. Thus, despite some popular historical examples to the contrary (Alexander the Great, Napoleon, Hitler, deGaulle), most of the research evidence does not support the "Great Man theory" that a particular constellation of physical and psychological traits will produce a renowned leader regardless of the circumstances or opportunities (Gibb, 1969; Hollander, 1985).

Behavior in the Group. If potential leaders cannot be selected reliably on the basis of physical and personal characteristics, can they be identified by their behavior in the group? The work of Bales (1958, 1970) would certainly suggest that they might. Especially when compared with the inconsistency of the trait research, the consistent differentiation between task specialists and social–emotional specialists in Bales' experimental groups indicates that effectiveness in those two domains of behavior might discriminate between leaders and followers. In an attempt to measure the varieties of leader behavior, Hemphill (1950) and his associates (Halpin, 1966) constructed questionnaires designed to assess several a priori dimensions of leadership activity. They then administered these questionnaires to a large group of subjects and factor-analyzed the responses to describe the results.

Consideration and Initiating Structure. This factor analysis revealed four different aspects of leadership behavior, two of which accounted for nearly 85% of the variance in the ratings. These two were *consideration*, the extent to which the leader is considerate of the feelings of the followers; and *initiating structure*, the extent to which the leader organizes the group, its activities, and his or her relationship to the group. Items that contributed to these two factors have been grouped into the Leadership Behavior Description Questionnaire, or LBDQ (Halpin, 1966), consisting of 30 descriptive statements, 15 for each factor. The consideration items deal with the leader's openness, warmth for the followers, and willingness to consult with the followers before taking action. The initiating structure items deal with the maintenance of standards of performance, the clarity of rules and expectations, and the guidance of individual responsibilities in the achievement of group goals.

If these two factors sound familiar to you, they should. They are for a formal group with a designated leader virtually the same behaviors we have seen before in the social–emotional specialist and task specialist found in the leaderless groups. The dimensions of consideration and initiating structure do seem to be independent, although the leaders of highly successful groups often show ability in both areas. Apparently the leaders of formal groups, like those of informal groups, can be identified by their actions.

A Model of Leadership Effectiveness

The early search for personality characteristics that would be associated with effective leadership did not prove to be productive because of the wide variety of situations in which leadership must be exercised, and because of the differences in leader behavior that are often called for. The shift to investigation of leader behavior provided a more accurate picture of formal leadership styles – consideration and initiating structure – but that research was only suggestive for the issue of leadership effectiveness. It is easy to think of situations in which a leader who was high on consideration but low on initiating structure might be ineffective (such as an Army infantry captain in combat). In the same way, situations exist in which a structure-initiator with little consideration would be ineffective (such as a "brainstorming" designed to create new products, or a group discussion of problems in personnel administration). When the question is effectiveness rather than leader behavior, it would make better sense to consider both the leader's style and the constraints imposed by the situation. This is just what Fiedler's (1964, 1971) **contingency model** of leadership effectiveness attempts to do, by assuming that the success of any personal style will be contingent upon certain specifiable characteristics of the situation.

The Leader's Attitudes Toward Co-Workers. The contingency model of leadership effectiveness takes a slightly different approach to the measurement of leader characteristics from that employed by Hemphill (1950) and his associates. Their LBDQ is completed not by the leader, but by his or her subordinates. Consequently, what is actually measured is the collective perceptions of the leader's actions and characteristics, not a direct measure of the leader's behavior (for example, as it might be observed by a researcher who actually watched the leader in action over an extended period of time). What this means, of course, is that those subordinates whose own actions receive approval from the leader are likely to evaluate his or her characteristics more positively than are subordinates whose own actions have not been rewarded by the leader (this potential bias is likely to be exaggerated if the leader being evaluated has just replaced a leader who had just the opposite view of the actions of the various subordinates).

Hoping to avoid some of these sources of possible distortion, Fiedler tried to obtain a measure of the leader's own attitudes. Because so many of the LBDQ items are socially desirable, it would hardly have made sense to ask the leaders to use that scale to describe themselves. In fact, any direct questions about a leader's behavior toward particular subordinates would be similarly affected by social desirability. Because of these problems, Fiedler decided on an indirect measure of the leader's attitudes toward subordinates in general, on the assumption that those attitudes would be reflected in the leader's behavior. Even this attitude scale was designed to make negative statements socially acceptable. The leader is asked to think of all of the people with whom he or she has ever worked (the kind of review of past relationships that is implicit in the exchange theory principle of the comparison level), and to select the one who was the most difficult to get along with. This person is the leader's *least preferred co-worker* (to put it mildly).

The leader is asked to describe this target person on a series of bipolar adjective scales. The Least-Preferred Co-worker (LPC) scale includes items such as pleasant–unpleasant, distant–close, and productive–unproductive, with each item scored on an 8-point scale where high scores indicate positive qualities. Some leaders will find positive qualities even in the people they dislike, and these leaders will have high LPC scores. Other leaders will be less charitable toward their least preferred coworkers, and they will have low LPC scores. In the terms we have used earlier, the high LPC leader is a social–emotional specialist, high in consideration, whereas the low LPC leader is likely to be "all business." Thus, the LPC scale—administered to the leaders, themselves–can be used to categorize leaders along one of the two major dimensions in the LBDQ.

The Favorability of the Situation. But the categorization of leaders is only half of the task of measuring leadership effectiveness. The other half is categorization of the situations, and Fiedler (1964) suggests that three different aspects of the setting should be taken into account. These are (a) the *affective relations* between the leader and the members, (b) the degree of *task structure* inherent in the work to be accomplished by the group, and (c) the *position power* of the leader. The affective relations factor is presumed to be the "most important single determinant of group processes which affect team performance" (Fiedler, 1964, p. 159). A leader who is liked and accepted by the subordinates (whether this acceptance is for the leader's good ideas, or for his or her social–emotional abilities) can get the maximum performance from those subordinates under a wide variety of conditions. The second factor, task structure, refers to the clarity or ambiguity of the task. When the group's task is a highly specific one, such as assembling part of an automobile or exercising a standard play in a football game, the leader's job is easier than when the task is ambiguous (discussing the social implications of a novel, or developing a policy to increase company profits). Finally, the third factor is what French and Raven (1959) would call *legitimate power* (see chapter 11)–the leader's traditionally recognized authority.

Three Dimensions for Situations.   To keep the theory to a manageable size, Fiedler considers each situational component as a dichotomy. Leader–member relations are divided into those that are good and those that are moderately poor, assuming that if the leader–member relations are very poor, the group will disintegrate (we return to this point later). The task is regarded either as structured or unstructured, and the leader's position power is classified as either strong or weak. These dichotomous factors can be combined into what amounts to a factorial design (2 × 2 × 2) to produce eight different characterizations of the situation, as shown in Fig. 12.2. Each characterization, or *octant* is thus a combination of three situational factors. You will notice that Fig. 12.2 shows nine octants, instead of the eight produced by the combinations of factors. This ninth octant, called V-A, had to be added to the conceptual model after it became clear that with a high degree of task clarity, a leader with a great deal of legitimate power could get subordinates to perform quite well even though the affective relations between leader and subordinates were terrible (instead of just moderately poor). If you are being paid on a "piece rate" for producing some good or performing some service, and your supervisor is legitimately the only person who checks to see how much you have accomplished, whether you also like that person will have only a slight bearing on your performance.

The octants are ordered (I through V-A) according to their overall *favorability toward the leader.* The best situation for a leader is one in which affective relations are good, the task is clear, and the leader's legitimate power is strong (octant I). The three factors affecting the situation are listed in the figure in the order of their importance, with the least im-

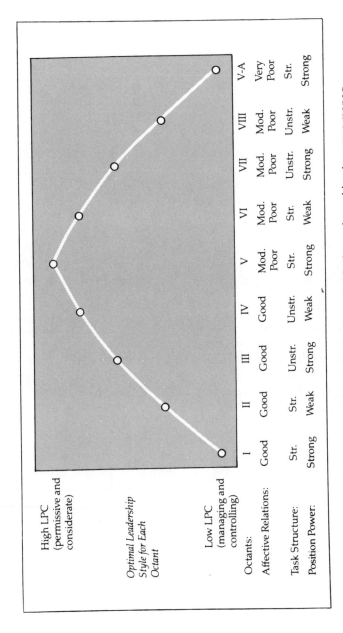

FIGURE 12.2 Curve indicating the optimal leadership style (permissive and considerate versus managing and controlling) required by each of several situations, as predicted by the contingency model of leadership effectiveness (adapted from Fiedler, 1964).

portant (position power) alternating from octant to octant. The differences in importance can be seen if we examine changes away from the best possible circumstances (octant I) in a single factor at a time. If the affective relations remain good and the task remains clear, a change in position power from strong to weak only changes the octant by one step (I to II). If affective relations remain good and now power remains strong, a change in the task from structured to unstructured changes the octant number by two steps (I to III). But if the affective relations change from good to moderately poor as the other two factors remain constant, the octant number changes by *four* (I to V). Thus, affective relations are the most important factor, followed by task structure, and then by position power.

The Contingency Prediction. The fundamental hypothesis of the contingency model is that *"the type of leader attitude* [permissive and considerate as opposed to managing and controlling] *required for effective group performance depends upon the degree to which the group situation is favorable or unfavorable to the leader"* (Fiedler, 1964; p. 164). As the curve in Fig. 12.2 indicates, the low LPC leaders, who are managing, controlling, and highly directive, perform best in situations that are either very favorable or very unfavorable. In contrast, high LPC leaders, who are diplomatic, tactful, and sensitive, perform best under moderately unfavorable conditions.

A Reservation About the Evidence. To test the contingency model, Fiedler has conducted a great many studies correlating the LPC scores of leaders with the performance, productivity, or effectiveness of the groups involved. Over a period in excess of 20 years, a wide variety of studies has been completed, and a review of 125 of these by Strube and Garcia (1981) finds general support for the model. As impressive as much of this evidence appears, the contingency model is not without problems.

To begin with, most of the comparisons that support the model are correlations between LPC scores and group performance. In the moderately unfavorable octants (IV through VII), these correlations are positive, indicating that high LPC scores are associated with success by the group. In the very favorable octants (I, II, III) and the very unfavorable ones (VIII, V-A) the correlations are negative, indicating that low LPC scores are associated with group success. In most of the research, however, the individual correlations have not been statistically significantly different, even though they were in the directions predicted by the model. In his review, Hollander (1985) notes other criticisms, including an important reservation about what the LPC scale actually measures. Specifically, leaders who have had unfortunate experiences with really troublesome subordinates will obviously have lower LPC scores than will leaders who have been fortunate enough not to have supervised any obnoxious people. Despite these problems, Fiedler's contingency model remains important.

There is substantial support for many of the model's predictions, it has served as the foundation for other contingency models (see Hollander, 1985), and it has moved the discussion of leadership beyond the early "Great Man" notions to a much more sophisticated investigation of the joint influence of personality and situation on a fundamental social behavior, the exercise of leadership. Leaders are neither born nor made, and will become most effective only when their own personal talents are a good match to the demands of the situation.

GROUP DECISION PROCESSES

We have seen that the structure of communication in a group can influence member satisfaction and group efficiency, and that leadership effectiveness can best be evaluated by considering the relevant aspects of the situation as well as the interpersonal style of the leader. But a social group is more than a collection of individuals; it is a unit that must coordinate its activity in order to achieve its objectives. Not all of the group's decisions can be—or should be—made by the leader alone. Many times decisions about priorities, plans, and actions will be group decisions arrived at after discussion among the group members. What can social psychology tell us about these decisions?

Successful group activity depends on coordinated action taken by all members of the group, even by those who might have initially opposed the course of action to e taken. Because so few group activities will have unanimous support, the group will frequently be in the position of asking at least some of its members to set aside their own individual goals in favor of the group's goal. To understand why these members will usually comply, we must know why individuals join groups in the first place, and how they become socialized to the standards and objectives of the group.

Attraction to the Group

Social and Emotional Needs. Many of the sources of attraction to groups are the same as sources of attraction to individuals, discussed in chapter 9. Remember that Aronson and Mills (1959) and Gerard and Matthewson (1966) found that the more severe the initiation, the greater the liking expressed for a rather dull group. Certainly these were experimentally created groups, but it is reasonable to think that even with real social groups, the more you invest in your decision to join, the more attractive you are likely to find the group and the more committed to it you are likely to be. Another important illustration is the desire to join positive reference groups. Just as you will be attracted to individuals whose attitudes and interests are similar to yours, you will be attracted to groups with values and objectives that are compatible with your own. In chapters 2 and 5 we described the Seekers group (Festinger, Riecken, & Schachter, 1956), which believed that the world was doomed, but that a small number of the faithful would be saved by a spaceship that would carry them to a better place. Admittedly, this group had limited appeal, but many groups today – from dieting groups to religious cults – do attract members through their strong belief systems. Finally, you may seek social comparison with a group of people in much the same way that you would seek it with an individual. In chapter 7, we discussed Schachter's (1959) research on the social reduction of fear. In those experiments, subjects who were anxious over the impending experimental treatment chose to wait with others who were in the same state, and a nonexperimental analog to this is the group treatment of people who are afraid to fly.

These examples illustrate one major category of reasons for attraction to social groups: those groups can serve social and emotional needs. Attraction can follow dissonance reduction, discovery of similar beliefs, or successful social comparison. In addition, participation in a group can provide prestige, a sense of self-definition, or the feelings of belonging that are necessary to overcome loneliness. Group membership may simply be an end in itself. To the extent that this is true, attraction toward the group may parallel the reasons for attraction to individuals.

The Instrumental Functions of Groups.   But participation in a group may serve more than social-emotional needs; it may also serve the instrumental function of enabling the individual to achieve goals that he or she would not be able to attain alone. Farmers organize cooperatives in order to purchase supplies at reduced rates; workers join unions in order to improve their bargaining position with employers; many people join political and charitable organizations to bring about ends that would be difficult for individuals to accomplish alone. Groups that concentrate on the social-emotional needs of their members will be concerned primarily with group maintenance activities, whereas groups that are formed to achieve instrumental goals will emphasize task-oriented activities. Which sort of leadership is more appropriate for the group will, of course, depend on the nature of the group itself.

In the same way that the two kinds of leadership are found to varying degrees in most groups, the two different sources of attraction are also typically found together in the same setting, often by intent of the group. For example, most enlightened business organizations will strive to have their employees satisfy some of their emotional needs through identification with the company. They will provide security, status, and individual recognition as well as a salary. The employees will then come to develop a "company loyalty" that extends beyond the remunerative relationship that exists between an organization and the people whose wages it pays. Businesses that take the position that all they need to provide for their

employees is a paycheck place their workers in a relationship that exchange theory (Chapter 8) would describe as dependence, rather than attraction. In so doing, they risk high absenteeism, frequent turnover of personnel, and a high proportion of mistakes in the production of goods or
services.

Not only employers, but also voluntary organizations (social clubs, interest groups, political parties) should provide a variety of ways for members to satisfy their emotional needs as well as to achieve their task objectives. In terms of field theory, each inducement provided by the group is a
different *force* acting on the individuals to keep them in the group. When
the group asks its members to forego some of their individual objectives in
order to achieve the group goal, the forces acting on individuals to keep
them in the group will become of paramount importance. A politician who
is more interested in running for office than in the principles his or her
party stands for will switch parties after losing a nomination. An executive
whose company has not attended to his or her psychological needs may
leave the company rather than move to an undesirable location, even
though the move would be a promotion. In general, the smaller the total of
forces acting to keep the individual in the group (relative to the demands
the group makes on its members), the more likely it is that dissatisfied individuals will leave the group.

Group Cohesiveness

Cohesiveness as Mutual Attraction.   The attraction of individuals to
the group and their tendency either to stay or to leave are ideas that make
intuitive sense. But how can these be measured more precisely? The examples we have used suggest that attraction can be described in terms of exchange theory. An individual would be attracted to a group that provided
outcomes above his or her comparison level (CL), and would be dependent
on any group that provided outcomes below CL but still above the comparison level for alternatives (CL_{alt}). Thus, in terms of exchange theory, attraction to a relationship with a group would have exactly the same determinants as attraction to a relationship with another individual. At first this
seems a satisfactory solution to the problem, but it has a significant draw-
back: it does not adequately describe the relationship among all the members of the group.

What we really need to know is how closely knit the entire group
might be, not how attractive it might seem to a single person. For this reason most social psychologists (for example, Cartwright & Zander, 1968)
use the term **cohesiveness** to describe the members' commitment and attraction to their social group. Cohesiveness is not an element of the relationship between one member and the group; it is a property of the entire
group. And it is more than the attractiveness of the group to an outsider; it

also takes into account the extent to which participation in the group satisfies the individual's own needs. Thus, for example, militant groups either on the far left or the far right of the political spectrum may be highly cohesive, although most of us would not find either sort attractive.

Sociometric Measurement of Cohesiveness. Although social psychologists can infer cohesiveness from a variety of scaling procedures (such as the multidimensional scaling methods used in the Forgas, 1978, study of a research group), they typically assess it with some variant of the sociometric technique described in chapter 9 (Moreno, 1934). Even though sociometric methods produce only one dimension at a time, and so are not adequate for complete characterization of members' opinions about the group, the one dimension of mutual attraction is usually satisfactory for the determination of cohesiveness. When researchers use sociometric methods for friendship choice, the dependent variable of interest might be the number of times that a particular individual was chosen (popularity). In the same way, Bales (1955) used frequency of choice to establish emergent social–emotional leaders (with the question phrased in terms of "best-liked" person) and emergent task leaders (person with the "best ideas").

In contrast, when researchers use sociometric methods to establish the cohesiveness of the group as a whole, the dependent variable is a comparison between collective choices made within the group and choices made outside the group. For example, in their study of friendship patterns in a housing development (described in chapter 9), Festinger, Schachter, and Back (1950) used the ratio of friendship choices made within an apartment unit to friendship choices made outside the unit as an index of the cohesiveness of the unit. Another way to use sociometric methods to compare the cohesiveness of different groups is to determine the number or proportion of reciprocated choices within the group, assuming that the highly cohesive groups should have a high proportion of reciprocated choices. However, cohesiveness is measured, the greater the cohesiveness, the more demands the group can place on its members before they drop out of the group.

Socialization of Group Members

Commitment and Role Transitions. You will recall from the discussion of friendship in chapter 9 that a good deal of early work on interpersonal attraction can best be described as a "snapshot" taken at a particular time in the relationship between two people. The same limitation has characterized traditional research on group cohesiveness. Although there has been a long-standing interest in the mutual attraction among members of a group, only recently have social psychologists begun to examine how that cohesiveness might influence the relationship that a group member might have with the group over time.

According to an analysis by Moreland and Levine (1983) the mutual commitment of member and group involves three different judgments that follow the general idea of a comparison level for alternatives. Each is a comparison between the "rewardingness" (or in terms we have used before, the goodness of the outcomes) of the current relationship and the rewardingness of available alternatives. Thus, for the individual, each standard is provided by other groups to which the person might give allegiance; for the group, each standard is the performance of other (present or potential) members. There is one of these comparisons for the present relationship between member and group, one for the past relationship as each party remembers it, and one for the future relationship anticipated by both. The comparison for the present is equivalent to the standard judgment of attraction against the CL_{alt}, whereas the judgments about past and future also involve elements more appropriately considered part of the CL (which is, after all, the average value of all past outcomes).

The reciprocal *commitment* between individual and group is held to be the sum of the three comparisons (past rewardingness minus past alternatives, plus present rewardingness minus present alternatives, plus future rewardingness minus future alternatives). Including the time dimension permits both the individual and the group to consider some present or past costs incurred merely to be "investments" for the future. As the individual's commitment to a group increases or decreases, group membership will become, respectively, more important or less important to the person. As the group's commitment to the individual increases or decreases, that member will be seen, respectively, as either more valuable or less valuable.

Until now, this model is merely an elaboration of earlier principles of goodness of outcomes and group cohesiveness. What it adds to our understanding of the relationship between an individual and a group is the idea that mutual commitment will be reflected in what Moreland and Levine call *role transitions*. A person's relationship to a group can be described in one of three ways: the person can be a nonmember, a quasi-member, or a full member of the group. There are four possible transitions from one of these roles to another. First, a prospective member can become a new member of the group. Then after a suitable period of mutual examination, the new member can become a full member. If the member's objectives begin to diverge from those of the group, the full member becomes a marginal member. Finally, if no accommodation is possible, the marginal member becomes an ex-member. What produces each of these role transitions? The mutual commitment of individual and group. In short, neither commitment nor group membership is regarded as dichotomous (committed or not; member or not); both are considered dimensions on which the relationship between an individual and a group can be described.

Passage Through a Group.   An individual's association with a group through time, as outlined by Moreland and Levine (1983), is shown in Fig. 12.3. Let us discuss this model of group socialization in terms of a familiar example–participation in a college fraternal organization. Almost as soon as you arrive at a college or university, you discover that many freshmen are considering joining a fraternity or sorority. Is such a move for you, or would you be happier to remain independent? At this point you are a prospective member, in the *investigation* phase of participation. The group is engaging in recruitment, inviting freshmen to take part in "rush." You as an individual are engaging in reconnaissance, perhaps asking people you know whether they are going to go through rush, examining the housing alternatives provided by the university, and inquiring about the reputation of various fraternal organizations. If at this point you decide that the future costs of joining outweigh the future benefits (no past or present

FIGURE 12.3 A model describing an individual's passage through various stages of association with a group (adapted from Moreland & Levine, 1983).

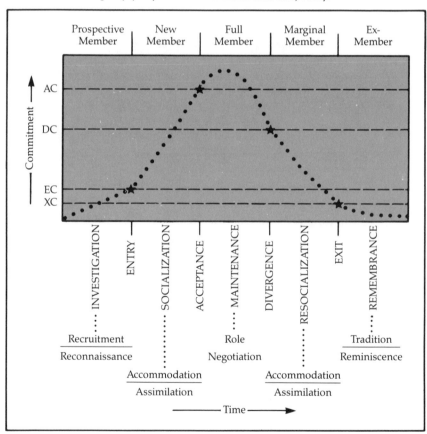

comparisons are possible), then you will never reach what Moreland and Levine (1983) call the *entry criterion* (EC in the figure).

If, on the other hand, you participate in formal rush, and join a fraternity or sorority, you will enter the *socialization* phase of participation. You are a "pledge," and during this socialization phase the organization will try to teach you what it considers "appropriate" behaviors for new members (and for full members) of the group. To the extent that the fraternity or sorority is successful in this endeavor, you will assimilate its norms. To the (more limited) degree that you are able to alter the group's expectations to take account of your individual needs and objectives, you will cause the group to accommodate to you. If the group's commitment to you (indicated in this example by its continued support for you) and your commitment to it (often indicated by your willingness to undergo some indignities of initiation) rise to the acceptance criterion (AC) for each, you will undergo the role transition to full membership.

This full membership will continue during your undergraduate career, unless at some point you decide that such full participation is no longer in your interest. As a full member in the *maintenance* phase of your relationship with the group, you will try to define your role in the organization in whatever way maximizes the likelihood of your achieving your own personal goals. For its part, the organization will attempt to define a specialized role for you that makes the best use of your talents to achieve the entire group's goals. If this role negotiation proves unsatisfactory to one party or the other, then that party's *divergence criterion* (DC) will be reached, and there will be efforts devoted toward *resocialization*. Should that resocialization process fail, then the *exit criterion* (XC) will be passed, and you will change from being a marginal member to being an ex-member. Whether or not there has been any marginal membership, upon graduation you will pass from being an "active" member to being an "alum." Although you may still have some psychological ties to the organization (and it probably hopes that you will have some financial ones), your participation as a full member has ended, to be replaced with *remembrance*.

This process of interchange over time between an individual and a group is not limited to voluntary organizations (such as fraternities and sororities). Before you graduate from college you will begin the investigation phase for employment or further schooling, and upon entry to a corporation or graduate school your socialization to what that organization considers "appropriate behavior" will begin all over again. The maintenance phase of your participation in a business organization will, if anything, involve much more role negotiation than a fraternal organization would have, because there are many more alternatives. Once you have been initiated into one fraternity or sorority, no others would consider your application, but full membership in a business does not prevent you from actively seeking other professional opportunities. A better offer from a competing firm is an important divergence criterion, and the counteroffer from your present employer is an attempt at resocialization. If that counteroffer is insufficient, you become an ex-member of the corporation, with remembrance taking the form of a line on your résumé. A great deal of "snapshot" research on the relations between a group and its members is consistent with the socialization model (Moreland & Levine, 1983), although the model has as of this writing not received the longitudinal test that it really needs. Keeping some of its principles in mind, we now turn to a more detailed examination of the concomitants of full membership in a group.

Pressure Toward Uniformity of Opinion

Social Reality and Group Locomotion. In an early analysis of social communication within small groups, Festinger (1950) distinguished between two different sources of pressure toward uniformity of opinion within social groups: social reality and group locomotion. It is consistent with Festinger's analysis for us to describe these two sources in terms we have been using throughout the chapter. Groups that exist primarily to serve social–emotional needs will be most successful if they can create an atmosphere, a social reality (as contrasted with objective reality), that validates the opinions of the members. Through the process of social comparison with the opinions of other members of this positive reference group, members can learn that they are indeed attractive, important, and useful human beings. Satisfaction among the members of a social–emotional group can be maintained only as long as the social reality has some basis in fact, or as long as there are no dissenting voices. But if the group is infiltrated by a subversive who insists that the emperor is truly wearing no clothes, the social reality will eventually collapse. To preserve its view of reality, the group must insist on uniformity of opinion, at least on relevant issues. The pressure toward uniformity is no less strong in a task-oriented group, but here its source is the need for *group locomotion* – movement toward the group goal. Achievement of task objectives requires coordinated and concerted effort on the part of all members of the group, and once the group has reached a decision about a plan of action, those who continue to maintain conflicting positions will simply get in the way.

Effects of Cohesiveness: An Experimental Demonstration. In both the social–emotional group and the task group, it is presumed that the greater the cohesiveness of the group is, the greater the pressure will be on full members to maintain uniformity of opinion. This direct relationship between cohesiveness and pressure toward uniformity, even in an informal group with a limited existence, was first demonstrated in a now classic study by Schachter (1951). Suppose that you had been a subject in this experiment. You would have volunteered to participate in a "club" and would have arrived for the first meeting of the group. After some preliminaries, you and the four or five other people in the group would be asked to discuss the Johnny Rocco case described earlier, and to arrive at a consensus about the punishment that should be imposed for Johnny's violations of the law. To begin the discussion, the experimenter would ask each of you to state a position on the question of punishment, in much the same way that subjects in an Asch-type conformity experiment are asked to make their choices of the proper comparison line. So you each state a position, and the last person to do so takes a stand that is as far as possible away from the opinion of the rest of the group. By now you have guessed (although the real subjects did not) that this *deviate* was in fact a confederate of the experimenter.

How do people react to this programmed deviate? The answer depends on the cohesiveness of the group, and on the degree to which the entire issue posed by the case is relevant to the ostensible purpose of the club. The experiment contained two levels of cohesiveness, determined by whether the subjects had been assigned to a club of their choice or to one in which they were not especially interested. Thus, cohesiveness was manipulated by varying the extent to which the club met the needs and desires of its members (and thus represented their within-group choices). The experiment was a factorial design, so that within each level of cohesiveness, half of the subjects had been given descriptions of the club that would have made discussion of the case seem appropriate, whereas the other half of the subjects would have been in "clubs" for which the discussion was irrelevant.

Now let us turn to the treatment of the deviate. As the discussion progressed in each experimental group, observers recorded the nature and frequency of communications directed to the deviate. At the end of the study, sociometric rankings were gathered from all participants. In the High Cohesive-Relevant groups communication to the deviate increased sharply at the beginning of the meeting, but then fell off when it became clear that he was not going to change his position. In all of the other conditions there was a gradual increase in communication to the deviate throughout the meeting.

A group will try to change the position of a deviate, in order to achieve uniformity of opinion, either for social–emotional reasons or reasons of group locomotion. In this experiment, of course, the requirement that there be a unanimous recommendation about what to do with Johnny Rocco provided a specific goal for the group to reach. What happens if one group member consistently refuses to participate in the group consensus? The sociometric rankings show the outcome: With relevance held constant, the more cohesive the groups were the more they rejected the deviate. In addition, with cohesiveness held constant, the more important the issue was, the more the deviate was rejected. And finally, the greatest rejection occurred, not surprisingly, in the High Cohesiveness-Relevant condition. The more important the issue and the more cohesive the group, the less tolerance there will be for disagreement. In terms of the Moreland and Levine (1983) analysis, the more commitment there is among full members of a group, the less the group will be willing to negotiate some nonstandard role for any full member. Requests for nonstandard treatment are likely to produce an immediate transition to marginal member, and any such member who cannot be resocialized in short order will be cast out of the group.

The Development of Groupthink

Silence Gives Consent. Rejection of the deviate in Schachter's (1951) experiment has important implications not only for psychological theory, but also for social policy decision-making processes. To avoid rejection by the others in a group, a member may conform or remain silent, hiding reservations about an important group decision precisely when he or she should be voicing those reservations. The consensus achieved under these circumstances will be a false consensus, with the apparently uniform social reality dangerously out of touch with objective reality outside the group. The group then becomes a victim of what Janis (1972) has called **groupthink**, a group preoccupation with unanimity that renders ineffective any critical evaluation of the situation.

As an example of groupthink in social policy decision making, Janis (1972) describes in detail the abortive Bay of Pigs invasion of Cuba, planned and conducted in 1961 by then-President John F. Kennedy and his advisors. In the invasion attempt, approximately 1,400 poorly equipped Cuban exiles landed at the Bay of Pigs in Cuba, expecting (as did Kennedy and his advisors) that a minimal show of force would be all that was necessary to begin a popular rebellion against Cuba's dictator, Fidel Castro. Some 1,200 of the invading exiles were captured and later ransomed by the United States government for $53 million in food and drugs. From the standpoint of the United States, everything about the operation went as badly as it possibly could have.

This is not an isolated instance, only a well documented one, and for the policymaker and the social scientist alike, the crucial question is how such gross miscalculations could have been made. Why did none of these intelligent people correctly anticipate an outcome that, in hindsight, seemed so obvious? Illustrating his argument with material from transcripts of the development of the invasion plan, Janis (1972) argues that groupthink is the most plausible explanation, an argument supported in a thorough study by Tetlock (1979) of public statements made by some of the participants in the decision. According to the theory, groupthink is probable whenever (a) the decision-making group is a highly cohesive one, (b) the group is insulated from outside opinion, and (c) the policy under consideration has been strongly endorsed by the leader of the group. Under such circumstances, what group member would be willing to risk status (or even full membership) in the group by pointing out flaws in the leader's reasoning? The resulting collective silence gives consent to a bad decision.

Reducing the Illusions.   Once groupthink has arisen on an issue, the reluctance of members to voice their objections leads to an *illusion of unanimity*, a false consensus that does not veridically reflect even social reality. This false consensus can lead to an *illusion of invulnerability*: after all, if none of the bright and capable people in this group, familiar with the issues as they are, can see any flaws in the plan, then that plan must be correct. Once critical thinking has been suspended, the group tends to ignore whatever contradictory information may become avaiable from outside the group. For example, Janis notes that even after newspapers began printing rumors of the impending invasion, President Kennedy and his advisors remained convinced that the invasion could be kept secret from the Cuban government and armed forces. The group merely hardens its position, perhaps to resolve dissonance created by the conflicting information, just as the Seekers began to proselytize after the anticipated doomsday passed uneventfully. The group thinks in simplistic and stereotyped terms about the problem, and develops whatever rationale is needed to justify its actions.

Although the Bay of Pigs invasion may be the best known example of groupthink in action, it is by no means the only one. A number of historical case studies described by Janis (1972), the ill-fated attempt by the Nixon administration to cover up the Watergate break-in, and the decision in 1985 by the Philadelphia police department to drop explosives from a helicopter onto the roof of a building occupied by a radical group (which ultimately resulted in the destruction of over 60 residences) might also qualify as examples of groupthink. Nor is the problem limited to governmental decisions. Decisions made by businesses, universities, and informal social groups often show the characteristics of groupthink as well.

How can this distortion of the decision-making process be avoided? Janis (1972) makes a number of specific suggestions, including bringing in outside experts who are encouraged to challenge the views of the group, having one member of the group play devil's advocate on any questions of importance, and teaching the leader of the group to accept criticism and refrain from stating his or her own position on the issue. Explicit procedures for the expression of disagreement and reservations must be institutionalized in the group in order to overcome the all-too-natural pressures toward uniformity of opinion.

Group Polarization of Individual Choices

As we have just seen, the pressures toward uniformity of opinion among full members of a group may lead to groupthink if a highly cohesive group with a strong, opinionated leader is insulated from outside opinion. But even if the group is essentially leaderless, even if there is full discussion of the issues, and even if the group is not isolated from outside opinion, it may make a group decision that would differ from the individual decisions made privately by its members. This is one conclusion from and extensive series of experimental studies originally called the *shift to risk*, or *risky shift*, later described in broader terms as a **choice shift** in group discussion (Pruitt, 1971), and now generally regarded as indicating **group polarization** of individual choices or attitudes (Moscovici & Zavalloni, 1969; Myers & Lamm, 1976).

The Choice Dilemmas. The phenomenon can best be illustrated by asking you to imagine that you are a member of a small, leaderless experimental group that has been formed to discuss a number of decision problems. Each of these decision problems, or *choice dilemmas* (Wallach & Kogan, 1959), describes a choice that must be made by a stimulus person. For example, one of these persons must decide whether to leave a steady job with a modest salary for a potentially more rewarding position with a newly formed company whose future is uncertain. Another must choose between attending a high prestige graduate program whose standards he might not be able to meet, and attending a school of much lower prestige from which he would certainly receive a degree. Still another must decide whether to marry a particular person after a marriage counselor suggests that the couple's marriage might be a good one, but that happiness is not assured. There are 12 choice dilemmas such as these, and your task is to serve as an advisor to the central person in each story. In each case you are asked to indicate the lowest probability of success that you would require before you would encourage the stimulus person to choose the risky but more desirable alternative (in these examples, the riskier alternatives are, respectively, taking the new job, attending the high prestige university, and getting married). The amount of risk that you are willing to take on each choice dilemma is simply the probability estimate that you give. If you are willing to accept a probability of success of 1 chance in 10, you are obviously more risky than if you would insist on a probability of success of 5 chances in 10.

It is clear that the probability level you require is a measure of your willingness to encourage others to take risks, but what exactly is the "risky shift?" That shift is a group-produced effect, in some ways similar to the convergence around a common judgment made in Sherif's (1936) studies with the autokinetic phenomenon. The risky shift was first observed by Stoner (1961), who was interested in group decisions on the choice dilemma problems. Small groups of subjects were brought together and presented with the choice dilemmas. Each member of the group first recorded a private estimate of the probability of success required, then the group discussed the issue, and finally each member recorded a second private opinion. Interestingly enough, the results showed that for most of the 12 choice dilemmas, the group's probability of success was lower (riskier) than the average of the original private opinions, and this shift to risk during the group discussion was in many cases retained in the subsequent private judgments. Just as in the autokinetic situation, group discussion produced a convergence of opinion that was to some degree maintained in later private estimates.

Implications of Convergence. But there are two crucial differences between convergence on the choice dilemmas and convergence in the autokinetic situation. First, the choice dilemmas describe situations that have value connotations–taking business risks, competing in contests of various sorts, or making decisions that can affect future life–whereas the autokinetic situation is a relatively value-free perceptual judgment. Second, and more important, convergence on the choice dilemmas was preponderantly in a particular direction, with more risky decisions apparently made by groups than by individuals. Prior to the publication of these findings, it had been assumed that if a decision had to be made on a controversial or uncertain issue, a decision-making committee would typically arrive at a more conservative solution than would a single person acting alone. The risky shift found by Stoner (1961) and subsequently replicated by others suggested that just the opposite was true. This possibility carried such important implications for group decision making in a variety of contexts that a great deal of effort was devoted to attempts to explain the risky shift.

Diffusion of Responsibility. An obvious possibility is that the subjects in the experiment are perfectly willing to make risky decisions for some other person, but would not do so if they were to suffer the consequences of failure themselves. This artifact of the procedure was quickly ruled out by having subjects decide on their own chances of experiencing noxious physical effects, such as nausea from smelling a chemical (Bem, Wallach, & Kogan, 1965).

The first theoretical explanation to receive attention was the idea that in the group setting, each member is less personally responsible for the outcome, and consequently less blameworthy for a potential failure. With this *diffusion of responsibility* (Wallach, Kogan, & Burt, 1967) among its members, the group can afford to make a riskier decision. You may remember from chapter 9 that Latané and Darley (1970) suggested that diffusion of responsibility for aiding a victim might contribute to bystander unresponsiveness in an emergency. They argued that diffusion of responsibility produced a failure to take the risk of intervening, whereas here it is argued that a similar process should produce a greater likelihood of risky action. The two are obviously contradictory, but fortunately for conceptual clarity, the diffusion-of-responsibility explanation of the risky shift has not been supported by most of the evidence (Pruitt, 1971).

Risk as a Cultural Value. A second explanation, suggested by Brown (1965), was that our culture places a positive value on taking reasonable risks, especially if they are entrepreneurial or competitive risks. As it happens, 9 of the 12 items in the set of choice dilemmas deal with just this sort of risk. The value explanation suggests that in the course of normal self-presentation, the members of the group desire to make public statements that indicate that they subscribe to this positive view of reasonable risk. During the group discussion, the "conservatives" realize that they have not gone far enough, and they shift in the risky direction in order to regain stature within the group.

Perhaps the most important contribution of the value theory was its implication that the shift ought to be greatest on those items that are most entrepreneurial or competitive in tone. This implication caused investigators to look more closely at the specific items, discovering to their surprise that a few of the items, such as the marriage item, produced consistent conservative shifts. Whether the group's opinion was more or less risky than the opinion of the individuals in the group thus seemed to depend on the content of the issue being discussed. Consequently, it became more appropriate to refer to the group induced changes as a choice shift, rather than a shift in a particular direction.

The discovery that some choice dilemma items produce conservative shifts and the finding that shifts occur on attitude dimensions (Moscovici & Zavalloni, 1969) as well as on the risk dimension made the choice shift less of a novelty, and brought the question of its causes back into the realm of the mutual social influence that occurs in the group setting (Cartwright, 1971). Individuals come to a group with preexisting attitudes and values, and the social reality within the group is created from these different initial positions. If in constructing social reality, the members discover that a preponderance of them share a direction on the attitude issue or choice to be made, group discussion will *polarize* the individual positions. What this view suggests is that the "risky" items in the CDQ produce shifts that differ from those found on the "conservative" items not so much because of the content of the items, themselves, as because of the initial positions that subjects hold on those items. What the items do is tap different predilections subjects bring with them into the laboratory.

Social Comparison on the Issue. This analysis in terms of reciprocal social influence is best represented in the two predominant explanations now offered for the group polarization effects. The first of these is the familiar process of social comparison. How is a person to determine what value the group places on risk (or on conservatism)? There is no objective standard, so the only alternative is to attend carefully to the opinions of other members of the group, especially to those who appear to be similar to the self. Indeed, the very fact of group membership may be all the similarity that is required.

According to a recent review by Isenberg (1986), there are two different mechanisms that have been invoked by proponents of the social comparison explanation of group polarization effects: "one emphasizing the removal of pluralistic ignorance [lack of knowledge about the group's position], and the other emphasizing one-upmanship (bandwagon effects)" (p. 1142). These two accounts can be seen as representing, respectively, the two senses of the "drive to evaluate" one's opinions and abilities. If "evaluate" is thought of as "locate," and a person's initial opinion is not regarded as permanently fixed, then discovery of the group's central tendency will produce change in that direction. The individual position becomes assimilated to the group view, not for reasons of self-promotion, but only because the group position becomes a new anchor for the individual. In contrast, if "evaluate" is considered "place a value upon," then it is important for individuals to present themselves as having views that not only support, but even extend, the group position. Isenberg (1986) notes that there has been empirical support for both aspects of the social comparison explanation.

Persuasive Arguments Theory. The second predominant explanation for occurrence of group polarization effects is the **persuasive arguments** theory of Vinokur and Burnstein (1974; Burnstein & Vinokur, 1977). When you are asked to state your position on the first choice dilemma (or on each succeeding one), it stands to reason that you will not have thought of all the arguments either for or against the hypothetical decision to be made. But during the group discussion of the question, or as part of the information you receive from other sources when no group discussion occurs, you learn of other arguments that you might not previously have considered. Some of these will be more persuasive than others, and a truly persuasive but unusual argument can change the course of the entire discussion.

To test this formulation, Vinokur and Burnstein (1974) first had subjects generate all of the pro and con arguments they could think of for each of the choice dilemmas. The proportion of people who listed a given argument was then taken to represent the probability that any single individual would have thought of the argument prior to group discussion. From this probability value, together with the number of subjects in the group, the researchers could compute a derivative probability value that reflected the number of participants in the discussion who would not have been aware of the argument before the discussion. Next, the subjects were asked to estimate the cogency or persuasiveness of every argument generated in the first step. Then the impact of each argument was determined by multiplying its persuasiveness times the derivative number of people who would have been unaware of it. Finally, a value for the total impact of a set of arguments was computed, and this *mean total impact* was used to predict whether discussion would produce a risky shift or a conservative one. Persuasive arguments theory has accurately predicted the outcome of group discussion in a number of studies. Isenberg (1986) concludes that on balance persuasive arguments theory has enjoyed greater support than the social comparison explanation, although both kinds of processes do seem to be involved in the production of group polarization.

Once Again, the Importance of the Individual

One reason that the risky shift first attracted the attention of social psychologists was that it seemed to be a legitimate *group phenomenon.* Both in the laboratory, where it was studied extensively, and in the social upheavals of the 1960s, to which it was generalized, the risky shift at first appeared to be a revival of the "group mind" notion (LeBon, 1895)—the idea that members of a group will lose their individuality (much like the notion of deindividuation discussed in chapter 7) and engage in acts that as rational individuals they would ordinarily avoid. But the consistent failure to demonstrate any diffusion-of-responsibility effects, the discovery of conservative shifts, and finally the individually based social comparison and persuasive arguments explanations, all indicate that this particular group phenomenon is most probably the consequence of the various contributions to discussion made by individual participants.

This analysis of group polarization does not deny the existence of all group-related effects. Social groups may indeed make decisions that will differ from those made by individual persons. In part, these differences will depend on the structure of communication processes within the group, in part they will be determined by the emergent and formal leadership of the group, and in part they will be the result of the group's cohesiveness and the resulting pressure toward uniformity of opinion. Participation in a group, regardless of the phase of the relationship, is an excellent example of the mutual contingency of social influence. Each full member brings individual social perceptions, attitudes, and social motives to the group. Through role negotiation, these individual characteristics influence the "plan" of the group, both in setting its objectives and in accomplishing the group locomotion needed to reach those objectives. By the same token, these group processes will affect the individual's "plan," occasionally requiring the alteration of some personal attitudes and the relinquishing of some personal goals.

As we have noted so often, the task of scientific social psychology is to develop theories and conduct research that will increase our understanding of human social behavior. Much of that behavior can be regarded as individual action, but some of it can also be thought of as the result of social exchange between the individual and various social groups. How do we account for these social exchanges? One approach is to adopt the viewpoint of the group and ask how groups produce various sorts of self-presentations, how they affect the self-concepts and attitudes of their members, and how their norms influence the individual's behavior in subtle ways as well as through explicit demands for conformity. Such an approach focuses on the group and its characteristics, placing the individual group members in the background. This concentration upon group processes was characteristic of early work in social psychology, and it continued to be a dominant theme throughout the 1950s. A different approach concentrates on the individual, relegating group influences to a secondary role. Here the focus is on the internal causes of social behavior—ways of integrating perceptual information, processes of social attribution, needs for cognitive consistency and self-esteem, rewards and costs of social exchange as viewed by the participants in a relationship. This latter approach has been the dominant theme of recent social psychology, and it is obviously inherent in our definition of the discipline as the study of the personal and situational factors that affect individual social behavior. Having just considered the consequences for those individuals of the social environment of the group, we next turn to consideration of the effects that the physical environment can have on human social behavior.

SUMMARY

A **social group** (p. 412) is a collectivity that has psychological implications for the individual. Such groups can be characterized by the degree to which they provide social–emotional rewards for their members, and by the degree to which they attempt to achieve well defined group goals. The functioning of the group and the place of the individual in that group will be affected by the communication structure of the group, the nature of the leadership, the members' socialization within the group, and the processes involved in group decision making.

The flow of communication within a group can be described in terms of various **communication networks** (p. 430) including such models as the chain, the circle, the Y, and the wheel. The communication *distance* (p. 430) between members will differ depending on the pattern of the network, as will the **relative centrality** (p. 431) of each position in the structure. Measures of group efficiency and member satisfaction are usually rank-ordered according to the degree of centralization in the communication network: More centralized networks are more efficient for the group but less pleasing to the individual. In addition, peripheral members of any network express less satisfaction than do the more central members.

Regardless of the structure of communication, the content of that communication can be examined through use of **Interaction Process**

Analysis (p. 434). In groups without formal structure or established leadership, most of the communication among members is related to the task objectives of the group, with the next most frequent communication consisting of group maintenance activities. Two different roles – the *task specialist* and the *social–emotional specialist* (p. 436) typically emerge in a group, and these are usually occupied by different people. When the group does have an established leader, those leaders who show *consideration* (p. 438) toward group members, and who *initiate structure* in the group's activities (p. 438) will be the most successful. Their effectiveness, however, will also depend on characteristics of the situation, as described by the **contingency model** (p. 438), which takes into account both the leader's style and the nature of the setting.

Successful group activity requires that at least some decisions be made by the group as a whole rather than exclusively by the leader, and a variety of factors will affect these group decision processes. Groups can serve social–emotional functions and/or instrumental functions for their members, and the degree to which a group meets all of its members' needs will determine the **cohesiveness** (p. 445) of the group. From the time they begin investigating a group to the time they become full members, prospective participants in a group will be *socialized* (p. 446) to the group's view of appropriate attitudes and behaviors. The more cohesive the group is, the more *pressure toward uniformity of opinion* (p. 450) there will be, and the more likely the group will be to expel any member who consistently takes a deviant position. An extreme example of this effect can be seen in the phenomenon of **groupthink** (p. 452): members of a highly cohesive group insulated from outside opinion may accept without question a policy strongly endorsed by the group leader. Because the social reality in such a group may be seriously out of touch with objective reality, disastrous miscalculations can occur. Even in a leaderless group with full discussion of the issues, the group setting may induce a **choice shift** (p. 454) in courses of action that individuals would have undertaken without any influence from the group. Discovery that such shifts occur on attitude dimensions as well as on courses of action has led to reconceptualization of choice shifts as one kind of **group polarization** (p. 454) of individual predilections, a polarization that seems to occur as a result of a combination of social comparison among group members and the identification during discussion of **persuasive arguments** (p. 457) that produce change.

SUGGESTED ADDITIONAL READINGS

CARTWRIGHT, D., & ZANDER, A. (Eds.). (1968). *Group dynamics: Research and theory.* New York: Harper & Row. This is an excellent collection of classic studies in group dynamics, including material on cohesiveness, group standards, communication, and leadership. Each section begins with an introduction by the editors.

COLLINS, B. E., & RAVEN, B. H. (1969). Group structure: Attraction, coalitions, communication, and power. In G. Lindzey & E. Aronson (Eds.), *Handbook of social psychology* (2nd ed., Vol. 4, pp. 102-204). Reading, MA: Addison-Wesley. A comprehensive review of communication networks, theories of group structure, and coalition formation in small groups.

HOLLANDER, E. P. (1985). Leadership and power. In G. Lindzey & E. Aronson (Eds.), *Handbook of social psychology* (3rd. ed., Vol. 2, pp. 485-537). New York: Random House. A thorough review of the various theories of leadership. This chapter takes the position that power is the ability to produce change in other people's behavior, and examines the ways in which leaders are able to accomplish that end. Intended for a professional audience, but still quite accessible to interested undergraduates.

CHAPTER THIRTEEN

THE ENVIRONMENT AND SOCIAL BEHAVIOR

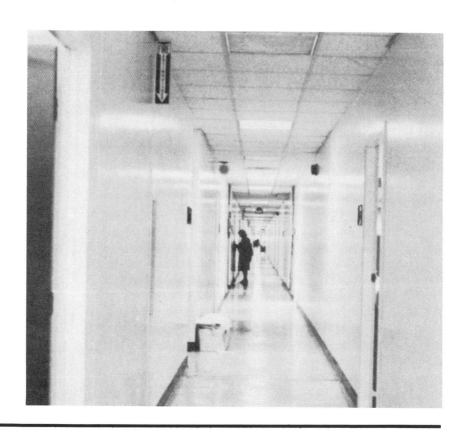

CONTENTS

PREVIEW

Features of the physical environment, and the way in which those features are perceived and understood, will affect the quality of social behavior. The individual brings to social interaction certain requirements for personal space, an understanding of the social meaning of interpersonal distance, and cognitive processes necessary for representing the natural and built environment. The physical environment sets limits on human interaction, and the social environment–represented in the theory of staffing–also places constraints on action. In his or her interpersonal behavior, an individual will attempt to control access to the self. This privacy regulation is an optimization process in which negative effects are associated with either too much or too little privacy. One aspect of the lack of privacy– crowding–has received special attention from social psychologists.

Imagine for a moment that you are in a mountain lodge overlooking crystal-blue lake nestled in the lush green of an alpine meadow. It is a crisp day in early summer, and although the meadow is dotted with wildflowers, you can see occasional patches of snow in the deep shade. Next, think of yourself as one of the people crowded shoulder to shoulder on a subway during the evening rush hour. It has been a sweltering summer day, and the train is presently stopped between stations, with the lights off, in a part of the tunnel that passes under the river. Finally, think of returning to your own dormitory room or apartment. It is shortly after the winter break, and the second term begins tomorrow.

Each stop on this imaginary trip involves a feature of the *built environment*: that part of the physical environment that has been altered by people. The lodge, the subway, and your residence were all constructed by people, but if your experience is typical, you will have different emotional reactions in each setting, and different behaviors would be appropriate (or ruled out) in each place. This imaginary excursion illustrates several fundamental principles of the newly emerging field of environmental psychology, and suggests why social psychologists have been quick to see the importance of environmental constraints on social behavior.

PRINCIPLES OF ENVIRONMENTAL PSYCHOLOGY

Situations and Persons

At numerous times throughout this book, we have noted that social psychology is the scientific study of the personal and situational factors that affect individual social behavior. Neither person alone nor environment alone can account for the complexity of human action. Rather, social behavior is the consequence of a dynamic interaction between the two. We have seen this to be true in such things as the formation of social attitudes, the decisions people make about intervention in emergencies, or the joint influence of achievement motivation and task difficulty upon the choice of an achievement task. In each of the settings just described, the natural environment has been altered by people, and in the case of your dormitory or apartment room, you can make further changes in the building, decorating it to suit your tastes. You do not, however, have complete freedom in changing the physical characteristics of your room, and you have still less opportunity to affect the physical environment of the subway (although some theorists, notably Sommer, 1974, argue that graffiti and vandalism can be regarded as evidence of the attempt to "humanize" the forbidding architecture of the subway). In this chapter we consider various aspects of the interaction between person and environment, including the construction of and adaptation to the built environment, establishment of personal space boundaries, regulation of privacy, and adjustment to life in the city.

As individuals and as members of organized social groups, we can make both temporary and permanent alterations in the natural environment. But as a society, we are becoming increasingly conscious that such changes can have long-term effects on our social behavior. In part because of the fact that environmental problems often lead to social problems, and in part because environmental studies emphasize the interchange between person and situation, social psychologists have been a dominant force in the development of the field of environmental psychology.

Research and Theory

A second major theme of this book, the concentration upon theory and research, can also be seen in the contributions that social psychologists have made to the study of environmental issues. The research methods of social psychology, including both naturalistic observations and laboratory experiments, overlap to a substantial degree with those designed specifically for environmental research (see discussions of environmental research methods by Ittelson, Proshansky, Rivlin, & Winkel, 1974). Some investigators disagree about the potential of social-psychological methods for the study of environmental questions, but some excellent examples of the kinds of application possible are given in a recent review by Darley and Gilbert (1985).

To note opportunities presented by the methods of social psychology is not to claim that they are perfectly suited for the study of environmental questions. Research in environmental psychology must necessarily be more concerned with external validity than with internal validity, for two different reasons. First, many research questions have arisen from attempts to solve pressing social and environmental problems such as urban decay, crowding, or uncontrollable noise and pollution. So that their work will have the greatest applied benefit, environmental researchers have made certain that their studies will generalize to the problems, even if that external validity has to be achieved through some sacrifice of control over the experimental setting. Second, by almost any standard, the scientific study of the relationship between environment and behavior is in its infancy; the first comprehensive text on the subject was published in 1974 (Ittelson et al., 1974). Consequently, the goal of the research is to build a body of data on which future theories can be founded, rather than to test precise derivations from well established theoretical models.

What theoretical formulations do exist in environmental psychology tend to be stated at the level of particular problems, such as crowding (Baum & Epstein, 1978; Freedman, 1975), the establishment and regulation of privacy (Altman, 1975), or urban stress (Glass & Singer, 1972). These theories, and many of the others we consider, have been contributed by social psychologists, and the imprint of traditional social psychological theory and analysis is a strong one. You will recall that in chapter 8 we distinguished between theories about internal processes—social perception, attribution, attitude organization—and those describing interpersonal behavior—social learning, exchange, equity. Because the latter attempt to account for larger units of human behavior, their explanatory principles are typically simpler, and the same is true for the theories of environmental psychology presented in this chapter. These theories not only attempt to describe the behavior of people engaged in social interaction, but also try to consider the physical boundaries within which that interaction takes place. This important addition has several consequences that can be illustrated by returning to our earlier example.

Dimensions of a Place

A mountain lodge, a subway, and a dormitory room are all features of the built environment, but they differ along some fundamental dimensions. The social *purpose* of the mountain lodge is primarily recreation, although people could certainly conduct an occasional business or professional retreat there. In contrast, the purpose of the subway is to provide travel facilities for commuters, shoppers, students, and others. The residence serves primarily as a housing unit, although some mixture of business and pleasure can occur there as well.

The *time of use* of the mountain lodge might be the most limited, because it might be open only during the summer. In contrast, the subway is in operation (barring mechanical failure) throughout the year, but peak times and slack times occur, and the system may not be operating 24 hours per day. An academic residence can be used whenever the university is in session, but only when its occupants are not attending classes or involved in extracurricular activities outside the building.

The *administrative organization responsible* for the lodge might be the National Park Service, a federal government agency. A local transit authority or city government controls the subway, whereas the residence is managed by a university administration that answers either to a state government or to a private board of directors. Users report problems respectively to park rangers, local or transit police, and campus or state police; the responsiveness of these various law enforcement officers will depend as much on their jurisdiction as on their sympathy for the victim.

Finally, each place imposes *limits on the behavior* that is appropriate (or possible). You cannot see the sky from a subway, and you may get claustrophobia while you are stopped in the tunnel. You must travel by automobile or bus to reach the mountain lodge, and, depending on your personal tastes, you may feel uplifted or bored out there in the wilderness. Only in the residence are you allowed to make alterations in the decor, although how you feel about your room may be more significantly affected by what else has happened during the day than by the room itself.

A Multidisciplinary and Systems Approach

Because of social purpose, time of usage, administrative responsibility, and other dimensions of places, thorough study of environmental psychology requires a multidisciplinary approach (Altman, 1975; Ittelson et al., 1974). The environment of the subway, for example, is only partly determined by the architects and engineers who actually supervised the construction. The design of the stations and cars should also have taken into account the safety needs, individual differences in waiting in lines (called queueing behavior), personal space requirements, and mechanical aptitude of passengers (all topics within the province of the psychologist). Placement of the stations and routes would have involved demographic and use patterns (the interest of the sociologist and urban planner), but would have required final approval by a variety of local governing boards (the actions of which are the concern of political scientists). Naturally, some decisions affect the psychological environment of the subway more directly than others, but a complete understanding requires the participation of representatives from various traditional disciplines. Our objective in this chapter is the more limited one of introducing you to some of the social-psychological contributions to environmental psychology, but even those are characterized by a somewhat broader reliance upon other areas of inquiry than we have seen to this point.

A second feature of the environmental approach that distinguishes it from many of the social-psychological theories we have considered before is its emphasis upon the person and environment as an interacting *system*.

You can alter your personal surroundings, often within quite broad limits, by changing your location, by varying the time of your visits to particular places, or, in some cases, by modifying the physical structure itself. But no change you make can eliminate the effects of the environment (in its original or altered form) on your behavior. For simplicity in exposition, we discuss separately those theories that concentrate on the features of places, those that deal with individual differences in cognitive abilities and use of space, and those primarily focused on aspects of the interaction between people and their environment. Throughout these discussions, however, you should remember that the goal of environmental psychology, like the goal of conceptions of social influence discussed in chapters 11 and 12, is to explain a system of reciprocal influence.

DESCRIPTIONS
OF THE PHYSICAL ENVIRONMENT

The Choice of Units of Analysis

We have seen studies of naturally occurring social behavior in a number of earlier chapters, and one of these studies at first seems to be an example of environmental psychology. You will recall from chapters 2 and 9 that Festinger, Schachter, and Back (1950) observed the development of friendship patterns in a married students' residence unit. They found that the likelihood that two couples would develop a friendship, to a large degree, depended on physical proximity within the residence unit, and this result does represent an effect of environment on behavior. But for two reasons it is not characteristic of studies in environmental psychology. First, and most important, Festinger, Schachter, and Back were interested in the conceptual variable of proximity (conveniently varied by the features of the building), not in a conceptual variable of residence, variations in which would have required using different sorts of buildings. Second, they made no attempt to relate the physical features of the building to different patterns of behavior. True, the investigators noted that a stairway was roughly equivalent in "functional units" to passing another doorway, but they did not examine the reasons for such equivalence. The physical environment was a source of variation to be minimized, not a dimension to be included in the analysis.

The first extensive study of social behavior in a natural context that did expressly include the physical environment was conducted by Barker and his colleagues at the Midwest Field Station in Kansas over a period of 25 years (Barker, 1968; Barker and Associates, 1978). The most serious problem confronting the researcher who attempts to conduct systematic observations of an entire community is the creation of an appropriate unit of analysis. Think for a moment about how you might try to solve this problem. Given your interest in the physical environment's effects on behavior, you might first think of all buildings as possible units. There could be, for example, high school behavior, hospital behavior, or church behavior. But is only one sort of behavior performed in each of these places? Are the places equivalent in the amount of behavior they encompass? What about all of the social interaction that takes place outdoors? Is it possible to retain physical setting as part of a definition and still account for the variety of actions that need to be documented?

Settings for Behavior

According to Barker (1968), the answer to this last question is affirmative, and is represented in the concept of the **behavior setting**: a structural and dynamic combination of place and activity. The behavior setting is defined by several different characteristics (Barker, 1968; Wicker & Kirmeyer, 1977). First, the activity must be a regularly occurring one, with definite place and time boundaries. Second, it must be independent of the specific individuals involved. Third, the activity must be coordinated with aspects of the physical environment, but it must be independent of adjacent places and activities. Finally, there must be a hierarchy of social roles or positions for people who influence or have responsibility for the setting; the setting itself must have the capacity to generate the forces necessary for its own maintenance.

Let us turn these criteria into a specific example. Your class in Social Psychology is a behavior setting. It meets regularly, at a consistent time and in a scheduled place, and would continue whether or not you personally were involved. The class requires a room, chairs, a chalkboard, and a particular subject matter. The single class meeting on January 22 is not a behavior setting, because that class occurs only once, on the specified day. The Social Psychology class can be distinguished from the behavior setting of the Physics class (even if the two meet in the same building at the same time) by virtue of differences in room and content area. The role of teacher and the role of student occur, and the mutual responsibility for holding class can maintain the setting, even though on a beautiful spring day, both teacher and students might prefer to be somewhere else.

According to the set of criteria, a high school is a building containing numerous behavior settings, one of which might be a Geometry class and one of which might be basketball practice. A hospital also contains numerous behavior settings, one of which might be appendectomies. A church would not be a behavior setting, but a worship service (even one that occurred regularly once a year) would be. Thus a behavior setting is a unique conjunction of activity and place that can serve as one unit of analysis for environmental psychology.

Setting and Behavior:
A Theory of Staffing

Creation of a unit of analysis is only the first task for the environmental psychologist. The goal, as noted earlier, is explanation of the reciprocal influence of environment and behavior. This dynamic interchange is represented in Barker's (1968) theory of *manning*, which holds that an optimal number of participants are evident in any behavior setting (the idea of optimization is also part of the predominant conception of privacy regulation discussed later). The original theory describes departures from optimum as "undermanning" or "overmanning," but it has been revised by Wicker and his associates (Wicker & Kirmeyer, 1977), who have changed some of the fundamental terms to make them less gender-biased. In the remainder of this section, we concentrate on the theory as revised. Departures from optimum affect the actions of the remaining participants in a variety of ways. The theory is most explicit about the problems of too few participants – the condition of **understaffing** – and notes that under these circumstances, participants will have to assume roles and tasks they might otherwise have ignored, will have to work harder to accomplish those tasks, will have a lower standard of best performance, and will reduce the requirements for admission to the setting as a participant. When there are too many participants – the condition of **overstaffing** – participants may compete for important roles, all participants can afford to reduce their level of effort, and the admission standards for participants will be raised.

Elements of the Theory.   Concentrating on behavior settings in which a service of some sort is delivered – a college class, a quick-copy service, an automobile repair shop, a dentist's office, a restaurant – Wicker and Kirmeyer (1977) first distinguish between the *staff* and the *clients*. This distinction follows Barker's division of the participants into *performers* (people who have assigned tasks in the setting) and *nonperformers* (people who may be consumers of the service, but who do not have assigned roles in the maintenance of the setting). The basic principle of staffing theory is then applied to each class of participants in order to determine the level of staffing of the setting. The critical condition for continuation of the setting is the *maintenance minimum*; if it has too few staff (*understaffed*) or too few clients (*underpopulated*), the setting will terminate. Consider the example of your Social Psychology class. Especially on days right before holidays, class attendance may drop significantly, but if there are still even a few students present the professor will consider the class *adequately populated*. But if the professor happens to be absent on one class day, the setting would immediately be understaffed. The *capacity* of the behavior setting is the maximum number of persons that the setting can accommodate, and a setting can become either *overpopulated* (so many students attempt to enroll in the class that you have to watch a taped lecture on a remote video monitor) or *overstaffed* (four different instructors desire to teach Social Psychology, but only one of them can do so). Finally, the revised theory talks about the *program* for the setting: the time-ordered sequence of events that must occur. Changes away from adequate staffing and/or adequate population often adversely affect the program for the setting.

The Restaurant Business: An Example of Staffing Theory. Two things need to be noted about the reformulation of manning theory. First, the concentration on settings in which some service is provided excludes from consideration family units and voluntary organizations (bridge clubs, automobile clubs, fraternal orders) in which no distinction is possible between staff and clients. Given the large number of service settings in our social lives, this is not a critical limitation of the theory. Second, the division of participants into two groups leads to three possibilities for a setting: (a) understaffed–overpopulated (for example, one secretary handing out folders at freshman registration), (b) adequately staffed and populated, and (c) overstaffed–underpopulated (for example, a transatlantic airplane flight with a full complement of flight attendants but only a few passengers).

In almost any service behavior setting, changes will occur in the population pattern. Sometimes these variations will occur from year to year, but occasionally they will take place from moment to moment, so a primary goal of the staff is to maximize the condition of adequate staffing and population. Let us consider the example of a restaurant. As a regularly occurring, standing pattern of activity with a defined place and time, a unit unto itself and distinguishable from adjacent buildings or activities, a restaurant satisfies the conditions of being a behavior setting. The participants can be separated into diners and staff, and a clearly defined hierarchy of roles is evident among the staff. Some people prepare the food; some people take orders and serve the food; others clean up empty tables; others take reservations, greet diners, and accept payments; still others prepare drinks or serve them. One obvious dimension on which restaurants differ is the number of occupants of each of these staff roles; a lunch counter in which one person serves in all positions is obviously different from a posh city restaurant with several people in each staff role (and with the roles differing according to the individual occupant's experience).

The service setting's attempt to regulate the flow of patrons begins with initial contacts between the restaurant and potential customers. In the heavy seasons, or on weekend nights, the restaurant may require reservations, thus raising the standards for admission. In contrast, during the off-season or on Mondays and Tuesdays, the restaurant may close entirely, advertise specials that are available only on these otherwise slow nights, or offer other inducements to potential diners (such as a free bottle of wine with two dinner entrees). Not only does the restaurant regulate the flow of patrons ("Your table is almost ready, would you care to wait in the bar?"), but it also adjusts the size of the staff in an attempt to maintain an optimal level of staffing. Naturally, in a business operated for profit, this optimal level is influenced by financial considerations, whereas in nonprofit service settings the size of an "adequate" staff is likely to be larger. (Some would argue that one trouble with "big government" is that the staffing does not seem responsive to reductions in the clientele; on the contrary, the clientele is continually expanded to justify the existing staff.) Finally, the wages received by many of the staff members are contingent on the client–staff ratio (the tips of waiters, waitresses, and to a lesser extent some others). As a result, the financial rewards increase as the setting approaches being poorly staffed (the low end of adequate staffing), so that the staff remains equitably compensated – its increased responsibilities per unit time are matched by increasing pay.

Tests of the Theory. The original theory of manning and the reformulation of the theory into staffing/populating have been tested in a variety of contexts. The 25 years' worth of observational data gathered at the Midwest Field Station serve primarily to catalogue the great diversity of behavior settings, but these data also provide support for the central proposition of manning theory – that optimal use of a behavior setting requires achieving and maintaining a balance between the population of clients and the staff available (Barker & Associates, 1978). Wicker and his associates have tested the staffing theory through analysis of archival records of churches, laboratory studies of slot-car racing, and observational research on responses to overpopulated settings in Yosemite National Park (Wicker & Kirmeyer, 1977).

Staffing theory touches on a number of concerns that we have discussed earlier, from the attributions that a person might make about the reasons for a particular client–staff ratio ("Is nobody here because the food is bad?"), through decisions about whether the ratio is an equitable one (for either client or staff member), to the instigation to aggression that all too often accompanies extreme scarcity in either resources or staff. These examples are drawn from traditional concerns of social psychology, and they are further illuminated by the dynamic properties of staffing theory.

THE INDIVIDUAL
AND ENVIRONMENTAL BEHAVIOR

Although the idea of the behavior setting contributes to our understanding of the effects of environment on social behavior, it has one element that reduces its influence within social psychology. You will recall that the definition of social psychology in chapter 1 included a reference to the individual person: unique human beings are not considered interchangeable, and social behavior is a product of their particular characteristics as well as a function of the ongoing environment. But one of the defining features of the behavior setting is that the setting will remain unchanged regardless of the individuals who participate. True, a social psychology class is still a course in social psychology if all of the students are different, but any instructor will tell you that there are good classes and bad classes (just as there are good professors and poor ones). The setting is consistent, but the experience of the people involved may be quite different. In this section, we consider some of the personal attributes that affect an individual's perception of and use of the environment.

Personal Space

As unobtrusively as you can, take a look at other people's behavior in a crowded elevator. You will discover that as people enter they move to the rear, turn around to face the front, and carefully direct their eyes straight at the lighted panel indicating which floors are being reached. If you dare, turn to another passenger and try to begin an innocuous conversation. Soon you will begin to feel an oppressive silence, and you will probably stop talking. Why should everyone resent a little pleasant conversation? Why do people carefully avoid looking at each other (until they start looking daggers at you)? One reason is that in a crowded elevator, everyone's personal space is being violated, and there are implicit norms (which you've had the bad manners to ignore) against interaction under these circumstances.

Public and Social Distances. The social implications of various physical distances were first fully documented by Hall (1959), who coined the term **proxemics** to refer to the study of those distances. Hall identified four levels of personal distance, each with a *close phase* and a *far* phase, and catalogued the social behaviors most prevalent and appropriate at each distance. Beginning with distances away from the person, the far phase of *public distance* (more than 25 feet) is found most typically in the case of public figures, or an interaction between a speaker and members of an audience. It is characterized by a clear status difference between stimulus person and observers; only one-way communication is really possible, and even then the speaker's voice must often be amplified. It is not just the number of other students in the class that inhibits your asking questions in a large lecture; it is also the distance between you and the lecturer. In the close phase of public distance (25 to 12 feet), it is possible to carry on a conversation, but only if both participants use formal and syntactically correct speech, and raise their voices slightly. Again, status differences are common between participants at this distance.

   At the far phase of *social distance* (12 to 7 feet), conversation can be sustained by eye contact between the participants, but only with mutual consent. Status differences begin to blur, but the voice must still be raised slightly, and there is often some formal relationship between the two parties. This distance is typical between receptionists and visitors to an office, because it is close enough for the receptionist to determine the visitor's identity and purpose, but not so close that the visitor will begin an informal conversation that would take the receptionist away from other duties. In the close phase of social distance (7 to 4 feet), the usual behavior is informal business, with no status or dominance differences.

Personal and Intimate Distances. A little closer to the person, we find the far phase of *personal distance* (4 to 2.5 feet). This distance marks the boundary of the "bubble" around a person, known as **personal space**: the area that a person considers his or her own (Sommer, 1969). At this distance, two parties can touch, but only by mutual consent, because the people are still an arm's length apart. The personal space bubble is not a perfect circle, but tends to be egg-shaped, larger at the front and rear than at the sides. In the close phase of personal distance (2.5 feet to 1.5 feet), touching is possible without mutual consent, and the distance must be "explained" by some form of social relationship between the parties in order for them to be comfortable with it.

Finally, the last zone is not surprisingly called *"intimate distance"* (far phase from 1.5 to .5 feet, close phase 6 inches to zero). Now we discover why the people in the elevator reacted as they did. In a crowded elevator people are in bodily contact, but (as opposed to a crowded party) they are strangers in a public, businesslike, setting. Behaviors that are appropriate for the interpersonal distance are wholly out of keeping with the level of acquaintance, so to ease the discomfort, people try to ignore the physical proximity. Each person carefully faces forward, and everyone watches the floor designations (which, for most people, are outside intimate distance). These implicit norms minimize psychological contact and permit each person to maintain an illusion of personal comfort. Because conversation in the close phase of intimate distance is usually a prelude to lovemaking, you are invading the privacy of the person you address, and you are forcing others to invade your privacy by watching. No wonder everyone hopes that the next floor will be your stop!

Culture, Personality, and Personal Space. Taken together, the physical space available in a setting and the number of people who must use that space will contribute to the opportunities for, and limitations of, social interaction. But because people have different requirements for personal space, their individual characteristics can influence the social environment of others. One of the central elements of Hall's (1966) analysis of personal distances is that people who are raised in "contact" cultures — Middle Eastern, Mediterranean, Latin — not only will tolerate, but will prefer social distances that are more intimate than those found comfortable by northern Europeans and Americans. In a thorough review of over a hundred studies in which interpersonal distances had been measured carefully, Altman and Vinsel (1977) tested this and other aspects of Hall's ideas. They found that more than 65% of everyday social behavior among people who are standing occurs in the far phase of intimate distance, and the close phase of personal distance, roughly from 18 to 24 inches. By contrast, less than 10% occurs in the close phase of intimate distance.

Although the consistent use of a limited distance range testifies to the generality of interpersonal spacing, important differences based on culture, personality, and nature of the relationship also appear. Both in cross-national comparisons and in studies of different American ethnic groups, researchers have found support for Hall's notion of the contact culture, with Middle Eastern and Latin ethnic subgroups showing smaller personal distances than those maintained by northern Europeans or Americans (Altman & Chemers, 1980). But as Altman and Chemers note, these conclusions must be qualified. Contradictory findings do exist, and there is the possibility that some of the results may have been confounded by differences in education or socioeconomic status. Research involving the nature of the relationship is more conclusive, with physical closeness positively related to liking, friendship, or other positive experiences (Altman & Vinsel, 1977). Close friends tend to use the far phase of intimate distance, whereas more casual encounters occur in the close phase of personal distance.

Invasions of Personal Space. Finally, there is evidence that people maintain greater distances from those who have physical handicaps or are socially stigmatized in some other way. Altman and Chemers (1980) note that people do not come as close to others who have some stigmatizing condition—either a physical handicap or a negative social label such as *criminality.* A study by Kinzel (1970) may provide a rationale for the latter. This research showed that federal prisoners who had a history of personal violence required substantially more personal space than did other prisoners. Certainly being in prison would make you guard your personal space more jealously, but Kinzel's study suggests that an assaultive prisoner's violent behavior might be a consequence of a perceived violation of personal space. This kind of prisoner might perceive as an intrusion into intimate distance what for most people would be an acceptable level of personal distance, and would greet the intrusion with an attack. In most cases, of course, one person's use of personal space would not have such serious consequences for others in the vicinity, but the individual differences in use of personal space can be a significant influence on social behavior.

Environmental Cognition

We have seen that interpersonal distances, like the physical features of the environment, can affect social interaction. It is important to emphasize that in a fundamental sense, all of these effects of the environment on behavior depend on cognition. Your behavior can differ from the mountain lodge to the subway to your residence because you as an individual recognize the limits and opportunities inherent in each setting. But you have to learn those limits and opportunities. On your first visit to the mountain lodge, you know as little about the hiking trails as you did about the ways to traverse the city on your first excursion into the subway system. As you gain experience in a new setting, you build up a representation of the critical features of the environment, you form sets of expectations for buildings, routes, and travel times; these expectations influence your subsequent actions just as the stereotypes (Chapter 4) you hold affect your behavior toward people identified as members of one or another social group.

The Cognitive Map. What is the northernmost point in the contiguous 48 states? The westernmost? Which is farther west, the western border of Indiana, or the western border of Tennessee? How far is it from the post office that serves your hometown to the nearest bank? In which of the 50 states would you like to live permanently? Have you ever been there? If not, what is the reason for your choice? All of these questions deal with your **cognitive map**: your organized representation of some part of the spatial environment (Downs & Stea, 1977). That cognitive map is a product, the result of your collection, organization, storage, recall, and manipulation of information about the spatial environment, so it is subject to the same variations in ability and experience (and to the same distortions) that affect other sorts of information processing.*

Images of Cities. In an early study of cognitive mapping, Lynch (1960) asked residents of Boston, Jersey City, and Los Angeles about the images they had of their cities. These people were asked to draw rough sketches of sections of the central business districts of their cities, to provide directions for a number of trips within the districts, to identify distinctive features of the environment, and to describe in detail the route they normally took home from work. On the basis of these structured interviews, and directions asked of passersby in the three cities, Lynch abstracted five key elements that seemed to be involved in the mental images of cities. The first three—paths, edges, and districts—can be regarded as linear components of the mental image, whereas the other two—nodes and landmarks—can be thought of as discrete points on the cognitive map.

Paths, Edges, and Districts. According to Lynch (1960), *paths* are "channels along which the observer customarily, occasionally, or poten-

---

*By the way, the answers to the first three questions, respectively, are Lake of the Woods, Minnesota; Cape Alava, Washington; and Tennessee.

tially moves" (p. 47). Paths can be streets, hiking trails, railroads, or short cuts through the woods, and for most people they were the predominant element of the description. In contrast, *edges* are "the linear elements not used or considered as paths by the observer" (p. 47). Edges mark boundaries between features of the physical environment, and consist of such aspects as the shoreline of a lake, a wall, or the explicit boundary of a development. Because these features are defined from the viewpoint of the observer, it is clear that the same physical structure could serve as either a path or an edge: if you are traveling along an interstate highway, it is a path; if you are on foot and attempting to cross the same highway, it is an edge. Finally, *districts* are the "medium to large sections of the city, conceived of as having two-dimensional extent, which . . . are recognizable as having some common identifying character" (p. 47). Examples of districts would be an exclusive subdivision enclosed by a wall, the theater district in New York, or Chinatown in San Francisco.

Nodes and Landmarks. Paths, edges, and districts are defined by their function to the observer, not by their actual physical dimensions, and the same is true for nodes. *Nodes* are "strategic foci into which the observer can enter, typically either the junctions of paths, or concentrations of some characteristic" (p. 72). Thus, a node can be a traffic circle, like Dupont Circle in Washington, D.C.; a place that, like Paradise Lodge in Washington state, serves as the point of origin for numerous hiking trails; or a collection of buildings like an airport (try flying almost anywhere across the country without going through the Chicago airport, or anywhere in the Southeast without going through the Atlanta airport). In all of these examples the node serves as a junction, but as the concentration of a characteristic it can also be the core of a district—Bourbon Street in New Orleans, Fisherman's Wharf in San Francisco, the corner of Wall and Broad Streets in New York. The final elements in the image of the city, *landmarks*, are "the point references considered to be external to the observer" (p. 78)), and are usually buildings that stand out from the surrounding environment because of their scale. Examples would be the Arc de Triomphe in Paris, the Washington Monument, or the Gateway Arch in St. Louis. There is, however, no requirement that a landmark be large. Like the other elements, its function for the observer is the distinguishing feature; as long as it contrasts with the immediate background, it can serve as a point of reference.

Although Lynch (1960) considered his work to be pilot research, the methods he developed and the five elements he identified have heavily influenced cognitive mapping research and theory. Lynch pointed out that his sample was too small (30 respondents in Boston, 15 in each of the other two cities) and unrepresentative (a convenience sample of educated, middle-class respondents). In addition, because the data were responses to structured interview questions, it is possible that Lynch's training as a city planner led him to concentrate on physical features to a greater extent than would another interpreter (for example, an environmental or social psychologist). Nevertheless, more recent empirical work on cognitive maps of cities (Appleyard, 1970; Milgram, 1976) is generally quite consistent with Lynch's analysis. Indeed, even though they note that the results so far are limited to Western cities, Altman and Chemers (1980) suggest that the five elements might be used as dimensions on which to classify the "personalities" of cities.

Individual Differences in Environmental Cognition. Thus, our current knowledge of cognitive mapping indicates that paths, edges, districts, nodes, and landmarks play an important role in people's representations of urban environments. The five elements can be seen in the descriptions provided by a variety of Western national groups, and although the scheme has not been explicitly tested in nonurban settings, it may prove quite descriptive there as well. In the face of these regularities, it is important to point out (as do Altman & Chemers, 1980; Downs & Stea, 1977) that wide individual differences occur in cognitive maps. The complexity of a cognitive map will depend on the individual's familiarity with the area, and this may be a function of such things as socioeconomic status, occupation, or personal interest. More important, the cognitive map embodies evaluations, beliefs, and values as well as spatial features. What parts of the city are dangerous? Do particular settings evoke pleasant memories? Was your initial impression formed from an automobile, from a train, or on foot? What stereotypes did you hold about the city before your first visit? How important to you are the cultural activities that a city can provide? Similar questions can be asked about preconceptions, memories, modes of acquaintance, and personal values held regarding small towns and rural locations. The answers will be reflected in variations in environmental cognition, because the physical world, like the social world, is often changed in the eye of the beholder.

PERSON-ENVIRONMENT INTERACTION

We have seen that in some important respects, the physical environment can be relatively independent of specific individuals, who, in turn might be affected only minimally by their physical surroundings. Neither the physical environment nor the behavior setting is truly immune to influence from people (even the wilderness cannot remain so without a legislative mandate), but both treat individual persons as interchangeable. For their part, people's requirements for personal space and their cognitive processes for representing the environment are both relatively independent of the specific physical surroundings. Intimate distance may be inappropriate in public places, but the public setting does not change the number of inches involved in that interpersonal distance; principles of cognitive mapping can, in theory, be applied across diverse physical settings. In this final section of the chapter we turn from these relatively independent components of the interaction between environment and behavior to the thoroughly interdependent processes of privacy regulation and responses to crowding.

Privacy as Access to the Self

You will recall from our discussion of the self (Chapter 7) that two opposing processes are involved in public behavior – self-presentation and self-disclosure. In any social interaction, you attend to the impression you are making (self-monitoring) and you choose either to reveal intimate features of your self (self-disclosure) or to do no more than participate in the face and line established for you in the interaction. The choice between concealment and disclosure is not an irrevocable one, and indeed, you may shift from one activity to the other at several points during an interaction, with the change being influenced by your own goals and by the actions of other participants. When it involves use of the physical environment as well as manipulation of social conditions, this regulation of access to the self is at the heart of several definitions of **privacy** (Altman, 1975; Westin, 1970).

Privacy: Four Types. When you first think of privacy, you are likely to imagine a person secluded from all outside interference, alone in the woods or a room with his or her thoughts. In fact, one of the first systematic discussions of privacy (Westin, 1970) does include this sort, calling it *solitude*. But Westin notes that individual freedom from outside interference can also be achieved in the presence of other people. You can find *anonymity* in a public place if there are enough other people around so that you do not stand out as distinctive. Even when you are engaged in an interaction with another person, you can achieve *reserve* by withdrawing psychologically from the contact. Many social interactions can proceed mindlessly (Langer, 1978), requiring so little concentration on your part that you are able to think about other things of more personal interest to you. In the terms used in chapter 11, you have shifted the interaction from one of mutual contingency to an asymmetric pseudocontingency: the other person is following a plan and responding to you, but your actions just follow a script (Schank & Abelson, 1977) for the interchange. Finally, there is a kind of privacy, called *intimacy*, that describes the behavior of a small group, usually a mixed-sex dyad who desire to be "alone together." These four different types of privacy broaden our understanding of the concept to include more than a single individual, and to encompass states of isolation that can be achieved despite the presence of others.

Three Functions of Privacy. What purposes might this isolation serve? Westin (1970) outlined four possible functions of privacy, but we agree with Altman (1975) that these can be reduced to three general goals, ordered in terms of their closeness to the self. The outermost of the three, the *interpersonal function*, is concerned with regulation of interactions with others in the social environment. Through a variety of environmental manipulations, such as closing doors, turning off telephones, or taking a weekend retreat, groups and individuals can protect themselves from intrusions by others. This corresponds to Westin's (1970) idea of limited and protected communication – the opportunity to share confidences with a restricted, small group of other people. At the next closest level, the boundary between the self and others, is what Westin called the *self-evaluation function.* Some privacy is required to engage in social comparison (Chapter 7), because not just any person can serve as an adequate comparison other. Privacy is also required at this level to reflect on past interactions and to make plans for the future. Other people are important sources of information, but they are selectively chosen. Finally, at the closest level, *self-identity*, withdrawal from interaction permits the person to achieve the emotional release that follows removal of the public mask. In addition, a person can have a degree of personal autonomy when alone that is simply not possible in the presence of others. There is time for self-observation, for reflection on one's capabilities and failings, for reexamination of one's goals, or for the kind of talking to oneself that would be thought quite strange if it were observed by others. It is interesting to note that technology has now provided a means of achieving complete withdrawal from interaction even in the presence of others: the personal stereo. Indeed, perhaps the least expensive way to "get away from it all" is to wear one of these personal cassette players while jogging on a well-traveled path in the park. No automobiles to worry about, enough company to be safe, but virtually no need even for exchanging the briefest greetings with other people.

Dynamic Interchange Between Person and Environment. As this example suggests, privacy can be attained only by exercising some control over both the physical and social environment. The amount of control possible, as we have seen earlier, will depend on characteristics of the physical world as well as on personal choice, so the regulation of privacy is an excellent example of the dynamic interchange between the person and the environment. Such an interchange is at the heart of Altman's (1975) comprehensive theory of privacy. The theory views privacy as a universal human need, and rests on three fundamental assumptions: (a) privacy is a dialectic entity involving opposing forces, (b) it is obtained and maintained through boundary regulation, and (c) it is an optimization process. Let us take a closer look at each of these assumptions.

In everyday discourse, we often speak of privacy as if it were a state to be achieved ("Go away and let me have some privacy!"). In contrast, Altman's theory takes the position, common among environmental theories, that privacy is a *process* that unfolds through the interplay of two opposing forces. Altman notes that the root of this idea is the ancient Chinese conception of yin and yang:

> The world is made up of opposites and tensional forces that, because of their very opposition, provide unity and meaningfulness to a whole. . . . Day has no meaning without night, and vice versa. . . . So it is that we view privacy as a series of opposing forces toward being open and being closed toward others, not one or the other force alone. (Altman & Chemers, 1980, p. 78)

Seen in this light, the processes of self-presentation and self-disclosure are not mutually exclusive, but can exist side by side within the same person. The appropriate question then changes from "Is behavior mask or reality?" to "How *much* of behavior is mask, and how much is honest self-disclosure?"

Boundary Regulation. The two opposing forces—being open toward others and being closed toward others—find expression in mechanisms of *boundary regulation.* Whether they are features of the built environment (walls, fences) or aspects of social behavior (personal distance, verbal prohibitions), our personal boundaries are rarely fixed. Walls and fences have gates, verbal prohibitions can be lifted, and through such changes in the permeability of our boundaries, we can affect the level of privacy we achieve.

Altman's theory describes four different mechanisms for privacy regulation. The first of these is a set of *cultural practices,* formal rules and informal norms that govern intrusions into the lives of others. In contemporary American culture, people are permitted to drop in on close friends, but not late at night, early on weekend mornings, or just in time for dinner. A second set of mechanisms can be found in those aspects of the *environment* under our control. The electrically-operated front-door lock on an apartment is an excellent example of a feature of the environment that can be used for regulation. Visitors must identify themselves, and on the basis of that identification and our mood at the time, we can choose either to release the lock or not. In the business world, executives frequently have their secretaries (sometimes several "layers" of secretaries) accomplish the same sort of screening. On an individual level, our *nonverbal* behavior—use of a personal stereo, daydreaming indifference to a persistent bore, rapt attention to every word of a lover—can indicate our accessibility. Finally, our *verbal* behavior can indicate the degree of our willingness to engage in social interaction.

It is possible, of course, that inconsistencies will arise among these four sets of cues to potential intruders. An obnoxious peer in the company can feel free to visit my office, can pass unquestioned by my secretary, and can even ask me a question to which I will respond. But unless he or she is wholly insensitive to nonverbal behavior, the action will not be repeated very often. At other times, a very open and positive response can make comfortable an unexpected old friend who had to convince the secretary that no appointment was really needed.

Privacy as Optimization. The final assumption of Altman's model flows from the previous two. To consider privacy as a process influenced by opposing forces of being open and being closed, a process that takes place through the regulation of personal boundaries, is to assert that in any circumstances an optimal level of privacy can be reached. If you are frantically trying to complete a term paper before your deadline, even a short interruption by your best friend will be an intrusion on your privacy. But without the pressure of the deadline, you would welcome an interchange of much longer duration. The amount of privacy you desire (as a result of the conflicting forces toward being open and being closed) can be compared to the amount of privacy actually achieved through boundary regulation. As long as the amounts are equal—regardless of whether they are both low, moderate, or high—you will be satisfied with the result. If the amount of solitude you achieve is greater than you desire, you will feel alone, isolated, or left out. By contrast, if the level of privacy you achieve is less than you desire, you will feel interrupted, harassed, or overstimulated.

The College Dormitory

Halls and Suites. An excellent illustration of the failure of privacy regulation can be seen in the research by Baum and Valins and their associates (Baum & Valins, 1977) on the behavioral effects of living in various sorts of college dormitories. Although there are numerous versions of the basic designs, many college residence halls can be grouped into two general categories. There are the long-corridor designs such as the one shown in Fig. 13.1, with individual rooms arranged on both sides of a long corridor. Each floor usually has a single common lounge, and one or two centrally located bathrooms. Each bedroom is shared by two roommates. The other general category of dormitory, shown in Fig. 13.2, is the short-corridor or suite dormitory, in which a limited number of bedrooms share both a bathroom and a small lounge area. Again, individual bedrooms are shared by two roommates. Because the bedrooms of both dormitories are of equivalent size, and because the total amount of space on each floor is also roughly comparable on a per-resident basis, the physical densities of these two environments are equal.

But the *social* densities of the two dormitories are radically different, and these differences have important implications for the regulation of in-

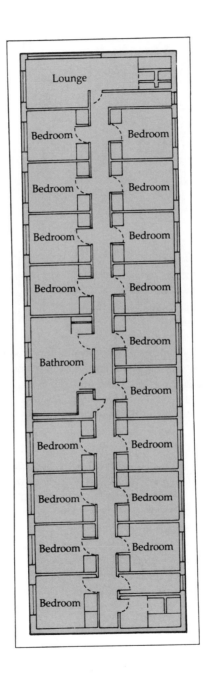

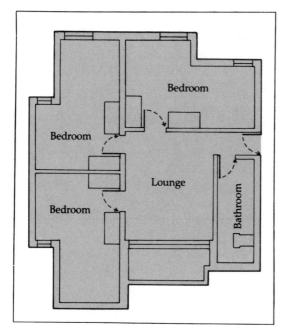

FIGURE 13.2 Design of a short-corridor or suite college dormitory

dividual privacy. Sharing a bathroom and a common lounge with 30 to 40 other people is very different from sharing a bathroom and common lounge with 6 to 12 others, even if the actual amount of space per person (or the number of lavatory facilities per person) are the same. Residents of long-corridor dormitories more frequently encounter people they do not know well, and do not have such encounters on a basis that is regular enough that friendships can develop. People passing in front of the doorway to your room in a long-corridor dormitory are less likely to be visiting someone you know, and the hallway belongs to no one. Because encountering strangers is more of an invasion of personal privacy than is encountering friends, residents of long-corridor dormitories suffer the distress that accompanies loss of control over privacy regulation.

Cognitively Mediated Social Withdrawal. In the early stages of the work, the researchers were able to study only residents who had already been living in a dormitory of one kind or another. They found that residents of long-corridor dormitories had fewer friends in the dormitory, tended to leave the dormitory more frequently, and reported feeling more crowded, with less personal control over unwanted interaction, than residents of suite dormitories did. In later research, with the cooperation of the university administration, Baum and Valins were able to assign entering freshmen to the two kinds of dormitories on a random basis, and these studies replicated all of the previous findings. Even more significant was the finding that the dormitory effects carried over into other aspects of the students' lives. In a variety of laboratory tasks, residents of long-corridor dormitories were more reserved and withdrawn, purposely avoiding contact with others, and these withdrawal responses increased over time, reaching a high level as early as 7 weeks into the first term (Baum, Gatchel, Aiello, & Thompson, 1980).

What makes these findings an illustration of interactive environmental effects rather than an example of direct environmental influence on behavior? In their review, Baum et al. (1980) argue that the dormitory effects are cognitively mediated. As long as a long-corridor dormitory resident attributes his or her lack of control and privacy to personal failings ("I cannot seem to control my interactions with others"), he or she will attempt to achieve control. Only when the attribution for lack of privacy is an external one ("This excess contact goes with the territory; there is nothing I can do about it"), will the social withdrawal and avoidance occur. Residents who take this view have failed to optimize their level of personal contact will reestablish their privacy in the only way under their control—withdraw.

The idea of optimization of interaction is not, as Altman (1975) points out, a novel idea in social psychology. It is quite similar to the maximization-of-outcomes notion inherent in much of social exchange theory (chapter 8), especially to Thibaut and Kelley's (1959; Kelley & Thibaut, 1978) concept of the comparison level as a standard against which outcomes can be evaluated. What is different about the theory is its explicit inclusion of manipulations of the environment (and limitations imposed by that environment) as well as social actions usually considered to be under the individual's control. The theory has yet to be thoroughly tested, but its environmental perspective gives it some additional promise over existing theories of social exchange.

The Problem of Crowding

One of the questions suggested by an optimization of interaction principle is "What happens when there are simply too many people in all settings?" Because of the increasing urbanization of American society, because of traditional distrust of the "group mind" of the crowd, and because of ethological (for example, Calhoun, 1962) and sociological (Galle, Gove, & McPherson, 1972) equating population density with social pathology, the effects of **crowding** on human behavior have been of concern to social psychologists for a number of years. This concern has accelerated with the growth of environmental approaches, producing numerous laboratory and field studies of crowding (reviewed by Baum & Epstein, 1978; Sundstrom, 1978). Our limited purpose here is to outline some of these recent developments.

Population Density. Imagine yourself in a dimly lit room, accompanied by many more people than the room can comfortably hold, assaulted by an ambient sound level so high that you have to shout in order to communicate with a person who is standing right next to you. As long as you remain in the room, you have no control over the stimulus conditions. Do you feel "crowded?" Unfortunately, the answer cannot be determined from the physical characteristics of the setting alone. If these conditions are found in a subway car, they are unpleasant; if they are found in a popular nightclub, they are enjoyable. Certainly there is a difference between noise and music, but because of this difference, merely knowing the decibel level of the sound is not sufficient. Just as certainly, there is a difference between being close to others on the subway and being close in a nightspot. For this reason, merely knowing the number of people per unit of available space is also not sufficient.

In much of the early sociological and psychological research on the antecedents of crowding, this subjective and psychologically aversive state was equated with population density. Social pathology in the inner city was thought to be the result of the large ratio of inhabitants to units of land area; the milder social pathology demonstrated in some laboratory experiments was thought to confirm this effect of density. It fell to Stokols (1972) to distinguish the physical parameter of density from the subjective experience of crowding. At the same time, Galle, Gove, and McPherson (1972) differentiated the gross density in the urban environment into two components. The first of these was *neighborhood density* (based on the number of dwellings per unit of land area) and is what Zlutnick and Altman (1972) called *outside density*. The second component was *household density* (based on the number of people per dwelling room), what Zlutnick and Altman called the *inside density*. The difference between the two is illustrated by the difference between an expensive 15-story condominium and a block of two-story dilapidated apartments. The former has much greater density per unit of land, but that measure is meaningless in the context of a multiple story building; the latter has a much higher density per room. Not surprisingly, Galle, Gove, and McPherson found inner-city social pathology most clearly related to the person-per-room measures of social density. Obviously, these density measures are highly correlated with numerous other facttors—education, employment, socioeconomic status—that will affect people's ability to achieve desired goals through socially acceptable means. But that is simply another way to state the point: sheer density alone will not necessarily produce antisocial behavior (Altman, 1975; Sundstrom, 1978).

Loss of Control. Indeed, a series of laboratory experiments by Freedman (1975) suggested that a high density would intensify whatever affective tone had previously existed in the setting; adding more passengers to the subway car makes the experience more noxious, but adding patrons in the nightclub makes the experience more enjoyable. Some researchers have expressed reservations about generalizing from laboratory experiments to real urban settings, but most agree that density alone cannot account for the negative experience of crowding.

What does seem to be important in the production of crowding is stress, itself often the consequence of the individual's loss of control over the environment (Altman, 1975; Baum, Aiello, & Calesnick, 1978; Rodin, Solomon, & Metcalf, 1978). From our perspective, this notion of loss of control is what makes the study of crowding one involving true interaction between the individual and the social and physical environment. You cannot influence the decibel level and social density in the nightclub any more than you can influence them in the subway car, but the opportunity to do so is only important to you in one of the places. In the subway, you are trying to get somewhere in the most efficient manner, and you know that if the subway is crowded, you will also have to fight for a place on the connecting bus. You may have to make this trip every day, so it is important to you to be able to exert as much control over your daily destiny as possible. By contrast, you have gone to the nightclub for relaxation. There is nowhere else you are trying to go, you can leave whenever you want to (an exercise of control), and you can freely decide never to return. Thus, although you have no power over the physical characteristics of the setting, your ability to depart (and your own mood at the time those characteristics are experienced) render that particular lack of control unimportant. Whether you experience crowding will depend on the interaction between the stimulus properties of the physical environment and the personal factors involved, such as mood, choice of a setting, and reasons for making that choice.

Adaptation Through Time.   One additional point needs to be made about this interaction between physical and personal characteristics: it is a process that occurs through time. When confronted by a potential loss of control over their surroundings, people will at first attempt to reestablish that control (Wortman & Brehm, 1975). Only if such attempts to maintain or reestablish control fail will they suffer from crowding, or worse, become completely helpless in dealing with the physical or social environment (Abramson, Seligman, & Teasdale, 1978; Seligman, 1975). Like the regulation of privacy discussed earlier, the development of the subjectively aversive state of crowding requires person–environment interchange over time, and this process is represented in a model by Sundstrom (1978).

The model begins with the presumed antecedents of crowding—those physical stimuli, social conditions, and personal characteristics that have been thought to be related to environmental stress. Among the physical elements are high density, an absence of partitions to separate people from each other, a complicated or disorderly setting that creates stimulus overload, and excessive, unpredictable noise. Social conditions that contribute to crowding might be invasions of personal space, understaffing of a behavior setting, and increased competition for scarce resources. Personal characteristics that could affect responses to adverse social conditions include size of personal space zones, individual differences in generalized expectancies about the extent of personal control (external versus internal locus of control), and gender (with males presumably more affected by brief exposures to high densities). After a thorough review of the literature, Sundstrom (1978) concluded that strong support existed only for the hypothesized effects of social density and personal space invasions, with other presumed antecedents receiving only partial or tentative support.

The next stage in the model concerns the psychological responses that an individual might have to the antecedent conditions. Three possible reactions–stress, adaptation, and changes in liking for other participants–have received attention. There is evidence that both psychological discomfort and physiological arousal accompany exposure to the antecedents of crowding, so stress can be regarded as one response. How well do individuals adapt to this stress? The research reviewed by Sundstrom (1978) indicates that although people seem to develop tolerance for long-term changes in their living patterns, they do not adapt with any success to brief exposures to high density. People who come from small towns find a given environment more crowded than do people who come from large cities, but if the conditions are sufficiently aversive, neither group will adapt successfully. Moreover, the residence-hall research mentioned earlier shows that developing a tolerance is not necessarily the same thing as maintaining effective behavior. Finally, does the stress inherent in the environment generalize to opinions of others present? Here the most consistent finding is an interaction between gender annd density, at least when the exposure to high density is brief. All-male groups like each other more in low density settings, whereas all female groups like each other more in high density settings. When exposure to high density is long term, this gender difference disappears, with liking decreasing for all.

The last step in the model deals with the presumed interpersonal consequences of crowding, and in so doing returns to the condition of social pathology with which this discussion began. Among the possible consequences are immediate behavioral reactions, such as antagonistic interpersonal actions or poor performance on tasks; and cumulative effects, such as aggression, withdrawal from society, ill health, and reduced effectiveness in occupations. Research on the immediate effects of crowding does not produce a clear picture, because some studies show performance decrements and increased hostility, whereas others fail to find these effects. As Sundstrom (1978) notes, more work needs to be done on this possible consequence of crowding. The research on general social pathology is more frequently correlational; it does not directly measure the presence of stress, and it often involves quite different definitions of density. Despite these problems, three cumulative effects–poor health, crime or aggression, and social withdrawal (among males) are reliably associated with high density. It remains the task of future environmental research to specify more closely all of the dynamics that are involved in the relationship between density and social pathology.

SUMMARY

Because of social psychology's emphasis on the personal and situational factors that affect human behavior, social psychologists have been heavily involved in the development of the emerging field of environmental psychology. The attempt to account for human action in an environmental context is reflected in the concept of a **behavior setting** (p. 469), a structural and dynamic combination of place and activity. The activity must be a regularly occurring one, independent of particular individuals, and coordinated with the physical setting. Any behavior setting has an optimal number of participants, and deviations from this optimum are known as **understaffing** or **overstaffing** (p. 470). The condition critical for the continuation of a behavior setting is the *maintenance minimum* (p. 470), and with either too few staff or too few clients the setting will terminate.

Whatever the setting, individuals bring with them requirements for **personal space** (p. 474), and the study of these interpersonal distances is known as **proxemics** (p. 473). Personal space marks the boundary or "bubble" around a person, the area that the person considers his or her own, and there are a number of cultural and individual differences in the use of this space. In addition to requirements for personal space, individuals bring with them particular **cognitive maps** (p. 476), their representations of features of the spatial environment. When these cognitive maps describe cities, they often include *paths, nodes,* and *landmarks.*

The spatial environment and the individual's capacities combine in the process of **privacy** (p. 479) regulation. Privacy can serve an interpersonal function, a self-evaluation function, or a self-identity function, with optimum privacy being obtained through boundary regulation (p. 481). The failure to achieve an appropriate balance between contact and isolation can lead to withdrawal from social contact. This loss of control over boundary regulation can also be seen in the problem of **crowding** (p. 485), with psychologically aversive consequences usually associated with the inability to adapt to extremes of social density. In all of these formulations from environmental psychology, the person-situation emphasis from social psychology is an essential ingredient. Aspects of the environment set limits for behavior, but the environment itself can be altered by the actions of people. Personal dispositions affect the manner in which settings are perceived or privacy is maintained, but these dispositions are influenced by the social and physical environment.

SUGGESTED ADDITIONAL READINGS

ALTMAN, I., & CHEMERS, M. (1980). *Culture and environment.* Monterey, CA: Brooks/Cole. This readable book summarizes much of Altman's earlier ideas about privacy, territoriality, and crowding, while placing the study of environmental psychology in a broader cultural context.

ITTELSON, W. H., PROSHANSKY, H. M., RIVLIN, L. G., & WINKEL, G. H. (1974). *An introduction to environmental psychology.* New York: Holt, Rinehart & Winston. The first textbook in environmental psychology, and still an excellent place to begin further study of the area.

STOKOLS, D. (Ed.). (1977). *Perspectives on environment and behavior: Theory, research, and applications.* New York: Plenum. This is a collection of professional papers covering the entire range of environmental questions. The selection will give students a good view of the relationships among theory, research, and practical applications in environmental psychology.

CHAPTER FOURTEEN

SOCIAL PSYCHOLOGY AND CRIMINAL JUSTICE

CONTENTS

PREVIEW

As the study of the personal and situational factors that influence individual social behavior, social psychology has a natural affinity for criminal justice – a system of rules and procedures designed to regulate the actions of individuals. Not only does the law set limits on what behavior is acceptable for ordinary citizens, it also prescribes limits for the decisions made by public officials. Within these constraints, officers of the court are permitted the discretion of action needed to ensure a flexible and individualized system of justice. It is, however, important to note that the actions of a public official exercising discretion are better described by principles of social psychology than by legal precedent. For example, two fundamental issues for the law are the determination of individual guilt and the maintenance of justice. These can be illuminated, respectively, by attribution theory and by equity theory. On a more specific level, familiar social psychological processes can be seen to operate at every stage of the criminal justice system, from the decision by victims to report crimes, through arrest and prosecution, through trial and sentencing, to incarceration and parole. Thus the law serves not only as an excellent laboratory for the application of principles of social psychology, but also as an instructive example of the more general social constraints on individual social behavior.

Most industrialized societies that take pride in fairness place the burden of achieving that objective on their legal systems. Indeed, in the United States it is virtually an article of faith that the government consists "of laws, not men." How justified is this belief? This chapter applies the principles of social psychology in an attempt to answer that question. We have just seen (Chapter 13) that the physical environment can place limits on social behavior, and that human action can change the face of that physical landscape. In much the same fashion, a person's social behavior is constrained by the requirements of a larger social system, and that system is shaped by the collective desires of individuals. In this concluding chapter, we consider one element of that larger social system in detail.

Few social institutions affect individual behavior more than does the law, and that influence begins early in life. In most states children are required to attend school until they are 16 years old; this prescription structures their social interaction for most of the day, usually for 180 days a year. Even on the other 185 days a year, with the variables of proximity, similarity, and familiarity being as important as they are, much of a child's social activities will revolve around his or her school friends. School would be this important for many children even without compulsory attendance, but the nature of the educational system, and its effects on participating children, might be radically different. In school or out, the law regulates other aspects of social activity. There is a legally specified age for driving and a different one for drinking alcoholic beverages. Regardless of their personal views on the matter, few college students would argue that recent increases in the age for the latter had no effect on social behavior. The law affects limits techniques of attitude change that advertisers can employ to induce us to purchase their products; it explicitly recognizes some interpersonal relationships while prohibiting others; it provides protection for "good samaritans" who try to help out at the scenes of accidents; it defines the circumstances under which various aggressive responses are, or are not, acceptable; and it specifies procedures through which a person may be deprived of that most critical aspect of a social self—individual liberty.

As these examples indicate, the law—especially the criminal law—constrains and regulates a great deal of everyday social behavior, and that fact alone would lead social psychology to be concerned with the operation of the legal system. There are, however, at least two other reasons for social psychology's interest in legal issues. The first of these is that the two disciplines share three fundamental assumptions: acceptance of the person as unit of analysis, the idea that there can be multiple descriptions of any given action, and the view that human behavior is generally rational (Darley & Shaver, 1983). The second is that the legal system is operated by individual people, whose freedom of action in exercising their official duties takes their actions out of the realm of the law and into the realm of social psychology (Shaver, Gilbert, & Williams, 1975). We consider each of these major reasons in turn.

Three Shared Assumptions

Emphasis on the Individual. Throughout the book I have argued that scientific social psychology is the study of the personal and situational factors that influence individual social behavior. Although processes of social perception, social cognition, and attitude formation and change exist within a person, they are of interest to social psychology because of the implications they have for that person's social actions. Similarly, although interpersonal attraction, aggression, and group decision making involve numerous people, the theories social psychology uses to account for these activities are stated in terms of one person's actions. Indeed, as noted in chapter 1, concentration on the person as the unit of analysis is what distinguishes social psychology from experimental psychology on the one hand and sociology on the other. As Darley and Shaver (1983) have noted, this emphasis on the behavior of the individual is also a central element of the criminal justice system. A crime is committed against one person, even though after such occurrences it is "the state" that brings the formal charges. Individual offenders are brought to the bar of justice, tried, and either acquitted or found guilty. Those who are guilty are sentenced as individuals, and will (if the sentence permits) later be paroled based on their unique circumstances. Thus both social psychology and criminal justice concentrate on the actions of an individual person.

Multiple Interpretations of Events. In their analysis of the assumptions of psychology and the law, Darley and Shaver (1983) point out that in part because of the way each discipline concentrates on the actions of a single person, both recognize that there can be multiple interpretations of events. The principal justification for studying processes of social cognition is that a person's actions will be determined by the social world, as that world appears to the individual. And each person's view will lead to a slightly different conclusion. In experimentation, the idea of demand characteristics reflects the fact that what the subject sees as the purpose of the research is not necessarily the study's true objective. In social perception, people have different implicit personality theories; these and other cognitive schemata lead to differences in the way people construe the social world. In interpersonal behavior, two people engaged in a zero-sum game will naturally interpret each other's actions in different ways ("I am merely defending myself; but you are attacking me"); problems can arise in close relationships when the participants see the world from their different vantage points; and the pressure toward uniformity of opinion in a group can obscure the legitimate differences that may exist in each person's definition of the task at hand. All of these outcomes depend involve, in one way or another, multiple interpretations of events.

In the law, especially the criminal law, recognition that there can be multiple interpretations of events is the fundamental assumption underlying the adversary system. The victim will have one view of the offense, a view that may or may not be shared entirely by the police and prosecutor. The defense will have a different interpretation, and determining whose construction of the events prevails is the function of the adversary system. If a defendant is not convicted, it may be because the jury or presiding judge has still a third view of the alleged offense. If the defendant is convicted, the notion of multiple interpretations of events leads to the possibility that a judge or jury may (a) find the defendant guilty of some charges but not others, and (b) impose a sentence that, itself, varies according to the perceived seriousness of the crime. So the criminal law, like social psychology, assumes that participants in social events may have different perspectives on what has actually happened.

Rational Actors. A third assumption shared by social psychology and the law is that individuals will, with a few notable exceptions, act rationally to accomplish their ends (Darley & Shaver, 1983). Our impressions of, and attributions about, other people are constructed in a manner designed to give us the most information possible for the least amount of cognitive effort. Our attitudes about objects and other people are structured in a highly logical way, and even the cognitive consistency theories of attitude change involve what can easily be regarded as a highly rational component: the reduction of the discomfort that accompanies inconsistency. In the interpersonal realm, the influence of rationality is even stronger, represented most obviously in the fundamental proposition of social exchange theory: people seek to maximize their outcomes. Desires for equitable treatment, evaluation of the costs and rewards associated with helping in an emergency situation, and the matching principle in interpersonal attraction all reflect this tendency to maximize outcomes. Even when group decision-making processes lead to the development of groupthink, that undesirable outcome occurs not because group members want to be wrong, but precisely because they do not want to assert a position that others may consider overly pessimistic. So a consistent thread through much of social psychological theory and research is that people act in ways designed to further their own interests, in short, they act rationally.

This same assumption that individuals will behave in a manner designed to maximize their outcomes and minimize their losses can be seen in the law. Indeed, one of the reasons that people in an adversary proceeding can be expected to have different views of the same situation is that each person has slightly different personal goals to achieve. The victim wants restitution, or retribution; the prosecution wants to deter similar behavior by other potential offenders; the defense attorney wants to do the best job possible for his or her client; and that client wants to minimize the losses that the court proceeding might impose.

Not only does the adversary system recognize the possibility of each person's desire to maximize his or her individual outcomes (or minimize losses), most of the sentencing structure is designed with rational objectives in mind. Treatises on criminal law typically recognize four different purposes that might be served by imposing a sentence: *removal, retribution, rehabilitation,* and *deterrence.* The first three of these are typically applied to the particular offender, whereas the fourth also involves other people who might themselves consider stepping outside the law. Removal (also called "incapacitation") refers to the physical relocation of the convicted person, which relocation makes it impossible for the person to commit any further offenses during the period of incarceration. Retribution is embodied in the principle that more serious crimes typically deserve stiffer sentences. Rehabilitation expresses society's hope that the sentence imposed will change the offender's fundamental attitudes and behavior enough so that when he or she is released there will be no resumption of criminal activities. Finally, the sentence is supposed to serve as society's warning to other potential offenders of the dire consequences that await them if they choose activities outside the law. Of the four purposes, retri-

bution embodies a principle of fairness that depends on rational consideration of what punishments truly fit which crimes, rehabilitation presumes
that people can change their behavior to fit new circumstances, and deterrence presumes that before deciding to embark upon criminal activity a potential offender will balance the possible rewards to be gained against the
punishment that could ensue. If people were not thought to act in a generally rational way to maximize their outcomes, none of these sentencing
purposes could be served.

The Principle of Discretion

One of the characteristics of the law that makes it different from other
forms of social control is that it regulates the behavior of the people who
administer the system, as well as the behavior of the people affected by
that system. Given the three major assumptions just outlined, how should
the law accomplish this task? To begin with, the emphasis on the person as
the unit of analysis can be seen as leading to the notion of *individualized
justice*–the idea that the legal system should be flexible enough to take
into account the particular circumstances of each case. What about the assumption that there can be multiple interpretations of events? Although
the adversary system permits these multiple interpretations to compete
with one another, it does not magically yield "the truth." Some legal decision maker must weigh the evidence and reach a single conclusion. And the
assumption of rationality, when applied to such a decision maker, suggests
that the person should be given enough freedom of action so that the decision can be made on the basis of that decision maker's best, thoughtful
judgment.

A Definition of Discretion.   Thus, together the three assumptions can
be seen as leading to a fundamental principle of the law, that of **discretion**,
defined by Black's (1968) legal dictionary as the "power or right" conferred
by law upon public officials to act "according to the dictates of their own
judgment and conscience, uncontrolled by the judgment or conscience of
others." Discretion is considered to be "bounded by rules and principles of
law, and not arbitrary, capricious, or unrestrained." No written system of
justice could hope to incorporate every conceivable aspect of the circumstances surrounding an offense, no computer program could infer the
motives and intent of the people involved, and no mechanical device would
have the experience to decide whether the evidence against a defendant
had proven guilt beyond a reasonable doubt. In short, if there is to be individualized justice, there is no substitute for providing an individual decision maker with the discretion to follow the dictates of conscience.

The Social Psychology of Criminal Justice.   What has just been described is the way that the principle of discretion is supposed to operate

when it works well. There are, however, two features of the principle that need further comment. First, Shaver, Gilbert, and Williams (1975) have argued that the behavior of a public official who is exercising discretion is better described by theories of social psychology than by theories of law. The law sets the limits, but it does not tell us what factors in the offender's behavior, the circumstances of the offense, or the decision maker's experience might affect the outcome. For example, imagine that you have just been stopped by the state police, who caught you in a radar trap on the interstate. The actual infraction is defined by the extent to which your speed exceeded the legal limit. Is there anyone who believes that a belligerent response – compared to a pleasant and contrite response – on your part is not going to increase the likelihood that you will get a ticket? The officer's impression of you, attribution for your obnoxious behavior, and general attitudes toward college students will almost certainly affect his or her use of the discretion permitted by the law. But attributions, attitudes, and the consequences of interpersonal behavior are part of social psychology, not the law. Your actions do not change the actual infraction, so the law would dictate that you should get a ticket in either case. What we have learned in social psychology, however, would predict that contrite offenders might occasionally get warnings, whereas belligerent offenders would always get tickets. Not surprisingly, a comprehensive study of police discretion (LaFave, 1965) reveals several social psychological variables, such as the officer's private opinion about the statute in question and his or her view of the community's desire for enforcement, that affect decisions to take suspects into custody. As we see in later sections, similar social psychological variables affect discretionary decisions made by prosecutors, judges, juries, and parole boards.

Unfortunately, the fact that legal decisions are susceptible to influence from social psychological factors leads to the second feature of discretionary justice: What was established in principle as a way to ensure that each defendant received fair and individualized treatment is, in practice, too frequently an opportunity for the exercise of unconscious or conscious unfairness. For example, Frankel (1972), himself a federal judge, recounts an incident in which he was presiding over the trial of a government official charged with corrupt behavior and perjury (lying under oath). The trial received a good deal of attention, and Frankel received numerous letters suggesting what should be done with the offender (who was later convicted only on the perjury charge. One was from a state trial judge, who lamented the lax sentences often imposed by federal judges, and went on to say

> Accordingly, as an individual, as a Judge in the State Court, as a father of a young man serving upon the High Seas of the country as an enlisted man, and as the step-father of a drafted Army Private on Asiatic soil, and as an individual who has served honorably for five years in the service of the United States Navy in wartime, let me strongly urge upon you that you impose the maximum sentence as provided by law upon the above Defendant, and upon

any other individuals who would tend to destroy and demoralize our nation's government from within. (Frankel, 1972, p. 20)

As Frankel notes, these remarks demonstrate that all too often the broad criminal penalties permit justice to be individualized not to the offender, but to the judge: "The evidence is conclusive that judges of widely varying attitudes on sentencing . . . mete out widely divergent sentences where the divergences are explainable only by the variations among the judges, not by material differences in the defendants or their crimes" (p. 21). Similar effects of social psychological variables can be seen in every phase of the criminal justice system. Thus both the principle of discretion and its abuse in practice provide a challenge to social psychological theory and research, a challenge the discipline has recently accepted.

INDIVIDUAL GUILT
AND ATTRIBUTION PROCESSES

Why have a criminal justice system at all? If one is truly necessary, what form should it take? These questions have been the subject of moral, social, and philosophical arguments for centuries, so it would make little sense to claim that there are social psychological justifications for the present structure of the criminal justice system. There are, however, principles from social psychology that help illuminate the nature and operation of that system of social control.

Involuntary Suffering. Recall the notion of usable power from the discussion of power and influence in chapter 11. The social power of a group or individual is defined as that agent's capacity to affect another's behavior, or, in terms of Thibaut and Kelley's (1959) exchange theory, the range of outcomes through which the powerful agent can move the target of influence. In the social relationships we have considered to this point, that power to affect another's outcomes is limited by the target person's comparison level for alternatives (CL_{alt}). If my attempts to control your actions become too odious, you will leave our relationship for another. Consequently, the lower limit of my usable power – the control I can exercise without causing you to leave the relationship – is defined by your CL_{alt}.

It is important to emphasize that this conception of usable power, as well as the power of a social group or the group's appointed or emergent leader (Chapter 12) is limited to a instances in which your participation in the interaction is voluntary. If you are not free to leave, then the CL_{alt} is no longer the lower boundary of the influencing agent's power, so in principle there is no limit to the punishment that the agent could make you suffer. Now, in social psychological terms, what is a criminal offender? A person who is willing and able to use coercive means to prevent your leaving a "relationship" in which there is a perfect negative correspondence of outcomes (the offender's gains are achieved entirely at your expense). As an individual, you personally cannot deter the offender, so the society must attempt to do so collectively, giving rise to a system of criminal justice.

The establishment of a criminal justice system reflects society's recognition that there are some individuals who will use coercive means to maximize their own outcomes. And unfortunately, society must employ coercion to prevent coercion. The difference, of course, is that the criminal justice system embodies procedures designed to protect citizens (whether or not those citizens are, in fact, offenders) from the arbitrary or capricious exercise of coercive influence. This emphasis on what is called *procedural due process* distinguishes the exercise of coercive power by the legal system from the exercise of coercive power by individual offenders. In short, the criminal justice system must apply sanctions to those determined to be guilty of offenses, but must do so in a according to procedures that are generally regarded as just. These two objectives—determination of guilt and maintenance of justice—can, themselves, be described in familiar social psychological terms.

The Determination of Guilt

Criminal Acts. The first problem for the criminal justice system is to distinguish criminal offenses from behaviors that are (merely) socially disapproved. How much of ordinary conduct should be regulated by the criminal law? The answer will differ from one society to another, and within a nation, even from one jurisdiction to another (laws imposing criminal penalties for everything from selling school supplies on Sunday to particular kinds of private sexual conduct between consenting adults are examples of the latter). Usually the boundary is drawn on the basis of imminent danger, either to an individual person or to the society at large, but the lines are not always as clear as we would like for them to be. Detailed consideration of the boundary between socially disapproved behavior and criminal behavior is beyond the scope of this chapter, so the examples chosen will involve offenses that are almost unanimously regarded as criminal activity.

With only a few legally defined exceptions, criminal acts must contain two distinct elements (Williams, 1953). The first of these, called the *actus reus*, is an overt action that is willfully performed, occurs in specified circumstances, and results in certain harmful consequences. No doubt you can think of numerous activities that are willfully performed and result in harmful consequences, yet only a small fraction of these become the concern of the criminal law. Why? Because the positive social goals of individual liberty and free expression of ideas dictate that the law's coercive power should be limited to those instances in which it is the only plausible solution. As noted in Mill's (1859) influential work on liberty, "the only purpose for which power can be rightfully exercised over any member of a civilized community, against his will, is to prevent harm to others" (p. 13). Thus, lying to your friend about the condition of your automobile becomes a matter for the law only if you are in the process of trying to sell the car.

Guilty Minds. The second element of a criminal act is called the *mens rea*, a "guilty mind" with which the *actus reus* was performed. In order to determine the presence of *mens rea*, the actor's capacities, intentions, and free exercise of will must be taken into account. A person who did not have the capacity to distinguish right from wrong at the time of commission of the prohibited action is not considered legally liable for the outcome (this, of course, is the substance of various versions of the "insanity defense"). A person who should have known the consequences of his or her actions, but did not intend for the harmful outcome to result may be guilty of a lesser offense (e.g., manslaughter rather than murder), or may not be guilty of any crime at all (e.g., sloppy preparation of an income tax form vs. intentional fraud). Finally, a person who intentionally engaged in illegal activity, but did so because of an external threat, may be relieved of some or all of the legal burden by virtue of the external coercion. In this sense, the free exercise of will is slightly different from the "willful" that is part of the *actus reus*, and the difference can best be described by examining the opposite in each case. In the case of the act, itself, the opposite of willful would be "unintentional" or "accidental"; in the case of the *mens rea*, the opposite would be "forced."

The Importance of Attributions

For a person to be found guilty of criminal activity, both the *actus reus* and the *mens rea* must typically – though not always – be present. A notable exception is found in the doctrine of "strict liability" (Hart, 1968), by which a person can be found guilty of criminal behavior without guilty intent. For example, suppose that you had the misfortune to be arrested for driving erratically after having a few drinks. In many states your conviction for driving under the influence would be virtually automatic if your blood contained more than some specified percentage of alcohol; no one would even so much as inquire whether you intended to drive while intoxicated. These and similar cases aside, in the large majority of criminal matters the offender's *intent* is a critical element in the ultimate acquittal or conviction, and that intent is inferred through the attribution processes we have considered in chapter 4. Indeed, you may recall that a jury decision was used as the initial example of how an attribution is made. The defendant's criminal activity is either reported firsthand by witnesses, or is reconstructed from the available evidence. Next the jury considers whether the outcome could have been brought about by chance, carelessness, or as the unintended side-effect of some intended action. Having decided that the action is intentional, the jury then searches for alternative explanations or mitigating circumstances. If there are none, then there is an attribution of guilt, and that attribution together with the performance of the act, leads to the imposition of sanctions.

Covariation or Schemata? Conviction for a criminal offense requires that either the judge or the jury consider the defendant "guilty beyond a reasonable doubt." As we see later, there is some disagreement over what, precisely, is meant by reasonable doubt. But the attributional processes involved will be the same, regardless of the specific criterion. You will remember from chapter 4 that, according to Kelley's (1967, 1973) attribution theory, there are two general approaches to the determination of what might have been the cause of an event (in this case, a criminal act). The first approach involves multiple observations of a correlation between presumed cause and effect. In this covariation model the perceiver first examines the entities that occur (i.e., the criminal act and other behaviors in which the stimulus person might engage). If the criminal act is distinctive, unlike other acts that could have been undertaken to reach the same general goal, the perceiver (the judge or jury) will begin to suspect that the criminal act reflects some underlying disposition of the stimulus person (the offender). Next the perceivers will observe the offender in a variety of different contexts (changes in what the theory calls time and modality) to see if the behavior remains stable. If it does stay consistent across circumstances, then those changed circumstances can be ruled out as a possible cause (an offender can be forgiven for a single transgression, but multiple offenses across time show the offender for what he or she really is). Finally, according to the model, the perceiver will compare his or her view with that of other people to make certain that the offense is not in the eye of the beholder (this search for consensus among observers is obviously more appropriate for a jury trial than for a trial conducted before a single judge). If everyone agrees that the defendant's actions are distinctive from other possibilities, and are consistent across time, then an attribution for the criminal activity will be made to the defendant.

The major difficulty with applying the covariation model to criminal activity is that in any given trial there is only likely to be a single instance of the prohibited behavior. True, a defendant may be charged with multiple offenses—several burglaries, writing dozens of bad checks, more than a single brutal assault—but in many instances there is only one encounter between offender and victim that is serving as the basis for any attributions drawn. What will happen in such cases? Again, according to the theory, the perceiver (judge or jury) will use some form of cognitive schemata to "fill in" for the missing data that would have been included had multiple observations been possible. Indeed, unless there are multiple charges filed or the defendant takes the stand, a defendant's past criminal history is explicitly excluded from that phase of the trial designed to determine guilt or innocence (it may be brought in, upon a finding of guilty, prior to sentencing).

Multiple Causes and Discounting. In practice, what the judge or jury must do is to assess the likelihood that the defendant is the major, if not the sole, cause of the occurrence. Without covariation information, this decision will be based on some form of cognitive schema, and which one is employed may depend on the nature of the decision to be made. For example, in order to make a plausible case against a defendant, prosecutors need to show that the defendant had both the opportunity to commit the crime and a motive to do so. Thus, motive and opportunity are what the theory would call *multiple necessary causes*: both must be present. Clearly the crime did take place (after all, there is a victim and there are witnesses to testify that a crime occurred), but if the defendant on trial can be shown to have an alibi that places him or her somewhere else, the opportunity is gone, and the jury will not be likely to believe that the defendant in question committed the crime.

When the decision to be made is considered from the vantage point of the judge or jury (rather than from that of the prosecutor), the emphasis on proof beyond a reasonable doubt calls forth a different schema, that of *multiple sufficient causes*. How might the occurrence of the crime be accounted for other than by attributing it to the defendant? As a practical matter, this question leads to a search for other possible perpetrators (or for accomplices of the defendant on trial), and to an examination of the factors of intent and coercion. For example, considering the case of a pedestrian killed by a car while crossing the street, there are numerous alternatives. Someone other than the defendant on trial might have killed the pedestrian, perhaps at the defendant's behest, but perhaps after having stolen the defendant's automobile. The defendant might have hit the pedestrian by accident, panicked, and fled from the scene, not reporting the accident to the police. The defendant might have hit the pedestrian intentionally, but only because a passenger in the defendant's car was holding a loaded pistol to the defendant's side during the entire episode. Each of these possibilities is sufficient to have brought about the demise of the victim. To the extent that the other alternatives are plausible, the prosecution's charge of murder in the first degree (with intent and premeditation) will be *discounted* by the legal decision makers. In an important sense, the prosecution will be trying to induce the judge or jury to attribute according to multiple necessary causes, whereas the defense will be attempting to get the same decision makers to employ the multiple sufficient causes schema, thus producing "reasonable doubt." Each side, however, is clearly trying to direct the attribution processes by which the decision makers find the defendant either guilty or not. Thus the social psychological processes of attribution play an important role in the major procedural task of the criminal justice system—the determination of guilt.

THE MAINTENANCE OF JUSTICE

Searching for an Equitable Outcome

Distributive and Rectificatory Justice. Most modern treatments of justice, whether framed in the context of the law or in the realm of interpersonal behavior can be traced to Aristotle's (1952) examination of the concept in his *Nicomachean Ethics.* Where "distributions of honour or award" (p. 378) are concerned, Aristotle argues for a principle of *proportionality*: two people will have been treated justly if each person's rewards are proportional to his or her merit. What is equal (and therefore just) is not equality of the awards, but equality between the ratios of honor to merit. This principle of distributive justice is, obviously, the concept on which the modern equity theory (described in chapter 8) is based.

But Aristotle recognized that justice might also require a third party to rectify an injustice perpetrated by one person against another. When two people are in a relationship that produces ill-gotten gains for one of the two, what Aristotle called "rectificatory justice" (1952, p. 380) will come into play. It does not matter whether the relationship is involuntary—as between a criminal offender and his or her victim—or voluntary. In either case, society will have an interest in returning each person to the original state that existed before the "transaction." In modern parlance, this is the principle of restitution, illustrated in the criminal law by a judicial requirement that a vandal pay for the damage he or she produced. It is important to note that this view of rectificatory justice does not include any retribution the offender might suffer beyond the requirement to compensate the victim.

Outcome or Process? Quite clearly, Aristotle's concept of rectificatory justice, and the modern conception of justice as equity, concentrate on the outcome of the legal intervention designed to provide redress. This view of justice sounds quite reasonable in the abstract, but is often difficult to apply to a specific case. Let us consider an example. Suppose that you are walking down a dark and deserted side street in a metropolitan area, and you get accosted by three youths brandishing large switchblade knives. After taunting you for a few moments, the youths threaten to "cut you up" if you don't hand over your watch and your money. To show you that they mean business, one of them takes a swipe at you, cutting through your clothes and making a shallow, but painful, wound in your shoulder. You try not to shake as you quickly comply with their demands, hoping that you will have had enough money to satisfy them, and that they will simply take it and leave. One takes the watch, another takes your money, looks at your credit cards but dumps them on the ground, and the third, who has been going through your other belongings menacingly says your name and then says "I guess that's enough for now." The three then swagger away. As soon as they disappear around a corner, you hurriedly pick up your credit cards and a few really important personal belongings and run to the nearest well populated place, where you hope to be relatively safe while you gather yourself together and try to decide whether to report the incident to the police. There will be other variations on this example in later sections, but for now suppose that you do decide to report the incident, the police find the perpetrators, a trial is held, and the perpetrators are found guilty. Now, the question is what sentence should be imposed?

As it was originally stated, Aristotle's principle of rectificatory justice would argue that you and the three offenders should be returned to the state that existed for each of you prior to the transaction. But what, exactly, would that (or any equivalent modern equity notion) require? Is it even possible literally to return you to the preattack state? Will the return of your watch and money balance the books? Should you not also receive some compensation over and above restitution for the pain and trauma you have suffered, and for the time you have lost from work while pursuing the case? Assuming that you should receive some additional compensation, how should the amount be decided? It is certainly possible to add up your actual hospital expenses, and the money you have lost while being absent from work, but it is much more difficult to specify in the abstract how much you should receive for psychological suffering both past and future. It is even more difficult to obtain agreement about what other factors might be relevant: Does your own personal wealth enter into how much you should receive; does what you were doing in that relatively unsafe part of town matter?

What about the offenders? Is returning them to the state in which they were prior to the attack really just? Suppose that they have taken your money, bet it on the numbers, and won five times the original amount. Should they be permitted to keep the winnings? Even if they just broke even on the numbers, so that there is no extra money to divide, is it really just for them not to suffer some additional penalty so that they will have lost more than they gained (and presumably will learn a lesson for the future)? In assessing the extent of some monetary penalty, should the court consider the offenders' ability to pay? What about their social circumstances and lack of education? Regardless of their background, these toughs have not only attacked you, in so doing they have also attacked civilized society. Does society deserve some retribution as well? If so, should it be given to you (in the form of a larger monetary payment), or should it be collected by society (in the form of some kind of sentence)?

Substantive versus Procedural Due Process. Regardless of the way in which a particular judge or jury might answer all of these questions, the fact that the questions can be asked indicates that the law cannot specify, either in advance or in general, what is called *substantive due process* – an equitable outcome. This fairness of outcome remains the goal in theory, but in practice is replaced by what the law can more plausibly guarantee in advance and in general, namely *procedural due process*. Irrespective of the facts of a particular case, the law presumes that fairness of procedures will, by permitting each side to make its most persuasive arguments, give the decision makers (judge or jury) the facts with which to make a substantively fair decision. This emphasis in practice on procedural due process rests, of course, on two of the fundamental assumptions noted earlier: there can be multiple interpretations of events, and decision makers will rationally consider those conflicting interpretations in order to arrive at a substantively equitable outcome. Social psychological theory and research are helpful in illuminating both the objective of substantive due process and the procedural means for achieving that end.

The Role for Equity Theory

Classes of Crimes. The idea that substantive due process cannot be specified in advance, or in the abstract, finds support in the revision of equity theory first outlined by Walster, Berscheid, and Walster (1973), and later applied specifically to the law by Austin, Walster, and Utne (1976). This version of equity theory begins by acknowledging that "individuals will try to maximize their outcomes" (p. 164), and then notes that in order to maximize collective reward, groups (in the present instance, society at large) must evolve systems that make "it more profitable to behave equitably than inequitably. Thus, groups will generally reward members who treat others equitably and generally punish . . . members who treat others inequitably" (p. 164). The theory "makes it clear that ultimately, equity is in the eye of the beholder" (p. 165). Thus a defendant can be expected to have a view of the substantive outcome that is different from that of the victim, and both of those may be different from that of the prosecutor and decision maker (judge or jury). It is precisely these potential differences and the variations in the specifics of a particular offense that make it impossible to construct an exhaustive list of what would constitute the equitable outcome of every conceivable offense.

Rather than attempt to enumerate all the elements of such a catalogue, the criminal justice system only sets forth classes of crimes and penalties, and endows selected individuals with the discretion to decide the issues involved, within the boundaries prescribed by the class. The law assumes that these individuals will make a rational decision based on the evidence, and includes controls against bias. For example, the defendant's constitutional right to a jury trial is a guarantee that a defendant could, in principle, even participate in the selection of the people whose discretionary judgments will decide his or her fate. Moreover, were a jury trial held, both the defense and the prosecution could reject potential jurors whose judgment might be colored in one way or another. Jury trials seldom occur in practice, with anywhere from 75% to 90% of the guilty verdicts being achieved through plea negotiation prior to the actual trial (Greenberg & Ruback, 1982). But the existence of the opportunity for such a choice is all that matters for our present purposes.

How will the legal decision maker—whether it be a judge or a jury—evaluate the evidence, determine whether any mitigating circumstances existed, and render a "fair" judgment? More precisely, is there a psychological principle that might guide this search for discretionary and individualized justice? The answer, of course, is affirmative: the re-establishment of equity. The decision maker(s) will listen to the best arguments that can be provided by prosecution and defense, define some features of the setting as relevant and others as irrelevant, and then decide whether fairness demands a conviction. If there is a conviction, then equity concerns will lead the rational decision makers to select a punishment that in some rectificatory fashion "fits the crime."

Distress, Compensation, and Justification. Although equity theory is no better than is the law at stating in advance what outcome is the correct one for a particular crime, it does suggest several factors that the decision makers might consider in making that judgment. According to equity theory, a harm-doer (in this case a criminal offender) will suffer two kinds of distress after having exploited a victim: self-concept distress, and retaliation distress. Self-concept distress arises because having treated another person inequitably is inconsistent with the harm-doer's personal belief that people should be fair in their dealings with others. Retaliation distress is the anxiety the harm-doer experiences at the thought that the victim, the victim's associates, the legal system, or God will restore equity to the relationship by punishing the harm-doer. Both sorts of distress are argued to have their roots in childhood socialization, and there may be wide individual differences in the degree to which a particular harm-doer experiences either or both (Walster, Berscheid, & Walster, 1976). For the criminal offender, retaliation distress is probably the more likely, especially if there is any personal history of prior offenses (such a history is a rather strong denial of the possible influence of self-concept distress).

Assuming for the moment that the harm-doer experiences at least some retaliation distress, how might that distress be reduced or eliminated? The first method for direct reduction of distress is *compensation* of the victim, returning money stolen, offers to provide still more money, and claims of a desire "to make it up to you." The second direct means for restoring equity is *self-deprivation*, which might be reflected in an offender's "desire to be caught" (and presumably punished). Voluntary criminal confessions would certainly be an instance of the latter means of direct reduction of distress. Unfortunately, neither of these seems very likely in the example. It is as difficult to imagine the three young toughs offering compensation or turning themselves in as it is to imagine their suffering pangs of self-concept distress from having frightened and robbed you.

In the absence of any direct reduction of the retaliation distress, the harm-doer may resort to one of three fundamental strategies to restore psychological equity. The first of these is derogation of the victim, a technique of minimization reported by Sykes and Matza (1957). Their research showed that juvenile delinquents often convinced themselves (or at least attempted to convince the interviewer) that their victims were really bums, or homosexuals, who deserved the treatment they had received. A second strategy is to minimize the victim's actual suffering, and that is one of the primary possibilities for our example. In the lives of the three toughs, getting threatened (or even cut) with a knife may be frequent enough that the youths would consider that "no big deal." Additionally, although they, themselves, might have no storehouse of cash, they might be able to convince one another that you did have plenty of money. Indeed, they could come to think that you might have had so much that the mere losses you suffered in the "transaction" with them would be of minor importance to you. After all, they left you with your credit cards!

The third strategy for restoration of psychological equity is *denial of responsibility* for the act, and this is another possibility in the example. If the youths can convince themselves (or even the legal decision maker) that the true fault lies with the deplorable social and economic conditions in their neighborhood, then the initial loss of equity will not be seen as quite so serious as it was. Similarly, if the youths can successfully claim (to themselves or others) that the occurrence was really your responsibility (you should have known better than to be there in the first place), then you have contributed some negative inputs for which your negative outcome was a just reward.

Restoration of Equity by the Legal System

If the offenders in our example – and many other offenders as well – suffer any distress at all, it is not self-concept distress, but rather retaliation distress. The power of retaliation distress is suggested by the question, "Who is the safest person on the street?" and the answer "the little old lady who carries cash for the mob." Those of us who are not "protected" from street crime by organized crime have to depend on the retaliation distress that is engendered by the law. In our example, the original offense was not only against you as an individual, it was also an offense against society at large.

The police and prosecutor do not represent you, personally; they represent society. Your formal complaint is needed to begin the process (unless the act happened to be witnessed by a police officer), but at that point the system assumes full responsibility for attempting to restore equity, specifically prohibiting you from taking revenge on the offenders yourself. The public acclaim bestowed on victims, both real and fictional, who "take matters into their own hands" gives some indication of just how unsatisfying to many people is this requirement that the law assume complete responsibility for the restoration of equity. One reason for this dissatisfaction, of course, is that the legal system must provide procedural fairness for the defendant, as well as substantive equity for society and the victim.

Seriousness of the Crime.   Putting the procedures aside for the moment, equity theory suggests several factors that will affect the severity of the legal sanctions eventually applied to a defendant. The most relevant input is, of course, the seriousness of the crime. The greater the gravity of the original offense, the more severe the penalty must be in order to restore equity. As Von Hirsch (1976) has noted, using desert (what others would call "retribution") as the basis for a punishment to be imposed differs from using any of the other three rationales (removal, rehabilitation, deterrence). Desert is a "backward-looking" criterion that is based on the defendant's actual past behavior, whereas the other three justify punishment on the basis of its presumed value for the future. Because it deals with known inequities, instead of predicted but unknowable benefits, desert is a criterion especially appropriate for consideration in an equity analysis of sentencing.

As important as the seriousness of the crime is, its application in the legal system is far from perfect. The principle of desert is most clearly employed in connection with crimes against persons: penalties for the "serious" crimes of murder, rape, aggravated assault, and robbery are differentiated from one another on the basis of the gravity of the original offense. But beyond the person crimes the principle of desert frequently does not apply as precisely. Most person crimes carry penalties that are more harsh than the penalties associated with property crimes or "victimless" crimes (e.g., drug possession, prostitution), but there are some jurisdictions in which this is not the case. And in the so-called "white collar" crimes, the principle occasionally seems to apply in the reverse: An individual embezzler might be convicted and sentenced, but the officers of a corporation that has in effect stolen millions from consumers might never even be prosecuted.

Restoration Through Suffering.   Equity theory suggests that in addition to the seriousness of the crime, the judicial decision makers should consider the actual restoration of equity that might have occurred by the time of the trial. Where seriousness would add to the punishment of the defendant, that defendant's own suffering, or the compensation provided to the victims, ought to lessen the imposed punishment. One of the most routine ways in which prior suffering by the defendant is taken into account occurs in large metropolitan jurisdictions that have long delays between initial arraignment (determination that sufficient evidence exists to "bind the defendant over" for trial) and trial. A defendant who cannot make bail, and whose attorney cannot interest the prosecution in a plea bargain, might spend nearly as much time in jail prior to the trial as he or she would have spent in jail upon conviction. In such cases, a judge who finds the defendant guilty may well impose a sentence equivalent to the time already served, thus recognizing the defendant's prior suffering.

Procedural Judges and Substantive Juries. Defendants whose criminal activity causes them to lose something very dear to them may be even more likely to be acquitted if the verdicts are reached by juries than if by judges. For example, a person whose carelessness in handling a loaded pistol causes the death of a dearly loved spouse is technically guilty of a crime (the criterion on which a judge would have to decide the case), but is so clearly distraught that the jury believes a legally imposed punishment to be unnecessary. This kind of difference between the behavior of judges and juries is illustrated in the landmark work of Kalven and Zeisel (1966).

In their research, conducted as part of what is still known as the (University of) Chicago (Law School) Jury Project, Kalven and Zeisel (1966) asked judges throughout the country to describe jury trials over which they had presided, describe the decision rendered by the jury, and indicate whether or not they would have reached the same conclusion (stating reasons for any differences that arose). The responses showed that the judges would have agreed with the jury verdict in approximately 80% of the cases examined. What is most interesting for our purposes here is that in the roughly 20% of cases on which there would have been disagreement, the judges would have convicted when the jury acquitted. And as Ellison and Buckhout (1981) have noted, the juries might have been more lenient "because they are allowed to take into account and respond to commonsense equities" (p. 134) not permitted to influence the behavior of a judge bound by rules of the system. In short, if forced to choose between procedural and substantive due process, judges must follow procedures, whereas juries can elect to emphasize substance.

In terms of the methodological controls described in chapter 2 and the Methodological Appendix, Kalven and Zeisel's research is weighted more heavily toward external validity than internal validity. The data were all provided by judges – not by a combination of judges and juries – so the results represent the judges impressions of the jury's reasoning process. Despite this difficulty, and several others also recognized and discussed by the authors, the large number of cases reviewed (over 3,500) has made the study a valuable resource for social scientists and legal scholars alike.

Some of the concern for substantive outcomes suggested by the judge–jury disagreements in Kalven and Zeisel's (1966) research has increasingly been incorporated into specific procedures. Rather than restore equity solely through punishment of the offender (reduction of that person's outcomes), more courts are attempting to restore equity in part by providing compensation to victims. Victim compensation is most likely, of course, when the crime has involved theft of property, not bodily injury. Such compensation is driven in part by a growing recognition that victims have traditionally been slighted in legal proceedings, and in part by a need for "creative" alternatives to incarceration. Sentences for nonviolent crime that concentrate on restitution and community service rather than on incarceration can help to restore equity through a direct transfer of resources from the offender to the victim.

Blaming the Victim.   Where the crime is a serious one, there is no suffering by the defendant, and adequate compensation of the victim is impossible, equity theory suggests that there may be some psychological restoration of equity in addition to the contributions made by a sentence imposed on the defendant. Unfortunately, this psychological restoration of equity too often involves blaming the victim for the occurrence. The classic example of victim blaming is in the case of rape. Nobody would think it reasonable to ask a victim of car theft, "Why did you keep your car looking so terrific? If you had just let it accumulate mud and trash, no thief would have been interested in it?" Or "Have you ever let anyone borrow the car? How many times?" But in jurisdictions that do not have so-called "shield laws" to protect rape victims, those victims can expect to be asked conceptually equivalent questions about their choice of clothing and makeup, and their past sexual history. In equity terms, this line of questioning suggests both that the victim might have been partially responsible for her victimization and that she was a morally unworthy individual who in some way deserved to suffer. The real tragedy is that the victims, themselves, too frequently seem to accept some of the fault.

ACHIEVING DUE PROCESS

Discussion of the potential for blaming the victim of a crime makes it clear that equity theory, like attribution theory, contains explanatory principles that can describe the discretionary action of legal decision makers. The overall substantive goal is the maintenance of justice, and in many circumstances the participants in the legal system achieve that goal. There are, however, times when personal motives (conscious or not) can adversely affect the decisions actually reached. For this reason as well as for the obvious reason that the parties are likely to disagree about the quality of the outcome, the legal system does not try to guarantee that any participant will receive substantive due process. What it does guarantee (through appeal, if necessary) is adherence to a standard of procedural due process. From the standpoint of social psychology, this standard of procedural due process is very much like the standards for research: Conclusions should be reached on the basis of methods that are as free as possible from confounding artifacts. Consequently, in addition to studying procedural justice in its own right, social psychologists have examined a wide variety of *extralegal* factors that might compromise the decision-making process. We consider each of these two areas in turn.

Procedural Justice

Requirements for Fairness. Most of us do not contemplate committing crimes, so our natural tendency is to side with the crime victim, and to wonder why the criminal justice system is "taking so long" to dispense the punishment we believe the defendant richly deserves. Indeed, if the only complaint about the criminal justice system were that it routinely took too long to accomplish the purpose, the system would probably be much more highly regarded than it is. What, then, is the source of public frustration? It may be the consequence of a failure to distinguish between substantive and procedural due process. Almost every daily newspaper will contain an article about a defendant who was acquitted "on a technicality," although it is stated (or at the very least implied) that the person was "guilty."

This kind of comment reveals two misimpressions about the criminal justice system. First, it equates being tried with being guilty. In fact, a defendant is presumed to be innocent until proven guilty. The attribution of "guilt" is to be made to a defendant only after the appropriate judicial process—either some form of plea negotiation or a formal trial—has been completed. Prior to that time, every defendant is to be considered innocent. So although it may be statistically true that virtually all of the defendants who are charged, arraigned, and bound over for trial are ultimately determined to be guilty, that statistical regularity is not supposed to be translated into a prediction of guilt for a particular defendant. The second misconception is that the "technicalities" are impediments to the achievement of a just outcome. Nothing could be further from the truth. As noted earlier, the criminal law does not even pretend to guarantee a just outcome, only fair procedures by which that outcome will be reeached. The converse of this guarantee, of course, is that no outcome can be considered fair if the procedures used to produce it are flawed. Thus, in a critical sense, the "technicalities" *are* the process.

The Veil of Ignorance.   To understand fully the need for procedural protections, we need to be able to leave the psychological shelter provided by our beliefs that we would never be defendants in a criminal trial. Just how this can be done is suggested by Rawls (1971), a philosopher who has written extensively on justice as fairness. Rawls recognizes that when asked to determine whether specific procedures are fair, rational people will choose as the most fair those procedures that favor their established position. To counter this natural tendency, Rawls argues that we must debate the fairness of a procedure from behind a "veil of ignorance." Participants in such a debate should know the facts about society that might affect their choice of principles of justice—general features of economic and social organization, principles of human motivation—but should not know their own place in that society.

The Effects of Advantage.   In an important psychological study of procedural justice, Thibaut and Walker (1975) used the idea of the veil of ignorance as a methodological tool. Specifically, they asked subjects to participate in a legal decision making task to resolve a dispute between two men, Adams (the defendant) and Zemp (the victim). Subjects were to assume the role of one man or the other, and then would participate in a hearing to settle the dispute. After the hearing, that person who had assumed the role of the party who won the dispute was to be paid $5 (the subject who had assumed the role of the loser would be paid nothing). As the story went, Adams was charged with assault for using excessive force to defend himself against attack by Zemp. The case materials given the subjects contained 14 items of evidence, 10 of which supported Zemp's claim that the response was excessive, and 4 of which supported Adams's version of the incident. Subjects were told that "in the interest of fairness they would be allowed to choose the type of hearing procedure they wished to be used to settle the dispute" (p. 104).

After reading the case materials, subjects were asked to select from among five different settlement methods, and given the manipulation involving the veil of ignorance. Those who were to be "behind" the veil were told that thhey were to choose from among the dispute resolution methods without knowing to which role they would ultimately be assigned. Those who were to be "in front of" the veil were told that they had been assigned to one role or another by a flip of the coin. Thus there were three experimental conditions: in front advantaged (the subjects assigned to the role of Zemp), in front disadvantaged (subjects assigned to the role of Adams), and behind the veil of ignorance (not yet assigned to either role).

Five Alternative Procedures.   The five dispute resolution procedures were inquisitorial, single investigator, double investigator, adversary, and bargaining. In the inquisitorial procedure, modeled after judicial proceedings in West Germany, the legal decision maker is a single judge who controls both the pretrial and trial proceedings, and actively participates in the discovery and interpretation of evidence. In the single investigator procedure, a somewhat less activist decision maker is assisted by an investigator whose role as an impartial truth-seeker is established and maintained by the judge. This procedure is typically found in Congressional investigations in the United States. In the double-investigator procedure, the legal decision maker is still less active, now assisted by two investigators, one of whom is assigned to obtain all of the information possible from each party to the dispute (e.g., the defendant and the victim). According to Thibaut and Walker (1975) the military court martial in the United States is a partial illustration of this model. The adversary model differs from the first three generally inquisitorial models in two crucial respects. First, the representatives for each side of the dispute (usually attorneys) are openly biased toward the position claimed by the individuals they represent; no claim is made that either adversary is an objective seeker after truth. Second, most of the control over the process shifts from the judge to the advocates, and through them, to the disputants. The judge is a relatively passive participant until it is time to rule on the issue. The final procedure, bargaining, excluded all parties (decision maker, investigators, advocates) except the two disputants, who were to discuss the issue and reach some kind of agreement.

Preference for Control, but with Help.   The five dispute resolution procedures can be ordered in terms of the control each provides to the disputants, themselves. The inquisitorial model gives the disputants the least amount of control, an amount not materially increased with a single investigator, and increased slightly with two investigators. The adversary model gives the disputants much more control, but permits them to have their positions represented by professional advocates, whereas the bargaining condition requires that the disputants settle the issue entirely on their own. Subjects in the study were asked to indicate their preferences among these models, and the overwhelming choice was for an adversary model. The double investigator model was a distant second, followed by the inquisitorial and single investigator models, with the bargaining model being the least favorite choice.

Within these overall preferences, however, there were also some important effects based on knowledge of one's relative advantage or disadvantage. Compared to the subjects who knew they were disadvantaged, the participants who knew they were advantaged preferred the inquisitorial and single investigator models. If you know the facts are on your side, you are more ready to accept the decision that would be made by an "impartial" inquisitor. In contrast, compared to the disadvantaged subjects, the advantaged ones placed much less stock in the bargaining method. Perhaps despite peoples' desires to maximize their own outcomes, they are reluctant to appear as "pushy" as necessary to obtain their full shares of benefit in a dispute. In each of these three cases (inquisitorial, single investigator, bargaining), the preferences expressed by subjects still behind the veil of ignorance fell in between the preferences expressed by the two groups who already knew the side to which they had been assigned.

What is most important for our purposes, however, is the relative judgments of the value of the adversary model. The advantaged subjects expressed less of a preference for this model than did either the disadvantaged subjects or those still behind the veil of ignorance. Even so, the disadvantaged subjects preferred the adversary model to any of the other alternatives. In other words, when you do not know whether you are likely to become a defendant or a victim, your view of the adversary system matches the view held by those who know that they are in the weaker position. Although Thibaut and Walker do not make this claim, their results suggest that the protections we so frequently dismiss as "technicalities" are essential ingredients of the procedural justice required for an outcome that equitably serves the ends of all the participants.

Extralegal Influences on Legal Decisions

No matter how carefully the legal system specifies the procedural safeguards to be included in criminal proceedings, from social psychology's standpoint there are still two major sources of potential error. First, the officers of the court who are responsible for translating the law's prescriptions into specific activities in the context of an individual case must have the discretion to make those translations as they see fit. But the very exercise of discretion presents opportunities for the influence of extralegal factors. For example, the judge whose remarks to Frankel (1972) were described earlier sees his own beliefs and military service as relevant in the determination of sentencing, and that overall approach could be expected to carry over to procedural issues as well. Other judges who disagreed with the initial premise (and most would disagree) might decide the same outcome and procedural questions differently.

The second source of potential error is the lack of correspondence frequently observed between the legal rules and the psychological realities. Consider the example of a defense attorney who asks a key prosecution witness, "Why have you suddenly become so moralistic against my client? Isn't it true that you, yourself, have attended parties at which people were openly sniffing cocaine?" Immediately the prosecutor rises, objecting to the question as immaterial to the issue before the court. The judge agrees with the prosecutor, sustains the objection, and says "The jury is to disregard that question." That is the legal reality. The psychological reality is that the jury will always have some nagging doubt about the credibility of this witness, a doubt that they will not even be able to discuss and resolve, because they have been instructed to disregard the entire episode. Does anyone seriously believe that a sophisticated defense attorney thought the question would be allowed? Or that the jury would really be able to disregard it? There are numerous similar instances in which legal proceedings fail to take account of psychological realities, our discussion of procedural due process concludes with two representative examples.

Demand Characteristics and Leading Questions. In preceding chapters the systematic observational and experimental methods of scientific social psychology have often been distinguished from the haphazard observations people ordinarily make about their social worlds. One basis for drawing that distinction is the social psychologist's careful attempt to remove artifacts that could otherwise compromise the results. This consistent concern for internal validity can be seen in keeping experimenters blind to conditions, attempts to minimize demand characteristics and evaluation apprehension, design and testing of attitude scale items, and numerous other procedural controls. Most of these controls are needed because the participants who take an interest in the research are assumed to be trying to find the "correct" answers. Any research method that involves asking questions of subjects will produce responses that are composed of at least four different elements. First, there is the "true score," that portion of the response that reflects the subject's honest answer, the answer that would be obtained if somehow it were possible to read the subject's mind without his or her awareness. Second, there is measurement error, that portion of the response produced by imprecision in the questions asked, or by limitations of the scale used to record the answer. Third, there is random variation, both across subjects and within a subject across time. A person might give somewhat different responses to the same question asked at different times, because of differences in immediate past experience, mood, or physical condition (hunger, thirst, fatigue). And fourth, there is the component based on reactivity. Different subjects will be differentially willing to help the investigator, differentially aware of social desirability constraints on action, or differentially interested in self-presentation.

What the researcher wants, of course, is for the response actually given to be composed mainly of true score, with as little interference as possible from other sources. Random variation can be estimated through statistical analysis of the data, reactivity is minimized with proper experimental controls (e.g., disguise of the researcher's true interest), and measurement error can be reduced through standard procedures for constructing the questions, presenting them to the subjects, and scoring the responses. The more committed the researcher is to the desired or predicted outcome, the greater is that investigator's responsibility to minimize the various artifacts, because the goal is to obtain the best estimate of "the truth." This process can be likened to Thibaut and Walker's (1975) inquisitorial model for a legal proceeding. The investigator is the "decision maker," and is responsible for considering the plausible alternatives to the hypothesis of interest and for objectively gathering the evidence necessary to evaluate the persuasiveness of all competing explanations.

This approach contrasts sharply with the adversarial model common to criminal justice. Each advocate (prosecutor or defense attorney) is ethically bound to present the very strongest case possible for *only one side* of the issue being decided. To be fair, many prosecutors would decline to prosecute a case they believed to be insufficient, but once the decision to go forward has been made, no prosecutor would intentionally expose the weaknesses in his or her case during the courtroom presentation. The "truth" is supposed to be what remains intact after each side has presented its own strongest arguments and made concerted efforts to weaken or destroy the arguments advanced by the other side.

An adversarial method of achieving the truth is no less effective, in principle, than is the scientific method, but it will only work well in practice if the opposing advocates are of roughly comparable skill. Where the scientist will attempt to eliminate demand characteristics, evaluation apprehension, and socially desirable responding, the advocate will structure his or her questions so as to build in all of those factors. Witnesses and the defendant will be told how to dress, how to respond to questions in order to create the most credible and positive impressions, and how to avoid responding naturally (i.e., defensively, or emotionally) to attacks by the other side.

As a specific example of the difference, consider the questions asked during the examination of a witness. Where the scientist will ask questions designed to eliminate measurement error, the advocate will employ questions designed to maximize the measurement error in favor of his or her side of the argument. Recall, for a moment, the example of your being mugged by the three knife-wielding youths. The way to find out what actually happened, with a minimum of measurement error, would be to ask you to think very hard about the incident, and to take your time to describe in your own words as precisely as possible exactly what happened. What the prosecutor will actually ask you, however, will be designed to paint the defendants in the worst light possible (questions like "What were you doing when these three defendants accosted you, threatened you with grievous bodily harm, and robbed you?" and "Which one mercilessly stabbed you in the shoulder, even though you were cooperating?"). For his or her part, the defense attorney would ask "What business did you have in the neighborhood where my clients found you?" and "Which of the defendants cut your coat?" The information (corresponding to the true score) sought by each set of questions comprises (a) your reason for being in that place at that time, and (b) the identity of the person who actually used a knife on you. The difference between the two sets is measurement error specifically introduced to support the claims made by each side. The problem is that unless the two advocates are equally skilled at using the language to (their own) extreme, the legal decision maker's impression may be unduly influenced by the form of the questions, a factor that ought to be external to the issues being decided.

Cognitive Processing and Eyewitness Testimony. As noted earlier, one of the fundamental assumptions that the law and social psychology share is that people are rational actors who use information about the world to make choices that will maximize their own outcomes. That capacity for rational decision making, in turn, presumes cognitive processes that veridically represent the external social world. Our study of social perception (Chapter 3), social cognition (Chapter 4), and attitude organization (Chapter 5) presents a picture of the person as a generally effective information processor. It should be emphasized, however, that "usually accurate" is not the same as "always accurate," and compared to social psychology, the law has not been as quick to recognize some of the important limitations in cognitive processing.

Determination of an individual defendant's guilt frequently requires a matter of months, and involves all of the principal actors in the criminal justice system, from the victim who makes a complaint to the judge or jury that ultimately assigns legal responsibility. Despite the time required and the number of participants, this determination is an attribution, one that can potentially be compromised by a variety of errors in social inference. Recall some of the possibilities. First, there is the constructive process in social perception: As each participant in the system forms an impression of the victim and the defendant, he or she does so against a personal background of attitudes and expectations. The attitudes may include stereotypes about particular classes of individuals that will obscure essential individual differences; the expectations held by the perceivers may be self-fulfilling, generating the behavior that has been expected. Once actions have occurred, there is the potential for a "fundamental attribution error": the tendency to overattribute actions to the underlying personal dispositions of the actor, rather than to the situational factors that might be governing the actor's behavior. This error might lead any of the participants to minimize mitigating circumstances. Because there is no possibility for repeated observations of an offense, every participant's belief about the true causes of the event will be affected by his or her causal schemata. Even if these tendencies can be countered successfully, there are the motivational factors to consider—the need to believe in a just world, defensive attribution, or any of the principles of cognitive consistency (such as dissonance). The need to believe in a just world could contribute to erroneous victim-blaming; defensive attribution could lead a decision maker to minimize the responsibility of a perpetrator who was personally similar to the decision maker; needs to reduce or avoid dissonance would lead witnesses to stick with their initial identification of a possible perpetrator, regardless of how tentative that identification had been when first uttered. These are by no means all of the possibilities, but the list is already long enough to make the point that where critical case information is concerned, every participant in the process is better regarded as an interpreter than as a recorder.

Unfortunately, the criminal justice system does not attend sufficiently to the limits of human information processing, and nowhere is this more true than in the case of eyewitness testimony. The *probative value* of any evidence is its usefulness in determining guilt or innocence, and few classes of evidence are given more weight than eyewitness testimony. Ballistics tests could identify a weapon that fired a fatal shot, fingerprints and other physical evidence could place the defendant at the scene, but neither of these is quite as convincing as the testimony of an eyewitness who can describe the actual murder in detail. Early in chapter 2, in the discussion of implicit theories of social psychology, I noted that for each of us nothing is more real than our own experience of events in the social world. We generalize this subjective validity to others, according an eyewitness more credibility than is always justified. Thus, notwithstanding the law's recognition that the prosecution and defense will have different perspectives on the crime, and despite reservations expressed by some legal professionals (e.g., see reviews by Levine & Tapp, 1982; Loftus, 1979; Wells, 1980), eyewitness testimony continues to be taken largely at face value.

The Reluctant Eyewitness.   The extent to which this confidence is misplaced can be illustrated by considering just what an eyewitness might do. Suppose that, unbeknownst to the three youths who accosted you, I had seen the incident from across the street. I would have thought you to be "minding your own business" when you were stopped, and would have noticed their menacing manner. As I was trying to decide whether to do anything about it, I saw the knives drawn and watched in horror as one of them jabbed at your shoulder. Rather than intervene directly, I now decided that the appropriate course of action would be to call the police. I looked up and down the block for a telephone booth, or for a store that might have a phone. By the time I ascertained that there was no available telephone, you were handing over your watch and wallet, they strutted away, and you ran in the other direction out of sight and, I presumed, to safety. Now they were gone, and you were gone, so I decided there was no point in my "getting involved."

Two days later I read about the attack in the newspaper, realized that the police were searching for the culprits, and decided to do my civic duty and report what I had seen to the police. The officer in charge of the investigation first wondered why it had taken me so long to come forward, and then asked for a physical description of the assailants—race, sex, height, weight, build, and clothes. Next the police artist asked me to help construct a composite sketch of their facial features (I did not stop to wonder why there was not already a set of composites, made from your descriptions). From time to time during the creation of the sketches, the artist asked me about particular features ("Should the nose be wider or narrower?"). When the sketches were completed, the artist thanked me and explained that the police would contact me again. Several days later they did so, asking me to come look at a lineup to see whether I could identify any of the assailants. As I looked at the group of six people, one of them looked vaguely familiar. The officers had each person step forward, and the first two did not look familiar to me. The third did, but I hesitated to say anything, until the officer supervising the lineup told me to take my time. So I looked more carefully at this person, and finally said that he looked familiar. When the lineup was completed, the police again thanked me and said that I would hear from them again. The next I heard was 6 months later, when the case came to trial. As I was seated on the witness stand, I noticed the person I had identified during the lineup was seated with two other people and an attorney at the defense table. When the prosecutor asked me if I saw any of the perpetrators present in the courtroom today, I confidently pointed to the one I had identified.

Recollection or Construction? Someone who had only seen my court testimony would conclude that I was close to the attack, had a good view of the attacker, and was certain that the defendant was that person. But is any of that really true? How much of my testimony is accurate recollection, and how much is a construction produced in my interactions with the authorities? To answer these questions, we need to return to the scene of the crime and examine the conditions as objectively as possible. It was dark; I was across the street (obviously far enough away so that the defendants didn't see me, even though the street was deserted); and I was undergoing the mixture of fear of the attackers, responsibility to try to do something to help, and desire to avoid having to get involved that is typical of the bystander's reaction to an emergency (Chapter 9). So neither the physical conditions nor my psychological state contributed to careful scrutiny of the attackers. When the attack was over, I had no intention of reporting the incident, so did not try to hold any of the details in mind.

I volunteered to testify when my reluctance was overcome by guilt, guilt that was enhanced by the attitude of the investigating officer, and this made me want very much to "do the right thing." In other words, my psychological state that day at the police station would have generated a degree of evaluation apprehension and sensitivity to demand characteristics (both discussed in chapter 2) substantially greater than that possessed by the normal experimental subject. Knowing that the police had already begun the investigation, I would think that they might have some suspects, and I would know that you must have provided them with a description before they talked to me. The last thing I would want would be to contradict anything you might have said, so I would take the slightest hint from the investigating officer or the police artist as a cue for the "correct" response, generating a description and picture as much theirs as mine. If this were experimentation, such demand characteristics would be avoided by having two artists, one of whom interviewed you, one of whom interviewed me, with each one independently preparing a sketch of the offender. But the few police departments that could afford to have more than a single artist on the payroll would probably not think this normal research precaution necessary.

I would still have been sensitive to the suggestions (intentional or unintentional) of the police at the time of the lineup. The third person in the lineup looked familiar, but I would not stop to ask myself whether that was because I had seen the person attacking you, or whether it was because that person's face matched the picture constructed by the police artist. I would have taken the supervising officer's caution to "take my time" as a cue that this must, indeed, be the perpetrator, and then would have made the identification. Finally, I would have only a vague recollection of the person's face by the time of the trial 6 months later, but who else would be sitting at the defense table? By now it should be apparent that my "recollection" might be mostly "construction," with that construction heavily influenced by the preconceptions of the police. So there is a strong possibility that my identification is of a person the police already suspected, not of the person who actually participated in the attack on you.

It should be emphasized that each of the participants in this fallible process of identification is acting from the best of motives. I am trying to help bolster the accusations made by a crime victim, and the police are trying to solve an unprovoked attack on a citizen. Nor have there been any obvious errors in the procedure, such as the construction of a lineup using the suspect and five people with very different physical characteristics (as in some of the instances reported by Ellison & Buckhout, 1981). What has happened is that the legal process has run its course without sufficient recognition of the psychological realities.

THE SYSTEM OF CRIMINAL JUSTICE

Given the principle of discretion, social and psychological factors can affect virtually every aspect of criminal justice. In this final section of the chapter we trace through the criminal justice system, briefly noting some of the social psychological processes implicated at each major step. The first thing to understand is that, with the exception of crimes committed on federal government reservations (military installations, Indian reservations, national parks), or crimes such as a kidnaping that would involve crossing state lines, nearly all crimes committed in America against persons will come under the jurisdiction of the states. Although states have developed relatively standard procedures for the investigation and adjudication of alleged offenses, there are still some differences among them. Perhaps for this reason there has only been one major attempt to specify the general structure of the criminal justice system (President's Commission, 1967), and a simplified diagram of that structure appears in Fig. 14.1.

Decisions and Consequences

The diagram illustrates the major choice points in the criminal justice system, and at each of these decision nodes (Ebbesen & Konečni, 1982) the proportion of defendants continuing to the next stage is roughly indicated by the width of the solid line. From left to right, these decision nodes are (a) the reporting of a crime to the police (or the witnessing of such a crime by a police officer), (b) an arrest made by the police, either immediately or after investigation, (c) prosecutorial review of the arrest to determine whether

FIGURE 14.1 Simplified model of the criminal justice system, showing percentage of offenders retained at each step toward felony conviction and sentence. Adapted from President's Commission on Law Enforcement and Administration of Justice (1967) and Ebbesen & Konečni (1982).

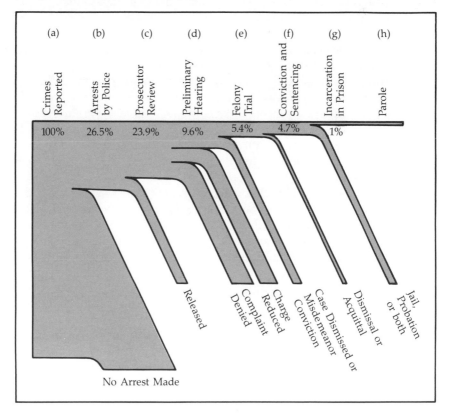

to proceed with prosecution, (d) the arraignment or preliminary hearing, at which among other things it is determined whether reasonable grounds existed for the original arrest and bail is set, (e) the actual trial on the felony charge, either before a judge or jury, (f) conviction of the defendant and sentencing, (g) incarceration in prison, and ultimately (h) parole and return to society. The system is partially closed, with the principal entry point being that at which the police learn of the occurrence, either by witnessing the crime directly or by receiving a report of the crime from a victim or witness. There are other possible entry points not shown on the diagram (e.g., the prosecutor can initiate investigation of a person thought to have committed crimes, whether or not any formal complaint has yet been lodged with the police), but these account for a relatively small fraction of the offenses that come to the attention of the authorities.

Three aspects of this diagram should be noted. First, for ease of presentation, some nodes outlined by the President's Commission (1967) have been omitted, and others have been combined. For example, the diagram shows the progression of a felony, a serious crime such as murder, rape, assault, or robbery, omitting misdemeanors committed by adults and all crimes committed by juveniles. Conviction and sentencing, often considered separately, have been combined here because in many jurisdictions the use of "sentencing guidelines" dramatically reduces the judge's sentencing discretion once the defendant has been found guilty.

A second thing to notice about the diagram is that it begins with crimes reported to the police, not with crimes actually committed. But studies of the extent of crime victimization (e.g., Census Bureau, 1977) show that slightly less than half of the instances of victimization for many crimes (the survey included rape, robbery, assault, burglary, personal and household larceny) are ever reported to the police. Thus one of the most critical decisions—that by the crime victim to report the incident—is omitted from the diagram. So you should keep in mind that the solid line begins with only those crimes known to the police.

The third thing that will be apparent from the diagram is that only a small fraction of the offenders ever find themselves serving time in state penitentiaries. By combining information from the President's Commission (1967) with data collected by Ebbesen and Konečni (1982) it is possible to estimate the final proportion of offenders confined to prison. Of the 100% of offenders reported to police, only 1% are ultimately sentenced to prison. A word of caution is in order: the data reported by Ebbesen and Konečni (1982) are limited to California, and are specific to the year 1977. There is, however, no reason to believe that data from other jurisdictions would be substantially different. Even if the final number were in error by a factor of 5, the proportion of imprisoned defendants would still be insignificant relative to the number reported to police. Thus, although it is certainly true that many defendants leave the system by being convicted of misdemeanors along the way, or by receiving sentences other than prison for felony convictions, not very many offenders must suffer the severe consequence of imprisonment for their initial decision to commit a crime.

Overload and Review

It might seem that the offender's progression through the criminal justice system is like a trip down a one-way street, leading either to a side turn or to the penitentiary. And it is certainly true that only those offenders retained under the system's control at one decision node will be dealt with at the succeeding one. The behavior of any set of participants other than the offender, however, is heavily influenced by expectations about what will happen at later stages of the process. Consider just two examples. The penitentiaries of most states are currently overcrowded, with conditions so deplorable in some that courts have had to order reductions in the inmate census. Many states have begun building more prison facilities, but new maximum security institutions can cost from $50,000 to $200,000 *per inmate* to construct. Suppose that the criminal justice system suddenly became more effective, and tripled the number of offenders ultimately sentenced to prison terms. Would the same state legislators who call for increased sentences and "crackdowns on crime" be willing to impose the increases in state taxes necessary to triple the number of prison beds available? In many jurisdictions the court calendars are so full that a defendant's right to a speedy trial exists in name only. What would happen if, thanks to a new computerized crime information system, the police forces were able to double the number of arrests made? Or if the 75% to 90% of defendants who now plead guilty all demanded their constitutionally-guaranteed jury trials? Where would the system find all the judges, and the courtrooms, that would be needed?

Questions like these have been considered for years in the criminal justice literature (e.g., see a book of readings by Cole, 1972), and it is difficult to imagine that any individual participant's personal answers to them will not affect his or her discretionary behavior. The overload already present in the system acts as a pressure on police to investigate only the most serious crimes, or to set dollar or kind-of-crime limits on the deployment of the department's resources (Ellison & Buckhout, 1981). The same pressure may lead a prosecutor to dismiss charges, or to plea bargain when ideally he or she would not have done so; it may increase a judge's likelihood of convicting the defendant on a misdemeanor rather than on the felony charge, or of imposing a sentence that includes jail and probation instead of than penitentiary time.

The extent to which system pressures, rather than case factors, will affect discretionary decisions is limited by one other feature of the criminal justice system: the opportunity for review. Even though an accused's progress through the system may appear to him or her like a one-way ticket, the other participants will be well aware that their own discretionary actions will be scrutinized by decision makers later in the process. Police officers rightly complain about having to make split-second decisions that will later be reviewed, and occasionally found in error, by state and then federal courts, up to and including the Supreme Court. Prosecutors can have cases they have presented denied by grand juries who refuse to return indictments, or by judges who deny complaints at preliminary hearings. The actions of trial judges are, in principle at least, reviewable by higher state courts and (through the appeals process) by federal courts as well. It is precisely this kind of review that is designed to keep the exercise of discretion at all levels from becoming "arbitrary, capricious, or unrestrained." You should keep the pressures from overload, and the potential for review, in mind as we trace through the system.

Social Decisions in Criminal Justice

Reporting of Crimes.   Assuming for the moment that the criminal justice system would be able to absorb the extra work with no change in efficiency, the public could double the number of convictions by reporting crimes. Why don't we do so? One of the principal reasons is fear of "secondary victimization" by the system, itself. Depending upon the nature of the crime, this victimization can begin almost immediately upon the victim's initial contact with the police. The rape victim who must give a detailed report to an unsympathetic male officer is one of the most distressing such examples, if not the only one. Police facilities are built for security, not for comfort of a victim; police training understandably concentrates on obtaining the most complete information possible, not on preserving the emotional well-being of a victim.

Once a victim has made a formal complaint, the state then becomes the victim of record (indeed, in some instances prosecutors can proceed against an accused offender with or without the cooperation of the actual victim). Victims may not be informed of case progress, and may lose time away from work in order to make identifications, discuss the case at the prosecutor's convenience, or appear in court. If the alleged offender is caught (and remember, only a quarter of crimes reported actually lead to arrest), that person may be free on bail pending the trial, and able to harass the victim into deciding not to testify. Should the defendant be found guilty at trial, the victim is rarely consulted before sentence is rendered, and even more infrequently consulted by a parole board considering release of an offender who has "done the time." Given the relatively low probability of conviction, the unknown likelihood that the offender will hold a grudge against the victim, and the victimizing nature of the process itself, it is not too surprising that only half of the incidents of victimization are reported. What is important for our purposes is that these failures to report frequently have to do not with questions of legal policy, but with issues of social exchange: "Is the vindication that I may obtain from the law greater than the pain I will suffer from participating in the process?" Thus, the failure to report is an excellent object for study by social psychology, and such studies have already begun (Greenberg & Ruback, 1984).

The Decision to Arrest. Training manuals for police officers direct that all laws should be enforced, and that all violations should lead to arrest, a position that Goldstein (1960) has called "full enforcement." Some of the laws still present in many state criminal codes outlaw practices (such as private heterosexual intercourse between consenting, but unmarried, adults) that are now so widely accepted that their full enforcement would cost the police dearly in public support. Other laws (such as those against drug trafficking) could not be enforced if all violations, no matter how minor, led to prosecution. Whether they are operating undercover or in uniform, police are frequently able to obtain information about major drug violators only by "trading" nonarrest for that information. (This discretionary decision, unlike many others that are made in the criminal justice system, is not reviewable by any later actors in the system.) What is important for our purposes is that any discretionary deviation from full enforcement will be determined in part by the police department's informal position on the issue in question, in part by the individual officer's own attitudes, and in part by the behavior of the offender. Again, these are social psychological matters, not legal ones.

Apprehension of offenders is only one of the services that society expects from the police, and notwithstanding television portrayals of police work, is not one of the most dangerous. Ask a police officer what he or she fears most, and the answer will be "domestics"—those calls in which it is the officer's job to intervene in a dispute between a cohabiting couple (who may or may not be married). This apprehension on the officer's part is a thoroughly justified response to the fact that more police officers are killed in situations of domestic violence than by any other single cause. For example, Bard (1970) found that 20% of police deaths and 40% of injuries on duty were sustained during intervention in family disputes. In part to try to reduce these figures, and in part to help provide psychological services to families in need, Bard established a training procedure to teach police tactics of conflict management. The training was designed to enable police to mediate the conflict, diverting people from the criminal justice system. The conflict management approach, however, has recently come under attack from advocates for battered women who argue that a physical assault is cause for arrest, whether it has been administered by a stranger or by a spouse (Dierking, 1978). As a consequence of this criticism, many departments now direct their officers to make arrests if there is any sign of physical violence. The change first from ignoring family violence to attempting to mediate the dispute, and the subsequent change from mediation to arrest, both reflect the influence of general social attitudes on the discretionary behavior of police.

Prosecution. There is general agreement among legal scholars (e.g., Davis, 1971; Gelman, 1982) that in American criminal justice the prosecutor possesses the greatest degree of discretion. Like police, prosecutors can decide that no further action is warranted against a particular defendant, but unlike police the prosecutors can also initiate investigation–often in the glare of publicity–of people against whom no credible evidence has yet been amassed. In recognition of the prosecutor's power, both the American Bar Association (1971) and the National District Attorneys Association (1977) have recommended guidelines for the *screening decision*: the decision of whether to continue or drop a case. To a large degree both sets of recommendations overlap, and some of their elements have a distinctly legal flavor, such as the likelihood of prosecution by another jurisdiction or a history of local nonenforcement of the particular statute. Other guidelines in both sets, however, have a decidedly social psychological ring: reluctance of the victim to proceed or testify, the prosecutor's personal doubts about the validity of the case, and possible improper motives on the part of a victim or witness.

Once the screening decision has been made in the affirmative, the prosecutor has virtually complete control over that part of the system that ultimately produces most of the sentences: plea negotiation. The prosecutor can set the charges and may "overcharge" in order to have something to bargain away. With or without overcharging, the prosecutor can choose whether or not to initiate or invite a plea negotiation, and then whether or not to accept an offer or counteroffer from the defense attorney. As part of his or her normal duties, the prosecutor makes a recommendation during the preliminary hearing about whether the defendant should be released on bail, and if so, what the amount of that bail should be. The bail recommendation and the plea negotiation can, of course, interact. A defendant who is unable to make bail, and who is facing a wait of 10 months in jail prior to trial, will be tempted to take a plea bargain that reduces a felony charge to a misdemeanor, whether he or she is actually guilty or not. Why? Because in most jurisdictions the actual sentence served is roughly one third that actually imposed by the judge, and misdemeanors typically carry a maximum of 1 year in jail. Thus from the defendant's point of view, the plea is a virtually certain 4 months, whereas the wait for trial (at which conviction is still possible) is a guaranteed 10 months. Most prosecutors are elected officials, and so their actions in screening, plea negotiating, and recommending bail are supposed to reflect the standards important to their communities. But the processes by which prosecutors come to know these standards, as well as the factors that affect the exercise of discretion in an individual case, are easily described in terms of impression formation, attribution, judgment of equity, and bargaining, all familiar topics in social psychology.

Adjudication.   Having discussed the adversary process, eyewitness testimony, and sentencing in some detail earlier, we will not consider the preliminary hearing, the actual trial, and the imposition of a sentence separately. It is important to point out, however, that a great deal of social psychological research on the criminal justice system concentrates on the selection and behavior of members of trial juries, and that research is almost as controversial within social psychology as it's applications are in the law.

If a defendant demands a jury trial, the jury will actually be selected in some variant of the following procedure. The process begins with a partial list of members of the community – a list of registered voters is the one typically employed. Most jurisdictions by statute exempt certain categories of people, such as doctors, attorneys, or even mothers of preschool children, from jury duty, and the names of these people will be removed from the lists. When juries are needed names will be randomly selected from the remaining names (the jury pool), and individuals will be summoned to jury duty, sometimes with the opportunity to refuse the summons on the basis of one of several legally prescribed hardships. Unless the case has had unusual circumstances or publicity, 20 to 40 people will be summoned to appear in court. There they will undergo a process called *voir dire*, in which the presiding judge (and occasionally the defense and prosecuting attorneys) will ask each juror a series of questions. These questions often include whether the prospective juror is related by blood or marriage either to the defendant or to a person employed in law enforcement, whether the candidate has formed an opinion about the case, and whether he or she can render an impartial verdict after all of the evidence has been presented. A prospective juror who answers any of these questions unsatisfactorily can be excused "for cause," leaving a group still larger than the 12 that normally constitutes a jury in a criminal case. Finally the prosecutor and defense attorney are permitted to remove through *peremptory challenges* a limited number of the remaining people, leaving 12 jurors and a few alternates.

Exactly how this jury selection takes place depends a great deal on the nature of the trial. Judges have discretion over how many peremptory challenges will be allowed, and they may or may not let the prosecution and defense each contribute questions to be asked of the prospective jurors. Social psychologists first became involved in jury selection during the Vietnam War, when John Mitchell, then Attorney General in Richard Nixon's administration, brought criminal conspiracy charges against a large group of antiwar activists. The government chose Harrisburg, Pennsylvania as the site for what many people regarded as trial designed only to silence political opposition to the war. In what they believed was a counter to outrageous behavior on the part of the government, several social scientists joined in the defense of the "Harrisburg 7."

After conducting demographic and attitude surveys in the community, the social scientists (Schulman, Shaver, Colman, Emrich, & Christie, 1973) provided defense attorneys with a series of questions to ask prospective jurors in order to lay the foundation for dismissal for cause, or at least to provide information that would be useful in deciding on peremptory challenges. If the trial outcome is any indication, this application of social science methods to jury selection was a resounding success: the defendants were acquitted by a jury drawn from a community known to be strongly opposed to the defendants' position. Scientific jury selection procedures have since been used in a wide variety of cases, although as Ellison and Buckhout (1981) note, the method has been criticized as giving the defendant an unfair advantage.

Although scientific jury selection has received the most publicity outside the discipline, most of the social psychological criticism of jury research deals not with selection but with *simulation* (e.g., see a review by Diamond, 1979). In some of the early studies "mock jurors" (usually college undergraduates) were given brief "case materials" and asked to make decisions, without actual deliberation, about the guilt or innocence of a particular (often hypothetical) criminal defendant. The case materials normally contained variations in a factor, such as seriousness of the offense, that might legitimately affect the outcome of a real trial, or variations in some extralegal source of bias, such as the physical attractiveness of a defendant.

There are, of course, two main objections to this research technique. First, it is easy to question the extent to which college undergraduates using limited case materials can approximate the decisions that would be made by real members of the jury pool after having listened to a full criminal trial. In the context of the limited case materials, the manipulated factor (be it legally relevant or extralegal) is quite likely to have an effect out of proportion to the importance it would assume in an actual trial. A good deal of the recent research incorporates much more realistic stimulus materials—videotaped trials, frequently involving real legal professionals as the participants, subjects chosen from jury rolls, actual deliberations prior to rendering of verdicts—so the first objection to simulation of legal processes is not as persuasive as it was in the early days of social psychology's interest in legal processes. It is worth noting, for example, that much of what we know about the extralegal influences on such things as eyewitness testimony comes not from real trials, but from just such simulations of judicial decision making, and many of these findings obtain regardless of the specific research technique employed.

The second criticism centers around a more serious question. Can the responses of any group of people, whether they are college students or actual members of a jury pool and whether they are reading prepared hypothetical case materials or listening to all of the testimony in an actual criminal trial, truly simulate the behavior of a jury whose verdict will either free or incarcerate a real defendant? Most social psychologists would either think that the answer to this question is negative, or at best would argue for very cautious generalization from research to reality. Where they would disagree is on whether the required caution leaves anything of value for simulated jury research to accomplish. Those who believe that external validity is all important (e.g., Konečni & Ebbesen, 1982) argue against simulation of this or any other legal process, claiming that only the methods of social psychology can be employed to help illuminate what occurs in criminal justice. Others who believe as I do that case factors must be isolated to be understood (e.g., Ellison & Buckhout, 1981) argue that despite its obvious limits simulation research has its proper place. Indeed, much of the material in this chapter, and the applications of social psychological theory to the law both here and elsewhere (e.g., Greenberg & Ruback, 1982; Saks & Hastie, 1978) presumes that careful simulation can be informative. What is clear is that because of the legal prohibitions against studying the deliberations of actual juries, the disagreement over the value of simulated juries will have to be settled on social psychological grounds, not on legal grounds.

Incarceration and Parole.   Once a felony defendant has been convicted, that person is sentenced to imprisonment in a state penitentiary. For anyone who has had the sobering experience of visiting, or conducting research in, such a facility—especially one that is nearly a hundred years old and overcrowded—two things become immediately apparent. First, it is extremely difficult to imagine how imprisonment can be "rehabilitative" in any normal sense of the word. Indeed, as Ellison and Buckhout (1981) suggest, very little in the way of rehabilitation took place in the one prison explicitly designed with this objective in mind. This prison, in Patuxent, Maryland, had been created in the 1950s to apply psychological principles of behavior modification to offenders found guilty of repeated instances of violence against others. The prison was run not by the usual warden, but by a psychiatrist and a staff of psychological professionals; the inmates were given *indeterminate* sentences (no year limits specified) and were "encouraged" to participate in group therapy that would correct their antisocial activities. Although inmates quickly learned that participation in therapy was far from voluntary (release was conditioned entirely on the judgment that an offender was "cured"), the average sentences were longer than they were for comparable offenders at institutions employing the more standard determinate sentences. The prison was closed by the state of Maryland in 1975 after a number of class-action lawsuits brought by prisoners, and in a context of strident criticism from some in the psychological community (e.g., Opton, 1975) of the behavior modification procedures.

The second strong impression created in the prison visitor is that the psychological effects of court-imposed denial of liberty cannot be simulated. You will remember from chapter 7 that psychologists at Stanford (Haney, Banks, & Zimbardo, 1973) conducted a simulation of the prison environment, with people randomly assigned to the role of prisoner or guard. Within the space of 6 days, the subjects assigned to be prisoners became listless and helpless, and the subjects assigned to be guards became sadistic, suggesting the power that the two roles can have over individual behavior and perhaps providing some insight into the problems experienced at Patuxent. Correctional officials have criticized this resarch as naive (Ellison & Buckhout, 1981), and even it did not include the racism and forced homosexuality that are common in prison. Certainly a prison is a self-contained social system, and as such should involve many of the processes common to similar social systems on "the outside." But because of the problems that arise in attempts to conduct social psychological research in the prisons (e.g., Gilbert & Shaver, 1975), thorough investigation of the deindividuating effect of prison life remains a challenge for future research.

One aspect of imprisonment that has been the subject of study by social psychologists is the decision process that leads to parole (Carroll & Payne, 1976; Greenberg & Ruback, 1982; Wilkins, 1982). According to Greenberg and Ruback (1982), this process involves four separate stages once enough prison time has been served to make an inmate eligible for consideration. First the prison staff, typically including the inmate's counselor, makes a report to the prison administration that describes the inmate's behavior and activities and often contains a recommendation about parole. Next, the report is passed to a member of the parole board's staff, often called a "case analyst," who independently reviews the inmate's activities and examines the inmate's plan for living arrangements and employment if parole is granted. Third, if there is a positive recommendation from the case analyst, a subgroup of the members of the parole board will conduct a hearing of the case, involving the inmate as well as relevant correctional personnel. If the hearing examiner(s) recommend parole, that recommendation is considered by the full parole board, which makes the final decision.

Of the four steps, the hearing presents the most easily accessible material for social psychological analysis because it is frequently recorded. Thus the contributions to the recommendation that are made by each individual hearing officer, as well as the inmate's answers to specific questions, can be examined. In one important study of the hearing process, Carroll and Payne (1976) found that a large proportion of the questions and comments initiated by hearing examiners could be classified as attributions about the causes of the inmate's original criminal activity and behavior while in prison. If these attributions identify stable causes of prior criminal behavior, then recidivism risk (likelihood that the offender will return to prison convicted of other crimes committed upon release) is estimated to be higher, and the parole decision is more likely to be negative. In addition to the attributions involved in parole hearings, Greenberg and Ruback (1982) have identified a number of social exchange considerations inherent in parole decision making, including the interaction the parole board has with the public, as well as with the inmate. The discretionary behavior of parole decision makers, like that of so many other actors in the criminal justice system, is affected as much by social psychological factors as by legal requirements.

THE PERSON AND THE SOCIAL SYSTEM

As the study of the personal and situational factors that influence individual social behavior, social psychology has a natural affinity for criminal justice – an example of rules and procedures that are designed to regulate interpersonal behavior. The rules inherent in the law and other social organizations provide an environment for social interaction just as surely as features of the physical world limit and guide that interplay between individuals. Limits imposed by the social environment, like those present in the physical environment, can be altered by human actions, as in the case of discretionary decisions made in the criminal justice system. One final point should be emphasized. The study of social psychology is an examination of the process of human behavior. This study of ongoing social process began in social psychology with Sherif's (1936) research on social influence in the autokinetic situation (Chapter 1) and it continues today in work on social cognition, social exchange, and criminal justice.

Throughout the book, I adhered to an individualistic viewpoint, turning to a person's interactions with others only after considering that person's social cognition, attitudes, self-concept, and social motivation. Given an individualistic definition of social psychology, the present chapter is a logical conclusion to our progression from simpler, internal processes to more complex, interpersonal ones. The study of a social system such as the law is as far as we can venture without losing sight of the individual. But it would be a mistake to think that this conclusion to social psychology as we have defined it marks the end of significant influences on social behavior. From here the trail simply leads to other disciplines: to sociology, which concentrates on human groups and institutions, and to anthropology, which places those institutions in their proper cultural context. The material presented in this chapter should be regarded as an introduction to other fields, as well as a conclusion to this one.

SUMMARY

Social psychology and the law share three fundamental assumptions about the nature of human behavior: That the unit of analysis should be the individual person (p. 495), that participants in an interaction may have different perspectives (p. 496) on the events that take place, and that people generally behave rationally (p. 496) in order to accomplish their goals. These shared assumptions, when coupled with the fact that legal officials are permitted to exercise **discretion** (p. 498) in the performance of their duties, provide a natural affinity between social psychology and criminal justice.

The establishment of a criminal justice system relfects society's recognition that there are some individuals who will use coercive means to maximize their own outcomes. Such a criminal justice system must determine individual guilt (p. 501) based on the proof of an *actus reus* (p. 501) in the presence of guilty intent, or *mens rea* (p. 501). This determination of individual culpability is heavily influenced by processes of social attribution (p. 502) including schemata (p. 503) for multiple necessary causes and multiple sufficient causes. In making determinations of guilt, the criminal justice system must also maintain justice (p. 505), attempting to ensure *substantive due process* (p. 507) through *procedural due process* (p. 507). This search for an equitable outcome may consider **self-concept distress** (p. 508) and **retaliation distress**, as well as equity-restoring distortions such as blaming the victim (p. 509). Achieving due process requires knowledge of principles of fairness (p. 513), often established by placing decision makers behind a *veil of ignorance* (p. 514) about their personal place in the system, and minimization of *extralegal* influences on legal decision making, such as those that adversely affect eyewitness testimony (p. 519).

In the United States the criminal laws are enforced by statutes that may differ from one state to another, but there are decision nodes (p. 523) common to all of the systems. These include the reporting of crimes by witnesses and victims (p. 526); the arrest decisions (p. 527) made by police officers; the screening decisions made by prosecutors (p. 528), who also control the controversial process of plea bargaining (p. 528), and the adjudication (p. 529) decisions made by judges and juries. Social scientists have participated in scientific jury selection (p. 530), and have given a great deal of attention to simulation research on jury decision making (p. 530). Once a convicted felon has been sentenced, he or she will typically be incarcerated (p. 531) in prison until ultimately released on parole (p. 532).

The criminal justice system serves not only as an excellent laboratory for the application of principles of social psychology, but also as an instructive example of the more general social constraints on individual social behavior.

SUGGESTED ADDITIONAL READINGS

ELLISON, K. W., & BUCKHOUT, R. (1981). *Psychology and criminal justice*. New York: Harper & Row. This is a general introduction to the field that takes a positive view of the contributions that social psychologists in particular can make to criminal justice. Topics covered include the police, eyewitness identification, and expert testimony provided by psychologists. There is a thorough discussion of jury research, and the book concludes with resource files designed for psychologists who are interested in legal issues, although the level of writing is geared for undergraduates.

GREENBERG, M. S., & RUBACK, R. B. (1982). *Social psychology of the criminal justice system*. Monterey, CA: Brooks/Cole. This book is a specific application of attribution theory and social exchange theory to all areas of criminal justice, including crime reporting by victims, the actions of police, pretrial and trial tactics, sentencing, incarceration, and parole. The most theoretically based introduction to social psychology and the law, this book is readable and interesting. Highly recommended.

KONEČNI V. J., & EBBESEN, E. B. (1982). *The criminal justice system: A social psychological analysis*. San Francisco: Freeman. This is a collection of chapters written for a professional audience. Topics include victimization, police activities and the gathering of evidence, an analysis of bail setting and the decision to prosecute, and descriptions of jury trials, sentencing, and parole decision making. In introductory theoretical and methodological comments the authors set forth their preference for externally valid study of the legal system as opposed to laboratory research on legally-relevant problems. A strong statement of an important theoretical and methodological position that should be considered by anyone planning research in the area.

METHODOLOGICAL APPENDIX: RESEARCH PROCEDURES IN SOCIAL PSYCHOLOGY

MEASUREMENT AND DESIGN

>Numbers and Scales
>Finding the Regularities
>The Importance of Control

DISCOVERING COGNITIVE STRUCTURES

>Implicit Personality Theory
>Attitude Measurement

ANALYSIS OF INTERPERSONAL BEHAVIOR

>Student-Initiated Research
>Influences on Attraction
>Collecting the Data
>Interpreting the Results
>A Word of Caution, A Note of Optimism

In its attempt to identify the factors that influence individual social behavior, scientific social psychology has developed procedures for discovering these underlying personal and situational regularities. There are the general methods of archival analysis, observation, and experimentation discussed in chapter 2, and more specific techniques for such things as the assessment of implicit personality theories (Chapter 4), the scaling of social attitudes (Chapter 6) and the analysis of ongoing social interaction (Chapter 12). The purpose of this Appendix is to illustrate some of these latter techniques, and to show how the general principles of measurement and control can be brought to bear in the design of a research project planned and conducted by students in a first course in social psychology.

MEASUREMENT AND DESIGN

Numbers and Scales

How much power does one person have over another? How effective will a persuasive communication be in changing an individual's attitude? How cohesive is a group? These and other questions of interest to social psychology all involve measurement: the numerical representation of a social behavior. Whether the question is asked at the level of an individual or at the level of a group of people, the answer will explicitly or implicitly involve a comparison. The power of an influencing agent must be described in the same numerical terms as the power of a target person in order to determine their relative positions. An individual's attitude must be assigned some numerical value before the persuasive communication is delivered, and that value must be compared to a value obtained after the communication has been received. The forces acting to keep members of a group together can only be understood if they can be compared either to the forces acting to split the group apart, or to the forces acting to pull the members into other groups. To understand the problems of measurement in any of these areas, you need to know a little about the various numerical scales that can be employed to make the needed comparisons.

The Nominal Scale. Let us consider, for example, the numerical scales that could be involved in the measurement of a social attitude. Suppose that we wanted to measure an individual's degree of racism. At the most basic level, we could simply ask "Are you a racist?" Ruling out uncertain responses ("I don't know," or "What do you mean by that?") and refusals ("What business is it of yours?"), we would be left with two possible answers, "Yes," and "No." If we were planning to try to change the respondent's attitude with a persuasive communication, we would want to assign some numerical value to each of these responses, so that the effect of our communication could later be measured. It might be appropriate to assign a value of zero to the negative answer, but what value should be assigned to the affirmative one. One, 50, 100, or what? Merely asking this question indicates that true numerical values are not justified for the answers to this question. What we have done is to classify respondents into two groups, but there is no necessary numerical relationship between the groups. In more formal terms, the responses are characterized by a *nominal scale*: a scale of measurement by which the observations can be classified, but not ordered.

The hypothetical responses of six subjects are shown in the first row of Table A.1. These responses fall into two categories—"yes" and "no." We could assign numbers to the two groups just for purposes of identification, but these numbers would not indicate anything about the classes except that they were different. Other examples of the use of nominal scales include a grouping of subjects into females and males, a division of survey respondents according to their own race, or a split of criminal offenders into those who have committed misdemeanors and those who have committed felonies.

The Ordinal Scale. At the next highest level of measurement, we could use a classification scheme that would permit us to order the groups or individuals involved. Instead of asking whether a person is or is not a racist, we might try to infer his or her racial attitudes from, say, political participation. We could ask whether he or she belongs to a number of political organizations, such as the National Association for the Advancement of Colored People (NAACP), the Democratic Party, the Republican Party, the John Birch Society, the American Independent Party, and the Ku Klux Klan. Then we would guess the person's attitudes on the basis of organizational membership. On the average we would expect that a member of the NAACP would less racist attitudes than would a member of the Democratic Party. A Democrat, in turn, should hold less racist attitudes than a

TABLE A.1 Scales of Measurement: Hypothetical Responses of Six Subjects to Different Questions about Racism

	Person A	Person B	Person C	Person D	Person E	Person F
			Nominal Scale			
"Are you racist?"	No	No	No	No	No	Yes
			Ordinal Scale			
Membership	NAACP	Democ.	Repub.	Birch	Am. Ind.	Klan
Rank order	6	5	4	3	2	1
			Interval Scale			
Attitude score	5	15	25	50	70	80
Transformed score	−30	−20	−10	15	35	45

Republican, who should hold less racist attitudes than a member of the John Birch Society, and so on. In short, given what we believe (perhaps erroneously) about these various groups, we should be able to arrange their members in a logical order of increasing racism. When data can be rank ordered in this fashion, they constitute what is known as an *ordinal scale* of measurement. Such a rank order is indicated in the second row of Table A.1. The ranks shown in the table are arranged in the usual manner, with the most positive score given the rank of 1 (keep in mind that the attitude being assessed here is racism, so the "most positive" score is the one that represents the highest degree of that attitude, whether or not the attitude described by the scale would normally have a positive social value).

You can probably think of the two principal difficulties with this rank order procedure. First, the groups have been arranged on as groups, and there is no guarantee that individual group members will subscribe to the organization's position on the issue. It is possible – even likely – that "liberal Republicans" will hold attitudes that are more egalitarian than those held by "conservative Democrats." This potential for reversals on an individual level is enhanced when the organizational categories are broad and the issue of race is only one of many concerns important to group members (like the two major political parties), as compared to the case of narrow categories with race the central issue (the NAACP or the Klan). The second problem is that there is no way to know how much difference there might be between the groups themselves, even on an aggregate basis. The difference between an average Democrat's views and an average Republican's views might be equal to the difference between an American Independent Party member and a Klansman, or it might be larger, or it might be smaller. We simply have no information on which to base such a judgment.

Consequently, although we can assign numbers to the groups that represent an ordinal scale, we cannot legitimately perform arithmetic operations on the numbers. It is important to note that the attitudes of a person whose rank is 4 are not necessarily the same distance from those of a person whose rank is 2 as they are from the attitudes of a person whose rank is 6. There are methods for determining whether two sets of ranks are significantly different, but these do not assume (and therefore do not permit us to conclude) anything about the distances between the ranked objects or people.

The Interval Scale.   When the numbers that are assigned to identify observations do reflect the distances between observations (while also representing a logical order), those numbers are said to constitute an *interval scale* of measurement. Attitude scales strive for this level of measurement, as do most of the dependent variables used in social psychological research, so it is important to discuss the properties of an interval scale more fully. First, and most fundamentally, the intervals between the numbers assigned are presumed to be equal regardless of the actual unit of measurement. This requirement is best described by an example. Suppose that instead of asking our six respondents about their memberships in political organizations, we devised an attitude questionnaire to measure racism. This attitude questionnaire, consisting of several different items, would yield a total score for each subject.

Some hypothetical attitude scores that might be obtained are shown in Table A.1, in the first row under the designation "interval scale." You will notice that rejection of black people, as measured by this attitude scale does follow the rank order obtained with the ordinal scale. But what about the distances between the scores? Person E has a score that is 20 points above that of Person D, but only 10 points below that of Person F, and great mathematical skill is not required to observe that these distances are different, not equal. The point is that an interval scale requires equal intervals between the numbers used to form the scale, not between the scores that happen to be achieved by respondents who answer the questions. Thus the difference between the scores of Persons E and D is $70 - 50 = 20$ scale units, and the difference between the scores of Persons A and C is $25 - 5 = 20$ scale units. What the interval scale assumes is that these identical numerical differences represent identical degrees of psychological difference. Thus, to meet the assumptions of the interval scale, the E–D difference in rejection of blacks must be psychologically identical to the A–B difference in rejection.

The second property of the interval scale is that it has an arbitrary zero point, and this feature makes it quite appropriate for representing attitudes and other social psychological variables. Until now we have been speaking of the attitude of racism as if it were a *unipolar* dimension: one running from a minimum value of zero to a maximum value of extreme presence of the variable in question. For example, the amount of sunlight present in a spot in the desert will vary from a total absence (night) to a maximum present at high noon. But social psychological variables are unlikely to have absolute zero points. In terms of our example, is it not more accurate to characterize a member of the NAACP as having a positive attitude toward black people than as having zero racism? Not surprisingly, many social psychologists would argue that attitude dimensions ought to be *bipolar*, running from extremely favorable to extremely unfavorable, with a zero point in the center of the scale that represents either uncertainty or neutrality, not the total absence of an attitude.

Specifically, on a dimension of racism the scores of the NAACP member, the Democrat, and the Republican ought to be negative (indicating varying degrees of favorability toward black people), whereas the attitudes of the Bircher, the American Independent Party member, and the Klansman ought to be represented by positive scores, indicating varying degrees of racism. This change in the original scale could be accomplished by subtracting a constant value of 35 from each attitude score. The resulting *transformed* scores are shown in the last row of Table A.1, and you can see that this transformation makes no difference in the essential property of the interval scale. The distance between Persons A and C remains 20 units, as does the distance between Persons D and E, and these identical scale differences are still presumed to represent equal psychological distances.

The Ratio Scale. If an absolute zero point is added to an interval scale, the scale then becomes a *ratio scale.* Perhaps the best illustration of a familiar ratio scale is the scale used to measure length (or height). Whether the units of this scale are described in terms of inches and yards or in terms of centimeters and meters, the scale begins from an absolute zero point of no length at all. Because of its absolute zero point, we can legitimately compare the ratios between points on the scale: 6 feet is twice as long as 3 feet. We cannot make this kind of statement about interval scale data (100 is not twice as hot as 50, an attitude of 50 is not necessarily twice as racist as an attitude of 25).

The ratio scale, like an interval scale, is unchanged by division or multiplication by a constant, but its properties—unlike those of the interval scale—are altered by the addition or subtraction of a constant. For example, add 1 foot to the amounts just noted, and you can see that although 6/3 = 2, 7/4 ≠ 2. Because social psychological variables can almost never be expressed in ratio scales, we cannot be in a position to say, for example, that one person's attitude is so many times more favorable than another person's attitude. But what is lost in precision is gained in flexibility. Because of its arbitrary zero point, an interval scale can be used to represent a quasi-unipolar variable (e.g., the amount of responsibility that a stimulus person might bear for producing a negative outcome) or a true bipolar variable (an attitude toward black people). Moreover, the values obtained can be subjected to whatever linear transformations are psychologically appropriate without changing the essential properties of the scale. Finally, any dependent variables that are interval scales can be subjected to a variety of arithmetic operations and statistical procedures without violating the assumptions underlying such tests.

Finding the Regularities

Suppose that instead of arbitrarily arranging the six organizations in Table A.1 according to the presumed views of their members we were interested in discovering the actual views of most of the people identified with each organization. It would obviously not be sufficient to locate a single individual representing each organization, give that person an attitude scale, and draw conclusions about the organization's position on the basis of the one individual's responses. Nor is it possible for us to poll every member of each organization and then average all of those responses. The underlying regularity that represents the organization's position will have to be *inferred* on the basis of the attitude scores of a subgroup of each organization's members.

Statistics and Common Sense.   Whether the task at hand is identifying the position of a political organization, measuring the attitude change produced by a persuasive communication, or determining the effect of a particular experimental variable, the discovery of underlying regularities in social behavior depends on two things: knowledge of procedures of statistical inference, and good common sense in the use of that knowledge. Neither is sufficient alone, as can be illustrated by something as simple as the selection of individuals whose attitudes are to be used to infer the organization's position. Two questions arise immediately. How many people are needed from each organization? What about individuals who belong to more than one group? The first of these is a purely statistical question, the answer to which can be obtained by application of an appropriate formula.

But the second question cannot be answered so mechanically. The actual statistics involved will be exactly the same whether the individuals in the sample belong to one organization or to several. What will differ is the group of people to which the results will *generalize*. So if you want to say something about the "pure" members of each organization – members who belong only to that group – then the people selected for the sample must be members of only one group. If you want the findings to reflect the attitudes of people whose primary allegiance is one organization or another (regardless of the number to which they belong), then the sample should consist of people who meet that criterion of primary allegiance. Lastly, if you want to estimate the likely diversity present in each organization, you should first determine the proportion of single memberships to multiple memberships within the organization, and then make certain that your sample consists of the same proportional representation. No statistical procedure can help you make these choices. Like the research techniques to be discussed in this appendix, statistical techniques are tools in the service of thinking, not substitutes for thinking.

Estimating the True Score.   Suppose that you have decided to sample only the "pure types" from each organization. You administer your attitude scale, obtaining a number (presumably at the level of an interval scale) for each person in the sample. Now this number is a composite of at least three different elements. First, there is a *true score*, the actual racism that would be discovered (a) if the subject knew his or her own racism, (b) if that self-knowledge could be tapped by an omniscient observer, (c) using some perfect measuring procedure of which the subject was completely unaware. The second element contributing to the score you actually obtain will represent *individual differences* between subjects. Even if each group member's true score could be assessed, there would be differences among those scores because now two people have identical life experiences. Finally, the third element of the composite is *measurement error*. No matter how carefully you have constructed your scale, you cannot achieve perfection in measurement. The words you have used to ask the questions will mean different things to different people, the social desirability implications of the questions you ask may lead some respondents to "fudge" their answers, and there is no guarantee that the gradations present in your scale will completely capture the fine shadings that might be present in the underlying attitudes of some of your subjects.

Obviously no present methods – and none anticipated in the future – can directly assess true scores on social behaviors, so those true scores must be estimated by attempts to minimize the other two components. Measurement error can be reduced by many of the techniques discussed in chapter 2: standardization of scales and procedures; inclusion of controls for experimenter effects, demand characteristics, and response biases; and by multiple operationism that broadens the methodological base for the conceptual conclusions drawn. Individual differences can be taken into account by combining data across subjects in a way that permits estimation of that portion of the variability attributable to the personal characteristics of the subjects This is the essence of the statistical procedures to which we now turn.

Two Descriptions of a Sample.   Employing all the procedural controls you can, you measure the attitudes of 100 randomly selected members of the Democratic Party. For each individual, there will be a single score that represents racism as measured by your scale, so there will be a *distribution* of 100 of these scores in this particular group of subjects. Whether your aim is to describe the group to other investigators, or to make inferences about the differences that might exist between this group of Democrats and the samples drawn from the other organizations, you will need some summary of the distribution. Although as many as four features of distributions are occasionally employed, only two of these need to be discussed here – measures of the *central tendency* of the distribution and measures of the *dispersion* or variability inherent in the scores.

The central tendency of the distribution is that feature that describes the general location of the distribution along the number scale, and as such represents an estimate of the likely location of the true scores of individuals in the group. The central tendency is typically defined in one of three ways. The *mode* is the one score that occurs most frequently, the *median* is the point (not necessarily an actual score obtained) above which exactly half of the scores lie, and the *mean* (also not necessarily an actual score obtained) is the arithmetic average of all of the scores. Which of these measures of central tendency is the most informative depends on the purpose to which it is going to be put. A person describing the earned income of a group of employees would probably use the median, because it is not susceptible to distortion by a few very high or very low scores. A teacher trying to eliminate items from a multiple choice test might examine the mode in order to exclude any questions that produce *bimodal* distributions (everyone who read the material got the question right, everyone who did not do the reading missed the question). And if the entire test were that way, the instructor would have only two grading choices – A and F. A researcher interested in comparing the scores of two groups of subjects would use the mean, because of the way in which it relates to the other characteristic of the distribution, the dispersion.

The dispersion of a distribution is its variability, and can be thought of as an estimate of the deviations from the true score, which deviations are based either on individual differences or on measurement error. One measure of the variability is the *range*, which is simply the value of the highest score minus the lowest score. But the range only uses these two pieces of information, without attending to the variability inherent in the remainder of the sample. Specifically, for example, a sample consisting of 24 scores of 25, 50 scores of 26, 24 scores of 27, one score of 10 and one score of 60 would have a range of $60 - 10 = 50$. So would a sample consisting of two scores each of every number between 10 and 60, but this second distribution would obviously contain much greater variability than the first.

Because of this limitation of the range, it is desirable to have a measure of dispersion that considers every score in the distribution. One such measure could be constructed by finding the difference between any observed score and the mean of the distribution. For example, if the mean score for the sample of Republicans is 25 on the attitude scale, an individual Republican whose score was 30 would have a positive *deviation score* of $30 - 25 = 5$ points. Similarly, another individual Republican whose raw score was 15 would have a negative deviation score of $15 - 25 = -10$. Every other Republican's own raw score could similarly be expressed as a deviation from the Republican mean score. With R_i representing each individual Republican score, and M_R representing the mean of the sample of Republican scores, each deviation score, D_R can be written as

$$D_R = R_i - M_R$$

and the sum of these deviation scores would be written as

$$\Sigma D_R = \Sigma (R_i - M_R)$$

Constructing deviation scores in this manner has the advantage of using every score in the distribution, but it still has one disadvantage: the overall sum of the deviation scores, ΣD_R, will always be equal to zero. Recall that the mean is the arithmetic average of the scores in the group. So by definition the sum of the positive deviation scores (each score above 25 has 25 subtracted from it, and then all of the resulting differences are added together) will be equal to the sum of the negative deviations (the sum of all the scores less than 25, with 25 subtracted from each such score), and combining the two will always produce zero.

To counter this problem while still using all of the information, each deviation score is squared to make its sign positive before it is added to the other deviation scores. Thus a raw score of 32 (7 points more than the mean of 25) and a raw score of 18 (7 points less than the mean of 25) would each have a squared deviation score of 49. The sum of these squared deviation scores is called the **sum of squares**, and it obviously increases (a) as the distances between raw scores and the mean score increase, and (b) as the total number of such observations increases. To correct for the number of scores, the sum of squares is divided by the quantity $(N - 1)$, where N is the total number of scores in the distribution. The resulting quantity is the **variance** of the distribution. This variance, and its square root, the **standard deviation**, are both measures of the dispersion present in a set of scores.

Analysis of Differences. By now you have given your attitude scale to members of every one of the six organizations, and you have a distribution of scores for each group. You have calculated the mean score for each group, from the sum of the squared deviations about the mean of each group you have calculated the variance of each group, and then you have taken the square root of the variance to obtain the standard deviation for each group. The higher the mean score for a group, the farther toward the racist end of the scale the group falls. The higher the standard deviation for a group, the more widely dispersed are the scores in the group. A graphic representation of these two principles is presented in Fig. A.1. The hypothetical data shown in the figure would indicate that the two major political parties, the Democrats and the Republicans contain members with widely differing views on the topic of race (both distributions are relatively flat, and there is a great deal of overlap between the two). In contrast, the hypothetical distributions for the special interest organizations, the NAACP

FIGURE A.1 Hypothetical distributions of racial attitudes for six political groups.

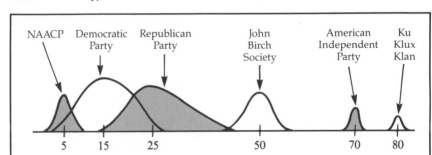

and the Ku Klux Klan, are quite narrow, which would suggest that on the question of race, each of these groups has a very specific and well-defined position.

Which groups have attitudes that are truly different from one another? If you answered this question literally, you have made a mistake. To say that one group is "truly different" from another is to suggest that you have been able to compare the true scores made by individuals in one group to the true scores made by individuals in another group. But you cannot ever measure the true scores directly; all you can do is assess the distributions of reported scores. So the question about group differences must be translated into statistical terms to take into account the underlying regularities in each distribution. Specifically, for example, if you were to wonder whether the attitudes of Democrats and Republicans were different, you would need to consider both the mean score for each of these distributions and the dispersion of the two distributions.

How exactly is this to be done? Imagine that you came across a score for a person whose party affiliation you did not know. This person's score was a 24. If you look at the distributions in Fig. A.1, you can be virtually certain that the person is not a member of the NAACP, because none of the scores you have for NAACP members is any higher than 10 on the scale. Similarly, you can be pretty certain that the person is not a member of the John Birch Society (the lowest available score for which is a 35), the American Independent Party (the lowest available score for which is a 60), or the Klan (the lowest score for which is a 75).

This leaves you with only two real possibilities: the person is either a Democrat or a Republican. The person's mean score is certainly closer to that of the Republicans, so on mean score alone you might be tempted to claim that the person is a Republican. But the two major party distributions overlap to such a degree that it is impossible to tell for certain. In conceptual terms, what the standard deviation of each distribution does is let you estimate the *probability* that the person really belongs in one distribution as opposed to the other. When two distributions have central tendencies that are close to one another, your certainty about the correct placement of an unidentified individual will depend on the size of the standard deviations. In contrast to the case of the Democrats and Republicans, imagine for a moment that the NAACP and the Klan were separated by only 10 scale points. The standard deviations of these two are small enough that there would still be virtually no overlap, so you could be very certain of the correct placement on the basis of mean score alone. But with the Democrats and Republicans, the standard deviations are so large that your placement of the unidentified individual will mostly be guesswork.

Statistical Significance. Under normal circumstances, of course, you are not in the position of trying to place an unidentified individual into one distribution or another. What you are attempting to do is determine whether two distributions are different from one another. The central tendency of each distribution is an estimate of the "true score" that would be achieved by individuals in that group. In effect, the standard deviation of each distribution is an indication of the lack of precision—traceable either to individual differences or to errors of measurement—with which those true scores have been estimated. So determining whether two groups differ requires you to consider both the mean of each distribution and its dispersion. The greater the dispersion of the two distributions, the farther apart their means must be for the groups to be regarded as different.

Unfortunately, the statistical question actually asked may strike you as backwards: "Given the level of precision I have been able to achieve, what is the likelihood that the means would be this far apart if there were *really no difference* between the two ?" In short, the statistical test requires you first to assume the truth of what is known as the *null hypothesis*: the hypothesis that there is really no difference between the groups on any psychologically meaningful dimension; that the observed difference is due only to individual differences and measurement error. The statistical test that is then performed, using information from both the central tendencies and the dispersions, permits you to estimate the likelihood of achieving such a large mean difference in the samples if the null hypothesis was true. Psychologists usually consider groups to be *statistically significantly different* if the odds are less than 1 in 20 that the mean difference actually obtained could have been reached merely by chance. So the original question of whether the Democrats are "truly" less racist than the Republicans becomes in statistical terms, a question of whether the two group mean scores are statistically significantly different. Thus the underlying regularities in social behavior are inferred, rather than measured directly. It is for this reason that scales of measurement and statistical methods are such an important part of methodology in scientific social psychology.

The Importance of Control

As noted earlier, the number that you obtain from an individual on a behavior of social interest will be a composite consisting of true score, individual differences, and measurement error. The random variations among people, and random fluctuations in measurement, can be estimated through statistical analysis, but inferences about the true score can still be complicated by systematic errors that may inadvertently have been built into the research. Ways to avoid some of these errors were first described in chapter 2, but they bear repeating here.

Internal Validity.   Regardless of whether the research conducted is archival, observational, or experimental, social psychologists strive for internal validity in their work. You will recall that internal validity is a measure of freedom from artifacts; the degree to which the findings of research represent real psychological differences. In archival research the real psychological differences can be obscured by any or all of three difficulties. Beginning with the initial construction of the records, there may be selective deposit, with some records kept more fully and more faithfully than others. Once the records have been established, there may be selective survival, the natural decay or deliberate destruction of some records but not others. Lastly, if the researcher is not careful in the choice of records for analysis, there may be selective sampling. Each of these threats to the validity of an archival research design can be minimized by increasing the investigator's control over the collection and analysis of the data.

Suppose, for example, that you wanted to find out what attitudes toward black people were held by members of the Democratic Party, but were unable to measure those attitudes yourself. You might be tempted to examine past issues of your hometown newspaper, looking for stories dealing with the topic. After much searching, you find only a few such articles, most of which suggest that the Democratic Party is uniformly more pro-black than the NAACP. How much confidence can you place in this result? You know that the newspaper has a Republican-leaning editorial policy, so you guess that it might be engaging in a bit of selective deposit: reporting stories that will lead its readers to become suspicious of the Democratic Party. You also discover that although the newspaper has thorough files for every election year, its collection of past papers is not quite so complete for the intervening years. Because of this selective survival, only those articles written in the "heat of the election" are available to contribute to your conclusion. Finally, the files of the paper are not computerized, and because your time is limited, you decide that you are able to search only the front page, the editorial page, and the front of the business section in each day's paper. What this selective sampling omits, of course, are routine articles—the ones that are buried on inside pages because the editor did not consider them sufficiently important to give them a prominent play.

Throughout the process, your judgment of what is important has been replaced by the editor's judgment, producing a result that may be politically useful, but is scientifically suspect. You would have done much better to spend a shorter time examining the results of national opinion polls on the views of registered Democrats. In contrast to the articles in the paper, the polls are conducted with scientific precision, by people who have no particular viewpoint to put forward, and who routinely keep excellent records for periods of years after the initial questions have been asked. Even if you examine poll results, you would not have exerted the control over the process yourself. But you would have placed your trust in people who did exercise appropriate control when the data were gathered and stored. What you can control, of course, is the choice of source for the information you seek, and this choice should be made with the goal of internal validity in mind.

Minimizing Artifacts in Observation. Your degree of control over the process increases dramatically in the case of observational research, because you are collecting the data yourself, rather than relying on another person or organization to have done so. With this more direct participation on your part, however, comes the major threat to internal validity in observational research: the subject's awareness of being tested. Imagine, for a moment, that it is a beautiful spring day. You and a friend are sitting in a quiet corner of the campus having a casual but private conversation. Suddenly a person appears from nowhere and watches the two of you intently for a few minutes. You and your friend become self-conscious, the topic of your conversation shifts, and each of you asks the other what is going on. Neither of you knows, so your self-consciousness turns to anger at having your privacy invaded. Now the observer makes notes on a piece of paper attached to a large clipboard, takes a picture of the two of you, and then begins to walk away. Is there any one of us who would not stop this intruder to find out what he or she was doing? Although you and your friend were in a public place, you still want to know exactly why your actions were being recorded. That is precisely the way that any subject in a study involving simple observation would feel. The awareness of being tested changes a person's behavior, focuses his or her attention on the process of observation, and engenders suspicion and even anger.

To control for the awareness of being tested, observational researchers resort to concealment and participation. The objective is to place the observer close enough to the subject for the behavior of interest to be recorded, without raising the subject's suspicion. Concealment can be accomplished only if the researcher has control over the setting in which the behavior occurs (hiding in an automobile, or in part of a building that does not belong to you is quite likely to produce frequent calls to the police, as well as data). Participation also requires control, but of time rather than place. In order to keep fairly regular notes about the interaction taking place, you need to be able to structure your time with the group in a manner that allows you occasional breaks by yourself. Not only is this kind of control difficult to achieve without raising suspicion, it also raises serious ethical questions first noted in chapter 2. Will the observer's participation lead the group to do anything illegal that might not have been done without the additional group member (you)? Will your participation keep a group going that might otherwise dissolve of its own weight? Is the problem sufficiently important to justify the failure to give subjects the opportunity to consent to participate? These questions need to be answered to the satisfaction of appropriate reviewers before the observational research can begin.

Apprehension, Demands, and Experimental Realism. If the methodological objective in observational research is to avoid letting the subjects know that they are being tested, the objective in experimental research is to construct a highly controlled setting in which the effects of this knowledge can be minimized. Like the person whose public behavior is clumsily observed, the experimental subject becomes careful not to reveal anything intimate (the problem of evaluation apprehension discussed in chapter 2), and tries to ascertain the researcher's true objectives (the problem of demand characteristics, also discussed in chapter 2). How, exactly, can these twin problems be minimized in the experimental setting?

The specific answers offered in chapter 2 were, respectively, avoid indicating what the "typical" response is supposed to be, and arrange the setting to minimize the likelihood that the subject will identify the true hypothesis of the research. The first of these involves assurances to the subjects that their behavior will be confidential or anonymous, that there are "no right or wrong answers" to any questions asked, and careful avoidance of any information about the behavior of other participants. The second involves, at minimum not telling the subjects what is the point of the research, and at maximum actively deceiving subjects about the true purpose. The latter, of course, raises ethical issues nearly as serious as those presented by concealed participant observation. If there is to be deception, ethical practice requires (a) that the benefits of the research outweigh the risks posed by deceit, (b) that the research be reviewed by appropriate institutional officials, and (c) that a gradual and thorough debriefing be conducted. Recall that the debriefing has the dual purposes of explaining the true purposes of the research and restoring some of the self-confidence the subject may have lost by "falling for" the deception in the first place. Incorporating all of these specific procedures will contribute to an experiment that, although ethically acceptable, helps to minimize the reactive effects arising from the subject's awareness of being tested.

In addition to including specific procedures designed to minimize reactivity, there is one more thing an experimenter can do to reduce the systematic error introduced by awareness of being tested: increase the subject's involvement in the task. What does it mean to talk of involvement when experiments are so often accused of being "artificial?" Are not the two terms mutually incompatible? Fortunately for researchers, the answer to this question is probably negative. Let us examine what "artificial" actually means in the experimental context, by comparing that laboratory setting to the "natural" behavior that occurs in the real social world outside the laboratory. Return for a moment to the conversation you were having with your friend. What had been a natural interchange was suddenly made artificial by the presence of an obtrusive observer. You and your friend change from concentrating on each other to concentrating on the unwelcome guest who is invading your "turf." Short of concealment or participation, nothing the observer can do will make his or her presence any less distracting.

What happens in an experiment? To begin with, you are on the experimenter's "turf," and in this context his or her presence is quite natural. Only your behavior is likely to be forced, but that may be a more tractable problem. Unlike the observer, the experimenter is not interested in having all of your behavior be free of outside contamination. Rather, the experimenter's concern is limited to the collection of particular dependent variables that have been specified in advance. These dependent measures will be gathered in the context provided by some experimental task, and the goal is to make that task as involving as possible. If a task, and the rationale provided for it, have a great deal of impact on the subject, the research is said to possess a high degree of **experimental realism** (Aronson & Carlsmith, 1968). In this sense, Milgram's (1963) research on destructive obedience was high in experimental realism. The reports of observers, and the film that was made of some of the experimental sessions, make it quite clear that the subjects became highly involved in the research. Indeed, some of the ethical questions raised about the study (e.g., Baumrind, 1964) arise because of the very power the situation seemed to have. If "artificial" is taken to mean "has no real effect on the subject's actions," the label does not apply in this instance. Paradoxically, the contrived nature of the experiment permits a degree of control sufficient to lead participants to "behave naturally," instead of behaving like subjects.

Despite its impact on subjects, the situation was, in a way, thoroughly artificial (how many of us have been asked to teach another person a series of word pairs by giving the person steadily increasing shocks for mistakes?). In terms suggested by Aronson and Carlsmith (1968), the experiment lacked **mundane realism**: the task required of participants was unlike anything they had experienced in their normal lives. It is important to note that lack of mundane realism is much more likely to affect external validity than to reduce internal validity. What generalizes from Milgram's research is the principle that people can be induced to follow orders that conflict with their moral codes, not their absolute performance on the task. An ideal experimental task, of course, would be high in both experimental and mundane realism, thus enhancing both the internal and external validity of the design.

Examples of Measurement and Control.   The reason to establish control in research procedures is, ultimately, the same as the reason to insist on careful attention to measurement issues: to permit more accurate inferences about important aspects of social behavior. Whether the research technique is archival, observational, or experimental, and regardless of the particular question under investigation, the thorough explanation of behavior that scientific social psychology seeks to provide can only be achieved through conscious attention to matters of methodology. This concern for methodology arises in part because there are very few "standard" techniques available; almost every phenomenon of social behavior could be measured in a variety of ways. For purposes of comparison, consider other subfields of psychology. In perception, the details of presentation time and response time were worked out years ago. In physiological research with animals, there is only one preferred thickness for brain sections, and only a limited set of stains that can be applied to the resulting slides. Even in clinical psychology, with a multitude of new tests produced every year, the American Psychological Association can publish a Diagnostic and Statistical Manual (DSM-III, American Psychological Association, 1980) that contains specific behavioral components of all the major emotional disorders.

In social psychology, however, there is no "established" way to define friendship, to determine whether a person's facial expression reflects a true underlying emotional state (as opposed to representing only the social display rules in effect at the time), or to describe the cognitive structures that are so important in guiding interpersonal behavior. So social psychologists concentrate on the more general principles of measurement and control, and attempt to build those principles into their research. The next section of the chapter presents examples of measurement, describing the assessment of implicit personality theories and social attitudes; the final section presents an example of a field experiment showing how the necessary control can be implemented even in the study of a topic often regarded as the proper subject only for poets—romantic attraction in an initial encounter.

DISCOVERING COGNITIVE STRUCTURES

Implicit Personality Theory

Correlational Methods. To what degree will a person's impression of another individual's personality be inferred from the target person's behavior, and to what degree will the impression be "given" by the perceiver's own cognitive structure? This is the fundamental question addressed in the study of implicit personality theory. In other words, to what extent do we see what is actually "out there," instead of seeing merely what we expect to find? It stands to reason that a perceiver with an extensive and rigid implicit personality theory will be less open to the real information contained in a target person's actions than will a perceiver whose implicit personality theory is less fixed, so it is important to be able to determine how strong the links are. As noted in chapter 4, the perceiver's set of expectations about which personality traits might be mutually associated can be assessed using any of several techniques, including the general correlational method (Wishner, 1960), the trait implication method

(Bruner, Shapiro, & Taguiri, 1958), and the peer nomination method (Passini & Norman, 1966).

Bipolar rating scales. Although these techniques differ in the means used to produce the trait adjectives, they share a statistical procedure by which the co-occurrences of the adjectives is assessed. This procedure can best be explained by including a little more detail in the example from chapter 4, the assessment of the implicit personality theories of a few of your friends. You would begin by having each of these people evaluate a set of stimulus persons (people your friends would all know, or at least know of), such as mutual acquaintances, professors, or national politicians. Each stimulus person would be described by a series of rating scales such as the following

$$\text{good} : \underline{7} : \underline{6} : \underline{5} : \underline{4} : \underline{3} : \underline{2} : \underline{1} : \text{bad}$$
$$\text{weak} : \underline{1} : \underline{2} : \underline{3} : \underline{4} : \underline{5} : \underline{6} : \underline{7} : \text{strong}$$

A similar 7-point scale would be provided for every adjective pair you chose to include. Each of your subjects would be instructed to place a mark on each scale in the division that bests represents his or her opinion of the stimulus person. Every scale consists of a pair of *bipolar adjectives* (constructed to be psychological antonyms). The numbers shown in the boxes do not normally appear on the scales actually given to subjects, but the scales are typically scored as shown, with higher numbers indicating more of the positively valued element of the adjective pair.

Correlations Among Ratings. Each of your subjects will make a rating for each of several stimulus persons, and an example is shown in Table A.2. This table includes the ratings on two dimensions – the evaluative dimension of good–bad, and the potency dimension of strong–weak – for each of four stimulus persons that were made by five different subjects. You can compute a variety of scores from these 40 ratings, depending on your particular interest. The first thing you might wonder is whether the two rating dimensions covary for a single subject; in the proper statistical terms, are the rating dimensions *correlated* with each other? Look first at the ratings made by Subject #1. As this person's ratings on the evaluative dimension increase across stimulus persons, his ratings on the potency dimension also increase. In fact, for this subject the ratings are identical and represent a *perfect positive correlation* between the two sets of scores. If we were to compute a statistical measure of this association, the **correlation coefficient** (represented by the symbol r), we find that the value of $r = +1.00$ (as shown in the last column of Table A.2.

In the case of Subject #2, the correlation is positive (the scores vary in

TABLE A.2 Trait Ratings on Two Dimensions for Four Hypothetical Stimulus Persons

Subject and Dimension	Hypothetical Stimulus Persons				Subject's Mean Rating	Correlation Between Dimensions
	Politician	Professor	Acquaintance	Friend		
Subject #1						
good–bad	1	3	5	7	4.0	+ 1.00
strong–weak	1	3	5	7	4.0	
Subject #2						
good–bad	1	2	5	6	3.5	+ .95
strong–weak	4	5	6	7	5.5	
Subject #3						
good–bad	1	2	6	7	4.0	0.00
strong–weak	5	3	3	5	4.0	
Subject #4						
good–bad	1	2	3	4	2.5	– .96
strong–weak	6	4	3	1	3.5	
Subject #5						
good–bad	1	3	5	7	4.0	– 1.00
strong–weak	7	5	3	1	4.0	
Mean Rating for Each Stimulus Person (M)						
good–bad	1.0	2.4	4.8	6.2		+ .05
strong–weak	4.6	4.0	4.0	4.2		

the same direction, with one set increasing as the other increases), and the degree of association is quite high (r = .95), but not perfect. Subject #3 has scores on the evaluative dimension that are *independent* of the scores on the potency dimension, because the correlation between the two sets of ratings for this subject is zero. Finally, the scores for Subject #4 and Subject #5 show that the correlation between two variables can be a negative one, with ratings on one dimension decreasing as the ratings on the other increase. Once again, these negative correlations can have different values for r, ranging from 0.00 to -1.00 (a perfect negative correlation).

To return to the issue of implicit personality theory, we might say that Subjects #1 and #2 share an implicit personality theory that associates goodness and strength: a person described as better is also likely to be described as stronger. In contrast, Subjects #4 and #5 share an opposite implicit personality theory. For both of these people, weakness is better. Lastly, in Subject #3's implicit personality theory, strength and goodness are independent. The fact that five different subjects can have such widely divergent perceptions of the relationship between goodness and strength within four different stimulus persons is an indication that what is driving the ratings is the cognitive structure of the perceiver, not the actual character or behavior of the stimulus person. This is especially obvious in the case of the individual (the politician) whose behavior has never been personally observed by any judge.

Generalizations Across Perceivers.   We have seen that the data in Table A.2 can be used to assess the implicit personality theories of individual perceivers. A second question that can be dealt with using those same data is the broader one, "To what degree do the implicit personality theories of people in general suggest a relationship between strength and goodness?" To answer this question, you would combine the ratings made by all five of the subjects, in effect (although not in actual statistical procedure) averaging the ratings on each dimension across perceivers.

To give you an indication of what this overall correlation would show, the mean scores on both rating dimensions have been included at the bottom of Table A.2. These scores, arithmetically averaged over subjects, show that the evaluation of the stimulus persons increases from the politician to the friend, whereas the estimate of strength does not vary greatly from one stimulus person to another. And, not surprisingly, the overall correlation coefficient is virtually zero (r = .05). From this result we would conclude that there is no generally shared implicit personality theory regarding the relationship between strength and goodness. Of course, in the example, the absence of an overall correlation arises because the positive associations found for Subjects #1 and #2 are canceled out by the negative associations found for Subjects #4 and #5. This is an unusual situation, because in most cases involving no significant overall correlation, individual subjects also show no relationship between the variables being considered.

Despite the unusual nature of the individual subject correlations in the example, it is still fair to conclude that there is no generally shared expectation about the relationship between strength and goodness.

Trait Implication and Peer Nomination. Instead of providing your subjects with a set of rating scales on which they are to describe a specified group of stimulus persons, you might generate the correlations shown in Table A.2 in one of two other fashions (both described in chapter 4). In the trait implication method, there would be no stimulus persons involved at all. You would merely provide a subject with a series of *cue traits* and ask that he or she say to what extent each of these implies the presence of various *response traits*. Specifically, for example, "A person is good. To what degree is that person also strong?" The major advantage of this method is, as noted in chapter 4, that it permits you to make estimates of the degree to which the presence of one trait really causes the other. If the good–strong combination produces a likelihood estimate of .23, whereas the strong–good combination produces a likelihood estimate of .87, then an observed correlation between evaluation and potency is probably observed because the strength judgment produces a corresponding change in evaluation.

You may recall that in the peer nomination method, individuals are brought together in a small group, and asked to say which members of the group (other than themselves) best represent each end of a series of bipolar scales. Specifically, in this example, the five subjects would each be asked to say which two persons in the group are "strong" and which two are "weak," then to say which two persons are "good" and which two are "bad." It is important to notice that the accuracy of these various interpersonal judgments is not at issue. The critical information is whether the subject chooses the *same* person to represent "good" and "strong," or chooses *different* people to represent these two endpoints. In the first instance, the perceiver would associate the two traits together, whereas in the second instance, the perceiver would think the two traits independent.

Whether the actual procedure used involves the application of rating scales to real (or hypothetical) stimulus persons, measurement of the degree to which particular traits imply others, or the nomination of peers to represent endpoints of bipolar scales, it is possible to establish patterns of correlation among trait ratings. These can be analyzed to describe either the individual's own implicit personality theory, or a more generalized implicit personality theory shared by numerous individuals. Our expectations about another's social behavior will be influenced in part by the personal characteristics we think that person possesses. Careful measurement of a perceiver's implicit personality theory can help us to determine the extent to which the perceiver's "impressions" are based on his or her own cognitive structure rather than on the actual data provided by the target person's behavior.

Attitude Measurement

A person's impressions about the personal characteristics possessed by others, as well as that person's other beliefs about the social world, will be reflected in the perceiver's attitudes, and as shown in chapters 5 and 6, attitudes are an extremely important contributor to social behavior. Because of their practical implications as well as their crucial place in theory, attitudes have been the object of research for years, and a substantial portion of this work has been directed toward the general topic of attitude measurement. Although new methods continue to be developed, the three major techniques discussed in this section – Thurstone scaling, Likert scaling, and semantic differential scaling – have been the most prominent through the years.

The Thurstone Scale

As noted in chapter 5, it is useful to consider attitudes as having a cognitive, an affective, and a behavioral component. The major contribution that social psychology, as compared to other disciplines, has made in the attitude area is to show how the three components might be measured, and the first such attempt was presented by Thurstone (1928). In this influential paper, Thurstone asserted that "attitudes can be measured" and provided a method for constructing an attitude scale that approximated the interval level of measurement. Thurstone expanded and tested this method, using attitudes toward the church, and reported his procedure and results in a book co-authored by Chave (Thurstone & Chave, 1929).

Selection of Items. The first step in the construction of a **Thurstone scale** is the gathering of attitude and opinion statements from various sources (for example, newspaper editorials on the attitude issue, assertions on the topic made by public figures, or items written by the researchers, themselves). These initial attitude or opinion statements constitute the **item pool** from which the statements later to be included in the attitude questionnaire will be selected. After the item pool has been amassed (usually about 100 elements), it is presented to a large group of individuals for the purpose of determining the scale values of the items.

The individual judges are asked to sort the attitude statements into 11 piles ranging from the one most favorable toward the attitude object (11) through no characterization of the attitude object one way or another (6) to the one most unfavorable toward the object (1). It should be emphasized that the judges are instructed to place the the statements according to the apparent favorability toward the object *of the statement itself*, not on the basis of the judge's own opinion on the issue. Unfortunately, the social judgment theory of attitude change discussed in chapter 6 suggests that this may be very difficult for the judges to do. You will recall that social judgment theory divides the range of possible opinions into a latitude of acceptance, a latitude of noncommitment and a latitude of rejection. A judge who has a strong personal view on the attitude issue being scaled is likely to make the distinctions demanded by the 11-category sorting task only on those items that fall into his or her latitude of noncommitment. Items in the judge's latitude of acceptance may be displaced toward the favorable end (assimilated), whereas items in the judge's latitude of rejection are likely to be displaced toward the unfavorable end (contrasted).

Item Analysis. Assuming for the moment that the sorting task can be accomplished reasonably well (perhaps by individuals who do not have a strong personal position on the topic in question), how can the item pool be reduced to some manageable number? Any individual item will have been placed in several categories by the judges, producing a distribution of category placements just like the distributions of attitudes discussed earlier. Rather than taking the mean of this distribution, the Thurstone procedure calls for assigning to each item the median value of its placements. A number of possible items, taken from the Thurstone–Peterson scale of attitudes toward war, are illustrated in Table A.3. The scale value shown is the median of the category placements, such that the 4.6 for statement B, "We want no more war if it can be avoided without dishonor," indicates that placements by 50% of the judges were above (and below) a hypothetical point .6 of the way through Category 4.

At this time in the procedure, three criteria suggested by Thurstone (1928) are employed to reduce the size of the item pool. First, the statements in the final scale should be selected so that they constitute an evenly graded series of scale values. In other words, the final set should cover the entire range of favorability (1–11), and should be approximately equally spaced across that range. The items shown in Table A.3 would satisfy this criterion. Second, items should be eliminated if the category judgments show them to be ambiguous. We can measure the ambiguity of an item in just the same way as the dispersion of attitudes within political organiza-

TABLE A.3 Sample Statements from the Thurstone–Peterson Scale of Attitudes Toward War

Scale Value		Attitude Statement
Least Favorable		
1.4	A.	War is a futile struggle resulting in self-destruction.
4.6	B.	We want no more war if it can be avoided without dishonor.
7.8	C.	War is sometimes necessary because right is more important than peace.
11.0	D.	War is glorious.
Most Favorable		

Note: *Adapted from Thurstone (1932).*

tions was identified earlier. In short, we compute the standard deviation of each item, and discard items whose standard deviation is so large as to indicate that the item is ambiguous. The third criterion is one of irrelevance. If the category judgments appear to have been affected by factors other than the attitude being measured (for example, if an item is out-of-date, erroneously worded, or obviously distorted by response biases), then the item should be discarded.

Use of the Scale. Once the items have been selected, the order of the statements in the scale is randomized to avoid order or progression effects that might arise from beginning with positive (or negative) statements and then moving gradually to the other extreme. The scale is preceded by directions to the subjects instructing them to agree or disagree with each item in the set (the median scale values shown on the scale in Table A.3 are not included in the version given the subjects). To determine a person's score, the researcher identifies all of the items with which the person has agreed, and then finds the median of these endorsed items. That midpoint is taken as the subject's attitude, and for convenience is usually indicated by the particular item that is closest in scale value to the subject's position. So, for example, a person whose median for endorsed items was 8.0 might have his or her position summarized by statement C in Table A-3, which indicates that war may sometimes be a necessary evil.

Difficulties with the Method. Although the Thurstone scaling method does yield data approximating an interval scale of measurement, a more stringent criterion than that met by many other scaling procedures, it is not without some conceptual and methodological problems. The conceptual problem, already noted, is that the judges who assign category placements to items may not be able to do so independent of their own positions on the issue, no matter hhow explicitly the instructions tell them to do so. The methodological problem is the sheer complexity of the procedure. Thurstone (1928) suggests that the item pool consist of roughly 100 statements, all of which are to be sorted initially by some 300 judges. These recommendations are designed to produce stable estimates of the sorting, estimates that suffer from a minimum of contamination by individual differences among judges in attitude toward the issue in question. Although smaller numbers of judges are acceptable (Green, 1954), the procedure still requires a large number of willing judges, and a long period of time per judge. Such an expenditure of time and effort is essential for someone interested (as Thurstone was) in thoroughly describing the properties of an attitude scale; it is impractical for a researcher who is simply looking for a dependent measure on which experimental treatments are to be compared.

Summated Agreement: The Likert Scale

For these methodological and conceptual reasons, the Thurstone scale has been supplanted in contemporary attitude measurement by the **Likert scale,** a method that asks for a respondent's degree of agreement with a set of statements. In the course of research on liberalism and conservativism, Likert (1932) developed a new method of attitude measurement that differed from the Thurstone technique in two important respects. First, Likert's procedure did not require initial category sorting by judges, although judges were recommended for item selection and refinement. Thus, a researcher who was quite familiar with the attitude domain in question could simply omit the first step in scale construction. Second, the subject's response alternatives were not restricted to a dichotomous choice of agree or disagree. Instead of this two-choice answer, Likert required subjects to indicate for each attitude item both the direction of his or her response (agree or disagree) and the degree of that choice.

Thus, in the original Likert scale, five responses were allowed for each item: strongly agree, agree, undecided, disagree, and strongly disagree, as shown in Table A.4. The resulting 5-point scale could be represented by numbers ranging from $+2$ to -2. To find the individual's overall attitude, the researcher would simply add all of these numbers together. On a 10-item questionnaire, the possible range of the resulting summated ratings of agreement would be from a low value of -20 (representing consistent strong disagreement) to a high value of $+20$ (representing consistent strong agreement).

Construction of a Likert Scale. As was the case with the Thurstone scale, the first task in constructing a Likert scale is to ensure that all the items measure the same underlying attitude continuum. For an attitude dimension unfamiliar to the researcher, the best way to accomplish this is to give a large pool of items to a number of judges and ask those individuals to

TABLE A.4 Adaptation of Two Items from the Thurstone–Peterson Attitudes-Toward-War Scale to a Five-Alternative Likert Scale Format

Attitude Statement	Response Alternatives and Numerical Scores					Scale Range
Five-alternative format (with a neutral or undecided point)						
"War is a futile struggle	SA	A	U	D	SD	
resulting in self-destruction."	-2	-1	0	$+1$	$+2$	(-2 to $+2$)
"War is glorious."	SA	A	U	D	SD	
	$+2$	$+1$	0	-1	-2	($+2$ to -2)

SA = strong agreement; A = agreement; U = undecided; D = disagreement; SD = strong disagreement. The numerical values are arranged so that higher numbers represent an attitude of greater favorability toward war on the respondent's part.

indicate their own attitudes using the five alternatives that will later be used with the subjects. Notice that this is different from the Thurstone procedure, in which the initial category sorting is supposed to be done independent of one's own attitude.

After the judges' ratings have been obtained, the items in the pool are subjected to a procedure called **item analysis**: the scores on all items are intercorrelated with each other and with the total score for the scale. Items that do not correlate with the total score (when that total is adjusted to remove the score for the particular item being compared) do not represent the same attitude dimension and should be discarded. This procedure for item analysis, in conjunction with checks for irrelevance and ambiguity, can be used to reduce the number of items to a set appropriate for the final questionnaire (20 or so). Unlike the Thurstone scale, the Likert scale does not have the additional requirement that the items be distributed across the range of the attitude continuum: the needed variation is provided by the different response alternatives available to the subject.

Interpreting Strong Disagreement. Likert scales are so common in social psychological research that most of you will have seen one in your introductory course, and at the time you might have had the reaction, "Why are all of these statements so extreme? Who could agree with this?" By now you may have an inkling about the answers to these questions. In constructing a Likert scale, care must be taken to avoid possible misinterpretation of a subject's response of "strong disagreement." Consider the attitude item "Women deserve to have the same employment opportunities that men have." We know what strong agreement with this item would mean. But does strong disagreement represent male chauvinism ("I disagree because I believe that better jobs should go to men; after all, they have families to support"), or does it reflect ardent feminism ("I disagree because I believe that to make up for past discrimination, women should be given the better jobs now")?

We have absolutely no way of knowing which of these quite different attitudes actually led to the strong disagreement with the item. The problem can be alleviated to some extent by writing items that are themselves clearly worded in one direction or the other, such as "Women deserve better employment opportunities than those men have." Now the feminist would agree, but the male chauvinist would disagree. But the person who believed in a total lack of discrimination would also disagree. On items of this sort, the best solution is to let the subject select the modifier, instead of requiring the person to agree or disagree with a modifier provided by the researcher. The statement could now read as follows:

Women should have employment opportunities that are

_____ much greater than those that men have.　　(+2)
_____ greater than those that men have.　　　　　(+1)

_____ the same as the ones men have.   (0)
_____ fewer than those that men have.   (−1)
_____ much fewer than those that men have. (−2)

On an item like this the subject simply checks the response alternative that represents his or her opinion, and we have a very clear idea of the individual's position on the issue. This is an alternative format used by Likert (1932), and has the other properties of a Likert scale.

Elimination of the Neutral Point. One other change from the direction-degree five-alternative response format is often needed. When a person is asked to express attitudes about a controversial issue, his or her use of the "undecided" alternative shown in Table A.4 is likely to be inflated. It is not that the subject truly has no attitude on the topic, but rather that the person just does not want the researcher to discover what that attitude is (especially if the subject knows that his or her position is an unpopular one). To counteract this tendency for people to take refuge in the neutral point, many investigators using Likert scales _eliminate_ the neutral point and often expand the response possibilities accordingly. Now instead of five alternatives, there would be the six—strongly, moderately, and slightly agree; slightly, moderately, and strongly disagree—shown in Table A.5.

Elimination of the neutral point forces the subject to make his or her position known, but the addition of the "slightly" category on each side of that eliminated neutral value permits the subject to save some face. Such a format is _scored as a 7-point scale,_ because the neutral point is assumed to be part of the underlying continuum even though it is precluded as a response possibility. Thus, the distance from slightly agree to slightly disagree is two scale points, as shown in Table A.5. The properties of this format are the same as those of other Likert scales, and it could be argued

TABLE A.5 Adaptation of Two Items from the Thurstone–Peterson Attitudes-Toward-War Scale to a Six-Alternative Likert Scale Format

Attitude Statement	Response Alternatives and Numerical Scores						Scale Range
Six-alternative format (without neutral point)							
"War is a futile struggle	STA	MA	SLA	SLD	MD	STD	
resulting in self-destruction."	−3	−2	−1	+1	+2	+3	(−3 to +3)
"War is glorious."	STA	MA	SLA	SLD	MD	STD	
	+3	+2	+1	−1	−2	−3	(+3 to −3)

STA = strong agreement; MA = moderate agreement; SLA = slight agreement; SLD = slight disagreement; MD = moderate disagreement; STD = strong disagreement. The numerical values are arranged so that higher numbers represent an attitude of greater favorability toward war on the respondent's part.

that the psychological intervals represented by the six alternatives are even more likely to be equivalent than are the intervals contained in the original five-alternative format.

The Problem of Summation.   As useful as it is, the Likert scale is not without some difficulties. The most important of these is the problem of interpreting the summated score. Consider now a 10-item Likert scale with six response alternatives (to be scored as a 7-point scale). There is only one way to obtain a total score of $+30$ (or $+70$ if all response alternatives are given positive scores ranging from 1 to 7), and that is to "strongly agree" with every item. Similarly, there is only one way to achieve a score of -30 (or 10, with all positive scores), and that is to "strongly disagree" with each item. But what about a score of zero (or 40, with all positive items)? Such a score cannot be achieved by responding "uncertain" on all items, because that alternative is not available. But it could be achieved by a balanced distribution of five "slight agreement" answers ($+5$) and five "slight disagreement" answers (-5), or by five "strong agreement" answers ($+15$) and five "strong disagreement" responses (-15).

Without looking at the two patterns of answers, we would conclude from the total scores that the two people who made these scores of zero had the same attitude. The truth, however, is different. One person was fundamentally indifferent to the topic, and was being forced to answer one way or the other, whereas the other person had very strong but conflicting feelings about the issue. Is it really proper to assume that these two individuals have equivalent attitudes? Probably not, and the inability of the Likert scale to discriminate between them (without requiring the researcher to evaluate every item for individuals who have moderate scores) is an important limitation of the method.

The Semantic Differential Scale

Part of the difficulty with the Thurstone scale and the Likert scale is that both of these attitude measures constrain the subject to a limited set of possible answers. Even people who understand the reasons for the structure inherent in the two techniques believe that such scales may not represent the true complexity of a subject's response to an attitude object. One of the primary criteria involved in the construction of either a Thurstone scale or a Likert scale is that the statements represent a unidimensional attitude. Indeed, the very purpose of the item analysis performed in each case is to remove items that do not significantly correlate with the total score. Unfortunately, all too often the exclusion of uncorrelated items produces a scale that measures only one aspect of the single attitude. Many of our important social attitudes are multidimensional in nature, and it would be desirable to have a technique that could deal with this complexity. The **semantic differential**, originally designed by Osgood and his colleagues

(Osgood, Suci, & Tannenbaum, 1957) as a measure of the connotative meaning of language, is just such a technique.

Construction of a Semantic Differential Scale. Rather than providing the subject with a preselected series of statements with which to agree or disagree, the semantic differential method presents a concept to be evaluated, along with a series of 7-point bipolar adjective scales on which that concept is to be judged. A sample set of scales for the concept "war" is shown in Table A.6. You will notice that four of the bipolar scales—futile-productive, honorable-dishonorable, unnecessary-necessary, humble-glorious—pertain to issues raised by each of the statements from the Thurstone-Peterson attitudes toward war scale discussed earlier. Instead of asking the subjects to agree or disagree about the futility of war, the semantic differential technique has them rate the concept "war" on a scale of futility to productiveness. Instead of including the idea of national honor in a statement, the semantic differential assesses the subject's opinion of that idea by means of an additional rating scale (honorable dishonorable). This parallel can be extended to nearly all the issues posed in either a Thurstone or a Likert scale dealing with attitudes toward war. The rating scales are scored as 7-point scales (ranging either from +3 to −3 as shown in Table A.6, or from 7 to 1 for all positive numbers), and the numbers are arranged so that higher scores represent more favorable evaluations of the concept. As is the case with the Thurstone and Likert scales, the numbers shown in the table are not normally printed on the questionnaires given subjects, to avoid the distortions based on evaluation apprehension that might result if the respondents knew which direction produced the higher scores (on the assumption that higher scores are "better").

Three Dimensions of Attitude Judgments. The other rating scales shown in Table A.6—good-bad, strong-weak, active-passive—deserve

TABLE A.6 Evaluation of the Concept of War Through the Semantic Differential Method of Attitude Assessment

	Concept to be Evaluated: "War"	
futile	: −3 : −2 : −1 : 0 : +1 : +2 : +3 :	productive
honorable	: +3 : +2 : +1 : 0 : −1 : −2 : −3 :	dishonorable
good	: +3 : +2 : +1 : 0 : −1 : −2 : −3 :	bad
unnecessary	: −3 : −2 : −1 : 0 : +1 : +2 : +3 :	necessary
active	: +3 : +2 : +1 : 0 : −1 : −2 : −3 :	passive
humble	: −3 : −2 : −1 : 0 : +1 : +2 : +3 :	glorious
strong	: +3 : +2 : +1 : 0 : −1 : −2 : −3 :	weak

further comment. You have seen the first two of these in the description of implicit personality theory, and they represent dimensions that Osgood, Suci, and Tannenbaum (1957) called, respectively, *evaluation* and *potency*. In a large number of studies in over 20 different cultures, Osgood and his associates found that these two dimensions and the third (called *activity*) accounted for most of the variance in the ratings of most concepts. These dimensions were not specified in advance, but were abstracted from the ratings subjects made using extensive sets of bipolar scales. Subjects were asked to use these extensive sets of adjective pairs to rate concepts dealing with social issues or with social roles appropriate to the culture. The resulting ratings were then intercorrelated to determine (in much the same fashion as with implicit personality theory) both how an individual rater might use the rating scales to describe different concepts, and how different raters might use the scales to describe the same concept. The intercorrelations were subjected to a statistical procedure known as **factor analysis** in order to reduce the number of dimensions needed to describe the ratings. For example, scales such as good–bad, valuable–worthless, and beautiful–ugly can typically be accounted for by an underlying factor of evaluation. Most of the factor-analytic studies on connotative meaning have found that three factors, evaluation, potency, and activity, account for a large proportion of the variance in the scores on individual rating scales. In other words, if we know how a person uses the scales good-bad, strong-weak, and active-passive to describe an attitude object, we can predict pretty well what his or her ratings would be on a large number of other bipolar scales. Of the three factors, the evaluative one seems to be the most important, and corresponds quite well to the conception of an affective component of an attitude.

Problems with Semantic Differential Scaling. Although the semantic differential scale makes many subjects happier with their rating task by not "forcing" them to answer prepared questions, it does have some disadvantages. One of the major reasons we try to measure people's attitudes toward various social objects is that we hope such attitude scores will enable us better to predict the individual's social behavior. This hope is based on the premise that what people think and feel about an attitude object (or, as noted in chapter 5, what behavioral intentions they have toward the object) will have some implications for their behavior toward the object. The connection between the internal components of cognition and affect and the externally observable behavior is not as strong as we might like, however, and use of the semantic differential to assess the internal components may weaken the link still further.

For example, if an individual indicates by endorsing a Thurstone or a Likert scale item that he or she considers affirmative action employment programs to be a serious mistake, that response may tell us a great deal about the person's choice of congressional candidates (provided one candidate endorses affirmative action and the other opposes it). But to know that a person considers the concept "affirmative action" to be bad, active, and strong (especially because in other circumstances strength and activity might have positive connotations) leaves us less certain about the individual's probable voting behavior.

At this point in the discussion of attitude scaling methods, you might expect the suggestion that a new attitude measurement technique be devised that would include the advantages of Thurstone, Likert, and semantic differential scaling while at the same time avoiding the limitations associated with each. Unfortunately, your expectation would overestimate the discipline's ability to solve the problem of attitude measurement. In part because of the importance to scientific social psychology of the concept of attitude, and in part because of a continuing search for a "perfect" method, investigators have developed a great profusion of attitude measurement techniques, of which the three discussed here are only the most prominent. But although each of these methods may solve a problem inherent in another technique, each also raises a new problem of its own. In attitude scaling, as in other social psychological research methods, there is no "established" way of doing business. All we can do as researchers is continue to concentrate on the twin objectives of measurement and control, in the hope of continually improving the techniques presently available.

ANALYSIS OF INTERPERSONAL BEHAVIOR

Student-Initiated Research

In the last section of this appendix we turn from measurement to control, showing how aspects of experimentation can be incorporated into a student-initiated study of the effects of attractiveness on initial social encounters. Before describing the research itself, I should say something about the reasons for conducting the study. One of the exciting features of social psychology is the ease with which students untrained in the discipline can draw on their experience for ideas that can be tested. This is not to say that personal experience is a substitute for scientific research, because as noted in chapter 2 each individual's view will be somewhat different. What one's own perspective can provide, however, is a rich source of "hunches" that can be integrated into existing theory. Consequently, to help demonstrate the research process I have had my classes originate a class project during the first 2 weeks of the semester (I have the luxury of classes limited to 40 students, about the maximum number at which such a project is feasible).

The projects always start small, with each student asked to state just the name of an "aspect of social behavior" that he or she would like to know more about. During the first class period these brief ideas are written on the board, and through successive rounds of elimination voting, the list (which usually includes some 20 or 30 different ideas in a class of 40 students) is winnowed to a single topic. Then each student is asked to come to the next class period with either (a) some idea of a factor that might influence the social behavior of interest, increasing or decreasing its likelihood, or (b) a single candidate for a nuisance variable that might complicate the study of the behavior. During the second class meeting the students are divided into small groups of six or seven people per group, and are asked to discuss among themselves either the potential independent variables or the potential confounds. These group discussions produce similar—but not always identical—short lists of variables to be considered in designing the research, and then each of the distinct variables is discussed briefly by the entire class.

By now students have read chapter 1, and have begun chapter 2, so for the next class period they are asked to bring in an operationalization of one independent variable, or a very precise suggestion of how to control one of the nuisance variables. Again, small groups discuss and refine these manipulations or controls, and then the entire class discusses the project as a whole. Throughout the process, the instructor's role is limited to one of a technical expert on issues of measurement and control, with the substance of the project being developed as much as possible by the class alone. Once the class has agreed on the specifics of the project, the instructor takes care of any remaining technical aspects of the methodology, and then after the research is approved by the institutional review officials, the entire class participates in collecting the data. The instructor analyzes the results and writes a brief report given to members of the class, and to any subjects who might have wanted to find out what happened in the study. You should remember in the discussion to follow that the critical aspects of the content of the project were developed by students, at the very beginning of a social psychology course.

Influences on Attraction

The Matching Principle.   You will recall from chapter 9 that a person's physical attractiveness is one of the elements of interpersonal attraction and friendship formation. Indeed, the matching principle (Berscheid, Dion, Walster, & Walster, 1971; Huston, 1973) argues that, because of the fear of rejection, people seek dates with partners who are roughly equivalent to themselves in physical attractiveness. And a recent study by Folkes (1982) found this matching principle to hold among adults involved in a metropolitan dating service, even though the participants had previously received information about each other's education, occupation, and personality characteristics. Interpersonal attraction is a topic of natural interest to undergraduates, so it is not surprising that one recent class project attempted to determine what factors might influence attraction in an initial encounter that did not have the explicit romantic content that would be present among people involved in a dating service.

Physical Attractiveness. During the initial discussions of the idea in class, the students—who did not yet know about the matching principle—wondered whether a person's attraction to another would be based primarily upon the target person's physical attractiveness or on that individual's "personality." Through refinement of these ideas in the small groups, students became convinced that at the very beginning stages of an encounter, before there had been much chance for significant interaction, physical attractiveness would probably account for most of the interest that one interaction partner would show toward another. But how can attractiveness be either manipulated or measured so that its effects can be determined?

There are two general kinds of answers to this question, and the choice between them must be dictated by the same attempt to balance internal versus external validity that affects so many procedural decisions. The most precise way to study the effects of attractiveness is to use still photographs (or slides) of a female whose clothing and makeup are altered to make her appear either as attractive or as repulsive as possible. Why a female, and why the same person in two different makeup/clothing conditions? The choice of a female stimulus person is dictated by the greater agreement among subjects (both male and female) about what constitutes attractiveness for females than for males, and by the fact that a female's appearance can be varied through a wider range of possibilities than can that of a male. The same person should be used in both an attractive and a sloppy condition to control for the natural differences in features, posture, and hairstyle that would be introduced in the design if different stimulus persons were used. This manipulation of the attractiveness of a single stimulus person, in still photographs that eliminate any effects associated with actual behavior, is the way to achieve the greatest internal validity. But the problem is that such a manipulation does not generalize well to real social situations (outside of the dating choices that might be made by participants in a dating service), especially to the kind of initial encounters of interest in the present research. It would have been possible to employ a number of experimental confederates whose appearance had been varied in attractiveness, but that, too, would have changed the research from the class's interest in a real social encounter.

If in the particular study being planned a variable of interest cannot successfully be manipulated, the only other solution is to construct a design that will permit the variable to be considered statistically instead of experimentally. Fortunately, where physical attractiveness is concerned, this is relatively easily accomplished. How? You probably guessed. Have observers rate the attractiveness of the participants. There are three design problems associated with this choice. First, the attractiveness ratings must be made for both female and male subjects in the research if the matching principle is to be tested. Second, these ratings must be collected by more than a single observer, so that individual differences across observers in perceptions of what constitutes attractiveness can be averaged out. And third, the attractiveness ratings must be done without the subjects becoming aware that it was happening. We will discuss later how each of these problems was solved in the study actually conducted.

The Structure of the Interaction. We know from the research described in chapter 9 that a number of other factors influence interpersonal attraction, but many of these were effectively controlled in the study constructed by the class. For example, all of the participants were in the same degree of proximity to one another, and all could assume the relative homogeneity of attitudes and interests that characterizes a college population. What could not be assumed to be similar in advance was built into the design of the research. Specifically, theories of social exchange suggest that the more rewards you receive from another person, the more you will like that individual. The problem, of course, is to keep these factors under control while at the same time permitting the participants in the study to engage in an interaction that provides some basis for the questions later to be asked as dependent variables.

The class's solution was to have pairs of subjects in the study play a "get acquainted" game in which people are given a limited amount of time to talk to one another, and there is a standard list of information to be obtained. As the class developed this procedure, it was to begin with the usual first-encounter questions typical of college students: name, hometown, major, year in school. Next, each partner in the interaction was to obtain information on one of the other's preferences, either a "favorite class this semester," a "favorite leisure time activity," or a "favorite musical group." Finally, to give the interaction a greater degree of substance, the class decided that the partners should obtain from one another a brief description of a "value conflict" that each had experienced recently. This value conflict could be "between two positive, but mutually exclusive, objectives, or a goal that is positive but may be prohibited." The interacting partners were to be given 10 minutes to obtain this information from one another.

Collecting the Data

Designing the Setting. Having an entire class of students collect data poses some problems not ordinarily associated with research in social psychology, and the most critical of these is coordination of schedules so that as many students can take part as possible. To keep participation at a maximum while also minimizing the likelihood that "the word would get out" about the research, the students decided to conduct the study in one session, to be held in the late afternoon on a midweek day. Once the time was set, a place had to be chosen. The classrooms or experimental laboratories in which a great deal of social psychological research is conducted would not be suitable for this study, because of the requirement that there be a large open space in which the subjects (and the observers who were making attractiveness ratings) could "circulate" surrounded by tables on which questionnaires could be completed by the subjects. As an inducement to potential participants, there were also to be punch and "munchies," so the building had to be one in which food and drinks were permitted. The perfect site turned out to be a ballroom in the student union building, and a few members of the class were assigned the "job" of arriving early to help set out the tables. Each member of the class had been asked to donate a dollar to a fund for purchasing the groceries, and several people were assigned the job of buying the food, and arriving early to set it up.

In addition to the arrangements of the physical setting, it was essential to the research to provide some social constraints on the behavior of the subjects. The whole idea was to examine the influences on attraction that affect a first encounter, so none of the subjects could be permitted to "encounter" one another prior to the time during the research when that became appropriate. This control on prior knowledge began with subject recruitment. Well over half the class members were assigned the task of bringing with them one male and one female (so that there would be an equal number of males and females among the subjects), making certain that (a) the two people did not know one another prior to the day of the experimental session, and (b) they did not talk to one another before the session began. Even during the experimental session, the subjects were not supposed to talk to one another except during the 10-minute periods specified by the experimenter (the instructor). To try to minimize the awkwardness of having so many people standing around saying nothing to anyone, the subjects were permitted to talk to members of the class, and to distinguish class members from subjects, every subject was given a nametag, whereas class members did not have nametags. Once in the session subjects were told not to talk to anyone wearing a nametag, unless it was during one of the "get acquainted" periods.

The Assessment of Attractiveness. The nametags not only served to distinguish class members from subjects, they also served a much more critical function. Think about the problem of measuring the attractiveness of the subjects. It is hardly possible to ask each subject, "Would you just step up here in front of our judges, please, so we can all rate you for physical attractiveness?" At the beginning of the study such a request would substantially increase the reactivity of the research, and even at the conclusion of the study subjects would find the request insulting. But to permit study of the matching principle every subject must be rated for attractiveness, by at least one male and one female class member. How can you be sure to cover every subject at least these two times? The obvious answer is to assign "observers" to subjects by name. To minimize the time required for these assignments during the experimental session, each class member who was to bring two subjects was asked to provide the subjects' names in advance. A master list of subjects was constructed from this set of names, and nametags were prepared for these subjects (this also had the effect of minimizing the time required for subjects to stand in line, without being permitted to talk, in order to receive a nametag). Last minute changes in subjects were accommodated by having two class members prepare nametags for people who had not been on the list, and update the lists. Each member of the class who was bringing a pair of subjects was instructed to come at precisely the beginning time of the study, so that all of the changes could be finished immediately, and subjects who were more than 5 minutes tardy were not permitted to take part. Finally, as soon as the master list was completed, while the experimenter gave the initial instructions to the assembled subjects, one of the class members took that list and had a photocopy made for each observer.

Ten members of the class (5 male, 5 female) had been assigned the job of being observers, and each one was to rate the attractiveness of 12 subjects (a total of 60 subjects, 2 each per class member assigned to bring subjects, had been planned). Each observer was given one of the copies of the final list of subjects on which had been designated the particular subjects to be assessed by the observer. Observers circulated among the subjects during the roughly 40 minutes required for the research, and wrote ratings of the attractiveness of their target subjects (the familiar 1–10 scale) next to the subject's name on the list. These sets of ratings were later averaged over observers in order to create a composite attractiveness score for each participating subject (despite the global nature of the ratings, there was surprising agreement among both male and female observers about the physical attractiveness of the subjects).

The Manipulation of Pairings. The matching principle argues that people actively choose those whose attractiveness matches their own, and that this choice affects later ratings of personal characteristics other than attractiveness (e.g., personality, intelligence). But it may be that these subsequent ratings are influenced not by the matching choice, but by the fact of the interaction produced by the choice. In other words, if people were forced to interact for a comparable period with people they might not have chosen, their ratings of these nonchosen partners might also be quite positive just on the basis of the shared experience. To test this possibility explicitly, the project was a true field experiment, comparing the ratings made by people who had been assigned to one another to ratings made by people who were permitted to choose their partners.

You will remember that the subjects were asked to play three rounds of the "get acquainted" game with one another. The first of these involved same-sex partners who had been randomly paired with one another on the basis of the master list. The study had been described in recruiting instructions as involving "social interaction," and the class felt that it would be too obviously male–female interaction if the first round of the game involved cross-sex partners. In addition, this first round gave subjects the opportunity to learn the procedure, and to fill out the questionnaires (so that any ambiguities could be cleared up on a "practice" trial prior to the collection of the major dependent variables). For the second round of the game, the subjects were split into cross-sex dyads on the basis of a random assignment of partners that had been constructed prior to the experimental session. Finally, for the third round of the game, subjects were given the opportunity to choose their cross-sex partners for the third round of the game, with the restriction that it could not be a person to whom they had already talked in the second round. All of the third-round choices were to be made at the same time, when that time was announced by the experimenter, to prevent those who were able to choose early from having more time to talk to each other than did those who could not make rapid selections. A 2-minute period just prior to the third round was designated as a time when the subjects could move around so that the subjects could "make a real choice" not merely have to choose a person who happened to be near following the second round. This period of time for circulation obviously also gave an opportunity for the matching principle to come into play: To make sure that your first offer will be accepted, you should place yourself near someone of approximately equivalent attractiveness.

Dependent Variables. After the "getting acquainted" questionnaire had been completed for the third round, each subject was asked to respond to a number of questions comparing the three partners, such as:

> Please rate the overall favorability of the impression that each of your partners made on you:

Answers to this and other questions were to be made on scales using the semantic differential format:

	Not at all							Extremely
Person 1:	Favorable :____:____:____:____:____:____:____:							Favorable

	Not at all							Extremely
Person 2:	Favorable :____:____:____:____:____:____:____:							Favorable

	Not at all							Extremely
Person 3:	Favorable :____:____:____:____:____:____:____:							Favorable

Notice that these are unipolar scales, that run from a total lack of favorability (not a presence of "unfavorability") to a high degree of favorability. On this and the other ratings, the scores increased from 1 to 7 from left to right. Although as noted earlier, the absence of reversals in wording might permit confounding from a position preference, that was not a problem in this study because the idea was to discover the difference between ratings of Person 2 (the assigned cross-sex partner) and ratings of Person 3 (the chosen cross-sex partner), not the absolute prevalence of some impression or rating. And there is no reason to believe that the position effect would operate differentially across these two comparisons.

In addition to being asked about the overall favorability of the impression made by each partner, subjects were asked how comfortable they felt during each conversation, how much they would be interested in having each partner for a friend, how much they had in common with each partner, how much they believed each partner enjoyed talking with them, how much eye contact each partner made with them, how much they, themselves, had carried the conversation, and (for Persons 2 and 3 only) how romantically attracted they were to the partner, and how interested they would be in dating the partner. Even without knowing the social exchange literature, the class had thought that attraction might be mediated by such things as common interests, eye contact, and mutual enjoyment of the conversation.

Interpreting the Results

Subjects' Own Attractiveness. If the matching hypothesis is correct, then there should have been a greater correspondence between the subject's own attractiveness and that of the chosen partner than between the subject and a randomly paired partner. The mean scores for attractiveness, along with the mean scores for some other dependent variables of particular interest, are presented in Table A.7. For purposes of the analysis, the subjects were split into two groups, depending on whether their composite attractiveness (averaged over the number of observers who rated it) was above or below the midpoint of the attractiveness scale (a numerical value of 6.5 for the scale from 1–10). This classification is shown in the second row of the header for the table, and indicates that among the 21 female subjects, 11 were rated below and 10 were rated above the midpoint, whereas for male subjects 12 were rated below and 9 were rated above the midpoint (on balance, the males were considered a little less attractive than the females, by both male and female observers).

Test of the Matching Hypothesis. All of the data in Table A.7 were analyzed by the statistical technique of analysis of variance, specifically by an analysis set up as a 2 × 2 × 2 (Subject Gender × Subject Attractiveness

TABLE A.7 Mean Scores for Romantic Attraction and Aspects of Conversations

Rating	GENDER: Att: Part:	FEMALE				MALE			
		Below (n = 11)		Above (n = 10)		Below (n = 12)		Above (n = 9)	
		Assn.	Pick	Assn.	Pick	Assn.	Pick	Assn.	Pick
Attractiveness		6.36	5.54	5.75	6.62	6.92	6.20	6.46	7.40
Romantic liking		2.45	2.45	2.20	2.70	3.00	3.75	3.22	4.11
Interest in dating		2.45	2.64	1.80	3.20	2.83	3.75	2.67	3.44
Other favorability		4.55	5.09	5.50	6.20	5.00	5.25	6.00	6.56
Own comfort		5.18	5.36	5.60	6.20	5.17	5.42	6.11	6.11
Other enjoyment		4.64	4.91	4.70	5.40	4.83	5.08	6.11	6.00
Other eye contact		3.91	4.72	5.50	5.40	4.92	4.92	6.33	6.22

× Presence of Choice) factorial design. This design had what is known as "repeated measures" on the last factor—the experimental manipulation of whether partners had been assigned or were chosen—because each subject participated in both conditions.

As noted earlier, the matching hypothesis would predict that, compared to the attractiveness of assigned partners, the attractiveness of chosen partners would more closely approximate own attractiveness. Specifically, the less attractive subjects should have chosen partners that were less attractive than their assigned partners, whereas the more attractive subjects should have chosen partners that were more attractive than their assigned partners. This, of course, is a predicted statistical *interaction*, and such a significant interaction was, indeed, obtained. For both male and female subjects, the below-midpoint individuals ended up with chosen partners who were lower in attractiveness (the mean, $M = 5.88$) than were their assigned partners ($M = 6.64$), whereas the above-midpoint subjects ended up with chosen partners who were more attractive ($M = 6.99$) than those they had been assigned ($M = 6.09$). The statistical test showed that such a pattern of mean scores would have been obtained fewer than 1 time in 100 simply by chance, suggesting that people were in fact choosing partners whose attractiveness matched their own. As often happens in research, however, there was a complication. Random assignment produces rough equivalence in the long run, not necessarily in the short run, and it just happened that in this study the group of females above the midpoint had been randomly assigned partners who were substantially below the overall attractiveness range (the mean of their attractiveness as shown in Table A.7 is 5.75). So the significant interaction must be interpreted with caution. But even looking at the mean scores for the males only shows evidence of the same matching tendency.

Not only does the matching hypothesis argue that people will choose to become romantically involved with others of roughly equivalent physical attractiveness, it also implies that people will be more satisfied with such a choice than they might have been with a more attractive (but for the below-midpoint individuals, a less similar) person. The next three measures shown in Table A.7 provide evidence in support of this position as well. First, when asked to rate whether they were romantically attracted to either partner of the opposite sex, the analysis revealed a strong trend for the manipulation of partner choice. Although the absolute scores were low, both male and female subjects expressed more romantic interest in chosen partners ($M = 3.23$) than in assigned partners ($M = 2.71$). There was a significant gender effect on this question in the direction that you would expect, with males expressing more romantic attraction ($M = 3.50$) toward female partners (assigned or chosen) than the females expressed toward assigned or chosen male partners ($M = 2.45$).

Second, the strong trend for the effect of choice on romantic attraction became significant when the subjects were asked to rate "how much you would be interested in *dating*" either partner of the opposite sex. Again the overall scores were quite low (especially in light of the overall high attractiveness of the participating subjects), but the effect of choice was clear. Female and male subjects both expressed a greater interest in dating those partners in the "choice" round ($M = 3.26$) than those in the "assigned" round ($M = 2.45$).

Ratings of Overall Favorability. These effects for romantic attraction and dating interest were echoed in the findings for general favorability of the impression created by the partner. As noted earlier, the first item on the questionnaire asked subjects to "rate the overall favorability of the impression that each of your partners made on you." This question applied to all three partners (including the same-sex partner assigned in the first round of the game), but the only responses scored were those having to do with opposite-sex partners. Again, there was a main effect for partner selection, with all subjects preferring chosen partners ($M = 5.71$) to assigned partners ($M = 5.21$). Interestingly enough, the analysis of this question also revealed a significant main effect for own attractiveness. Regardless of their gender, subjects above the midpoint on attractiveness said their partners made a more favorable impression ($M = 6.05$) than did subjects below the midpoint on attractiveness ($M = 4.98$), $F(1, 38) = 18.99, p \neq 001$. Keep in mind that this greater rated favorability is for partners who (according to the ratings made by class members) are less physically attractive than those doing the ratings of favorability.

Alternatives to Choice, Itself. Not only does the social psychologist need to measure carefully the dependent variables of interest, he or she must also include in the design checks on alternative explanations for any results that might be obtained. So the need for control does not end with the experimental design, or even with the implementation of the procedures. Taken together, the results so far suggest that people are more romantically inclined toward others when choice is involved than when it is not. Can any features of the interaction, itself, account for this influence of choice? Three obvious possibilities are the degree to which people feel comfortable in the interaction, the presumed degree to which one's partner enjoyed talking to one, and the amount of eye contact made by chosen partners. Mean scores for these three variables are also shown in Table A.7, but in no case was there an effect for partner selection that corresponded to the effects found on measures of romantic attraction.

To begin with the subject's own comfort in the interaction, responses to the request to "rate how comfortable you felt in the interaction" showed only a main effect for own attractiveness. Subjects whose attractiveness was above the midpoint were more comfortable ($M = 5.99$) than were subjects below the midpoint on attractiveness ($M = 5.28$). When asked how much they thought their partner "enjoyed talking to you," subjects whose attractiveness was above the midpoint thought (probably realistically) that their partners enjoyed talking to them more ($M = 5.52$) than did subjects whose attractiveness was below the midpoint ($M = 4.86$). Finally, the quite explicit possible mediator of romantic attraction, "how much eye contact each partner made with you during the time of the conversation" also showed no effects having to do with choice. There was a significant effect of own attractiveness, with partners of subjects above the midpoint claimed to have made more eye contact ($M = 5.83$) than partners of subjects below the midpoint ($M = 4.63$). Thus none of the presumed mediators of the effect of choice – comfort, enjoyment, or even eye contact – showed any influence of the manipulation of possibility of partner selection. Nor were there any differences of any kind on measures of how much the subject and the various partners had in common, how much the subject believed that he or she had carried the conversation, or even an unobtrusive measure of interest in the topic (an average word count of the length of the written descriptions of the "value conflicts"). It is almost as though the act of choosing – independent of any matters of style or content of the resulting conversation – accounts for nearly all of the influence that choice seems to have on romantic attraction. And one important precursor of that choice seems to have been the physical attractiveness of the partner to be selected.

A Word of Caution, A Note of Optimism

Within the limits of the procedures and design, the findings of this study support nearly all of the predictions that would be made on the basis of the matching principle. Subjects given a choice of partners became paired with people whose level of attractiveness was more like their own than was the case when the partner assignments were randomly made by the experimenter. Moreover, despite the fact that roughly half the subjects in the choice condition end up with partners who were less physically attractive than their assigned partners had been, there was, on the average, greater expressed romantic liking and interest in dating the partner than there had been when the partner had been assigned. The act of choice itself, not aspects of the style or content of the conversation, was the critical element in producing these differences, and it seems likely that similarity in physical attractiveness—matching—helped to produce these choices.

Before making too much out of these findings, one important caution is in order. The assignment-choice manipulation was necessarily confounded with time order. Assignments were made for the second round of the get-acquainted game, choices were made in the third round. Consequently, it could be argued that the partner selection difference was nothing more than an expression of greater personal comfort, and greater willingness to consider the possibilities of romantic attraction, as the process became more familiar to the subjects. On the other hand, it is difficult to see how this change would not have produced corresponding differences in rated comfort (which did not occur).

An unexpected finding that deserves some comment is the consistent main effect for own attractiveness. People whose own attractiveness was above the midpoint of the distribution reported greater comfort in the interaction, more frequent eye contact by their partners, and greater enjoyment by their partners. At first glance this all sounds quite egotistical. But if one takes the view that interaction is a social exchange, and if one recognizes that attractive people have "more to exchange," then the outcome may be nothing more than an accurate report of the situation.

However the findings might be interpreted, the study demonstrates that it is possible to produce theoretically relevant results in a student-initiated class project. Especially with the use of multiple observers of attractiveness (none given any specific guidance about characteristics to consider, or to ignore, in making the ratings), with more communication between the subjects than had been planned (it was virtually impossible to keep subjects from talking to one another completely in the nametag lines and in between the 10-minute scheduled periods), and with the lack of experimental control that accompanies use of multiple, untrained, experimenters, the successful completion of this study should stand as an encouragement to students. It also serves as a cause for optimism that the social psychologist's requirements for measurement and control can be satisfied in research that still remains highly involving for students just learning the discipline.

GLOSSARY

Acquiescence The *response set** representing a tendency to agree with attitude statements regardless of their content. (45).

Aggression Intentional action directed toward the injury of another person. (See *catharsis hypothesis, excitation-transfer theory,* and *frustration-aggression hypothesis.*) (375).

Altruism Intentional self-sacrificing behavior that benefits other people. (See *objective altruism, reciprocity norm,* and *social responsibility norm.*) (306).

Ambiguous Mediation In social perception, the case in which an individual's action might reflect any one of several *personal dispositions.* (See *synonymous mediation.*) (78).

Anticonformity The counterforce to *conformity* that represents an active attempt to sabotage the group's objectives. (See *independence.*) (413).

Artifact In research, a spurious finding resulting not from real psychological differences but from procedural errors. (40).

Associative Bond In *congruity theory,* an assertion of a connection between a source and an object. (See *dissociative bond.*) (172).

Assumed Desirability In the *correspondent inference* theory of *attribution,* the degree to which a choice by a stimulus person is valued by the subgroup to which that stimulus person belongs. (See *noncommon effects.*) (131).

Asymmetric Contingency A social interaction in which one person's responses are determined by an internal plan, while the other person's responses are entirely contingent on the actions of the first person. (See *mutual contingency, pseudocontingency,* and *reactive contingency.*) (421).

---

*Words in italics indicate other glossary entries.

Attitude An organized predisposition to respond in a favorable or unfavorable manner toward a specified class of social objects. (152).

Attraction A complex *attitude* of favorability toward a person, often with components of emotion and commitment absent from attitudes toward other social objects. (See *complementarity* and *law of attraction*.) (325).

Attribution Processes The cognitive processes through which perceivers interpret the actions of other people (and in some cases their own actions as well). (125).

Attributional Criteria The attributional criteria are distinctiveness, consistency, and consensus. An attribution will be made to a distinctive entity when the response to that entity is consistent over time and when there is consensus among observers about the response. (134).

Balance Theory A *cognitive consistency* theory of attitude organization that posits two primary relations—liking and *unit formation*—between cognitive elements. Imbalance in the system is presumed to be unpleasant and to motivate the person to make whatever attitudinal changes are necessary to restore balance. (165).

Balanced Replication An experimental design that includes both the conditions necessary to reproduce earlier findings thought to be *artifacts* and the conditions needed to eliminate the effects of those artifacts. (184).

Behavioral Intention In the *information-processing model* of attitude organization, a specific response tendency reflecting the more general predisposition toward the attitude object. (161).

Behaviorism The approach to psychology that explain behavior entirely in terms of observable stimuli and observable responses rather than, for example, in terms of intervening cognitive process inferred from overt behavior. (278).

Behavior Setting The structural and dynamic combination of place and activity that is the unit of analysis in environmental psychology. The activity must be regularly recurring, independent of the specific individuals involved, and coordinated with aspects of the physical environment. The social *roles* of the individuals involved must help to maintain the setting. (469).

Belief Premise In the *syllogistic model* of attitude organization, the premise that states the person's beliefs about the non*criterial attributes* of the attitude object. (156).

Belief Strength In the *information-processing model* of attitude organization, the respondent's subjective probability that an attitude object actually possesses a characteristic in question. (161).

Catharsis Hypothesis The hypothesis that suggests that the observation of aggression will decrease later aggressive behavior. (See *frustration-aggression hypothesis, social learning theory, and vicarious reinforcement*.) (385).

Central Traits In impression formation, the important characteristics or traits (such as warm–cold) that seem to exert an organizing influence on other traits involved in the impression. (82).

Choice Shift Originally described in the more limited terms of a "risky shift," this is the tendency of a group to make a collective decision after discussion that differs from the decision that would have been made by pooling the individual, private decisions of group members. (454).

Coercive Power The *social power* derived from an ability to provide a target person with negative outcomes. (See *expert power, legitimate power, referent power, and reward power.*) (396).

Cognitive Consistency Model   Any of several models of attitude organization— for instance, *balance, cognitive dissonance, or congruity*—based on the assumption that people seek to maintain consistency among their attitudes, or between their attitudes and their behavior. (154).

Cognitive Dissonance Theory   A *cognitive consistency* theory of attitude organization that posits three possible relations between pairs of cognitive elements—consonance, irrelevance, and dissonance. Dissonance arises when one element implies the opposite of another, and this dissonance serves as a motivation for attitude change. (174).

Cognitive Evaluation Theory   A theory of intrinsic motivation that argues that an individual's concern for competence will lead the person to distinguish between the informational value and the control value of any extrinsic reward. (254).

Cognitive Labeling Theory   An outgrowth of *social comparison theory* that holds that the experience of an emotion requires both internal physiological arousal and cognitive label (derived either from experience or from the present surroundings) for that arousal. (250).

Cognitive Map   An organized representation of some part of the spatial environment. (476).

Cognitive Schema   A relatively specific cognitive structure that acts as a template for perceptual experience. Schemata provide expectations about objects, and will fill in for missing sensory data. (135).

Cohesiveness   The mutual commitment and attraction of members to their *social group*; the sum of forces that bind the group together. (445).

Communication Network   A pattern of communication flow among members of a *social group*. (430).

Comparison Function   The function served by a *reference group* when that group is used as an example either of what attitudes and behavior should be (a positive reference group) or what they should not be (a negative reference group). (See *normative function.*) (241).

Comparison Level (CL)   In *exchange theory*, one standard for evaluating the *goodness of outcomes*; the average value of all outcomes known to the person, each weighted by its momentary salience. (See *comparison level for alternatives.*) (285).

Comparison Level for Alternatives (CL$_{alt}$)   In *exchange theory*, one standard for evaluating the *goodness of outcomes*; the level of outcomes prevailing in the best currently available alternative to the present relationship. (See *comparison level.*) (285).

Competition   An interaction in which each participant, by striving to achieve his or her individual goals, makes it less likely that other participants will achieve their goals. A situation characterized by a low *correspondence of outcomes*. (352).

Complementarity   The principle that states that long-term (such as marital) relationships may be based as much on the complementary personality characteristics of the participants as on *attitude* similarity. (See *law of attraction.*) (340).

Compliance   Observable change in behavior in the direction advocated by an influencing agent. This overt change need not be accompanied by any internal attitude change. (See *identification and internalization*.) (199).

Conceptual Replication A test of a single conceptual idea using procedures that differ from those employed in preceding tests of the same idea. (See *empirical replication*.) (38).

Conformity A change in belief or behavior toward a group as a result of real or imagined group pressure. (See *anticonformity* and *independence*.) (413).

Congruity Theory A *cognitive consistency* theory of attitude organization that describes both sources of statements and objects of those statements on a seven-point evaluative scale. Unless the source and the object have the identical positions on this scale, the incongruity between them will serve as a motivation for attitude change. (171).

Constructive Process In the lens model of social perception, the perceiver's interpretation of a *proximal stimulus*. (77).

Contingency Model A theory of leadership effectiveness that holds that the efficacy of various leadership styles will depend on the characteristics of the situation. Situations are described in terms of the affective relations between leader and group members, the structure of the task, and the position power of the leader. Leader characteristics are described on a dimension of management style that ranges from managing and controlling to permissive and considerate. (438).

Contingent Strategy A strategy for repeated plays of the *Prisoner's Dilemma Game* or other *mixed-motive games* characterized by a low *correspondence of outcomes*. In this strategy the player's move on any given trial depends on the other player's move on the preceding trial. (358).

Correlation Coefficient A statistical measure of the association between two variables. Represented by the symbol r, the correlation coefficient can range from a numerical value of $+1.00$ (a perfect positive relationship between the two variables) through a value of 0 (no relationship between the variables) to a value of -1.00 (a perfect inverse relationship). (554).

Correspondence of Inference The degree to which a stimulus person's actions and the *personal disposition* presumed to account for the action can be described in the same terms. The greater the correspondence, the greater the perceiver's certainty about the *attribution*. (132).

Correspondence of Outcomes In an interaction described by *exchange theory*, the degree to which one person will increase (high correspondence) or decrease (low correspondence) the other person's rewards by pursuing his or her own goals. (289).

Counterattitudinal Advocacy Public advocacy, usually as a consequence of *forced compliance*, of a position inconsistent with one's own private *attitude* on the issue. Counterattitudinal advocacy is usually presumed to produce *cognitive dissonance*, which, in turn, produces attitude change in line with the position advocated. (176).

Covariation The attributional principle that holds that an effect will be attributed to the presumed cause that is present when the effect is present but absent when the effect is absent. (See *attributional dimensions*.) (133).

Credibility The believability of a person who attempts a persuasive communication. Usually credibility is thought to be based on the communicator's expertise and trustworthiness. (215).

Criterial Attribute An essential attribute of an object or person that helps to define the superordinate category to which that object or person belongs. For example, having a child is a criterial attribute for membership in the category "parent." (118).

Crowding In environmental psychology, the negative affective response to a variety of environmental stresses, particularly those associated with social density, invasions of *personal space*, and loss of control. (485).

Debriefing The postexperimental interview designed to ascertain an experimental subject's suspicions, reveal and explain any deceptions, and remove residual effects of the manipulations. (66).

Deindividuation The decreased concern for social evaluation (either self-evaluation or evaluation of the self by others) brought about by anonymity, altered states of consciousness, or diffusion of responsibility for action among members of a group. This loss of identity is reflected in lowered restraints against inappropriate, negative, or hostile behavior. (268).

Demand Characteristics The sum total of all the cues that convey an experimental hypothesis (not necessarily the correct hypothesis) to a subject. (43).

Dependent Variable The measured response in an experiment; the behavior expected to change as a result of changes in the *independent variable*. (8).

Determinism The philosophical principle that holds (a) every event has a cause, and (b) complete specification of the causal structure of the universe at one point in time will permit infallible prediction of all future states. (29).

Differential Accuracy A perceiver's ability to identify the degree to which different individuals possess varying amounts of various personality traits. The only true "accuracy" score in judgment of others. (101).

Discretion The power or right conferred by law upon public officials to act in their official capacities according to the dictates of their own judgment or conscience. (498).

Displacement A Freudian defense mechanism thought to involve the shifting of id impulses (often *aggression*) away from their primary target and toward a similar, but less inhibiting, second person (or animal, or inanimate object). (377).

Dissociative Bond In *congruity theory*, the denial of a connection (or the rejection of a connection) between a source and an object. (See *associative bond*.) (172).

Distal Stimulus In perception, a physical object or social entity external to the perceiver. (See *constructive process, proximal stimulus*.) (76).

Distributive Justice A principle for evaluating the fairness of a comparison of rewards from interaction. If the ratio of one person's profits to investments is equal to the ratio of the other person's profits to investments, then distributive justice is said to occur. (See *equity theory*.) (292).

Dyadic Effect The fact that in an interaction the amount of personal information disclosed by one participant will be positively correlated with the amount disclosed by the other participant. (264).

Effect Dependence In socialization, the fact that nearly all a young child's rewards and punishments are mediated by the parents. (See *information dependence*.) (196).

Ego-Defensive Function People will develop *attitudes* that have the effect of shielding them from conscious recognition of their own inadequacies and failings. (See *instrumental function, knowledge function,* and *value-expressive function.*) (202).

Electromyography   The measurement, using extremely sensitive surface electrodes, of the minute electrical potentials that initiate contraction of a muscle. (96).

Emergent Leadership   In an informal *social group,* the gradual assumption by one or more members of the social *role* of group leader. (436).

Empathy   The state of experiencing the emotion felt by another person. (100).

Empirical Replication   A research study in which all procedures are kept as nearly identical as possible to procedures employed in a preceding study. (See *conceptual replication.*) (37).

Equity Theory   A theory that expands on the principle of *distributive justice,* and states that equity occurs between participants in an interaction when each person's outcomes are proportional to that person's inputs. Inputs must be relevant and recognized, and inequity can be reduced by alteration of inputs or outcomes, by cognitive distortion of inputs or outcomes, or by the dissatisfied person's leaving the situation. (293).

Evaluation Apprehension   An experimental subject's concern about attaining a positive evaluation of his or her behavior from the experimenter, usually by trying to behave in a "typical" manner. (43).

Evaluative Premise   In the *syllogistic model* of attitude organization, the premise that states the person's affective emotional, or evaluative reaction to the characteristics associated with the attitude object in the *belief premise.* (156).

Exchange Theory   A theory of interpersonal behavior that holds that (a) social encounters can best be described as exchanges of rewards and punishments among participants, and (b) in such encounters people seek to maximize their pleasure and minimize their pain. (281).

Excitation-Transfer Theory   A *cognitive labeling* theory of the facilitation of aggressive behavior. The theory holds that once there has been an instigation to *aggression,* adding to the instigated person's arousal by other (nonaggressive) means will enhance the aggressive response. (380).

Expectancy-Value Models   Models of social impression formation or attitude organization in which the final impression or attitude is obtained by summing the products of the value placed on each element times the expectancy that the object possesses each element. (162).

Experimental Realism   The degree of psychological impact that the experimental setting and manipulations have on the subject. (See *mundane realism.*) (552).

Experimenter Expectancy   An *artifact* in experimental research based on the experimenter's unintentional communication to the subject of the results anticipated for the research. (44).

Expert Power   The *social power* derived from skills or knowledge that the target person lacks. (See *coercive power, legitimate power, referent power,* and *reward power.*) (397).

External Validity   The extent to which the findings of research will generalize beyond the confines of the particular setting or procedures. (See *internal validity.*) (40).

Face   In the analysis of self-presentation in social interaction, the positive social value that each participant claims for himself or herself. (261).

Facial Feedback Hypothesis The assertion that the facial expression of a posed emotion, or the exaggeration or inhibition of the facial expression of a spontaneous emotion, will alter the subjective emotional experience. (95).

Factor Analysis A statistical procedure for determining the number of fundamental dimensions underlying a set of ratings or personality traits. The procedure is designed to explain the greatest amoung of variation in the ratings in as few basic dimensions as possible. (556).

Factorial Design A research design, usually an experiment, in which there are systematic variations in more than one *independent variable*. Each independent variable thus becomes one factor in the experimental design. (60).

False Consensus Effect The tendency to overestimate the proportion of people who agree with one's position (regardless of the direction of that position) on an *attitude* issue. (102).

Fate Control In *exchange theory*, the degree to which one interactant's outcomes can be affected by the whims of the other, while that other remains indifferent to the first person's behavioral choices. (See *mutual behavior control* and *reflexive control*.) (288).

Field Experiment An observational method in which a manipulation controlled by the experimenter is performed on subjects unaware that they are participating in research. (55).

Field Theory The general theory of human motivation that holds that a person's behavior will be determined by a total field of personal desires and environmental factors. (See *life space*.) (394).

Forced-Choice Format A format for an attitude or personality scale consisting of item pairs (or occasionally triads). The respondent produces a self-description by choosing between the elements of each pair. These elements are matched in *social desirability*, but only one of each pair is keyed for the attitude or personality characteristic in question. (404).

Forced Compliance The experimental procedure used to induce *cognitive dissonance* by making a subject perform a *counterattitudinal* behavior while leaving the subject with the illusion that he or she has freely chosen to perform the behavior. (176).

Frustration–Aggression Hypothesis The hypothesis that suggests that all aggressive behavior is the product of frustration, and that frustration inevitably leads to *aggression*. (See *catharsis hypothesis* and *social learning theory*.) (197, 378).

Gestalt An organized perceptual whole, or unit. (75).

Goodness of Outcome In *exchange theory*, the psychological representation of a person's profit (reward–cost) for any particular behavior. (See *comparison level* and *comparison level for alternatives*.) (284).

Group Locomotion Movement of a *social group* toward its collective goal. A source of pressure toward uniformity of opinion within the group. (434).

Group Maintenance Actions by members of a *social group*, which actions are directed toward facilitation of pleasant interaction among the members of the group. (434).

Group Polarization Group-produced enhancement of an individual member's initial position based on the individual's discovery of the group's position (usually through discussion). If there is a predominant directional tendency in the private positions of individual group members, *social comparison* processes and *persuasive arguments* will shift the individual positions. (See *choice shift*.) (454).

Groupthink Within a *social group*, a preoccupation with unanimity of opinion (usually in order to facilitate achievement of a group goal) that renders ineffective any critical evaluation of the proposed decision. (452).

Hedonistic Calculus Bentham's early analysis of human motivation in terms of a fundamental desire to seek pleasure and avoid pain. The analysis included dimensions – for example, duration, intensity, certainty – that could characterize sources of pleasure and pain. (277).

Horizontal Structure In the *syllogistic model* of attitude organization, the number of different syllogistic chains leading to exactly the same attitudinal conclusion. (See *vertical structure*.) (158).

Hypothetical Construct A conceptual principle that serves as the explanation for an aspect of observable behavior. The construct itself is not observable. (12).

The I That part of the *self* that is pure ego – thinker, knower, organized stream of conscious awareness. (See *the Me*.) (234).

Ideal Self In some measures of self-esteem, the list of personal characteristics that the respondent considers desirable. This contrasts with the *real self*, the characteristics the respondent claims to possess. (257).

Identification Private acceptance of influence based on a satisfying self-defining relationship between the influenced person and the influencing agent. (See *compliance* and *internalization*.) (199).

Implicit Personality Theory A perceiver's set of expectations about which personality traits will be mutually associated. (140).

Incentive Theory An *attitude* change theory, based on the principle of *reinforcement*, that holds that attitude change should increase with increases in external rewards for change. This view contrasts with the position of *cognitive dissonance theory*. (180).

Independence A counterforce to *conformity* representing a refusal to comply with the objective of a *social group* (either by maintaining one's own position or by leaving the group). (See *anticonformity*.) (413).

Independent Variable The variable selected or manipulated by an experimenter in order to determine its effects on behavior. The independent variable may be under the experimenter's direct control, or it may be a characteristic of the subjects (for instance, gender) expected to affect behavior in the experimental setting. (See *dependent variable*.) (59).

Index Numbers Numbers that have been corrected for the base rate of occurrence of the phenomena they represent. Although there would be more blue-eyed people in a large group than in a small group, the percentage (an index number) should be nearly the same in both groups. (48).

Information Dependence In socialization, the fact that most of a child's knowledge about the social world is derived from information provided by the parents. (See *effect dependence*.) (196).

Information Integration Theory A mathematical model of impression formation that holds that both the scale value (positivity) and the normalized weight of every adjective involved in a description of a stimulus person combine to produce the final impression of the person. (145).

Informational Social Influence The *social power* of persuasion that produces private acceptance by providing the target person with the information needed to make a wise decision. (See *normative social influence*.) (401).

Information-Processing Model A model of attitude organization that describes a social attitude as a combination of belief strength and evaluation. (161).

Informed Consent An ethical guideline for psychological research that holds that a subject should agree to participate only after receiving a description of the risks that might be associated with the research. (67).

Inoculation An *attitude* consolidation technique based on an analogy to medicine. If a person can be exposed to a weakened version of possible counterpropaganda, the person will become resistant to any effects from that later counterpropaganda. (213).

Instrumental Function Favorable *attitudes* will be developed toward people and objects that facilitate the achievement of goals; unfavorable attitudes will be developed toward people and objects that frustrate goal attainment. (See *egodefensive function, knowledge function,* and *value-expressive function*.) (201).

Insufficient Justification A conceptual explanation for the attitude change that follows *counterattitudinal advocacy*. The minimal external rewards for such behavior are insufficient to justify having performed the action, and the resulting *cognitive dissonance* leads to change. (176).

Interaction Matrix In *exchange theory*, the set of interaction alternatives formed by the conjunction of one person's possible behaviors with the other person's possible behaviors. (282).

Interaction Process Analysis A method for coding the content of the interaction among members of a *social group*. The method is used to distinguish between contributions to the group's task (*group locomotion*) and contributions to the positive feelings of the group members (*group maintenance*). (434).

Intermittent Reinforcement The provision of reward not for every occurrence of an action, but only occasionally (often according to a prearranged schedule). (280).

Internal Validity The extent to which the findings of research reflect the actual psychological differences thought to be measured; freedom from confounding or from *artifacts*. (See *external validity*.) (40).

Internalization Private acceptance of influence based on the influenced person's belief that the position advocated is congruent with his or her own value system. (See *compliance* and *identification*.) (199).

Interpersonal Simulation A technique devised to test the *self-perception theory* of attitude change. In this technique the simulating subject is given information about the situation confronting a person in a *forced compliance* experiment, and is asked to predict that person's *attitudes*. (182).

Item Analysis Any of several procedures for determining the suitability of an individual item for inclusion in an attitude scale. One such procedure measures the degree to which each item in the scale correlates with the total score (less that item) on the scale. (562).

Item Pool The complete set of attitude or opinion statements (often ranging up to 100 such statements) from which items to be included in a *Thurstone scale* or a *Likert scale* are to be selected. (558).

Kinesic Cues Cues in social perception arising from the body movements—posture, gestures, facial expressions—of a stimulus person. (85).

Knowledge Function People will develop *attitudes* that help bring structure and organization to their social worlds and help to explain social events. (See *ego-defensive function, instrumental function,* and *value-expressive function.*) (201).

Latitude of Acceptance   In the *social judgment theory* of *attitude* change, that portion of the attitude dimension that is slightly discrepant from the target person's position. (See *latitude of noncommitment* and *latitude of rejection.*) (207).

Latitude of Noncommitment   In the *social judgment theory* of *attitude* change, that portion of the attitude dimension that is moderately discrepant from the target person's position. This area encloses all messages that will be neither immediately accepted nor immediately rejected. (See *latitude of acceptance* and *latitude of rejection.*) (207).

Latitude of Rejection   In the *social judgment theory* of *attitude* change, that portion of the attitude dimension that encloses all messages so far from the target person's position that they will be rejected out of hand. (See *latitude of acceptance* and *latitude of noncommitment.*) (207).

Law of Attraction   The proposition that states that *attraction* toward an object or person is a positive linear function of the positive *reinforcements* received from that object or person. A typical experimental procedure equates positive reinforcements with degree of similarity in *attitudes.* (See *complementarity.*) (338).

Law of Effect   The first psychological representation of hedonism (see *hedonistic calculus*), which holds that behavior leading to pleasure would be "stamped in," while behavior leading to pain would be "stamped out." (277).

Legitimate Power   The *social power* derived from acceptance by the target person of the authority inherent in the influencing agent's social *role.* (See *coercive power, expert power, referent power,* and *reward power.*) (397).

Level of Aspiration   A self-imposed expectation for task performance that will determine whether the self-evaluation following actual task performance is positive or negative. (256).

Life Space   In *field theory,* the total field of environmental factors and personal desires that are perceived by the person at any given moment in time. (394).

Likert Scale   An *attitude* scale that requires respondents to indicate their degree of agreement or disagreement with a set of statements about the attitude object. The respondent's score is the sum of his or her responses to the individual statements. (561).

Limiting Conditions   Factors in the environment that place restrictions on causal relationships specified by theory. (3).

Looking-Glass Self   The proposition from *symbolic interactionism* that holds that one's self-concept will be determined in large part by one's imagined social value to others. (240).

Machiavellianism   The interpersonal style characterized by the manipulation of other people, especially in face-to-face interactions where there is latitude for improvisation and the opportunity to introduce irrelevant affect into the process. (404).

Matching Principle   A statement of the fact that people tend to select dates whose physical attractiveness is close to their own. (342).

The Me   The *self* as an object of reflection, consisting of the material possessions, psychological faculties, social behaviors, and the emotions to which these elements give rise. (See *the I.*) (234).

Mixed-Motive Game An interaction in which there is a low *correspondence of outcomes*, such that if both participants pursue their own immediate goals, they will both lose. The very best outcome for each also carries the greatest risk. (289, 354).

Multidimensional Scaling A statistical technique for constructing a spatial configuration of stimuli, on the basis of the judged similarity between the elements of all possible pairs of those stimuli (90).

Multiple Operationism In a single research study, the use of very different operations to measure a single concept. A way to enhance the *internal validity* of a research design. (39).

Mundane Realism The degree of correspondence between the actions required of a subject in an experiment and the actions that subject might perform in everyday life outside the laboratory. (See *experimental realism*.) (226, 552).

Mutual Behavior Control In *exchange theory*, the degree to which each person's outcomes depend on the mutual choices that are made, a measure of the true interdependence in an interaction. (See *fate control* and *reflexive control*.) (288).

Mutual Contingency A social interaction in which each participant's actions are partly determined by an internal plan and partly determined by the other's actions. (See *asymmetric contingency, pseudocontingency,* and *reactive contingency*.) (423).

Naive Psychology The systematic *attribution* theory that attempts to account for the way in which an untrained (naive) observer might explain the causes of behavior. (128).

Natural Experiment An experiment in which the manipulation is accomplished by an environmental or situational change not under the experimenter's control. (54).

Noncommon Effects In the *correspondent inference* theory of *attribution*, the effects produced by one behavioral choice but not by an alternative choice. (See *assumed desirability*.) (131).

Nonverbal Leakage The information from a stimulus person's nonverbal behavior that conflicts with his or her verbal message. (86).

Nonzero-Sum Game A social interaction in which one person's gain is not necessarily the other person's loss. Includes cooperation as well as some *mixed motive games*. (See *zero-sum game*.) (352).

Norm A set of expectations for behavior in a particular situation, regardless of the social *roles* held by the participants. (12, 309).

Normative Function The function served by a *reference group* when the group establishes rules (*norms*) for behavior and provides rewards and punishments to enforce those rules. The normative function is usually limited to cases in which the target person holds (or desires) membership in the reference group. (See *comparison function*.) (241).

Normative Social Influence The *social power* of reward and punishment that produces behavioral *compliance* but may not produce any private acceptance of the position advocated. (See *informational social influence*.) (401).

Objective Altruism Voluntary action that benefits another person with no external rewards for the actor. (See *altruism, reciprocity norm,* and *social responsibility norm*.) (307).

Objective Self-Awareness Heightened recognition of the *self* as a social object, brought about by focusing attention on oneself. (266).

Operational Definition   A definition of a conceptual variable stated in terms of the operations performed. "Twelve hours since the last meal" is an operational definition of hunger. (3, 36).

Oversufficient Justification   External reward for something that the person would normally have done without that reward. Used as a test of the *self-perception theory* of attitude change. Contrasts with *insufficient justification.* (185).

Paralinguistic Cues   In social perception, cues to a stimulus person's characteristics that are contained in the person's manner of speaking. These cues include, for example, dialect, loudness, and rate of speech. (97).

Participant Observation   The recording of behavior by an observer who also takes part in the activities of the individual or *social group* being observed. Participant observation may be partially concealed (the subjects know the observer is there, but do not know which behaviors are being recorded) or completely concealed (subjects are unaware that any record is being kept of their activities). The latter method raises serious ethical concerns. (See *simple observation.*) (52).

Peer Nomination Method   A method for studying a perceiver's *implicit personality theory.* A number of rating dimensions (for example, weak–strong) are presented to the perceiver, who nominates a specific person to represent each end of every dimension. The traits attributed to a single stimulus person are then considered to be associated. (142).

Percept   The phenomenal experience of an object, person, or situation; the way that object, person, or situation appears to the perceiver. (73).

Personal Disposition   An enduring personality characteristic, behavioral style, or other stable reason for acting. (See *attribution processes.*) (123).

Personal Norms   In a two-factor theory of altruistic action, the expectations for one's own behavior in a specific situation (as contrasted with a more general social *norm.* (See *responsibility denial.*) (316).

Personal Reference Scale   An individualized scale of social judgment or *attitude* that takes into account both the psychological distance from one end of the scale to the other and the number of categories or divisions within that distance. The latter distinctions are accomplished through the use of an *unlimited response language.* (210).

Personal Space   The spatial area immediately surrounding a person that the person considers to be his or her own. (474).

Persuasive Arguments Theory   An analysis of *choice shifts* that suggests that the shift occurs because the group discussion raises persuasive arguments not previously considered by many of the members of the *social group* (See *group polarization.*) (457).

Phenomenological Experience   An individual's internal perception of the world; a construction the perceiver creates from sensory data. (32).

P-O-X Triad   In *balance theory*, a triad consisting of the person (p), whose viewpoint is taken, another person (o), and an object (x) associated in some positive or negative way with both people. Such a triad would be balanced if, for example, p and o both like each other and also like x. (See *unit formation.*) (169).

Primacy Effect   In impression formation or persuasive communication, the tendency for material presented at the beginning of a sequence to have a greater effect than the material presented at the end of the sequence (81).

Priory Entry Effect In social categorization, the error that results from the fact that early information contributes more to the formation of a category than later information will contribute to change in that category. (119).

Prisoner's Dilemma Game A *mixed motive game* in which the payoffs for joint *competition* and joint cooperation fall between the payoffs for the combination of cooperation by one participant (who loses the most) and *competition* by the other participant (who gains the most). (353).

Privacy In environmental psychology, the dynamic process of regulation of access to the self. (479).

Probabilogical Model Any of several models of attitude structure (such as the *syllogistic* and *information-processing* models) that assume cognitive functioning to occur according to the laws of probability and logic. (154).

Proxemics The study of the social meanings of various interpersonal distances. (473).

Proximal Stimulus in perception, the local and immediate representaion of a *distal stimulus* at the sense organs. (See *constructive process.*) (76).

Pseudocontingency The limiting case of social interaction in which participants who appear to be responding to each other are really following their own internal plans. An example is a group of actors engaged in a discussion dictated by a script. (See *asymmetric contingency, mutual contingency,* and *reactive contingency.*) (421).

Reactance The specific negative motivational state directed at restoring lost decision freedom. (211).

Reactive Contingency A social interaction in which each participant's behavior is entirely dependent on the immediately preceding action of the other. (See *asymmetric contingency, mutual contingency,* and *pseudocontingency.*) (421).

Reactivity The extent to which research findings are distorted by the subjects' knowledge that they are participating in research. (See *internal validity.*) (41).

Real Self In some measures of self-esteem, the personal characteristics that the respondent claims to possess. This contrasts with the *ideal self,* those characteristics considered desirable. (257).

Reciprocity Norm The social *norm* that requires that (1) people should help those who have helped them, and (2) people should not injure those who have helped them. (See *social responsibility norm.*) (309).

Reference Group Any *social group* used as a standard for self-evaluation or attitude formation. The group may be used either as an example to follow (a positive reference group) or as an example to avoid (a negative reference group). (See *comparison function* and *normative function.*) (241).

Referent Power The *social power* derived from the target person's desire for *identification* with the powerful agent. (See *coercive power, expert power, legitimate power,* and *reward power.*) (397).

Reflexive Control Within *exchange theory,* a person's ability to alter his or her own outcomes by the choices made, independent of the other person's choices. (See *fate control* and *mutual behavior control.*) (287).

Reinforcement (Principle of) The representation in modern *behaviorism* of the early *law of effect*: Behavior followed by positive consequences will be more likely to recur (positive reinforcement), as will behavior that is followed by the removal of aversive stimuli (negative reinforcement). (175).

Relative Centrality In a *communication network,* the importance of a particular position is measured by dividing total sum of distances from all positions to all others by the sum of distances from the position being considered. (431).

Relative Deprivation   A principle of fairness in social *exchange* that suggests that an individual will resent receiving an outcome that is less than the person (a) wants, (b) believes possible (especially through the example of another person's receiving the outcome desired), and (c) feels entitled to, when the person (d) does not think the failure to achieve better is his or her fault. (See *distributive justice* and *equity theory*.) (292).

Representativeness   Similarity in psychological characteristics or experience between subjects in research and the population from which those subjects were drawn (or to which the researcher hopes to generalize). (See *external validity*.) (41).

Response Set   A systematic tendency to answer questions in a way determined not by the content of the question, but by its form or by the characteristics of the possible answers. (See *acquiescence* and *social desirability*.) (45).

Responsibility Denial   In a two-factor theory of altruistic action, the individual's tendency to rationalize away personal responsibility for the consequences of behavior. (See *personal norms*.) (317).

Resultant Achievement Motivation   The strength of the motive to approach success (usually measured by a version of the Thematic Apperception Test) minus the motive to avoid failure (usually measured by the Test Anxiety Questionnaire). (364).

Retaliation Distress   According to *equity theory*, one of the two sorts of distress felt by a harm-doer; fear that the victim or some outside agency will restore equity by punishing the harm-doer. (See *self-concept distress*.) (315).

Reward Power   The *social power* derived from the ability to provide a target person with positive *reinforcements*. (See *coercive power, expert ower, legitimate power,* and *referent power*.) (396).

Role   The set of behavioral expectations for a person who performs a particular social function. Examples would be "student" or "supervisor." (See *norm*.) (238).

Role Conflict   Perceived incompatibility of the expectations inherent in several simultaneously occupied social *roles*. (238).

Selective Deposit   In archival methods, the possibility that some records will have been kept more fully than others, either because of deliberate action by the record-keepers, or because of contemporary social custom. (48).

Selective Sampling   In archival methods, the possibility that the records chosen for analysis will not adequately represent the population from which a sample is taken. (49).

Selective Survival   In archival methods, the possibility that some records will not last as long as others, either because of natural decay or because of deliberate destruction. (47).

Self   The totality of answers to the question "Who am I?" including, for example, inner experience, awareness, observable abilities, and material possessions. (See *the I, ideal self, the Me,* and *real self*.) (232).

Self-Concept Distress   According to *equity theory*, one of the two sorts of distress felt by a harm-doer; the loss of self-esteem that accompanies behavior inconsistent with equity and fairness. (See *retaliation distress*.) (315).

Self-Perception Theory   A theory that holds that people learn of their own *atti-*

tudes and reasons for acting by observing their behavior in much the same way that another person might observe them. In the area of attitude change, this view contrasts with that of *cognitive dissonance theory*. (181).

Self-Presentation The creation and maintenance of a public *self*. (104).

Semantic Differential A scaling technique that employs a series of bipolar adjective pairs to measure the connotative meaning of words and concepts, or to assess social *attitudes*. (564).

Simple Observation The recording of the public behavior of subjects, without their awarness and without any interference in the situation by the observer. (See *participant observation*.) (51).

Social Comparison Theory A theory of self-evaluation that holds that (a) people have a drive to evaluate their opinions and abilities, (b) in the absence of objective standards this evaluation will occur through social comparison with others, and (c) such social comparisons will usually be made with similar people. (243).

Social Desirability The *response set* representing a tendency to respond in a socially approved manner regardless of the content of the behavior requested or the questions asked. (45).

Social Group A collectivity that has psychological implications for the individual, based on the person's awareness of the other group members, his or her membership (or desired membership) in the group, and the emotional significance of the group. (412).

Social Influence Attitudinal or behavioral change brought about by the application of *social power*. Social influence is a result, whereas social power is a capacity. (394).

Social Judgment Theory A theory of *attitude* change that considers the position advocated in relation to the target person's initial position on the issue. Persuasive communications falling in the *latitude of acceptance* will be assimilated, those falling in the *latitude of noncommitment* are most likely to produce real change, and those falling in the *latitude of rejection* will produce no change. (206).

Social Learning Theory A theory of interpersonal behavior that emphasizes the role of *reinforcement* in the development and maintenance of social interaction patterns. Some social learning theories concentrate on imitation and *vicarious reinforcement*, others deal with expectancy and value, but all share the view of social development as a learning process. (279).

Social Power The capacity of a person or group to affect the behavior of another person or group. In terms of *exchange theory*, the range of outcomes through which one person can move another. Implicit in the definition is "other things being equal." (See *social influence*.) (393).

Social Psychology The scientific study of the personal and situational factors that affect individual social behavior. (18).

Social Reality The consensus about a situation or *attitude* issue derived from *social comparison* among the members of a *social group*. (414).

Social Responsibility Norm A social *norm* that holds that people should help anyone in a dependent position. (See *objective altruism* and *reciprocity norm*.) (310).

Sociogram A diagram showing the interpersonal relationships among members of a *social group*. Often such diagrams illustrate friendship choices or co-worker preferences, showing both reciprocated and nonreciprocated choices. (328).

Speaker-State Signal   The nonverbal and *paralinguistic cues* that together indicate that a listener desires to take a turn at speaking. (97).

Standard Deviation   A measure of the variability in a distribution of scores, computed from the sum of the squared deviations (*sum of squares*) around the mean of the distribution. The sum of squares is divided by the quantity $(n - 1)$, where n is the number of observations, to produce the *variance*, and the standard deviation is the square root of this variance. (546).

Sublimation   A Freudian defense mechanism that holds that some unacceptable id impulses (such as *aggression*) can be channeled into socially acceptable behaviors. (377).

Sum of Squares   A measure of the variability in a distribution of scores. The sum of squares is computed by first finding the mean (arithmetic average) of the distribution, then subtracting the mean from each of the observations, and squaring the resulting differences. The sum of these squared deviations (sum of squares) is used in computation of the *variance* and *standard deviation*. (546).

Syllogistic Model   A model of attitude organization that describes a social *attitude* as the syllogistic conclusion of the two premises: a *belief premise* representing opinions about the object's characteristics, and an *evaluative premise* reflecting the person's affective reaction to the object. (156).

Symbolic Interactionism   A theory of social behavior that describes social encounters in terms of their symbolic meaning and the value of that meaning to the participants in the encounter. (See *looking-glass self*.) (239).

Symbolic Self-Completion   A theory of *self-presentation* that suggests that people will, through use of symbols (such as language or possessions), attempt to compensate for weaknesses they see in their self-definitions. (263).

Synonymous Mediation   In social perception, the case in which an individual's action unequivocally reflects a single underlying *personal disposition*. (See *ambiguous mediation*.) (78).

Thurstone Scale   An *attitude* scale made up of statements with known scale values. These scale values have been determined previously in a sorting procedure designed to produce *equal-appearing intervals*. A respondent's *attitude* is taken to be the midpoint of the scale values of all items agreed with. (558).

Trait Implication Method   A method for studying a perceiver's *implicit personality theory* that assesses the extent of the perceiver's belief that the presence of one trait (such as "warm") implies the presence of another trait (such as "sociable"). (140).

Understaffing/Overstaffing   In the environmental psychology theory of optimum use of *behavior settings*, the conditions, respectively, of too few and too many staff members for the number of clients available. (470).

Unfreezing/Moving/Refreezing   The process of attitude change presumed to occur as a consequence of group discussion of an issue anchored in the *social group*. A communicator using this process would first unfreeze the group's *attitude*, then move the group to a new position, then refreeze the attitude in the new position (15, 223).

Unit Formation   In *balance theory*, the relationship of association–through kinship, proximity, similarity, formal organizations, owning, or other factors— between cognitive elements. (165).

Unlimited Response Language In the measurement of a social *attitude* using a *personal reference scale*, a response continuum with no fixed or apparent categories. An example would be the size or weight of small piles of sand used to assess favorability toward a number of attitude objects. (210).

Usable Power The *social power* that an influencing agent is willing to exercise. Because the target of influence can typically provide the powerful person with some aversive stimuli, or simply leave the relationship altogether, usable power is often less than actual social power. (398).

Value-Expressive Function People will develop *attitudes* that are consistent with and expressive of their broader value systems. (See *ego-defensive function, instrumental function,* and *knowledge function.*) (201).

Variance A measure of the dispersion in a distribution of scores. The quantity obtained by dividing the sum of squared deviations around the mean score (the *sum of squares*) by the quantity $(n - 1)$, where n is the number of observations in the distribution. The square root of the variance is the *standard deviation*. (546).

Veridicality The extent to which a *percept* corresponds to objective reality. (74).

Vertical Structure In the *syllogistic model* of *attitude* organization, the length of any single syllogistic chain leading to an attitudinal conclusion. (158).

Vicarious Reinforcement In *social learning theory*, the process of increasing the likelihood of recurrence of an action by permitting the actor to observe a model's being rewarded for the same action. (281).

Zero-Sum Game An interaction in which there is a perfect negative *correspondence of outcomes*: one person's gains are identical in magnitude to the losses of the other. (See *mixed motive game, nonzero-sum game.*) (289, 352).

Z-Score A statistically derived measure of the degree to which an observation or response differs from the mean score of a relevant group of observations after taking into account the variability inherent in the distribution of observations. Computed by subtracting the mean score from the observation, and dividing this quantity by the *standard deviation* of the distribution. (364).

REFERENCES

ABELSON, R. P. (1968). Psychological implication. In R. P. Abelson, E. Aronson, W. J. McGuire, T. M. Newcomb, M. J. Rosenberg, & P. H. Tannenbaum (Eds.), *Theories of cognitive consistency: A sourcebook* (pp. 112–139). Chicago: Rand McNally.

ABRAMSON, L. Y., SELIGMAN, M. E. P., & TEASDALE, J. D. (1978). Learned helplessness in humans: Critique and reformulation. *Journal of Abnormal Psychology, 87,* 49–74.

ADAMS, J. S. (1965). Inequity in social exchange. In L. Berkowitz (Ed.), *Advances in experimental social psychology* (Vol. 2, pp. 267–299). New York: Academic Press.

ADAMS, J. S., & JACOBSEN, P. R. (1964). Effects of wage inequities on work quality. *Journal of Abnormal and Social Psychology, 69,* 19–25.

ALLEN, V. L. (1965). Situational factors in conformity. In L. Berkowitz (Ed.), *Advances in experimental social psychology* (Vol. 2, pp. 133–175). New York: Academic Press.

ALLEN, V. L. (1975). Social support for nonconformity. In L. Berkowitz (Ed.), *Advances in experimental social psychology* (Vol. 8, pp. 2–43).

ALLPORT, F. H. (1955). *Theories of perception and the concept of structure.* New York: Wiley.

ALLPORT, G. W. (1954). *The nature of prejudice.* Reading, MA: Addison-Wesley.

ALLPORT, G. W. (1958). *The nature of prejudice* (Abr. ed.). New York: Doubleday, Anchor Books. (Original work published 1954).

ALLPORT, G. W. (1968). The historical background of modern social psychology. In G. Lindzey & E. Aronson (Eds.), *Handbook of social psychology* (2nd ed., Vol. 1, pp. 1–80). Reading, MA: Addison-Wesley.

ALLPORT, G. W., & KRAMER, B. M. (1946). Some roots of prejudice. *Journal of Psychology, 22,* 9–39.

ALTMAN, I. (1975). *The environment and social behavior.* Monterey, CA: Brooks/Cole.

ALTMAN, I., & CHEMERS, M. (1980). *Culture and environment.* Monterey, CA: Brooks/Cole.

ALTMAN, I., & TAYLOR, D. A. (1973). *Social penetration processes: The development of interpersonal relationships.* New York: Holt.

ALTMAN, I., & VINSEL, A. M. (1977). Personal space: An analysis of E. T. Hall's proxemics framework. In I. Altman & J. F. Wohlwill (Eds.), *Human behavior and environment: Advances in theory and research* (Vol. 2, pp. 181–259). New York: Plenum.

American Bar Association Project on Standards for Criminal Justice. (1971). *Standards relating to the prosecution function and the defense function*. New York: American Bar Association.

ANDERSON, N. H. (1968). A simple model for information integration. In R. P. Abelson, E. Aronson, W. J. McGuire, T. M. Newcomb, M. J. Rosenberg, & P. H. Tannenbaum (Eds.), *Theories of cognitive consistency: A sourcebook* (pp. 731–743). Chicago: Rand McNally.

ANDERSON, N. H. (1974). Cognitive algebra: Integration theory applied to social attribution. In L. Berkowitz (Ed.), *Advances in experimental social psychology* (Vol. 7, pp. 1–102). New York: Academic Press.

ANDERSON, N. H., & HUBERT, S. (1963). Effect of concomitant verbal recall on order effects in personality impression formation. *Journal of Verbal Learning and Verbal Behavior, 2,* 379–391.

APFELBAUM, E. (1974). On conflicts and bargaining. In L. Berkowitz (Ed.), *Advances in experimental social psychology* (Vol. 7, pp. 103–156). New York: Academic Press.

APPLE, W., STREETER, L. A., & KRAUSS, R. M. (1979). Effects of pitch and speech rate on personal attributions. *Journal of Personality and Social Psychology, 37,* 715–727.

APPLEYARD, D. (1970). Styles and methods of structuring a city. *Environment and Behavior, 2,* 100–118.

ARISTOTLE (1952). Nicomachean ethics (W. D. Ross, Trans.). In R. M. Hutchens (Ed.), *Great books of the western world* (Vol. 9, pp. 335–436). Chicago: Encylopaedia Brittanica.

ARONSON, E. (1969). The theory of cognitive dissonance: A current perspective. In L. Berkowitz (Ed.), *Advances in experimental social psychology* (Vol. 4, pp. 2–35). New York: Academic Press.

ARONSON, E., & CARLSMITH, J. M. (1968). Experimentation in social psychology. In G. Lindzey & E. Aronson (Eds.), *Handbook of social psychology* (2nd ed., Vol. 2, pp. 1–79). Reading, MA: Addison-Wesley.

ARONSON, E., & MILLS, J. (1959). The effect of severity of initiation on liking for a group. *Journal of Abnormal and Social Psychology, 59,* 177–181.

ARONSON, E., WILLERMAN, B., & FLOYD, J. (1966). The effect of a pratfall on increasing interpersonal attractiveness. *Psychonomic Science, 4,* 227–228.

ASCH, S. E. (1946). Forming impressions of personality. *Journal of Abnormal and Social Psychology, 41,* 258–290.

ASCH, S. E. (1951). Effects of group pressure upon the modification and distortion of judgments. In H. Guetzkow (Ed.), *Groups, leadership, and men* (pp. 177–190). Pittsburgh: Carnegie Press.

ATKINSON, J. W. (Ed.). (1958). *Motives in fantasy, action, and society*. Princeton, NJ: Van Nostrand.

ATKINSON, J. W. (1964). *An introduction to motivation*. Princeton, NJ: Van Nostrand.

AUSTIN, W., & SUSMILCH, C. (1974). Comment on Lane and Messé's confusing clarification of equity theory. *Journal of Personality and Social Psychology, 30,* 400–404.

AUSTIN, W., WALSTER, E., & UTNE, M. K. (1976). Equity and the law: The effect of a harmdoer's "suffering in the act" on liking and assigned punishment. In L. Berkowitz & E. Walster (Eds.), *Advances in experimental social psychology, Vol. 9. Equity theory: Toward a general theory of social interaction* (pp. 163–190). New York: Academic Press.

BALES, R. F. (1950). *Interaction process analysis*. Cambridge, MA: Addison-Wesley.

BALES, R. F. (1955). How people interact in conferences. *Scientific American, 192,* 31–35.

BALES, R. F. (1958). Task roles and social roles in problem solving groups. In E. E. Maccoby, T. M. Newcomb, & E. L. Hartley (Eds.), *Readings in social psychology* (3rd ed., pp. 437–447). New York: Holt, Rinehart & Winston.

BALES, R. F. (1970). *Personality and interpersonal behavior*. New York: Holt, Rinehart & Winston.

BANDURA, A. (1973). *Aggression: A social learning analysis.* Englewood Cliffs, NJ: Prentice-Hall.

BANDURA, A., & WALTERS, R. (1963). *Social learning and personality development.* New York: Holt, Rinehart & Winston.

BARD, M. (1970). *Training police as specialists in family crisis intervention.* Washington, DC: U.S. Government Printing Office.

BARKER, R. G. (1968). *Ecological psychology: Concepts and methods for studying the environment of human behavior.* Stanford, CA: Stanford University Press.

BARKER, R. G., and Associates. (1978). *Habitats, environments, and human behavior.* San Francisco: Jossey-Bass.

BARON, R. A., & BELL, P. A. (1977). Sexual arousal and aggression by males: Effects of type of erotic stimuli and prior provocation. *Journal of Personality and Social Psychology, 35,* 79–87.

BATESON, G., JACKSON, D. D., HALEY, J., & WEAKLAND, J. H. (1956). Toward a theory of schizophrenia. *Behavioral Science, 1,* 251–264.

BAUM, A., AIELLO, J. R., & CALESNICK, L. E. (1978). Crowding and personal control: Social density and the development of learned helplessness. *Journal of Personality and Social Psychology, 36,* 1000–1011.

BAUM, A., & EPSTEIN, Y. M. (Eds.). (1978). *Human response to crowding.* Hillsdale, NJ: Lawrence Erlbaum Associates.

BAUM, A., & GATCHEL, R. J., AIELLO, J. R., & THOMPSON, D. (1980). Cognitive mediation of environmental stress. In J. H. Harvey (Ed.), *Cognition, social behavior, and the environment* (pp. 513–533). Hillsdale, NJ: Lawrence Erlbaum Associates.

BAUM, A., & VALINS, S. (1977). *Architecture and social behavior: Psychological studies of social density.* Hillsdale, NJ: Lawrence Erlbaum Associates.

BAUMRIND, D. (1964). Some thoughts on the ethics of research: After reading Milgram's "Behavioral study of obedience." *American Psychologist, 19,* 421–423.

BAVELAS, A. (1950). Communication patterns in task-oriented groups. *Journal of the Acoustical Society of America, 22,* 725–730.

BEM, D. J. (1965). An experimental analysis of self-persuasion. *Journal of Experimental Social Psychology, 1,* 199–218.

BEM, D. J. (1972). Self-perception theory. In L. Berkowitz (Ed.), *Advances in experimental social psychology* (Vol. 6, pp. 2–62). New York: Academic Press.

BEM, D. J. (1970). *Beliefs, attitudes, and human affairs.* Belmont, CA: Brooks/Cole.

BEM, D. J., WALLACH, M. A., & KOGAN, N. (1965). Group decision making under risk of aversive consequences. *Journal of Personality and Social Psychology, 1,* 453–460.

BENNETT, E. B. (1955). Discussion, decision, commitment, and consensus in "group discussion." *Human Relations, 8,* 251–274.

BENTHAM, J. (1879). *An introduction to the principles of morals and legislation.* Oxford: Clarendon. (Original work published 1789)

BERGLAS, S., & JONES, E. E. (1978). Drug choice as a self-handicapping strategy in response to noncontingent success. *Journal of Personality and Social Psychology, 36,* 405–417.

BERKOWITZ, L. (1962). *Aggression: A social psychological analysis.* New York: McGraw-Hill.

BERKOWITZ, L. (Ed.). (1969). *Roots of aggression: A re-examination of the frustration-aggression hypothesis.* New York: Atherton.

BERKOWITZ, L. (1975). *A survey of social psychology.* New York: Holt, Rinehart and Winston.

BERKOWITZ, L., & DANIELS, L. (1963). Responsibility and dependency. *Journal of Abnormal and Social Psychology, 66,* 429–436.

BERKOWITZ, L., & GEEN, R. G. (1967). Stimulus qualities of the target of aggression: A further study. *Journal of Personality and Social Psychology, 5,* 364–368.

BERKOWITZ, L., KLANDERMAN, S. B., & HARRIS, R. (1964). Effects of experimenter awareness and sex of subject and experimenter on reactions to dependency relationships. *Sociometry, 27,* 327–337.

BERLYNE, D. E. (1970). Novelty, complexity, and hedonic value. *Perception and Psychophys-*

ics, 8, 279–286.

BERSCHEID, E. (1985). Interpersonal attraction. In G. Lindzey & E. Aronson (Eds.). *Handbook of social psychology* (3rd ed., Vol. 2, pp. 413–484.). New York: Random House.

BERSCHEID, E., DION, K. K., WALSTER, E. H., & WALSTER, G. W. (1971). Physical attractiveness and dating choice: A test of the matching hypothesis. *Journal of Experimental Social Psychology, 7,* 173–189.

BERSCHEID, E., & PEPLAU, L. A. (1983). The emerging science of relationships. In H. H. Kelley, E. Berscheid, A. Christenson, J. H. Harvey, T. L. Huston, G. Levinger, E. McClintock, L. A. Peplau, & D. R. Peterson, *Close relationships* (pp. 1–19). San Francisco: Freeman.

BERSCHEID, E., & WALSTER , E. H. (1969). *Interpersonal attraction.* Reading, MA: Addison-Wesley.

BERSCHEID, E., & WALSTER, E. H. (1974a). A little bit about love. In T. L. Huston (Ed.), *Foundations of interpersonal attraction* (pp. 356–382). New York: Academic Press.

BERSCHEID, E., & WALSTER, E. H. (1974b). Physical attractiveness. In L. Berkowitz (Ed.), *Advances in experimental social psychology* (Vol. 7, pp. 157–215). New York: Academic Press.

BERSCHEID, E., & WALSTER, E. H. (1978). *Interpersonal attraction* (2nd ed.). Reading, MA: Addison-Wesley.

BICKMAN, L. (1971). The effect of another bystander's ability to help on bystander intervention in an emergency. *Journal of Experimental Social Psychology, 7,* 376–379.

BILLS, R. E., VANCE, E. L., & McLEAN, O. S. (1951). An index of adjustment and values. *Journal of Consulting Psychology, 15,* 257–261.

BIRNBAUM, M. H., & STEGNER, S. E. (1979). Source credibility in social judgment: Bias, expertise, and the judge's point of view. *Journal of Personality and Social Psychology, 37,* 48–74.

BLACK, H. C. (1968). *Black's law dictionary* (4th ed.). St. Paul, MN: West.

BORGATTA, E. F. (1962). A systematic study of interaction process scores, peer and self-assessments, personality and other variables. *Genetic Psychology Monographs, 65,* 219–291.

BORGIDA, E., & HOWARD-PITNEY, B. (1983). Personal involvement and the robustness of perceptual salience effects. *Journal of Personality and Social Psychology, 45,* 560–570.

BREHM, J. W. (1966). *A theory of psychological reactance.* New York: Academic Press.

BREHM, J. W., & COHEN, A. R. (Eds.). (1962). *Explorations in cognitive dissonance.* New York: Wiley.

BREHM, J. W., GATZ, M., GOETHALS, G. R. McCRIMMON, J., & WARD, L. (1970). *Psychological arousal and interpersonal attraction.* Unpublished manuscript, Duke University.

BREHM, M. L., BACK, K. W., & BOGDANOFF, M. D. (1964). A physiological effect of cognitive dissonance under stress and deprivation. *Journal of Abnormal and Social Psychology, 69,* 303–310.

BREHM, S. S., & BREHM, J. W. (1981). *Psychological reactance: A theory of freedom and control.* New York: Academic Press.

BRIGHAM, J. C. (1971). Ethnic stereotypes. *Psychological Bulletin, 76,* 15–38.

BRISLIN, R. W., & LEWIS, S. A. (1968). Dating and physical attractiveness: Replication. *Psychological Reports, 22,* 976.

BROWN, R. (1965). *Social psychology.* Glencoe, IL: Free Press.

BRUNER, J. S. (1957). Going beyond the information given. In J. S. Bruner, E. Brunswik, L. Festinger, F. Heider, K. F. Muenzinger, C. E. Osgood, & D. Rapaport (Eds.), *Contemporary approaches to cognition.* Cambridge, MA: Harvard University Press.

BRUNER, J. S., SHAPIRO, D., & TAGUIRI, R. (1958). The meaning of traits in isolation and in combination. In R. Taguiri & L. Petrullo (Eds.), *Person perception and interpersonal behavior* (pp. 277–288). Stanford, CA: Stanford University Press.

BRUNER, J. S., & TAGUIRI, R. (1954). The perception of people. In G. Lindzey (Ed.), *Handbook of social psychology* (Vol. 2, pp. 634–654). Reading, MA: Addison-Wesley.

BRUNSWIK, E. (1934). *Wahrnemung und Gegenstandwelt*. Leipzig and Vienna: Deuticke.

BRYAN, J. H., & TEST, M. A. (1967). Models and helping: Naturalistic studies in aiding behavior. *Journal of Personality and Social Psychology, 6*, 400–407.

BURNSTEIN, E., & VINOKUR, A. (1977). Persuasive argumentation and social comparison as determinants of attitude polarization. *Journal of Experimental Social Psychology, 13*, 315–332.

BURNSTEIN, E., & WORCHEL, P. (1962). Arbitrariness of frustration and its consequences in aggression in a social situation. *Journal of Personality, 30*, 528–541.

BUSS, A. H. (1961). *The psychology of aggression*. New York: Wiley.

BYRNE, D. (1961). Interpersonal attraction and attitude similarity. *Journal of Abnormal and Social Psychology, 62*, 713–715.

BYRNE, D. (1971). *The attraction paradigm*. New York: Academic Press.

CACIOPPO, J., & PETTY, R. (1983). *Social psychophysiology: A sourcebook*. New York: Guilford.

CALDER, B. J. (1977). An attribution theory of leadership. In B. M. Staw & G. R. Salancik (Eds.), *New directions in organizational behavior* (pp. 179–204). Chicago: St. Clair Press.

CALHOUN, J. B. (1962). Population density and social pathology. *Scientific American, 206*, 139–148.

CAMPBELL, A. (1971). *White attitudes toward black people*. Ann Arbor, MI: Institute for Social Research.

CAMPBELL, D. T., & FISKE, D. W. (1959). Convergent and discriminant validation by the multitrait-multimethod matrix. *Psychological Bulletin, 56*, 81–105.

CAMPBELL, D. T., SIEGMAN, C., & REES, M. B. (1967). Direction-of-wording effects in the relationships between scales. *Psychological Bulletin, 68*, 293–303.

CANNON, W. B. (1927). The James-Lange theory of emotions: A critical examination and an alternative theory. *The American Journal of Psychology, 34*, 106–124.

CANTOR, N., & MISCHEL, W. (1979). Prototypes in person perception. In L. Berkowitz (Ed.), *Advances in experimental social psychology* (Vol. 12, pp. 3–52). New York: Academic Press.

CARDUCCI, B. J., COZBY, P. C., & WARD, C. D. (1974). Sexual arousal and interpersonal evaluations. *Journal of Experimental Social Psychology, 14*, 449–457.

CARLSMITH, J. M., COLLINS, B. E., & HELMREICH, R. L. (1966). Studies in forced compliance: I. The effect of pressure for compliance on attitude change produced by face-to-face role playing and anonymous essay writing. *Journal of Personality and Social Psychology, 4*, 1–13.

CARROLL, J. D., & CHANG, J. (1970). Analysis of individual differences in multidimensional scaling via an N-way generalization of "Eckart-Young" decomposition. *Psychometrika, 35*, 238–319.

CARROLL, J. S., & PAYNE, J. W. (1976). The psychology of the parole decision process: A joint application of attribution theory and information processing psychology. In J. S. Carroll & J. W. Payne (Eds.), *Cognition and social behavior* (pp. 13–32). Hillsdale, NJ: Lawrence Erlbaum Associates.

CARTWRIGHT, D. (1959). A field theoretical conception of power. In D. Cartwright (Ed.), *Studies in social power* (pp. 183–220). Ann Arbor, MI: Institute for Social Research.

CARTWRIGHT, D. (1971). Risk-taking by individuals and groups: An assessment of research employing choice dilemmas. *Journal of Personality and Social Psychology, 20*, 361–378.

CARTWRIGHT, D. (1979). Contemporary social psychology in historical perspective. *Social Psychology Quarterly, 42*, 82–93.

CARTWRIGHT, D., & HARARY, F. (1956). Structural balance: A generalization of Heider's theory. *Psychological Review, 63*, 277–293.

CARTWRIGHT, D., & Zander, A. (Eds.). (1968). *Group dynamics: Research and theory* (3rd. ed.). New York: Harper & Row.

CARVER, C. S., & SCHEIER, M. F. (1981). *Attention and self-regulation: A control-theory approach to human behavior*. New York: Springer-Verlag.

CATER, D., & STRICKLAND, S. (1975). *TV violence and the child: The evolution and fate of the Surgeon General's report.* New York: Russell Sage Foundation.

CHAPMAN, L. J. (1967). Illusory correlation in observational report. *Journal of Verbal Learning and Verbal Behavior, 6,* 151–155.

CHAIKIN, A. L., DERLEGA, V. J., BAYMA, B., & SHAW, J. (1975). Neuroticism and disclosure reciprocity. *Journal of Consulting and Clinical Psychology, 43,* 13–19.

CHRISTIE, R., & GEIS, F. L. (Eds.). (1970). *Studies in Machiavellianism.* New York: Academic Press.

CIALDINI, R. B. (1985). *Influence: Science and practice.* Glenview, IL: Scott, Foresman.

CLARK, K. B., & CLARK, M. P. (1947). Racial identification and racial preference in Negro children. In T. M. Newcomb & E. L. Hartley (Eds.), *Readings in social psychology* (pp. 169–178). New York: Holt.

CLARK, R. D., & WORD, L. E. (1974). Where is the apathetic bystander? Situational characteristics of the emergency. *Journal of Personality and Social Psychology, 29,* 279–287.

COCH, L., & FRENCH, J. R. P., JR. (1948). Overcoming resistance to change. *Human Relations, 1,* 512–532.

COHEN, A. R. (1962). An experiment on small rewards for discrepant compliance and attitude change. In J. W. Brehm & A. R. Cohen (Eds.), *Explorations in cognitive dissonance* (pp. 73–78). New York: Wiley.

COLLINS, B. E., & RAVEN, B. H. (1969). Group structure: Attraction, coalitions, communication, and power. In G. Lindzey & E. Aronson (Eds.), *Handbook of social psychology* (2nd ed., Vol. 4, pp. 102–204). Reading, MA: Addison-Wesley.

COLE, G. F. (Ed.). (1972). *Criminal justice: Law and politics.* Belmont, CA: Wadsworth.

COOK, S. W., KIMBLE, G., HICKS, L., McGUIRE, W. J., SCHOGGEN, P., & SMITH, M. B. (1973). *Ethical principles in the conduct of research with human participants.* Washington, DC: American Psychological Association.

COOLEY, C. H. (1902). *Human nature and the social order.* New York: Scribner's.

COOPER, J., & FAZIO, R. H. (1984). A new look at dissonance theory. In L. Berkowitz (Ed.), *Advances in experimental social psychology* (Vol. 17, pp. 229–266). New York: Academic Press.

COOPERSMITH, S. (1967). *The antecedents of self-esteem.* San Francisco: Freeman.

CRANDALL, V. C., KATKOVSKY, W., & CRANDALL, V. J. (1965). Children's beliefs in their control of reinforcements in intellectual academic achievement behaviors. *Child Development, 36,* 91–109.

CRONBACH, L. J. (1955). Processes affecting scores on "understanding of others" and "assumed similarity." *Psychological Bulletin, 52,* 177–193.

CROSBY, F. (1976). A model of egoistical relative deprivation. *Psychological Review, 83,* 85–113.

CROWNE, D. P., & MARLOWE, D. (1964). *The approval motive.* New York: Wiley.

CROYLE, R. T., & COOPER, J. (1983). Dissonance arousal: Physiological evidence. *Journal of Personality and Social Psychology, 45,* 782–791.

DARLEY, J. M., JR., & BERSCHEID, E. (1967). Increased liking caused by the anticipation of personal contact. *Human Relations, 20,* 29–40.

DARLEY, J. M., & GILBERT, D. T. (1985). Social psychological aspects of environmental psychology. In G. Lindzey & E. Aronson (Eds.), *Handbook of social psychology* (3rd. ed., Vol. 2, pp. 949–991). New York: Random House.

DARLEY, J. M., & GOETHALS, G. R. (1980). People's analyses of the causes of ability-linked performances. In L. Berkowitz, (Ed.), *Advances in experimental social psychology* (Vol. 13, pp. 1–37). New York: Academic Press.

DARLEY, J. M., JR., & LATANÉ, B. (1968). Bystander intervention in emergencies: Diffusion of responsibility. *Journal of Personality and Social Psychology, 8,* 377–383.

DARLEY, J. M., & SHAVER, K. G. (1983). *Psychology and the law: An analysis of assumptions.* Unpublished manuscript, Princeton University, Princeton, NJ.

DARWIN, C. (1872). *The expression of the emotions in man and animals.* London: John

Murray.

DAVIDSON, A. R., & JACCARD, J. J. (1979). Variables that moderate the attitude-behavior relation: Results of a longitudinal survey. *Journal of Personality and Social Psychology, 37,* 1364–1376.

DAVIS, K. C. (1971). *Discretionary justice: A preliminary inquiry.* Urbana, IL: University of Illinois Press.

DEAUX, K., & EMSWILLER, T. (1974). Explanations of successful performance on sex-linked tasks: What is skill for the male is luck for the female. *Journal of Personality and Social Psychology, 29,* 80–85.

DECI, E. L., & RYAN, R. M. (1980). The empirical exploration of intrinsic motivational processes. In L. Berkowitz (Ed.), *Advances in experimental social psychology* (Vol. 13, pp. 39–80). New York: Academic Press.

DEJONG, W. (1979). An examination of self-perception mediation of the foot-in-the-door effect. *Journal of Personality and Social Psychology, 37,* 2221–2239.

DERMER, M., & PYSZCZYNSKI, T. A. (1978). Effects of erotica upon men's loving and liking responses for women they love. *Journal of Personality and Social Psychology, 36,* 1302–1309.

DERMER, M., & THIEL, D. L. (1975). When beauty may fail. *Journal of Personality and Social Psychology, 31,* 1168–1176.

DEUTSCH, M. (1960). The effect of motivational orientation upon threat and suspicion. *Human Relations, 13,* 122–139.

DEUTSCH, M. (1969). Socially relevant science: Reflections on some studies of interpersonal conflict. *American Psychologist, 24,* 1076–1092.

DEUTSCH, M., & GERARD, H. B. (1955). A study of normative and informational social influences on individual judgments. *Journal of Abnormal and Social Psychology, 51,* 629–636.

DEUTSCH, M., & KRAUSS, R. M. (1960). The effect of threat on interpersonal bargaining. *Journal of Abnormal and Social Psychology, 61,* 181–189.

DEUTSCH, M., & KRAUSS, R. M. (1962). Studies of interpersonal bargaining. *Journal of Conflict Resolution, 6,* 52–76.

DIAMOND, S. S. (Ed.). (1979). Simulation research and the law. *Law and Human Behavior, 3*(1/2).

DIENSTBIER, R. A. (1977). Sex and violence: Can research have it both ways? *Journal of Communication, 27,* 176–188.

DIERKING, A. (1978). What should the police do in spouse abuse cases? *Social Action and the Law, 4,* 8.

DILLEHAY, R. C. (1973). On the irrelevance of the classical negative evidence concerning the effect of attitudes on behavior. *American Psychologist, 10,* 887–891.

DION, K. K. (1972). Physical attractiveness and evaluations of children's transgressions. *Journal of Personality and Social Psychology, 24,* 207–213.

DION, K. K., BERSCHEID, E., & WALSTER, E. H. (1972). What is beautiful is good. *Journal of Personality and Social Psychology, 24,* 285–290.

DION, K. K., & STEIN, S. (1978). Physical attractiveness and interpersonal influence. *Journal of Experimental Social Psychology, 14,* 97–108.

DOLLARD, J., DOOB, L. W., MILLER, N. E., MOWRER, O. H., & SEARS, R. R. (1939). *Frustration and aggression.* New Haven, CT: Yale University Press.

DONNERSTEIN, E., & BERKOWITZ, L. (1981). Victim reactions in aggressive-erotic films as a factor in violence against women. *Journal of Personality and Social Psychology, 41,* 710–724.

DOWNS, R. M., & STEA, D. (1977). *Maps in minds: Reflections on cognitive mapping.* New York: Harper & Row.

DUNCAN, S., JR., & NIEDEREHE, G. (1974). On signaling that it's your turn to speak. *Journal of Experimental Social Psychology, 10,* 234–247.

DUVAL, S., & WICKLUND, R. A. (1972). *A theory of objective self-awareness.* New York: Academic Press.

DYCK, R. J., & RULE, B. G. (1978). Effect on retaliation of causal attributions concerning attack. *Journal of Personality and Social Psychology, 36,* 521–529.

EBBESEN, E. B., & KONEČNI, V. J. (1982). Social psychology and the law: A decision-making approach. In V. J. Konečni & E. B. Ebbesen (Eds.), *The criminal justice system: A social psychological analysis* (pp. 3–23). San Francisco: Freeman.

EDWARDS, A. L. (1957). *The social desirability variable in personality assessment and research.* New York: Holt.

EISER, J. R., & STROEBE, W. (1972). *Categorization and social judgement.* New York: Academic Press.

EKMAN, P. (1965). Communication through nonverbal behavior. In S. S. Tomkins & C. E. Izard (Eds.), *Affect, cognition, and personality* (pp. 390–442). New York: Springer.

EKMAN, P., & FREISEN, W. V. (1974). Detecting deception from the body or face. *Journal of Personality and Social Psychology, 29,* 288–298.

EKMAN, P., & OSTER, H. (1979). Facial expressions of emotion. In M. R. Rosenzweig & L. W. Porter (Eds.), *Annual reviews of psychology* (Vol. 30, pp. 527–554). Palo Alto, CA: Annual Reviews.

ELDER, G. H., JR. (1969). Appearance and education in marriage mobility. *American Sociological Review, 34,* 519–533.

ELIG, T. W., & FRIEZE, I. H. (1975). Measuring causal attributions for success and failure. *Journal of Personality and Social Psychology, 37,* 621–634.

ELLISON, K. W., & BUCKHOUT, R. (1981). *Psychology and criminal justice.* New York: Harper & Row.

ELMS, A. C. (1967). Role playing, incentive, and dissonance. *Psychological Bulletin, 68,* 132–148.

ELMS, A. C., JANIS, I. L. (1965). Counter-norm attitudes induced by consonant versus dissonant conditions of role-playing. *Journal of Experimental Research in Personality, 1,* 50–60.

ENZLE, M. E., HANSEN, R. D., & LOWE, C. A. (1975). Causal attribution in the mixed-motive game: Effects of facilitory and inhibitory environmental forces. *Journal of Personality and Social Psychology, 31,* 50–54.

EXLINE, R., THIBAUT, J. W., HICKEY, C. B., & GUMPERT, P. (1970). Visual interaction in relation to Machiavellianism and an unethical act. In R. Christie & F. L. Geis (Eds.), *Studies in Machiavellianism* (pp. 53–75). New York: Academic Press.

FAZIO, R. H., & ZANNA, M. P. (1978). Attitudinal qualities relating to the strength of the attitude-behavior relationship. *Journal of Experimental Social Psychology, 14,* 393–408.

FEHRENBACH, P. A., MILLER, D. J., & THELEN, M. H. (1979). The importance of consistency in modeling behavior upon imitation: A comparison of single and multiple models. *Journal of Personality and Social Psychology, 37,* 1412–1417.

FELLER, W. (1968). *An introduction to probability theory and its applications* (3rd ed.). New York: Wiley.

FENIGSTEIN, A., SCHEIER, M. F., & BUSS, A. H. (1975). Public and private self-consciousness: Assessment and theory. *Journal of Consulting and Clinical Psychology, 43,* 522–527.

FESHBACH, S., & SINGER, R. (1971). *Television and aggression.* San Francisco: Jossey-Bass.

FESTINGER, L. (1950). Informal social communication. *Psychological Review, 57,* 271–282.

FESTINGER, L. (1954). A theory of social comparison processes. *Human Relations, 7,* 117–140.

FESTINGER, L. (1957). *A theory of cognitive dissonance.* Stanford, CA: Stanford University Press.

FESTINGER, L., & CARLSMITH, J. M. (1959). Cognitive consequences of forced compliance. *Journal of Abnormal and Social Psychology, 58,* 203–210.

FESTINGER, L., RIECKEN, H. W., & SCHACHTER, S. (1956). *When prophecy fails.* Minneapolis: University of Minnesota Press.

FESTINGER, L., SCHACHTER, S., & BACK, K. (1950). *Social pressures in informal groups: A study of human factors in housing.* New York: Harper.

FIEDLER, F. E. (1964). A contingency model of leadership effectiveness. In L. Berkowitz

(Ed.), *Advances in experimental social psychology* (Vol. 1, pp. 149–190). New York: Academic Press.

FIEDLER, F. E. (1971). Validation and extension of the contingency model of leadership effectiveness: A review of empirical findings. *Psychological Bulletin, 76,* 128–148.

FINCHAM, F., & JASPARS, J. (1979). Attribution of responsibility to the self and others in children and adults. *Journal of Personality and Social Psychology, 37,* 1589–1602.

FISHBEIN, M., & AJZEN, I. (1975). *Belief, attitude, intention, and behavior: An introduction to theory and research.* Reading, MA: Addison-Wesley.

FISKE, S. T., & TAYLOR, S. E. (1984). *Social cognition.* Reading, MA: Addison-Wesley.

FOLKES, V. S. (1982). Forming relationships and the matching hypothesis. *Personality and Social Psychology Bulletin, 8,* 631–636.

FORGAS, J. P. (1978). Social episodes and social structure in an academic setting: The social environment of an intact group. *Journal of Experimental Social Psychology, 14,* 434–448.

FOSS, R. D., & DEMPSEY, C. B. (1979). Blood donation and the foot-in-the-door technique: A limiting case. *Journal of Personality and Social Psychology, 37,* 580–590.

FRANKEL, M. E. (1972). *Criminal sentences: Law without order.* New York: Hill & Wang.

FREEDMAN, J. L. (1970). Transgression, compliance, and guilt. In J. R. Macaulay & L. Berkowitz (Eds.), *Altruism and helping behavior* (pp. 155–161). New York: Academic Press.

FREEDMAN, J. L. (1975). *Crowding and human behavior.* New York: Viking.

FREEDMAN, J. L., & FRASER, S. C. (1966). Compliance without pressure: The foot-in-the-door technique. *Journal of Personality and Social Psychology, 4,* 195–202.

FRENCH, J. R. P., JR., & RAVEN, B. (1959). The bases of social power. In D. Cartwright (Ed.), *Studies in social power* (pp. 150–167). Ann Arbor, MI: Institute for Social Research.

FREUD, S. (1933). *New introductory lectures on psychoanalysis.* New York: Norton.

FREUD, S. (1950). Why war? In J. Strachey (Ed.), *Collected papers* (Vol. 5, pp. 273–287). London: Hogarth Press.

GALLE, O. R., GOVE, W. R., & MCPHERSON, J. M. (1972). Population density and pathology: What are the relationships for man? *Science, 176,* 23–30.

GALLO, P. S., & MCCLINTOCK, C. G. (1965). Cooperative and competitive behavior in mixed-motive games. *Journal of Conflict Resolution, 9,* 68–78.

GAMSON, W. A. (1968). *Power and discontent.* Homewood, IL: Dorsey.

GEEN, R. B., & QUANTY, M. B. (1977). The catharsis of aggression: An evaluation of a hypothesis. In L. Berkowitz (Ed.), *Advances in experimental social psychology* (Vol. 10, pp. 1–37). New York: Academic Press.

GELMAN, A. M. (1982). Prosecutorial decision-making: The screening process. In V. J. Konečni & E. B. Ebbesen (Eds.), *The criminal justice system: A social psychological analysis* (pp. 235–255). San Francisco: Freeman.

GERARD, H. B., CONOLLEY, E. S., & WILHELMY, R. A. (1974). Compliance, justification, and cognitive change. In L. Berkowitz (Ed.), *Advances in experimental social psychology* (Vol. 7, pp. 217–248). New York: Academic Press.

GERARD, H. B., & MATTHEWSON, G. C. (1966). The effects of severity of initiation on liking for a group: A replication. *Journal of Experimental Social Psychology, 2,* 278–287.

GERGEN, K. J. (1969). *The psychology of behavior exchange.* Reading, MA: Addison-Wesley.

GERGEN, K. J. (1984). Theory of the self: Impasse and evolution. In L. Berkowitz, (Ed.), *Advances in experimental social psychology* (Vol. 17, pp. 49–115). New York: Academic Press.

GIBB, C. A. (1969). Leadership. In G. Lindzey & E. Aronson (Eds.), *Handbook of social psychology* (2nd ed., Vol. 4, pp. 205–282). Reading, MA: Addison-Wesley.

GILBERT, G. M. (1951). Stereotype persistence and change among college students. *Journal of Abnormal and Social Psychology, 46,* 245–254.

GILBERT, M. A., & SHAVER, K. G. (1975, April). *Seriousness of crime, race of prisoner, characteristics of interviewers, and attribution of blame for incarceration.* Paper presented at the meeting of the Southeastern Psychological Association, Atlanta.

GILLIG, P. M., & GREENWALD, A. G. (1974). Is it time to lay the sleeper effect to rest? *Journal of Personality and Social Psychology, 29*, 132–139.

GLASS, D. C., & SINGER, J. E. (1972). *Urban stress.* New York: Academic Press.

GOFFMAN, E. (1959). *The presentation of self in everyday life.* Garden City, NY: Doubleday.

GOLDMAN, A. I. (1970). *A theory of human action.* Englewood Cliffs, NJ: Prentice-Hall.

GOLDSTEIN, J. (1960). Police discretion not to evoke the criminal process: Low visibility decisions in the administration of justice. *Yale Law Journal, 69*, 543–557.

GOULDNER, A. (1960). The norm of reciprocity: A preliminary statement. *American Sociological Review, 25*, 161–178.

GREEN, B. F. (1954). Attitude measurement. In G. Lindzey (Ed.), *Handbook of social psychology* (Vol. 1, pp. 335–369). Cambridge, MA: Addison-Wesley.

GREENBERG, M. S., & RUBACK, R. B. (1982). *Social psychology of the criminal justice system.* Monterey, CA: Brooks/Cole.

GREENBERG, M. S., & RUBACK, R. B. (Eds.). (1984). Criminal victimization. *Journal of Social Issues, 40*(1).

GROSS, N., MASON, W. S., & MCEACHERN, A. (1957). *Explorations in role analysis: Studies of the school superintendency role.* New York: Wiley.

GRUDER, C. L., COOK, T. D., HENNIGAN, K. M., FLAY, B. R., ALESSIS, C., & HALAMAJ, J. (1978). Empirical tests of the absolute sleeper effect predicted from the discounting cue hypothesis. *Journal of Personality and Social Psychology, 36*, 1061–1074.

HALL, E. T. (1959). *The silent language.* New York: Fawcett.

HALL, E. T. (1966). *The hidden dimension.* New York: Doubleday.

HALL, J. (1978). Gender effects in decoding nonverbal cues. *Psychological Bulletin, 85*, 845–857.

HALPIN, A. W. (1966). *Theory and research in administration.* New York: Macmillan.

HAMILL, R., WILSON, T. D., & NISBETT, R. E. (1980). Insensitivity to sample bias: Generalizing from atypical cases. *Journal of Personality and Social Psychology, 39*, 578–589.

HAMILTON, D. L. (Ed.). (1981). *Cognitive processes in stereotyping and intergroup behavior,* Hillsdale, NJ: Lawrence Erlbaum Associates.

HAMILTON, D. L., DUGAN, P. M., & TROLIER, T. K. (1985). The formation of stereotypic beliefs: Further evidence for distinctiveness-based illusory correlations. *Journal of Personality and Social Psychology, 48*, 5–17.

HANEY, C., BANKS, C., & ZIMBARDO, P. G. (1973). Interpersonal dynamics in a simulated prison. *International Journal of Criminology and Penology, 1*, 69–97.

HANSON, D. J., & VLEEMING, R. G. (1982). Machiavellianism: A bibliography. *JSAS Catalog of Selected Documents in Psychology, 12*, 21 (Ms. No. 2448).

HARDING, J., KUTNER, B., PROSHANSKY, H. M., & CHEIN, I. (1969). Prejudice and ethnic relations. In G. Lindzey & E. Aronson (Eds.), *Handbook of social psychology* (2nd ed., Vol. 5, pp. 1–76). Reading, MA: Addison-Wesley.

HARRISON, A. A. (1977). Mere exposure. In L. Berkowitz (Ed.), *Advances in experimental social psychology* (Vol. 10, pp. 39–83). New York: Academic Press.

HART, H. L. A. (1968). *Punishment and responsibility.* New York: Oxford University Press.

HEIDER, F. (1958). *The psychology of interpersonal relations.* New York: Wiley.

HEMPHILL, J. K. (1950). *Leader behavior description.* Columbus: Ohio State University Personnel Research Board.

HOLLANDER, E. P. (1985). Leadership and power. In G. Lindzey & E. Aronson (Eds.), *Handbook of social psychology* (3rd ed., Vol. 2, pp. 485–537). New York: Random House.

HOLTON, G. (1973). *Thematic origins of scientific revolutions.* Cambridge, MA: Harvard University Press.

HOMANS, G. C. (1961). *Social behavior: Its elementary forms.* New York: Harcourt Brace.

HORNER, M. (1972). Toward an understanding of achievement-related conflicts in women. *Journal of Social Issues, 28*, 157–175.

HOVLAND, C. I. (Ed.). (1957). *The order of presentation in persuasion.* New Haven, CT: Yale University Press.

HOVLAND, C. I., JANIS, I. L., & KELLEY, H. H. (1953). *Communication and persuasion.* New Haven, CT: Yale University Press.

HOVLAND, C. I., & ROSENBERG, M. J. (Eds.). (1960). *Attitude organization and change.* New Haven, CT: Yale University Press.

HOVLAND, C. I., & WEISS, W. (1951). The influence of source credibility on communication effectiveness. *Public Opinion Quarterly, 15,* 635–650.

HUSTON, T. L. (1973). Ambiguity of acceptance, social desirability, and dating choice. *Journal of Experimental Social Psychology, 9,* 32–42.

HUSTON, T. L. (Ed.). (1974). *Foundations of interpersonal attraction.* New York: Academic Press.

HUSTON, T. L., & LEVINGER, G. (1978). Interpersonal attraction and relationships. *Annual Review of Psychology, 29,* 115–156.

HYMAN, H. (1942). The psychology of status. *Archives of Psychology,* No. 269.

INSKO, C. A. (1984). Balance theory, the Jordan paradigm, and the Wiest tetrahedron. In L. Berkowitz (Ed.), *Advances in experimental social psychology* (Vol. 18, pp. 89–140). New York: Academic Press.

ISENBERG, D. J. (1986). Group polarization: A critical review and meta-analysis. *Journal of Personality and Social Psychology, 50,* 1141–1151.

ITTELSON, W. H., PROSHANSKY, H. M., RIVLIN, L. G., & WINKEL, G. H. (1974). *An introduction to environmental psychology.* New York: Holt, Rinehart & Winston.

IZARD, C. E. (1971). *The face of emotion.* New York: Appleton-Century-Crofts.

IZARD, C. E. (1977). *Human emotions.* New York: Plenum.

JACOBS, R. C., & CAMPBELL, D. T. (1961). The perpetuation of an arbitrary tradition through several generations of a laboratory microculture. *Journal of Abnormal and Social Psychology, 62,* 649–658.

JAMES, W. (1892). *Psychology: The briefer course.* New York: Holt.

JAMES, W., & LANGE, G. C. (1922). *The emotions.* Baltimore: Williams & Wilkins.

JANIS, I. L. (1968). Attitude change via role-playing. In R. P. Abelson, E. Aronson, W. J. McGuire, T. M. Newcomb, M. J. Rosenberg, & P. H. Tannenbaum (Eds.), *Theories of cognitive consistency: A sourcebook* (pp. 810–818). Chicago: Rand McNally.

JANIS, I. L. (1972). *Victims of groupthink: A psychological study of foreign policy decisions and fiascoes.* Boston: Houghton-Mifflin.

JANIS, I. L., & FIELD, P. (1959). Sex differences and personality factors related to persuasibility. In C. I. Hovland & I. L. Janis (Eds.), *Personality and persuasibility* (pp. 55–68). New Haven, CT: Yale University Press.

JANIS, I. L., & GILMORE, J. B. (1965). The influence of incentive conditions on the success of role playing in modifying attitudes. *Journal of Personality and Social Psychology, 1,* 17–27.

JASPARS, J., HEWSTONE, M., & FINCHAM, F. D. (1983). Attribution theory and research: The state of the art. In J. Jaspars, F. D. Fincham, & M. Hewstone (Eds.), *Attribution theory and research: Conceptual, developmental and social dimensions* (pp. 3–36). London: Academic Press.

JOHNSON, R. N. (1972). *Aggression in man and animals.* Philadelphia: Saunders.

JONES, E. E. (1964). *Ingratiation: A social-psychological analysis.* New York: Appleton-Century-Crofts.

JONES, E. E. (1979). The rocky road from acts to dispositions. *American Psychologist, 34,* 107–117.

JONES, E. E. (1985). Major developments in social psychology since 1930. In G. Lindzey & E. Aronson (Eds.), *Handbook of social psychology* (Vol. 1, pp. 47–107). New York: Random House.

JONES, E. E., & DAVIS, K. E. (1965). From acts to dispositions: The attribution process in person perception. In L. Berkowitz (Ed.), *Advances in experimental social psychology* (Vol. 2, pp. 219–266). New York: Academic Press.

JONES, E. E., & GERARD, H. B. (1967). *Foundations of social psychology.* New York: Wiley.

JONES, E. E., & McGILLIS, D. (1976). Correspondent inferences and the attribution cube: A comparative reappraisal. In J. H. Harvey, W. J. Ickes, & R. F. Kidd (Eds.), *New directions in attribution research* (Vol. 1, pp. 389–420). Hillsdale, NJ: Lawrence Erlbaum Associates.

JONES, E. E., & NISBETT, R. E. (1972). The actor and the observer: divergent perceptions of the causes of behavior. In E. E. Jones, D. E. Kanouse, H. H. Kelley, R. E. Nisbett, S. Valins, & B. Weiner (Eds.), *Attribution: Perceiving the causes of behavior* (pp. 79–94). Morristown, NJ: General Learning Press.

JONES, E. E., & PITTMAN, T. S. (1982). Toward a general theory of strategic self-presentation. In J. Suls (Ed.), *Psychological perspectives on the self* (pp. 231–262). Hillsdale, NJ: Lawrence Erlbaum Associates.

JONES, J. M. (1972). *Prejudice and racism.* Reading, MA: Addison-Wesley.

JONES, R. A., LINDER, D. E., KIESLER, C. A., ZANNA, M. P., & BREHM, J. W. (1968). Internal states or external stimuli: Observers' attitude judgments and the dissonance/self-perception theory controversy. *Journal of Experimental Social Psychology, 4,* 247–269.

JOURARD, S. (1964). *Self-disclosure and well-being.* Princeton, NJ: Van Nostrand.

JOURARD, S. (1971). *Self-disclosure: An experimental analysis of the transparent self.* New York: Wiley.

JUNG, C. G. (1953). *The collected works of C. G. Jung. Vol. 12: Psychology and alchemy.* New York: Pantheon.

KAHLE, L. R., & BERMAN, J. J. (1979). Attitudes cause behaviors: A cross-lagged panel analysis. *Journal of Personality and Social Psychology, 37,* 315–321.

KAHNEMAN, D., & TVERSKY, A. (1973). On the psychology of prediction. *Psychological Review, 80,* 237–251.

KALVEN, H., JR., & ZEISEL, H. (1966). *The American jury.* Boston: Little, Brown.

KAPLAN, M. F. (1975). Information integration in social judgment: Interaction of judge and informational components. In M. F. Kaplan & S. Schwartz (Eds.), *Human judgment and decision processes* (pp. 139–172). New York: Academic Press.

KARLINS, M., COFFMAN, T. L., & WALTERS, G. (1969). On the fading of social stereotypes: Studies in three generations of college students. *Journal of Personality and Social Psychology, 13,* 1–16.

KATZ, D., & BRALY, K. W. (1933). Racial stereotypes of one hundred college students. *Journal of Abnormal and Social Psychology, 28,* 282–290.

KATZ, D., & KAHN, R. L. (1966). *The social psychology of organizations.* New York: Wiley.

KATZ, D., & STOTLAND, E. (1959). A preliminary statement to a theory of attitude structure and change. In S. Koch (Ed.), *Psychology: Study of a science* (Vol. 3, pp. 423–475). New York: McGraw-Hill.

KAUFMANN, H. (1970). *Aggression and altruism.* New York: Holt, Rinehart & Winston.

KELLEY, H. H. (1950). The warm-cold variable in first impressions of persons. *Journal of Personality, 18,* 431–439.

KELLEY, H. H. (1952). The two functions of reference groups. In G. E. Swanson, T. M. Newcomb, & E. L. Hartley (Eds.), *Readings in social psychology* (2nd ed., pp. 410–414). New York: Holt, Rinehart & Winston.

KELLEY, H. H. (1967). Attribution theory in social psychology. In D. Levine (Ed.), *Nebraska symposium on motivation 1967* (pp. 192–238). Lincoln, NE: University of Nebraska Press.

KELLEY, H. H. (1973). The processes of causal attribution. *American Psychologist, 28,* 107–128.

KELLEY, H. H., BERSCHEID, E., CHRISTENSEN, A., HARVEY, J. H., HUSTON, T. L., LEVINGER, G., McCLINTOCK, E., PEPLAU, L. A., & PETERSON, D. R. (1983). *Close relationships.* San Francisco: Freeman.

KELLEY, H. H., & THIBAUT, J. W. (1969). Group problem solving. In G. Lindzey & E. Aronson (Eds.), *Handbook of social psychology* (2nd ed., Vol. 4, pp. 1–101). Reading, MA: Addison-Wesley.

KELLEY, H. H., & THIBAUT, J. W. (1978). *Interpersonal relations: A theory of interdepend-*

ence. New York: Wiley.

KELMAN, H. C. (1961). Processes of opinion change. *Public Opinion Quarterly, 25,* 57–78.

KENNY, D. A. (1979). *Correlation and causality.* New York: Wiley-Interscience.

KENRICK, D. T., CIALDINI, R. B., & LINDER, D. E. (1979). Misattribution under fear-producing circumstances: Four failures to replicate. *Personality and Social Psychology Bulletin, 5,* 329–334.

KERCKHOFF, A. C., & DAVIS, K. E. (1962). Value consensus and need complementarity in mate selection. *American Sociological Review, 27,* 295–303.

KIDDER, L. H., & JUDD, C. M. (1986). *Research methods in social relations* (5th ed.). New York: Holt, Rinehart & Winston.

KIESLER, C. A., & KIESLER, S. B. (1969). *Conformity.* Reading, MA: Addison-Wesley.

KIHLSTROM, J. F., & CANTOR, N. (1984). Mental representations of the self. In L. Berkowitz, (Ed.), *Advances in experimental social psychology* (Vol. 17, pp. 2–47). New York: Academic Press.

KINZEL, A. (1970). Body buffer zone in violent prisoners. *American Journal of Psychiatry, 127,* 59–64.

KLOPFER, P. H. (1969). *Habitats and territories.* New York: Basic Books.

KOGAN, N., & WALLACH, M. A. (1965). *Risk-taking: A study in cognition and personality.* New York: Holt.

KOMORITA, S. S. (1984). Coalition bargaining. In L. Berkowitz (Ed.), *Advances in experimental social psychology* (Vol. 18, pp. 183–245). New York: Academic Press.

KONEČNI, V. J., & EBBESEN, E. B. (1982). *The criminal justice system: A social psychological analysis.* San Francisco: Freeman.

KRAUT, R. E., & JOHNSTON, R. E. (1979). Social and emotional messages of smiling: An ethological approach. *Journal of Personality and Social Psychology, 37,* 1539–1553.

KREBS, D. L., & MILLER, D. T. (1985). Altruism and aggression. In G. Lindzey & E. Aronson (Eds.), *Handbook of social psychology* (3rd ed., Vol. 2, pp. 1–71). New York: Random House.

KUHN, M. H., & MCPARTLAND, T. S. (1954). An empirical investigation of self-attitudes. *American Sociological Review, 19,* 68–76.

KUHN, T. S. (1962). *The structure of scientific revolutions.* Chicago: University of Chicago Press.

LABOV, W. (1970). The logic of nonstandard English. In F. Williams (Ed.), *Language and poverty: Perspectives on a theme* (pp. 153–189). Chicago: Markham.

LAFAVE, W. R. (1965). *Arrest: The decision to take a suspect into custody.* Boston: Little Brown.

LAIRD, J. D. (1974). Self-attribution of emotion: The effects of expressive behavior on the quality of emotional experience. *Journal of Personality and Social Psychology, 29,* 475–486.

LAIRD, J. D. (1984). The real role of facial response in the experience of emotion: A reply to Tourangeau and Ellsworth, and others. *Journal of Personality and Social Psychology, 47,* 909–917.

LANGER, E. J. (1978). Rethinking the role of thought in social interaction. In J. H. Harvey, W. Ickes, & R. F. Kidd (Eds.), *New directions in attribution research* (Vol. 2, pp. 36–58). Hillsdale, NJ: Lawrence Erlbaum Associates.

LANZETTA, J. T., CARTWRIGHT-SMITH, J., & KLECK, R. E. (1976). Effects of nonverbal dissimulation on emotional experience and autonomic arousal. *Journal of Personality and Social Psychology, 33,* 354–370.

LAPIERE, S. T. (1934). Attitudes vs. actions. *Social Forces, 13,* 230–237.

LARSEN, O. N. (Eds.). (1968). *Violence and the mass media.* New York: Harper & Row.

LASSWELL, H. D. (1948). The structure and function of communication in society. In L. Bryson (Ed.), *The communication of ideas.* New York: Harper.

LATANÉ, B., & DARLEY, J. M., JR. (1970). *The unresponsive bystander: Why doesn't he help?* New York: Appleton-Century-Crofts.

LEAVITT, H. J. (1951). Some effects of certain communication patterns on group performance.

Journal of Abnormal and Social Psychology, 46, 38–50.

LeBon, G. (1985). *Psychologie des foules* [The crowd]. Paris: F. Olean.

Lefcourt, H. M. (1976). *Locus of control: Current trends in theory and research*. Hillsdale, NJ: Lawrence Erlbaum Associates.

Lefcourt, H. M. (Ed.). (1981). *Research with the locus of control concept* (Vol. 1). New York: Academic Press.

Lepper, M. R., & Greene, D. (Eds.). (1978). *The hidden costs of reward*. Hillsdale, NJ: Lawrence Erlbaum Associates.

Lepper, M. R., Greene, D., & Nisbett, R. E. (1973). Undermining children's intrinsic interest with extrinsic rewards: A test of the overjustification hypothesis. *Journal of Personality and Social Psychology, 28*, 129–137.

Lerner, M. J., & Miller, D. T. (1978). Just world research and the attribution process: Looking back and ahead. *Psychological Bulletin, 85*, 1030–1051.

Lerner, M. J., & Simmons, C. H. (1966). Observers' reaction to the "innocent victim": Compassion or rejection? *Journal of Personality and Social Psychology, 4*, 203–210.

Leventhal, G. S., & Michaels, J. W. (1969). Extending the equity model: Perception of inputs and allocation of reward as a function of duration and quantity of performance. *Journal of Personality and Social Psychology, 12*, 303–309.

Leventhal, H. (1974). Emotions: A basic problem for social psychology. In C. Nemeth (Ed.), *Social psychology: Classic and contemporary integrations* (pp. 1–51). Chicago: Rand McNally.

Levine, F. J., & Tapp, J. L. (1982). Eyewitness identification: Problems and pitfalls. In V. J. Konečni & E. B. Ebbesen (Eds.), *The criminal justice system: A social psychological analysis* (pp. 99–127). San Francisco: Freeman.

Levinger, G. (1964). Note on need complementarity in marriage. *Psychological Bulletin, 61*, 153–157.

Levinger, G. (1983). Development and change. In Kelley, H. H., Berscheid, E., Christensen, A., Harvey, J. H., Huston, T. L., Levinger, G. McClintock, E., Peplau, L. A., & Peterson, D. R. (1983). *Close relationships* (pp. 315–359). San Francisco: Freeman.

Lewin, K. (1933). Environmental forces. In C. Murchison (Ed.), *A handbook of child psychology* (2nd ed., rev., pp. 590–625). Worcester, MA: Clark University Press.

Lewin, K. (1942). Field theory of learning. In National Society for the Study of Education *Yearbook* (Vol. 41, pt. 2, pp. 215–242). Washington, DC: Author.

Lewin, K. (1947). Frontiers in group dynamics: Concept, method, and reality in social science; social equilibria and social change. *Human Relations, 1*, 5–42.

Lewin, K. (1951). Problems of research in social psychology. In D. Cartwright (Ed.), *Field theory in social science: Selected theoretical papers by Kurt Lewin* (pp. 155–169). New York: Harper & Row.

Lewin, K. (1958). Group decision and social change. In E. E. Maccoby, T. M. Newcomb, & E. L. Hartley (Eds.), *Readings in social psychology* (3rd ed., pp. 197–212). New York: Holt, Rinehart & Winston.

Lewin, K., Dembo, T., Festinger, L., & Sears, R. S. (1944). Level of aspiration. In J. McV. Hunt (Ed.), *Personality and the behavior disorders* (Vol. 1, pp. 333–378). New York: Ronald Press.

Lewin, K., Lippitt, R., & White, R. K. (1939). Patterns of aggressive behavior in experimentally created "social climates." *Journal of Social Psychology, 10*, 271–299.

Liebert, R. M., Neale, J. M., & Davidson, E. S. (1973). *The early window: The effects of television on children and youth*. New York: Pergamon.

Likert, R. (1932). A technique for the measurement of attitudes. *Archives of Psychology*, No. 140, 5–53.

Linder, D. E., Cooper, J., & Jones, E. E. (1967). Decision freedom as a determinant of the role of incentive magnitude in attitude change. *Journal of Personality and Social Psychology, 6*, 245–254.

Lindzey, G., & Aronson, E. (Eds.). (1968–1969). *Handbook of social psychology* (2nd ed.,

Vols. 1–5). Reading, MA: Addison-Wesley.

LINDZEY, G., & ARONSON, E. (Eds.). (1985). *Handbook of social psychology* (3rd ed., Vols. 1–2). New York: Random House.

LIPPMAN, W. (1922). *Public opinion.* New York: Harcourt, Brace.

LOFTUS, E. F. (1979). *Eyewitness testimony.* Cambridge, MA: Harvard University Press.

LORENZ, K. (1966). *On aggression.* New York: Harcourt, Brace, & World.

LOTT, A. J., & LOTT, B. E. (1960). The formation of positive attitudes toward group members. *Journal of Abnormal and Social Psychology, 61,* 297–300.

LUCE, R. D., & RAIFFA, H. (1957). *Games and decisions.* New York: Wiley.

LUCHINS, A. S. (1957). Primacy-recency in impression formation. In C. I. Hovland (Ed.), *The order of presentation in persuasion* (pp. 33–61). New Haven, CT: Yale University Press.

LYNCH, J. G., JR., & COHEN, J. L. (1978). The use of subjective expected utility theory as an aid to understanding variables that influence helping behavior. *Journal of Personality and Social Psychology, 36,* 1138–1151.

LYNCH, K. (1960). *The image of the city.* Cambridge, MA: MIT University Press.

MACAULAY, J. R. (1970). A shill for charity. In J. R. Macaulay & L. Berkowitz (Eds.), *Altruism and helping behavior* (pp. 43–59). New York: Academic Press.

MACAULAY, J. R., & BERKOWITZ, L. (Eds.). (1970). *Altruism and helping behavior.* New York: Academic Press.

MACHIAVELLI, N. (1952). The prince (W. K. Marriott, Trans.). In R. M. Hutchins (Ed.), *Great books of the western world* (Vol. 23, pp. 3–37). Chicago: Encyclopaedia Britannica. (Original work published 1532)

MAHL, G. F. (1957). *Speech disturbances and emotional verbal content in initial interviews.* Paper presented at the meeting of the Eastern Psychological Association.

MAHONE, C. H. (1960). Fear of failure in unrealistic vocational aspiration. *Journal of Abnormal and Social Psychology, 60,* 253–261.

MALAMUTH, N. M., & DONNERSTEIN, E. (1982). The effects of aggressive-pornographic mass media stimuli. In L. Berkowitz (Ed.), *Advances in experimental social psychology* (Vol. 15, pp. 103–136). New York: Academic Press.

MANDLER, G., & SARASON, S. (1952). A study of anxiety and learning. *Journal of Abnormal and Social Psychology, 47,* 166–173.

MARLOWE, D., GERGEN, K. J., & DOOB, A. N. (1966). Opponent's personality, expectation of social interaction, and interpersonal bargaining. *Journal of Personality and Social Psychology, 3,* 206–213.

MARROW, A. J. (1969). *The practical theorist: The life and work of Kurt Lewin.* New York: Basic Books.

MASLOW, A. (1961). Peak experiences as acute identity-experiences. *American Journal of Psychoanalysis, 21,* 254–260.

MCARTHUR, L. A. (1972). The how and the what of why: Some determinants and consequences of causal attribution. *Journal of Personality and Social Psychology, 22,* 171–193.

MCCALLUM, D. M., HARRING, K., GILMORE, R., DRENAN, S., CHASE, J. P., INSKO, C. A., & THIBAUT, J. W. (1985). Competition and cooperation between groups and between individuals. *Journal of Experimental Social Psychology, 21,* 301–320.

MCCAULEY, C., & STITT, C. L. (1978). An individual and quantitative measure of stereotypes. *Journal of Personality and Social Psychology, 36,* 929–940.

MCCLELLAND, D. C., ATKINSON, J. W., CLARK, R. A., & LOWELL, E. L. (1953). *The achievement motive.* New York: Appleton-Century-Crofts.

MCDOUGALL, W. (1908). *An introduction to social psychology.* London: Methuen.

MCGUIRE, W. J. (1960). A syllogistic analysis of cognitive relationships. In M. J. Rosenberg & C. I. Hovland (Eds.), *Attitude organization and change* (pp. 65–111). New Haven, CT: Yale University Press.

MCGUIRE, W. J. (1964). Inducing resistance to persuasion: Some contemporary approaches. In L. Berkowitz (Ed.), *Advances in experimental social psychology* (Vol. 1, pp. 191–229). New York: Academic Press.

McGuire, W. J. (1966). The current status of cognitive consistency theories. In S. Feldman (Ed.), *Cognitive consistency: Motivational antecedents and behavioral consequents* (pp. 1–46). New York: Academic Press.

McGuire, W. J. (1968). The structure of human thought. In R. P. Abelson, E. Aronson, W. J. McGuire, T. M. Newcomb, M. J. Rosenberg, & P. H. Tannenbaum (Eds.), *Theories of cognitive consistency: A sourcebook* (pp. 140–164). Chicago: Rand McNally.

McGuire, W. J. (1985). Attitudes and attitude change. In G. Lindzey & E. Aronson (Eds.), *Handbook of social psychology* (3rd ed., Vol. 2., pp. 233–346). New York: Random House.

McGuire, W. J., McGuire, C. V., & Winton, W. (1979). Effects of household sex composition on the salience of one's gender in the spontaneous self-concept. *Journal of Experimental Social Psychology, 15,* 77–90.

McGuire, W. J., & Papageorgis, D. (1961). The relative efficacy of various types of prior belief-defense in producing immunity against persuasion. *Journal of Abnormal and Social Psychology, 62,* 327–337.

Mead, G. H. (1934). *Mind, self, and society.* Chicago: University of Chicago Press.

Mehrabian, A. (1968). Inference of attitudes from the posture, orientation, and distance of a communicator. *Journal of Consulting and Clinical Psychology, 32,* 296–308.

Mehrabian, A. (1969). Measures of achieving tendency. *Educational and Psychological Measurement, 29,* 445–451.

Merton, R. K. (1948). The self-fulfilling prophecy. *Antioch Review, 8,* 193–210.

Merton, R. K. (1957). *Social theory and social structure* (rev. ed.). Glencoe, IL: Free Press.

Messé, L. A., & Lane, I. M. (1974). Rediscovering the need for multiple operations: A reply to Austin and Susmilch. *Journal of Personality and Social Psychology, 30,* 405–408.

Messé, L. A., & Sivacek, J. M. (1979). Predictions of others' responses in a mixed-motive game: Self-justification or false consensus? *Journal of Personality and Social Psychology, 37,* 602–607.

Mill, J. S. (1956). *On liberty.* Indianapolis, IN: Bobbs-Merrill. (Original work published 1859)

Miller, N. E. (1941). The frustration-aggression hypothesis. *Psychological Review, 48,* 337–342.

Milgram, S. (1963). Behavioral study of obedience. *Journal of Abnormal and Social Psychology, 67,* 371–378.

Milgram, S. (1964). Issues in the study of obedience: A reply to Baumrind. *American Psychologist, 19,* 848–852.

Milgram, S. (1965). Some conditions of obedience and disobedience to authority. *Human Relations, 18,* 57–76.

Milgram, S. (1976). Psychological maps of Paris. In H. M. Proshansky, W. H. Ittelson, & L. G. Rivlin (Eds.), *Environmental psychology: People and their physical settings* (2nd ed.). New York: Holt, Rinehart & Winston.

Monahan, L., Kuhn, M., & Shaver, P. (1974). Intrapsychic vs. cultural explanations of the "fear of success" motive. *Journal of Personality and Social Psychology, 29,* 60–64.

Montagu, M. F. A. (Ed.). (1968). *Man and aggression.* London: Oxford University Press.

Moreland, R. L., & Levine, J. M. (1983). Socialization in small groups: Temporal changes in individual-group relations. In L. Berkowitz (Ed.), *Advances in experimental social psychology* (Vol. 15, pp. 137–192). New York: Academic Press.

Moreno, J. L. (1934). *Who shall survive?* Washington, DC: Nervous and Mental Diseases Monograph, No. 58.

Morris, J. L. (1966). Propensity for risk taking as a determinant of vocational choice: An extension of the theory of achievement motivation. *Journal of Personality and Social Psychology, 3,* 328–335.

Moscovici, S. (1985). Social influence and conformity. In G. Lindzey & E. Aronson (Eds.), *Handbook of social psychology* (3rd ed., Vol. 2, pp. 347–412). New York: Random House.

Moscovici, S., & Zavalloni, M. (1969). The group as a polarizer of attitudes. *Journal of Personality and Social Psychology, 12,* 125–135.

Moyer, K. E. (1967). *Kinds of aggression and their physiological basis.* (Report No. 67-12.)

Pittsburgh, PA: Carnegie-Mellon University, Department of Psychology.

MURCHISON, C. (Ed.). (1935). *Handbook of social psychology*. Worcester, MA: Clark University Press.

MURRAY, H. A. (1938). *Explorations in personality*. New York: Oxford University Press.

MURSTEIN, B. I. (Ed.). (1971). *Theories of attraction and love*. New York: Springer.

MYERS, D. G., & LAMM, H. (1976). The group polarization phenomenon. *Psychological Bulletin, 83*, 602–627.

National District Attorneys Association. (1977). *National prosecution standards*. Washington, DC: Author.

NEMETH, C. (1972). A critical analysis of research utilizing the Prisoner's Dilemma paradigm for the study of bargaining. In L. Berkowitz (Ed.), *Advances in experimental social psychology* (Vol. 6, pp. 203–234). New York: Academic Press.

NEWCOMB, T. M. (1943). *Personality and social change*. New York: Dryden.

NEWCOMB, T. M. (1961). *The acquaintance process*. New York: Holt, Rinehart & Winston.

NEWCOMB, T. M. (1978). The acquaintance process: Looking mainly backward. *Journal of Personality and Social Psychology, 36*, 1075–1083.

NISBETT, R. E., & SCHACHTER, S. (1966). Cognitive manipulation of pain. *Journal of Experimental Social Psychology, 2*, 227–236.

NISBETT, R. E., & VALINS, S. (1971). Perceiving the causes of one's own behavior. In E. E. Jones, D. A. Kanouse, H. H. Kelley, R. E. Nisbett, S. Valins, & B. Weiner (Eds.), *Attribution: Perceiving the causes of behavior* (pp. 63–78). Morristown, NJ: General Learning Press.

NOVAK, D., & LERNER, M. J. (1968). Rejection as a consequence of perceived similarity. *Journal of Personality and Social Psychology, 9*, 147–152.

OPTON, E. M. (1975). Institutional behavior modification as a fraud and a sham. *Arizona Law Review, 17*, 20–28.

ORNE, M. T. (1959, September). *The demand characteristics of an experimental design and their implications*. Paper presented at the meeting of the American Psychological Association, Cincinnati.

ORNE, M. T. (1962). On the social psychology of the psychological experiment: With particular reference to demand characteristics and their implications. *American Psychologist, 17*, 776–783.

OSGOOD, C. E., SUCI, G. J., & TANNENBAUM, P. H. (1957). *The measurement of meaning*. Urbana, IL: University of Illinois Press.

OSGOOD, C. E., & TANNENBAUM, P. H. (1955). The principle of congruity in the prediction of attitude change. *Psychological Review, 62*, 42–55.

OSKAMP, S. (1972). Effects of programmed strategies on cooperation in the Prisoner's Dilemma and other mixed-motive games. In L. S. Wrightsman, J. O'Conner, & N. Baker (Eds.), *Cooperation and competition: Readings on mixed-motive games* (pp. 147–189). Monterey, CA: Brooks/Cole.

PARKE, R. D., BERKOWITZ, L., LEYENS, J. P., WEST, S. G., & SEBASTIAN, R. J. (1977). Some effects of violent and nonviolent movies on the behavior of juvenile delinquents. In L. Berkowitz (Ed.), *Advances in experimental social psychology* (Vol. 10, pp. 135–172). New York: Academic Press.

PASSINI, F. T., & NORMAN, W. T. (1966). A universal conception of personality structure? *Journal of Personality and Social Psychology, 4*, 44–49.

PAULHUS, D. (1983). Sphere-specific measures of perceived control. *Journal of Personality and Social Psychology, 44*, 1253–1265.

PEPLAU, L. A. (1983). Roles and gender. In H. H. Kelley, E. Berscheid, A. Christensen, J. H. Harvey, T. L. Huston, G. Levinger, E. McClintock, L. A. Peplau, & D. R. Peterson, *Close relationships* (pp. 220–264). San Francisco: Freeman.

PETTIGREW, T. F. (1967). Social evaluation theory: Convergences and applications. In D. Levine (Ed.), *Nebraska symposium on motivation 1967* (Vol. 15, pp. 241–311). Lincoln, NE: University of Nebraska Press.

PETTIGREW, T. F. (1971). *Racially separate or together?* New York: McGraw-Hill.

PETTY, R. E., & CACIOPPO, J. T. (1981). *Attitudes and persuasion: Classic and contemporary approaches.* Dubuque, IA: W. C. Brown.

PILIAVIN, I. M., RODIN, J., & PILIAVIN, J. A. (1969). Good samaritanism: An underground phenomenon? *Journal of Personality and Social Psychology, 13,* 289–299.

PILIAVIN, J. A., & PILIAVIN, I. M. (1972). Effects of blood on reactions to a victim. *Journal of Personality and Social Psychology, 23,* 353–361.

PILIAVIN, J. A., PILIAVIN, I. M., LOEWENTON, E. P., MCCAULEY, C., & HAMMOND, P. (1969). On observers' reproductions of dissonance effects: The right answers for the wrong reasons? *Journal of Personality and Social Psychology, 13,* 98–106.

PLUTCHIK, R. (1980). *Emotion: A psychoevolutionary synthesis.* New York: Harper and Row.

PORIER, G. W., & LOTT, A. J. (1967). Galvanic skin responses and prejudice. *Journal of Personality and Social Psychology, 5,* 253–259.

President's Commission on Law Enforcement and Administration of Justice. (1967). *The challenge of crime in a free society.* Washington, DC: U. S. Government Printing Office.

PRUITT, D. G. (1968). Reciprocity and credit building in a laboratory dyad. *Journal of Personality and Social Psychology, 8,* 143–147.

PRUITT, D. G. (1971). Choice shifts in group discussion: An introductory review. *Journal of Personality and Social Psychology, 20,* 339–360.

RAWLS, J. (1971). *A theory of justice.* Cambridge, MA: Belknap Press.

RIGGIO, R. E., & FRIEDMAN, H. S. (1983). Individual differences and cues to deception. *Journal of Personality and Social Psychology, 45,* 899–915.

RODIN, J., SOLOMON, S. K., & METCALF, J. (1978). Role of control in mediating perceptions of density. *Journal of Personality and Social Psychology, 36,* 988–999.

ROETHLISBERGER, F. J., & DICKSON, W. J. (1939). *Management and the worker: An account of a research program conducted by the Western Electric Company, Hawthorne Works, Chicago.* Cambridge, MA: Harvard University Press.

RORER, L. G. (1965). The great response-style myth. *Psychological Bulletin, 63,* 129–136.

ROSENBAUM, M. E. (1986). The repulsion hypothesis: On the nondevelopment of relationships. *Journal of Personality and Social Psychology, 51.*

ROSENBERG, M. J. (1965). When dissonance fails: On eliminating evaluation apprehension from attitude measurement. *Journal of Personality and Social Psychology, 1,* 28–42.

ROSENBERG, M. J. (1968). Hedonism, inauthenticity, and other goads toward expansion of a consistency theory. In R. P. Abelson, E. Aronson, W. J. McGuire, T. M. Newcomb, M. J. Rosenberg, & P. H. Tannenbaum (Eds.), *Theories of cognitive consistency: A sourcebook* (pp. 140–164). Chicago: Rand McNally.

ROSENHAN, D. L. (1972). Learning theory and prosocial behavior. *Journal of Social Issues, 28*(3), 151–163.

ROSENTHAL, A. M. (1964). *Thirty-eight witnesses.* New York: McGraw-Hill.

ROSENTHAL, R. (1966). *Experimenter effects in behavioral research.* New York: Appleton-Century-Crofts.

ROSS, E. (1908). *Social psychology: An outline and source book.* New York: Macmillan.

ROSS, L., GREENE, D., & HOUSE, P. (1977). The "false consensus effect": An egocentric bias in social perception and attribution processes. *Journal of Experimental Social Psychology, 13,* 279–301.

ROSS, L. D. (1977). The intuitive psychologist and his shortcomings. In L. Berkowitz (Ed.), *Advances in experimental social psychology* (Vol. 10, pp. 173–220). New York: Academic Press.

ROTTER, J. B. (1954). *Social learning and clinical psychology.* Englewood Cliffs, NJ: Prentice-Hall.

ROTTER, J. B. (1966). Generalized expectancies for internal versus external locus of control of reinforcement. *Psychological Monographs, 80,* 1–28.

RUBIN, Z. (1970). Measurement of romantic love. *Journal of Personality and Social Psychol-*

ogy, 16, 265–273.

RUBIN, Z. (1973). *Liking and loving: An invitation to social psychology*. New York: Holt.

RUBIN, Z. (1974). From liking to loving: Patterns of attraction in dating relationships. In T. L. Huston (Ed.), *Foundations of interpersonal attraction* (pp. 383–402). New York: Academic Press.

RUSSELL, J. A., & BULLOCK, M. (1985). Multidimensional scaling of emotional facial expressions: Similarity from preschoolers to adults. *Journal of Personality and Social Psychology, 48*, 1290–1298.

SAHAKIAN, W. (1974). *Systematic social psychology*. New York: Chandler.

SAKS, M. J., & HASTIE, R. (1978). *Social psychology in court*. New York: Van Nostrand Reinhold.

SARNOFF, I., & ZIMBARDO, P. G. (1961). Anxiety, fear, and social affiliation. *Journal of Abnormal and Social Psychology, 62*, 597–605.

SCHACHTER, S. (1951). Deviation, rejection, and communication. *Journal of Abnormal and Social Psychology, 46*, 190–207.

SCHACHTER, S. (1959). *The psychology of affiliation*. Stanford, CA: Stanford University Press.

SCHACHTER, S. (1964). The interaction of cognitive and physiological determinants of emotional state. In L. Berkowitz (Ed.), *Advances in experimental social psychology* (Vol. 1, pp. 49–80). New York: Academic Press.

SCHACHTER, S., & SINGER, J. E. (1962). Cognitive, social, and physiological determinants of emotional state. *Psychological Review, 69*, 379–399.

SCHANK, R. C., & ABELSON, R. P. (1977). *Scripts, plans, goals, and understanding*. Hillsdale, NJ: Lawrence Erlbaum Associates.

SCHLOSBERG, H. (1952). The description of facial expressions in terms of two dimensions. *Journal of Experimental Psychology, 44*, 229–237.

SCHOPLER, J. (1965). Social power. In L. Berkowitz (Ed.), *Advances in experimental social psychology* (Vol. 2, pp. 177–219). New York: Academic Press.

SCHROEDER, D. A., & LINDER, D. E. (1976). Effects of actor's causal role, outcome severity, and knowledge of prior accidents upon attributions of responsibility. *Journal of Experimental Social Psychology, 12*, 340–356.

SCHULMAN, J., SHAVER, P., COLMAN, R., EMRICH, B., & CHRISTIE, R. (1973). Recipe for a jury. *Psychology Today, 6*, 37–44, 77–84.

SCHWARTZ, S. (1977). Normative influences on altruism. In L. Berkowitz (Ed.), *Advances in experimental social psychology* (Vol. 10, pp. 221–279). New York: Academic Press.

SCHWARTZ, S., & CLAUSEN, G. T. (1970). Responsibility, norms, and helping in an emergency. *Journal of Personality and Social Psychology, 16*, 299–310.

SCOTT, J. P. (1966). Agonistic behavior of mice and rats: A review. *American Zoologist, 6*, 683–701.

SELIGMAN, M. E. P. (1975). *Helplessness: On depression, development, and death*. San Francisco: Freeman.

SENSENIG, J., & BREHM, J. W. (1968). Attitude change from an implied threat to attitudinal freedom. *Journal of Personality and Social Psychology, 8*, 324–330.

SHANTEAU, J., & NAGY, G. F. (1979). Probability of acceptance and dating choice. *Journal of Personality and Social Psychology, 37*, 522–533.

SHAPIRO, E. G. (1975). Effect of expectations of future interaction on reward allocations in dyads: Equity or equality? *Journal of Personality and Social Psychology, 31*, 873–880.

SHAVER, K. G. (1970). Defensive attribution: Effects of severity and relevance on the responsibility assigned for an accident. *Journal of Personality and Social Psychology, 14*, 101–113.

SHAVER, K. G. (1975). *An introduction to attribution processes*. Cambridge, MA: Winthrop.

SHAVER, K. G. (1985). *The attribution of blame: Causality, responsibility, and blameworthiness*. New York: Springer-Verlag.

SHAVER, K. G., GILBERT, M. A., & WILLIAMS, M. C. (1975). Social psychology, criminal justice, and the principle of discretion: A selective review. *Personality and Social Psychology Bulletin, 1,* 471–484.

SHAVER, K. G., PAYNE, M. R., BLOCH, R. M., BURCH, M. C., DAVIS, M. S., & SHEAN, G. D. (1984). Logic in distortion: Attributions of causality and responsibility among schizophrenics. *Journal of Social and Clinical Psychology, 2,* 193–214.

SHAW, M. E., & SULZER, J. L. (1964). An empirical test of Heider's levels in attribution of responsibility. *Journal of Abnormal and Social Psychology, 69,* 39–46.

SHERIF, M. (1936). *The psychology of social norms.* New York: Harper and Row.

SHERIF, M., & HOVLAND, C. I. (1961). *Social judgment: Assimilation and contrast effects in communication and attitude change.* New Haven, CT: Yale University Press.

SHERIF, M., & SHERIF, C. W. (1969). *Social psychology.* New York: Harper & Row.

SHOTLAND, L. R., & HUSTON, T. L. (1979). Emergencies: What are they and do they influence bystanders to intervene? *Journal of Personality and Social Psychology, 37,* 1822–1834.

SIGALL, H., & OSTROVE, N. (1975). Beautiful but dangerous: Effects of offender attractiveness and nature of the crime on juridic judgment. *Journal of Personality and Social Psychology, 31,* 410–414.

SKINNER, B. F. (1953). *Science and human behavior.* New York: Macmillan.

SLETTO, R. F. (1937). *A construction of personality scales by the criterion of internal consistency.* Hanover, NH: Sociological Press.

SMITH, W. P., & ANDERSON, A. J. (1975). Threats, communication, and bargaining. *Journal of Personality and Social Psychology, 32,* 76–82.

SNYDER, M. (1979). Self-monitoring processes. In L. Berkowitz (Ed.), *Advances in experimental social psychology* (Vol. 12, pp. 85–128). New York: Academic Press.

SNYDER, M. (1984). When belief creates reality. In L. Berkowitz (Ed.), *Advances in experimental social psychology* (Vol. 18, pp. 247–305). New York: Academic Press.

SNYDER, M., & TANKE, E. D. (1976). Behavior and attitude: Some people are more consistent than others. *Journal of Personality, 44,* 510–517.

SNYDER, M., TANKE, E. D., & BERSCHEID, E. (1977). Social perception and interpersonal behavior: On the self-fulfilling nature of social stereotypes. *Journal of Personality and Social Psychology, 35,* 656–666.

SOMMER, R. (1969). *Personal space: The behavioral basis of design.* Englewood Cliffs, NJ: Prentice-Hall.

SOMMER, R. (1974). *Tight spaces: Hard architecture and how to humanize it.* Englewood Cliffs, NJ: Prentice-Hall.

SPENCE, J. T., DEAUX, K., & HELMREICH, R. L. (1985). Sex roles in contemporary American society. In G. Lindzey & E. Aronson (Eds.), *Handbook of social psychology* (3rd. ed., Vol. 2, pp. 149–178). New York: Random House.

SPENCE, J. T., & HELMREICH, R. L. (1972). Who likes competent women? Competence, sex-role congruence of interests, and subjects' attitudes toward women as determinants of interpersonal attraction. *Journal of Applied Social Psychology, 2,* 197–213.

STAUB, E., & SHERK, L. (1970). Need approval, children's sharing behavior, and reciprocity in sharing. *Child Development, 41,* 243–253.

STEPHAN, W. G. (1985). Intergroup relations. In G. Lindzey & E. Aronson (Eds.), *Handbook of social psychology* (3rd. ed., Vol. 2, pp. 599–658). New York, Random House.

STOKOLS, D. (1972). On the distinction between density and crowding: Some implications for future research. *Psychological Review, 79,* 275–277.

STOKOLS, D. (Ed.). (1977). *Perspectives on environment and behavior: Theory, research, and applications.* New York: Plenum.

STONER, J. A. F. (1961). *A comparison of individual and group decisions including risk.* Unpublished master's thesis, Massachusetts Institute of Technology, School of Industrial Management, Boston, MA.

STORMS, M. D., & NISBETT, R. E. (1970). Insomnia and the attribution process. *Journal of Personality and Social Psycholgy, 16,* 319–328.

STOTLAND, E., SHERMAN, S., & SHAVER, K. G. (1971). *Empathy and birth order: Some experi-*

mental explorations. Lincoln, NE: University of Nebraska Press.

STOUFFER, S. A., SUCHMAN, E. A., DEVINNEY, L. C., STARR, S. A., & WILLIAMS, R. M., JR. (1949). *The American soldier: Adjustment during army life* (Vol. 1). Princeton, NJ: Princeton University Press.

STRAUS, M. A., GELLES, R. J., & STEINMETZ, S. (1980). *Behind closed doors: Violence in the American family*. Garden City, NY: Anchor Press-Doubleday.

STRICKER, L. J., MESSICK, S., & JACKSON, D. N. (1970). Conformity, anticonformity, and independence: Their dimensionality and generality. *Journal of Personality and Social Psychology, 16*, 495–507.

STRUBE, M. J., & GARCIA, J. E. (1981). A meta-analytic investigation of Fiedler's contingency model of leadership effectiveness. *Psychological Bulletin, 90*, 307–321.

STRYKER, S. (1983). Social psychology from the standpoint of a structural symbolic interactionism: Toward an interdisciplinary social psychology. In L. Berkowitz (Ed.), *Advances in experimental social psychology* (Vol. 16, pp. 181–218). New York: Academic Press.

SUNDSTROM, E. (1978). Crowding as a sequential process: Review of research on the effects of population density on humans. In A. Baum & Y. M. Epstein (Eds.), *Human response to crowding* (pp. 32–116). Hillsdale, NJ: Lawrence Erlbaum Associates.

SULZER, J. L. (1971, July). *Heider's "Levels model" of responsibility attribution*. Paper presented at the Symposium on Attribution of Responsibility Research, Williamsburg, VA.

SYKES, G. M., & MATZA, D. (1957). Techniques of neutralization: A theory of delinquency. *American Sociological Review, 22*, 664–670.

TANNENBAUM, P. H. (1968). The congruity principle: Retrospective reflections and recent research. In R. P. Abelson, E. Aronson, W. J. McGuire, T. M. Newcomb, M. J. Rosenberg, & P. H. Tannenbaum (Eds.), *Theories of cognitive consistency: A sourcebook* (pp. 52–72). Chicago: Rand McNally.

TANNENBAUM, P. H., & ZILLMAN, D. (1975). Emotional arousal in the facilitation of aggression through communication. In L. Berkowitz (Ed.), *Advances in experimental social psychology* (Vol. 8, pp. 149–172). New York: Academic Press.

TAYLOR, S. E. (1975). On inferring one's attitudes from one's behavior: Some delimiting conditions/. *Journal of Personality and Social Psychology, 31*, 126–131.

TETLOCK, P. E. (1979). Identifying victims of groupthink from public statements of decision makers. *Journal of Personality and Social Psychology, 37*, 1314–1324.

THIBAUT, J. W., & KELLEY, H. H. (1959). *The social psychology of groups*. New York: Wiley.

THIBAUT, J. W., & WALKER, L. (1975). *Procedural justice: A psychological analysis*. Hillsdale, NJ: Lawrence Erlbaum Associates.

THORNDIKE, E. L. (1898). Animal intelligence: An experimental study of the associative process in animals. *Psychological Review*, Monograph Supplement No. 8.

THURSTONE, L. L. (1928). Attitudes can be measured. *American Journal of Sociology, 33*, 529–554.

THURSTONE, L. L. (1932). *The measurement of social attitudes*. Chicago: University of Chicago Press.

THURSTONE, L. L., & CHAVE, E. J. (1929). *The measurement of attitude*. Chicago: University of Chicago Press.

TOMKINS, S. S. (1962). *Affect, imagery, and consciousness* (Vol. 1). New York: Springer.

TVERSKY, A., & KAHNEMAN, D. (1974). Judgment under uncertainty: Heuristics and biases. *Science, 185*, 1124–1131.

UPSHAW, H. S. (1969). The personal reference scale: An approach to social judgment. In L. Berkowitz (Ed.), *Advances in experimental social psychology* (Vol. 4, pp. 315–372). New York: Academic Press.

U. S. Bureau of the Census. (1977). *Statistical abstract of the United States, 1977*, (98th ed.). Washington, DC: U.S. Government Printing Office.

U. S. Department of Justice. (1985). *Crime in the United States*. Washington, DC: U.S. Government Printing Office.

VALINS, S. (1966). Cognitive effects of false heart-rate feedback. *Journal of Personality and Social Psychology, 4,* 400–408.

VALINS, S., & RAY, A. A. (1967). Effects of cognitive desensitization on avoidance behavior. *Journal of Personality and Social Psychology, 7,* 345–350.

VINOKUR, A., & BURNSTEIN, E. (1974). Effects of partially shared persuasive arguments on group-induced shifts: A group problem-solving approach. *Journal of Personality and Social Psychology, 29,* 305–315.

VON HIRSCH, A. (1976). *Doing justice: The choice of punishment.* New York: Farrar, Straus, & Giroux.

WAGNER, C., & WHEELER, L. (1969). Model, need, and cost effects in helping behavior. *Journal of Personality and Social Psychology, 12,* 111–116.

WALLACH, M. A., & KOGAN, N. (1959). Sex differences and judgment processes. *Journal of Personality, 27,* 555–564.

WALLACH, M. A., KOGAN, N., & BURT, R. (1967). Group risk taking and field dependence-independence of group members. *Sociometry, 30,* 323–339.

WALSTER, E., BERSCHEID, E., & WALSTER, G. W. (1973). New directions in equity research. *Journal of Personality and Social Psychology, 25,* 151–176.

WALSTER, E., BERSCHEID, E., & WALSTER, G. W. (1976). New directions in equity research. In L. Berkowitz & E. Walster (Eds.), *Advance in experimental social psychology. Vol. 9, Equity theory: Toward a general theory of social interaction* (pp. 1–42). New York: Academic Press.

WALSTER, E. H., WALSTER, G. W., & BERSCHEID, E. (1978). *Equity: Theory and research.* Boston: Allyn & Bacon.

WARR, P. B., & KNAPPER, C. (1968). *The perception of people and events.* London: Wiley.

WEARY, G., & ARKIN, R. M. (1981). Attributional self-presentation. In J. H. Harvey, W. Ickes, & R. F. Kidd (Eds.), *New directions in attribution research* (Vol. 3, pp. 223–246). Hillsdale, NJ: Lawrence Erlbaum Associates.

WEBB, E. J., CAMPBELL, D. T., SCHWARTZ, R. D., & SECHREST, L. (1966). *Unobtrusive measures: Nonreactive research in the social sciences.* Chicago: Rand McNally.

WEINER, B. (1972). *Theories of motivation: From mechanism to cognition.* New York: Markham.

WEINER, B. (1974). *Achievement motivation and attribution theory.* Morristown, NJ: General Learning Press.

WEINER, B., FRIEZE, I. H., KUKLA, A., REED, L., REST, S., & ROSENBAUM, R. M. (1972). Perceiving the causes of success and failure. In E. E. Jones, D. E. Kanouse, H. H. Kelley, R. E. Nisbett, S. Valins, & B. Weiner (Eds.), *Attribution: Perceiving the causes of behavior* (pp. 95–120). Morristown, NJ: General Learning Press.

WEINER, B., RUSSELL, D., & LERMAN, D. (1978). Affective consequences of causal ascriptions. In J. H. Harvey, W. Ickes, & R. F. Kidd (Eds.), *New directions in attribution research* (Vol. 2, pp. 59–90). Hillsdale, NJ: Lawrence Erlbaum Associates.

WELLS, G. L. (Ed.). (1980). Eyewitness behavior. *Law and Human Behavior, 4*(4).

WEST, S. G., WHITNEY, G., & SCHMEDLER, R. (1975). Helping a motorist in distress: The effects of sex, race, and neighborhood. *Journal of Personality and Social Psychology, 31,* 691–698.

WESTIN, A. (1970). *Privacy and freedom.* New York: Atheneum.

WICKER, A. W. (1969). Attitudes versus actions: The relationship of verbal and overt behavioral responses to attitude objects. *Journal of Social Issues, 25,* 41–78.

WICKER, A. W., & KIRMEYER, S. (1977). From church to laboratory to national park: A program of research on excess and insufficient populations in behavior settings. In D. Stokols (Ed.), *Perspectives on environment and behavior: Theory, research, and applications* (pp. 69–96). New York: Plenum.

WICKLUND, R. A. (1974). *Freedom and reactance.* New York: Academic Press.

WICKLUND, R. A., & BREHM, J. W. (1976). *Perspectives on cognitive dissonance.* Hillsdale, NJ: Lawrence Erlbaum Associates.

WICKLUND, R. A., & GOLLWITZER, P. M. (1982). *Symbolic self-completion.* Hillsdale, NJ: Lawrence Erlbaum Associates.

WIEST, W. M. (1965). A quantitative extension of Heider's theory of cognitive balance applied to interpersonal perception and self-esteem. *Psychological Monographs, 79,* Whole No. 607.

WILDER, D. A. (1986). Social categorization: Implications for creation and reduction of intergroup bias. In L. Berkowitz (Ed.), *Advances in experimental social psychology* (Vol. 19, pp. 291–355). New York: Academic Press.

WILKINS, L. T. (1982). Parole decisions. In V. J. Konečni & E. B. Ebbesen (Eds.), *The criminal justice system: A social psychological analysis* (pp. 367–392). San Francisco: Freeman.

WILLIAMS, G. L. (1953). *Criminal law: The general part.* London: Stevens & Sons.

WILSON, W. C., & GOLDSTEIN, M. J. (Eds.). (1973). Pornography: Attitudes, use, and effects. *Journal of Social Issues, 29*(3).

WINCH, R. F. (1958). *Mate-selection: A study of complementary needs.* New York: Harper and Row.

WISHNER, J. (1960). Reanalysis of "Impressions of personality." *Psychological Review, 67,* 96–112.

WISPÉ, L. G. (Ed.). (1972). Positive forms of social behavior. *Journal of Social Issues, 28*(3).

WOODWORTH, R. S. (1938). *Experimental psychology.* New York: Holt.

WORTMAN, C. B., & BREHM, J. W. (1975). Responses to uncontrollable outcomes: An integration of reactance theory and the learned helplessness model. In L. Berkowitz (Ed.), *Advances in experimental social psychology* (Vol. 8, pp. 277–336).

WRIGHTSMAN, L. S., & COOK, S. W. (1965). *Factor analysis and attitude change.* Paper presented at the meeting of the Southeastern Psychological Association, Atlanta.

YNGVE, V. H. (1970). On getting a word in edgewise. *Papers from the sixth regional meeting, Chicago Linguistic Society,* 567–577.

ZAJONC, R. B. (1968). The attitudinal effects of mere exposure. *Journal of Personality and Social Psychology Monograph Supplement, 9,* Part 2, 1–27.

ZANDER, A. (1979). The psychology of group processes. In M. R. Rosenzweig & L. R. Porter (Eds.), *Annual Review of Psychology, 30,* 417–451.

ZANNA, M. P., & COOPER, J. (1974). Dissonance and the pill: An attribution approach to studying the arousal properties of dissonance. *Journal of Personality and Social Psychology, 29,* 703–709.

ZILLER, R. C. (1973). *The social self.* New York: Pergamon.

ZILLMANN, D. (1978). Attribution and misattribution of excitatory reactions. In J. H. Harvey, W. Ickes, & R. F. Kidd (Eds.), *New directions in attribution research* (Vol. 2, pp. 335–368). Hillsdale, NJ: Lawrence Erlbaum Associates.

ZILLMANN, D. (1979). *Hostility and aggression.* Hillsdale, NJ: Lawrence Erlbaum Associates.

ZIMBARDO, P. G. (1970). The human choice: Individuation, reason, and order versus deindividuation, impulse, and chaos. In W. J. Arnold & D. Levine (Eds.), *Nebraska symposium on motivation, 1969* (pp. 237–307). Lincoln, NE: University of Nebraska Press.

ZIMBARDO, P. G., EBBESEN, E. B., & MASLACH, C. (1977). *Influencing attitudes and changing behavior* (2nd ed.). Reading, MA: Addison-Wesley.

ZLUTNICK, S., & ALTMAN, I. (1972). Crowding and human behavior. In J. F. Wohlwill & D. H. Carson (Eds.), *Environment and the social sciences: Perspectives and applications.* Washington, DC: American Psychological Association.

ZUCKERMAN, M., KOESTNER, R., & ALTON, A. O. (1984). Learning to detect deception. *Journal of Personality and Social Psychology, 46,* 519–528.

ZUCKERMAN, M., & REIS, H. T. (1978). Comparison of three models for predicting altruistic behavior. *Journal of Personality and Social Psychology, 36,* 498–510.

ZUCKERMAN, M., & WHEELER, L. (1975). To dispel fantasy about the fantasy-based measure of fear of success. *Psychological Bulletin, 82,* 932–946.

AUTHOR INDEX

SUBJECT INDEX